Archaeology in Hertfordshire

Tony Rook (photograph: Kris Lockyear).

Archaeology in Hertfordshire

Recent Research

A *FESTSCHRIFT* FOR TONY ROOK

Edited by
KRIS LOCKYEAR

HERTFORDSHIRE PUBLICATIONS
an imprint of
University of Hertfordshire Press

First published in Great Britain in 2015 by
Hertfordshire Publications
an imprint of
University of Hertfordshire Press
College Lane
Hatfield
Hertfordshire
AL10 9AB

British Library Cataloguing in Publication Data
A catalogue record for this book is available from the British Library

ISBN 978–1-909291–42–3

Design by Arthouse Publishing Solutions Ltd
Printed in Great Britain by Charlesworth Press

Publication has been made possible by generous grants from the
Marc Fitch Fund and from Institute of Archaeology, University College London

MARC FITCH FUND

Contents

Figures

Plates

Tables

Abbreviations

ABT	Laws of Æthelberht of Kent
AHRC	Arts and Humanities Research Council
BL	British Library
CAGG	Community Archaeology Geophysics Group
DWWS	*Dig Where We Stand: Developing and Sustaining Community Heritage*
EG	Laws of Edgar, King of England
HADAS	Hendon and District Archaeological Society
HALS	Hertfordshire Archives and Local Studies
HER	Historic Environment Record
HHA	Hatfield House Archives
HHER	Hertfordshire Historic Environment Record
Hl	Laws of Hloþhere and Eadric of Kent
HLF	Heritage Lottery Fund
HSCAP	Hendon School Community Archaeology Project
HU	Hundred Ordinance
ICP-MS	inductively coupled plasma mass spectroscopy
LAS	Lockleys Archaeological Society
ME	Middle English
OE	Old English
OSL	Optically Stimulated Luminescence
PAS	Portable Antiquities Scheme
RCUK	Research Council UK
SAHAAS	St Albans and Hertfordshire Architectural and Archaeological Society
SFB	sunken-featured building
TNA:PRO	The National Archives: Public Record Office
UCL	University College London
VCH	Victoria County History
WAS	Welwyn Archaeological Society

Preface

Kris Lockyear

This volume has its origin in a conference held by the Welwyn Archaeological Society (WAS) on 14 July 2012 to mark Tony Rook's 80th birthday. Some of the speakers have known Tony for many years, others know him only through his work, but all the contributors recognise his contribution to the archaeology and history of Hertfordshire. This book contains all the papers given on that day along with additional papers – those by Burleigh, Moorhead, Rook and Lockyear, Williamson and Wythe – solicited afterwards to round out the theme of the volume. For example, as Tony was the Director of the Welwyn Archaeological Society – originally the Lockleys Archaeological Society (LAS) – from its foundation in about 1964 until 2009, it seemed appropriate to include a 'personal history' of the Society based on Merle Rook's diaries (Rook and Lockyear, this volume). Although it has taken a couple of years to bring this book to fruition, the work is still very much recent – and in some cases still ongoing.

Tony was born on 12 July 1932 in Burnt Barn Farm, Leeds, Kent, to Reginald and Cecilie Rook, although his parents were universally known as Curly and Haggis. He went to the Judd School in Tonbridge, Kent. Tony's first experience of excavation was at the age of sixteen, when he helped Sheppard Frere excavate in the bomb-damaged areas of Canterbury. The following year, he worked on the first season of the excavations at Lullingstone Roman villa. Tony won a Higher Exhibition and wanted to use the award to study archaeology, but was told that 'boys were expected to study something useful'. In 1951 Tony joined the RAF and was trained as a radar fitter and posted to the Black Forest in Germany. On leaving the RAF in 1954 he obtained a place at Leicester University to study Maths, Chemistry and Physics. It was there, in his first term, that he met Merle. After graduation in 1957 Tony obtained a post in Southall undertaking building research for George Wimpey, at that time the largest building contractor in the world. Merle and Tony married in 1959, and in 1960 he was offered a post with the Chalk, Lime and Allied Industries Research Association (CLAIRA), based in Welwyn. Thus began Tony and Merle's long association with Hertfordshire (see Rook and Lockyear, this volume).

Tony and Merle's first daughter, Kate, was born in 1962. In the following year Tony was offered the post of Head of Science at Sherrardswood School, Lockleys, Welwyn, and moved into the Lodge of Lockleys House. The following year their second daughter, Sylvia, was born. During the 1960s and early 1970s Tony and the LAS/WAS members undertook a series of 'rescue' excavations. Tony also edited the *Hertfordshire Archaeological Review*, which ran from 1970 to 1975. In 1973 he began his MPhil on Roman bath houses at the Institute of Archaeology, supervised by Donald Strong. He was awarded his MPhil in 1975 and for the next seven years taught extramural classes for University College London (UCL). He also ran distance learning courses for Cambridge and Essex. In that same year the Rook family moved to the Old Rectory in Welwyn, which became the hub of the activities of the Welwyn Archaeological Society, and where Tony still lives (Rook 1979).

From then on Tony was a tutor on many extramural and adult education courses, as well as being a freelance researcher and a prolific author – a selection of his publications is listed below. Even since the conference Tony has had no fewer than three volumes published – *Roman Building Techniques* (2012), *Welwyn and Welwyn Garden City Through Time* (2013) and *The River Mimram* (2014) – an astounding achievement.

As editor of this volume I would like to thank the authors for submitting such an interesting range of papers. A number of people helped with images and queries and I would like to thank all those who helped, especially Isobel Thompson of the Hertfordshire Historic Environment Record. I would also like to thank the members of the Welwyn Archaeological Society, including Clare Lewis, Jenny Searle, Daphne Goddard, Alasdair Campbell, Jon Wimhurst, John Bright and Nick Tracken, for all their help with both the conference and the running of the Society and its fieldwork. Jane Housham, of the University of Hertfordshire Press, has been extremely patient with the many delays to this volume, and is also due my thanks. Lastly, I would like to thank my wife, Ellen Shlasko, not only for her efforts during the conference and with various archaeological events and activities but also for her patience while I was editing this book.

A select bibliography

Rook, Tony (1968a), 'Investigation of a Belgic Occupation Site at Crookhams, Welwyn Garden City', *Hertfordshire Archaeology* 1, pp. 51–65.

– (1968b), 'Romano-British Well at Welwyn', *Hertfordshire Archaeology* 1, pp. 117–18.

– (1968c), 'A Belgic ditched enclosure at Nutfield, Welwyn Garden City', *Hertfordshire Archaeology* 1, pp. 121–3.

– (1968d), *Welwyn Beginning*, 1st edn (Welwyn).

– (1968e), 'A note on the "rediscovery" of a Belgic chieftain burial', *Hertfordshire Past and Present* 8, pp. 17–18.

– (1968f), 'The Romano-British cemetery at Welwyn. Obiit 1967', *Hertfordshire Past and Present* 8, pp. 32–7.

– (1970a), 'A Belgic and Roman site at Brickwall Hill', *Hertfordshire Archaeology* 2, pp. 23–30.

– (1970b), 'Investigation of a Belgic site at Grubs Barn, Welwyn Garden City', *Hertfordshire Archaeology* 2, pp. 31–6.

– (1971a), 'Lockleys Archaeological Society', *Hertfordshire Archaeological Review* 4, pp. 63–4.

– (1971b), 'Ayot St Lawrence', *Hertfordshire Archaeological Review* 4, pp. 77–8.

– (1972), *Strange Mansion* (London).

– (1973), 'Excavations at the Grange Romano-British Cemetery, Welwyn, 1967', *Hertfordshire Archaeology* 3, 1–30.

– (1974), 'Welch's Farm – a success for the fieldworker', *Hertfordshire Archaeological Review* 9, pp. 170–74.

– (1976), 'Beaten by the Bounds', *Hertfordshire's Past* 1, pp. 8–10.

– (1978), 'The development and operation of Roman hypocausted baths', *Journal of Archaeological Science* 5/3, pp. 269–82.

– (1979), 'History begins at home: the Old Rectory, Welwyn', *Hertfordshire's Past* 7, pp. 34–7.

– and Henig, M. (1981), 'A bronze cockerel from a late Romano-British context at Aston, Hertfordshire', *Antiquaries Journal* 61, pp. 356–9.

–, Lowery, P.R., Savage, R.D.A. and R.L. Wilkins (1982), 'An Iron Age Bronze Mirror from Aston, Hertfordshire', *Antiquaries Journal* 62, pp. 18–34.

– (1983), *The Labrador Trust* (London).

– (1984), *A History of Hertfordshire*, 1st edn (Chichester).

–, Walker, S. and Denston, C.B. (1984), 'A Roman Mausoleum and Associated Marble Sarcophagus and Burials from Welwyn, Hertfordshire', *Britannia* 15, pp. 143–62.

– (1983-6), 'The Roman Villa Site at Dicket Mead, Lockleys, Welwyn', *Hertfordshire Archaeology* 9, pp. 79–175.

– (1986), *Of Local Interest, a Book of Welwyn Pubs* (Welwyn).

Scott, V.G. and – (1989), *County Maps & Histories: Hertfordshire* (London).

– (1992), *Roman Baths in Britain* (Princes Risborough).

– (1994a), 'The fishponds at Digswell', *Hertfordshire Past* 36, pp. 1–7.

– (1994b), *Before the Railway came. Welwyn 1820–1850* (Welwyn).

– (1995a), *Welwyn. A Simple History* (Welwyn).

– (1995b), *Welwyn Beginning*, 3rd edn (Welwyn).

Rook, K. and – (1996), *St Mary's Church, Welwyn. A History and Guide* (Welwyn).

– (1997a), *A History of Hertfordshire*, 2nd edn (Chichester).

– (1997b), 'The view from Hertfordshire', in R.M. Friendship-Taylor and D.E. Friendship-Taylor, *From Round House to Villa*, (Northampton) pp. 53–7.

– (2001), *Welwyn Garden City Past* (Chichester)

– (2002), *The Story of Welwyn Roman Baths* (Welwyn).
– (2004), 'The construction of the Welwyn Viaduct: fact and fiction', *Herts Past & Present* 3, pp. 24–7.
– (2005), *I've Come About the Drains. An adventure in architecture* (Welwyn).
– (2012), *Roman Building Techniques* (Stroud).
– (2013), *Welwyn & Welwyn Garden City Through Time* (Stroud).
– (2014), *The River Mimram* (Stroud).

CHAPTER 1

Archaeology in Hertfordshire

Kris Lockyear

1.1 The historical and institutional context

In 1939 Arthur Mee, in his introduction to *Hertfordshire: London's Country Neighbour*, was able to write:

> It is country as it should be, unspoiled by the heavy hand of industry. Its four hundred thousand people on their four hundred thousand acres are all country folk, loving their small rivers and their little hills, so near to town that they can come to London when they will, always going back. (Mee [1939] 1991: 1)

In 1999, however, Simon Jenkins wrote:

> One of the smallest English counties, Hertfordshire finds excitement hard to come by. Its rolling chalk hills have been overwhelmed by suburban development, with little concern for landscape conservation. Everywhere are roads, housing estates, industrial zones and new towns. Such corners of green belt as survive seem to be gasping for breath. (Jenkins 1999: 279)

These two quotations illustrate nicely a number of key factors to be considered when investigating the history and archaeology of the county. Firstly, Hertfordshire has lain in the shadow of London almost since the foundation of that city in the early Roman period. Verulamium, the Roman city at St Albans, was the third largest settlement in the province, but Londinium was the largest. The main Roman roads – Watling Street and Ermine Street – ran through the county, connecting Londinium to the rest of Britannia (Thompson 2011a).

Secondly, until relatively recently, Hertfordshire was a 'county of small towns', to borrow the title of a recent volume on the subject (Slater and Goose 2008).

Although there were some industries, such as straw plaiting (Gróf 1988; Rook 1997a: 110–12), most were light and many, such as brewing (Whitaker 2006), were tied to agricultural production. The county was also the chosen location for many smaller landed estates owing to its location close to the capital, and many of those changed hands rapidly (Prince 2008: 1). As a result, the county has a rich garden history (Rowe 2007; Spring 2012).

Thirdly, population growth has had a considerable impact. Since the end of the nineteenth century the population of Hertfordshire has increased rapidly (Fig. 1.1). From 1901 to 1931 the population rose by just under 143,000, but in the years between 1931 and the start of the Second World War the population grew by another 166,000. During the 1940s growth was, unsurprisingly, slower, but the desperate need to replace housing destroyed during the War led to the growth of the 'New Towns' during the 1950s (Hertfordshire Publications 1990), and the population leapt by over 223,000 between 1951 and 1961. My parents, who moved from London to Welwyn Garden City in 1958, are typical of this growth. As my father had obtained a job at the De Havilland aircraft factory in Hatfield they were entitled to a newly built council house – so new, in fact, that they were not allowed to paint the walls and the road was little more than a muddy track in a building site. Although population growth slowed in the 1960s and 1970s and did not begin to pick up once more until the new millennium, the twentieth century as a whole saw the county's population quadruple to more

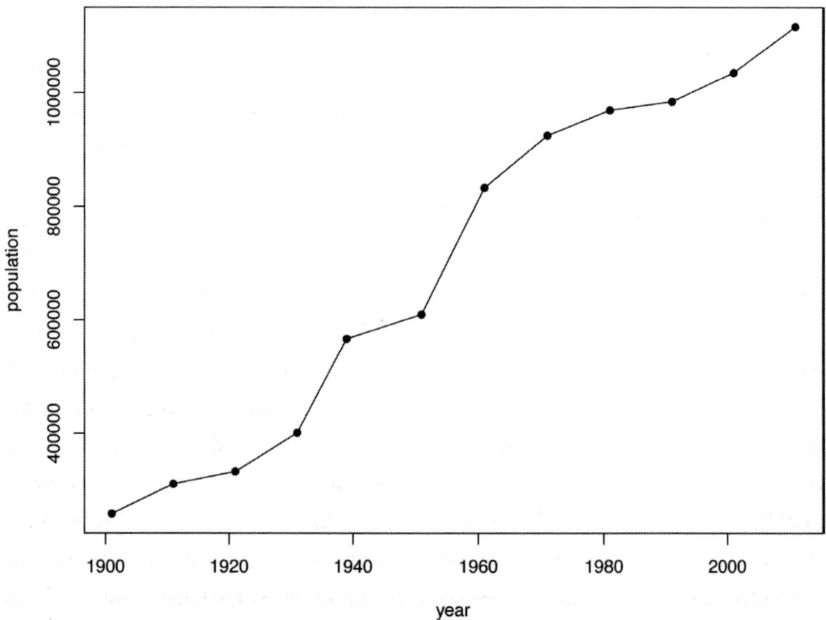

Figure 1.1: Population growth in Hertfordshire.

than a million. Accompanying this growth has been a major social change, from a county principally reliant on agriculture (Agar 2005), to one in which a significant proportion of the population commute to work in London.

Lastly, Hertfordshire is a county that tends to hide its light under a bushel. For many outside the county it is the last glimpse of countryside before London seen from the car or train window, the home of new towns and Shredded Wheat. As Jenkins' quote illustrates, many are ignorant of what Hertfordshire has to offer. The 'small rivers and ... little hills' are still to be found by those willing to explore the delightful but understated countryside that still exists, not all of which is 'gasping for breath'.

How, however, does all of this relate to the archaeology of the county? The lack of natural resources needed for heavy industry resulted in a county where agriculture was, until recently, the dominant occupation and the principal form of wealth. The evidence of this is dug, literally, into the landscape. For example, the recognition that at least some of the field systems that survived until the mechanisation of agriculture in the second half of the twentieth century may be many centuries old, if not pre-Roman, is but one important discovery (Catt *et al.* 2010: 245–6; Rowe and Williamson 2013; Williamson 2000: 144–52; Williamson, this volume). Indeed, one classic example lies in the area that has long been the focus of the work of WAS (Williamson 2000: fig. 27; Rook and Lockyear, this volume).

The huge growth in population should have created many opportunities for archaeological research (see Bryant, this volume, Plate 3.2). In some cases this is true – Tony Rook's work in Welwyn and Welwyn Garden City in the 1960s and John Moss-Eccardt's work in Letchworth are two excellent examples – but in general this was not the case. Although Tony's work was preceded by the Welwyn and District Regional Survey Association, much would appear to have been missed. Unfortunately, the massive growth in settlement and infrastructure in Hertfordshire took place before the development of commercial archaeology, as can be clearly demonstrated by the information held in the Hertfordshire Historic Environment Record (HHER). On a map of all archaeological 'events' one can see, for example, the route of the A10 mapped out as archaeological investigations that took place in advance of the recent widening of the road. Notably harder to discern, however, are the routes of the M1, A1(M) and M25, which preceded, as noted by Bryant (this volume), modern planning controls, notably the introduction of Planning Policy Guidance Note 16 (PPG16) in 1990. We can only guess at the wealth of information lost during the massive building programmes of the 1950s and 1960s (see, for example, Rook 1968a). Much of the valuable information gained since PPG16, however, is not easily available, as it lies in a multitude of grey literature reports. It is particularly welcome, therefore, that many of the papers in this volume, especially those by Bryant, Burleigh, Thompson and West, draw on this treasure trove of data.

For the casual visitor, the view expressed by Renn (1971: 1) that Hertfordshire's castles are 'a disappointment' could be extended to cover many periods of archaeology. The lack of good building stone means that we do not have a Stonehenge, a Maes Howe, a Hadrian's Wall or a Harlech. For much of the prehistoric period, visible, visitable remains are few and far between. The long and round barrows of Therfield Heath are one exception. Only in the late Iron Age do we get more dramatic features, such as the Devil's Dyke in Wheathampstead or Beech Bottom Dyke in St Albans. For the Roman period, Verulamium is probably the star attraction, with its walls, theatre and hypocaust building, although most of the best material is in the Museum. Hertfordshire had many Roman villas but only the bath house at Welwyn, which lies in a vault under the A1(M), can be visited (Plate 1.1; Rook 1983-6, 2002). For the medieval period, the abbey at St Albans and the castle at Berkhamsted are possibly the highlights. These, however, are the 'tourist attractions', somewhat lacking in the excitement that Jenkins desired. To those with a less superficial interest, however, Hertfordshire does indeed have a great deal to offer, and this will be explored in more detail below.

It has been pointed out to me that, even for specialists, it has been difficult to work on Hertfordshire material (D. Perring, pers. comm.). Many English counties have strong societies with a long tradition of publication and archaeological research: the Kent Archaeological Society, for example, was founded in 1857 and has just published volume 135 of *Archaeologia Cantiana*; the Sussex Archaeological Society was founded in 1846 and has published 150 volumes of the *Sussex Archaeological Collections*. Our county society – the St Albans and Hertfordshire Architectural and Archaeological Society (SAHAAS) was founded in 1845 (Moody 1995) and initially published individual articles later followed by volumes of *Transactions* from 1883 until the new journal *Hertfordshire Archaeology* started in 1968. The East Herts Archaeological Society (EHAS) was founded in 1898 by R.T. and W.F. Andrews partly, according to R.T. Andrews, because SAHAAS had 'left this side of the county somewhat out in the cold' (cited by Perman 1998: 9). Indeed, the 1895–6 volume of the *Transactions* was the first to add 'and Hertfordshire' to the name of SAHAAS. EHAS then proceeded to publish its own series of *Transactions*, starting in 1899, again ceasing publication with the creation of *Hertfordshire Archaeology*. This new journal, however, has never succeeded in becoming an annual publication; only 16 volumes have been published to date. Why is this so? Several suggestions can be made. Firstly, the impact of London on the transport system of the county made it much easier to travel north–south than it ever was to travel east–west. This may have contributed to the lack of cohesion in the archaeological community of the late nineteenth century. Later, during the second half of the twentieth century, a plethora of local societies were formed, including a new 'Hertfordshire Archaeological Society', which was founded at the start of 1969[1] but, as far as I am aware, lasted only a few years. An attempt at cohesion was made via the Hertfordshire Archaeological Council, which, through the 1970s, held a very successful series of conferences. The Council, however, no longer exists.

Secondly, many of the more successful county societies are relatively wealthy, presumably as the result of bequests, and that wealth is used to ensure regular publication of the county journal. Hertfordshire during the nineteenth century was, as noted above, a county of many smaller landed estates which often changed hands, with a small number of notable exceptions, such as the Cecil family and Hatfield House. Perhaps these families did not have the ties to the county that led to the bequests seen elsewhere?

Whatever the reasons – and the current *Hertfordshire Archaeology* team are, obviously, not at fault – the lack of an annual journal is detrimental to the rapid publication of archaeological projects. This is especially true for those projects which are too small to merit a monograph but are nonetheless important, such as the paper by Boyer *et al.* (this volume). In recent years SAHAAS, although very active in local research, has undertaken far less archaeological work than it did in the past, to the extent that in 2009 it polled its members about changing its name to *The St Albans and Hertfordshire History Society* (SAHAAS Newsletter 172: 2). Following a lively AGM the proposal was rejected by 84 votes to 57 (SAHAAS Newsletter 174: 1). One reason cited for the rejection was the dropping of 'Archaeological' from the Society's name.

In other ways, the county has suffered from being ahead of the game. The *Victoria County History* for Hertfordshire was one of the earlier ones to be published (Page 1902, 1908, 1912, 1914),[2] which are, naturally, less detailed and rigorous than the more recent volumes. The *Inventory of Historical Monuments* for the county was also one of the earlier volumes (RCHME 1910) and is now available online.[3] The Royal Commission for the Historical Monuments of England (RCHME) – now subsumed into English Heritage – also used the county as one pilot study for its aerial photographic National Mapping Programme (NMP) (RCHME 1992), which did not become generally available until 2011. As a pilot study it, naturally, does not benefit from the experience and methodology now applied in the NMP (*cf.* Ingle and Saunders 2011). The county is also surprisingly lacking in volumes of collected papers (*cf.* that by Ellis 2001 for Wiltshire); the volume edited by Holgate (1995) is one of the exceptions, if not specifically for Hertfordshire.

Recently, however, two valuable volumes have been published. The *Historical Atlas of Hertfordshire* (Short 2011) is a very useful collection of maps and short summaries on a wide variety of topics. The chapter by Catt *et al.* (2010) in *Hertfordshire Geology and Landscape* is an equally useful overview of the pre-Roman archaeology of the county. The greatest aid to the archaeological researcher in recent years, however, must be the variety of sources of data now available on the Internet: the HHER monument data is now available via the Heritage Gateway;[4] finds made by members of the public, principally metal detectorists, are recorded by the Portable Antiquities Scheme;[5] at least some grey literature reports are available via the Archaeological Data Service;[6] and some projects maintain blogs giving summary accounts of the results.[7]

Although in many ways using a relatively modern county boundary as a region for archaeological research seemingly makes no sense, the surprisingly varied institutional context of each county – as discussed above – makes the practicalities more straightforward. One can also argue that the erratic border of the county is no less a valid means of defining a study zone than a rectangular transect across the south of England.

1.2 The archaeological context

1.2.1 Prehistory to the middle Iron Age

Catt *et al.* (2010: 227–35) summarise the evidence for the Palaeolithic period in the county. The principal sites are mainly located in the far west: Long Valley Wood, Croxley Hall Wood and Mill End, all gravel pits. The nationally important sites around Caddington now lie across the border in Bedfordshire, although prior to the rationalisation of the county boundaries in 1897 they lay within the county. The distribution of Palaeolithic material is widely scattered, and the pattern is likely to be more a result of geology and gravel extraction than early human behaviour.

With the rapid warming of the climate at the start of the Holocene, Britain was rapidly repopulated. Even so, the population of Hertfordshire was probably in the hundreds, rather than the thousands, but the long time span involved, some 5,000 years or so, has resulted in a number of Mesolithic sites being known (Catt *et al.* 2010: 235–9), although the majority belong to the later Mesolithic. There is a marked distribution of these sites along the river valleys, especially the Colne and the Ver (Catt *et al.* 2010: fig. 8.7). Published sites include those around Cuffley (Lee 1977; 1983–86), Stanstead Abbots (Davies *et al.* 1980–82), Aldwickbury (West 2006–8: 8–9; Turner-Rugg 2006–8), Redbourne (West 2004–5), Old Parkbury (Niblett 2001) and the M1, Junction 9 (Simmonds 2012: 65–8; Mullin and Devaney 2012).

The early Neolithic is poorly represented in Hertfordshire, the only long barrows being Therfield Heath and Knocking Knoll, which lies on the Hertfordshire–Bedfordshire border (see Burleigh, this volume). The latter was almost entirely destroyed in 1856 (Rook 1997a: 22). One possible causewayed camp has been identified from aerial photographs at Sawbridgeworth (Palmer 1976: 184), and unpublished excavations at Bragbury End may represent another (HHER 4391). One remarkable find was that of a burnt log boat containing cremated bones at Old Parkbury (Niblett 2001). The only reasonably certain cursus is that discussed by Fitzpatrick-Matthews (this volume), although some others are suspected from aerial photographs. From the later Neolithic a small number of henges are suspected from aerial photographic data (RCHME 1992 [2011]: 15–16), but the henge from Norton is the only one with good-quality information (Fitzpatrick-Matthews, this volume). An interesting late Neolithic square burial enclosure was excavated on the route of the Baldock Bypass (Phillips 2009: 11–15; see also Plate 4.1). The distribution of Neolithic sites contrasts with those of the Mesolithic in that they lie on lighter, more easily cultivable soils rather than along the valleys (Catt *et al.* 2010: 242).

Very little from the Beaker period has been recovered in the county. The Bronze Age is much better represented, with perhaps the most prolific remains from the earlier Bronze Age being round barrows and ring ditches, the former concentrated on the chalk uplands in the north of the county and the latter often representing the ploughed-out remains of barrows (Catt *et al.* 2010: 243–4 and fig. 8.10). Some 443 were identified by the NMP (RCHME 1992 [2011]: 16–17). The ring ditch at Witchcraft near Ayot St Lawrence is probably a typical example (Rook 1971) although the Neolithic material contained in its upper fills was thought to be residual. A number of barrows were excavated on the route of the Baldock bypass (Phillips 2009: 23–7). The later Bronze Age and early Iron Age is marked by flint-tempered pottery (Barrett 1980) found on sites such as Great Humphreys, site X (Fig. 1.2; HHER 6312; Lockyear 1987: 6; Rook and Lockyear, this volume).

An overview of the evidence for the mid-Bronze to the mid-Iron Age periods is given by Bryant (this volume), and Thompson deals with the problem of 'the missing middle Iron Age' (this volume) – readers are directed to those papers for details.

1.2.2 Late Iron Age and Roman

Although the evidence for the middle Iron Age is more common than once thought (Thompson, this volume), it is nonetheless true that the late Iron Age sees a massive growth in the evidence available to us. Major settlement foci

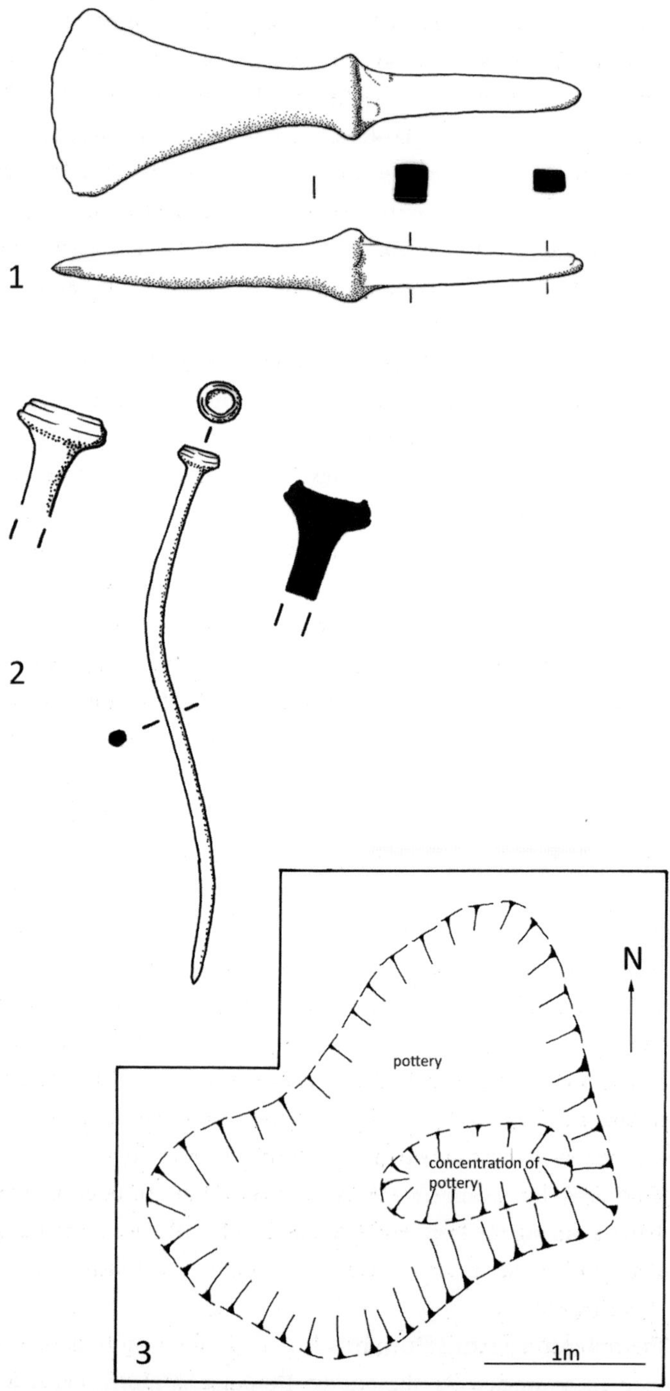

Figure 1.2: Finds from the Bronze Age 'site X' at Great Humphreys. 1. Chisel (lifesize); 2. Pin (lifesize, details 2x); 3. Plan of the feature. Objects drawn by Frances Saxton, plan from Lockyear (1987). For location of the site see Fig 9.1.

developed at Baldock (Burleigh 1995; Burleigh, this volume), Wheathampstead (Wheeler and Wheeler 1936: 16–22; Saunders and Havercroft 1980–82; West, this volume), Verulamium (Wheeler and Wheeler 1936: 6–16, 22–4, 40–49; Niblett and Thompson 2005: 23–40), Braughing/Skeleton Green (Partridge 1981; Potter and Trow 1988) and Cow Roast/Ashridge (Morris and Wainright 1995). It must be said, however, that the map of these concentrations (e.g., Bryant and Niblett 1997: fig. 27.2) is uncomfortably similar to the distribution of active archaeological societies (Bryant and Niblett 1997: 280), especially during the massive expansion of housing and infrastructure that took place in the 1950s and 1960s, as noted above. Bryant has recently suggested that the dyke systems associated with Verulamium may represent processional ways rather than defensive works, for which purpose they seem ill-suited (Bryant 2007).

In addition to the major settlements, large numbers of 'enclosures' are known, of which Hunn (1996) has provided a corpus. Without excavation or field survey it is impossible to date them precisely, although Hunn (1996: 8) argues that the external ditches go out of use towards the end of the first century AD. Great Humphreys is a good example (Lockyear 1987; Lockyear and Rook, this volume): here the large enclosure ditch was dug in the late pre-Roman Iron Age, weathered-in during the first and second centuries AD, and was then used as the burial site for babies in the third century and for the dumping of rubbish in the fourth. Other excavated examples include Stanborough School, Welwyn Garden City (Hunn 2009) and the Broom Hall Farm site, Watton-at-Stone (Lockyear, this volume).

Another notable feature of the late Iron Age of the county is the so-called 'Welwyn-type chieftain burials'. Named after the original find of two rich burials during the digging of a cutting in Welwyn in 1906 (Smith 1912), these include additional discoveries made in Welwyn Garden City (Stead 1967), Mardleybury (Rook 1968b), Baldock (Stead and Rigby 1986: 51–61) and Hertford Heath (Hussen 1983). Other cemeteries with an important Iron Age component are those at Baldock (Burleigh and Fitzpatrick-Matthews 2010) and King Harry Lane (Stead and Rigby 1989), as well as the mirror burial from Great Humphreys, Aston (Rook *et al.* 1982; Rook and Lockyear, this volume).

Hill (2007) brings these various strands together to offer an explanation of the changes during the late Iron Age that involves the migration of people into the area who then adopt new lifestyles in order to differentiate themselves from neighbouring groups.

The transition from Iron Age to Roman in the county is now seen as less dramatic than previously. The important burial at Folly Lane, for example, is dated to a few years *after* the Roman invasion (Niblett 1999). Papers in this volume by both Thompson and West address this crucial issue.

The main Roman settlement in the county is the city of Verulamium, which is an extremely important site for a number of reasons. Firstly, it is the largest Roman town in Britain which does not have a modern city built upon it. Major excavation campaigns at the site in the 1930s by Kenyon (1935) and the Wheelers (1936), and then in the late 1950s and 1960s by Sheppard Frere (1972, 1983, 1984), resulted in the sequence for the town becoming the model for the development of urbanism in the province. Frere's (1972: 10–12) suggestion that the early building in Insula XIV was constructed by the Roman military was part of a widespread belief in the role of the Roman state in the creation of towns in the province, a belief which was challenged by Millett (1990) and is decidedly out of favour now. Indeed, there really is no evidence for Roman military involvement in Verulamium and it is more common now to regard the Roman town as a development of the late Iron Age settlement (West, this volume).

For the later Roman period, Wheeler's description of the town as bearing 'some resemblance to a bombarded city' (Wheeler and Wheeler 1936: 28) led to a general belief in the dramatic decline in urbanism in the later province, whereas Frere's (1983: 193–228) discovery of a late sequence in his excavations led to a reassessment and a widespread attempt to identify fifth-century features in the towns of the province. Reece (1980) believed that by the fourth century towns had turned into administrative villages and that the evidence from Verulamium was the exception that proves the rule. Recently, Neal (2003) has challenged Frere's dating, although this is not universally accepted (Frere and Witts 2011). The emphasis on preservation *in situ* in recent years has resulted in most of the more recent work either being of a smaller scale (e.g., Niblett *et al.* 2006) or of a rescue nature (see West, this volume). Magnetometry, resistance and ground penetrating radar (GPR) surveys of Verulamium Park by members of the Community Archaeology Geophysics Group have contributed significantly to our knowledge of the plan of the city.[8] For both the Iron Age *oppidum* and the Roman town, the invaluable volume by Niblett and Thompson (2005) is a major resource.

There are a number of Roman 'small towns' in the county. Some are inferred from other evidence, such as Welwyn, where we know very little of the actual town but the density of cemetery evidence clearly indicates the existence of a settlement (Rook 1968a; 1973; Rook *et al.* 1984). Perhaps the best known of these are Baldock, in the north of the county (see Burleigh, this volume, and references therein), and Braughing (Partridge 1977; 1980–82; Potter and Trow 1988). The GlaxoSmithKline factory site at Ware overlies a Roman small town (O'Brien and Roberts 2004–5) and a major project by KDK Archaeology is underway to write up the results of numerous unpublished excavations at the site.

A number of Roman villas have been excavated in Hertfordshire, including Lockleys (Ward-Perkins 1938), Park Street (O'Neil 1945; Saunders 1961), Latimer (Branigan 1971), Dicket Mead (Rook 1983–6), Gadebridge Park (Neal 1974), Northchurch and Boxmoor (Neal 1974–6), Gorhambury (Neal *et al.* 1990) and, most recently, Turners Hall Farm (West, this volume). Although the Lockleys and Park Street excavations are often used as examples of continuity of occupation from the late Iron Age into the Roman period (e.g., Jones and Mattingly 1990 [2002]: map 7:7), they are actually rather inconclusive and atypical for the area. Gorhambury, however, is a valuable example as not only were the main villa buildings excavated but also a significant area around them that included enclosures and subsidiary buildings. As Rook (1997b) notes, the classic 'roundhouse to villa' sequence is generally not found in Hertfordshire; for example, Skeleton Green has rectangular buildings in the late Iron Age. Gorhambury is the exception that proves the rule in having a pre-invasion roundhouse, but, curiously, more round structures are built well into the Roman period. The slow diffusion of the Roman conquest is discussed by both Thompson and West (this volume).

Non-villa rural sites must have outnumbered villas by a considerable degree, but fewer have been published; examples include the site at Boxfield Farm (Going and Hunn 1999) and Leavesden Aerodrome (Brossler *et al.* 2009). This is partly because each *individual* rural settlement often has very little of note, and as a result many have only a grey literature report. The ongoing Roman Rural Settlement Project, however, is one of the most exciting developments in recent years.[9] By collating the evidence from thousands of grey literature reports across the country the Project is able to see patterns in the data that would not be visible otherwise. The final report is likely to be a huge advance in our understanding.

Applied numismatics, the study of coin use and coin-loss, features in the current volume in papers by Moorhead and Wythe that build on the work of Richard Reece, who has worked on coins from Cow Roast (1980–82), Dicket Mead (1983–86), Verulamium (1984) and other sites in the county (1991).

1.2.3 Early medieval

The transition from late Roman Britain to early Anglo-Saxon England is a period which is still controversial and not well understood (see Gerrard 2013 for a recent study). The problems that beset our general understanding are multiplied in Hertfordshire owing to the lack of evidence. This lack is so marked that Wheeler (1935) proposed that there was a 'sub-Roman triangle' from which Saxon settlers were excluded, an idea developed further by Rutherford Davis (1982). Wingfield (1995) gives a review of the evidence for the early period, and Baker (2006) examines both the archaeological and place-name evidence in detail. Early sites include the Saxon phase at Foxholes Farm (Partridge 1989) and at Old Parkbury (Niblett 2001), the Saxon phase of the cemetery at King Harry Lane (Agar 1989) and at Broadwater, Stevenage (HHER 455), which was excavated by Irene Traill in the early 1960s assisted by members of WAS (Rook and Lockyear, this volume). The recent discoveries at Watton-at-Stone are an important addition (Boyer *et al.*, this volume).

From the mid-Saxon period onwards the quantity of evidence, both archaeological and historical, improves greatly. Williamson's *The Origins of Hertfordshire* (2000, 2010) is the key work for this period. The recent *Landscapes of Governance* project combines evidence from place-names and landscape archaeology to reconstruct the administrative system of this period, and Baker (this volume) provides an excellent case study from Hertfordshire. Sadly, little remains of the Anglo-Saxon churches of Hertfordshire (Smith 1973) as they have been largely destroyed by later rebuilding. Many of the county's parish churches, such as the probable minster churches at Wheathampstead (Plate 1.2; Saunders and Havercroft 1980–82) and Welwyn (Rook and Rook 1996), must, however, have Anglo-Saxon origins, as shown, in both cases, by burial evidence. The abbey at St Albans certainly had an Anglo-Saxon predecessor (Biddle and Kjølbye-Biddle 2001).

1.2.4 Medieval and later

The evidence for this period, both historical and archaeological, is far too large a topic for a short summary such as this and the following selection is necessarily very incomplete. It is also in this period that a truly interdisciplinary approach is needed. Archaeology, by the very nature of its evidence, is a *local* study, even if the evidence generated is then used for more wide-ranging research. Some of the most fruitful studies are those which combine the best of archaeology with the best of local history.

The study of the landscape was pioneered in Hertfordshire by Munby (1977), building on the work of W.G. Hoskins (1955). Rowe and Williamson (2013) have brilliantly developed this theme and their papers in this volume continue this study. Renn (1971) gave us an overview of the castles in the county, and Rutherford Davis (1973) and Thompson (2011b) examined deserted settlements. Of these, Caldecote, in the north of the county, was extensively excavated in the 1970s and has recently been published (Beresford 2009). Parks were also a major part of the Hertfordshire landscape, as shown by their prominence on early maps. Rowe (2009) has dealt with early parks, and Prince (2008) with those from post-1500. The houses of the county were subject to an extensive study by J.T. Smith (1992, 1993) and the development of many of the older towns is addressed by papers in the volume edited by Slater and Goose (2008). Branch Johnson's (1970) volume on industrial archaeology has been updated with a booklet by Smith and Carr (2004). The newer towns, especially the Garden Cities of Letchworth and Welwyn Garden City, have also been the subject of study (Busby 1976; Filler 1986; Miller 1989; Rook 2001).

1.3 Conclusion

In this chapter I have attempted to provide an archaeological and institutional context for the papers that follow. I realise that others might choose different themes, or different publications to highlight, and that the selection here is far from complete or representative. I hope, however, that readers will find my comments and select bibliography a helpful introduction to the archaeology of the county.

1.4 References

Agar, B.M. (1989), 'The Anglo-Saxon cemetery', in Stead and Rigby (1989), pp. 219–39.

Agar, N.E. (2005), *Behind the Plough: agrarian society in nineteenth-century Hertfordshire* (Hatfield).

Baker, J.T. (2006), *Cultural Transition in the Chilterns and Essex Region, 350 AD to 650 AD* (Hatfield).

Barrett, J. (1980), 'The pottery of the Late Bronze Age in Lowland England', *Proceedings of the Prehistoric Society* 46, pp. 297–320.

Beresford, G. (2009), *Caldecote: The Development and Desertion of a Hertfordshire Village* (Leeds).

Biddle, H. and Kjølbye-Biddle, B. (2001), 'The origins of St Albans Abbey: Romano-British cemetery and Anglo-Saxon monastery', in M. Henig and P. Lindley (eds), *Alban and St Albans: Roman and Medieval Architecture, Art and Archaeology*, British Archaeological Association Conference Transactions 24 (Leeds), pp. 45–75.

Branch Johnson, W. (1970), *Industrial Archaeology of Hertfordshire* (Newton Abbot).

Branigan, K. (1971), *Latimer: Belgic, Roman, Dark Age and Early Modern farm* (Bristol).

Brossler, A., Laws, G. and Welsh, K. (2009), 'An Iron Age and Roman Site at Leavesden Aerodrome, Abbots Langley', *Hertfordshire Archaeology and History* 16, pp. 27–56.

Bryant, S.R. (2007), 'Central places or special places? The origins and development of "oppida" in Hertfordshire', in Haselgrove and Moore (2007), pp. 62–80.

Bryant, S.R. and Niblett, R. (1997), 'The late Iron Age in Hertfordshire and the Chilterns', in A. Gwilt and C.C. Haselgrove, *Reconstructing Iron Age Societies* (Oxford), pp. 270–81.

Burleigh, G.R. (1995), 'A late Iron Age *oppidum* at Baldock, Hertfordshire', in Holgate (1995), pp. 103-12.

Burleigh, G.R. and Fitzpatrick-Matthews, K.J. (2010), *Excavations at Baldock, Hertfordshire, 1978-1994. Volume 1: An Iron Age and Romano-British Cemetery at Wallington Road*, North Hertfordshire Museums Archaeology Monograph 1 (Letchworth Garden City).

Busby, R.J. (1976), *The Book of Welwyn* (Chesham).

Catt, J., Perry, B., Thompson, I. and Bryant, S. (2010), 'Prehistoric archaeology and human occupation of Hertfordshire', in Catt (ed.)(2010), *Hertfordshire Geology and Landscape* (Welwyn Garden City), pp. 226–55.

Davies, A.G, Gibson, A.V.B and Ashdown, R.R. (1980–82), 'A Mesolithic Site at Stanstead Abbots, Hertfordshire', *Hertfordshire Archaeology* 8, pp. 1–10.
Ellis, P. (ed.) (2001), *Roman Wiltshire and After* (Devizes).
Filler, R. (1986), *Welwyn Garden City* (Chichester).
Frere, S.S. (1972), *Verulamium Excavations*, vol. 1 (London).
Frere, S.S. (1983), *Verulamium Excavations*, vol. 2 (London).
Frere, S.S. (1984), *Verulamium Excavations*, vol. 3 (Oxford).
Frere, S.S and Witts, P. (2011), 'The Saga of Verulamium Building XXVII 2', *Britannia* 42, pp. 212–26.
Gerrard, J. (2013), *The Ruin of Roman Britain: An Archaeological Perspective* (Cambridge).
Going, C.J. and Hunn, J.R. (1999), *Excavations at Boxfield Farm, Chells, Stevenage, Hertfordshire*, Hertfordshire Archaeological Trust Report No. 2 (Hertford).
Gróf, L. (1988), *Children of Straw. The story of a vanished craft and industry in Bucks, Herts, Beds and Essex* (Buckingham).
Haselgrove, C.C. and Moore, T. (eds) (2007), *The late Iron Age in Britain and Beyond* (Oxford).
Hertfordshire Publications (1990), *Garden Cities and New Towns. Five lectures* (Hertford).
Hill, J.D. (2007), 'The dynamics of social change in Later Iron Age eastern and south-eastern England *c.*300 BC–AD 43', in Haselgrove and Moore (2007), pp. 16–40.
Holgate, R. (ed.) (1995), *Chiltern Archaeology: Recent Work. A handbook for the next decade* (Dunstable).
Hoskins, W.G. (1955), *The Making of the English Landscape* (London).
Hunn, J.R. (1996), *Settlement Patterns in Hertfordshire: a review of the typology and function of enclosures in the Iron Age and Roman landscape*, British Archaeological Reports British Series 249 (Oxford).
Hunn, J.R. (2009), 'Excavation on the First-Century Enclosure at Stanborough School, Welwyn Garden City', *Hertfordshire Archaeology and History* 16, pp. 5–26.
Hussen, C.-M. (1983), *A Rich Late La Tene Burial at Hertford Heath, Hertfordshire* (London).
Ingle, C. and Saunders, H. (2011), *Aerial Archaeology in Essex: the role of the National Mapping Programme in interpreting the landscape,* East Anglian Archaeology 136 (Chelmsford).
Jenkins, S. (1999), *England's Thousand Best Churches* (London).
Jones, B. and Mattingly, D. (1990 [2002]), *An Atlas of Roman Britain*, (Oxford).
Kenyon, K. (1935), 'The Roman theatre at Verulamium, St Albans', *Archaeologia,* second series 84, pp. 213–61.
Lee, J.W.C. (1977), 'Mesolithic and Neolithic sites at Cuffley, Herts', *Hertfordshire Archaeology* 5, pp. 1–12.
Lee, J.W.C. (1983–86), 'A Mesolithic site at Thorntons Farm, Cuffley', *Hertfordshire Archaeology* 9, pp. 1–7.
Lockyear, K. (1987), 'A survey of the antiquities of Great Humphreys and their relation to other sites in Hertfordshire.' BA dissertation (University of Durham).
Mee, A. ([1939] 1991), *Hertfordshire: London's Country Neighbour* (Otley).
Miller, M. (1989), *Letchworth. The First Garden City* (Chichester).
Millett, M.J. (1990), *The Romanization of Britain* (Cambridge).
Moody, B. (1995), *The Light of Other Days. A Short History of the St Albans and Hertfordshire Architectural and Archaeological Society 1845 to 1995* (St Albans).

Morris, M. and Wainright, A. (1995), 'Iron Age and Romano-British settlement, agriculture and industry in the upper Bulbourne valley, Hertfordshire: an interim interpretation', in Holgate (1995), pp. 68–75.

Mullin, D. and Devaney, R. (2012), 'Flint', in D. Stansbie, P. Booth, A. Simmonds, V. Diez and S. Griffiths, *From Mesolithic to Motorway. The Archaeology of the M1 (Junction 6a–10) Widening Scheme, Hertfordshire* (Oxford), pp. 91–8.

Munby, L.M. (1977), *The Hertfordshire Landscape* (London).

Neal, D.S. (1974), *The Excavation of a Roman Villa in Gadebridge Park, Hemel Hempstead, 1963–8* (London).

Neal, D.S. (1974–6), 'Northchurch, Boxmoor, and Hemel Hempstead Station: The excavation of three Roman buildings in the Bulbourne valley', *Hertfordshire Archaeology* 4, pp. 1–135.

Neal, D.S. (2003), 'Building 2, Insula XXVII from Verulamium: A reinterpretation of the evidence', in P. Wilson (ed.), *The Archaeology of Roman Towns* (Oxford), pp. 193–202.

Neal, D.S., Wardle, A. and Hunn, J. (1990), *Excavation of an Iron Age, Roman, and Medieval Settlement at Gorhambury, St Albans*, English Heritage Archaeological Report 14 (London).

Niblett, R. (1999), *The Excavation of a Ceremonial Site at Folly Lane, St Albans* (London).

Niblett, R. (2001), 'A Neolithic dugout from a multi-period site near St Albans, Herts, England', *The International Journal of Nautical Archaeology* 30/2, pp. 155–95.

Niblett, R., Manning, W. and Saunders, C. (2006), 'Verulamium: Excavations within the Roman Town 1986–88', *Britannia* 37, pp. 53–188.

Niblett, R. and Thompson, I. (2005), *Alban's Buried Towns. An assessment of St Albans' archaeology up to AD 1600* (Oxford).

O'Brien, L. and Roberts, B. (2004–5), 'Excavations on Roman Ermine Street at the New Restaurant Facility, GlaxoSmithKline, Ware', *Hertfordshire Archaeology* 14, pp. 3–39.

O'Neil, H.E. (1945), 'The Roman villa at Park Street, near St Albans, Hertfordshire', *Archaeological Journal* 102, pp. 21–110.

Page, W. (ed.) (1902), *VCH Hertford*, vol. 1 (London).

Page, W. (ed.) (1908), *VCH Hertford*, vol. 2 (London).

Page, W. (ed.) (1912), *VCH Hertford*, vol. 3 (London).

Page, W. (ed.) (1914), *VCH Hertford*, vol. 4 (London).

Palmer, R. (1976), 'Interrupted ditch enclosures in Britain: the use of aerial photography for comparative studies', *Proceedings of the Prehistoric Society* 42, pp. 161–86.

Partridge, C.R. (1977), 'Excavations and Fieldwork at Braughing 1968–73', *Hertfordshire Archaeology* 5, pp. 22–108.

Partridge, C.R. (1980–82), 'Braughing, Wickham Kennels 1982', *Hertfordshire Archaeology* 8, pp. 40–59.

Partridge, C.R. (1981), *Skeleton Green. A late Iron Age and Romano-British site*, Britannia Monographs 2 (London).

Partridge, C.R. (1989), *Foxholes Farm. A multi-period gravel site* (Hertford).

Perman, D. (1989), 'The birth of a society' in D. Perman (ed.) *A Century of Archaeology in East Herts* (Ware), pp.9–12.

Phillips, M. (ed.) (2009), *Four millennia of activity along the A505 Baldock Bypass, Hertfordshire*, East Anglian Archaeology 128 (Bedford).

Potter, T.W and Trow, S.D. (1988), 'Puckeridge-Braughing, Herts.: The Ermine Street Excavations, 1971–1972', *Hertfordshire Archaeology* 10.

Prince, H. (2008), *Parks in Hertfordshire since 1500* (Hatfield).

RCHME (Royal Commission for the Historical Monuments of England) (1910), *An Inventory of the Historical Monuments in Hertfordshire* (London).

RCHME (1992 [2011]), *Crop Marks in Hertfordshire. A report for the National Mapping Programme*, PDF version 2011 available from <https://www.english-heritage.org.uk/professional/research/landscapes-and-areas/national-mapping-programme/hertfordshire-nmp/>, accessed 18 August 2014.

Reece, R. (1980), 'Town and country: the end of Roman Britain', *World Archaeology* 12/1, pp. 77–92.

Reece, R. (1980–82), 'The coins from Cow Roast, Herts. – a commentary', *Hertfordshire Archaeology* 8, pp. 60–66.

Reece, R. (1983–86), 'The coins', in Rook (1983–86), pp. 143–5.

Reece, R. (1984), 'The coins', in Frere (1984), pp. 3–17.

Reece, R. (1991), *Roman coins from 140 sites in Britain*, Cotswold Studies IV, provisional edition (Cirencester).

Renn, D.F. (1971), *Medieval Castle in Hertfordshire* (Chichester).

Rook, K.L. and Rook, T. (1996), *St Mary's Church, Welwyn. A History and Guide* (Welwyn).

Rook, T. (1968a), 'The Romano-British cemetery at Welwyn. Obiit 1967', *Hertfordshire Past and Present* 8, pp. 32–7.

Rook, T. (1968b), 'A note on the "rediscovery" of a Belgic chieftain burial', *Hertfordshire Past and Present* 8, pp. 17–18.

Rook, T. (1971), 'Ayot St Lawrence', *Hertfordshire Archaeological Review* 4, pp. 77–8.

Rook, T. (1973), 'Excavations at the Grange Romano-British Cemetery, Welwyn, 1967', *Hertfordshire Archaeology* 3, 1–30.

Rook, T. (1983-6), 'The Roman Villa Site at Dicket Mead, Lockleys, Welwyn', *Hertfordshire Archaeology* 9, pp. 79–175.

Rook, T. (1997a), *A History of Hertfordshire*, 2nd edn (Chichester).

Rook, T. (1997b), 'The view from Hertfordshire', in R.M. Friendship-Taylor and D.E. Friendship-Taylor (eds), *From Round House to Villa* (Northampton), pp. 53–7.

Rook, T. (2001), *Welwyn Garden City Past* (Chichester)

Rook, T. (2002), *The Story of Welwyn Roman Baths* (Welwyn).

Rook, T., Lowery, P.R., Savage, R.D.A. and R.L. Wilkins (1982), 'An Iron Age Bronze Mirror from Aston, Hertfordshire', *Antiquaries Journal* 62, pp. 18–34.

Rook, T., Walker, S. and Denston, C.B. (1984), 'A Roman Mausoleum and Associated Marble Sarcophagus and Burials from Welwyn, Hertfordshire', *Britannia* 15, pp. 143–62.

Rowe, A. (ed.) (2007), *Hertfordshire Garden History. A miscellany* (Hatfield).

Rowe, A. (2009), *Medieval Parks of Hertfordshire* (Hatfield).

Rowe, A. and Williamson, T. (2013), *Hertfordshire: A Landscape History* (Hatfield).

Rutherford Davis, K. (1973), *The Deserted Medieval Villages of Hertfordshire* (Chichester).

Rutherford Davis, K. (1982), *Britons and Saxons: The Chiltern Region 400–700* (Chichester).

Saunders, C. (1961), 'Excavations at Park Street 1954–57', *The Archaeological Journal* 118, pp. 100–135.

Saunders, C. and Havercroft, A.B. (1980–82), 'Excavations on the line of the Wheathampstead By-Pass 1974 and 1977', *Hertfordshire Archaeology* 8, pp. 11–39

Short, D. (ed.) (2011), *An Historical Atlas of Hertfordshire* (Hatfield).

Simmonds, A. (2012), 'Junction 9', in D. Stansbie, P. Booth, A. Simmonds, V. Diez and S. Griffiths, *From Mesolithic to Motorway. The Archaeology of the M1 (Junction 6a–10) Widening Scheme, Hertfordshire* (Oxford), pp. 63–83.

Slater, T. and Goose, N. (eds) (2008), *A County of Small Towns. The development of Hertfordshire's urban landscape to 1800* (Hatfield).

Smith, J.T. (1992), *English Houses 1200–1800: The Hertfordshire Evidence* (London).
Smith, J.T. (1993), *Hertfordshire Houses: Selective Inventory* (London).
Smith, R. (1912), 'On late Celtic antiquities discovered at Welwyn, Herts.', *Archaeologia*, second series 63, pp. 1–30.
Smith, T.P. (1973), *The Anglo-Saxon Churches of Hertfordshire* (Chichester).
Smith, T. and Carr, B. (2004), *A Guide to the Industrial Archaeology of Hertfordshire and the Lea Valley* (Leicester).
Spring, D. (ed.) (2012), *Hertfordshire Garden History vol. II: Gardens pleasant, groves delicious* (Hatfield).
Stead, I.M. (1967), 'A La Tène III Burial at Welwyn Garden City', *Archaeologia*, second series 101, pp. 1–62.
Stead, I.M. and Rigby, V. (1986), *Baldock: The Excavation of a Roman and Pre-Roman Settlement, 1968–72*, Britannia Monograph Series 7 (London).
Stead, I.M. and Rigby, V. (1989), *Verulamium: The King Harry Lane Site*, English Heritage Archaeological Report 12 (London).
Thompson, I. (2011a), 'Roman Roads', in Short (2011), pp. 36–7.
Thompson, I. (2011b), 'Abandoned Settlements', in Short (2011), pp. 152–3.
Turner-Rugg, A. (2006–8), 'The chipped stone', in West (2006–8), pp. 15–19.
Ward-Perkins, J.B. (1938), 'The Roman Villa at Lockleys, Welwyn', *Antiquaries Journal* 18, pp. 340–76.
West, S. (2004–5), 'A Mesolithic and later prehistoric site in Redbourn, *Hertfordshire Archaeology and History* 14, pp. 1–2.
West, S. (2006–8), 'A multi-period landscape at Aldwickbury Golf Course, near Harpenden', *Hertfordshire Archaeology and History* 15, pp. 5–20.
Wheeler, R.E.M. (1935), *London and the Saxons* (London).
Wheeler, R.E.M. and Wheeler, T.V. (1936), *Verulamium. A Belgic and two Roman Cities*, Research Reports of the Society of Antiquaries of London 11 (Oxford).
Whitaker, A. (2006), *Brewers in Hertfordshire. A historical gazetteer* (Hatfield).
Williamson, T. (2000), *The Origins of Hertfordshire* (Manchester and New York).
Williamson, T. (2010) *The Origins of Hertfordshire*, 2nd edn (Hatfield).
Wingfield, C. (1995), 'The Anglo-Saxon settlement of Bedfordshire and Hertfordshire: the archaeological view', in Holgate (1995), pp. 31–43.

Notes

1 Minutes of the HAS dated 17 January 1969, Bernard Barr archive, Harlow Museum.
2 Some volumes are available online: < http://www.british-history.ac.uk/catalogue.aspx?type=1&gid=16>, accessed 26 August 2014.
3 < http://www.british-history.ac.uk/source.aspx?pubid=1304>, accessed 26 August 2014.
4 <http://www.heritagegateway.org.uk/>
5 <finds.org.uk>
6 <http://archaeologydataservice.ac.uk/archives/view/greylit/index.cfm>
7 e.g., the 'Sensing the Iron Age and Roman Past' project: <http://hertsgeosurvey.wordpress.com/>
8 <http://hertsgeosurvey.wordpress.com/>
9 <http://www.reading.ac.uk/archaeology/research/roman-rural-settlement/>, accessed 24 August 2014.

CHAPTER 2

The Welwyn Archaeological Society 1960–1998: a personal history

Merle Rook[†] *and Kris Lockyear*

2.1 Introduction

Archaeologists have long been interested in the history of their own subject. Glyn Daniel's *One Hundred and Fifty Years of Archaeology* (1976) is a classic of the genre and, more recently, volumes discussing *Great Excavations* (Schofield 2011) and *Great Archaeologists* (Bahn 2008) have been published. Biographies and autobiographies are not uncommon, e.g., Sir Mortimer Wheeler's memoir *Still Digging* (1955) and Jacquetta Hawkes' biography of him, *Adventurer in Archaeology* (1982). Organisations also have their celebratory histories; for example, *Building on the Past* (Vyner 1994) was published to celebrate 150 years of the Royal Archaeological Institute and *Visions of Antiquity* (Pearce 2007) marked 300 years of the Society of Antiquaries of London. Smaller societies, such as the East Herts Archaeological Society (Perman 1998) or the St Albans and Hertfordshire Architectural and Archaeological Society (Moody 1995), have also published histories. More recently, oral history has become an extremely popular method of research (e.g., Perks and Thomson 1998) and this, combined with the continued growth of the Internet as a means of publication, has led to the development of the *Personal Histories Project* (Smith 2011).

In parallel with this has been an increasing interest in putting the people back into archaeology (S. Hamilton, pers. comm.). Nineteenth-century reports were often personal and diary-like, whereas the sterilised, emotion-free reports that developed as part of the systemisation of excavation recording in the 1960s and 1970s lack any of the wonder or excitement of discovery. Both the

Leskernick Project (Bender *et al.* 1997) and Boxgrove (Pitts and Roberts 1998) have tried to redress the balance, and Everill (2008) has examined the life and work of commercial field staff.

Merle Rook and I originally discussed writing a history of the Welwyn Archaeological Society (WAS) back in 2009, when I took over the directorship of the Society from her husband, Tony Rook. One problem we faced is that the Society has never kept a log of its activities, although there is an archive of newspaper cuttings as well as reports, finds and photographs. The only continuous history was contained within Merle's personal diaries (Plate 2.1). Merle spent many hours copying copious relevant extracts from her journals for the history, a project she was working on when she passed away in 2012. The result is a stack of notebooks 9 inches high!

'The history' of the Society is still a work-in-progress, but Merle's abstracts inspired the telling of a more personal 'history'. In reality, it is three personal histories: principally Merle's, which is inevitably entwined with Tony's, but also at times mine. I joined the Society in December 1975 at the age of 11 and first appear in the diary, when I excavated at Chapel Wood on 25 April 1976, as 'another boy …'

As pleasurable as trips down memory lane are, this paper has a deeper purpose. Small archaeological societies such as WAS are not uncommon. Many of them started in the early 1960s; for example, the Chess Valley Archaeological and Historical Society and the North Herts Archaeological Society, as well as WAS, were started in 1960. Selkirk (2014) sees the 1960s and 1970s as 'the golden age of archaeology' because of this rise of local societies. He bemoans, however, the fact that many have become 'lectures-and-outings societies'. Hertfordshire was particularly rich in active local societies in the 1960s and 1970s, to the extent that the annual conference of the now defunct Hertfordshire Archaeological Council managed to fill a whole day with reports on fieldwork projects. Some of those societies, such as the Hatfield and District Archaeological Society, no longer exist. What, then, makes a local group like WAS prosper? What are the ingredients for a successful 'community heritage group', to use the current jargon? What lessons can we learn from the history of a small group?

In the remainder of this paper I will examine a number of themes through the entries in Merle's notebooks with the aim of addressing these questions in the final section.

2.2 The origins of the Society

The Welwyn Archaeological Society, known originally as the Lockleys Archaeological Society, was less founded than came into being. As a result, placing a date on its creation is difficult. The date most often used is 1960, the year in which Tony and Merle Rook moved to Hertfordshire, although other dates are possible, such as 1964 (when the Society became affiliated with the Council for British Archaeology [CBA]) or 1965 (when it finally gained a constitution in order to open a bank account so that a reward cheque could be cashed [Rook, 1971]). At first – archaeologically at least – life was quiet.

> **9 May 1960:** Cycled to Chequers site to look for Roman pottery. Nothing special.
> **14 May 1960:** Looked at earthworks at Digswell. Nothing.

At this time, however, Merle and Tony began building contacts with others involved in the archaeology of the county.

> **28 May 1960:** St Albans again. 2.30 lecture by Dr Ilid Antony on Pre-Roman and Roman Countryside in Hertfordshire. She introduced us to Branch Johnson who invited us to visit him the next evening.

Ilid Antony was at that time the Curator of Verulamium Museum and Director of Excavations for SAHAAS, although she later moved to South Wales to take up a post there. W. Branch Johnson was a notable scholar and author of several books on the county, including *The Industrial Archaeology of Hertfordshire* (1970).

The Rooks continued to explore, keeping an eye on construction at the new Welwyn bypass:

> **16 July 1960:** To new by-pass to look for 'bits.' No luck.

Then finds started to turn up:

> **26 July 1960:** Tony found remains of Roman hypocaust [corn drier].
> **30 July 1960:** Tony to the by-pass at 10.0. A number of diggers turned up to help.
> **31 July 1960:** Off again to by-pass at 10.0. A few pieces of pottery.
> **1 August 1960:** Dig again. Tony and Peter MacT[aggart] made a plan, watched by Branch. Spent the evening washing pottery.

The finds were sufficient to warrant an article in the local paper – the *Welwyn Times and Hatfield Herald* – on 5 August 1960 entitled 'Roman villa?' (reproduced in Rook 2002: 23) and a fuller article in the *Herts Advertiser and St Albans Times* on 12 August. The site was published as part of the report on the bath house (Rook 1983–6: 105–6). More importantly, it drew attention to the archaeology of the area and a group of volunteer diggers began to form. The key find came later in the year:

> **30 October 1960:** Dressed in boots and anoraks, up to lab for wood which Tony sawed and then down to the Mimram where he paddled. He found more pieces of tile on the further bank so I crossed the bridge to help dig out some pieces of pottery, watched by a little girl. In the evening, after washing, drying and gluing Tony produced a quarter of a large dimpled pot.

These were the first finds from what is now known as the Dicket Mead Roman villa (Rook 1983-6). April of the following year saw excavations in 'the policeman's garden', but in June permission was granted to excavate trial trenches at Lockleys/Dicket Mead:[1]

> **10 June 1961:** … Also called on Mr Godsmark at Lockleys and got permission to dig a hole.
> **15 June 1961:** Tony stayed out late digging at Lockleys, Grids 1 and 3.
> **21 June 1961:** Tony brought home a bone pin and a large heavy coin with Britannia on it – profile of a bearded emperor facing right.
> **28 June 1961:** There are ten grids – I, III, V, VB, VI, VII. VIII, IX and X. Large flints and tiles wedged together, particularly in VB and only 3 coins so far and sherds of pottery. 'Rather a puzzle.' Helped with barrow for a bit. Peter took photo of VB. Looks like a path.
> **1 July 1961:** Collected 'Archaeology from the Earth' from the library. Spent about 5 hours on the dig. Peter watched Tony paddling. Keith Hornett traced Tony and the barrow and did some digging. John Lee looked in briefly in the evening. Then we visited Branch and met Reg Reed and a boy called Adrian and had drinks at the White Horse (noisy and raucous, records and singing). Pleasant to sit out on the grass in the late evening.

For the remainder of 1961 the team concentrated their efforts on Dicket Mead. Meanwhile, Tony continued to keep an eye on the development in Welwyn Garden City.

> **18 February 1962:** Tony and Peter to new housing estate and returned with bag full of Belgic pottery.
> **4 March 1962:** Picked up some Belgic pottery near Blytheway. Tony gave a talk with several slides to follow at Lockleys. Dined with Head and wife. Tea later with some of staff. Icy roads and snow.

The 'new housing estate' site is now known as Crookhams (Rook 1968a) and was excavated on and off during 1962. In April 1962 the team returned to Dicket Mead, but they also helped out elsewhere, working, for example, with Miss Irene Traill in Stevenage during June and July.[2]

> **6 August 1962:** Exhibition in Lockleys. Painted 'Welwyn Archaeological Group' to put along the mantelpiece.

This is the first mention of a name for the informal group that had coalesced around Tony and Merle. What Merle fails to mention is that at this point she was more than eight months pregnant.

> **5 September 1962:** Wheeled pram (and baby) to Lockleys, had tea with Mrs Godsmark and looked at the exhibition. Tony, Keith and Andy at DM in evening.

During the winter of 1962/3 much work was undertaken on the assemblage of late Iron Age grog-tempered pottery from Crookhams. Site visits continued:

> **10 March 1963:** Tony cycled to Crookhams in the morning and entertained Mr Moodey [from the EHAS], a young coin collector and a woman from the Record Office.

Despite the long winter – it snowed again on 11 April – work at Dicket Mead resumed in the spring of 1963. Tony, who had been working as a building technologist, was offered the post of Science Master for Sherrardswood School on 7 May. By the end of the year his position in the school was beginning to be felt:

> **3 December 1963:** Tony went to Dicket Mead and four boys got permission to help him instead of doing cross-country.

In 1964, however, the pace of work at Crookhams stepped up, with site visits taking place regularly from mid-February through to the end of June 1964:

> **19 April 1964:** John Moss [–Eccardt], five helpers and Julian came to dig. It rained. Also Hertford enthusiast with three children called to see pots. We stuck some fine grey decorated ware together.
> **25 April 1964:** Tony cycled to join new digger at 11.0 and home at 3.30 to ask Graham for help in transporting pottery. All drove to Crookhams with Mary,

Christopher and Kate and Tony photographed his oven-kiln, a fine site, or sight!
18 May 1964: Crookhams – Tony, Julian, and Mr and Mrs Golesworthy. Julian drove us to look and Mrs G. had dug up a delightful little straining pot, whole apart from a broken base where the hole was. Tony bought it home to wash and Mrs G. took the rest.
29 May 1964: Sylvia born in the study.
21 June 1964: Jim and Barbara Golesworthy took Tony to Crookhams. Jim returned at 6.30 and took us all to see the flint-lined stokehole/furnace Tony found on the other side of the kiln. A perfect bronze brooch and some fine pieces of Samian turned up today. Barbara found the brooch. Tony was hoping to find the base of the Samian bowl. The grey flint-lined furnace was 4' x 4'. The brooch looks quite modern despite the greenish tinge. Tony delighted.
1 July 1964: No more digging at Crookhams unless the mechanical diggers turn up something when the sewers are dug.

At the completion of Crookhams, work resumed at Dicket Mead through the summer of 1964. One innovation was an attempt at some early geophysics:

24 August 1964: Tony made his proton-magnetometer, went out into the middle of the cricket pitch and got the Home Service broadcasting 'Lark in the Clear Air'.

In 1965 the first of the LAS/WAS winter lectures was held:

17 January 1965: Tony gave his first archaeological talk in the pavilion [of Sherrardswood School] – alternate Fridays. He had about 20 children, the Golesworthys and two of the Holder-Vales, John and Edwin. Made coffees.

The winter lecture season continues to this day and is still held on alternate Fridays, accompanied by tea and coffee.

In March, an exciting find came to light:

29 March 1965: Disturbing letter from Gordon Moodey … about a pottery find between Welwyn and Panshanger. It was accompanied by a sketch of an amphora … It was written by a man called Mr Robertson in Stevenage. He had seen the amphora in the garage of a Gas Board employee called Mr Day who'd dug it up while laying pipes in a new estate not far from WGC High School.
2 April 1965: In evening Jim called and he and Tony drove to Stevenage to meet Mr Robertson. He gave them coffee and directions to find Mr Day. They found

two amphorae in his garage which he wanted for his garden, to grow plants in – or he might sell it for £10. They returned puzzled at what to do.

3 April 1965: They decided to photograph the pot and other pieces and Tony rang Gordon Davis. 8.30am Jim phoned and … arranged to look at the site suggested in a rough map drawn by Mr Day … 10.30 Tony and the Golesworthys off to find the site. 11.0 Mr Cheer arrived to photograph our robin's nest in a kettle, stayed for coffee and talked about moles. He writes the nature page in the Welwyn Times. 11.30 T and G's returned from site with bits of pot picked up from edge of new road. All the trenches had been filled in. Refreshments. 3.0 Golesworthys and Gordon arrived simultaneously. All piled in Jim's car, leaving boys with me, and off to Mr Day who remembered 'other bits of pottery on the other side of the road.' They returned to the site. 5.0pm Party returned with more pottery and ⅔ of a silver cup, rather crumpled – the same period as the Welwyn burial ones c. AD 50. It has little decorative borders and weighs 6 oz. Also the bottom of an amphora. Tony contacted the police because of Treasure Trove and coroner's inquest and an inspector arrived during supper, took a statement and insisted that Tony should come out to the site. He phoned Gordon Moodey later in the evening. The silver bowl was taken by the Inspector.

This site is now known as the 'Welwyn Garden City Chieftain burial' (Stead 1967) and is on display in the British Museum. Over the next few days, phone calls and meetings were had with the Development Corporation, the British Museum and other interested parties, and a metal detector was borrowed to help locate finds. The Ministry of Works initially offered the Society a grant of £100 to excavate the site, but this plan soon fell through:

7 April 1965: Ilid called with a Mr Stead and they looked at the maps and went on to the site.

9 April 1965: After breakfast Tony rang Mr MacKay [from the Ministry of Public Buildings and Works] who was out. Ian Stead told him that the excavation was his and he was starting next Monday with 12 diggers. Tony rang Gordon and Ilid (who'd gone on holiday), asking him who was in charge. Gordon rang, after 20 minutes discussion with Stead, and Stead rang to arrange a meeting for tomorrow.

10 April 1965: At 2.0 Mr and Mrs Stead and a bearded lecturer from Leicester arrived. Provided tea and they left with Tony for the site.

12 April 1965: Tony cycled to Panshanger at 2.0 but no diggers till 3.0 when the huts arrived. He surveyed a new road and returned before a terrific storm. All the scale plans, site records and aerial photos and contour maps now taken by

> Stead, without any discussion. Mr Day refused to relinquish his amphorae or to say who worked with him. Now he's the Min. of Works problem.

The Ministry of Works excavation lasted from 12 to 23 April, when Ian Stead had to attend a rescue excavation in Prae Wood, St Albans. Luckily they had a 'fibreglass transparent cover':

> **19 April 1965:** Rain, hail, snow and strong winds. Gordon Moodey arranged to come in the afternoon so Tony was able to have a brief glimpse of part of the excavated grave at Panshanger. Several pots and a dish there.

Excluded from the burial site, the Society turned its attention to other projects. Later that year excavations continued at Dicket Mead, but also on a Roman well in the centre of Welwyn (Rook 1968b), and further work took place on Late Iron Age sites in Panshanger, Welwyn Garden City, during which:

> **13 August 1965:** Tony on front page of Welwyn Times after finding a safe in a chalk pit.

A further article appeared on 20 August which stated that 'A local man walking by a pit in a field near Hern's Lane, WGC, at the weekend found an opened safe and a number of cheques lying about … WGC police were called and safe and cheques were taken away in a Black Maria for examination.'

The importance of this event for the Society is that a reward was given for the find, and in order to cash the cheque the Society needed to open a bank account, which required a constitution (Rook 1971). The Society was, at last, formally born:

> **24 September 1965:** AGM of Lockleys Archaeological Society 8.0–9.45. A new lady from Tunbridge Wells, now in Ayot St Peter, v. enthusiastic. Provided coffee. 1½lb biscuits, 4 pints milk, 30 spoonfuls of coffee and about ¾ packet of Demerara sugar did nicely – milk diluted by half.

2.3 Fieldwork

Fieldwork, and especially rescue excavation, played a major role in the formation of the Society. Commercial archaeology has taken away the 'rescue' element, but fieldwork remains part of the life of the Society. I have decided to concentrate on just one site, known, from the field name, as Great Humphreys (HHER 6280,

6309, 6312, 6313, 9983). This site lies in the countryside between Datchworth and Watton-at-Stone, where the Society has worked since the early 1970s. Sites investigated in this area included a medieval chapel in Chapel Wood (HHER 1987), a Roman cremation cemetery in Lower Rivers Field (HHER 6590) and, most recently, the Broom Hall Farm site (HHER 12898; Lockyear, this volume). Interest in Great Humphreys began in 1979:

> **13 May 1979:** Met Mr and Mrs Wallace and Diana for coffee. He's found a crumpled Iron Age mirror, damaged by ploughing. S [Tony] had a look at the site …
> **14 May 1979:** Tony to the British Museum with Mr Wallace's mirror. It's thought to be worth as much as £4000. He did some phoning in the evening as Mrs W thought the land it was found on belonged to Mr Clark but it in fact belongs to Mr Jeffries.
> **16 May 1979:** Tony cycled to see Mr Jeffries to persuade him to give the mirror to the BM [British Museum]. He had a flat tyre so had to be driven back! Mr J. said he would.

Although at this stage sadly missing its handle, the Aston Mirror is one of a small number of Iron Age bronze mirrors known and a significant find (HHER 6313; Rook *et al.* 1982). Nothing much could happen at the site until later in the year when the crop came off, at which point the search for the handle could begin in earnest.

> **30 August 1979:** Kate struggled with her history essay but left it at last to come out for a walk round THE field. Tony was pleased to meet Mr Clark the farmer by chance.
> **3 September 1979:** Tony phoned Ian Stead and arranged to go to Ashwell to collect the magnetometer so after lunch we went. 40 miles including delivery to the farm.
> **6 September 1979:** Tony and Richard [Balley] tired after all the cycling to Datchworth. They found some big horseshoes today.

Eventually surface finds of Roman pottery at the highest point in the field led to some test trenches being excavated (HHER 6309).

> **23 September 1979:** Kris rang at 10.0 to ask for a lift so left Sylvia behind when we set off for Datchworth. Returned for them at 4.20. It was drizzling. It took ages for them to pack up. Richard located [with the metal detector] and Kate

found two coins. Tony used the metal detector to find two lovely sheep bells – crotals (or maybe harness bells?).
30 September 1979: Did BH [bath house] duty … Left Sylvia to lock up and rushed back to collect Tony, Kate, Richard and Kris Lockyear from Datchworth plus surveying equipment and bucketful of pottery.

Excavation continued every Sunday for the next few weeks.

16 October 1979: Because there's to be a rail strike tomorrow, Tony arranged to meet Ashwell train at Welwyn North about 5.40, deliver the magnetometer to Ian Stead and receive two copies of the Iron Age mirror [made by the British Museum for the finders]. The copy is really splendid. Wish we had one.
21 October 1979: The ditch at Great Humphreys is down over 10 feet now. Tony brought home some hefty Iron Age pottery from it.

The trenches were put to bed for the winter and Sundays were taken up with winter walks. In the spring of 1980 the digging season opened with an opportunity to section part of the ditch in Well Wood.

9 March 1980: Kris played with his school band [in church] and came home for lunch – corned beef sandwiches. Diggers off after lunch. Collected them at 5.0. Kris caught his bus about 6.0 carrying the great silver tuba and a crash helmet!

At the end of April work resumed at Great Humphreys. The original 1m-wide test trenches were extended to enable a good-sized portion of the ditch to be excavated.

4 May 1980: Very windy at the dig. Chilly, too. Went late and didn't stay long. They're sieving the soil for a change.
11 May 1980: Took Tony, Kris and Richard to Datchworth. They were sitting in the sun in our garden. Mike found a bronze cockerel, beautifully modelled. John and Tony photographed it and Richard took it home. All came back for tea. Kris and Sylvia did four minutes recording for the Newspaper for the Blind.

The cockerel was published (Rook and Henig 1981) and is now in the British Museum. The excavation continued, mostly on Sundays, through the spring and summer (Plate 2.2). Once the crop was harvested the search for the missing mirror handle continued using a metal detector.

19 September 1980: Tony off with Jack Parker again and returned triumphant with the handle of the Iron Age mirror! Richard and Kris came to wash pottery. Richard returned to Baldock by train.
21 September 1980: Back from church to find Alec had taken Tony and Kate to the dig but Kris and friend had arrived later by bike so had to drive there anyway. Went to sleep for a bit but had to drive out there again as Tony wanted his camera, as he'd found something. Two pots and a pile of bones. A crowd of people came to look so Tony was fairly cagey.
22 September 1980: Tony excavated with Val Rigby most of the day. She took the pots and the handle back to the British Museum. Tony is soaking the cremated bones in the kitchen.
26 September 1980: Richard and Kris came and sorted the 'princess's' bones and Tony found a bear's claw. He rang Ian Stead's wife. She's a palaeopathologist and is going to examine them.

The excavation was put to bed for the winter and resumed the following spring.

31 May 1981: Drove to the dig at 4.15 and sat and listened to the skylarks and a cuckoo. Field a mass of bobbing yellow flowers …

By the summer we were through the Roman layers and into what seemed to be a sterile chalky fill when:

5 August 1981: Tony went digging with Jack and Diana Smith. Returned in evening to photograph 2 babies skeletons.
30 August 1981: Hurried home from church to go digging with Tony … It was a beautiful day. Richard found another baby and we took up the bones of all of them after measuring up.

There were at least 13 baby skeletons in the ditch fill. Great Humphreys had some other surprises:

18 October 1981: Took Tony to deliver the mirror to the farmer. He then had a class to take field-walking. They found Bronze Age pottery and a bronze pin which somebody snapped in half thinking it was plastic! He and four others returned for tea.
11 November 1981: Tony to London and delighted with reception of Bronze Age finds at B.M. [British Museum]

The finds included a Bronze Age chisel (Lockyear 1987: fig. 3; see also this volume, Fig. 1.2), but Merle's diary does not record the circumstances of the find. Work resumed in the spring of 1982.

> **2 May 1982:** … The ditch is narrowing rapidly. An unusual animal skull turned up and an 'Ali Baba' rim.
> **30 May 1982:** Jack called for Tony at 11.30. We went to look at the ditch later. It's 10 feet from the grass to the bottom. Peter was washing pigs' skulls and stripy pottery.
> **31 May 1982:** Took Kate to the station and Tony and Kris to the dig. Collected them and Richard at 4.30. They reached the bottom of the ditch and cleaned it up for a photograph.
> **6 June 1982:** Took Tony to the dig … The ditch looks very smart and tidy, though not yet finished … All back for drinks.

Having finished the first section of the ditch, a second length was opened up that autumn.

> **5 September 1982:** Took Tony to the dig – exactly 5½ miles. Returned at 3.0 when there was a sudden downpour. He had taken off some ploughsoil by then. In the morning the stubble was still burning and my feet got black. Spoke briefly to Bill Jeffries [the farmer] who was watching.

They also took the opportunity to return to the Bronze Age site (HHER 6312):

> **19 September 1982:** Tony to dig with Jack as I was making coffee for church. They dug up lots of thick Bronze Age pottery.

The season started late in 1983, as the Society conducted what we would now call 'an archaeological evaluation' at Parkside, Welwyn, which found nothing of archaeological interest.

> **12 June 1983:** Took Tony and Bill to Datchworth [i.e., Great Humphreys] … took sewing to the site and sat in the sun while Tony, Bill and Richard forked out the 'fill' of the ditch and Mike trowelled. He found a lovely coin of Constantine.

The latter part of 1983 was taken up with more evaluation work on the route of the Watton-at-Stone bypass, particularly plotting coin finds made by metal dectectorists. We were able, however, to do some more in the autumn.

> **23 October 1983:** We drove to the dig leaving Kate on her own. Walked around the field and then I spent the rest of the time picking up baby bones and putting them in a plastic bag. Joined by Richard, Mike and later Tony [...]. Delightful walk at lunchtime towards the coppice. Mike stayed behind and dozed. Bluest of skies, high con-trails from planes and rooks flying. All back for tea and we showed Tony2 [Lane] photos of the ditch as he wasn't there last summer.
>
> **27 November 1983:** Out for a walk with Tony, Mike and Tony2. Heavy mud. The canopy over the dig had come apart so helped undo the ropes etc. and Mike climbed the ladder to put it back together. He also folded the plastic and carted it off, muttering that it was what his navy training had been for.

The winter of 1983–4 saw WAS battling with cold and mud to excavate the Roman roadside settlement at Watton-at-Stone, which was going to be destroyed by the new bypass. Work resumed at Great Humphreys at the end of April:

> **29 April 1984:** Drove to the by-pass along the rough roadway and loaded the car with buckets, the barrow and plastic sheeting. Also brought back part of a Roman grindstone. Richard and Jack came too and fetched other objects and we drove across the paddock at the Homestead and deposited our loads in the hut. By then it was 1.0. Time for our picnic. Then we uncovered the site and tidied it and spent the rest of the day digging (after a short walk to the pond to see the newts diving). Bluebells and primroses out. Much coppicing done beyond the pond. Kris came back for a cuppa.
>
> **17 June 1984:** Off to the dig with Tony and Lewis. As we reached the stables, a terrific storm. Sheltered in the barn and talked to Mr Aylott and eventually located Jack in the hut. Soon Kris, Mike and Richard appeared. We put the canopy over the dig and excavated through lightning and thunder. The worst bit was taking off the canopy because of all the mud. Did a bit of baling with the shovel, a bit like 'It's a Knock-out'. Kris and Lewis came for tea and we looked at pots, Tony's little ones and my bits of clay.
>
> **15 July 1984:** Up in the field by 11.45. No girls this time. Kris late. He'd fallen off his bike and had a hole in his trousers and a bloody knee. Richard came without Mike who wasn't well. Jack there first. We baled out and later had to put the covers over to keep off a cloudburst. Hailstones in Welwyn. Then sky cleared and it was hot. Covers eventually removed about 4.0. Shifted about a foot of soil, very friable and nothing in it.
>
> **26 August 1984:** A hazy summer day of unexpected heat and beauty. As usual to the dig and took Lewis who enjoyed himself in a quiet sort of way. Tony and Richard spread out the covers and eventually shortened one and spread it over

the frame after we'd moved it along. I mostly trowelled and used a pick as the ground was so hard. Found a massive piece of rim.

2 September 1984: Tony, Richard and Jack spent the day cutting two slots near the fence to locate the ditch while Lewis and I trowelled very slowly across our patch and got hardly anywhere – no finds worth seeing. The field has been burnt off and ploughed. The polythene sheet flapped loudly till we rolled it up. When we got back home Kris had arrived so we had a long chat till nearly 6.30 when Lewis went for his bus.

In the autumn and for most of the following year the Society worked on the ring ditch at Ladylowe, followed by an excavation in the Grange in Welwyn, only returning to Great Humphreys in the autumn. I had also decided to do my undergraduate dissertation on the site (Lockyear 1987) and that winter enlisted the help of my fellow WAS members:

22 December 1985: Took Tony's present to the Wallace's and met all three by their bungalow before rejoining Richard and Mike and attracting Kris's attention by throwing stones at the hut. Spent the afternoon walking parallel across Great Humphreys, picking up sherds and putting them in plastic bags. Mike went home and we returned for tea.

29 December 1985: … enjoyed hurling stones through ice in a drainage ditch. Almost impossible to pick up anything as the ground was frozen hard. Kris worked on alone. Richard gave him and his bike a lift back here and we ate Christmas cake and drank tea.

1 January 1986: Met Richard for another field-walk, picking up pottery sherds and putting them in labelled plastic bags. It was cold and fairly dark when we left Great Humphreys and rain began while we were at home having tea.

3 January 1986: Kris called and drew small finds.

5 January 1986: Out with Lewis and Tony at 2.0. Very cold in the field and we stuck it for only an hour to Kris's dismay. He and Richard went early to measure it out and came back late.

12 January 1986: In the afternoon, Lewis called and we met Kris, Richard and Mike up at the site and made three separate journeys across the field with our plastic bags. Kris was very pleased and grateful.

Work on the site itself resumed in May.

15 June 1986: A perfect day – warm, breezy and a blue, blue sky. Tony anxious to be off as soon as I returned from church (confirmation service; read lesson).

Richard and Mike arrived to collect the ladders, my lunch was packed, I changed into a new white broderie anglaise blouse and we were off. A peaceful hour before lunch – good Emmental cheese sandwiches – and then walked to the pond where we saw a demoiselle fly and through the wood to look for purple orchids. They were nearly over. Lewis arrived as we returned, then a couple with three sons from Datchworth, a girl from Ware and then Bill. So quite a crowd. I left off trowelling and marked Milton essays instead. We trundled gently home at 5.30 and drank beer in the garden so spent rest of evening a bit hazy.

27 June 1986: Kris turned up before leaving for Devon. He brought us some aerial photographs with splendid Roman road on one, at Datchworth.

The photograph was from the Royal Commission on the Ancient and Historical Monuments of England (RCAHM(E)) collection then held in Fortress House that I had visited as part of my dissertation research. I had missed the road when I found the photograph, but thought I could see a ring ditch!

As part of my dissertation I undertook some resistance surveys at the site.

7 August 1986: Fetched Kris and took him and the 'instrument' to Datchworth after supper.

10 August 1986: Dug all afternoon, lots of finds and exercise … Kris stayed for supper … He and Tony sorted more pottery and he cycled off into a thunderstorm with only a rear light.

12 October 1986: Cloudy and cooler … Kris arrived soon after I got back and we had lunch at Great Humphreys. Mike arrived while Tony was preparing to cook the bratwurst … Finished reading 'Brat Farrar' in the hut with the door closed, and then wrote down Kris's readings on the resistivity meter.

2 November 1986: Home from church about 11.45 and straight out to Great Humphreys. Richard and Mike there before us. Stayed for toasted sandwiches and baked apples which Tony kept warm in newspaper. Kris was very tired still and his repeated survey was no better than the first one.

9 November 1986: At about 11.15, Tony and I to join Kris, Mike and Richard at Great Humphreys and measured out a grid to walk up and down in. The wind was buffeting us about … All lunched in … [the hut] – a tight fit with the drying frame in the way. Then walked up and down in my square and Tony's till it was time to take Kate to her rehearsal at the Barn Theatre … Kris was very tired, too …

4 January 1987: I joined Kris, Richard and Mike and we collected pottery till Kris had finished his square and then we walked to Chapel Wood and back … All very wet, muddy and windswept.

30 January 1987: WAS lecture by Kris Lockyear [on the Gubbio Project]. He phoned at 6.30. He handed his dissertation in at 1.0pm and caught the next train [from Durham]. He's only had six hours' sleep in the last three days so was a bit wound up. Richard drove him home.

Excavations at Great Humphreys resumed once more in April, taking place, as usual, most Sundays.

7 June 1987: New digger – Jenny [Searle]. We arrived before Richard and Mike and put up the covers as the weather was grey, cloudy and windy. Worked hard all day … Found a collection of little tacks, probably from an old sandal. All back for tea, exhausted.
12 July 1987: Lewis and Jenny arrived at exactly 11.0 and Kris just as we were leaving. Lewis found a curious collection of bones. They could have been in a bag. I found more pottery and swapped with Mike who found none, and then when he was dozing returned and found more. Jenny and I left the others to look for Kris's peg and crept down to the pond where Richard and Mike were silently watching a moorhen and four chicks. Back for beer and orange juice in the garden.
11 October 1987: The sun shone and it was much warmer so Tony and the gang – Richard, Andrew and Jenny – went digging. Mike joined them at 3.0 and hit the first baby. Tony found a superb coin of Vespasian AD 69.

Having put the site safely to bed for winter digging there was suspended, although other work took place at Hill Farm and in Welwyn. Work at Great Humphreys started again the following April.

24 April 1988: A glorious day after a chilly night. Not a cloud in the sky all day. Off to the dig with Andrew and Tony for 11.50 … Nothing much found … Primroses just finishing; violets in bloom; bluebells just coming out. John Wallace has planted a grove of cherry trees.
29 May 1988: Out to dig at 11.30, just us, Jenny, and Andrew. Ate lunch down the hole as the wind was chill and the clouds threatening. Then it rained so we covered the site and sat in the hut while Tony made Andrew a kite from a blue plastic sack and the handle of the fishing net.
12 June 1988: A beautiful, beautiful day. Sat by the pond before breakfast and smelled the pinks and watched the newts. Blue sky all day. To dig with Tony and Andrew. Richard later. A wild wind which ruffled the barley so it flowed round us. My arms are stippled with red dots after walking through it. Richard's shoulders went pink so put some sun lotion on them. Tony said I was an 'interesting mangle' which confused Andrew!

19 June 1988: Didn't go to the dig until nearly midday when Kris finally arrived … Jenny came, too. It was very hot. Went beetroot in the afternoon so lay in the barley and listened to the long-tailed tits and some animal grunting in the hedge. Saw a blue butterfly and a Burnet moth. A new foal was standing gangly next to its mother. Eventually, Andrew and I washed pottery which was pleasant. We finished it all. Tony found the remains of two Belgic pots and lots of bones. Andrew was thrilled. Shandy on the lawn afterwards, orange juice for Jenny and Richard had tea.

10 July 1988: … Richard … found two babies so all delighted …

17 July 1988: … Spent digging time on the baby – a very fiddly job. Its fingers and toes kept shifting in the soil. Tony did the other one which was much disturbed. Its arm seemed to be above its head. Tony photographed them both …

24 July 1988: A good day at the dig. I took up both babies and found some super Belgic pottery on the lower level …

7 August 1988: … Richard found another baby which he allowed Jenny to tidy up …

16 October 1988: Jenny couldn't come out today because of visitors so she missed the tidying and photographing of the site. Andrew, Lewis, Richard and I tidied the bottom and sides again and Tony did some shovelling and pulled up buckets … we ended up shifting all the buckets, bags, old tyres etc. for the photographs. Joan and Mike came to watch and Joan took photos and so did I. Richard and Lewis lashed together the two ladders against the sieving frame and Tony climbed to the top and so did I. Gorgeous view. All back for tea …

13 November 1988: Did plenty of picking and shovelling and emptying of buckets at the dig. Much earth-moving revealed the bend in the ditch – quite remarkable that it should be exactly where we left a division between two separate excavations … Rick turned up with his metal detector and found two Roman nails!

In 1989 the Society, as well as finishing off the sections of ditch from the previous seasons, began to excavate in the paddock next to Great Humphreys in the hope of revealing structures associated with the late Roman material that had been dumped into the top of the Iron Age ditch.

4 June 1989: By 11.0 Jenny, Lewis, and a girl called Belinda who's researching snails arrived and we all went to the dig … Very blustery at times and some heavy showers and hot sunshine. My transparent umbrella proved a blessing and then the spokes came through the plastic and it gave up the ghost. Belinda collected about 10 bags of soil plus molluscs and we helped carry them back. Then she drew a section of the ditch. My hands are sore from pulling up buckets

> of earth. The two sections of the ditch have now been joined. Jenny and Lewis eventually met at the bottom. Lewis found a fine piece of Belgic storage jar and Mike found a minute bronze coin in the patch in the paddock!

Once the crop came off we were able to bring in a JCB to both fill in the ditch and excavate test trenches through the plough soil to trace the line of the Iron Age enclosure.

In 1990 the excavation season was occupied with work at Hawbush Close in Welwyn. Work in 'the Paddock' next to Great Humphreys resumed at the end of March 1991 and continued through the summer:

> **7 July 1991:** Very hot all day. Left for dig at 11.15. The girls, Julie Chalk and Katherine Stevens came too. Brian-number-4 turned up and Frank brought a party of Belgians at 4.0. Bill came for an hour. Spent all day washing pottery, Bill and Tony helped. All sat in the garden and drank shandy afterwards, except for Jenny who had tea. The girls took her home.
>
> **11 August 1991:** Out to dig with Tony and Jenny. Cleared away burnt patch after general brushing down. Tony photographed the surface … Went off to see the Battle of Shiloh at Knebworth House in the afternoon … About 850 participants and very exciting cannons.

By the end of the summer the focus of attention had shifted to 'Oaks Cross Farm', the Hooks Cross Roman villa site. Other sites were tackled, including the Queen Victoria Memorial Hospital site in Welwyn and the fish ponds at Digswell (Rook 1994). It is unclear from Merle's diaries when the excavation at Great Humphreys was filled in. The Society returned to the site in 1997 to trace the line of the ditch in the paddock which lies to the west of Great Humphreys (*WAS News*, Summer and Christmas 1997). To this day, however, our two abandoned huts still stand on the edge of the paddock, slowly disappearing into the hedgerow.

2.4 Lectures, outings, parties and other things

As noted above, the first LAS/WAS lecture took place in January 1965. We have had 10 or 12 lectures a year since then, usually held fortnightly between October and April. The talks vary both in topic and in presenter, ranging from 'member's evenings' to lectures by well-known archaeologists. The following is a small sample:

> **25 October 1968:** LAS lecture on Roman Roads by Eddy Parrott. Late. He had a puncture … some pretty pictures of countryside around Rickmansworth. Sociable crowd. About 30 coffees.

16 February 1972: LAS lecture by Gareth Davis. Lots of slides of Bronze Age spears and some gold clasps and rings. Rushed over to FineFare as forgot biscuits.
October 22 1976: WAS lecture by [J.B.] Ward-Perkins [then Honorary President of the Society]. Very successful and an enormous crowd packed the lecture theatre with people sitting on the window sills and standing at the back. He told us about the trials of setting up the Pompeii 79 Exhibition which is due to open at the Royal Academy next month. He actually went out to select the exhibits himself, with one assistant, and it took three months to get the Italians moving. Rome said they'd be delighted to help if Naples would be responsible, and Naples said they'd be charmed as long as Rome gave permission. He is a very amusing speaker.
21 January 1983: WAS Member's evening. Five talks. Kris's very long and Mike Petterson was rather crowded out.
12 October 1984: WAS lecture on Wroxeter by Kate Pretty. She's in charge of the finds which are many and varied. Eric Balley stayed for a chat, and Liz Simmons and all the old ones like the Redhouses, Mr Keatley and the Holder-Vales, and both Rogers. Sold over 20 coffees and teas and B helped.
16 February 1996: WAS lecture interesting – bits about the holes dug by St Albans Field Officer, a pleasant young man called Simon West.
6 February 1998: WAS lecture by Jonathan Hunn. A leisurely stroll through boring landscapes in Lincolnshire and Stevenage. Also saw a ditch recently sectioned at Stanborough School full of Belgic pottery.[3]

Coach outings have also been a feature of WAS activities. Many of Merle's extracts are quite summary, although a few give a little more colour. They started in a modest way, but became more elaborate as time passed.

17 September 1967: Outing to Olney and Chellington. Eight cars. We went with Mr Nash. No Golesworthys – Barbara said she didn't feel too good.
7 April 1979: WAS outing to Avebury and Stonehenge, with pick-ups in Potters Bar and Wembley. Soon it began to rain. Avebury was mud. Couldn't reach West Kennett long barrow as the river had flooded. Stonehenge looked colourful despite icy, slanting rain. Old Sarum, however, was dry and breezy.
24 October 1987: WAS outing to Singleton Open-Air museum. Beautiful October sunshine. All went spinningly till Kris suggested detour to Compton Church. Here we found both delight (two-storey Norman chancel) and disaster. A fallen cedar had just missed the tower and the coach had a flat tyre. Enjoyed watching Mike on point duty and Richard and co struggling successfully with

wheel nuts. At Haselmere Museum we were given coffee, loos, an art exhibition and a guided tour.

Lunched at the Open Air Museum and wandered vaguely among the old houses and, with Andrew, looked at horses ploughing and a threshing machine hurling chaff in the air. On to Petworth House, lots of statues and a very up-market wedding.

29 April 1995: WAS outing to Chartwell and Knole. 45 passengers and 14 weren't National Trust. Collected £7.50 from each – £4.50 Chartwell and £3.00 Knole. Grey skies and rather cold. Coffee with Bryan and Jenny. Tea with Brian and Gillian. Australians chilled.

The annual Christmas parties were originally held in a variety of venues in the area, but since January 1976 they have been held in Tony and Merle's beautiful fifteenth-century home in Welwyn.

30 November 1968: LAS dig dinner at the Cowper Arms. Derek drove us there, with Tony's mother, and we walked home. Very pleasant.

4 December 1970: LAS dig dinner – a real Christmassy one. Alec not well enough to come. A smaller turn-out, about 20. Home by 10.15. Service slow and a bit expensive, £2 per head incl. wine.

13 December 1974: WAS party at North Star. Tony arranged some 'guess the picture' questions and Alec and Derek some slides to 'guess the place'. 25 people altogether. Ollie wore his silver Duke of Edinburgh award and Richard looked elegant in a narrow-waisted suit. Guy and Andrew came too …

24 January 1976: WAS Christmas party – at home. Sylvia collected French sticks from Algars and Tony made a magnificent coleslaw. Kate made mince pies which all went. Cut price cake, cheese, biscuits etc. from Welwyn Stores as well, and we made trifles. In all, spent £16 on food and £2 on paper plates and mugs. We had three large flagons of wine and borrowed glasses from the shop. Cider, too. Our 29 guests paid £1 a head. Quite a sedate affair with 'guess the adverts' and 'scrambled villages' competitions. By 11.15 the last had left – Derek with his record player. He said we could easily have had ten more people! The house looked very pretty in the snow. Tony took a photo.

12 December 1981: WAS party. Sylvia put up decorations and Kate did some and made 1½ batches of mince pies. So did I as some of hers burnt while we ate lunch. It took over an hour for Tony to carve the turkeys. He also 'starred' the tomatoes. We hoovered and put the Z-bed in the study. Kate wore a side plait, her new mini-skirt and gold boots. Sylvia wore trousers and a purple shirt. She did masses of serving out. Everyone except Richard had left by midnight.

> Jack and Edna couldn't come. Icy night so Richard slept – intermittently – in the living-room. We forgot to stop the clock so the chimes woke him.

There were various other celebrations, some held in the bath house, some in Tony and Merle's garden:

> **5 November 1987:** WAS fireworks celebration. Joan arrived first with a Black Forest gateau. Then Frank with a big bottle of wine, Bill with a small bottle of red, Mike with a box of fireworks, Richard ditto and later Jenny with some splendid individual ones from Shoplands. Just as we stopped to eat, Andrew and Mum arrived. She returned over an hour later for the second instalment and then we all had cocoa. Andrew was marginally more interested in roasting a turnip than watching the fireworks but he'd been to Lockley's first anyway.

In addition to strictly WAS activities, Tony and Merle were involved in a wide variety of other archaeological initiatives. For example, they edited and produced the *Hertfordshire Archaeological Review* between 1970 and 1975 and organised the Hertfordshire Archaeological Council's annual conference for many years.

> **18 March 1972:** HAC Conference at College of Further Education. Everyone pleased with the organization. Kept busy – made coffee for 45 helpers before it started, collected 75 dinner tickets from people who'd ordered food as they went into the refectory and made about 300 cups of tea in the afternoon. Sheila and her daughter helped. Bought 7lb biscuits from Welwyn Stores and the children set them out on big plates. We actually had some left over. Daphne sat at the entrance with tickets and publications. Collected 3 figurines from home and sold them all. Lots of tidying up later.

2.5 Conclusions

What can we conclude from this brief history of the Society? What makes a small group like this 'tick'? From the above, one can be forgiven for suggesting that the answer is 'tea'!

Firstly, it is clear that one key ingredient is leadership from a dedicated individual who can, and is willing to, spend a significant amount of time running excavations, leading walks, organising trips, writing reports and so forth. Larger societies, such as SAHAAS, have developed various smaller 'special interest groups' that, I presume, are again led by an individual with time and motivation. In the beginning of the Society, it was Tony and Merle's dedication that recorded so many sites in the area. As Thompson says (this volume): 'Where were the

Tony Rooks of Stevenage and Hemel Hempstead, when those New Towns were being built?'

Secondly, the range of activities attracts members with varied interests. Many do just want 'lectures and outings', as Selkirk states, but many are also attracted to excavation and fieldwork. Modern excavation, however, is an expensive business. Specialists in a commercial world are no longer able to write reports for free. Academics are by necessity driven by the need to obtain grants, the larger the better. In recent years, however, 'public outreach' and 'community engagement' have become increasingly important within the academic sector, creating opportunities for collaborations between archaeological societies and the universities (see Dhanjal *et al.*, this volume). Unfortunately, the number of individuals willing to help dig far exceeds those willing to help with post-excavation. This, inevitably, leads to our 'dedicated individual' having to take on this as well as all the other tasks.

The last factor, and I believe the most important one, brings us back to tea. The key element is a sense of *community*. Not the big-society, politically driven meaning of the word 'community', but the smaller scale, almost intimate meaning of the word. What keeps a society like WAS going is the sharing of interests in a group that develops friendships beyond the task at hand. Tony and Merle's seemingly unending willingness to make tea (or shandies) created a group around them with a sense of shared purpose and a high degree of camaraderie. Over the 50-plus years of the Society the members of that group came and went, but that core still persists.

But what of the future? Local societies of all types, not just archaeological, are declining in membership. I was fascinated to observe that many of the concerns discussed at recent WAS committee meetings were also discussed at the 2014 AGM of the East Herts Archaeological Society: how to attract younger members, the viability of outings and so on. Perhaps the growth of online fora and discussion groups as well as 'social media' is providing a way for busy individuals to be part of a virtual group, negating the need for traditional clubs and societies? Can we still run activities that will attract and keep members? There are challenging times ahead.

I hope that Merle would approve of the use I have made of her diary. Working through it has been, for me, both fascinating and emotional. I hope, however, that some sense of the life of the Society has come through the extracts I have chosen: the excitement of new finds, the tension at times of emergency, the fun of the parties and coach outings. I am sure she would approve of my dedicating this paper to all the members of WAS, past and present, in thanks for their efforts and their friendship.

2.6 References

Bahn, P. (ed.) (2008), *The Great Archaeologists* (London).

Bender, B., Hamilton, S. and Tilley, C. (1997), 'Leskernick: Stone Worlds; Alternative Narratives; Nested Landscapes', *Proceedings of the Prehistoric Society* 63, pp. 147–78.

Branch Johnson, W. (1970), *The Industrial Archaeology of Hertfordshire* (Newton Abbot).

Daniel, G.E. (1976), *A Hundred and Fifty Years of Archaeology* (London).

Everill, P. (2008), *The Invisible Diggers: A Study of British Commercial Archaeology* (Oxford).

Hawkes, J. (1982), *Mortimer Wheeler: Adventurer in Archaeology* (London).

Hunn, J.R. (2009), 'Excavation on the First-Century Enclosure at Stanborough School, Welwyn Garden City', *Hertfordshire Archaeology and History* 16, pp. 5–26.

Lockyear, K. (1987), 'A survey of the antiquities of Great Humphreys and their relation to other sites in Hertfordshire.' BA dissertation (University of Durham).

Moody, B. (1995), *The Light of Other Days. A Short History of the St Albans and Hertfordshire Architectural and Archaeological Society 1845 to 1995* (St Albans).

Pearce, S.M. (2007), *Visions of Antiquity: The Society of Antiquaries of London, 1707–2007* (London).

Perks, R. and Thomson, A. (1998), *The Oral History Reader* (London and New York).

Perman, D. (ed.) (1998), *A Century of Archaeology in East Herts* (Ware).

Pitts, M.W. and Roberts, M. (1998), *A Fairweather Eden: Life in Britain Half a Million Years Ago as Revealed by the Excavations at Boxgrove* (London).

Rook, T. (1968a), 'Investigation of a Belgic Occupation Site at Crookhams, Welwyn Garden City', *Hertfordshire Archaeology* 1, pp. 51–65.

Rook, T. (1968b), 'Romano-British Well at Welwyn', *Hertfordshire Archaeology* 1, pp. 117–18.

Rook, T. (1971), 'Lockleys Archaeological Society', *Hertfordshire Archaeological Review* 4, pp. 63–4.

Rook, T. (1983-6), 'The Roman Villa Site at Dicket Mead, Lockleys, Welwyn', *Hertfordshire Archaeology* 9, pp. 79–175.

Rook, T. (1994), 'The fishponds at Digswell', *Hertfordshire Past* 36, pp. 1–7.

Rook, T. (2002), *The Story of Welwyn Roman Baths* (Welwyn).

Rook, T. and Henig, M. (1981), 'A bronze cockerel from a late Romano-British context at Aston, Hertfordshire', *Antiquaries Journal* 61, pp. 356–9.

Rook, T., Lowery, P.R., Savage, R.D.A. and Wilkins, R.L. (1982), 'An Iron Age Bronze Mirror from Aston, Hertfordshire', *Antiquaries Journal* 62, pp. 18–34.

Schofield, J. (2011), *Great Excavations: Shaping the Archaeological Profession* (Oxford).

Selkirk, A. (2014), 'Local Societies and Grey Literature', *Current Archaeology* 293 (August), pp. 48–9.

Stead, I.M. (1967), 'A La Tène III burial at Welwyn Garden City', *Archaeologia* 101, pp. 1-62.

Smith, P.J. (2011), *The Personal Histories Project* <http://www2.arch.cam.ac.uk/personal-histories/> accessed 18 July 2014.

Vyner, B. (1994), *Building on the Past: papers celebrating 150 years of the Royal Archaeological Institute* (London).

Wheeler, R.E.M. (1955), *Still Digging: Interleaves from an Antiquary's Notebook* (London).

Notes

1 Lockleys, which became Sherrardswood School in 1950, was a minor stately home outside Welwyn. A Roman villa was excavated in its grounds in 1937 by J.B. Ward Perkins and is normally known as the Lockleys Villa. Dicket Mead, the name of the field, was adopted for the villa excavated by LAS/WAS to differentiate the two.

2 See HHER 455.

3 Now see Hunn (2009).

CHAPTER 3

A nice place to live: settlement and landscape in Hertfordshire from 1500 BC to 300 BC

Stewart Bryant

3.1 Redrawing the settlement map – the implications of the scale of new discoveries since 1993

This paper will review the evidence for settlement and landscape in Hertfordshire between *c.*1500 BC and *c.*300 BC – that is, from the beginning of the middle Bronze Age until the beginning of the middle Iron Age.

It is nearly 20 years since a review of the evidence for this period was undertaken for broadly the same study area by the author (Bryant 1995; Bryant and Burleigh 1995). It has therefore been very interesting and instructive to reflect on the changes, in both the archaeological issues and debates and also the range and quality of the evidence, that have taken place in the 20 years since that initial research was undertaken in 1993. Although most of the changes have been evolutionary rather than revolutionary, it is probably true to say that the sum of them has amounted to a step change in our understanding of the period.

The most obvious and dramatic change has been in the number and range of new settlements and other occupation sites discovered since 1993. In 1993 there were only about 20 known sites of the period in Hertfordshire, representing the accumulated endeavour of archaeologists from the nineteenth century onwards. Many of these sites were also either highly visible, including hillforts such as Wilbury Hill, Arbury Banks and Ravensburgh Castle, or well-known as a result of published reports, such as Blackhorse Road, Letchworth, and Foxholes Farm,

Hertford. However, in 2013 there is a total of 105 known sites that span the date range 1500 BC–300 BC, representing a fivefold increase.

Before looking in more detail at the range of new discoveries, their dynamics through time and the impact they are having on our understanding of the past, it is worth dwelling briefly on the reasons for this quite dramatic increase in the numbers of known sites. Plate 3.1 shows the number and distribution of sites known in 1993 (in black) and the new discoveries between 1993 and 2013 (in red) against the background of rivers and geology. It can be observed that the 2013 distribution of known sites is much more extensive, especially within the central clay areas of the county. The only areas without any known sites are the London Clay soils in the far south of the county and a large part of the boulder clay soils of east Hertfordshire. In contrast, the pre-1993 distribution is largely confined to the chalk areas along the Icknield belt in the north and to some of the major river valleys (the Lea, Colne and Stort).

The distribution shown in Plate 3.1 is likely to reflect some aspects of the real distribution of prehistoric settlement, but it is also influenced by the places where development has taken place in the past 20 years. Plate 3.2 shows all sites against the urban areas of Hertfordshire, the routes of new road schemes built since 1992 and the belt of gravel extraction. A comparison between these development themes and the distribution of archaeological sites shows some clear correlations, with a high proportion of sites occurring along the new roads, in areas of urban expansion and within the gravel extraction belt, with the cluster of sites around Bishop's Stortford at the right-hand side of the map being particularly marked. These patterns are a consequence of what is probably the most important policy development affecting archaeology within this period, the requirement for developers to ensure that archaeology is either protected or excavated in advance of development, a requirement which has meant that almost all excavations since 1990 have been funded by developers. Prior to 1990 and the publication of Planning Policy Guidance Note 16 (PPG 16) on planning and archaeology, only a relatively small proportion of archaeological excavation was funded in this way, and even as late as the early 1980s the construction of the M25 – the largest ever single development project in Hertfordshire – had almost no archaeological provision. Since 1990, however, almost all developments affecting archaeology have made provision for archaeological investigation and post-excavation of some kind, and many developments have been archaeologically evaluated prior to the granting of planning permission.

Most development within Hertfordshire between 1993 and 2013 has taken the form of mineral extraction, new road schemes (The Cole Green Bypass, The

A10 Wadesmill Bypass, The M1 Widening and the Baldock Bypass) or urban development around existing towns such as Bishop's Stortford. Plate 3.2 shows the routes of the new roads, with the addition of the A41 Kings Langley and Berkhamsted Bypass, which was constructed in 1992. The total area taken in by new development during this period amounts to between 32km^2 and 50km^2, or between 2 and 3 per cent of the county's total area of 1,600km^2. A simple calculation of the average density of later prehistoric sites reveals a rather high figure of three to four sites per square kilometre within the areas that have been developed. If this density were extrapolated for the whole county it would suggest a staggeringly high total number of sites in the range 4,800–6,400.

However, for the purposes of this study, the definition of 'site' has necessarily had to be very broad in order to accommodate the varying scope and quality of available evidence. Not all sites, therefore, necessarily represent settlements, even of a temporary nature; such non-settlement 'sites' include the late Bronze Age burnt mound at King Harry Lane St Albans (HHER 30093) and the landscape of late Bronze Age boundary features at Radwell, near Baldock (Armour 2000). The areas where new sites have been found have also tended to be in parts of the county where the settlement density was probably above average in any case, perhaps owing to the presence of light, easily cultivated soils in the gravel extraction areas and the tendency of new roads to run along the edge of river valleys, which would also have been favoured locations for settlement. The average of four sites per square kilometre in these areas is therefore likely to be significantly above the average for the county.

In contrast, there are large parts of the county that have much lower potential for settlement owing to poor soils and drainage. These include the 114km^2 London Clay region in the south, for which there are no known sites. If these and other areas of middling potential – such as the extensive clay-with-flints soils in the west of the county – are taken into account, the potential average density of sites falls to roughly within the broad range of 0.5–2 sites per square km (800–3,200 for the whole county). This figure is further reduced if assessing the potential for finding new sites is the objective of the exercise. Between 25 per cent and 30 per cent of the county has already been developed, mostly in the creation and development of Hertfordshire's 25 towns, and has a low potential for the discovery of new sites. The resulting very broad range of later prehistoric sites that may well be as yet undiscovered is therefore *c.*550–*c.*2400.

There are clearly many other factors that would need to be taken into account in attempting to make anything like an accurate prediction of the likely number and distribution of sites, including, crucially, how the term 'site' itself is defined. It is also acknowledged that the assumptions which have been made in producing even this very broad range of figures can also be easily challenged. However, the important overall conclusion is that, without doubt, there are large numbers of sites that have yet to be discovered – probably four to five times the number currently known, and possibly up to 20 times this figure. Support for this basic assertion has also been forthcoming from an aerial photographic assessment of the 2010 county-wide aerial survey by Chris Cox (2013) for the Hertfordshire Historic Environment Record, which has produced 675 new sites across the county. Many are likely to be of late Iron Age or Roman date, but the experience of the archaeological investigation of cropmark sites over the past 20 years is that a significant proportion of the 675 sites is likely to date between the middle Bronze Age and the middle Iron Age. This has important implications both when it comes to drawing conclusions about the period in question based on what is likely to be a very small and possibly unrepresentative sample, and also for the identification of where these currently unknown sites are and how they should be conserved and managed.

3.2 A chronological framework

The dating of almost all known late Bronze Age and early Iron Age sites in Hertfordshire up until 2000 was based on the evidence of pottery fabrics and styles for what have been termed 'post-Deverel-Rimbury ceramics' using the typology first introduced by Barrett (1980). In very simple terms, this distinguishes between earlier assemblages of plain ware jars and bowls in coarse, flint-gritted fabrics which generally date to between *c.*1200 BC and *c.*800 BC and later assemblages that include simple decoration and finer fabrics, including sand-tempered ones, that date to between *c.*850 BC and *c.*600 BC (Barrett 1980). It has also been assumed that the transition between the two types of assemblages was relatively gradual. However, the forms and fabrics of the two groups are quite similar and, as most site assemblages tend to consist of small numbers of mostly undiagnostic sherds, a generic late Bronze Age–early Iron Age date has historically been ascribed to most known sites of this period.

Since the mid-1990s there have been several important advances in absolute dating resulting from significant improvements in the usefulness of radiocarbon dating, especially for what has been the problematic calibration curve of the Iron Age, and from the application of Bayesian modelling techniques (see Whittle and Bayliss 2007). Several strategic radiocarbon dating programmes have also been initiated partly on the back of these developments, the most important of which for this study is the dating of the end of the Bronze Age from selected dating of over 40 key bronze artefacts (Needham *et al.* 1997). This has demonstrated that the end of the late Bronze Age, which is marked by a dramatic increase in the quantity of bronze being discarded, occurred around 800 BC, a century earlier than had previously been thought.

An analysis of the pottery and metalwork evidence has subsequently been undertaken by Needham (2007), which has confirmed that the change from the early plain ware post-Deverel-Rimbury pottery assemblages to the later decorated assemblages occurred around 800 BC and was a relatively rapid change that coincided with the end of the late Bronze Age and the collapse of what Needham refers to as 'the bronze standard'. There was also a marked increase in the quantity of the later decorated pottery in circulation after 800 BC, suggesting that pottery crafts and production may have taken on some of the social and political roles previously performed by bronze (Needham 2007). The period between *c.*850 BC and *c.*750 BC is therefore now thought to be a period of significant and quite rapid social change ('800 BC, the Great Divide' to quote the title of Needham's influential paper) that included the end of long-distance gift exchange by the elite and of the more widespread bronze-dependent culture within late Bronze Age society.

The following terminology, based largely on that proposed by Needham (2007: 55), will be used for this study to take account of the new chronology and also to address the varying levels of dating precision:

- late Bronze Age (1150–800 BC)
- earliest Iron Age (800–600 BC)
- early Iron Age (600–300 BC)
- middle Iron Age (300–100 BC)
- late Bronze Age/earliest Iron Age (850–750 BC)
- late Bronze Age–earliest Iron Age (1150–600 BC)
- late Bronze Age–early Iron Age (1150–300 BC)
- later prehistoric (1600–100 BC)

Unless otherwise stated, all quoted radiocarbon dates are with a 95 per cent or ± 2σ confidence interval.

3.2.1 Chronological issues with the Hertfordshire evidence

However, this dating mini-revolution for the late Bronze Age and Iron Age has so far had almost no impact in Hertfordshire. Unfortunately, for over 50 per cent of the sites that are the subject of this study it has not proved possible to distinguish early plain ware from the later decorated assemblages, and thereby to enable sites to be dated to the late Bronze Age, the earliest Iron Age or the early Iron Age. This is either because insufficient pottery analysis has been undertaken, as at small archaeological evaluations, or because not enough diagnostic sherds are present. There is also only a handful of radiocarbon dates spanning the late Bronze Age–early Iron Age date-range between 1150 BC and 300 BC. Only three sites of the total of 105 provide relatively unambiguous dates, in these instances for late Bronze Age pottery assemblages. We have two dates from charcoal at Gadebridge, Hemel Hempstead (1140–820 BC and 1055–885 BC), two from cremated bone at the M1 Junction 8 excavations (1370–1090 BC and 1130–900 BC) and two from Stocks, Albury (1050–900 BC and 1130–910 BC). These are clear late Bronze Age dates that fit in well with the typological dating of the plain ware pottery assemblages (Last and McDonald 2013; Stansbie *et al.* 2012; Hunn forthcoming). The dates from two other sites are more ambiguous. A single radiocarbon date from a pit at Buncefield Lane, Hemel Hempstead, which contained plain ware late Bronze Age type pottery, produced a date of 810–515 BC, which appears to place the context at the late Bronze Age/earliest Iron Age transition and into the earliest Iron Age (McDonald 1997–2003b). The site also produced a triangular loomweight more typical of the early Iron Age (McDonald 1997–2003a: 54), which indicates that the site may indeed straddle the two periods, although the evidence from this and the single radiocarbon date is not sufficient to draw any real conclusions. There is a similar situation with the unpublished site at Thorley, Bishop's Stortford, which has a pottery assemblage dated to the late Bronze Age and two radiocarbon dates of 785–380 BC and 1000–750 or 635–560 BC, which would seem to place the site within earliest Iron Age with possibly some overlap into the late Bronze Age (Last and McDonald 2004). Lastly, Half Hyde Lane, Turnford, has one very old and uncalibrated date of *c.*700 BC (HHER 6484).

Ironically, perhaps, probably the most important site for dating the late Bronze Age and the earliest–early Iron Age of Hertfordshire, and one which exemplifies the impact of current radiocarbon technology, lies just outside the county boundary at Fairfield Park, Stotfold, in Bedfordshire (Webley *et al.* 2007). Here, late Bronze Age occupation which comprised scattered pits and a cremation outside a large enclosure ditch was dated by radiocarbon from a cremation to 970–790 BC. The small pottery assemblage was of fairly undiagnostic late Bronze Age type. There followed a gap of more than 300 years in occupation before a substantial early Iron Age hamlet-type settlement appeared on the site by 500 BC. This phase is dated by a group of eight radiocarbon dates which fall within the date-range 500 BC–200 BC. It also includes a large assemblage of over 13,000 sherds (115kg) of the distinctive Chinnor/Wandlebury type pottery that is characteristic of the early Iron Age of the Chilterns and south Cambridgeshire (Cunliffe 2005).

The importance of Fairfield Park is that it demonstrates the value of radiocarbon dating in terms of both dating pottery assemblages – a small undiagnostic one in the case of the late Bronze Age phase, and what is probably the most important assemblage from the region in the case of the early Iron Age – and its potential for dating the Iron Age. The radiocarbon dates also provide clear evidence of a long gap in occupation between *c.*800 BC and *c.*500 BC, roughly the period of the earliest Iron Age following the end of the late Bronze Age. This has potential implications for the many sites in Hertfordshire that are the subject of this study and that are only loosely dated to the late Bronze Age–earliest Iron Age or late Bronze Age–early Iron Age. It is possible that at least some of these were subject to similar periods of abandonment or relocation during the earliest Iron Age (*c.*800–600 BC). More radiocarbon dates are urgently needed to inform this important issue, especially for those sites with large and diagnostic pottery assemblages.

3.3 Period summaries

3.3.1 The middle Bronze Age *c.*1600–*c.*1200 BC

The steadily accumulating evidence from south-east England and the south midlands is that the middle Bronze Age marks an important transition in prehistory from semi-nomadic farming communities for which landscapes devoted to ritual, ceremonial and burial appear to have been very important – in many cases since the early fourth millennium BC – to the beginnings of more settled farming communities that made much less direct use of the landscapes of ritual and burial. The middle Bronze Age also marks the appearance for the first time of extensive landscapes of fields, in some cases covering many hectares, notably the recently excavated landscape at Heathrow Terminal 5 (Brown *et al.* 2006).

However, all aspects of the middle Bronze Age – including settlement, burial and field systems – are either absent or very poorly represented in Hertfordshire, with only a handful of known or probable sites, most of which were discovered before the 1990s. This absence is at least partly due to the lack of diagnostic Deverel-Rimbury pottery from the county, especially domestic pottery in a settlement context, and also, crucially, the lack of radiocarbon dates. It is therefore possible that some known late Bronze Age sites also have unrecognised middle Bronze Age phases. Several recently discovered sites at Hatfield (Davis and Sygrave 2002), Harpenden (Miles 2006–2008), Park Lane, Waltham Cross (Morse 2006), Moles Wood, Thundridge (Ashworth and Turner 2007), and Dunmow Road, Bishop's Stortford (Last 1999, 2004), have also begun to extend the known extremely limited distribution of middle Bronze Age occupation sites. The site at Waltham Cross in the Lea valley is significant as it includes field systems and a probable ritual pit, suggesting settlement in the vicinity (Morse 2006).

As with the example of Fairfield Park, Bedfordshire (above), and its usefulness for the dating of the late Bronze Age and Iron Age of Hertfordshire, the most significant middle Bronze Age site for Hertfordshire that has been discovered in recent years is also just beyond the boundary of the county, in this case to the east, at Stansted in Essex. Here, the archaeological investigations in advance of the airport expansion between 1999 and 2003, revealed a complete and well-preserved middle Bronze Age settlement on the boulder clay close to the Pincey Brook, providing clear evidence that farming communities had begun to create permanent settlements in the extensive boulder clay landscapes of west Essex during the middle Bronze Age (Cook *et al.* 2008: 31–78). In addition, a small burial mound radiocarbon dated to the middle Bronze Age (1610–1430 BC) was found 400m from the settlement and had probably been constructed by its inhabitants. This suggests that the small communities may have been establishing their own new special places for burial.

The significance of the middle Bronze Age settlement at Stansted for Hertfordshire is that it has highlighted the potential for evidence of comparable settlements across the extensive and broadly similar chalky boulder clay areas of east Hertfordshire, a potential that may be beginning to be realised from the first tentative signs of Stansted-type middle Bronze Age evidence in east Hertfordshire. This has come in the form of the discovery of a small, well-preserved ring ditch that is similar in size and form to the Stansted barrow and is also radiocarbon dated to the middle Bronze Age, between 1669 BC and 1521 BC. It was found during an archaeological evaluation in advance of a large housing development on the other side of the Stort valley, on the boulder clay at Bishop's Stortford, roughly eight kilometres west of the middle Bronze Age settlement at Stansted (Fletcher 2013). However, the evaluation is of only a 3 per cent sample of the development and any further evidence of contemporary middle Bronze Age settlement in the area will have to await excavation and analysis of the site in advance of the development.

3.3.2 The late Bronze Age and earliest Iron Age *c.*1200–*c.*600 BC

In Hertfordshire – and also throughout much of southern England – the 600 years or so of the late Bronze Age–earliest Iron Age saw a substantial increase in both the number of known settlements and their variety in terms of form and size, including hillforts, ringworks and various forms of farmstead-type settlements. The area of known settlement also appears to have expanded considerably and included at least some of the extensive claylands of Hertfordshire. As of 2013, a total of 97 sites of this period is known from the county, compared with the 18 that were known in 1993. The steadily accumulating evidence is indicating that population numbers increased, probably quite significantly, during the period.

The variety of settlement types is also matched by a greater variety of structures and artefacts, including bronze metalwork, as well as extensive evidence for mixed agricultural production and widespread evidence for cremation burial and structured or ritual deposition within or close to settlements. The difficulty with this period, as mentioned above (Section 3.2), is that, for a majority of sites, it has not proved possible to assign them to either the late Bronze Age or the earliest Iron Age, or to identify the equally important category of sites that in fact continued to be occupied across 'the Great Divide' of 800 BC.

3.3.3 Hillforts

The largest and most visible prehistoric settlements in Hertfordshire are the three hillforts – Ravensburgh Castle, Hexton; Wilbury Hill, Letchworth; and Arbury Banks, Ashwell – which are located at intervals of around 10 to 15 kilometres along the Chiltern ridge. Wilbury Hill and Arbury Banks are similar, with a sub-circular plan and relatively simple and slight defences enclosing areas of between four and five hectares (for an aerial photograph of Arbury Banks hillfort see Fig. 5.3). Ravensburgh is a little larger, at six hectares, and has larger and more complex multiple defences and a sub-rectangular form. There is very little useful published evidence from which it is possible to date the construction and occupation of the three hillforts. Wilbury Hill has produced late Bronze Age pottery from the rampart ditch (Applebaum 1949), although this is clearly residual, and, given the absence of firm evidence for late Bronze Age hillfort rampart construction generally in southern England (Needham 2007: 55), it would seem more likely that the defences at Wilbury are Iron Age in date. There is also pottery and metalwork evidence from the rampart ditch at Wilbury to suggest that the site was occupied in some form from the late Bronze Age, throughout most of the Iron Age and into the early Roman period (Applebaum 1949). A find of late Bronze Age metalwork reported from Arbury Banks also suggests possible contemporary occupation on the site, but there has not been any confirmation of this from excavation or survey (HHER 26). No evidence of late Bronze Age or earliest Iron Age occupation has been recovered at Ravensburgh, but, as at Wilbury, the finds from the limited excavations indicate some occupation from the early Iron Age into the Roman period (Dyer 1976).

The function of hillforts within late prehistoric society has been reappraised since 1993 following the results of a number of investigations of hillforts and their wider landscape contexts, most notably the Danebury environs project (Cunliffe and Poole 1991). This has led to significant changes to the previously accepted interpretation of hillforts as being primarily for defence and as central places for the control of territories and resources. Rather, they are now thought of more as multifunctional communal monuments that serve a variety of roles relating to, for instance, the secure storage of agricultural produce and ceremonial activities, including communal feasting, that are related to key moments in the agricultural cycle (Hill 1996). Obviously, centralised control would be necessary for the construction and maintenance of the defences and there is evidence for substantial occupation within most hillforts, but it seems likely that in many cases such dense internal occupation – and also probably rampart construction and maintenance – was only seasonal. A function for hillforts that included communal ceremonial activities is also suggested by the close physical relationship between hillforts and earlier burial and ceremonial landscapes. Certainly, Wilbury Hill and Arbury Banks are both situated within earlier prehistoric landscapes of burial monuments (barrows) and other ritual monuments which would have been highly visible when the hillforts were first constructed.

Sharples (2007) has suggested that the construction of hillforts in parts of southern England can be seen as part of the wider changes in society that occurred following the collapse of bronze manufacturing and exchange at the end of the late Bronze Age at *c.*800 BC. It is clear that, in the earliest and early Iron Age, iron did not replace the enhanced social, economic and political role, including gift exchange by the elite, that bronze had performed in the late Bronze Age. In the earliest and early Iron Age, therefore, hillforts, as centres for a variety of ceremonies connected with agricultural production, may have taken on some of the social and political roles that in the late Bronze Age had been performed by bronze manufacturing and exchange.

3.3.4 Ringworks

An example of the diversity of settlements that is a feature of the late Bronze Age in particular is the 'ringwork' settlement, a dozen or so of which are now known from eastern England, including two from Hertfordshire. Their characteristic plan consists of one or two concentric circular enclosures with multiple entrances and one or more substantial central circular dwellings. They have provided evidence for a developed late Bronze Age social hierarchy associated with activities indicative of high social status, such as metalworking, craftworking and ritual feasting, and may have been the settlements of chiefs or religious leaders. However, the ringworks appear to be a relatively short-lived class of settlement dating to the end of the late Bronze Age in the tenth and ninth centuries BC, with some continuing for a little while in the eighth century, after which they all appear to have been abandoned (Needham 2007: 48–9; Yates 2007: 115).

The two known sites from Hertfordshire – Whiteley Hill, Royston, and Great Westwood, Watford – are also notable in including both the largest and one of

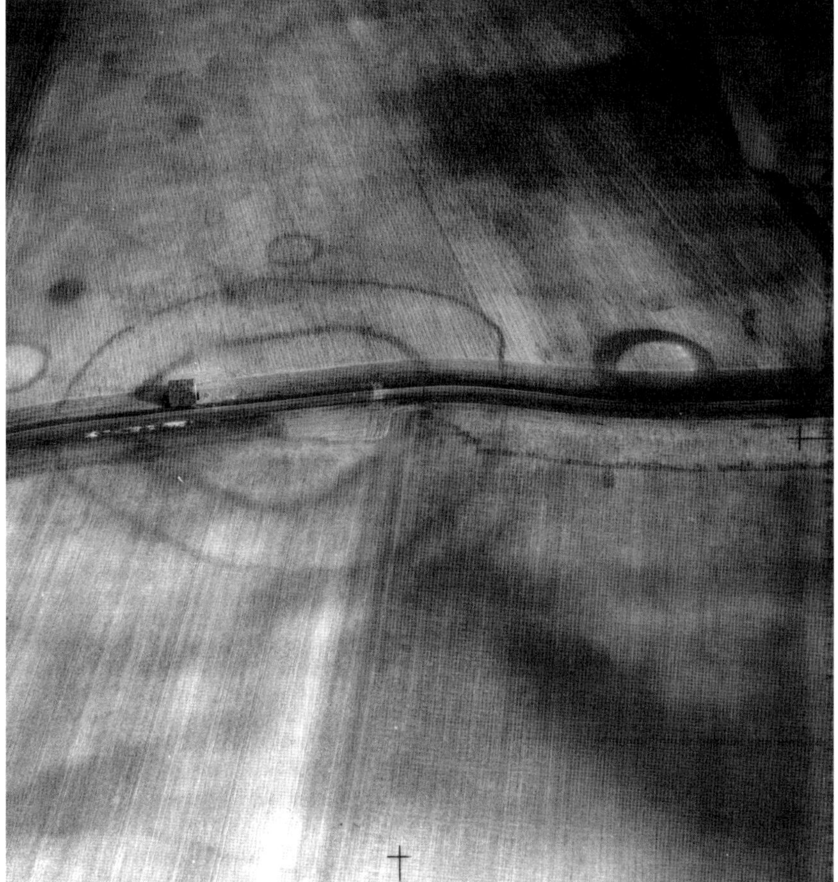

Figure 3.1: Aerial photograph of Whiteley Hill, near Royston, showing cropmarks of the late Bronze Age double-enclosure ringwork and plough-damaged burial mounds located just outside the outer enclosure. Reproduced by courtesy of Cambridge University Collection of Air Photographs, copyright reserved.

the smallest sites within the class of known ringworks. Whiteley Hill, at 1.4ha in area, is by far the largest of the known ringworks and, indeed, was thought to be a hillfort, partly because of its prominent hilltop location (Fig. 3.1). However, it is too small – the interior enclosure is less than one hectare – and the distance (30m) between the deeper inner ditch (2.8m) and shallower outer ditch (1.8m) is atypically large for a conventional hillfort. The published pottery is also in keeping with Barrett's late Bronze Age plain ware typology (Bryant 1993). Whiteley Hill does not have any clear evidence for a central structure, although there has been no geophysical survey of the interior. Like the later hillforts at Wilbury Hill and Arbury Banks, a notable aspect of the location of Whiteley Hill is its proximity to early prehistoric burial monuments, three of which are just outside the outer enclosure and close to the entrance. Such association with earlier prehistoric ritual and burial monuments is a feature of ringworks more generally and includes the proximity of the earlier Neolithic causewayed enclosure to the Springfield Lyons ringwork (Brown and Medlycott 2013). Great Westwood was excavated between 2000 and 2002 in advance of gravel extraction (Duncan *et al.* 2007) and has a single post-built roundhouse in the centre of a circular enclosure which has an outer ditch in the south-eastern half (Fig. 3.2). At 0.1 hectares it is less than one tenth the size of Whiteley Hill, and its closest parallels are probably in Essex, with the late Bronze Age ringworks at South Hornchurch (Guttmann and Last 2000) and Mucking North Rings, which itself was located one kilometre from the much larger double enclosure ringwork at Mucking South Rings (Bond 1988).

3.3.5 Other settlements and evidence of burial and occupation

The discovery of late Bronze Age–earliest Iron Age evidence in the form of pottery, pits, ditches, structures and, occasionally, human remains has become a common occurrence on development sites within Hertfordshire since 1993, with perhaps half a dozen new sites being found each year. However, most of this evidence is relatively small-scale and for only a very small proportion of sites is there evidence for the whole (or even the likely majority) of the settlement plan. The excavated evidence can be classified into the categories detailed in the paragraphs below.

Twenty-nine of the 97 sites are known only from fragmentary evidence revealed within trial trenches (usually 30–50m by 1.5–2m) which form part of archaeological evaluations undertaken in advance of planning permission, usually for housing or mineral extraction. Some of the evaluations comprise hundreds of trenches and cover very large areas in excess of a square kilometre, with excavated evidence often complemented by geophysical survey. It can take up to five years, and sometimes as much as 15 years, before these large development sites are given the go-ahead and any further archaeological work to define and interpret the archaeological sites is carried out. Currently there are five or six such prospective development sites in the county which include a number of late Bronze Age sites as well as sites of other periods.

Another significant group of 15 or so sites are those which have been fully archaeologically excavated but which have revealed only partial evidence of the site, either because the development was much smaller than the site or because much of the site extends beyond the limit of the development, as is often the case in linear developments such as roads and pipelines. This group includes Mangrove Road, Hertford (Boyer 2005), the Western Hills, Baldock (Phillips 2009), a group of three or four sites found on the route of the A10 Wadesmill, High Cross and Colliers End Bypass (Ashworth and Turner 2007) and an unusual site at

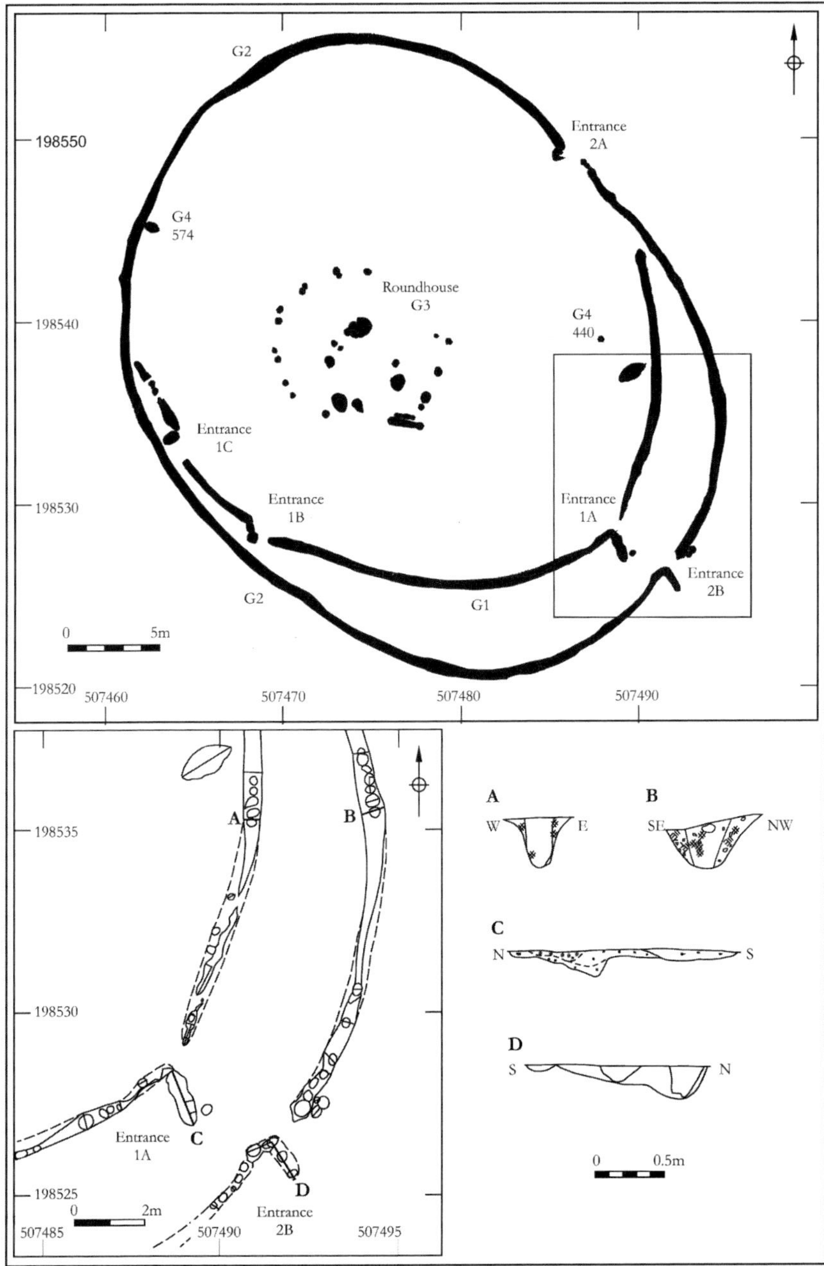

Figure 3.2: Plan of the late Bronze Age ringwork at Great Westwood Quarry, near Watford. Reproduced by courtesy of Albion Archaeology, copyright reserved.

Bengeo, Hertford (Brown 2012). The last of these, like Fairfield Park (Stotfold, Bedfordshire), has sections of what appear to be large empty enclosures that have associated late Bronze Age occupation and burials outside them.

By far the largest group – 50 or more sites – comprise groups of pits and ditches which contain pottery and animal bone, together with the occasional evidence for dwelling structures or other structures such as four-poster granaries and evidence for human remains. These sites vary widely in size, from 20m^2 to several hectares (*c.*30,000m^2), and their precise number is dependent upon the definition used for a site or 'occupation', both spatially and temporarily. For example, the large development at The University of Hertfordshire and Hatfield Business Park in the 1990s revealed at least six clusters of late Bronze Age pits, ditches and other assorted undiagnostic features; most were in clearly distinct groups or clusters, but others were less than 200m apart, and these have been classified as a single 'site' (Davis and Sygrave 2002). Also similarly classified as a single site are three clusters of occupation activity including a cremation burial and a probable field system excavated along a 600m length of the bypass route on the Western Hills in 2003–5 (Phillips 2009: 35–47). It is possible that this site – and a significant proportion of the sites within this general category – represents only temporary or seasonal occupation.

There have been few excavations in which complete or nearly complete settlement plans dating to the late Bronze Age–earliest Iron Age period have been revealed, but unfortunately only two have so far been fully published: Foxholes Farm (Partridge 1989) and Cole Green Bypass (McDonald 1997–2003a). However, these and the unpublished sites do reveal some clear patterns and are important in understanding the period.

Foxholes Farm and Cole Green lie five kilometres apart, both overlooking the Lea valley river complex either side of modern Hertford (for location see Plate 3.3). The Cole Green site spans a one-kilometre length of the route of the current Cole Green Bypass overlooking the river Mimram to the north. The main focus is at the eastern end, where an open settlement with post-built roundhouses and numerous other structures, pits and ditches lay within a wider system of fields in which a mixed farming economy was practised. Remains of one of the structures (Building 1) produced a large quality of late Bronze Age pottery (3kg, representing 37 per cent of the total from the site) and a spindle whorl. A small pit nearby also contained an urned cremation and a cylindrical loomweight (McDonald 1997–2003a: 8–10). Of particular interest was a hollow-way feature at the eastern end of the settlement which contained eroded late Bronze Age soils that also revealed evidence of manuring, indicating that a relatively intensive infield agricultural regime was being practised, but also that the soils were unstable and this regime was probably ultimately unsuccessful; this may have been a reason for the abandonment of the site (Macphail and Cruise 1997–2003).

Foxholes Farm was also an unenclosed late Bronze Age settlement excavated in the 1970s in advance of gravel extraction. Its range of roundhouses and other post-built structures was similar to that seen at Cole Green and, perhaps not unexpectedly for two adjacent settlements, there was also a similar range of late Bronze Age pottery types (Partridge 1989). However, no evidence of field systems was found at Foxholes, although several palisade boundary features were present. It is possible that the farming was less intensive at Foxholes Farm than at Cole Green, a suggestion which could be supported by the fact that, unlike Cole Green, the site was occupied subsequently in the Iron Age and Roman periods.

Fifteen kilometres further east at Thorley, 1.5km west of the river Stort valley (for location see Plate 3.3), the excavation in advance of a large housing development in 1994 revealed late Bronze Age settlement evidence extending over three hectares and comprising pits, ditches and four-post granary-type structures situated within a system of fields (Last and McDonald 2004). Subsequent to these excavations several other late Bronze Age sites have been found in the vicinity on the chalky boulder clay plateau and also to the north of Bishop's Stortford, close to the middle Bronze Age ring ditch mentioned above, and it would seem that the Stort valley and its environs was especially favoured for settlement in the late Bronze Age and earliest Iron Age.

A year earlier, in 1993, another excavation in advance of a large housing development of 2.6 hectares at Gadebridge, Hemel Hempstead, revealed a large late Bronze Age settlement and associated evidence (Last and McDonald 2013). The site location overlooked the Gade valley on the eastern edge of the extensive clay-with-flints plateau which forms the dipslope of the Chiltern Hills. The settlement was open, with no evidence for enclosures or field systems, but included numerous pits, gullies, circular post-built structures (including at least one dwelling), four-post structures, a range of other post-built structures and a linear ditch complex that may represent a droveway. As with Cole Green, a substantial proportion of the total weight of pottery (16kg) was located in features associated with the dwelling. A notable feature of the settlement was that cremated human remains were recovered from 14 features, 12 of which were located in two clusters of four and eight at the western and northern edges of the settlement respectively. This is the largest number of late Bronze Age cremations from Hertfordshire and is notable because cemeteries are relatively rare finds from late Bronze Age settlements generally. However, the fact that Gadebridge probably represents the most complete recovered plan of a late Bronze Age settlement in the county suggests that such small and relatively ephemeral clusters of cremations in pits might be expected to be more common at – or just beyond – the edges of other late Bronze Age settlements.

A notable and widely discussed aspect of late Bronze Age settlement is the presence of special or structured deposits variously of pottery, animal bone, charred organic material and occasionally human remains located within pits and other negative features, usually at specific locations such as entrances and routes. A number of such deposits have been excavated and reported from late Bronze Age sites in Hertfordshire, some of which are substantial in terms of the number, weight and range of artefacts. Particularly noteworthy examples, in addition to those at Cole Green and Gadebridge mentioned above, are a pit with 400 unused sherds of pottery and 274 pieces of struck flint from excavations at the John Warner School, Hoddesdon (McDonald n.d.) and a pit with 130 pottery sherds, mostly from a single vessel, from the M1 Junction 8 South excavations (Stansbie *et al.* 2012: 100).

The largest and most impressive structured deposit so far discovered in Hertfordshire was excavated in 2011 on the small but remarkable late Bronze Age settlement at Aldbury in west Hertfordshire. The excavated late Bronze Age evidence comprised five hearths, four pits and three postholes within an area 50m by 55m. Sixteen kilograms of pottery was recovered from the site, with 5.3kg from a single pit including a set of largely complete broken vessels of differing forms and sizes (Fig. 3.3). Also recovered from the pit was a small spindle whorl and quern stone fragments. Three postholes were located at one end of the pit and may have supported a small structure over it (Hunn forthcoming).

3.3.6 The early Iron Age (*c.*600–*c.*300 BC)

Only a handful of sites, mainly from the north of the county, can be dated with reasonable confidence to this period. Almost all have produced the distinctive Chinnor/Wandlebury fineware pottery (Fig. 3.4), including Ravensburgh Castle and Wilbury Hill hillforts, to which can probably be added a small and unusual site one kilometre to the south-west of Wilbury Hill consisting of several four-post structures and a dense complex of over 50 intercutting pits (Barlow and Newton 2013). The distribution of Chinnor/Wandlebury sites in Hertfordshire is much the same as it was when the pottery style and name was first coined by Barry Cunliffe in the 1960s (Cunliffe 1968). Given the large number of new sites discovered since that time and the distinctive nature of the pottery, its absence from the south and east of the county would suggest that it probably does indeed represent a regional type for the Chilterns and south Cambridgeshire. It is also possible to speculate that the pottery forms part of an early Iron Age Chilterns cultural package together with the distinctive archaeology of hillforts and multiple ditch systems (Bryant and Burleigh 1995).

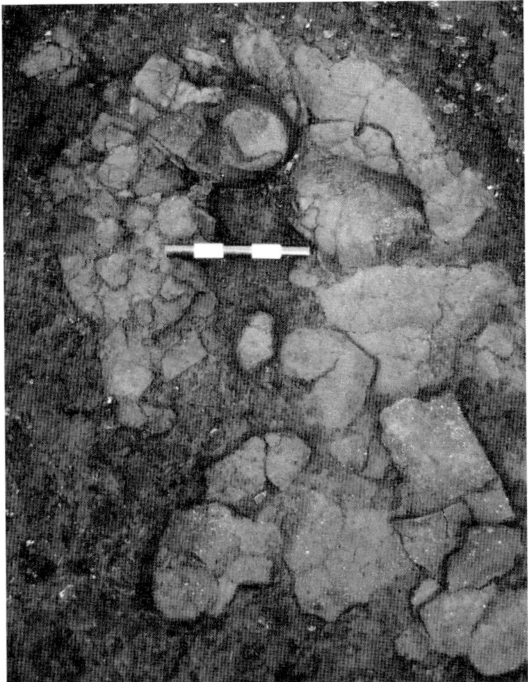

Figure 3.3: Late Bronze Age pottery deposit *in situ* within pit 88, Stock Golf Course, Aldbury. Photograph © Jonathan Hunn.

Figure 3.4: Decorated 'Chinnor-Wandlebury' bowl from Fairfield Park, Bedfordshire (after Webley *et al.* 2007, plate 3.1. Reproduced courtesy of Central Bedfordshire Council, copyright reserved).

3.4 Evidence of later prehistoric fields systems and land allotment

3.4.1 Coaxial field systems

An important advance in our understanding of late prehistory since 1993 has been the realisation that extensive landscapes of fields were created in the period after 1400 BC over much of southern England. The evidence is summarised by Yates (2007), who personally undertook much of the data collection from hundreds of archaeological investigations carried out in advance of development by dozens of different archaeological organisations. Some of the field systems, such as those at Heathrow, cover many hectares, but most are partial and relatively small scale. However, even such partial examples are rare in Hertfordshire and are only known associated with settlements such as Cole Green (McDonald 1997–2003a), the Western Hills, Baldock (Phillips 2009: 35–6), Park Lane, Waltham Cross (Morse 2006), and Thorley, Bishop's Stortford (Last and McDonald 2004). However, the interpretation of linear ditches and boundaries as 'fields' is generally dependent upon the investigation of large areas or the combining of excavation evidence with that of geophysical survey or cropmarks known from aerial photography. The lack of excavated evidence for late Bronze Age/earliest Iron Age fields is therefore almost certainly a reflection of the relatively small scale of most of the investigations in the county since 1993.

In contrast, the evidence for later prehistoric field systems revealed principally from landscape and historical survey is much more extensive in Hertfordshire. A relict landscape of 5km^2 of coaxial-type fields (a brickwork pattern with two dominant axes of orientation, one of which has much longer boundaries) survives as extant earthworks within Wormley and Bencroft Woods in south-east Hertfordshire, which is itself part of a much larger and less well-preserved area of at least 35km^2 (Bryant *et al.* 2006; see plate 3.3 for a plan of the area). A pre-Roman date for the origins of the field system is highly likely and a late or middle Bronze Age date is possible given the pollen profile of a buried soil beneath one of the banks (Wiltshire 1999). The morphology of the Wormley coaxial field systems is best suited for cattle farming, with each field having access to water and one of the principal east–west droveways. This is also in keeping with the conclusions of Yates that the late Bronze Age field systems show a consistent emphasis on livestock and pastoralism and invariably include droveways and waterholes (2007: 120). The generally marginal nature of the Wormley and Bencroft Woods area for agriculture and settlement is also the main reason why the field boundaries have survived intact and are currently located within protected ancient woodland.

Another even more extensive landscape of coaxial field with probable prehistoric origins is located in the west of the county on the clay-with-flints soils of the Chilterns dipslope to the north-west of Hemel Hempstead. The fields and routeways were also initially identified from historical mapping and have since been augmented with evidence from excavation undertaken advance of the construction of the Boxted–Friar's Wash water pipeline. This confirmed a Roman or earlier date for one of the main routeways and also provided indications of a possible Iron Age date, although this will need to be confirmed by analysis of the excavation results (HHER 16169). The full extent of the landscape of coaxial fields has recently been plotted by Rowe and Williamson (2013; see also Williamson, this volume). They have also superimposed on these field systems the known late Iron Age and Roman relict earthwork evidence of settlements, fields and linear boundaries at Ashridge, on the clay-with-flints plateau. Like the earthworks within Wormley and Bencroft Wood, these show a clear alignment with the wider coaxial landscape and provide further evidence of a likely pre-Roman origin.

The survival of such large areas of ancient field systems might seem unlikely to non-specialists – and indeed to many historians and archaeologists – given Hertfordshire's long history of intensive agriculture and settlement. However, a characteristic of the county is its diverse landscape and geology, which also results in a very wide variability in the potential of areas and landscapes for ancient settlement and agriculture. The London clays and related geology in particular, within which the Wormley and Bencroft field system lies, have a very low agricultural potential owing to the intractable nature of the soils. The topography of the Wormley area, which is dissected by brooks feeding into the river Lea, is nonetheless eminently suitable for low-intensity cattle farming of the type practised in later prehistory.

The clay-with-flints geology of the Chilterns dipslope, within which the larger western area of coaxial fields lies, has a higher agricultural potential than the London Clay area and much of the area is currently under arable cultivation. Before the twentieth century, however, cattle rearing was the dominant agricultural regime and – as with the Wormley and Bencroft Woods area to the east – its topography of upland clay landscapes dissected by river valleys is conducive to cattle rearing. Also, in contrast with much of the rest of the county, both landscapes were largely unaffected by landscape change before the twentieth century.

3.4.2 Linear boundaries

The extent of our understanding of the later prehistoric linear boundaries in Hertfordshire has not changed significantly since the last review (Bryant and Burleigh 1995). The boundaries are divided into two groups: the long linear boundaries that mostly follow the contours of the Bulbourne valley in west Hertfordshire and which are collectively known as 'Grim's Ditch'; and the shorter multiple ditch systems that occur at regular intervals along the Icknield Way between Ivinghoe Beacon hillfort in Buckinghamshire and Therfield Heath near Royston.

The Hertfordshire Grim's Ditch is at the eastern end of a system of linear ditches and 'dykes' thought to be of late Bronze Age–earliest Iron Age date that extend through Buckinghamshire, Oxfordshire and Berkshire and which have been argued to be territorial boundaries that delineate areas of pasture (e.g., Ford 1982). A short plough-damaged length of the Hertfordshire Grim's Ditch was excavated in 1991–2 in advance of the construction of the A41 trunk road near Hamberlin's Wood, Berkhamsted. It produced middle Iron Age (300–100 BC) pottery from the primary fill and remnants of the ploughed-out bank (Last 2001). This is much later than the dates for the Grim's Ditch further west (Bradley *et al.* 1994), although the quantity of pottery was small and does not appear to be from contexts that can securely date the monument. It is also possible that Grim's Ditch was re-cut during the middle Iron Age and/or late Iron Age (a quantity of late Iron Age pottery was also found from the excavations) as the Berkhamsted area – including Hamberlin's Wood – is within a known late Iron Age and early Roman settlement and industrial ironworking complex. There is also another length of Grim's Ditch on the other side of the valley at Berkhamsted Golf Course which cuts across the ridge rather than following the contours and is probably of late Iron Age date (Bryant 2007).

The multiple ditch systems cut across rather than follow the natural contours. They date from the middle Bronze Age to the late Iron Age, and are also thought to have a territorial/boundary function, an interpretation which is supported by their regular spacing at between 3.5km and 5.5km (Bryant and Burleigh 1995). A territorial boundary role by itself, however, does not explain the variety of situations in which they occur and their associations with other prehistoric monuments, including earlier prehistoric barrow cemeteries. It is therefore likely that the multiple ditch systems performed other communal and ceremonial functions and in some instances may have had a more prosaic role related to stock control.

3.5 Conclusions

3.5.1 The appearance of the first settled farming communities in Hertfordshire

The large number of new later prehistoric sites that have been discovered since 1993 is undoubtedly the most important development and one which has profound implications for our understanding of the period and the wider prehistory and history of Hertfordshire. Before the beginning of the late Bronze Age (*c.*1200 BC), the evidence in Hertfordshire is primarily from burial mounds and is concentrated on the chalk soils in the north of the county and along the larger river valleys. There is also only very limited evidence for settlement before this date and it is assumed that farming was based on temporary seasonal occupation. In contrast, after 1200 BC, the evidence is almost entirely from settlement and occupation, and it is clear that there was a marked expansion of settlement along the edges of the many river valleys of the county and also into some of the more fertile and easily farmed clay plateau areas. It is also clear that some of these settlements were occupied on a more permanent basis. From comparisons with other parts of south-east England, it is likely that the more intensive exploitation of these areas for farming and the founding of new settlements – both permanent and temporary – and the creation of field systems did begin and gather pace during the middle Bronze Age (1600–1200 BC), although the direct evidence of this early settlement phase is only slight at present in Hertfordshire.

There also appears to be significant differences in the density of later prehistoric settlement across the county and sometimes between adjacent areas. The clearest example of this is the very obvious difference between the chalky boulder clay area to the west of the river Stort between Bishop's Stortford and Harlow, which has revealed 25 sites within an area of approximately 10km^2, and the area of London Clay and related soils 5km to the south-west, which is 114km^2 in extent and has no known later prehistoric sites (see Plates 3.1 and 3.3). Even accounting for the biases created by development mentioned above and the relative difficulties of detecting archaeological sites on the London Clay from aerial photography and geophysical survey, the differences are striking. The relic landscape at Wormley, which lies within the London Clay area, provides a possible example of a less intensive pastoral economy based on seasonal exploitation that may have been more widespread across the London Clay and the extensive clay-with-flints landscapes in the west of the county.

3.5.2 Settlement form and morphology

Although much of the evidence described above for later prehistoric human occupation in Hertfordshire is small in scale, lacks chronological precision and is functionally unclear, there are nonetheless a number of significant patterns that can be discerned.

Enclosed settlements are relatively rare and those that are known (e.g., the hillforts, ringworks and a D-shaped enclosure) appear to be 'special' in terms of social status and the range of their activities and associations. The arcs of what appear to be large late Bronze Age enclosures at Bengeo and Fairfield Hospital that are devoid of internal features but which have evidence of external activity are also unusual (Webley *et al.* 2007: 14; Brown 2012).

The lack of enclosures does pose significant problems in terms of the interpretation of the spatial extent of sites and of some key aspects of their role and function. The presence of a substantial enclosure ditch can provide an indication of permanent settlement and also aspects of the role of that settlement, e.g., stock control. The lack of enclosures also means that remote sensing techniques such as geophysical survey, aerial photography and Light Detection and Ranging (LiDAR) are less useful for detecting sites than, for instance, in the succeeding middle and late Iron Age, in which settlement enclosures are much more common.

Post-built structures, especially four-posters, traditionally interpreted as granaries, are a characteristic feature of settlement from the ninth and eighth centuries BC onwards (Gent 1983; Needham 2007: 55) and they are present on almost all known sites of any size in Hertfordshire. Dwelling structures are less common, although they can be relatively difficult to identify from posthole evidence alone. Artefact-rich pits, including those with evidence of structured deposition, are often located within or close to known dwellings, as at Cole Green and Gadebridge, and can potentially be used as an indicator of habitation areas.

Pits are ubiquitous on almost all sites of the period, although there are few of the classic Iron Age storage pits before *c.*600 BC. Nonetheless, there is a large enough corpus of environmental data from plants and fauna to suggest that most sites were practising a mixed farming economy. This is also supported by the common occurrence of loomweights, spindle whorls, charred grain and animal bone, and the presence of four-posters (mentioned above). Abundant evidence for agriculture is indeed one of the defining characteristics of the archaeology of the period and is present on almost all known sites.

The ending of the active use of burial mounds and other ritual and ceremonial monuments of the earlier Bronze Age is another defining characteristic of the period, which coincides with the rise in the importance of agriculture. The single small ring ditch at Bishop's Stortford, which appears to be directly comparable to the nearby barrow at Stansted in Essex, may, however, represent a class of burial or ceremonial monuments that form part of the process of establishing new settlements and places on the chalky boulder clay areas of east Hertfordshire and west Essex in the middle Bronze Age. Human remains, mostly cremations, occur commonly on sites, especially during the late Bronze Age. Most are partial remains in shallow pits away from the main habitation areas. The presence of two small cemetery groups of un-urned cremations at Gadebridge is unusual, but may possibly represent evidence of a more widespread phenomenon.

3.5.3 The Lea valley in the late Bronze Age

There is accumulating evidence from landscape survey, metalwork finds and a number of excavations that the river Lea and its tributaries were a focus in the late Bronze Age and earliest Iron Age for settlement, large-scale field systems, bronze working and the ritual deposition of metalwork. Plate 3.3 shows the distribution of the evidence by type, including the concentration of sites around Hertford and Ware and the likely area of coaxial fields around Wormley on the west side of the Lea, based on the evidence of historic mapping. Yates (2007: 137–8) points out that late Bronze Age field systems tend to be at strategic locations, positioned alongside the long-distance trading networks, and are not always on the best soils, both of which criteria apply to the Lea valley and the Wormley area respectively.

Further evidence for late Bronze Age coaxial fields two kilometres to the south of the Wormley area has also recently been found at Park Lane, Waltham Cross, on one of the few large-scale excavations of later prehistoric occupation to be undertaken in the past 20 years. Several phases of long rectilinear fields interpreted as stock enclosures and extending over several hectares on the western edge of the Lea valley just north of the M25 have been dated to the middle and late Bronze Age (Morse 2006). The fields are on the same orientation as those at Wormley and, although not directly linked to them, are important in providing evidence of the type of boundaries that might be expected to be found in smaller-scale excavations along the Lea valley.

Yates also points out that such field systems are often associated with high-status settlements in the form of ringworks, D-shaped settlement enclosures and palisaded riverside settlements (2007: 115). Although there is no evidence for the latter along the Lea, the small unpublished excavation at Half Hyde Lane, Turnford, is in a lowland riverside location and produced evidence for bronze working that includes crucible fragment and clay moulds, possibly for swords. Pottery from the site was of the decorated post-Deverel Rimbury type, which, together with a single radiocarbon date of *c.*700 BC, would indicate a date at the beginning of the earliest Iron Age date (Stewart 1985). There are also two late Bronze Age enclosures, including a D-shaped enclosure at Rickneys, overlooking the river Bean at Hertford (Wallis 2006; Percival and Richmond 1997).

Ashworth and Turner (2007: 74–5) have briefly reviewed the evidence for late Bronze Age metalworking in the Lea valley, including the sites at Half Hyde Lane, Turnford, a possible metalworking complex at Foxholes Farm (Partridge 1989: 71–4), a group of late Bronze Age axes and a bun ingot from Prior's Wood, Hertford Heath (Partridge 1980), and the site found by Ashworth and Turner at Moles Wood overlooking the Rib valley, three kilometres north of Ware (Ashworth and Turner 2007: 74). The evidence for this comprised a series of inter-cutting pits containing the fragments of three ceramic crucibles and probable middle Bronze Age pottery. The crucible fragments also included evidence for re-melting in the form of surviving heavily leaded fragments of bronze (Gilmore 2007). The site was located at the very edge of the development area and therefore not all of it was excavated; in the absence of radiocarbon dating and given the small quantity of mostly undignostic sherds found, a more generic middle Bronze Age–earliest Iron Age date for the site is to be preferred. Lastly, Yates (2007: 113–14) also noted that there is a high concentration of high-status late Bronze Age metalwork in the river Lea – what he refers to as 'war gear' – which is likely to have been ritually deposited.

3.5.4 Priorities for the future

Assuming that many more new discoveries of settlements will be made in the future, and that most will be unenclosed and not especially well preserved, it will be necessary to identify the archaeological 'signatures' for types and activities and the role/s of settlement and other evidence of occupation in order to better understand how the landscape was settled and farmed. For instance, it will be necessary to distinguish between temporary and more permanent settlements and assess the size of settlements, their differing characteristics, the types of farming practised and the degree to which the landscape was exploited, using such evidence as that for manuring and soil erosion at Cole Green near Hertford. The ability to generally compare and contrast sites will also be a priority which will require more sophisticated archaeological sampling techniques, including targeted 100 per cent sampling of some pits and other features and the systematic recording of the volume of excavated soils, as advocated by Evans (2012).

Improving our understanding of this very important initial period of settlement and farming will also require more connections to be made between the settlements and occupation sites and the wider farmed landscapes. The relatively small-scale and partial nature of most archaeological investigations is likely to continue in future, which may mean, in some instances, prioritising the investigation of field boundaries and other 'off-site' evidence and also considering strategic environmental sampling programmes of buried soils and peat deposits. The relationship between settlement and the extensive relic landscapes of coaxial fields is also a priority, as is their relationship with linear monuments such as Grim's Ditch. Such relationships are notoriously difficult to date and will require further landscape research, including taking advantage of opportunities to investigate key relationships in these landscapes in instances when linear developments cut across these landscapes, as happened with the Boxted–Friar's Wash pipeline.

Finally, without doubt the most important priority for the future is to create a chronological framework for the period 1200–300 BC from which it is possible to date sites and key phases of occupation to within 200, or, preferably, 100 years. The assessment of potential for radiocarbon dating must be a research priority for all archaeological investigations and dating must also be mandatory where this potential exists, including the taking of multiple dates wherever possible. In addition, there is a need at the same time to reassess the dating of pottery assemblages, including regional variations in key diagnostic types.

3.6 References

Applebaum, E.S. (1949), 'Excavations at Wilbury Hill, an Iron Age Hillfort near Letchworth', *Bedfordshire Archaeology* 16, pp. 12–45.

Armour, N. (2000), 'Investigation of the archaeological landscape at MSA A1/A507, Radwell, Hertfordshire: phase 2, excavations'. Cambridge Archaeological Unit unpublished report.

Ashworth, H. and Turner, C. (2007) *Archaeology on the A10 Wadesmill, High Cross and Colliers End Bypass*, Heritage Network (Letchworth).

Barlow, G. and Newton, A.S. (2013), 'Hitchin Grade Separation, Hitchin, Hertfordshire: an archaeological excavation. Interim report and updated project design'. Archaeological Solutions unpublished report.

Barrett, J. (1980), 'The pottery of the Late Bronze Age in Lowland England', *Proceedings of the Prehistoric Society* 46, pp. 297–320.

Bond, D. (1988), *Excavation at the North Ring, Mucking, Essex*, East Anglian Archaeology 43 (Chelmsford).

Boyer, P. (2005), 'An assessment of an archaeological excavation at the former Ashbourne Hostels, Mangrove Road, Hertford'. CgMs Consulting unpublished report.

Bradley, R., Entwhistle, R. and Raymond, F. (1994), *Prehistoric Land Divisions on Salisbury Plain*, English Heritage Archaeological Reports 3 (London).

Brown, J. (2012), 'Archaeological excavations at Sacombe Road, Bengeo, Hertfordshire, May 2011'. Northamptonshire Archaeology unpublished report.

Brown, L., Lewis, J. and Smith, A. (eds) (2006), *Landscape Evolution in the Middle Thames Valley: Heathrow Terminal 5 Excavations Volume 1, Perry Oaks*, Framework Archaeology Monograph 1 (Salisbury).

Brown, N. and Medlycott, M. (2013), *The Neolithic and Bronze Age Enclosures at Springfield Lyons, Essex: Excavations 1981–1991*, East Anglian Archaeology 149 (Chelmsford).

Bryant, S.R. (1993), 'Whiteley Hill, near Royston: a Late Bronze Age Ringwork?' *Hertfordshire Archaeology* 11, pp. 26–9.

Bryant, S.R. (1995), 'The late Bronze Age to the middle Iron Age of the North Chilterns', in Holgate (1995), pp. 17–27.

Bryant, S.R. (2007), 'Central places or special places? The origins and development of "oppida" in Hertfordshire', in C.C. Haselgrove and T. Moore (eds), *The late Iron Age in Britain and Beyond* (Oxford), pp. 62–80.

Bryant, S.R. and Burleigh, G. (1995), 'Later prehistoric dykes of the eastern Chilterns', in Holgate (1995), pp. 92–5.

Bryant, S., Perry, B. and Williamson, T. (2006), 'A "relict landscape" in south-east Hertfordshire: archaeological and topographical investigations in the Wormley area', *Landscape History* 27, pp. 5–16.

Cook, N., Brown, F. and Phillpots, C. (2008), *From Hunter Gatherers to Huntsmen: a history of the Stansted landscape*, Framework Archaeology Monograph 2 (Salisbury).

Cox, C. (2013), 'Interpretation of aerial photographs for archaeology in Hertfordshire, 2010–2013 HER update; final report'. Air Photo Services unpublished report.

Cunliffe, B. (1968), 'Early Pre-Roman Iron Age Communities in Eastern England', *Antiquaries Journal* 48, pp. 175–91.

Cunliffe, B. (2005), *Iron Age Communities in Britain*, 4th edn (London).

Cunliffe, B. and Poole, C. (1991), *Danebury: an Iron Age hillfort in Hampshire. Volume 4: the excavations 1979–1988*. Council for British Archaeology Report 73 (York).

Davis, S. and Sygrave, J. (2002), 'Residential development, Hatfield Aerodrome, Hatfield: an interim report on the archaeological investigation', Museum of London Archaeology Service unpublished report.

Duncan, H.B. *et al.* (2007), 'A late Bronze Age ringwork and late Iron Age/early Roman enclosure system at Great Westwood Quarry, Watford'. Albion Archaeology unpublished report.

Dyer, J.F. (1976), 'Ravensburgh Castle, Hertfordshire', in D.W. Harding (ed.), *Hillforts: later prehistoric earthworks in Britain and Ireland* (London), pp. 153–9, 421–3.

Evans, C. (2012), 'Archaeology and the Repeatable Experiment: a comparative agenda', in A.M. Jones, J. Pollard, J. Gardiner and M.J. Allen (eds), *Image, Memory and Monumentality*, Prehistoric Society Research Paper No. 5 (Oxford), pp. 295–306.

Ford, S. (1982) 'Fieldwork and Excavation on the Berkshire Grim's Ditch', *Oxoniensia* 47, pp. 13–36.

Fletcher, T. (2013), 'Prehistoric, Anglo-Saxon and post-medieval remains on land at Hazel End, Bishops Stortford, Hertfordshire: archaeological evaluation'. Oxford Archaeology East unpublished report.

Gent, H. (1983), 'Centralised storage in in later prehistoric Britain', *Proceedings of the Prehistoric Society* 49, pp. 243–67.

Gilmore, B. (2007), 'Fragment of Crucible, Moles Wood', in Ashworth and Turner, (2007), pp. 47–8.

Guttmann, E.B.A. and Last, J. *et al.* (2000), 'A Late Bronze Age landscape at South Hornchurch, Greater London', *Proceedings of the Prehistoric Society* 66, pp. 319–59.

Haselgrove, C.C. and Pope, R. (eds) (2007), *The earlier Iron Age in Britain and the near Continent* (Oxford).

Hill, J.D. (1996), 'Hillforts and the Iron Age of Wessex', in T.C. Champion and J.R. Collis (eds), *The Iron Age in Britain and Ireland: Recent Trends* (Sheffield), pp. 95–116.

Holgate, R. (ed.) (1995), *Chiltern Archaeology: Recent Work. A handbook for the next decade* (Dunstable).

Hunn, J.R. (forthcoming), 'Archaeological Excavation: New Clubhouse, Stocks Golf Course Aldbury, Hertfordshire', *Hertfordshire Archaeology and History* 17.

Last, J. (1999), *Household waste site, Dunmow Road, Bishop's Stortford, Hertfordshire*. Hertfordshire Archaeological Trust publication draft.

Last, J. (2001), 'A41 Berkhamsted and Kings Langley Bypass Updated Project Design'. Hertfordshire Archaeological Trust unpublished report.

Last, J. (2004), 'Excavations at the new household waste site, Dunmow Road, Bishop's Stortford. Archaeological excavation report'. Archaeological Solutions unpublished report.

Last, J. and McDonald, T. (2004), 'Thorley: a multi-period landscape in east Hertfordshire'. Archaeological Solutions publication draft.

Last, J. and McDonald, T. (2013), 'Gadebridge: a late Bronze Age settlement near Hemel Hempstead, Hertfordshire: research archive report'. Archaeological Solutions unpublished report.

Macphail, R.I. and Cruise, G.M. (1997–2003), 'Soil investigation of Area A', in McDonald (1997–2003a), pp. 33–35.
McDonald, T. (n.d.), 'John Warner School, Hoddesdon, Hertfordshire: archaeological excavation final report'. Hertfordshire Archaeological Trust unpublished report.
McDonald, T. (1997–2003a), 'Archaeological Investigations in advance of the A414 Cole Green By-Pass, near Hertford', *Hertfordshire Archaeology* 13, pp. 3–46.
McDonald, T. (1997–2003b), 'Excavations at Buncefield Lane, Hemel Hempstead', *Hertfordshire Archaeology* 13, pp. 47–60.
Miles, R. (2006–2008), 'A Bronze Age Bucket Urn from Harpenden', *Hertfordshire Archaeology and History* 15, pp. 21–22.
Morse, C. (2006), 'An assessment of the potential for analysis of data from excavations at Project HAL Southern Site, land east of A10 at Waltham Cross'. L-P Archaeology unpublished report.
Needham, S., Ramsey, C.B., Coombs, D., Cartwright, C. and Pettit, P. (1997), 'An independent chronology for British Bronze Age metalwork: the results of the Oxford Radiocarbon Accelerator Programme', *Archaeological Journal* 154, pp. 55–107.
Needham, S. (2007), '800 BC, The Great Divide', in Haselgrove and Pope (2007), pp. 40–63.
Partridge, C. (1980), 'Late Bronze Age Artifacts from Hertford Heath, Hertfordshire', *Hertfordshire Archaeology* 7, pp. 1–9.
Partridge, C. (1989), *Foxholes Farm: A Multi-Period Gravel Site* (Hertford).
Percival, J. and Richmond, A. (1997), 'Report on an archaeological evaluation: Rickney's extension, north of Hertford, Hertfordshire'. Tempus Reparatum unpublished report.
Phillips, M. (2009), *Four Millennia of Human Activity Along the A505 Baldock Bypass, Hertfordshire*, East Anglian Archaeology 128 (Bedford).
Rowe, A. and Williamson, T. (2013), *Hertfordshire: A Landscape History* (Hatfield).
Sharples, N. (2007), 'Building communities and creating identities in the first millennium BC', in Haselgrove and Pope (2007), pp. 174–84.
Stansbie, D., Booth, P., Simmonds, A., Diez, V. and Griffiths, S. (2012), *From Mesolithic to Motorway: The Archaeology of the M1 (Junction 6a–10) Widening Scheme, Hertfordshire*, Oxford Archaeology Monograph 14 (Oxford).
Stewart, D.S. (1985), 'Turnford Half Hide Lane', *Hart Archaeological Unit Newsletter*, Autumn 1985.
Wallis, S. (2006), 'Proposed eastern extension, Rickneys Quarry, near Ware, Hertfordshire: an archaeological evaluation'. Thames Valley Archaeological Services unpublished report.
Webley, L., Timby, J. and Wilson, M. (2007), *Fairfield Park, Stotfold, Bedfordshire: Later Prehistoric Settlement in the Eastern Chilterns*, Bedfordshire Archaeology Monograph 7 (Bedford).
Whittle, A. and Bayliss, A. (eds) (2007), *Histories of the dead: building chronologies for five southern British long barrows*, Cambridge Archaeological Journal Supplement 17/S1 (Cambridge).
Wiltshire, P.E.J. (1999), 'Wormley Wood, Herts: palynological assessment of sediments and buried soil profiles associated with a linear earthwork'. unpublished report.
Yates, D. (2007), *Land, power, and prestige: Bronze Age field systems in southern England* (Oxford).

CHAPTER 4

The Baldock Bowl: an exceptional prehistoric landscape on the edge of the Chilterns

Keith J. Fitzpatrick-Matthews

4.1 Introduction

Tony Rook was a pioneer of landscape archaeology in Hertfordshire whose studies of late Iron Age sites around Welwyn were an early influence on my approach to the more northerly part of the county. I was inspired to think in terms of the settings of sites, rather than the sites as mere assemblages of excavated or surveyed data, by his attempt to work out the prehistoric landscape context of the enigmatic site at Welch's Farm, for instance (Rook 1974: 173; it remains the only archaeological paper I know to quote Truman Capote!). This approach of Tony's was one that was gaining ground at the time among so-called 'Economic Prehistorians' such as Eric Higgs.

Having grown up in Letchworth Garden City and then worked on Gil Burleigh's sites in and around Baldock in the 1980s, I already had an insight into the later prehistory of this fascinating area. However, it has been work in more recent years, carried out by the Norton Community Archaeology Group, to the north-west of Baldock, that has begun to push back the story of what I have termed the 'Baldock Bowl' into the fourth millennium BC.

The Bowl is a distinctive landscape feature (Fig. 4.1). Although not marked by dramatic hills and slopes, it is nevertheless a discrete unit that, from the springs of the river Ivel on the northern edge of Baldock, gives the impression of being enclosed by a ring of higher ground. Within this landscape there is a remarkable concentration of monuments, particularly of the Neolithic to

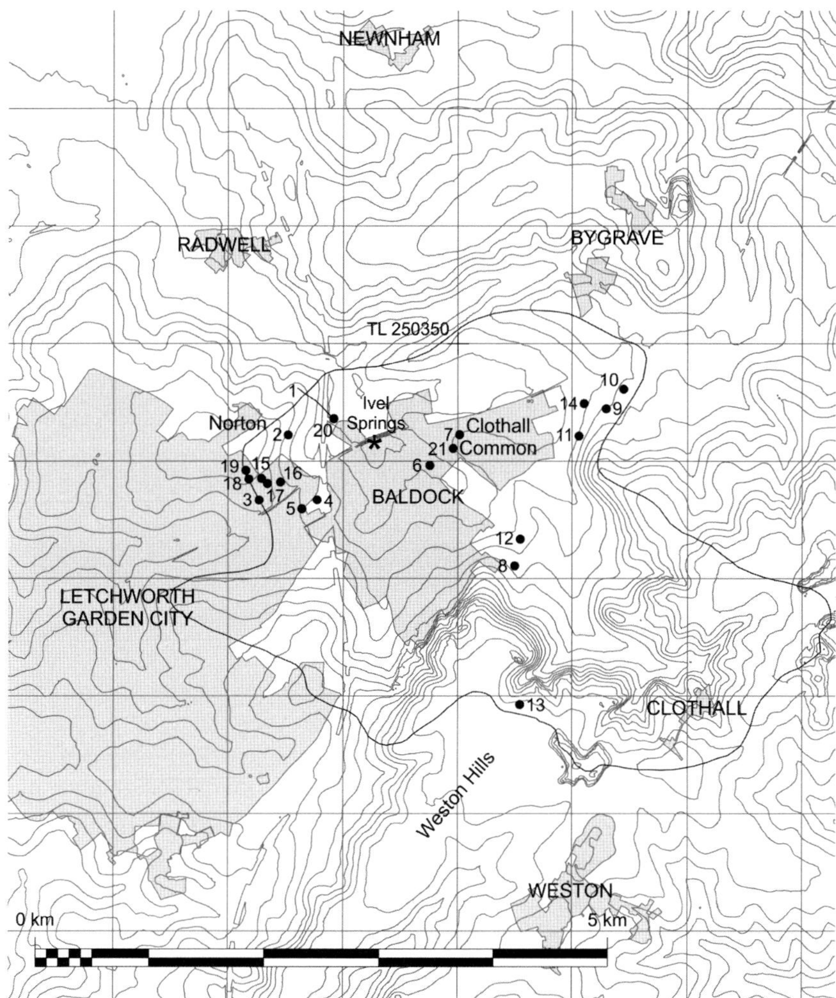

Figure 4.1: The Baldock Bowl: topography and modern settlements. 1: Nortonbury Cursus; 2: Norton Henge; 3: D-shaped enclosure, Blackhorse Road; 4: L-shaped enclosure, Works Road; 5: Hengiform monument, Works Road; 6: Baldock Telephone Exchange; 7: South of Royston Road, Clothall Common, Baldock; 8: pit containing aurochs horn core; 9: Baldock Bypass square enclosure; 10: Neolithic pit L127; 11: Neolithic Pit L147; 12: Neolithic pit L218; 13: Weston Hills henge; 14: Early Bronze Age roundhouse; 15: Blackhorse Road Iron Age enclosure 2; 16: Blackhorse Road Iron Age enclosure 4; 17: Blackhorse Road Iron Age enclosure 3; 18: Early Iron Age enclosure (Green Lane 1988); 19: Early Iron Age pit cluster; 20: Middle Iron Age triangular enclosure, Ivel Springs. Ordnance Survey data © Crown Copyright 2015 OS 100056350.

Roman periods. The purpose of this paper is to summarise what is known of the archaeology of the Bowl and to suggest reasons for this unusual density of sites, acknowledging my debt to Tony for his inspiration.

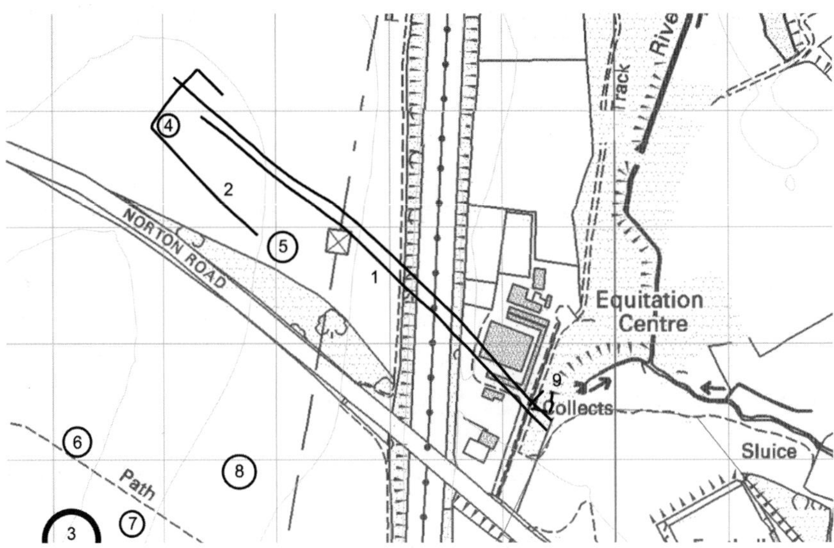

Figure 4.2: The Nortonbury cursus (plan). 1: Narrow cursus; 2: Possible broad cursus; 3: Norton henge; 4–8: Ring ditches. © Crown Copyright 2015 OS 100056350.

4.2 The Neolithic and early Bronze Age

4.2.1 The cursus

The earliest archaeology of the Bowl – apart from scattered Palaeolithic and Mesolithic finds – is represented by an unusually narrow cursus monument of presumably middle Neolithic date in the north-western part of the study area (Fig. 4.2; HHER 9449). It was discovered by John Moss-Eccardt of Letchworth Museum, who excavated several sections across it in 1963 on the line where the A1 motorway was to be built (Moss-Eccardt 1988: 49). The ditches, which cut the chalk bedrock, were 1.2m wide, 0.9m deep and generally around 7m apart; they had a U-shaped profile. There were traces of ploughed-out chalk banks between the ditches, while the centre of the monument remained blank, with the formation of a subsoil deposit between the remains of the banks. Only one section produced some evidence for postholes. These were cut into the filled ditches, meaning that they post-date the construction of the monument and have little bearing on its form or function. The ditches were traced for a distance of 244m and geophysical evidence indicates that they may be at least 500m long. To the south-east the course of the monument becomes lost beneath material dumped by Baldock Urban District Council at its former waste disposal site north of the Ivel Springs. However, the trend is towards the springs (it passes within a few metres of one of the outlying sources of the river), which probably formed the termination at this end. To the north-west the ditches have been traced on aerial

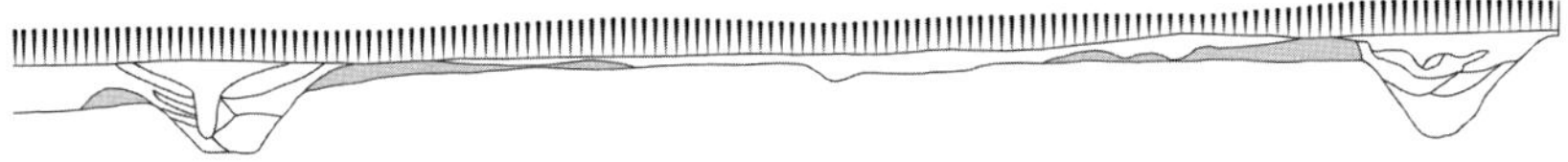

Figure 4.3: The Nortonbury cursus (section).

photographs and by geophysical survey to a point south of Nortonbury Farm. The monument's ultimate destination in this direction remains unknown.

The date of the ditches could not be assessed from their fills, as they contained no datable material. Instead, it was inferred from their cutting through the colluvium in a glacial hollow, one of the fills of which produced one sherd each of Impressed Ware, Grooved Ware and Rusticated Beaker as well as seven flint flakes (six blade-like, one with slight retouch) and a bipolar core. The sections from which this material was derived, however, lay some 13m east of the eastern ditch, so the stratigraphic relationship is not clear-cut. Moreover, the recorded sections do not indicate a clear relationship between the colluvium and the ditch; indeed, one appears to show the uppermost deposit of colluvium sealing a deposit through which the ditch had been cut (Fig. 4.3). The space between the ditches is very narrow for an early Neolithic cursus monument (the average is in the region of 20–60m) and more closely resembles the width of a Romano-British or later trackway. The excavator suggested that they might have formed 'a droveway rather than any ceremonial feature' (Moss-Eccardt 1988: 73), although the lack of surfaces, wear or rutting in the centre of the feature and the presence of two denuded banks immediately inside the ditches rules out this possibility.

4.2.2 The multi-phase henge at Hundred Acre Field

An early (or 'formative') henge, probably contemporary with the later use of the cursus, has recently been identified in Hundred Acre Field (also known as Stapleton's Field), Norton (Fig. 4.4; Fitzpatrick-Matthews 2013). Excavations between 2010 and 2013 suggest that it was first constructed in the later fourth millennium BC as a circular monument some 55m in diameter, with an outer ditch 5m wide and less than a metre deep, with near vertical sides and a flat base (Fig. 4.5). Its fills contained material only of early and middle Neolithic date, including pottery and lithics; the primary silt contained large quantities of animal bone. Deposits at its centre hint at activities involving the smashing of pottery (mostly Peterborough-type Wares), feasting and other ritual activities. Its entrance faced due east, toward the Ivel Springs and, perhaps not coincidentally, the equinox sunrises. A line of three pits, all backfilled with hard packed chalk and clay, lay in the centre of the entrance. Their function is obscure, although their fills would have prevented them from filling with water after heavy rain,

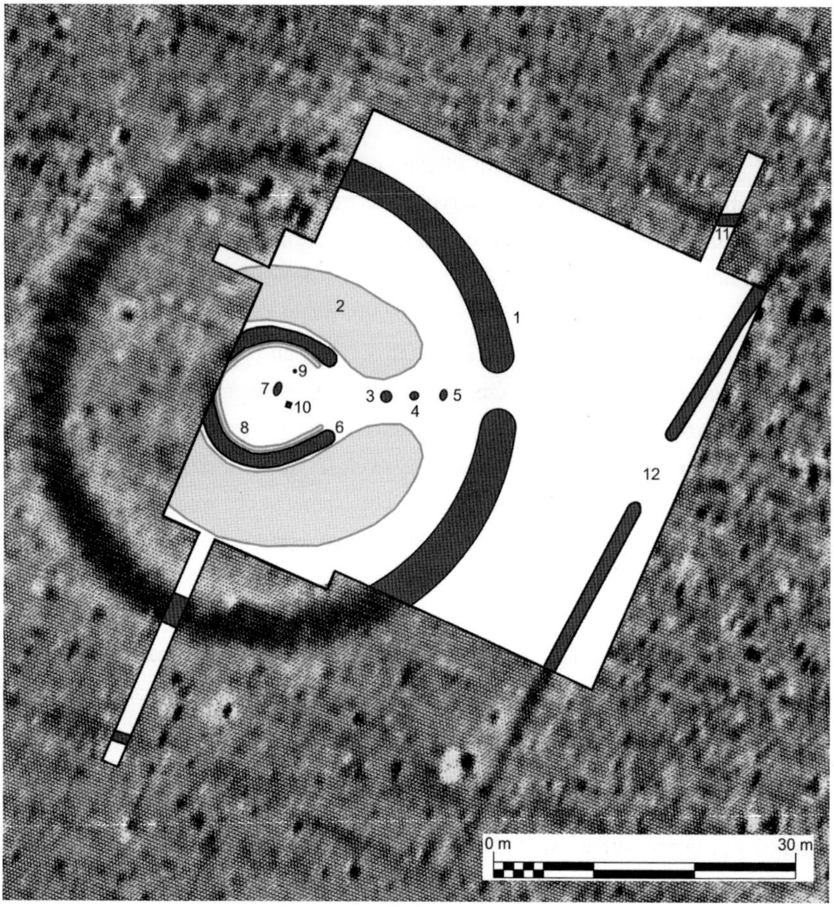

Figure 4.4: Norton henge (geophysics and excavated areas). 1: outer ditch; 2: chalk bank; 3–5: pits; 6: inner ditch; 7: cremation burial pit; 8: inner bank; 9: cremation burial pit; 10: pit containing miniature collared urn; 11: ring ditch; 12: Romano-British enclosure.

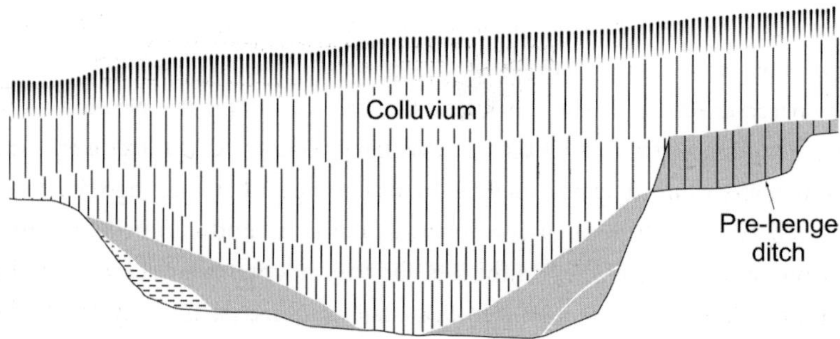

Figure 4.5: Section across the outer ditch of Norton henge.

a phenomenon noted during excavation in 2013. The henge bank, created from chalk excavated from the outer ditch, had been badly damaged by medieval and later ploughing, reducing its height to only a few centimetres. Intriguingly, at least three small plank-built houses were covered by the construction of the bank (Fig. 4.6); an earlier ditch cut by the henge outer ditch may be an enclosure surrounding these houses, none of which contained a hearth. The earlier ditch had a flattish base and was shallow. While it is tempting to suggest that this may have been part of a causewayed enclosure, this speculation goes way beyond the evidence presently available.

During the earlier third millennium BC the monument was altered by the digging of a horseshoe-shaped ditch inside the bank and the modification of the bank by cutting away part of it opposite the entrance to create a more oval form, transforming it into a classic henge. The ceramics associated with this phase continued to be Peterborough-type Wares but were now mixed with Grooved Ware forms. A chalk rubble paving was laid across the centre of the monument and through its entrance, the previous topsoil having worn down as a result of earlier activities, exposing the chalk bedrock in places. At the centre of the monument a large cremation pit was dug which contained the combined remains of a neonate, a child and at least one adult. In this respect, the early henge, like Stonehenge, was used as a place of burial.

In a third phase, probably towards the end of the third millennium, a massive post was set up close to its centre and a ring of posts erected on a low chalk bank constructed on the inner lip of the ditch. A square chalk platform was laid over the top of the cremation pit. Pottery of this phase appears to include a little Beaker material (albeit in small quantities) and Collared Urns, although Grooved Ware continued to be present. Towards the end of this phase the cremated remains of a child, aged perhaps eight to 10 years, were deposited just inside the entrance, while a complete miniature Collared Urn was placed in a shallow square pit close to the centre, unusually not accompanying a human burial. These appear to have been the last events in the history of the henge, which was subsequently abandoned.

The ceramics retrieved from the site were predominantly Neolithic (apart from later types from subsoils, colluvium deposits and cut features). There appear to be sand-tempered middle Neolithic types, Peterborough Wares and Grooved Ware, with small quantities of Beaker types and Collared Urns in the later phase deposits. Precise dating will depend on obtaining radiocarbon dates from organic materials retrieved from sealed deposits, particularly for the final phase, as the date at which Collared Urns first appeared is a matter for debate (Longworth 1984: 19).

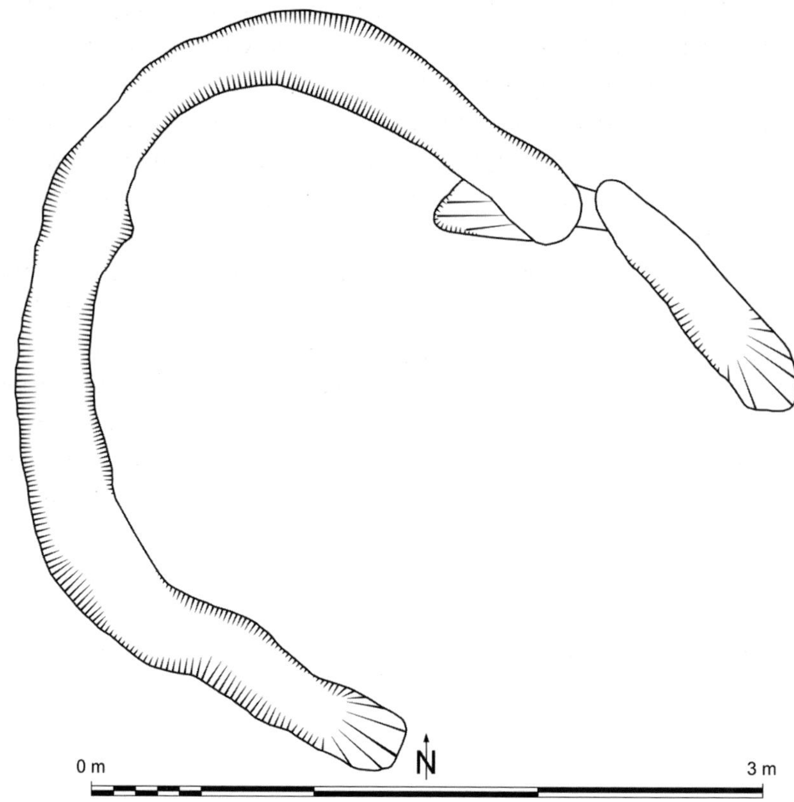

Figure 4.6: Middle Neolithic house, Hundred Acre Field, Norton.

Following small-scale exploratory work on the outer ditch during Easter 2013, a sample of pig bone from its base was submitted for radiocarbon dating. The result, 1910 ± 45 bp (IHME-2085, 1–230 Cal AD at 2σ), conflicts with the material culture retrieved from the fills, which was entirely of fourth millennium BC character. Contamination of the sample while in the ground is suspected – there was an animal burrow visible in section – and further samples will be needed to test the reliability of this date. This is in hand. It is of interest to note that a date obtained from organics in soil associated with the bone, 5940 ± 80 bp (IHME-2083, 5030–4610 cal BC at 2σ), suggests an earlier prehistoric date.

4.2.3 Blackhorse Road and Works Road

Excavations undertaken by Letchworth Museum during the development of the industrial estate at Blackhorse Road to the south-west of Hundred Acre Field in 1958–67 revealed evidence of occupation during the third millennium BC (Moss-Eccardt 1988: 44–7). A large D-shaped enclosure identified on the highest point of the site at Blackhorse Road and dated by its excavator to the Iron Age (Moss-Eccardt 1988: 67, Enclosure One) is more likely to be a Neolithic type (Fig. 4.7). No positive dating evidence for its construction was recovered during its investigation, although one of the palisade postholes produced unfeatured potsherds said to be of Iron Age character; these will need to be reassessed. Similar enclosures are known from south-west England, where they are of later Neolithic date.

A group of six large pits situated towards the south-west of the area investigated appear to have been quarries for fresh chalk or flint and their deliberate backfills contained an eclectic mixture of middle Neolithic to early Bronze Age ceramics, lithics and animal bones, for which anomalously young radiocarbon dates were obtained (see below). Although these pits may have been dug initially to extract chalk or flint, the nature of the artefacts recovered from them and their rapid filling suggests a ritual context; an early interim report stated that each had a dog burial in the base (CBA Group 10 1962: 11). At the eastern end of the site a posthole produced a flint-backed knife, a shallow pit contained an antler pick and a ditch contained bones of a bear.

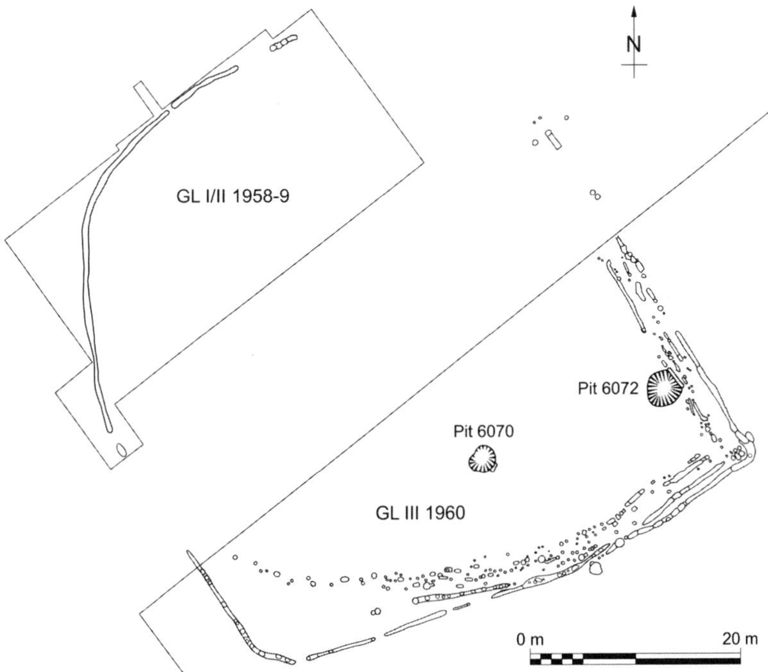

Figure 4.7: Late Neolithic D-shaped enclosure, Blackhorse Road, Letchworth Garden City (after Moss-Eccardt 1988).

A range of Neolithic pottery types was found across the site, including three styles of Peterborough Ware (Ebbsfleet, Fengate and Mortlake styles), Grooved Ware, six Rusticated Beakers and one Necked Beaker. One of the Beakers recovered from the deep pits was associated with carbonised wood that produced a radiocarbon date of 3590 ± 130 bp (BM-284; 2312–1608 cal BC at 2σ), while another pit containing Ebbsfleet pottery produced dates of 3520 ± 150 bp, 3310 ± 150 bp and 3830 ± 140 bp (BM-186, BM-187 and BM-283; 2271–1483 cal BC, 1975–1275 cal BC and 2666–1890 cal BC at 2σ). These dates are extremely late for Peterborough Wares, which are generally believed to have fallen from use by *c.*2400 cal BC, raising the possibility that the ceramics were residual in their contexts.

Nearby, an L-shaped enclosure was excavated by the Hertfordshire Archaeological Trust in 1997 at the east end of Works Road, about 250m to the south-east of Blackhorse Road (Fig. 4.8; Humphrey 1997a: 5). It was associated with lithics similar to those found at Blackhorse Road, many with the characteristic blue-white patination noted there. The ditch followed an earlier line of pits, suggesting that this was a long-lived boundary. Inside the enclosure were further pits and a group of postholes forming part of a rectangular structure. To its south-west, a small hengiform monument, with the crouched inhumation burial of a child at its centre, was cut by a late neolithic ring ditch, although the monument produced no directly datable material (Fig. 4.9; Humphrey 1997b: 11). North of the ring ditch were further pits and postholes, although it is not possible to recognise any definite structures in this area. The flint assemblage from this site has been compared with that from Blackhorse Road, suggesting that it was contemporary and the location of further occupation in the later third and earlier second millennia BC.

4.2.4 Baldock

An early Neolithic leaf-shaped arrowhead (Robinson 1986: 173, no. 750) was found in a gully (Stead and Rigby 1986: Feature C4) on the Telephone Exchange site that lay on a different alignment from the Iron Age and Romano-British gullies and ditches in this area. This may be evidence for earlier Neolithic activity in the lower part of the hollow in which the Iron Age settlement later developed. There is a general scatter of Neolithic material from the site of the town, so the occupation appears to have been extensive, if not intensive.

On the eastern edge of the Bowl in situ deposits of third millennium BC date were exposed in a large but shallow doline during the excavation of the Iron Age and Romano-British settlement complex south of Royston Road from 1986 to 1989 (Fig. 4.10). A flint working floor with numerous pieces of débitage was

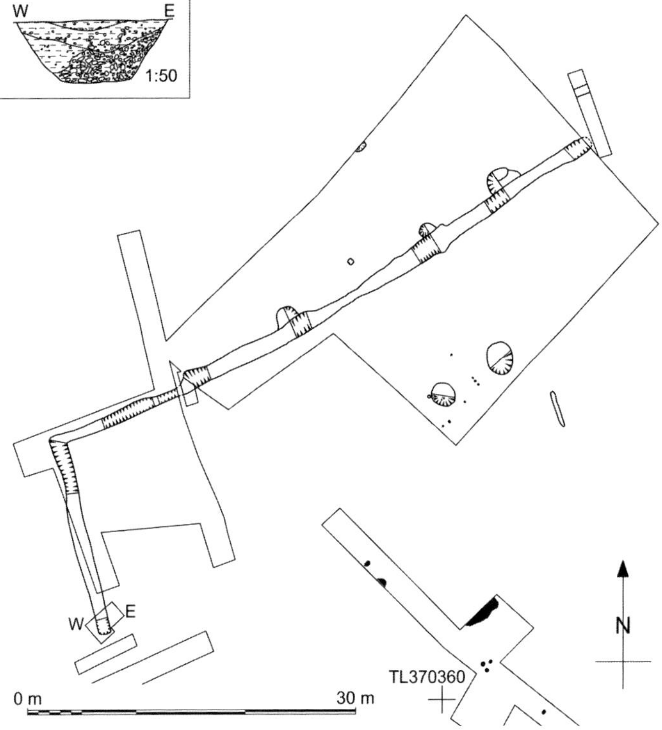

Figure 4.8: L-shaped enclosure, Works Road, Letchworth Garden City (after Humphrey 1997b).

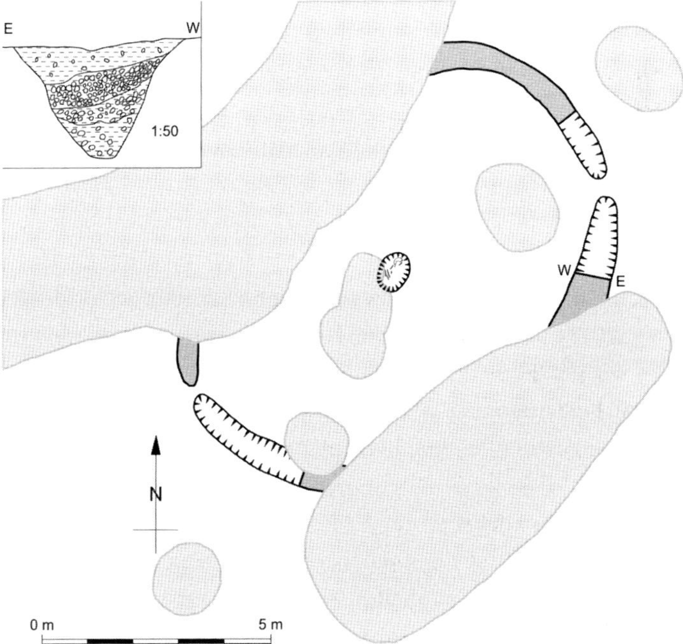

Figure 4.9: Hengiform enclosure, Works Road (after Humphrey 1997b).

associated with numerous fragments of Peterborough Ware on the northern edge of the hollow, while elements of a rectangular post-built structure were identified to the south (Fig. 4.11; Plate 4.1). The broad and shallow periglacial doline became the focus for a cremation cemetery in the first century AD. Although the late Neolithic soils in the hollow produced mollusc remains indicative of an open landscape, the fill of a nearby Neolithic pit was more suggestive of a shaded environment (Murphy 1990).

During excavations on the line of the A505 Baldock Bypass in 2003 a series of Neolithic features, including a pit containing a complete aurochs horn core, was encountered to the south-east of the town (Keir and Phillips 2009: 16). Towards the eastern edge of the bowl, south of Bygrave, a square enclosure with corners aligned roughly towards the cardinal points (Plate 4.2) contained the crouched skeleton of a mature adult male, aged over 50, laid on his right side with his head to the north-east (Mallows and Phillips 2009a: 13). Bone collagen produced a radiocarbon date of 4460 ± 40 bp (Beta-210616, 3414–2938 cal BC at 2σ), probably contemporary with the first phase at the Norton henge.

To the east of Baldock, three shaft-like pits resembling those at Blackhorse Road were discovered spread out over 1.7km. Unlike the pits at the latter site, however, they contained little datable material and there was no evidence for structured deposition; all appeared to have been only partly backfilled before being left to fill naturally in what mollusc remains suggest was a woodland environment (Mallows and Phillips 2009a: 11; Phillips 2009a: 16).

South of Baldock, on the north-eastern edge of the Weston Hills and on the skyline of the Bowl, a Class II henge monument was first identified from aerial photographs (Fig. 4.12), although it also survives as a low earthwork, which was scheduled in 1995 (HHER 3258). The earthwork is around 65m in diameter and is raised around 1m above the surrounding landscape, with an external ditch represented by a hollow up to 0.5m deep and varying in width between 7m and 10m. The eastern entrance is around 15m wide and the western around 20m. The monument sits towards the top of the southern side of a dry valley running down to the north-east, towards the Baldock–Braughing road. Aerial photographs show a macula in the centre of the henge, which is probably the site of a dene hole known as Jack o'Legs' Cave, filled in during the mid-twentieth century. Although undated by excavation, this is an oval henge of classic type and its construction presumably post-dates that of the henge in Norton. It is unclear, though, if the later phases at Norton overlapped with activity at the Weston henge.

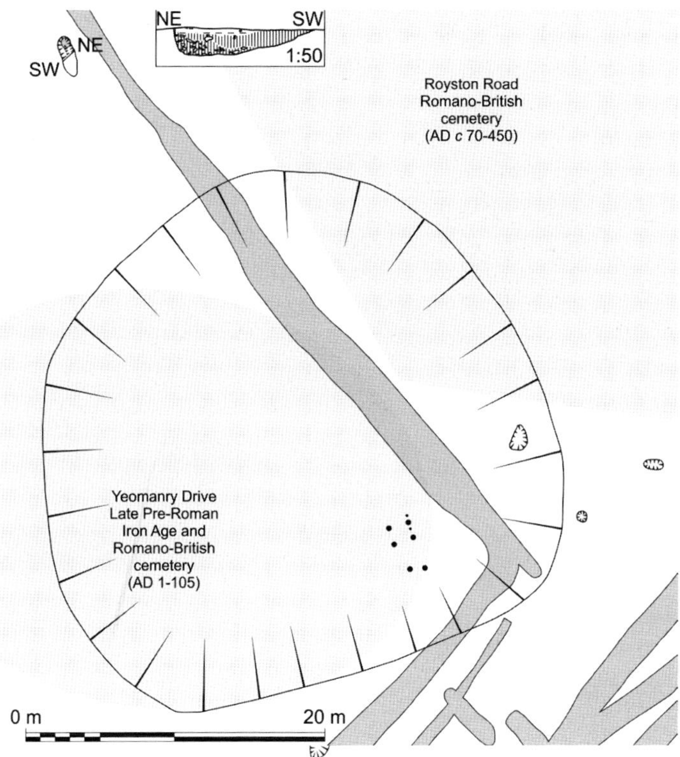

Figure 4.10: Third millennium BC activity at Clothall Common, Baldock.

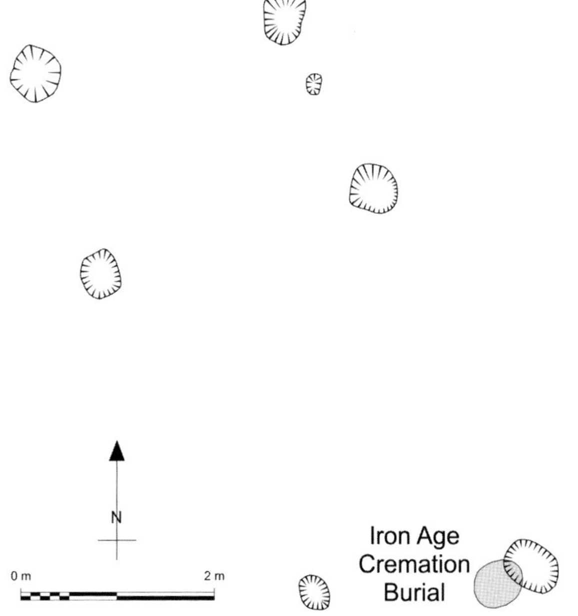

Figure 4.11: Post-built structure, Clothall Common.

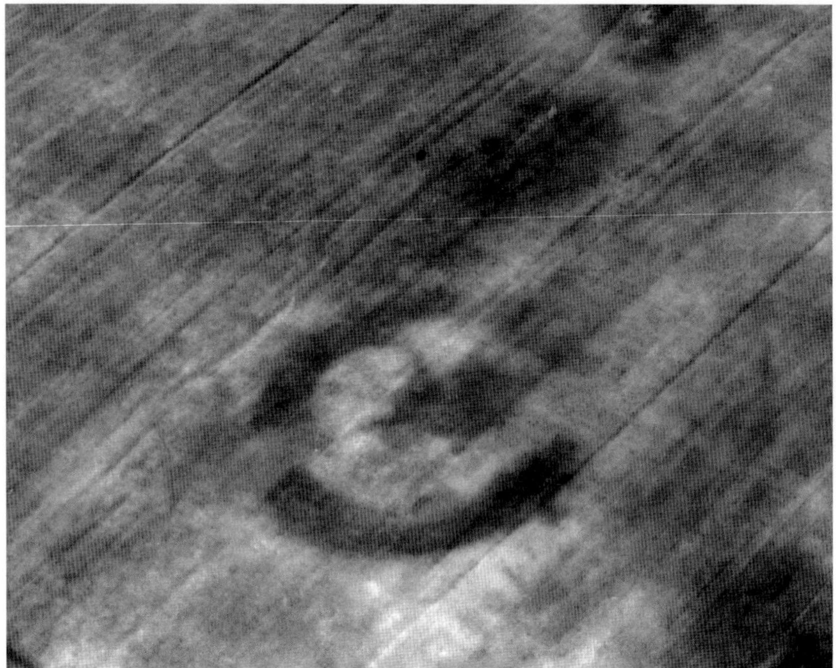

Figure 4.12: The henge at Jack o'Leg's Cave, Weston Hills, on 7 July 1960 (Cambridge University Collection of Aerial Photography ABU95, reproduced with permission).

4.2.5 The second millennium BC: burial mounds and a dearth of settlements

In 1959–61 John Moss-Eccardt excavated a ring ditch with a diameter of approximately 17m in Hundred Acre Field (HHER 1032). This is not reported in his (1988) publication of sites in the Letchworth area and it is understood that the site records were stolen around the time of the excavation (J. Moss-Eccardt, pers. comm.). Part of a biconical urn of middle Bronze Age date was found and, although its original context is not clear, if it derives from a central burial it suggests that the mound dates from about 1800–1600 BC. The site probably lay towards the north-eastern edge of the field, where there are unclear hints of ring ditches on aerial photographs and geophysical surveys. This was one of the areas where some early geophysical survey was carried out for Moss-Eccardt.

In 1963 Moss-Eccardt excavated a section through a second ring ditch, 30.5m in diameter, north of Norton Road (Fig. 4.2 no. 5; Moss-Eccardt 1988: 47–9; HHER 4765). A central pit, assumed to be the grave, contained only soil and appeared to have been re-dug on at least one occasion; four other pits and two postholes were also found inside the ditch. The fills of the ditch contained finds ranging from Peterborough Wares in the primary silts to Beaker and Collared Urn sherds in the subsequent layers.

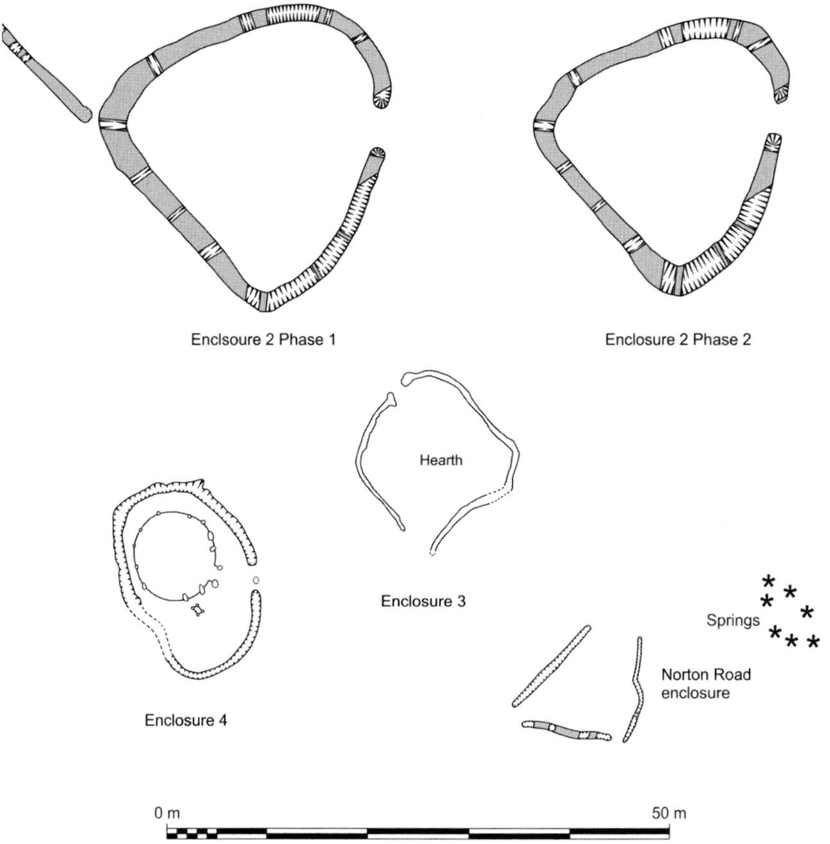

Enclsoure 2 Phase 1
Enclosure 2 Phase 2
Hearth
Enclosure 3
Enclosure 4
Springs
Norton Road
enclosure
0 m
50 m

Figure 4.13: Iron Age enclosures, Blackhorse Road (after Moss-Eccardt 1988).

0 mm 50 mm

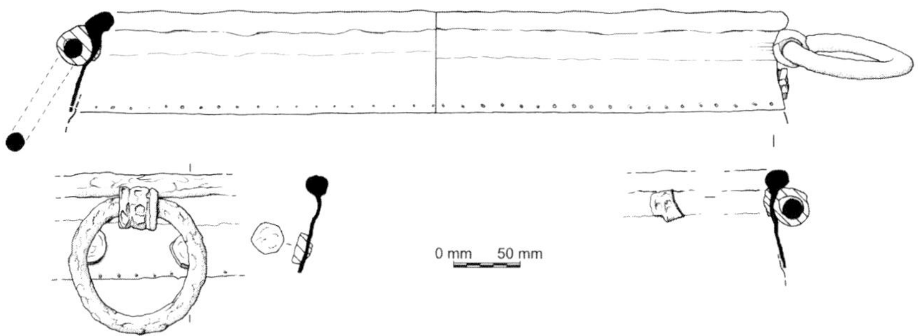

Figure 4.14: The Iron Age cauldron rim from Blackhorse Road (drawing by Frances Saxton).

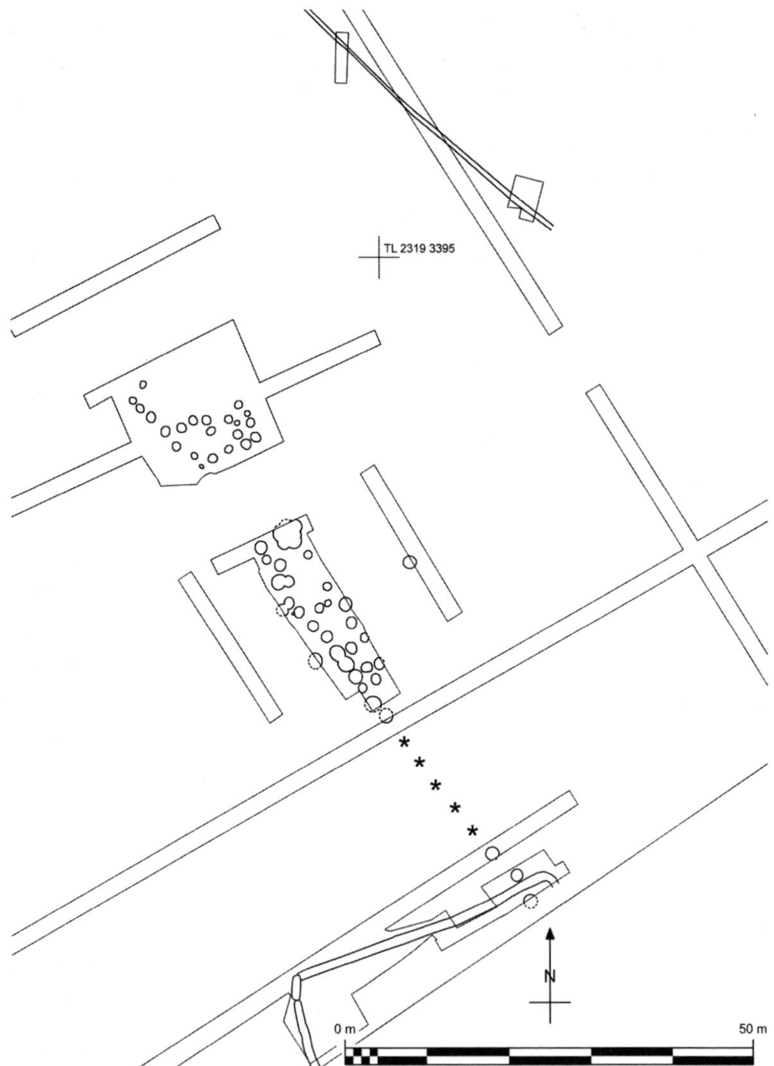

Figure 4.15: Early Iron Age pit cluster, Green Lane, Letchworth Garden City.

Part of another ring ditch, estimated to be around 20m in diameter, was excavated by the Hertfordshire Archaeological Trust in 1997 at the eastern end of Works Road, around 650m to the south of the Stapleton's Field henge in the historic parish of Willian (Humphrey 1997b: 12). Four separate episodes of ditch cutting were observed, the final being done in discrete segments.

At the eastern edge of the Bowl, beside the A505 south of Bygrave, a ploughed-out barrow cemetery consisting of six ring ditches and a pond 'barrow' was investigated during the construction of the Baldock Bypass.

Aerial photographs from 1968 show that the barrows survived as low mounds at that time; they were completely destroyed in the 35 years that preceded their excavation and the ditch fills were highly truncated (Mallows and Phillips 2009b: 23). Only two burials beneath the former mounds remained as a sad reflection on the destructive nature of everyday agricultural practices in the late twentieth century. They included, in the south-westernmost barrow of the group, a central cremation deposit under an inverted Collared Urn consisting of an infant and possibly a female young or mature adult. An unurned burial, located in the south-eastern quadrant of the northernmost and largest of the barrows, produced a radiocarbon date from the bone of 3400 ± 40 bp (Beta-210609, 1793–1605 cal BC at 2σ). Two other unurned cremation burials were found in the ditch fills. Environmental evidence suggests an open, probably grassland, landscape.

It is noteworthy that there is little evidence for second millennium BC activity at Blackhorse Road or Baldock, despite the numerous nearby ring ditches, many of which are presumably of this date, suggesting that contemporary settlement must have been located elsewhere. There are hints from unstratified lithic material at Clothall Common, Baldock, that activity continued in this area, although its focus has not been located. The probably early Bronze Age roundhouse found to the south of the A505 during the construction of the Baldock Bypass in 2003 (Mallows and Phillips 2009b: 27) suggests that the focus of settlement may have shifted further to the east.

4.3 The first millennium BC

4.3.1 Renewed activity at Blackhorse Road

At Blackhorse Road a series of at least four enclosures was built from the eighth century BC through to the Roman conquest (Moss-Eccardt 1988: 67–72; Matthews and Burleigh 1989: 27; Fig. 4.13). Each is thought to have been a single farmstead, with timber roundhouses and storage pits, occupied by perhaps just one extended family. The ceramics included early and middle Iron Age types. One of the most significant finds was the rim of an iron cauldron of La Tène II type dating from the second or third century BC (Fig. 4.14; Moss-Eccardt 1965: 177). As well as the domestic occupation, ritual activity is shown by the construction of an early Iron Age pit cluster to the north, partly excavated in 1988 (Fig. 4.15), which seems to have been backfilled almost immediately after it was dug.

During the investigation of the Nortonbury cursus in 1963, before construction of the A1 motorway, a triangular enclosure was partly investigated (Moss-Eccardt 1988: 72–3). The ditches, which were open at the corners, were characterised by fills of fine gravel. These appear to have been deposited during episodes of flooding; the north-eastern corner of the enclosure lies adjacent to one of the Ivel Springs and it is likely that they were the focus of the activity, as no structures were identified in the ditched area. Land molluscs indicate that the enclosure was built in an open, arable landscape. The ceramics were of middle Iron Age date and included two low-shouldered bowls with decorated rims.

Similar material was found nearby in the doline at Clothall Common, where the Neolithic activity had been located, but no evidence for structures was found. In another large doline to the south-west there is evidence that the hollow was used for the disposal of human bodies, perhaps by exposure. One of a number of residual bones found in late Iron Age deposits produced a radiocarbon date of 2380 ± 130 bp (HAR-5965, 508 ± 396 cal BC at 2σ), placing this activity within the middle Iron Age. So far, only this burial evidence has been identified and it is likely that these dells were seen as natural places for the disposal of the dead. There may be echoes of pond barrows and the ritual pit (Green 1986: 133) in their use as a means of accessing the underworld, a natural equivalent of the Greek βοθρός or the Roman *mundus*.

4.3.2 The Baldock *oppidum*

It was during the later part of the middle Iron Age that the next major development in the Bowl began: the growth of a large *oppidum* at Baldock, defined by linear ditches, pit alignments and a polyfocal settlement at its core. It is not the purpose of this paper to dwell on the *oppidum* at length, but it is worth pointing out that many of its features date from the second century BC, including its early Welwyn type burial (Stead and Rigby 1986: 51–61), which must date from before *c.*100 BC. It is evident from limited excavation that a proto-urban settlement had developed in Walls Field before the middle of the first century BC (Stead and Rigby 1986: 84; Burleigh and Fitzpatrick-Matthews forthcoming), making it arguably the earliest such site in Britain.

The *oppidum* became a Roman town of some size following the conquest, although it seems never to have been administratively important (Burleigh and Fitzpatrick-Matthews 2010: 27). Nevertheless, its unusual diversity of burials and cemeteries is noteworthy and suggests that it may have been more significant as a cult centre. Unusually for a Romano-British small town in eastern England, there is clear evidence for its continued existence into the fifth and even sixth centuries AD, based on both stratigraphic and artefactual evidence (Fitzpatrick-Matthews 2010: 138). There is no space here to explore this fascinating site, which is dealt with elsewhere in this volume by Gil Burleigh.

4.4 Understanding the landscape

Although, as already noted, this is not a dramatic landscape of mountains and deep valleys, it is nevertheless an unusual topographical feature in the north-eastern Chilterns, which is generally characterised by dry valleys. From the Ivel Springs, as indeed from most places within the Bowl, there is a distinct sense of being enclosed by hills. More obvious to the south, they include some very recognisable landforms, especially Bird Hill, Clothall. It is tempting to speculate that the bank of the Norton henge was designed, at least partly, to mimic this ring of low hills, creating a microcosm of the bowl on its north-western edge.

There appears to be a cycle of activity, in the terms of the *Annales* school of historiography's *longue durée*: the later fourth and earlier third millennia BC see the construction of ritual monuments, followed by occupation in the later third, then burial during the second millennium and domestic occupation in the first. In many ways, this is the story of later prehistory in Britain: Bronze Age settlement sites are notoriously difficult to recognise, while the same is true for Iron Age burials. Nevertheless, the rhythm of these changes is probably tied in to longer-term social changes and differing belief systems.

It is clear that in the Neolithic the Ivel Springs formed a focus for religious belief, with one end of the Nortonbury cursus apparently situated by the southernmost spring. Later in the middle Neolithic the entrance of the Norton 'formative' henge is certainly focused on the same area. Evidence of activity inside the henge, which evidently included the consumption of large quantities of meat, the subsequent smashing of animal bone and pottery, and the knapping of flint, suggests that gatherings were potentially boisterous and noisy. This matches the hypothesised Neolithic belief systems explored by David Lewis-Williams and David Pearce (2005), who present evidence for visions of a tiered cosmos induced by ritual and mind-altering substances. Andrew Jones (2007) has suggested that the role of rituals as performance was an important element in inscribing memories of the ancestors. Processions along the cursus and celebrations within the 'formative' henge were ways of connecting with an ancestral dreamtime, with the flow of the river perhaps a metaphor for the course of human life (Bradley 2007: 68), the springs representing birth and/or the mysterious origins of new life. Burial was restricted to places away from the springs, east of Baldock and at Works Road, Letchworth.

By the end of the third millennium, however, formerly ritual and domestic areas were either abandoned or given over to monuments for the dead. At Clothall Common activity in the doline ceased with the end of the use of Peterborough type Ware: there is no Beaker or later Bronze Age material from the site. At Blackhorse Road and east of Baldock the shafts, with their deliberate backfills containing much older (and perhaps curated) ceramics and selected animal bones, suggest a shift towards appeasing chthonic deities. The dead, on the other hand, were highly visible, their burial mounds colonising areas such as the Norton henge or the Works Road site, which had previously been the realm of the living. Perhaps this should be seen as a means of uniting them with the ancestors, colonising landscapes associated with those who first opened them up for farming.

During the Iron Age the springs once again became a focus for activity, while domestic occupation resumed in areas abandoned for more than a thousand years. The remarkable middle Iron Age triangular 'enclosure' at the head of one of the springs must be connected with the water source, while the presence of pond weed as a temper in at least some of the ceramics (Birley in Moss-Eccardt 1988: 83) suggests the use of material from the springs themselves in the production of pottery. The unprecedented developments at Baldock, in the centre of the bowl, from the late second century BC onward have usually been seen in terms of political development, but the role of the springs should not be overlooked. The survival of the Celtic river name 'Ivel' (derived from Brittonic **gablo-*, 'forked') suggests a continuing symbolic importance into the early medieval period.

4.5 Conclusion

The remarkable prehistory of this small landscape unit is without parallel in Hertfordshire or neighbouring areas, although clusters of monuments of a single period have been noted elsewhere, as at Cardington in the Ouse valley (Luke 2007: 38). One of the most compelling features is the ritual nature of many of the elements within the landscape: it may be suggested that one of the reasons for the apparent popularity of the Bowl for these activities is the presence of the Ivel springs, which were certainly a focus of prehistoric interest, although their status in the Roman period is more obscure. It is the long-term continuity not just of human settlement but also of a possible religious focus that is the most striking aspect of the Baldock Bowl: this is without doubt an exceptional landscape.

4.6 References

Bradley, R. (2007), *The prehistory of Britain and Ireland* (Cambridge).

Burleigh, G.R. and Fitzpatrick-Matthews, K.J. (2010), *Excavations at Baldock, Hertfordshire, 1978–1994, volume 1: an Iron Age and Romano-British cemetery at Wallington Road*, North Hertfordshire Museums Archaeological Monograph 1 (Letchworth Garden City).

Burleigh, G.R and Fitzpatrick-Matthews, K.J. (forthcoming), *Excavations at Baldock, Hertfordshire, 1978–1994, volume 2: the Iron Age oppidum and its cemeteries*, North Hertfordshire Museums Archaeological Monograph 2 (Letchworth Garden City).

CBA Group 10 (1962), *The Archaeologist in Essex, Hertfordshire, London and Middlesex 1960* (London).

Fitzpatrick-Matthews, K.J. (2010), 'Collapse, change or continuity? Exploring the three Cs in sub-Roman Baldock', in A. Moore, G. Taylor, E. Harris, P. Girdwood and L. Shipley (eds), *TRAC 2009: Proceedings of the Nineteenth Annual Theoretical Roman Archaeology Conference, Michigan and Southampton 2009* (Oxford), pp. 132–48.

Fitzpatrick-Matthews, K.J. (2013), 'The discovery of an early henge at Norton, Hertfordshire by local archaeologists', *Heritage Daily* 11 September 2013. Available at: <http://www.heritagedaily.com/2013/09/the-discovery-of-an-early-henge-at-norton-hertfordshire-by-local-archaeologists/98965>, accessed 26 September 13.

Green, M.J. (1986), *The Gods of the Celts* (Stroud).

Humphrey, R. (1997a), *Land to the east of Works Road, Letchworth, Hertfordshire: an archaeological excavation*, Hertfordshire Archaeological Trust Report 236 (Hertford).

Humphrey, R. (1997b), *Land to the east of Works Road, Letchworth, Hertfordshire: archaeological observation and recording*, Hertfordshire Archaeological Trust Report 270 (Hertford).

Jones, A. (2007), *Memory and Material Culture* (Cambridge).

Keir, W. and Phillips, M. (2009), 'Late Neolithic, Area 3. Neolithic, Area 1', in Phillips (2009b), p. 16.

Lewis-Williams, D. and Pearce, D. (2005), *Inside the Neolithic mind: consciousness, cosmos and the realm of the gods* (London).

Longworth, I.H. (1984), *Collared urns of the Bronze Age in Great Britain and Ireland* (Cambridge).

Luke, M. (2007), 'The Palaeolithic to early Bronze Age', in M. Oake, M. Luke, M. Dawson, M. Edgeworth and P. Murphy (eds), *Bedfordshire archaeology. Research and archaeology: resource assessment, research agenda and strategy*, Bedfordshire Archaeological Monograph 9 (Bedford), pp. 21–57.

Mallows, C. and Phillips, M. (2009a), 'Late Neolithic, Area 1', in Phillips (2009b), pp. 11–13.

Mallows, C. and Phillips, M. (2009b), 'Early Bronze Age', in Phillips (2009b), pp. 23–7.

Matthews, K.J. and Burleigh, G.R. (1989), 'A Saxon and early medieval settlement at Green Lane, Letchworth', *Hertfordshire's Past* 26, pp. 27–31.

Moss-Eccardt, J. (1965), 'An iron cauldron-rim from Letchworth, Herts.', *Antiquaries Journal* 45/2, pp. 173–7.

Moss-Eccardt, J. (1988), 'Archaeological investigations in the Letchworth area, 1958–1974', *Proceedings of the Cambridge Antiquarian Society* 77: 35–103.

Murphy, P. (1990), 'Land molluscs, carbonised cereals and crop weeds, charcoal, avian eggshell and coprolites from prehistoric and Roman contexts', North Hertfordshire Museums Field Archaeology Section unpublished report.

Phillips, M. (2009a), 'Late Neolithic, Area 2', in Phillips (2009b), pp. 13–16.

Phillips, M.,(ed.)(2009b), *Four millennia of activity along the A505 Baldock Bypass, Hertfordshire*, East Anglian Archaeology 128 (Bedford).

Robinson, P. (1986), 'The Flint Assemblage', in Stead and Rigby (1986), pp. 173–7

Rook, T. (1974), 'Welch's Farm – a success for the fieldworker', *Hertfordshire Archaeological Review* 9, pp. 170–74.

Stead, I.M. and Rigby, V. (1986), *Baldock: the excavation of a Roman and pre-Roman settlement, 1968–1972, Britannia* Monograph 7 (London).

CHAPTER 5

Burials, ditches and deities: defining the boundaries of Iron Age and Romano-British Baldock

Gil Burleigh

5.1 Introduction

This paper presents a hypothesis that the territorial boundaries of the pre-Roman and Roman town of Baldock may be defined by temples and temple treasure hoards, coin hoards, shrines, cult sanctuaries and elite burials, as well as by multiple ditches, originally with embankments. Part of the evidence for this idea comes from the work of Tony Rook in Welwyn and its hinterland. The opportunity is also taken here to write in some detail about the sites at Ashwell End, Hinxworth and Pegsdon in the belief that they deserve to be better known pending the completion of the final reports.

Writing in the second century AD, the Greek geographer and traveller Pausanias mentions temples, shrines and other sanctuaries sited on frontiers and the political boundaries between city states (*poleis*); likewise, the tombs of heroes (Levi 1971). As a result a number of modern authors postulate sanctuaries on frontiers and territorial boundaries in other Roman provinces, such as Gaul and Germania (R. Haeussler, pers. comm.; Spickermann 2008).

It has been convincingly argued that the origins of the Greek city state, from the eighth century BC onwards, was in large measure due to religion. The city states of classical Greece were defined as much by the boundaries of 'civilised' space as by its urban centres. The city took shape through what de Polignac (1995) calls a 'religious bipolarity', the cults operating both to organise social space and to articulate social relationships not only at the heart of the inhabited area but also on the edges of the territory. Together with the urban cults, these sanctuaries 'in the wild' identified the *polis* and its sphere of influence, giving rise to the concept of the state as a territorial unit distinct from its neighbours (de Polignac 1995).

Could a similar process have influenced the development of urban centres and their territories – all settlements require an economic and social hinterland – in other Roman provinces, including Britain? Urbanisation in Britain began in some cases before the Roman Conquest – possibly as early as the late second century BC at Baldock/C.Vic[1] (Burleigh 1995b; Burleigh and Fitzpatrick-Matthews 2010: 21–4; Fitzpatrick-Matthews and Burleigh 2007: 7), certainly by the mid-first century BC at Silchester/Calleva Atrebatum (Fulford 1993; Fulford and Timby 2000), and by around the last quarter of the first century BC at Colchester/Camulodunon (Hawkes and Crummy 1995: 3–61).

A significant number of Iron Age and Romano-British rural shrines and temples are located on or near the boundaries of tribal or *civitas* territories (Wait 1985: 176; Woodward 1992: 20). The idea of boundaries as places of sacred liminality was important and this will have helped determine the location of such sanctuaries (Smith 2001: 150). Examples include Woodeaton, Oxfordshire, on the boundary between the Catuvellauni and the Dobunni (Goodchild and Kirk 1954; Kirk 1949); Thetford, Norfolk, on the boundary between the Catuvellauni, Trinovantes and Iceni (Gregory 1992); Frilford, Berkshire, near the boundary of the *civitas* areas of the Atrebates, Catuvellauni and Dobunni (Bradford and Goodchild 1939); and Great Chesterford and Harlow, Essex, sited near the boundary of the Catuvellauni and Trinovantes (France and Gobel 1985). Frilford, Great Chesterford, Harlow and Thetford, at least, have Iron Age antecedents. Baldock, of course, lies well within the territory of the Catuvellauni.

Woodward (1992: 20) has suggested that such rural temples served a variety of economic and social as well as religious functions, including as centres for trade and exchange between tribal and *civitas* groups, for social contact, and for the administration of justice. It is known that many temples in Gaul are on boundaries and served multiple functions, and it is likely that the same diversity would have applied in Britain. A sanctuary's religious, economic, legal and social activities would have attracted people and led to settlement expansion, making what may have started as an isolated sanctuary become part of a larger community.

In addition, it is worth noting here that a number of temples are associated with older monuments, including hillforts (e.g., Chanctonbury, Croft Ambrey, Henley Wood, Lydney Park, Maiden Castle and Uley); Neolithic and Bronze Age barrows (Brean Down, Maiden Castle, Mutlow Hill and Uley) and other features (Wait 1985: 414; Williams 1998: 72). These *loci* may have inspired a sense of place and of the past, providing continuity and a link to the ancestors that would have exerted a powerful attraction for people seeking suitable settings for sacred sites (Smith 2001: 151).

Is it possible that individual late Iron Age and Romano-British settlements had territories defined by the placing of temples and shrines, as well as other boundary markers? After all, at least in Italy, and no doubt in other provinces too, an even smaller entity, estates, had boundaries defined with marker stones. Each February there was the festival of the *Terminalia*, when the boundaries were processed with various rituals and offerings to honour Terminus or Jupiter Terminus, the gods of boundaries and boundary markers. Perhaps the medieval and later custom of beating the parish bounds reflects a distant memory or a continuing echo of such rituals (Rook 1976: 8-10).

And what of the tombs of heroes? At Camulodunon (Colchester), an elite burial in a barrow is sited at Lexden, on the territorial boundary of the early town (*oppidum*), which is defined also by an extensive system of ditched and banked dykes. Peacock (1971: 179) suggested that the tomb, dating to *c.*10 BC, could possibly be that of the Iron Age ruler Addedomarus, known from his coins (see also Foster 1986: 187). The burial goods included a bronze cupid, boar and bull figurines, wine amphorae, furniture fittings, a folding stool, iron mail armour and a medallion of the Roman emperor Augustus.

In the next section I will discuss the sites which may be seen in the light of the hypothesis. The location of these sites is shown in Fig. 5.1.

5.2 Discussion and evidence

5.2.1 'Heroic' burials at Baldock

On the south-west edge of the putative late Iron Age town of Baldock an elite burial, probably once under a barrow, was discovered in 1967. It contained a wine amphora, two bronze-bound wooden wine-mixing buckets, a bronze cauldron, two iron fire-dogs, pig remains, bronze dishes and some claws from a bearskin (Stead and Rigby 1986). Dating from the early first century BC at the latest, it is the earliest Welwyn-type burial known. Around 30 BC another elite individual was buried on the north-east edge of the town, this time in an enormous square ditched enclosure, and originally under a square barrow, excavated in 1980–81 (Burleigh 1982; Burleigh and Fitzpatrick-Matthews 2010: 15–16). Like the earlier Baldock ruler, he took a bronze-bound wine-mixing bucket and pig carcasses into the after-life, as well as bronze jewellery, wooden furniture decorated with bronze studs, a pottery jar with a pedestal base and fragments of rare and skilfully crafted iron mail cut from a coat of armour. Fitzpatrick-Matthews suggested that this burial could be an alternative candidate for Addedomarus (Fitzpatrick-Matthews and Burleigh 2007: 5), although the dating may make this

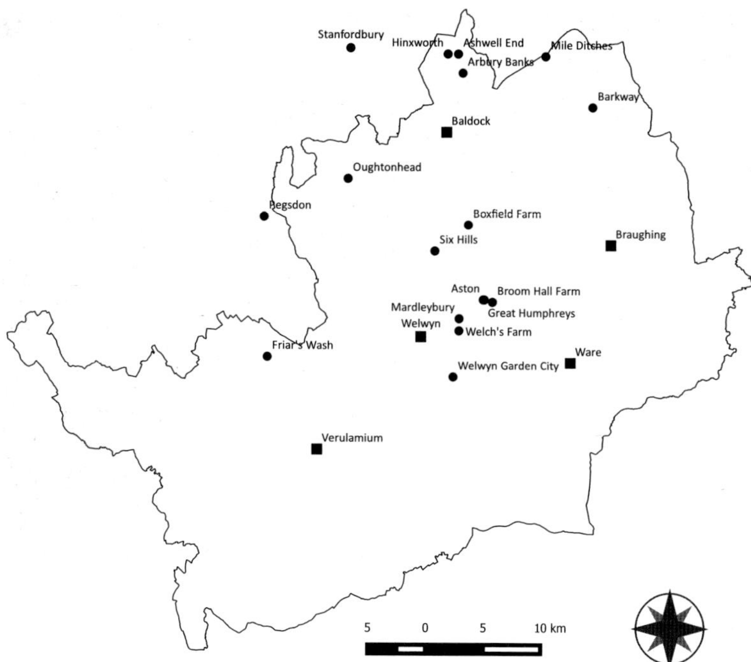

Figure 5.1: Location of the main sites discussed in this paper. Map by Ellen Shlasko. Contains Ordnance Survey data © Crown copyright and database right 2014.

debatable. A later chieftain, Andoco, who ruled from about 10 BC to AD 10, may also have been based in Baldock, as more of his coins have been found there than anywhere else, but his burial site has not been identified (Fitzpatrick-Matthews and Burleigh 2007: 5).

5.2.2 Multiple dykes

It has been argued elsewhere that the Iron Age *oppidum* of Baldock was partly defined by a series of multiple ditches with corresponding, now mostly levelled, banks. Along with pit alignments, these helped to define not only the core settlement area but also a wider territory extending for a number of miles around the settlement (Burleigh 1995a; Bryant and Burleigh 1995). Similarly, the Iron Age *oppida* and their territories of Calleva Atrebatum, Camulodunon, and Selsey, among others, were defined and protected by complex systems and sequences of dykes (Cunliffe 1971: 1; Fulford 1993; Fulford and Timby 2000; Hawkes and Crummy 1995: 3–61; Hawkes and Hull 1947).

Just to highlight one example here: the Mile Ditches, just to the west of Royston and about 9.5km east of Baldock, probably mark the eastern boundary of the Baldock *oppidum* (Fig. 5.2; Burleigh 1980). Originally a single bank and ditch in the second century BC, later two more ditches and three more banks

Figure 5.2: The Mile Ditches on Therfield Heath, Royston, Hertfordshire, from the SSW, taken by Major G. Allen, March 1934. © The Ashmolean Museum.

were added to create a formidable physical and symbolic barrier across the line of the Icknield Way. One might speculate that the additional ditches and banks may have been added by the community to celebrate a special religious or social event, such as a jubilee, anniversary or feast day (K. Fitzpatrick-Matthews, pers. comm.).

The excavated evidence demonstrated that the ditches silted up slowly over a very long period of time through the process of natural weathering. This process continued throughout the Roman, medieval and post-medieval periods, until the banks on the Cambridgeshire side were backfilled into the ditches at the time of enclosures in the early nineteenth century; this did not occur on the Hertfordshire side until the early 1940s, when the remaining banks were levelled into the ditches on Therfield Heath by Italian prisoners-of-war in order to assist local farmers in growing potatoes!

Not only were these multiple banks and ditches formidable physical boundaries but they may well also have had powerful religious and symbolic meaning for the local people, an association which may have continued for many hundreds of years after they were first constructed. For instance, it can be argued that the Mile Ditches, as one example of those around Baldock, were marking the boundary not only of the Iron Age *oppidum* but of the Roman town's *territorium* also, and may well have been a territorial boundary beyond the end of the Roman period.

It may be no coincidence that a hoard of eight Tealby silver pennies was buried in the westernmost of the Mile Ditches in the late twelfth century AD (Archibald and Cook 2001: 10–11), possibly in a superstitious ritual which retained a faint memory of the boundary's considerable significance in the distant past. This perhaps compares with the ritual burial of a decapitated male skeleton of Anglo-Saxon date in the Aves Ditch, a linear earthwork in Oxfordshire of late Iron Age origin that continued in use throughout the Roman and Anglo-Saxon periods, and which was constructed on the boundary between the Catuvellauni and the Dobunni (Sauer 2005: 47–57).

Beyond the settlement at Baldock, at the limits of its postulated *territorium* (Burleigh 1995a; 2008) a number of temples and shrines are known or suspected. All except one of these have evidence for origins in the late pre-Roman Iron Age.

5.2.3 Ashwell

It is proposed that, approximately 5–6km to the north of Baldock, the spring-line on the north edge of the chalk scarp, around Ashwell/Hinxworth, marks the limit of the Romano-British town's *territorium*, and of the late Iron Age *oppidum*. The area has a number of sites with definite or possible religious elements and their location is on the northern edge of the Icknield Belt routeway.

At the early Iron Age defended enclosure or hillfort of Arbury Banks, artefacts have been found indicating significant occupation both in the late Iron Age and throughout the Romano-British period (Burleigh 1995a). Aerial photographs taken in the 1960s by the University of Cambridge revealed, inside the defences, the cropmarks of a large circular building 12m in diameter with an entrance on the south-east, contained by a rectangular ditched enclosure, *c.*50m by 30m, with an entrance on its south side (Fig. 5.3). It is possible that this is a late Iron Age or Romano-British temple. Two Roman coin hoards reputedly found within the hillfort, one in 1820, the other before 1914 (Appendix 1, nos 51 and 38; Robertson 2000: 261), might further suggest a religious dimension to the site in the Roman period, and may represent votive deposits.

Around the spring-head in Ashwell village, the main source of the river Rhee, which flows north to become the Cam, finds of all periods, from prehistoric to post-medieval, have been unearthed, including a significant quantity of Romano-British finds that may indicate the site of a shrine (Burleigh *et al.* 1990; Burleigh and Stevenson 2000: 14).

5.2.4 Ashwell End

Below the chalk scarp, 6km north of Baldock, and to the north-west of Ashwell village, near the west bank of the river Rhee, a hoard of Romano-British temple

Figure 5.3: Cropmarks inside Arbury Banks, Ashwell, Hertfordshire, showing a possible circular temple within a ditched enclosure. Photograph from the SW by St Joseph, University of Cambridge, 1965. Cambridge University collection of Aerial Photographs AEE19.

treasure was found at Ashwell End by a metal detectorist in September 2002 (Jackson 2004a; 2004b). The Ashwell hoard sheds new light on the ritual of religion in Roman Britain. It comprises some 27 gold and silver objects: a hollow-cast silver-gilt figurine resembling Fortuna, with, separately, two silver-gilt arms of different construction to the rest of the figurine, one holding a libation dish, the other ears of corn; a suite of gold jewellery; and 20 votive 'leaf' plaques, seven of gold and 13 of silver. Many of the plaques depict the goddess Minerva and at least 10 of the plaques have inscribed texts, the majority of which are dedications to the goddess Senuna, a hitherto unknown Romano-Celtic deity.

Archaeological excavation of the find-spot and surrounding area from 2003 to 2006 was organised by the author, supported by the North Hertfordshire Archaeological Society, the Heritage Network, the British Museum, the BBC and Hertfordshire County Council. In the first season's excavation the silver base for the figurine, inscribed with the name Senuna, was found (Jackson 2003a, 2003b, 2004a, 2004b; Jackson and Burleigh 2007; Tomlin 2005).

Fieldwork has revealed a late Iron Age and Romano-British settlement extending mainly along the west bank of the river. At the hoard site the excavations exposed a circular open area approximately 14m diameter utilised at the end of the Iron Age and in the Romano-British period for rituals involving feasting, the deposition of votives and possibly the commemoration of the dead (Burleigh 2005; Jackson and Burleigh 2005; 2007). About 35m to the north of this feature geophysical survey located a 35m-square ditched enclosure of more than one phase that contained a timber building approximately 30m square (Plate 5.1). Could this be the temple from which came the hoard of gold and silver jewellery and decorated votive plaques?

Alternatively, the temple treasure may have been originally associated with a massive walled enclosure, at least 45m by 30m, located by geophysics in an adjacent field, a feature that might well have contained a temple building. This possibility is emphasised by the recovery, during some archaeological trial trenching at the location in the early 1970s, of a marble ornamental volute, perhaps from a composite capital of a column, which could have been a decorative architectural element on a Roman temple (R. Jackson, pers. comm.).

Excavation of the ritual open area has uncovered a curious sequence of events. A possibly natural hollow in the ground, now surviving up to 1m in depth, had been used for a variety of activities. Initially, at around the second quarter of the first century AD, topsoil on the south side of the hollow was stripped to the natural chalky clay and a fine flint gravel surface was laid. In the centre of the hollow topsoil was also stripped and a clay hearth built on the surface of the natural clay. This hearth was associated with abundant artefactual and ecofactual material, including a great quantity of very fragmentary calcined animal bone. There were also fragments of burnt bone pins. Several Bronze Age artefacts, including part of a sword blade and a double-ended awl, were arranged in an arc around the north-west side of this hearth. On its east side a small pit held a structured deposit of animal bone and pottery, including sherds of an imported fine ware beaker. The hearth proved to be the first in a series of hearths arranged in an ellipse around a central clay surface. On this surface lay debris from feasting, including abundant broken pottery, animal bone and oyster shell, and artefacts that may have been deliberately deposited as part of the rituals. These included two halves of a puddingstone quern, fragments of pipe-clay figurines, stone and pottery spindle whorls and metalwork such as Iron Age coins, iron nails and other unidentified iron objects, as well as items of personal dress. The westernmost hearth had part of a late Bronze Age sword blade built into its make-up. The last hearth in the sequence, on the east side of the arrangement, was possibly as late as the third century AD in date. It was cut by a shallow midden pit containing considerable quantities of ovicaprid bones and oyster shells and a large variety of broken pottery, including decorated and figured Samian, one sherd depicting a flying bird and a ram's head.

Cut through the central clay surface were several small pits, each containing calcined bone and ash. One, the largest and deepest, produced a number of artefacts, including potsherds, animal bone, part of a copper alloy bangle and, at the base, an Iron Age coin. Another pit also had an Iron Age coin at its base.

Apparently as a result of ritual feasting, an organic soil formed across the whole hollow and above the hearths and gravel surface. This soil is rich in artefacts and ecofacts, including pottery and glass sherds, nails, animal bones, oyster shells, calcined bone and many apparent votives deliberately deposited. These include large numbers of coins, mostly Iron Age, personal dress items such as brooches and pins, stone and pottery spindle whorls and a possible bone weaving shuttle, and some pipe-clay figurine fragments, including a Venus and a *Dea Nutrix*. Periodically, the organic soil deposits were sealed by the laying of a chalk pebble surface. Once this was done the ritual activities continued, organic soil continued to accumulate until another chalk pebble surface was laid, and so on. Altogether three extensive chalk pebble surfaces were laid to seal accumulated deposits of soil, artefacts, ecofacts and votives. After soil and materials formed over the last chalk pebble surface a flint gravel surface of two phases was laid on the west side of the area. This was immediately beneath the modern plough-soil. The entire sequence seems to run from the first to the third century AD. The temple hoard was deposited in the fourth century AD.

Five other Romano-British structured votive deposits have been recorded within the soils filling the hollow. One very extensive deposit contained the partly dismembered skeletons of numerous pigs, much broken pottery, apparently carefully placed, sometimes on edge, many late Iron Age coins, several pieces of Bronze Age metalwork, a large bone weaving shuttle and a headless pipe-clay figurine of Apollo holding a lyre. Another held three Iron Age coins, one each of gold, silver and bronze, and an iron spearhead. A third included Romano-British potsherds, three Roman and seven Iron Age coins, a bow brooch, calcined bone fragments, a Bronze Age spearhead, numerous cut fragments of iron mail armour and a pipe-clay head from a male figurine, apparently a character from Roman comedy. The fourth comprised a hoard of Bronze Age tools and weapons, including spearheads, axeheads, sword and knife fragments, gouges and awls. The fifth was a hoard of eight *asses*, Claudian copies of the mid-first century AD, which had probably been contained in a small bag of textile or leather (Appendix 1, no. 3).

Near the centre of the hollow the chalk rubble floor of a building 2.10m by 1.40m was associated with collapsed Roman roof tile and wall rubble. The badly disturbed chalk rubble floor of a structure of similar dimensions was close by. Considering the possible connection of the site with funerary rites (R. Jackson, pers. comm.) has suggested that perhaps these two structures were used for the laying-out of human corpses before cremation. Alternatively they may have housed cult statues, perhaps wooden, and other religious paraphernalia (Jackson and Burleigh forthcoming).

There are clear similarities between this feature at Ashwell End and the natural hollow adjacent to the Large Burial Enclosure in the Baldock settlement (Burleigh 1982: 7–14; Burleigh and Fitzpatrick-Matthews 2010: 15–16): both involve ritual activities centred on a hollow; both involve the apparent treatment and commemoration of the dead; both involve ritual feasting associated with hearths; both have small chalk-floored shrines or mortuary houses; and both seal earlier ritual deposits with carefully laid metalled surfaces. In detail, of course, there are also clear differences between these two broadly contemporary features, but that is to be expected if the rituals and purpose of each site were not identical. However, they do seem to belong to a similar native late Iron Age/Romano-British cultural and religious tradition. At Baldock the specific rituals seem to have developed from much earlier Iron Age antecedents and come to an end in the early Roman period.

At Ashwell End the feature and its rituals seem to originate at the very close of the Iron Age and continue throughout most of the Roman period. Here, the emphasis on the curation and eventual ritual deposition of antiquities – Iron Age coins and Bronze Age artefacts – is curious, and may be a tradition specifically associated with the Romano-Celtic goddess Senuna. Since she was clearly equated with the Roman Minerva, it seems sensible to assume that Senuna had similar powers to Minerva. Minerva was associated with crafts, healing, warfare, water and wisdom, and many of the finds from the Ashwell End feature could be taken to reflect these powers.

It may be no coincidence that the Ashwell End shrine and its rituals, and their association with Senuna, are situated on a spring-line and by a river. A document from the Roman period, the *Ravenna Cosmography* (Richmond and Crawford 1949), refers to a river somewhere in southern Britain with the name Senua. Stephen Yeates (2009) has controversially ascribed this to the river Rhee, which later in its course becomes the Cam, because of its association with the goddess Senuna, and based on place-name evidence. Keith Fitzpatrick-Matthews (2013) vigorously disputes Yeates's claim.

On the gold and silver plaques from the Ashwell End temple treasure hoard the following deities are represented: Minerva, equated with Senuna as evidenced by the votaries' inscriptions; Mercury; Victory; and Roma. The figurine and its inscribed base from the hoard clearly equates Fortuna with Senuna as well. Finds from the ritual site add the following to the list of deities venerated: Apollo; the *Dea Nutrix*; and Venus. The Romano-British community at Ashwell End was worshipping a pantheon associated with the temple building from which the hoard originated and the nearby excavated ritual feasting site.

Numerous metal-detected finds recorded over the last 20 years show that the settlement area extended a further kilometre to the north of the temple treasure hoard site, to the confluence of the Rhee, flowing northwards from the spring-head in Ashwell village, with another stream flowing north-eastwards from a spring in Hinxworth parish. It was at the confluence in 1876 that coprolite diggers found a hoard of more than 500 Roman silver coins in an iron or iron-bound container which had been buried in the late second century AD (Appendix 1, no. 11; Cussans 1881: 316; Robertson 2000: 48). It is suggested that this coin hoard may have been a religious offering at the highly significant location of the meeting of two rivers (Jackson and Burleigh forthcoming).

The nearest published parallel to Ashwell End is Hallaton, Leicestershire, in the territory of the Corieltavi (Score 2012). This was a Conquest period open-air ritual site on a hilltop defined by a polygonal ditch with an entrance 'guarded' by sacrificed dogs which had been ritually bound and buried. Multiple silver and gold coin hoards deposited in the ditch near the entrance totalled over 5,000 coins, the largest group of Iron Age coin hoards from Britain. Other votive deposits close by included an ornately decorated Roman silver-gilt helmet and the silver-gilt cheek-pieces of similar helmets, a unique silver bowl and items of military equipment. The activities on the hill involved feasting on sacrificed pigs, attested by a mass of bones buried by the entrance (Score 2012).

5.2.5 Hinxworth

At Hinxworth, on the spring-line at the foot of the chalk scarp, 1km west of the Ashwell End Romano-British settlement and on the west bank of the stream that has a confluence with the Rhee at the north end of the Ashwell End settlement, two features that are visible as crop and soilmarks on aerial photographs lie in close proximity. One is the severely plough-damaged masonry remains of a possible courtyard villa measuring 150m by 100m overall (HHER 1178). The other, nearby to the north, is a curious arrangement of three square narrow-ditched enclosures, the outer measuring 120m overall, each one set within the next so that each in turn is smaller than the enclosing one, like a nest of boxes (Fig. 5.4).

Strangely, this has been identified on the official record as a Roman fortlet (HHER 0181). Its location on low-lying ground is odd for a defensive work and it is in a region with few Roman military installations, other than the fort at Great Chesterford. Rather, it resembles the late Iron Age ritual ceremonial enclosure and temple excavated at Fison Way, Thetford (Gregory 1992; Burleigh 2008: 196; Burleigh and Jackson 2009: 63), which was of similar appearance and

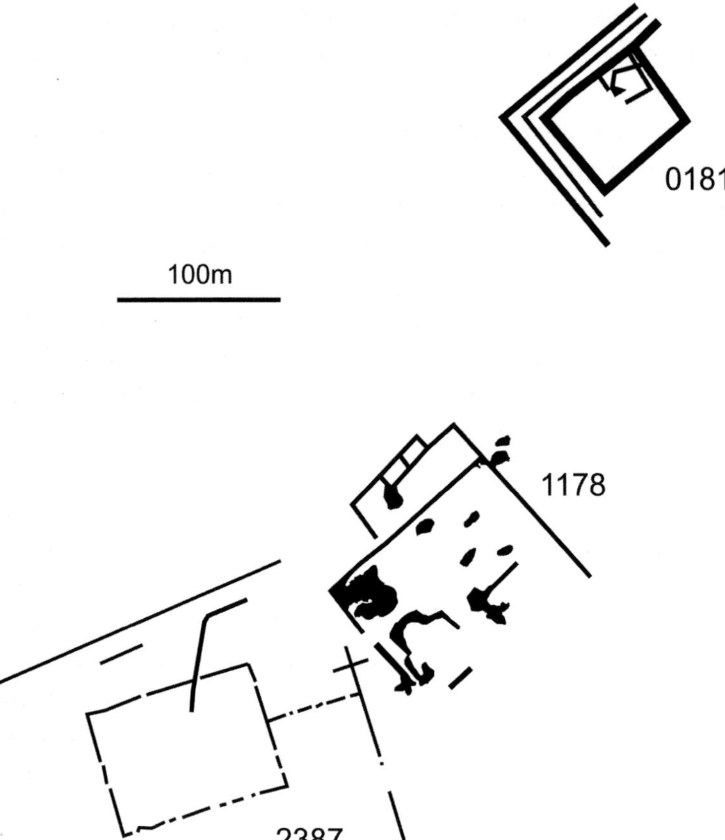

Figure 5.4: Plan of soilmarks of masonry buildings in a walled enclosure, HHER 1178, possibly a Romano-British temple complex; and a triple ditched enclosure, HHER 0181, possibly an Iron Age shrine, Middle Farm, Hinxworth. Redrawn from a Hertfordshire CC 1:10000 map and RCHME (1992) by Kris Lockyear.

dimensions, and is now thought to lie on the tribal boundary between the Iceni and Catuvellauni. Independently, the RCHME also thought that the Hinxworth site HHER 0181 was a temple because it resembled the plan of the Gosbecks temple and enclosure at Colchester (RCHME 1992; Lewis 1966: 196). A similar multi-ditched square enclosure visible on aerial photographs at Sparrow's End, near Saffron Walden, Essex, might be a temple too, although it shows a central pit that may be a burial (Ingle and Saunders 2011: 71, fig. 3.11). At a distance of about 6.5km and close to the river Granta or Cam, it could be on the southern boundary of the Iron Age settlement and Roman town of Great Chesterford.

Finds made by metal detectorists from the area of the features at Hinxworth consist almost entirely of Roman coins with a few Iron Age examples. Apart from much Romano-British pottery there are very few finds except a handful of

Romano-British personal civilian dress items and a well-preserved late Bronze Age spearhead of the same type as the numerous examples found in the Ashwell End ritual hollow.

In about 1911 a local antiquarian recovered a headless and armless marble Roman statue of Venus which was being used as a harrow weight on the local farm (Fig. 5.5). The statue may well have come from the site on this field (Burleigh and Jackson 2009: 63; Coombe *et al.* 2014, no. 10; Toynbee 1964: 82; Westell 1926: 270; 1938: 231). It is now on display in Ashwell Village Museum.[2]

Rather than being a Roman fortlet, it seems much more likely that this site is a religious and ceremonial one, probably closely connected to the Ashwell End site. Indeed, both sites might comprise one extensive sanctuary. The suggested courtyard villa at Hinxworth might instead be a Romano-Celtic temple complex within a walled enclosure.

In 2004 a very unusual Roman bronze figurine was found by a metal detectorist in the same field as the features just described. It was identified by the author with the help of Ralph Jackson of the British Museum. It depicts a standing female deity in Greco-Roman dress. On her head she wears a Greek-style helmet, which is pushed back to reveal her face and hair. On the top of the helmet the fixing for a crest is evident. Her face is very worn, comparatively, as if from fingering. On her torso is a cuirass of scale armour with traces of an aegis in the form of a gorgon's head on the breastplate. Underneath the cuirass she wears a long folded and draped dress which entirely covers her legs. Her left hand and crooked arm support a cornucopia, or horn of plenty, while her right arm is bent upwards at 90° from the elbow. The right hand is clenched, allowing a hole between fingers and palm, suggesting that the figure once held a spear in a throwing motion.

This figurine seems to represent an amalgamation of the Greek twinned deities, Athena–Tyche, and the Roman twinned deities, Minerva–Fortuna. The latter is a very unusual – perhaps unique – pairing. In view of the character of the figurine, the find-spot and its link with the Ashwell End cult site, it may be suggested that this unique figurine is another manifestation of the rediscovered goddess Senuna – in this case not simply Senuna–Minerva but Senuna–Minerva–Fortuna. This is paralleled by the silver Fortuna figurine from the Ashwell End hoard, discussed above, which had a silver base with an inscription to the goddess Senuna (Burleigh and Jackson 2009; Jackson and Burleigh forthcoming).

5.2.6 Stanfordbury

Approximately 9.5km to the west of Hinxworth and 12km north-west of Baldock, at Stanfordbury, Shefford, Bedfordshire, two late Iron Age Welwyn-

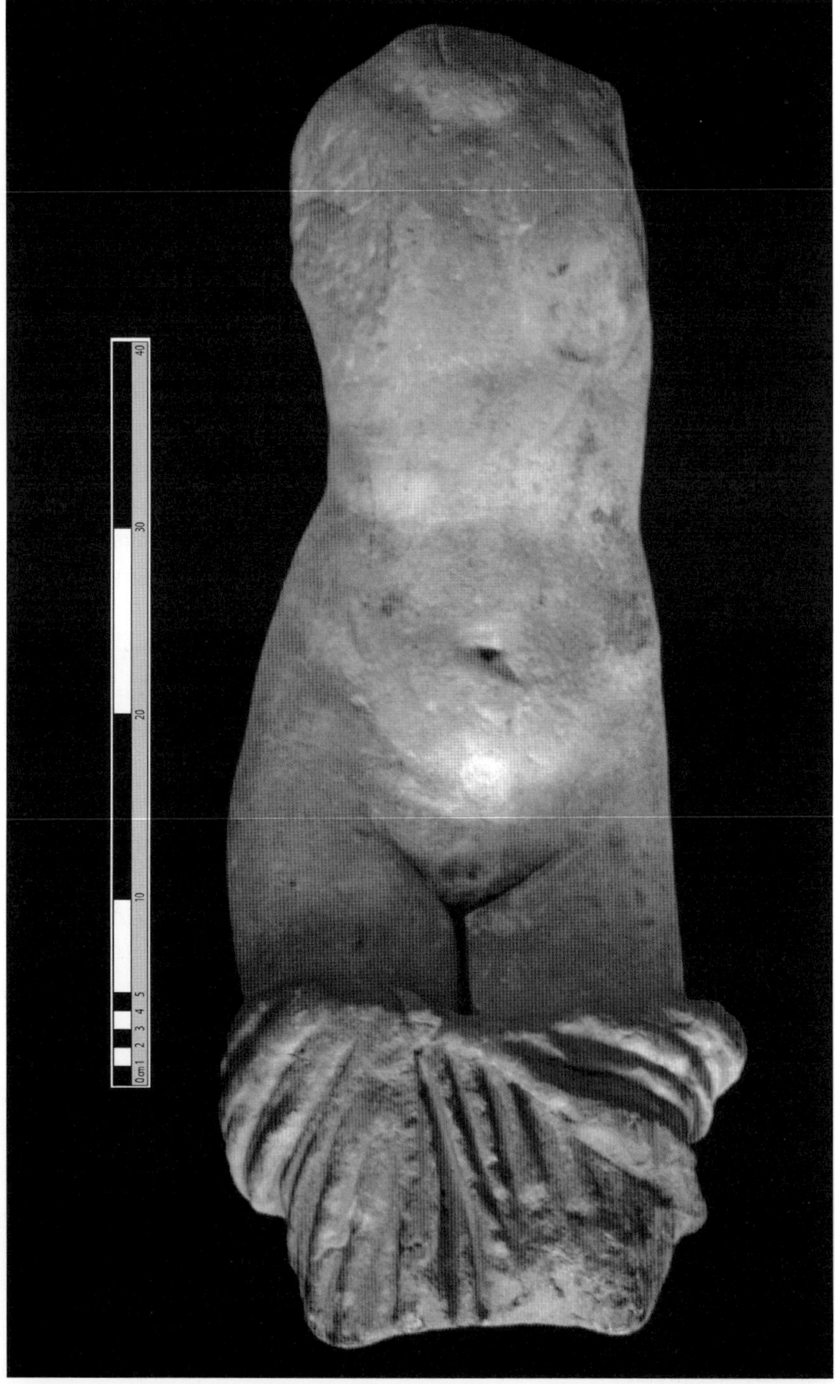

Figure 5.5: Marble Venus statue from Middle Farm, Hinxworth, in Ashwell Village Museum. Photograph by G.R. Burleigh.

type cremation burials were found in the early nineteenth century (Dryden 1845; Stead 1967: 55–6). One contained six amphorae, Samian vessels, a shallow bronze bowl, a bronze jug, a bronze patella, a bronze shield boss (it is very unusual to find weaponry in such burials), two pairs of iron fire-dogs, iron spits, an iron tripod, iron 'scales of armour', a bone 'flute' and five stone gaming pieces. The other contained two amphorae, Samian vessels, a silver buckle, a silver strap-end, a glass urn, a glass bowl, two glass bottles, four glass beads, two amber beads, a bronze handle, bronze box-fittings, a Roman coin, two bronze brooches, two iron bars and a shale bracelet (Stead 1967: 55–6). These two elite burials, like the Ashwell End/Hinxworth sanctuary complex, probably lay on the northern boundary of Baldock's extended territory, and perhaps on the southern boundary of the settlement at Sandy.

5.2.7 Pegsdon

Another site with religious and burial evidence of major significance is at Pegsdon Common Farm, in the parish of Shillington, Bedfordshire. The site is situated approximately 9km to the south of Stanfordbury and 11.5km west of Baldock. It may, therefore, mark the westernmost edge of Baldock's territory. It is also 14km from the Romano-British small town at Dunstable, which also lies on the Icknield Way, and could mark the north-east limit of its territory, although perhaps the multiple ditches and banks of Dray's Ditches (TL090266) are more likely, at least in the Iron Age.

Spectacular finds have been made at Pegsdon in recent years on the site of a Romano-British rural settlement known from aerial photographs and finds. The settlement lies on the Icknield routeway, on chalky clay colluvium over a solid geology of Lower Chalk at the foot of the chalk scarp of the Chiltern Hills. It extends between Kettledean Farm in the north and Pegsdon Common Farm to the south, centred at TL125313. It is on the spring-line and, historically, a stream, now ditched, rose on the uphill side of the settlement, just below the 65m contour line, and flowed north-west, then west, through the settlement, which grew up on its banks from at least the late pre-Roman Iron Age. The spring source issues from the mouth of a deep dry valley which is only about 600m in length and runs north-west down the scarp. The scarp itself rises to about 130m OD while the settlement is situated on relatively flat ground between the 65m and 60m contours. A second small stream, also now ditched, running north–south, also bisects the settlement. It emerges from the ground some 600m to the north.

The topography of this site, as we shall see below, is significant. On top of the scarp, approximately 200m north of the dry valley and 800m east of the settlement, is a Neolithic short-long burial mound, Knocking Knoll. Close to the head of the dry valley and 1km south-east of the settlement, on the scarp, lies a Bronze Age round barrow, Tingley Tumulus. At the mouth of the dry valley, on its north side, is a very prominent, rounded spur of natural hard chalk, Knocking Hoe. Looking from the settlement up and along the scarp, the chalk landscape is quite spectacular (Burleigh and Megaw 2007: 109–11).

Today, after nearly 5,000 years, Knocking Knoll long barrow still stands proudly on the skyline at the 120m contour; it must have been a dramatic sight when it was first constructed in the early third millennium BC, showing as a large mound of gleaming white chalk in the sunshine. By the late Iron Age/ Romano-British periods, after enduring the best part of 3,000 years of weathering and erosion and grassing over, it would have been still an impressive feature in the landscape. Even more visually dramatic are the Knocking Hoe spur, which rises to 107m, and the dry valley winding beneath it towards the settlement on the lower land. Knocking Hoe itself is particularly prominent and looks like a gigantic round burial mound, although it is entirely natural in origin.

Until the 1950s the land was used for grazing, having been common pasture for the hamlet of Pegsdon since the medieval period. Pegsdon lies some 4km south of the centre of Shillington village. Chance finds of archaeological material, including Roman pottery and puddingstone quern fragments, have been made on the site since the late 1950s (Thorpe and Wells 2003: 6) when the land was first ploughed up in modern times. Annual ploughing over the past half century has severely truncated underlying archaeological features. Aerial photographs taken in the summer of 1964 by the University of Cambridge show a complex of sub-rectangular and circular ditched enclosures and other linear ditches on the site (Thorpe and Wells 2003: 6). Fieldwalking by members of the Manshead Archaeological Society of Dunstable in the 1970s first identified the site as a Romano-British settlement with late Iron Age origins from the collection of Romano-British and some late post-Roman Iron Age potsherds and other artefacts. Metal detecting since the early 1990s has produced a substantial number of Roman and Iron Age coins and artefacts (see below; Burleigh and Megaw 2007: 111). In 2002 Albion Archaeology undertook a detailed field survey and study of nine hectares of the site on behalf of Bedfordshire County Council and English Heritage (Thorpe and Wells 2003).

A hoard of 127 Roman gold *aurei* was recovered from the settlement in October 1998 by two metal detectorists. The majority (111) of the coins were still in situ in a small pit cut into the chalky clay beneath the plough-soil (Burleigh and Megaw 2007: 111). The coins date from the emperor Tiberius (AD 36–7) through to Vespasian and Titus (AD 78–9). The latest coins show only slight wear, suggesting that the closing date lies in the early AD 80s

(Curteis and Burleigh 2002). The composition of the hoard would appear to be unique in Britain and examples from elsewhere in the empire are rare. In the near vicinity of this gold coin hoard a number of separate deposits were made of Roman silver *denarii*, amounting to 18 coins in total. They range in composition from late Republican to an issue of Hadrian dating to AD 128 (Curteis and Burleigh 2002).

Although later Roman coins have been found by metal detecting over much of the settlement, early finds are largely confined to the near vicinity of the coin hoards or an area approximately 150m to the east. The late Iron Age metalwork includes three bronze coins, bow brooches and a rare lyre shaped strap-link. Early Roman metalwork includes first and second century AD coins, brooches, a cosmetic mortar, dress pins, a nail cleaner and a knife hilt decorated with a bear's head (Burleigh and Megaw 2007: 111).

The study of the aerial photographs taken in 1964 reveals a multi-phased settlement extending over an area of approximately one square kilometre (Thorpe and Wells 2003). The resulting plot of features (Plate 5.2) was divided by Thorpe and Wells into eight 'complexes' labelled A–H. There are two possible round barrows with surrounding ditches and two possible short-long barrows, one apparently overlying the other (Thorpe and Wells 2003: 8). It is possible that the latter, given their low-lying position, represent a late Iron Age or Roman period barrow of two phases. The chalk rubble mound which can be seen on the 1964 photographs is now visible at ground level in the field as a chalky low rise surrounded by the darker soil of the ditches.

Within Complex B a massive ditched sub-rectangular enclosure cuts into the ditch of one of the possible round barrows. It measures *c.*70m across and has been proposed as a defended Iron Age enclosure (Thorpe and Wells 2003: 10). The rest of the settlement is represented by a palimpsest of linear features, presumably indicating boundaries, enclosures and trackways. The settlement features are concentrated on the west bank of the north–south stream. Within many of these enclosures are circular ditches or gullies, possibly indicating roundhouses, as well as some pits (Thorpe and Wells 2003, 8–13).

The dating of the multi-phased settlement revealed by aerial photographs to the Iron Age and Romano-British periods was confirmed by systematic surface collection (Thorpe and Wells 2003: 14–22 and figs 4–7) as well as the metal detector finds.

In November 2000 the same two metal detectorists who had found the gold and silver coin hoards in 1998, unearthed a decorated bronze Iron Age mirror together with a first-century BC silver brooch and fragments of a Late Iron Age pedestal urn and flat-based jars (Burleigh and Megaw 2007: 113–14 and fig. 4).

They reported their discovery to the author, then Keeper of Field Archaeology for the North Hertfordshire Museums Service, who visited the site with the finders and recorded the exact location of the find-spot. At that time it was not possible to archaeologically re-excavate the find-spot, although the author had realised immediately that the finds probably came from a disturbed grave. A small excavation of the find-spot was completed by the author, with the assistance of the finders, in September 2001.

Cut into the natural chalky clay was a very severely plough-truncated sub-rectangular pit 0.18m deep, with gently sloping sides forming a shallow bowl shape. The bulk of the soil filling the pit was backfill redeposited by the finders previously. On the north side of the pit a small patch of the original soil fill was in situ, from which was recovered four late Iron Age sherds from the same vessel and one fragment of calcined bone, presumed to be human (Burleigh and Megaw 2007: 113–14).

The excavation demonstrated that the mirror, brooch and associated pottery did indeed come from a grave that had contained a cremation burial. It is not now possible to say whether the cremated remains would have been in one of the pottery vessels or in a separate organic container or simply deposited on the floor of the grave, as with the Aston mirror burial (Rook *et al.* 1982). The finders reported that the mirror was lying on the chalk base of the grave pit, with the silver brooch and potsherds in the soil above. Many of the sherds retrieved by the finders must have come from the plough-soil, while some may have contaminated the disturbed grave fill by being introduced as a result of the ploughing. All the original pottery vessels in the grave, of which there were two or three, had been shattered into small sherds. The brooch was originally one of a pair, as shown by its attached linking chain, but it is not known if the pair was deposited in the grave at the time of burial or whether one of the brooches had been lost in antiquity before the burial. Intensive searching of the plough-soil by the detectorists, both in the immediate vicinity of the grave and over a much wider area of the field, has failed so far to find the other (Burleigh and Megaw 2007: 114–20).

The mirror burial does not seem to be an isolated instance of funerary practice at the settlement. The grave lay close to the large, possibly two-phased, Iron Age burial mound on its south-west side. The finders also detected a significant spread of Roman coins and metalwork extending in a belt northwards from the long mound through Complexes D and E (Plate 5.2). The same belt yielded a concentration of large sherds of Samian ware and other Roman pottery. These finds could suggest the presence of an underlying Romano-British cemetery. The plotted cropmarks indicate a trackway running between enclosures in this area and a cemetery may be extending alongside it.

Although the site displays many phases of settlement and activity, one can argue that one of those phases, stretching from the first century BC to the second century AD, included a major religious element. The deposition of a rare Roman first-century AD gold coin hoard can be seen as continuing the late Iron Age tradition of depositing gold coins on ritual sites, either in a hoard, as at Alton, Hampshire (Abdy 2002: 16), and Wanborough, Surrey (Cheesman 1994: 31–4), or singly, as at the Romano-British temple of Harlow, Essex (France and Gobel 1985), and the shrine at Ashwell End, Hertfordshire. (Burleigh 2005). The deposition of a series of silver coin hoards around the gold coin hoard is very unusual and likewise suggests ritual activity associated with a cult site (Abdy 2002: 19; Curteis and Burleigh 2002: 72). A Conquest period ritual site at Hallaton in Leicestershire had at least a dozen separate hoards containing coins of all denominations (Hobbs 2003: 65–8; Score 2012).

Of course, the deposition of single Iron Age coins of all denominations is apparent also at sanctuary sites, as at Ashwell End and Harlow. The single Iron Age coins found close to the Pegsdon gold coin hoard, as with many of the other single brooches, pins and other personal dress items, are probably votives associated with the site of a shrine. This compares closely with the excavated evidence for the deposition of similar votive objects at the shrine of Senuna at Ashwell End. At both sites these ritual customs continued well into the Roman period.

It is reasonable to conclude that the coin hoards and other votive objects were deposited in or close to a temple or shrine. On the aerial photographs there are several ring and penannular enclosures, as well as a large rectangular enclosure in Complex F, any one of which might be, or might have contained, a religious structure. To the south is the massive ditched sub-rectangular enclosure in Complex B that could conceivably be an Iron Age/Romano-British cult sanctuary. Without large-scale excavation to investigate these possibilities, it is impossible to say.

One can also argue that the topography discussed above, with earlier prehistoric monuments overlooking the site from the edge of the scarp slope, was important both for the location of the site and, possibly, in its rituals. The prehistoric burial mounds and the natural feature, Knocking Hoe, may have been involved in whatever rites and rituals were associated with the cult sanctuary sited below at the foot of the scarp. Metal detectorists have reported concentrations of late Iron Age and Roman coins and artefacts, as well as pottery, immediately around the two burial mounds. It may also be suggested that the dry valley and the stream flowing from its mouth may have been a link between the ancient mounds on the top of the scarp and the shrine or temple in the settlement. Disturbance of the soil by rabbits in the valley has unearthed casual finds of Romano-British artefacts, including at least one brooch. The valley may have been utilised as a processional way, as may other dry valleys in similar landscapes with similar monuments. It has been suggested (Bryant 2007: 71–2 and fig. 5) that a very much longer processional way ran from Wheathampstead via Beech Bottom dyke and a dry valley to the Roman temple at Folly Lane, Verulamium. There may also be connections here with the proposed artificially created processional way linking the late Iron Age settlement at Baldock with a shrine at its other end (Fitzpatrick-Matthews and Burleigh 2007: 4–5; Burleigh and Fitzpatrick-Matthews 2010: 16–17).

5.2.8 Oughtonhead, Hitchin

About 3km south-east of the Pegsdon sanctuary and 8.5km west of Baldock lies the source of the river Oughton which eventually flows into the Bedfordshire Ouse to the north. At the spring-head and from an area of several hectares to its south, many, probably thousands, of Roman coins have been found by metal detectorists over the last 40 years, although most have not been archaeologically recorded. The coins are predominantly small denomination third or fourth-century AD types, although there are earlier examples, including from the first century AD. In addition to some metal personal dress items, such as brooches, there have been few other Roman artefacts found apart from a general scatter of abraded potsherds.

In 1991 a detectorist uncovered two small bronze figurines from the bank at the spring source. One is a bust of Minerva wearing a crested helmet, the other is a male head – possibly a Satyr or a character from Roman comedy – similar to the example found at the Ashwell End site (see above). The finds suggest that there was a shrine or temple here in the Roman period. Close by, a handful of Iron Age coins and a heavily twisted bronze torc indicate that it may have had a pre-Roman antecedent. An HCC aerial photograph taken in May 1973 reveals the faint outline of a circular post-hole structure, *c.*30–*c.*40m in diameter, on the south bank of the spring-head which may be a later prehistoric or Romano-British open-air shrine. The location may mark the western limit of the Roman town's *territorium*. Interestingly, it is not far from a multiple-ditched dyke at Punch's Cross, Pirton, which bisects the line of the Icknield Way, here running on the north side of the river. The dyke may define the boundary of the late Iron Age *oppidum* (Bryant and Burleigh 1995: 93), at least in one phase.

5.2.9 Six Hills, Stevenage

The southern boundary of Baldock's postulated territory may be marked by the barrows at Six Hills Common, Stevenage, 9.5km to the south. There has been no modern scientific excavation of any of the Six Hills, although they have all been pillaged by curio seekers in past centuries with very little record of what was found. They possibly date to the first and second centuries AD, and may have been the tombs of one or more elite local families.

If they have been correctly dated (see Thompson, this volume, ftn 1), they form the most complete Roman barrow group in Britain. The comparable Roman barrow group at Bartlow Hills, Essex, is 7.5km away from the Roman small town at Great Chesterford, and may mark the eastern boundary of that town's territory.

5.2.10 Boxfield Farm, Chells, Stevenage

The third century AD coin hoard found in trial excavations at Boxfield Farm, Chells, Stevenage, in 1986, approximately 8km south of Baldock, may indicate the possible boundary at that period. The hoard was found in a pottery vessel and comprised 2,579 silver *denarii* and *antoniniani* dating to around AD 261 (Appendix 1, no. 19; Bland 1988; Bland in Going and Hunn 1999: 45–50). It was buried on a, by then, largely deserted farmstead (Going and Hunn 1999), perhaps at a religious ceremony as a votive offering to mark the boundary of Baldock's *territorium*.

5.2.11 Aston and Watton-at-Stone

In the first century BC, the southern boundary may have been indicated by the Iron Age decorated mirror from an elite burial found at Aston, near Stevenage (Rook *et al.* 1982). The boundary here may have been with the putative *oppidum* whose core apparently is situated around Welch's Farm (Rook 1974). The important late Iron Age and Roman settlement at Broom Hall Farm, Watton-at-Stone (Lockyear, this volume), lies a mere 700m from the mirror burial and the late Iron Age enclosure at Great Humphreys (Rook and Lockyear, this volume), and 3.5km north-west of Welch's Farm. The finds at Aston and Chells, at 11km and 12km respectively, could, therefore, mark the boundaries with Iron Age and Roman Braughing.

5.2.12 Barkway

In 1743 a Roman temple treasure hoard was found during small-scale quarrying on Periwinkle Hill near Barkway, 12.5km east of Baldock. The hoard consisted of decorated and inscribed silver votive plaques, a bronze figurine of Mars and the bronze handle of a patera. The leaf-shaped votive plaques, which are similar to, but in better condition and larger than the silver ones from the Ashwell End temple hoard, bear dedications to and images of Mars-Toutatis (a Celtic deity with similar attributes to Mars), Mars Alator (the Avenger), and the smith-god, Vulcan. It is probable that this hoard came from a temple located in the vicinity. The site is on a chalk ridge 1.5km to the east of Ermine Street in a position that could mark the eastern limit of the town of Baldock's territory (Walters 1921; Jackson and Burleigh forthcoming).

5.3 Boundaries of other settlements

Is it possible to identify territorial markers of the types here identified in relation to Baldock on the possible boundaries of other important contemporary settlements in the region? Several have been indicated above already. Below are some further possibilities.

5.3.1 Friar's Wash, Redbourn

At Friar's Wash, Redbourn, Hertfordshire, a sanctuary complex of four Roman temples lies within a *temenos* ditch, forming a sub-circular enclosure approximately 100m north-west to south-east, bounded to the south-west by the river Ver which here is a stream not far from its source (see West, this volume). Aerial photography by Verulamium Museum staff in 1976 and trial excavations in 2008 by *Time Team* staff revealed a pair of Romano-Celtic temples lying next to a circular temple or shrine, with a nearby rectangular temple building (Wessex Archaeology 2009). The pair of Romano-Celtic temples is unusual and similar in style to a pair of Gallo-Roman ones at Mont de Sene in Burgundy (Wilson 1980: 7–8 and fig. 1.1), while the adjacent circular shrine/temple compares with examples at Frilford, Berkshire (Drury 1980: 68–9), Hayling Island, Hampshire (King and Soffe 2008), and Wanborough, Surrey (Williams 2008).

The whole complex is bounded to the north by triple ditches, originally with parallel banks, of probable late Iron Age construction. This dyke is at least 100m in length and lies at right-angles to Roman Watling Street, running 400m to the south-west (Wessex Archaeology 2009). It is suggested here that this religious sanctuary complex might be situated at a point where the boundaries of the territories of Durocobrivae/Dunstable, 9.5km distant, and Verulamium/St Albans, 8km distant, meet. I doubt if the modern local place-name Verulam End is a clue or on reflection, simply a coincidence!

5.3.2 Welwyn

The late Iron Age and Romano-British settlement at Welwyn (Rook 1968a, 1968b, 1970a, 1970b, 1973, 1983–6), with its two elite late Iron Age burials containing feasting gear, amphorae, silver cups, bronze vessels, iron fire-dogs, imported and native pottery vessels, which gave rise to the definition of Welwyn-type burials, is very likely sited on the north-eastern boundary of the territory of Iron Age *Verlamion*. The fact that the two burials at Welwyn are 3.6km from the even richer one at Welwyn Garden City, containing five amphorae, 36 pots, a silver cup, bronze dishes, many bronze dome-headed studs, a triangular iron knife, and other objects (Stead 1967), only emphasises the likelihood of this being the boundary of Verulamium, between 12km and 14km away. Indeed, late Iron Age and Romano-British Welwyn may have been primarily a religious settlement and sanctuary on the boundary of Verlamion/Verulamium which did not possess a separate territory of its own, just as the substantial religious sanctuary settlement at Ashwell End/Hinxworth on the north-east boundary of Baldock's territory probably did not.

5.3.3 Mardleybury, Woolmer Green

An elite late Iron Age/early Roman burial with amphorae and other pottery vessels was discovered in 1904 during gravel quarrying near Swangley's Lane on the Mardleybury estate, near Woolmer Green, 'a few yards north of the northernmost railway tunnel', TL25811802. It lies about 40m from the ancient Verulamium to Braughing road and was possibly on the north-east boundary of Verlamion/Verulamium which lies about 16km away. It is 3.1km from the Welwyn burials. The cremation burial was in a pit measuring about 2.0m by 3.0m by 3.0m deep and contained at least three amphorae stood upright, one of which had inside it a small poorly fired coarse ware cup, and possibly other urns (Andrews 1911). From the surviving evidence, this burial was almost certainly of Welwyn type. It may well have contained other grave-goods, including metal vessels and iron feasting equipment, which were, for various reasons, not reported by the quarrymen at the time.

5.3.4 Mirror burials

We have seen above that elite cremation burials furnished with decorated bronze mirrors may be sited on Baldock's postulated territorial boundaries at Aston and Pegsdon. Four such mirror burials in Bedfordshire, at Bromham (Burleigh and Megaw 2007; 2011; Joy 2008a; 2008b; 2010), Ruxox in Maulden parish (Burleigh and Megaw 2011), and the two from Old Warden (Dyer 1966; Spratling 1970), might be on possible boundaries around local late Iron Age settlements; Sandy in the case of the latter two mirrors.

5.4 Conclusion

The hypothesis rehearsed here suggests that in south-east Britain, at least, just as in Greece and other Continental countries, many late Iron Age and Roman settlements, especially towns and cities, had a territorial hinterland for economic, legal and social reasons, with boundaries defined at special places, often topographic or sacred, by 'heroic' or elite burials, mostly in visible mounds or barrows; by temples, sometimes extensive religious sanctuaries, and by barriers, such as dykes, which were as much symbolic of power and authority as they were actually physical and controlling.

Baldock has been used as an example for this hypothesis because it does exhibit the features identified in positions which could indicate the existence of the town's territorial boundary. If the hypothesis seems speculative, or a circular argument, it surely cannot be denied that Baldock and surrounds has more than a typical share of remarkably unusual, even unique, sites and finds in relatively close proximity to its core, such as the Pegsdon and Ashwell End/Hinxworth proposed sanctuary complexes, the Ashwell End and Barkway temple treasure hoards, the Pegsdon first century AD Roman gold coin hoard, and the Stevenage Six Hills barrows. Perhaps they demonstrate that the small town of Baldock and its hinterland was a very special place, for whatever reasons, in the late Iron Age and Roman periods, well worthy of further research and investigation.

5.5 Acknowledgements

The following colleagues have been generous with their expertise and time in helping me prepare this paper by providing advice, information and references, for which I am truly grateful. Any errors or omissions remain my responsibility.

Prof. Miranda Aldhouse-Green, Cardiff University; Dr Stewart Bryant, HCC; Keith Fitzpatrick-Matthews, North Hertfordshire District Council (NHDC) Museums; Dr Ralph Haeussler, Lampeter University; Dr Ralph Jackson, British Museum; Dr Kris Lockyear, University College London; and Prof. Eberhard Sauer, Edinburgh University.

5.6 References

Abdy, R.A. (2002), *Romano-British Coin Hoards* (Princes Risborough).

Andrews, R.T. (1911), 'A Late Celtic cemetery at Welwyn', *The Antiquary* 47, pp. 6-10, 53–60.

Archibald, M.M. and Cook, B.J. (2001), *English Medieval Coin Hoards: I Cross and Crosslets, Short Cross and Long Cross Hoards*, British Museum Occasional Paper 87 (London).

Bland, R.F. (1988), 'Stevenage, Hertfordshire', in R.F. Bland and A.M. Burnett (eds), *The Normanby hoard and other Roman coin hoards from Roman Britain* (London), pp. 43-73.

Bradford, J.P.S. and Goodchild, R.G. (1939), 'Excavations at Frilford, Berks. 1937-8', *Oxoniensia* 4, pp. 1-70.

Bryant, S.R. (2007), 'Central places or special places? The origins and development of "oppida" in Hertfordshire', in C.C. Haselgrove and T. Moore (eds), *The late Iron Age in Britain and Beyond* (Oxford), pp. 62–80.

Bryant, S.R. and Burleigh, G.R. (1995), 'Late prehistoric dykes of the eastern Chilterns', in Holgate (1995), pp. 92–5.
Burleigh, G.R. (1980), 'The Mile Ditches, near Royston: Excavations, 1978', *Hertfordshire's Past* 8, pp. 24–9.
Burleigh, G.R. (1982), 'Excavations at Baldock, 1980–81', *Hertfordshire's Past* 12, pp. 3–18.
Burleigh, G.R. (1995a), 'A late Iron Age *oppidum* at Baldock, Hertfordshire', in Holgate (1995), pp. 103–12.
Burleigh, G.R. (1995b), 'The plan of Romano-British Baldock', in A.E. Brown (ed.), *Roman Small Towns in Eastern England and Beyond* (Oxford), pp. 177–82.
Burleigh, G.R. (2005), 'Romano-British remains on a site near Baldock, Hertfordshire', *CBA Mid-Anglia Newsletter*, Spring 2005, pp. 6–10.
Burleigh, G.R. (2008), 'Temples, shrines and deities in Iron Age and Romano-British Baldock and its territorium, Hertfordshire, GB', in J. d'Encarnação (ed.), *Divindades indígenas em análise – divinités pré-romaines, bilan et perspectives d'une recherché: actas do VII workshop FERCAN, Cascais, 25–27.05.2006* (Coimbra), pp. 189–219.
Burleigh, G.R. and Fitzpatrick-Matthews, K.J. (2010), *Excavations at Baldock, Hertfordshire, 1978–1994. Volume 1: An Iron Age and Romano-British Cemetery at Wallington Road*, North Hertfordshire Museums Archaeology Monograph 1 (Letchworth Garden City).
Burleigh, G.R. and Jackson, R. (2009), 'An Unusual Minerva-Fortuna Figurine from Hinxworth, Hertfordshire', *Antiquaries Journal* 89, pp. 63–7.
Burleigh, G.R. and Megaw, V. (2007), 'The Iron Age Mirror Burial at Pegsdon, Shillington, Bedfordshire: An Interim Account', *Antiquaries Journal* 87, pp. 109–40.
Burleigh, G.R. and Megaw, V. (2011), 'An Iron Age Mirror from Ruxox, Maulden, Bedfordshire', *Antiquaries Journal* 91, pp. 51–8.
Burleigh, G.R. and Stevenson, M.D. (2000), *A Decade of Archaeological Fieldwork in North Hertfordshire 1989–99*, North Hertfordshire District Council Archaeological Report 34 (Letchworth Garden City).
Burleigh, G.R., Colley, C. and Went, D. (1990), *A Catalogue of the Archaeological Finds from the Garden of 'The Steppes', Springhead, Ashwell, Hertfordshire*, North Hertfordshire District Council Archaeological Report 10 (Letchworth Garden City).
Cheesman, C. (1994), 'The coins', in M.G. O'Connell and J. Bird, 'The Roman temple at Wanborough, excavation 1985–6', *Surrey Archaeological Collections* 82, pp. 1–168, pp. 31–92.
Coombe, P., Grew, F., Hayward, K. and Henig, M. (2014), *Roman Sculpture from London and the South-East*, Corpus Signorum Imperii Romani Great Britain, Vol. 1, Fascicule 10 (Oxford).
Cunliffe, B.W. (1971), 'The Origin and development of Chichester', in A. Down and M. Rule, *Chichester Excavations 1* (Chichester), pp. 1–6.
Curteis, M. and Burleigh, G.R. (2002), 'Shillington A & B, Bedfordshire: 127 *aurei* to AD 78, 18 *denarii* to AD 128', in R.A. Abdy, I. Leins and J. Williams, *Coin Hoards from Roman Britain Volume XI* (London), pp. 65–74.
Cussans, J.E. (1881), *History of Hertfordshire, Volume III, Part 2. The Hundred of Cassio* (Hertford). Reissued 1972 by E.P. Publishing (Wakefield).
de Polignac, F. (1995), *Cults, Territory, and the Origins of the Greek City-State* (Chicago and London).
Drury, P.J. (1980), 'Non Classical Religious Buildings in Iron Age and Roman Britain: A Review', in Rodwell (1980), pp. 45–78.
Dryden, H. (1845), 'Roman and Romano-British Remains at and near Shefford, Co. Beds.', *Publications of the Cambridge Antiquarian Society* 1, no. 8, separately paginated.

Dyer, J.F. (1966), 'A second Iron Age mirror-handle from Old Warden', *Bedfordshire Archaeological Journal* 3, pp. 55–6.

Fitzpatrick-Matthews, K.J. (2013), *Britannia in the Ravenna Cosmography: a reassessment*, <https://www.academia.edu/4175080/BRITANNIA_IN_THE_RAVENNA_COSMOGRAPHY_A_REASSESSMENT>. Accessed 5 March 2015.

Fitzpatrick-Matthews, K.J. and Burleigh, G.R. (2007), *Ancient Baldock: the story of an Iron Age and Roman Town* (Letchworth Garden City).

Foster, J. (1986), *The Lexden Tumulus: a re-appraisal of an Iron Age burial from Colchester, Essex*, British Archaeological Reports British Series 156 (Oxford).

France, N.E. and Gobel, B.M. (1985), *The Romano-British Temple at Harlow* (Gloucester).

Fulford, M.G. (1993), 'Silchester: the early development of a civitas capital' in S.J. Greep (ed.), *Roman Towns: the Wheeler Inheritance. A review of 50 years' research*, Council for British Archaeology Research Report 93 (York), pp. 16–33.

Fulford, M.G. and Timby, J. (2000), *Late Iron Age and Roman Silchester: Excavations on the site of the Forum-Basilica 1977, 1980–86*, Britannia Monograph Series 15 (London).

Going, C.J. and Hunn, J.R. (1999), *Excavations at Boxfield Farm, Chells, Stevenage, Hertfordshire*, Hertfordshire Archaeological Trust Report 2 (Hertford).

Goodchild, R. and Kirk, J.R. (1954), 'The Romano-Celtic Temple at Woodeaton', *Oxoniensia* 19, pp. 15–37.

Gregory, A. (1992), *Excavations in Thetford, 1980-82: Fison Way*, East Anglian Archaeology 53 (Norwich).

Hawkes, C.F.C. and Crummy, P. (1995), *Camulodunum 2*, Colchester Archaeological Report 11 (Colchester).

Hawkes, C.F.C. and Hull, M.R. (1947), *Camulodunum, First Report on the Excavations at Colchester 1930–1939*. Society of Antiquaries of London Research Report 14 (Oxford).

Hobbs, R. (2003), *Treasure: Finding our past* (London).

Holgate, R. (ed.)(1995), *Chiltern Archaeology: Recent Work. A handbook for the next decade* (Dunstable).

Ingle, C. and Saunders, H. (2011), *Aerial Archaeology in Essex: the role of the National Mapping Programme in interpreting the landscape*, East Anglian Archaeology 136 (Chelmsford).

Jackson, R. (2003a), 'A new goddess for Roman Britain', *British Museum Magazine* 46, p. 49.

Jackson, R. (2003b), 'A new treasure and a new goddess for Roman Britain', *Lucerna* 26, pp. 2–4.

Jackson, R. (2004a), 'Baldock area, Hertfordshire: about 25 votive finds, including statuette, 19 plaques and jewellery', in Department of Culture, Media and Sport, *Treasure Annual Report 2002* (London), pp. 38-43.

Jackson, R. (2004b), 'A hoard of Roman gold and silver votives found near Baldock (G-B)', *Instrumentum* 20, pp. 10–11.

Jackson, R. and Burleigh, G.R. (2005), 'From Senua to Senuna', *British Museum Magazine* 52, pp. 32–5.

Jackson, R. and Burleigh, G.R. (2007), 'The Senuna treasure and shrine at Ashwell (Herts)', in R. Haeussler and A. King (eds), *Continuity and Innovation in Religion in the Roman West*, Journal of Roman Archaeology Supplementary Series 67 (Portsmouth, RI), vol. 1, pp. 37–54.

Jackson, R. and Burleigh, G.R. (forthcoming), *Dea Senuna: Treasure, Cult and Ritual at Ashwell, Hertfordshire* (London).

Joy, J. (2008a), 'Reflections on the Iron Age: biographies of Iron Age mirrors', PhD thesis (University of Southampton).

Joy, J. (2008b), 'Reflections on Celtic art: a re-examination of mirror decoration', in D. Garrow, C. Gosden and J.D. Hill (eds), *Rethinking Celtic Art* (Oxford), pp. 77–98.

Joy, J. (2010), *Iron Age Mirrors: a biographical approach*, British Archaeological Reports British Series 518 (Oxford).

King, A. and Soffe, G. (2008), 'Hayling Island: A Gallo-Roman Temple in Britain', in Rudling (2008), pp. 139–51.

Kirk, J.R. (1949), 'Bronzes from Woodeaton, Oxon.', *Oxoniensia* 14, pp. 1–45.

Levi, P. (tr.) (1971), *Pausanias. Guide to Greece* (Harmondsworth).

Lewis, M.J.T. (1966), *Temples in Roman Britain* (Cambridge).

Peacock, D.P.S. (1971), 'Roman amphorae in pre-Roman Britain', in M. Jesson and D. Hill (eds), *The Iron Age and its Hill-forts*, University of Southampton Monograph Series 1 (Southampton), pp. 161–88.

RCHME (Royal Commission for the Historical Monuments of England) (1992 [2011]), *Crop Marks in Hertfordshire. A report for the National Mapping Programme*, PDF version 2011 available from <https://www.english-heritage.org.uk/professional/research/landscapes-and-areas/national-mapping-programme/hertfordshire-nmp/>, accessed 18 August 2014.

Richmond, I.A. and Crawford, O.G.S. (1949), 'The British section of the *Ravenna Cosmography*', *Archaeologia*, second series, 93, pp. 1–50.

Robertson, A.S. (2000), *An Inventory of Romano-British Coin Hoards* (London).

Rodwell, W. (ed.) (1980), *Temples, Churches and Religion in Roman Britain*, British Archaeological Reports British Series 77 (Oxford).

Rook, A.G. (1968a), 'Investigation of a Belgic Occupation Site at Crookhams, Welwyn Garden City', *Hertfordshire Archaeology* 1, pp. 51–68.

Rook, A.G. (1968b), 'A Belgic ditched enclosure at Nutfield, Welwyn Garden City', *Hertfordshire Archaeology* 1, pp. 121–3.

Rook, A.G. (1970a), 'A Belgic and Roman site at Brickwall Hill', *Hertfordshire Archaeology* 2, pp. 23–30.

Rook, A.G. (1970b), 'Investigation of a Belgic site at Grubs Barn, Welwyn Garden City', *Hertfordshire Archaeology* 2, pp. 31–6.

Rook, A.G. (1973), 'Excavations at the Grange Romano-British Cemetery, Welwyn, 1967', *Hertfordshire Archaeology* 3, pp. 1–30.

Rook, T. (1974), 'Welch's Farm – a success for the fieldworker', *Hertfordshire Archaeological Review* 9, pp. 170–74.

Rook, T. (1976), 'Beaten by the Bounds', *Hertfordshire's Past* 1, pp. 8–10.

Rook, A.G. (1983–6), 'The Roman Villa site at Dicket Mead, Lockleys, Welwyn', *Hertfordshire Archaeology* 9, pp. 79–175.

Rook, T., Lowery, P.R., Savage, R.D.A. and Wilkins, R.L. (1982), 'An Iron Age Bronze Mirror from Aston, Hertfordshire', *Antiquaries Journal* 62, pp. 18–34.

Rudling, D. (ed.) (2008), *Ritual Landscapes of Roman South-East Britain* (Great Dunham and Oxford).

Sauer, E.W. (2005), *Linear Earthwork, Tribal Boundary and Ritual Beheading: Aves Ditch from the Iron Age to the Early Middle Ages*, British Archaeological Reports British Series 402 (Oxford).

Score, V. (2012), *Hoards, Hounds and Helmets: A Conquest Period Ritual Site at Hallaton, Leicestershire*, Leicester Archaeology Monograph 21 (Leicester).

Smith, A. (2001), *The Differential Use of Constructed Sacred Space in Southern Britain, from the Late Iron Age to the 4th Century AD*, British Archaeological Reports British Series 318 (Oxford).

Spickermann, W. (2008), *Germania Inferior, Religionsgeschichte des römischen Germanien II* (Tübingen).

Spratling, M.G. (1970), 'The late pre-Roman Iron Age bronze mirror from Old Warden', *Bedfordshire Archaeological Journal* 5, pp. 9–16.

Stead, I.M. (1967), 'A La Tene III burial at Welwyn Garden City', *Archaeologia* 101, pp. 1-62.

Stead, I.M. and Rigby, V. (1986), *Baldock: The Excavation of a Roman and Pre-Roman Settlement, 1968–72*, Britannia Monograph Series 7 (London).

Thorpe, R. and Wells, J. (2003), 'Land North of Pegsdon Common Farm, Shillington, Bedfordshire: Aerial Photograph Analysis and Fieldwalking', unpublished Albion Archaeology Report 2003/6 (Bedford).

Tomlin, R.S.O. (2005), 'Near Baldock, Hertfordshire', *Britannia* 36, p. 489.

Toynbee, J.M.C. (1964), *Art in Britain under the Romans* (Oxford).

Wait, G.A. (1985), *Ritual and Religion in Iron Age Britain*, British Archaeological Reports British Series 149 (Oxford).

Walters, H.B. (1921), *Catalogue of the Silver Plate (Greek, Etruscan and Roman) in the British Museum* (London).

Wessex Archaeology (2009), *Friars Wash, Redbourn, Hertfordshire. Archaeological Evaluation and Assessment of Results*, Wessex Archaeology Report 68735.01 (Salisbury).

Westell, W.P. (1926), 'Roman and pre-Roman antiquities in Letchworth Museum', *Transactions of the East Hertfordshire Archaeological Society* 7, pp. 258-81.

Westell, W.P. (1938), 'Roman and pre-Roman antiquities in Letchworth Museum', *Transactions of the East Hertfordshire Archaeological Society* 10, pp. 231-3.

Williams, D. (2008), 'The Wanborough Temple Site', in Rudling (2008), pp. 87–93.

Williams, H.M.R. (1998), 'The Ancient Monument in Romano-British Ritual Practices' in C. Forcey, J. Hawthorne and R. Witcher (eds), *TRAC 97: Proceedings of the Seventh Annual Theoretical Roman Archaeology Conference* (Oxford), pp. 71–86.

Wilson, D.R. (1980), 'Romano-Celtic temple architecture: how much do we actually know?' in Rodwell (1980), pp. 5–30.

Woodward, A. (1992), *Shrines and Sacrifice* (London).

Yeates, S. (2009), 'Senuna, goddess of the river Rhee or Henney', *Proceedings of the Cambridge Antiquarian Society* 98, pp. 65–8.

Notes

1 The full name of the Roman town at Baldock is unknown but lead seals with the text C.VIC on them probably incorporate the name of the town in the abbreviation (Fitzpatrick-Matthews and Burleigh 2007: 7).

2 Accession no. 1947.25.

CHAPTER 6

When was the Roman conquest in Hertfordshire?

Isobel Thompson

6.1 Background

This study developed from several strands. It was originally prompted by a short presentation compiled for a seminar on 'The Iron Age of the Thames Valley: regional and chronological perspectives', organised by the Prehistoric Society in February 2011. The current understanding of the Iron Age of London and Hertfordshire was covered by myself and Stewart Bryant, both of the Hertfordshire Historic Environment Unit. The presentation was necessarily short, but was based upon data in the two relevant Historic Environment Records and upon many years of research into the Iron Age of the region. It helped to crystallise our thoughts and it was clear that the work needed to be taken further. Along with presentations on the changes in ceramics to the Prehistoric Ceramics Research Group and the Study Group for Roman Pottery, this developed into a more general talk put together to address the transformation from 'late Iron Age' to 'Roman' in Hertfordshire and its surroundings, which posed the question of when this fundamental event took place. I was pleased to be asked to air this at the conference to mark Tony Rook's 80th birthday.

One of the points made was that Tony's active presence in Welwyn and Welwyn Garden City during the construction of housing estates produced vital information about one of the centres of late Iron Age Hertfordshire which, without him and WAS, would have been lost. He has done much other work, too, on the late Iron Age and Roman archaeology of the county. Where were the Tony Rooks of Stevenage and Hemel Hempstead when those New Towns were being built? As far as we know, neither was a late Iron Age centre, but there are many unanswered questions about the scattered Roman finds recorded in both places, and in particular the relationship of the Hemel Hempstead area with St Albans.

Underlying this review are the results of 20 years of developer-funded archaeology. The sheer quantity of new data, aptly called 'a breath-taking rise in the amount of evidence' (Haselgrove and Moore 2007b: 3), has transformed our knowledge base – or it should have. We have reached a point at which we have enough new material for fundamental reassessment of what we think we know, to test and add detail to the bigger picture. But synthesis is not keeping pace with the evidence and, in certain ways, is falling behind. The following illustrates this with an outline of middle and late Iron Age Hertfordshire and its possible relationship with the London basin and the foundation of Londinium.

6.2 The late Iron Age map

Hertfordshire has been known for its major late Iron Age sites since the work of Mortimer Wheeler in the early 1930s (Wheeler and Wheeler 1936). There are now hundreds of late Iron Age sites and finds on the Historic Environment Record, and this will increase. The map (Fig. 6.1) indicates a large population and several major centres. It also shows the known Roman road system[1] and the

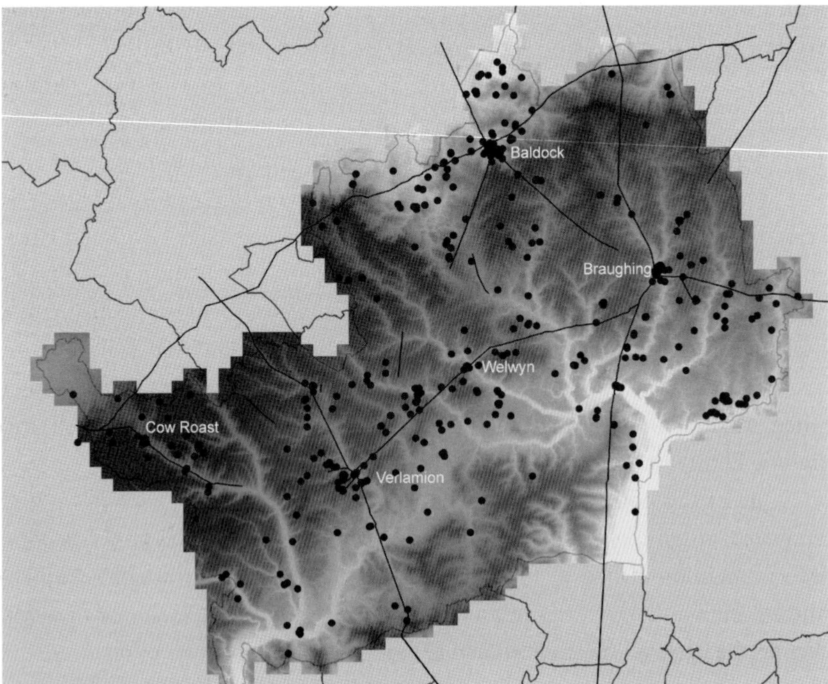

Figure 6.1: Late Iron Age Hertfordshire, with known Roman roads, the Icknield Way, and the main centres. The ironworking area at Cow Roast is also marked. Ordnance Survey data © Crown Copyright 2015 OS 100056350.

estimated course of the Icknield Way, along the Chiltern ridge, despite debate over its being a long-distance route either in prehistory or in the Roman period (Harrison 2003); it must have existed at least in part. The map implies that many of these Roman roads were in fact engineered versions of pre-Roman routes, connecting the major centres of Baldock, Verulamium, Welwyn, Braughing and east towards Colchester. The relief shows how the Verulamium to Braughing and Colchester route follows the edge of the higher ground, across the south-eastern ends of the many valleys running down from the Chilterns watershed, and avoiding the London Clay of southern Hertfordshire.[2]

6.3 The missing middle Iron Age

The basic cultural marker for the late Iron Age in Hertfordshire is pottery tempered with grog. At first hand-made, this distinctive fabric began to appear in the earlier first century BC, but sites with early examples are still rare. In the later first century BC the number of sites with this pottery begins to pick up, but the majority of late Iron Age sites, filling the map, are largely first century AD in date. This fabric, increasingly wheel-made and used for new forms, some very elaborate, is ubiquitous on late Iron Age sites, although it is often found with a small percentage of shell-tempered pottery as well as imported wares. The economics behind the exponential growth visible in the archaeological record are not understood, but clearly there was a period of rapid growth taking place in the later first century BC – at about the time when the continental imports begin to arrive – and the early first century AD.

What this exponential growth emerged from is still obscure. It has long been thought that there is very little which could be labelled 'middle Iron Age' in the county. Flint-tempered pottery had been ubiquitous for so long (from the Neolithic, at Gorhambury; Neal *et al.* 1990) that it is hard to date, although it lasts into the early Iron Age (perhaps to *c.*400 BC); abraded fragments of flint-gritted sherds are found, evidently residual, as background noise all over the county. Then, in the first century BC, late Iron Age Hertfordshire overwhelms what goes before. Other than a handful of sites on the east side (Foxholes Farm, Hertford) and northern edge of the county (Barley, Wilbury Hill, Blackhorse Road), there appeared to be no identifiable middle Iron Age. Only a few years ago it could be said in print that 'there is little evidence for middle Iron Age settlement in the St Albans area' (Haselgrove and Millett 1997: 283); in effect, late Iron Age Verlamion appeared to emerge from nothing.

But Figure 6.2 shows, across the centre of the county, a recently identified band of sites with the characteristic hand-made sandy wares of Little Waltham type (Drury 1978), which are distinctively middle Iron Age. The type site is to

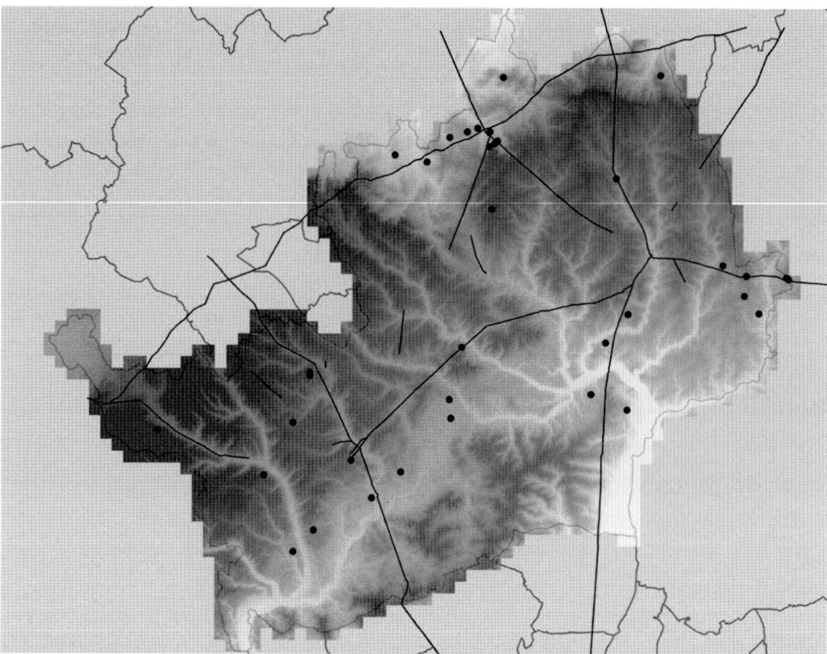

Figure 6.2: Middle Iron Age sites and finds in Hertfordshire (to early 2014), plotted against the known Roman road system and the Icknield Way. Ordnance Survey data © Crown Copyright 2015 OS 100056350.

the east, in Essex; it appears likely that use of these sandy wares, from *c.*400 BC to *c.*100 BC, was spread across Hertfordshire and west into Buckinghamshire.

Table 6.1 lists the main middle Iron Age sites shown on the map. Herein is a problem which needs to be addressed; virtually none of these sites is published. The middle Iron Age is hidden within grey literature reports, which are, in many cases, unsatisfactory: some reports include pottery fabric descriptions, but many do not, and some sites have been mistakenly attributed to the late Iron Age through a lack of familiarity on the part of archaeological contractors with the county's pottery. Partly, of course, this is a consequence of the lack of publication, as well as the self-perpetuating view that Hertfordshire has virtually no middle Iron Age sites. Illustrations are never included, so without detailed fabric descriptions it is impossible to tell from the text how accurate statements on type and date are. Without the presentation of the evidence conclusions on date are mere opinion, and potentially – sometimes actually – misleading. This is not a minor problem; it is something which has grown up with developer-funded archaeology, which has simultaneously provided huge quantities of data and begun to impede our understanding of it. The first step, of course, is awareness of the problem. At the very least, a digital photograph of the finds should be included as a matter of course in all these reports; this is still unusual.

Site	Features	Late Iron Age present?	State of reporting
Wilbury Hill	Roundhouses, pits, enclosure at hillfort	Yes	Old piecemeal publication, needs reassessment
Blackhorse Road, Letchworth	Enclosures, pits	Yes	Published, but needs reassessment
Barley	Enclosure, many pits, four-post structure	No	Published; needs some reassessment
Mayne Avenue, St Albans	Curvilinear enclosure	Yes	None (other than small-scale plan)
Foxholes Farm, Hertford	Enclosure ditches, hearth	Yes	Published
Hadham Hall, Little Hadham	Ditches, pits, postholes	Yes	Grey literature report
Thorley	Roundhouses within ditch system, pits, four-post structure	Yes	Draft publication
The Grove, Watford	Rectilinear enclosure, roundhouses	Yes	Draft in progress
Turners Hall Farm, Wheathampstead	Roundhouse etc.	Yes	Post-excavation work in progress
Manor Estate, Apsley	Roundhouse, four-post structures	Yes	Draft publication
Balls Park, Hertford	Curvilinear ditch	Yes	Draft publication

Table 6.1: The main middle Iron Age sites known to date.

Figure 6.2 shows the distribution of the sites and finds. Analysis of the main sites with middle Iron Age pottery makes it clear that in almost every case this was succeeded on the same site by late Iron Age (invariably a small amount of middle Iron Age sandy wares followed by large amounts of late Iron Age; at Mayne Avenue the totals were 2.2kg and 92kg, and at The Grove 1.5kg and 41kg). The two fabrics are never found together in the same context; there does seem to be a chronological succession, sometimes with grog-tempered sherds in the top fills of middle Iron Age ditches which were no longer functional. Interestingly, the recently recognised middle Iron Age sites lie on either side of the putative route connecting the late Iron Age centres which became one of the main Roman highways. It is possible, then, that this route is even older.

What was this route for? The main late Iron Age centres grew up along it, although one of them, Verulamium's predecessor, may be later than the others. It does not appear to have emerged as a place of importance until the beginning of the first century AD (Niblett and Thompson 2005), although a recent find in King Harry Lane indicates some earlier domestic occupation on the plateau. The axis shown on the map runs roughly from west (via the Bulbourne valley) to north-east; at present we still do not know if there was another route running south-west from Verlamion, as the so-called Silchester road has been lost (see note 2). It is an assumption of long standing that the road issuing from Roman Verulamium's south-west gate went to Silchester in Hampshire. It may be reasonable to suppose that such a route existed from the late Iron Age, when Silchester too was a central place within its region, but it is still only an assumption.

Niblett (2001: 48) suggests that the route through the Bulbourne valley, known now as Akeman Street, was used to carry iron ore from Cow Roast to Colchester, and that Verlamion emerged as a chieftain's power base where this route crossed the marshy valley of the river Ver. Iron ore was available from local ironpan in the vicinity of Cow Roast and the Ashridge estate, where there was intensive late Iron Age and Roman occupation. Certainly iron working was carried on here. Catt *et al.* (2010: 247), uncertain whether local deposits would be sufficient, considers that a 'more likely' source would be the ironstones of the Woburn Sand Formation of south Bedfordshire, 30km north and north-west of Verulamium, but late Iron Age exploitation of local iron-rich accretions has been identified in Kent, at Stockbury near Maidstone (Allen 2012). Similarly, the sandy heathlands of north-west Surrey also contain 'easily won and workable resources of iron' exploited by a major local ironworking industry which began in the middle Iron Age (Hayman *et al.* 2012: 14). Several iron smelting sites are known and others suspected near the confluence of the Thames and the Colne, to the extent that 'the ironworking district that encompasses north-west Surrey and perhaps the adjoining area of east Berkshire may have been the principal supplier for a far greater region' (Hayman *et al.* 2012: 14). Quite possibly ore was obtained from a variety of sources, near and far, for distribution to the major late Iron Age centres within a much larger network. Haselgrove (2011: 173) even suggests that one of Verulamium's sources lay in the 'ironstone deposits on the plateau flanking the Welland valley in the Corby area.'

6.4 The London basin in the Iron Age

Hertfordshire's relationship with the London basin has not been seriously considered, and London tends to be viewed as self-contained, which is a pity.

One reason for this is that south Hertfordshire and north London are both based on London Clay, which constituted a physical barrier between the populous parts of Hertfordshire and the gravel terraces along the Thames. Prehistoric, late Iron Age and even Roman sites are uncommon here, to say the least, and it remained sparsely settled until the twentieth century. It is good soil for trees, and in historic times for barley, but if there is any reasonable alternative people have always gone elsewhere. From early medieval times much of south Hertfordshire was land only fit for hunting parks and scattered assarts.

This might be thought a matter of chance, the archaeological evidence having been lost beneath twentieth-century development. Claylands elsewhere – such as in south Cambridgeshire – have only recently been found to have been densely settled in prehistory, and the London Clay might be thought comparable. But this does not appear to be the case. Iron Age sites are known across the London basin, many discovered as a result of developer-funded archaeology, and they occupied the better soils, not the London Clay. Greenwood (1997) compiled an invaluable list of those known, and more have been identified since. As in Hertfordshire, there is plenty of material, but it remains undigested.

Interestingly, in 1997 Greenwood noted that, in stark contrast to Hertfordshire, there are many more middle Iron Age sites in London than either early or late Iron Age. Research on more recent sites will confirm whether or not this is still the case; and the middle Iron Age of the London basin is still much more substantial than that of Hertfordshire. The distribution (Fig. 6.3) shows a linear landscape of farmsteads following the Thames. The river has settlement up and down it on the gravelly soils of the river terraces which is able to take advantage of a range of resources (likely to include timber on the London Clay). This linear landscape extends at least as far downriver as Mucking, with two substantial fortifications north and south of the Thames at Woolwich and Uphall Camp, Ilford.[3] The map also suggests that the Colne and Lea valleys linked this Thames-side landscape and the band of middle Iron Age sites across Hertfordshire.[4]

Greenwood (1997) also notes that the middle Iron Age pottery of sites in west London appears to have stylistic (and fabric) links different from those further east. Tyers (1996) pointed to a similar variety in the late Iron Age, and a lack of any distinctive ceramic identity in the London region. This tends to support the idea of the Thames being a busy routeway with links in many directions, including Hertfordshire. It may also imply that the London basin was in some way neutral territory, lying between, but not within, the powerful polities which emerged in the century before the conquest.

The transition from middle to late Iron Age along the Thames in the London basin evidently followed a different course from that of the lands to the north.

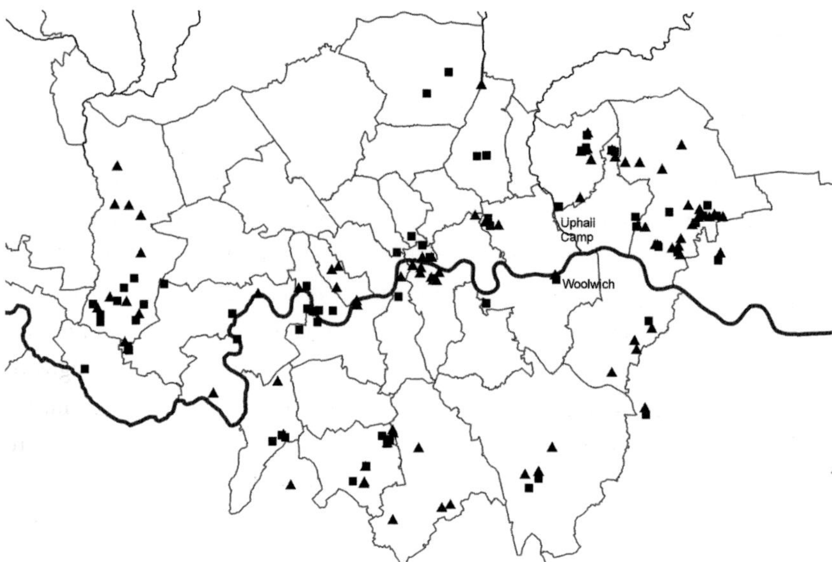

Figure 6.3: The Iron Age in Greater London. Data from Greenwood 1997, updated to 2013 largely from the Greater London Historic Environment Record. Squares represent 'middle Iron Age' and triangles 'late Iron Age' sites, although this distribution is not definitive. Some squares may be early rather than middle Iron Age, and it is not clear how many of the 'late Iron Age' sites are certainly pre-conquest. Ordnance Survey data © Crown Copyright 2015 OS 100056350.

In Hertfordshire middle Iron Age sites are comparatively sparse. To summarise, the earliest 'proto-late Iron Age' pottery appears in Hertfordshire in the earlier first century BC, and the century after Caesar's incursions is one of rapid change: the adoption of continental potting technology and vessel forms – some very elaborate – implying the acquisition, at certain levels of society, of new eating habits accompanied by imported ceramics and other goods; a huge increase in the numbers of known settlements; the emergence of major centres; and flamboyantly wealthy chieftain burials. The London basin, in contrast, remained a place of scattered farmsteads of no particular distinction that continued to utilise the better soils and the rivers.

The emergence of special places in Hertfordshire, with high-status imports and links with the continent and the Mediterranean, is also characteristic of Essex and Kent, and the late Iron Age pottery of all these areas is sufficient in quantity, quality and range to fall into distinct stylistic zones (Thompson 1982), each with at least one of these special places (Verlamion, Colchester, Canterbury) within it (Fig. 6.4). There is no 'special place' along the Thames in the late Iron Age. It may also be worth noting that the late Iron Age pottery style zones suggest that the river Lea was not a boundary at this time; this lay along the smaller Roding, to the east in Essex (see note 3). The inclusion of both banks of the river Lea within the Hertfordshire style zone implies its use as a routeway within a single polity that could control it.

6.5 The bigger picture

This is not the place to go into detail, but it would be worth considering further the complexities engendered by the gradual emergence of a 'Romanised' elite, presumably for the most part pro-Roman, and their 'special places'. These people generated obvious links, as shown by imported goods, with Gaul and the Mediterranean, but what about more local functions, not so readily recognisable? Are we just not thinking on a large enough scale? Places with similar signs of special functions and comparable ranges of material goods are apparent in, for instance, the Leicester region (Score 2011) and at Old Sleaford in Lincolnshire (Elsdon 1997). Were the production and distribution of iron ore and salt, in particular, organised on a much larger scale than hitherto envisaged, with regular traffic between the centres of the south-east and those much further north? And what was the relationship between Verlamion and Silchester, to the south-west?

6.6 The transition to 'Roman' in Hertfordshire

When was the Roman conquest in Hertfordshire? This is a serious question, as in archaeological terms there is no obvious answer. If we did not have the written record of the 'conquest' in AD 43 – describing events which take place elsewhere

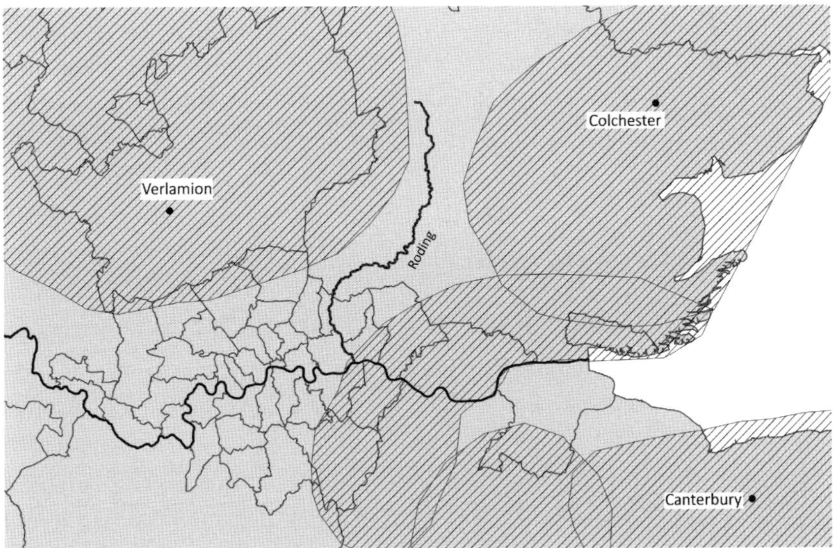

Figure 6.4: Late Iron Age ceramic style zones in Hertfordshire, Essex and Kent, with the major centres. Note the division marked by the river Roding. Ordnance Survey data © Crown Copyright 2015 OS 100056350.

– it would be very difficult to say when the 'late Iron Age' became 'Roman'. As seen above, it is easier, although it is still not clear-cut, to say when the 'late Iron Age' begins. The century between Caesar and Claudius is one of increasing 'Romanisation' in parts of south-eastern Britain (Creighton 2000, 2006), and Hertfordshire is at the forefront of this process. From a rural backwater in the mid-first century BC, which left only sparse archaeological traces, it appears to have taken perhaps two or three generations to transform the county into the major part of a dominant tribal territory in which chieftains flaunted their wealth and Mediterranean connections. Some of this wealth may have been due to control of the trade in iron ore (and other things), but the result was the emergence of central places at Verlamion, Welwyn, Braughing and Baldock, with an exponential growth in the numbers of farmsteads in the hinterlands of these centres and in the material goods available for use at all levels. This must imply an equally impressive rise in population. The differing proportions of the middle and late Iron Age pottery fabrics (see above) illustrate the point.

It is evident that connections were established between the Roman world and various different polities, especially in eastern Britain from Kent to Lincolnshire, during the century between Caesar and Claudius. Gradually details are emerging and gaining in clarity. Individual links must have been varied in nature and chronology, and the trajectory of events centred on Hertfordshire was only one story; it is certain that there were many different ones. What happened in Hertfordshire need not be the same at all as what happened elsewhere: north Essex, for example, with a comparable high-status focus at Colchester, has a very different history and was directly involved in the conquest, while south Essex, along the Thames, seems to have remained essentially untouched by the 'Romanisation' process – perhaps deliberately rejecting it – until after the conquest.

Was increasing 'Romanisation' in the late Iron Age in fact Caesar's long game plan? It seems quite possible. Creighton (2006: 16) points out that *obsides*, the word Caesar used for 'hostages', the sons of kings who surrendered to him in 54 BC, has more the meaning of 'fostering' than the taking of prisoners as guarantees of good behaviour. This meant that these boys were sent to Rome to receive a Roman education; and in due course they went home to succeed their fathers, but as tribal chiefs with a taste for a Mediterranean lifestyle and direct associations with Rome. In time their own sons would be sent to be educated in the same way. At this elite level they were literate, and belonged to a European network of men with similar backgrounds and connections; and they had served their turn in the Roman army. Awareness of this process sheds an interesting light on the contents of the rich chieftain burials which appear from the later first century BC. The Welwyn burials in particular (Smith 1911–12; Stead 1967) were furnished with articles which reflect the adoption by the elite of a 'package of continental and Roman culture', articles not previously seen in Britain. These include wine amphorae, Mediterranean tableware (jugs, cups and plates) and gaming counters, together with the new custom of burial with these appropriate grave-goods (Hall and Forsyth 2011). Wine and board games produce an image of tribal chiefs with an exotic lifestyle which was bound to impress; the observable consequence was the gradual filtering down through society of these new customs with the increased availability of new vessel forms, imports being copied and adapted by local potters.

At the same time the complexities and distinct character of the period are a reminder that 'there was no single, direct trajectory of social change that led inevitably to … the Roman conquest' (Hill 2007: 30–31). It is very clear that the elite adopted and adapted what they chose, from their Gaulish counterparts as well as the Mediterranean, and did not choose to copy a Roman lifestyle. But by the time of the official conquest, several generations later, Claudius would have been able to rely upon the support of friendly tribal leaders, or at least those powerful enough to quell any anti-Roman faction within their tribal territories.

Hertfordshire appears to have been the core of one of these reliable territories, where the chieftain burials culminated in that of the man buried at Folly Lane, St Albans. Niblett (1999: 394–400) shows that the closest parallels for the Folly Lane burial rite are not the local 'Welwyn' type burials, but the Stanway and Lexden burials at Colchester, and others in northern Gaul. Interestingly (in view of Creighton's proposition that the education of this elite included a period in the Roman army), his grave goods included, as well as native metalwork, the trappings of a Roman cavalry officer (Foster 1999) decorated with silver inlay in Roman style. Foster (1999: 176) points out that Roman cavalry consisted of 'Celtic' auxiliaries; as cavalry officers would have come from native elites it is no great step to see how such items came to be included among the Folly Lane grave goods. These included high-status pieces of local, Gaulish and Mediterranean origin that formed a distinctly cosmopolitan mix:

- Gear for a cavalry horse, with late Iron Age and Roman decoration;
- Nave band and cart pole end from a cart, with Roman decoration;
- Bronze pieces from a trumpet (possibly cavalry) or sceptre;
- Complete suit of chain mail, late Iron Age;
- Hobnails from at least two pairs of shoes or boots;
- Box with silver and bronze fittings, Iron Age decoration;
- Iron firedog, late Iron Age;
- Bronze fittings from a wooden chair;

- Ivory fittings from a couch, made in north Italy;
- Plates, bowls and jug imported from Gaul;
- Thirteen to seventeen south Gaulish Samian vessels;
- Six Italian amphorae;
- Some local pottery.

6.7 Verlamion – Verulamium

The discovery of the chieftain burial at Folly Lane in 1992 led to a radically new interpretation of the '*oppidum*' of Verlamion[5] and its replacement by Roman Verulamium (Niblett 1999), while the compilation of the Urban Archaeological Database for St Albans in the mid-1990s meant that all the evidence was re-examined (Niblett and Thompson 2005). At the time of the Roman conquest Verlamion was the dominant central place in Hertfordshire and beyond.

In the present context, the compelling fact about the Folly Lane burial is that it did not take place until the early 50s AD, perhaps 10 years after the conquest. Yet this was the burial of a native ruler, still regarded as having such quasi-mystical authority that to serve the Roman town a temple (in native Romano-Celtic form) was built over the site of his mortuary chamber later in the first century. This temple, like the burial site before it, overlooked the town in the valley from the hillside to the north-east, and continued to do so for two centuries.

Whoever this man was, his status after AD 43 must have been that of a 'friendly king'. He continued to rule during the laying out of Watling Street in the late 40s and the foundation of Londinium. Watling Street appears to have come first, linking Verlamion with the Thames and through north Kent to Richborough. It did not link Verlamion directly with Londinium, and the excavations at 1 Poultry in the City of London (Hill and Rowsome 2011: 258–60) suggested that the connecting road from Watling Street in the Westminster area to the new port may have been built from west to east, not the other way round. The implication is that the initial vital link was between Richborough and Verlamion (perhaps again following existing routes), the connection with Londinium following slightly later.

During the lifetime of this client king, Verlamion remained a high-status late Iron Age settlement. It was of an unusual kind, and it is probable that each of the other central places in late Iron Age Hertfordshire had its own unique character. The term '*oppidum*' no longer appears adequate as a label, as they are all different. Baldock, in the Chilterns, emerged as a focal point in the early first century BC. It had its own high-status burials and a demarcated burial zone, and continued to attract burials throughout the Roman period (Stead and Rigby 1986; Fitzpatrick-Matthews and Burleigh 2007; Burleigh and Fitzpatrick-

Matthews 2010); more people were buried there than could possibly have lived there. Braughing had its heyday in the later first century BC, with Mediterranean merchants bringing in exotic goods (Partridge 1981), but declined in importance as Verlamion rose; Welwyn had its rich later first-century BC chieftain burials (Smith 1911–12; Stead 1967), but appears to have declined at the same time as Braughing. There is a concentration of farmsteads in the vicinity, but the centre has not yet been found. It is a pity that not enough is yet known about either Braughing or Welwyn.

Much more is known about Verlamion in the mid-first century AD (Niblett and Thompson 2005). It was of a peculiar character, with ordinary domestic settlement kept on higher ground outside the centre, which was demarcated by Wheeler's Ditch along the edge of the plateau bordering the south-west side of the valley. Part of a ditch in a similar position on the north-east side was found in the Folly Lane excavations, again with domestic occupation beyond it. Burials are exclusively found within the area demarcated by these ditches, both on the slope and in the valley bottom. In the centre of the valley, on the south-west side of the river Ver, was a large central enclosure surrounded by a deep ditch. A trackway ran down the hillside, rounding the south-west corner of the enclosure ditch as it approached the river crossing. The purpose of this central enclosure is unknown, as it lies beneath the Roman forum-basilica and St Michael's Church, but this in itself indicates its importance as the focal point of Verlamion during the client king's lifetime. His death in the early 50s brought the first attempt to give Verlamion the elements of a Roman town, with an embryo street grid and new buildings, only for them to be destroyed a few years later in the Boudiccan revolt. So it was only in the 60s that Roman Verulamium began at last to take root. This is the period of real change, with contemporary abandonment of farmsteads in its hinterland resulting in substantial 'termination deposits' of pottery, as at Stanborough, Welwyn Garden City (Hunn 2009), implying a movement of population into the new town.

Pottery studies, however, show that, although 'Romanisation' had begun very early, it took even longer for some aspects of the transformation to be completed. Structural kilns making Roman wares appear at the same time as the construction of Watling Street and the foundation of Londinium, and were set up by continental specialist potters along Watling Street from Brockley Hill, by about AD 50, to Verulamium (Swan 1984). At the same time the native grog-tempered pottery went on being made into the Flavian period, and, in the case of some forms (such as large storage jars), into the second century. Interestingly, the change to Roman potting and firing technology was adopted only slowly by local producers. Grog-tempered pots in familiar late Iron Age forms continued to be made and fired in bonfire kilns. In contrast to developments elsewhere (notably at Mucking, on the Thames estuary in south Essex; Evans *et al.* forthcoming), only two experiments in firing grog-tempered late Iron Age forms in structural kilns (single flue updraught types) have been identified. These were at The Grove, Watford, and at junction 21A on the M25 4km south of Verulamium (see West, this volume). Even more interestingly, the kiln at The Grove, which was post-Boudiccan in date, was making particular vessel forms, including large cordoned jars, familiar from early contexts in Verulamium, but these types were not represented in the substantial assemblages of native pottery in contemporary ditches at The Grove (Thompson 2002). In other words, it appears that the kiln was built to make special forms for use at Verulamium, 10km away.

This unusual arrangement may be the result of a military order. No Roman fort has been identified at Verulamium (it is unlikely that one was needed), but a substantial group of distinctive imported pottery of the period AD 60–85, with strong military associations, was excavated in 1955 in the Museum car park (V. Rigby, pers. comm.). It implies the presence of military officials directing the post-Boudiccan reconstruction, and on reflection it is hard to see how the town could have recovered without it. Part of the process was the continued involvement of the surviving tribal elite, the client king's heirs. 'It seems likely that the tribal aristocracies were encouraged to channel their wealth and competitive energy into providing public buildings and public entertainments, rather than into the more traditional warfare and feasting' (Niblett and Thompson 2005: 42), and at Verulamium they presumably played a key role in the reconstruction.

In conclusion, is it possible to say when the 'Roman period' begins in Hertfordshire? Verulamium kept its chieftain, its 'friendly king', and an essentially late Iron Age layout and set of functions until at least AD 50. The king's death coincides with the early development of the new port of Londinium. The first attempt to develop elements of a 'Roman' town at Verulamium, in the 50s, was destroyed in AD 60. It may have been under military direction, with the support of the local elite, that the town was then laid out anew in the 60s and populated with people from farmsteads in the surrounding countryside. Somewhat similar circumstances and gradual change can be seen elsewhere, as at Fison Way, Suffolk, which remained a tribal centre of a distinct character until its dismantling *c.* AD 60 (Gregory 1991). But Fison Way represented a threat to the new authorities, and Verulamium and its tribal territory did not.

It could be argued, then, that in Hertfordshire the Roman period begins in the 60s. Again, 'conquest period' is not a helpful term. 'Transition period' is far more apt, as late Iron Age gradually became Roman. The sequence of events marking this transition appears at present to be as follows:

c.400 BC–c.100 BC Little Waltham-type sandy wares and ditched enclosures found in a band from central Essex, across central Hertfordshire and into Buckinghamshire.

Early first century BC Incipient grog-tempered pottery appears at Baldock.

55–54 BC Caesar's incursions, and his taking of 'hostages'; degree of disruption in Hertfordshire uncertain.

Second half of first century BC Emergence of early late Iron Age ceramic forms and fabric, including groups at what had been middle Iron Age sites; no real continuity (except at The Grove, Watford).

Late first century BC Exponential increase in sites and quantities of late Iron Age pottery; elite and trading links with the continent and the Mediterranean; imported goods and new customs; emergence of inscribed coinage; copies of imported forms in grog-tempered fabrics, including new vessel types such as plates and jugs.

Early first century AD Emergence of Verlamion; iron ore possibly carried along a key route from the Bulbourne valley (and points beyond) via Verlamion to Braughing and Colchester.

AD 43 Roman direct rule imposed; 'friendly king' continues to rule at Verlamion; Central Enclosure and burials in the centre of Verlamion.

c. AD 45–50 Watling Street laid out; Londinium founded.

AD 50–55 Death and burial of the 'friendly king'; embryo Roman street layout and buildings at Verulamium.

AD 60 Verulamium and Londinium destroyed by Boudicca.

AD 60s New, larger Verulamium laid out for new population, and farmsteads within its hinterland close down. This operation may have been under military direction.

AD 70–100 Temple built on the site of the client king's burial, overlooking Verulamium; late Iron Age pottery continues to be made in the town.

AD 79 Completion of the Forum-Basilica.

6.8 References

Allen, T. (2012), 'Late Iron Age iron smelting works found near Stockbury', *Kent Archaeological Society Newsletter* 91, (winter 2011–12), pp. 4–5.

Bowlt, C. (2008), 'A possible extension to Grim's Dyke', in J. Clark, J. Cotton, J. Hall, R. Sh. and H. Swain (eds), *Londinium and beyond: essays on Roman London and its hinterland for Harvey Sheldon*, Council for British Archaeology Research Report 156 (York), pp. 107–11.

Burleigh, G.R. and Fitzpatrick-Matthews, K.J. (2010), *Excavations at Baldock, Hertfordshire, 1978–94, vol.1: an Iron Age and Romano-British cemetery at Wallington Road* (Letchworth).

Catt, J., Perry, B., Thompson, I. and Bryant, S. (2010), 'Prehistoric archaeology and human occupation of Hertfordshire', in J. Catt (ed.), *Hertfordshire Geology and Landscape* (Welwyn Garden City), pp. 226–55.

Creighton, J. (2000), *Coins and Power in late Iron Age Britain* (Cambridge).

Creighton, J. (2006), *Britannia: the creation of a Roman province* (London).

Drury, P.J. (1978), *Excavations at Little Waltham 1970–71*, Council for British Archaeology Research Report 26, Chelmsford Excavation Committee Report 1 (London).

Elsdon, S.M. (1997), *Old Sleaford revealed*, Nottingham Studies in Archaeology 2 (Oxford).

Evans, C., Lucy, S. and Appleby, G. (forthcoming), *Mucking, Essex. Excavations by Margaret and Tom Jones (1965–78): Prehistory*, Cambridge Archaeological Unit Landscape Archives: Historiography and Fieldwork 2 (Cambridge).

Fitzpatrick-Matthews, K.J. and Burleigh, G.R. (2007), *Ancient Baldock: the story of an Iron Age and Roman town* (Letchworth).

Foster, J. (1999), 'The metal finds', in Niblett (1999), pp. 133–82.

Greenwood, P. (1997), 'Iron Age London: some thoughts on *Current knowledge and problems* 20 years on', *London Archaeologist* 8/6 (autumn 1997), pp. 153–61.

Gregory, T. (1991), *Excavations in Thetford, 1980-82: Fison Way*, East Anglian Archaeology Report 53 (Dereham).

Hall, M.A. and Forsyth, K. (2011), 'Roman rules? The introduction of board games to Britain and Ireland', *Antiquity* 85, pp. 1325–38

Harrison, S. (2003), 'The Icknield Way: some queries', *Archaeological Journal* 160, pp. 1–22.

Haselgrove, C.C. (2011), 'Beyond Hallaton: rewriting the early history of central Britain', in Score (2011), pp. 165–74.

Haselgrove, C.C. and Millett, M.J. (1997), 'Verlamion reconsidered', in A. Gwilt and C.C. Haselgrove (eds), *Reconstructing Iron Age societies: new approaches to the British Iron Age* (Oxford), pp. 282–96.

Haselgrove, C.C. and Moore, T. (eds) (2007a), *The later Iron Age in Britain and beyond* (Oxford)

Haselgrove, C.C. and Moore, T. (2007b), 'New narratives of the later Iron Age', in Haselgrove and Moore (2007a), pp. 1–15.

Hayman, G., Jones, P. and Poulton, R. (2012), *Settlement sites and sacred offerings: prehistoric and later archaeology in the Thames valley, near Chertsey* (Woking).

Hill, J.D. (2007), 'The dynamics of social change in later Iron Age eastern and south-eastern England *c.*300 BC–AD 43', in Haselgrove and Moore (2007a), pp. 16–40.

Hill, J. and Rowsome, P. (2011), *Roman London and the Walbrook stream crossing: excavations at 1 Poultry and vicinity, City of London*, Museum of London Archaeology Monograph 37 (London).

Hunn, J.R. (2009), 'Excavations on a first-century enclosure at Stanborough School, Welwyn Garden City', *Hertfordshire Archaeology and History* 16, pp. 5–26.

Margary, I. (1973), *Roman roads in Britain*, 3rd edn (London).

Neal, D.S., Wardle, A. and Hunn, J. (1990), *Excavation of the Iron Age, Roman and medieval settlement at Gorhambury, St Albans*, English Heritage Archaeological Report 14 (London).

Niblett, R. (1999), *The excavation of a ceremonial site at Folly Lane, Verulamium*, *Britannia* Monograph 14 (London).

Niblett, R. (2001), *Verulamium: the Roman city of St Albans* (Stroud).

Niblett, R. and Thompson, I. (2005), *Alban's Buried Towns. An assessment of St Albans' archaeology to AD 1600* (Oxford).

Partridge, C. (1981), *Skeleton Green: a late Iron Age and Romano-British site*, Britannia Monograph 2 (London).

Philp, B. (2010), *Woolwich Power Station site: SE London (formerly Kent); the major Iron Age riverside fort and Roman settlement* (Dover).

Score, V. (2011), *Hoards, hounds and helmets: a conquest-period ritual site at Hallaton, Leicestershire*, Leicester Archaeology Monograph 21 (Leicester).

Smith, R.A. (1911–12), 'On late Celtic antiquities discovered at Welwyn, Herts', *Archaeologia* 63, pp. 1–30.

Stead, I.M. (1967), 'A La Tene III burial at Welwyn Garden City', *Archaeologia* 101, pp. 1–62.

Stead, I.M. and Rigby, V. (1986), *Baldock: the excavation of a Roman and pre-Roman settlement, 1968-72, Britannia* Monograph 7 (London).

Swan, V. (1984), *The Pottery Kilns of Roman Britain* (London).

Thompson, I. (1982), *Grog-tempered 'Belgic' Pottery of South-Eastern England*, British Archaeological Reports British Series 108 (Oxford).

Thompson, I. (2002), 'Late Iron Age pottery at The Grove, Watford, Hertfordshire (site code GRO99)', AOC Archaeology unpublished report.

Tyers, P.A. (1996), 'Late Iron Age and early Roman pottery traditions of the London region', in J. Bird, M. Hassall and H. Sheldon (eds), *Interpreting Roman London: papers in memory of Hugh Chapman* (Oxford), pp. 139–45.

Viatores, The (1964), *Roman Roads in the South-East Midlands* (London).

Wheeler, R.E.M. and Wheeler, T.V. (1936), *Verulamium: a Belgic and two Roman cities*, Research Reports of the Society of Antiquaries of London 11 (Oxford).

Notes

1 The Viatores were a group of enthusiasts inspired by Margary (1973); in the late 1950s they set out to rediscover and map Roman roads. The routes they drew up came with a wealth of circumstantial detail for highways criss-crossing Hertfordshire and surrounding counties, but these are no longer held to be definitive. Fifty years of archaeology have failed to confirm them, and it is clear from the Viatores' own account (1964) that many of these routes relied on antiquarian assumptions which were then 'proved' by straightness of supposed line, extant footpaths, stony patches, the occasional excavated section and a resolute dismissal of the lack of dating. Archaeological evidence has since refined a few suggested routes and revealed some new ones; but the network for which there is good evidence remains very disconnected and much of it still consists of those roads which were never lost. The road through Stevenage typifies a problem inherent even now. One of the main arguments for its Roman origin is that it runs alongside a prominent row of barrows called the Six Hills. They are assumed to be Roman; but one of the arguments for this is that they lie alongside the road.

2 This pattern may indicate that the missing course of the so-called 'Silchester road' followed similar topography. It leaves the 'Silchester Gate' of Verulamium and its south-westwards course is plain for a mile or so, but thereafter it disappears. No archaeological trace of it has yet been found.

3 At the south end of the river Roding, a short distance north of where it runs into the Thames, was the large middle Iron Age fortified site known as Uphall Camp (Greenwood 1997: 157–8). This went out of use in the mid-first century BC. Opposite, on the south bank of the Thames, was the huge ditch at Woolwich (Philp 2010), also of middle Iron Age date, with a few decorated pieces of pottery suggesting that this

fortification, too, lasted until the early to mid-first century BC. Possibly neither site survived Caesar.

4 The substantial bank and ditch called Grim's Dyke, running intermittently along the north London ridge from Pinner to Watling Street at Brockley Hill and once thought to be Iron Age, is probably entirely post-Roman (Bowlt 2008) – a more likely context.

5 'Verlamion' is the name conventionally used (from letters on the inscribed coins) to distinguish the late Iron Age settlement from Roman Verulamium. See Niblett and Thompson (2005) for an explanation, although 'in fact there is considerable doubt about the actual spelling of the name in the Roman period, let alone in the pre-Roman' (Niblett and Thompson 2005: 24).

CHAPTER 7

A survey of Roman coin finds from Hertfordshire

Sam Moorhead

7.1 Introduction

This article is intended to provide an overview of Roman coins found in the county of Hertfordshire. The first group of finds comprises up to 48 coin hoards, containing over 12,600 coins, which have been recorded since the eighteenth century, four being added since the Treasure Act of 1996. The second group comprises single or site finds from two major sources. First are the finds of Roman coins made on excavations at Verulamium and a variety of other sites across the county in the last century or so. Secondly, there is the increasing volume of coin finds being recorded with the Portable Antiquities Scheme (hereafter PAS; <www.finds.org.uk>). I have managed to locate records for 15,807 site finds which are available for analysis. Therefore, this study of Roman coinage in Hertfordshire draws upon over 28,400 coins.[1]

7.1.1 Apologia

Analysis of these different types of finds can only be superficial in an article of this length. In the first instance the retrieval of coin hoards is often reliant in the most part on chance, although 25 of the hoards from Hertfordshire come from excavations. Excavation coins and those found in field or detector surveys can have very different profiles, for example, owing to the greater depth penetration of archaeological activity. However, there is no doubt that an overview of coin finds from a county or region can help to inform the history or archaeology of the area, even if the chosen county of Hertfordshire is a post-Roman construct. This has been shown in a number of cases before, where the data stimulates further comment and research from historians and archaeologists with a deeper understanding of the material culture of the region (Davies and Gregory 1991; Guest and Wells 2007; Moorhead 2001a; 2001b; Penhallurick 2009; Shotter 1990, 1995, 2000, 2011; Walton 2012). I have not attempted to make interpretations using other evidence, except for the late fourth century, where I have linked some Hertfordshire sites into a broader pattern across Britain. I am sure that those with deep knowledge of the county will present cogent reasons for any patterns or trends that I highlight. If nothing else, such a study provides *comparanda* for people writing up new hoards or groups of coins from excavation in the county.

7.2 Roman coin hoards from Hertfordshire

7.2.1 The material

The data for this section is provided in Appendix 1 (p. 335).[2]

Between 1759 and the present day 48 coin hoards have been recorded from Hertfordshire, which in total contain at least 12,600 coins. The information in Appendix 1 is gleaned from Anne Robertson's *Inventory of Romano-British Coin Hoards* (2000), which covered finds up to around 1990, and from subsequent volumes of *Coin Hoards from Roman Britain* and Treasure Reports kept on file at the British Museum. Over half of the hoards (25) have been found on excavation, 19 of these from or near to Verulamium. Four of the hoards have been recorded since the Treasure Act (1996). As is always the case when studying a corpus of coin hoards, there is often some uncertainty about the precise nature of a deposit (see Wythe, this volume). Some hoards are determined from a scatter of coins (no. 36), some might well actually be votive deposits from a longer time frame

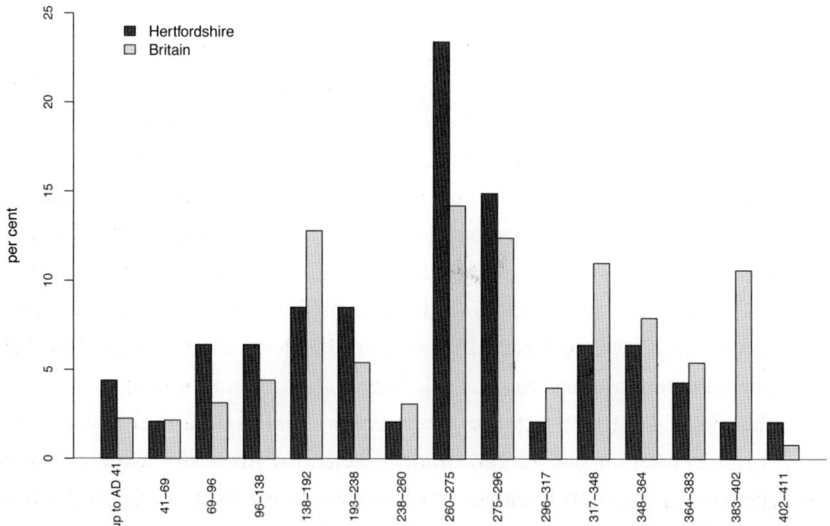

Figure 7.1: Bar chart showing the percentage of Roman coin hoards from Hertfordshire, compared with Britain.

(nos 41 and 47); certain groups of coins have been found in excavation which could be hoards or possible votive deposits (nos 9 and 10). Some finds have incomplete records which makes the determination of a *terminus post quem* difficult or impossible (no. 46). However, most of the finds are recorded to a sufficient level of detail to enable further study.

7.2.2 The chronological distribution

The 'earliest' hoard from Northchurch, near Cow Roast (no. 1), consists of two legionary *denarii* of Mark Antony, struck 32–31 BC in western Turkey or Greece just before the Battle of Actium. However, it is quite likely that these coins were deposited much later, certainly after the Claudian invasion of AD 43; because these coins were debased, they often remained in circulation until the early third century AD.[3] The Ayot St Lawrence hoard (no. 2), terminating with coins of Tiberius, was probably buried soon after the Claudian conquest. A recent find from Ashwell (no. 3) consists of eight Claudian copies, coins that were struck in enormous numbers in north-western Europe, probably until Nero's coinage reform of AD 64 (Harper 2010; Kenyon 1987: 1992; Walton 2012: 79–87). Of the six hoards ending with Vespasian to Hadrian (nos 4–9), four come from, or near to, Verulamium (nos 5–8). It could be argued that this shows how coins tended to be used more in an urban, rather than a rural, context at this time. Fig. 7.1 shows how Hertfordshire is relatively well represented by coin hoards up until the reign of Hadrian, which might be expected for a region that was to develop early in the history of the province.

Although Antonine hoards (AD 138–92) are common in Britain (see Table 7.1 and Fig. 7.1), there are only four from Hertfordshire (nos 10–13). However, one of these, from Hinxworth (Ashwell, no. 11; see Burleigh, this volume), is larger than average in size for the period, with over 500 coins. None of these hoards come from Verulamium; one was found at the top of a pit in excavations at Braughing (no. 10), two are in close proximity to Braughing (no. 12) and Baldock (no. 11), and the final one comes from an area where Roman activity has been attested (no. 13). In contrast, of the four Severan period (AD 193–238) hoards, three are from Verulamium (nos 15–17); the remaining hoard comes from Much Hadham (no. 14), to the east of Braughing and Ware. Another large hoard of silver *denarii* and radiates, from Brickendon, south of Ware (no. 18), has a *terminus post quem* in the reign of Trajan Decius (AD 249–51).

The major peak in Hertfordshire hoarding comes in the mid to late third century (AD 260–96; nos 19–36). Radiate hoards of this period are common in Britain, with over 610 recorded, representing 27 per cent of all Roman coin hoards from Britain. However, the 18 hoards from Hertfordshire represent 38 per cent of all hoards from the county. Excavations at Verulamium account for 10

	Period	Dates	Herts	%	Robertson†	%
1	Republican to Caligula	Up to AD 41	2‡	4.4	52	2.3
2	Claudius to Otho	41–69	1	2.1	62	2.3
3	Flavian	69–96	3	6.4	72	3.1
4	Nerva to Hadrian	96–138	3	6.4	101	4.4
5	Antoninus Pius to Commodus	138–192	4	8.5	293	12.8
6	Pertinax to Balbinus and Pupienus	193–238	4	8.5	124	5.4
7	Gordian III to Valerian I	238–260	1	2.1	71	3.1
8	Postumus to Aurelian	260–275	11	23.4	325	14.2
9	Tacitus to Allectus	275–296	7	14.9	285	12.4
10	Tetrarchy and early House of Constantine	296–317	1	2.1	91	4.0
11	House of Constantine	317–348	3	6.4	251	11.0
12	Late House of Constantine	348–364	3	6.4	180	7.9
13	Valentinian I to Gratian§	364–383	2	4.3	124	5.4
14	House of Theodosius	383–402	1	2.1	242	10.6
15	Late House of Theodosius and Constantine III	402–411	1	2.1	18	0.8
	Totals		**47**	**100.0**	**2291**	**100.0**

Table 7.1: Coin hoards from Hertfordshire and Britain. †These totals are taken from an initial draft of Roman hoards in Robertson (2000) and subsequent hoards drawn up by Eleanor Ghey and Sam Moorhead. ‡The two Mark Antony *denarii* from Northchurch were probably deposited after the Claudian invasion of AD 43. §Excluding Cheshunt (no. 46).

of these hoards (nos 23–4, 27, 30–36). Another comes from Ninesprings Villa at Wymondley (no. 28). We will see that this peak in hoarding in the radiate period is mirrored by high proportions of radiate coins found on most sites in the county.

If Hertfordshire is well represented in the latter part of the third century, the same cannot be said for the fourth century. Fig. 7.1 shows how, for most of the century, Hertfordshire lags behind the provincial average in all but one period. There is only one Tetrarchic hoard (no. 37) and three Constantinian hoards (nos 38–40) from the period AD 317–48. The Stag Lane hoard, from near Chorleywood, is the largest hoard found in the county, with 4,089 pieces (no. 39). Two hoards terminate with coins of Magnentius (AD 350–53; nos 41–42) and one ends with small module FEL TEMP REPARATIO coins (*c.* AD 355–64; no. 43). None of the hoards from the period AD 296–364 come from Verulamium, but two come from the nearby Roman villas at Gadebridge (no. 41) and Park Street (no. 43).

In the final years of the province Hertfordshire boasts the only major Valentinianic bronze hoard outside of the West Country, from Kings Langley (no. 44). I have excluded the Cheshunt hoard (no. 46) because the records are too vague. However, the three latest hoards in the county come from the environs of Verulamium (nos 45, 47 and 48). It is highly likely that no. 47 comprises in part votive offerings, but it does show the presence of late Theodosian bronze coins at Verulamium. What is highly significant is that none of the late hoards are of the very common class of silver *siliqua* hoards, of which there are over 150 from across Britain (Moorhead and Walton 2014). These hoards tend to be most numerous in the West Country, Midlands, East Anglia and up the east coast to East Yorkshire. The lack of such hoards in Hertfordshire might, therefore, not be so surprising, but it certainly deserves more consideration alongside other evidence (see below). That *siliquae* circulated in the county is shown by the 34 single finds recorded on the PAS database.

By way of recompense, in 2012 the second largest surviving hoard of late Roman gold coins from Britain, with 159 specimens, was found at Sandridge, St Albans (no. 48).[4] No silver coins or other artefacts were found in association with the hoard, which has a *terminus post quem* of AD 408. The hoard contains the last relatively common gold issues to arrive in Britain, although the odd later coin of Constantine III and Jovinus (AD 407–13) is found on our shores. The coins are in very fresh condition and it is very tempting to suggest that they were deposited in the upheaval caused by the British rebellion of AD 409, when Zosimus tells us the Roman authorities were ejected from Britannia (Zosimus, *New History*, 6.5.3; Moorhead and Stuttard 2012: 238).

7.2.3 The spatial distribution

The distribution of hoards is shown in Fig. 7.2. Twenty-one of the 48 hoards have been found in, or near to, Verulamium. Nineteen of these come from excavations in or just outside the Roman town (nos 5–7, 15–17, 23–4, 27, 30–36, 45, 47 and 48). Three hoards come from excavations of Roman villas, at Ninesprings Villa (no. 28), Gadebridge Villa (no. 41) and Park Street Villa (no. 43).

Close to the road running south-west from Verulamium are three hoards, two at Kings Langley (nos 20 and 44) and one at Scattersdell Wood (no. 37). Off the road running west (Akeman Street) is a cluster around Hemel Hempstead (nos 4, 21 and 41), and further west are three or four hoards near to Cow Roast (nos 1, 25, 26 and 29).[5]

To the north-east, in the vicinity of Welwyn, are two hoards (nos 2 and 22) and in the region around Baldock a further seven (nos 3, 9, 11, 19, 28, 38 and 42), of which five are from Ashwell (nos 3, 9, 11, 38 and 42). In the Braughing and Ware region to the east there are three hoards (nos 10, 12 and 40).

It is clear that the majority of hoards are in the northern and western part of the county, in the vicinity of the Chilterns, which are bounded by the Icknield Way and Stane Street (and its continuation, which runs south-west through Verulamium). In the region to the south and east – the London and Boulder Clay zones – there are only four outlying hoards (nos 13, 18, 39 and 46).

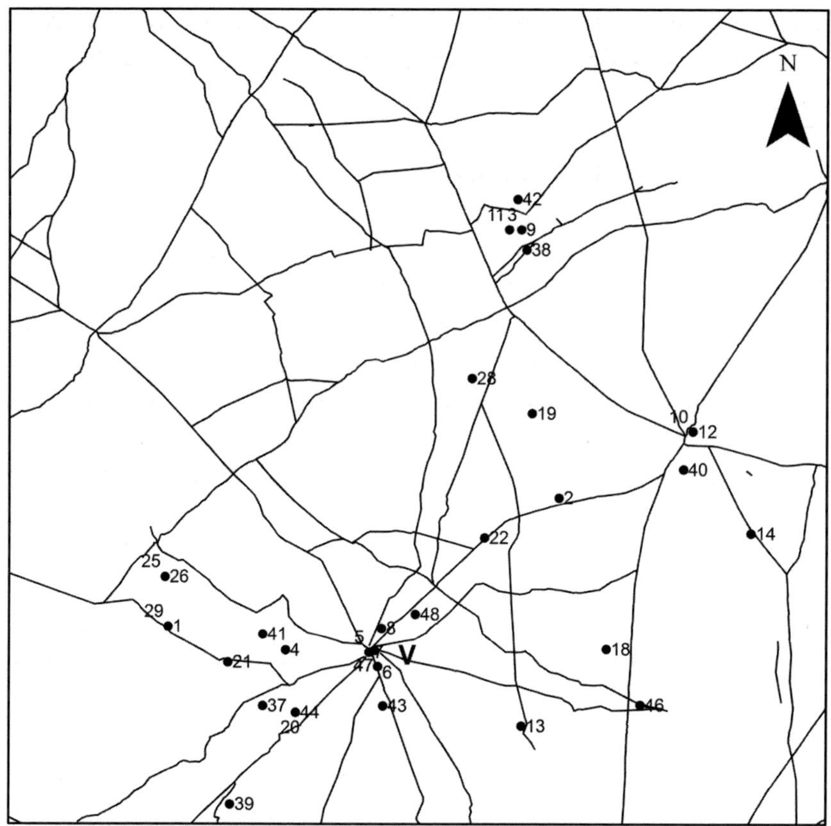

Figure 7.2: Map showing Roman coin hoards in Hertfordshire (numbered according to Appendix 1). V = Verulamium. Map © Philippa Walton.

Early hoards, with a *terminus post quem* up to *c.* AD 250, are found at Verulamium (nos 5–8 and 15–17), near Hemel Hempstead (no. 4), near the settlement at Cow Roast (no. 1), near Welwyn (no. 2), in the Baldock region (Ashwell, nos 3, 9 and 11), in the Braughing region (nos 10, 12 and 14) and at Potters Bar (no. 13). Therefore, most are at or near established centres in this period.

Radiate hoards (*c.* AD 250–94) are found at Verulamium (nos 23–4, 27, 30–36), Kings Langley (no. 20), near Hemel Hempstead (no. 21), near Cow Roast (nos 25–6 and 29), at Welwyn (no. 22) and south-west of Baldock (nos 19 and 28). There is one outlier south of Ware (no. 18). It is interesting to note that all of the radiate hoards circle Verulamium – there are none from Ashwell, nor any from the Braughing region.

Fourth-century hoards are found at Park Street Villa (no. 43), Chorleywood (no. 39), Scatterdell Wood (no. 37), Hemel Hempstead (no. 41), Ashwell (nos 38 and 42) and near Braughing (no. 40). The very latest hoards are found in close proximity to Verulamium (nos 45, 47 and 48), supporting an assertion that, in the very last period of coin use in Britain, circulation was centred mainly around major or nodal centres (Walton 2012: 109–10).

7.3 Excavation and PAS finds

7.3.1 The material

In Appendix 2 I list 54 groups of coins from Hertfordshire, providing a total number of 15,807 pieces for study. Twenty-seven of the groups come from good-quality excavation reports and provide the lion's share of the coins: 12,328 pieces (78 per cent). Four other groups, comprising a total of 198 coins, are reconstructed from summary lists in the *Victoria County History for Hertfordshire* (Page 1914; see nos 1.15, 5.3 and 5.5) or taken from secondary sources (no. 7.2). These reconstructions cannot be precise, but I believe them to be valid for the purposes of this study. Over 4,700 Roman coins have been recorded from 82 parishes on the PAS database, but I have chosen to include only 3,357 pieces, those which come from the 23 parishes which have more than 20 coins recorded.[6] There is enormous scope for a full study of all of these parishes to determine the nature of the Roman sites represented and I am well aware that my sampling method could be challenged. As we shall see, however, at a *high* level, the PAS data chime well with those from excavation.

I have decided to follow the broad regional divisions of Hertfordshire as used in Rosalind Niblett's (1995: 8) work *Roman Hertfordshire*, although my numbering is different and I combine the Braughing and Ware regions. In Appendix 2 I list the various groups of coins by region, including brief references to hoards found in the same areas. Statistics for the finds are provided in Tables 7.2 to 7.6.

For the analysis of site finds I have followed Richard Reece's (1972) method of dividing the Roman period into 21 phases:

1	Up until AD 41	12	AD 238–260
2	AD 41–54	13	AD 260–275
3	AD 54–69	14	AD 275–296
4	AD 69–96	15	AD 296–317
5	AD 96–117	16	AD 317–330
6	AD 117–138	17	AD 330–348
7	AD 138–161	18	AD 348–364
8	AD 161–180	19	AD 364–378
9	AD 180–192	20	AD 378–388
10	AD 192–222	21	AD 388–402
11	AD 222–238		

Site No.	Site name	Site type	REECE PERIODS 1	2	3	4	5	6	7	8
1.1	Verulamium	Verulam 7	15	16	11	50	32	37	37	31
1.2	Verulamium	Wheeler 8	15	33	27	58	30	26	33	22
1.3	Verulamium	Frere 6	31	46	33	97	40	30	30	17
1.4	Verulamium	Insula XIII	1	1	1	14	8	4	6	2
1.5	Verulamium	Insula II	0	0	0	2	1	2	0	0
1.6	Verulamium	Insula III	0	0	0	0	0	0	0	0
1.7	Verulamium	Theatre	2	3	3	13	25	26	25	4
1.8	King Harry Lane	Cemetery	1	3	6	29	6	23	18	5
1.9	Folly Lane	Cemetery	0	0	2	2	4	8	4	6
1.10	Branch Road	Bath House	0	1	0	4	5	1	9	2
1.11	St Michael	PAS	8	1	0	0	0	2	3	0
1.12	Gorhambury	Villa	4	8	4	9	9	6	5	3
1.13	Park Street	Villa	0	0	0	1	0	0	0	0
1.14	Gadebridge	Villa	0	0	0	5	3	6	3	3
1.15	Boxmoor	Villa (VCH)	1	0	1	3	1	2	0	1
1.16	Boxmoor	Villa (exc)	0	0	0	0	0	0	1	0
1.17	Hemel Hempstead	PAS	1	0	0	2	0	0	0	0
1.18	Redbourn	Temple	0	0	0	0	1	0	2	0
1.19	Redbourn	PAS	1	1	2	0	2	0	1	1
2.1	Sarratt	PAS	1	3	1	4	3	1	0	1
3.1	Cow Roast	Orchard	0	8	4	8	6	6	7	3
3.2	Cow Roast	Marina	0	2	1	8	2	2	2	2
3.3	Aldbury	PAS	0	0	0	0	0	0	0	0
3.4	Berkhamsted	PAS	1	1	0	1	0	0	1	0
3.5	Northchurch	Villa	0	0	0	0	1	0	1	1
4.1	Lilley	PAS	0	0	0	1	0	2	0	2
4.2	Offley	PAS	1	1	0	3	4	4	9	3
5.1	Baldock	Curnew	1	13	1	7	5	5	12	1
5.2	Baldock	Guest	0	13	2	7	5	6	9	2
5.3	Ninesprings 1884	Villa	0	0	0	0	0	0	0	0
5.4	Ninesprings 1921–2	Villa	0	0	0	0	0	0	1	0
5.5	St Mary's Church	Mounds	0	0	0	1	1	0	2	1
5.6	Boxfield Farm, Chells	S'ment	1	0	1	2	2	1	2	3
5.7	Lobs Hole	S'ment	0	0	0	0	0	0	0	0
5.8	Hinxworth	PAS	1	0	0	0	1	0	1	0
5.9	Ashwell	PAS	4	0	4	13	7	10	9	0
5.10	Clothall	PAS	4	2	1	4	2	4	2	1
5.11	Wallington	PAS	1	1	4	5	2	5	9	2
5.12	Buckland	PAS	0	0	0	0	1	0	0	0
5.13	Borley	PAS	2	0	0	1	0	2	3	0
5.14	Therfield	PAS	1	0	0	1	1	0	1	0
5.15	Buntingford	PAS	0	0	0	0	0	0	1	1
6.1	Puckeridge	S'ment	1	5	3	5	10	6	5	2
6.2	Foxholes Farm	S'ment	0	0	0	0	1	0	0	1
6.3	Braughing	PAS	0	0	0	1	0	1	1	1
6.4	Little Hadham	PAS	0	0	0	1	2	0	3	2
6.5	Much Hadham	PAS	1	1	0	4	2	0	5	3
6.6	Widford	PAS	1	0	0	2	1	0	2	1
6.7	Stanstead Abbots	PAS	0	0	0	0	0	1	1	1
7.1	Dicket Mead	Villa	0	1	0	2	0	0	3	5
7.2	Welwyn St Mary	S'ment	0	0	0	1	0	2	1	2
7.3	Lockleys	Villa	0	1	0	0	0	1	0	0
7.4	Watton-at-Stone	PAS	0	0	0	0	1	1	0	0
7.5	Ayot St Lawrence	PAS	2	0	1	1	1	1	1	0
Total			**103**	**165**	**113**	**372**	**228**	**234**	**271**	**138**

Table 7.2: Numbers of coins from Hertfordshire sites/parishes by Reece Periods.

REECE PERIODS													
9	**10**	**11**	**12**	**13**	**14**	**15**	**16**	**17**	**18**	**19**	**20**	**21**	**Tot**
10	34	17	10	505	627	29	69	594	262	160	4	52	2602
7	26	6	17	633	442	10	17	71	67	64	4	27	1635
6	18	13	14	382	291	14	38	257	147	96	0	36	1636
1	0	2	5	18	4	2	3	1	3	0	0	0	76
0	1	0	0	5	1	0	0	1	0	0	0	0	13
0	0	0	1	9	0	0	1	0	0	0	0	0	11
7	8	8	17	534	413	41	136	984	686	289	3	41	3268
0	4	3	2	4	2	0	1	4	3	0	0	0	114
0	4	2	0	14	16	0	0	2	1	1	0	0	66
0	2	0	0	5	4	0	0	1	0	0	0	0	34
0	0	0	2	12	6	0	4	16	6	2	2	1	65
2	3	2	2	86	73	7	31	21	3	4	0	0	282
1	0	0	0	6	8	0	1	12	33	0	0	0	62
0	1	1	0	43	31	2	31	125	16	16	0	7	293
0	1	2	1	21	8	2	5	13	10	3	0	1	76
0	1	0	0	38	31	8	9	10	5	0	0	1	104
1	0	0	0	5	3	1	0	5	2	1	0	0	21
0	1	0	0	8	15	2	1	10	1	2	0	1	44
0	0	0	1	2	4	2	0	8	2	2	0	1	30
2	2	0	0	0	1	1	5	5	0	1	0	0	31
0	2	2	0	26	45	3	11	50	31	51	0	29	292
4	4	1	1	23	27	3	4	17	2	19	1	3	128
0	0	0	0	12	7	0	2	10	3	1	0	0	35
1	3	0	1	8	3	5	1	1	0	0	0	1	28
0	1	0	1	11	3	0	2	3	1	0	0	0	25
1	0	0	0	13	17	1	5	14	12	7	0	0	75
4	3	1	2	102	48	16	19	96	15	43	1	1	376
4	5	4	4	43	36	14	16	87	51	85	11	44	449
3	6	1	2	30	25	10	17	46	39	61	13	43	340
0	1	0	0	12	4	1	3	5	2	3	0	2	33
0	2	0	1	17	8	1	3	17	5	6	2	1	64
0	0	0	0	6	1	1	2	1	1	0	0	0	17
0	2	5	11	78	25	1	5	48	10	50	0	7	254
0	0	0	0	6	3	0	0	2	0	2	0	2	15
0	0	1	2	23	6	2	5	20	1	18	1	3	85
7	15	4	13	324	149	19	42	145	56	125	0	8	954
2	8	2	4	84	72	9	19	66	17	58	0	5	366
3	5	1	8	150	61	12	17	142	47	59	1	5	540
0	0	1	0	0	6	2	5	16	2	3	0	0	36
0	2	0	1	4	3	1	1	4	1	0	0	0	25
0	2	0	3	1	7	1	3	20	5	1	0	0	47
0	1	0	1	13	5	1	4	3	2	0	0	0	32
0	3	1	1	47	14	2	3	28	13	2	1	8	160
0	0	0	0	3	5	1	1	9	3	8	0	2	34
0	0	0	0	5	3	0	2	4	0	0	0	0	18
1	1	2	4	23	14	9	9	22	9	2	0	0	104
1	0	1	2	29	29	4	23	68	13	19	1	0	206
0	2	0	1	18	14	0	0	9	2	13	0	2	68
1	1	0	1	12	11	4	7	33	10	3	0	0	86
5	9	4	2	70	76	2	6	42	9	1	0	0	237
1	0	0	0	14	5	1	1	26	7	11	0	0	72
0	0	0	0	2	1	0	1	4	2	2	0	0	14
1	1	1	1	21	7	6	9	32	12	6	0	0	99
0	0	0	0	6	7	1	3	5	1	0	0	0	30
76	**185**	**88**	**139**	**3566**	**2727**	**254**	**603**	**3235**	**1631**	**1300**	**45**	**334**	**15807**

Site No.	Site name	REECE PERIODS 1	2	3	4	5	6	7	8
1.1	Verulamium	6	6	4	19	12	14	14	12
1.2	Verulamium	9	20	17	35	18	16	20	13
1.3	Verulamium	19	28	20	59	24	18	18	10
1.4	Verulamium	13	13	13	184	105	53	79	26
1.5	Verulamium	0	0	0	154	77	154	0	0
1.6	Verulamium	0	0	0	0	0	0	0	0
1.7	Verulamium	1	1	1	4	8	8	8	1
1.8	King Harry Lane	9	26	53	254	53	202	158	44
1.9	Folly Lane	29	0	29	29	59	118	59	88
1.1	Branch Road	0	29	0	118	147	29	265	59
1.11	St Michael	123	15	0	0	0	31	46	0
1.12	Gorhambury	14	28	14	32	32	21	18	11
1.13	Park Street	0	0	0	16	0	0	0	0
1.14	Gadebridge	0	0	0	17	10	20	10	10
1.15	Boxmoor	13	0	13	40	13	26	0	13
1.16	Boxmoor	0	0	0	0	0	0	10	0
1.17	Hemel Hempstead	48	0	0	95	0	0	0	0
1.18	Redbourn	0	0	0	0	23	0	46	0
1.19	Redbourn	33	33	67	0	67	0	33	33
2.1	Sarratt	32	97	32	129	97	32	0	32
3.1	Cow Roast	0	27	14	27	21	21	24	10
3.2	Cow Roast	0	16	8	63	16	16	16	16
3.3	Aldbury	0	0	0	0	0	0	0	0
3.4	Berkhamsted	36	36	0	36	0	0	36	0
3.5	Northchurch	0	0	0	0	40	0	40	40
4.1	Lilley	0	0	0	13	0	27	0	27
4.2	Offley	3	3	0	8	11	11	24	8
5.1	Baldock	2	29	2	16	11	11	27	2
5.2	Baldock	0	38	6	21	15	18	27	6
5.3	Ninesprings 1884	0	0	0	0	0	0	0	0
5.4	Ninesprings 1921–2	0	0	0	0	0	0	16	0
5.5	St Marys Church	0	0	0	59	59	0	118	59
5.6	Boxfield Farm, Chells	4	0	4	8	8	4	8	12
5.7	Lobs Hole	0	0	0	0	0	0	0	0
5.8	Hinxworth	12	0	0	0	12	0	12	0
5.9	Ashwell	4	0	4	14	7	11	9	0
5.1	Clothall	11	6	3	11	6	11	6	3
5.11	Wallington	2	2	7	9	4	9	17	4
5.12	Buckland	0	0	0	0	28	0	0	0
5.13	Borley	80	0	0	40	0	80	120	0
5.14	Therfield	21	0	0	21	21	0	21	0
5.15	Buntingford	0	0	0	0	0	0	31	31
6.1	Puckeridge	6	31	19	31	63	38	31	13
6.2	Foxholes Farm	0	0	0	0	29	0	0	29
6.3	Braughing	0	0	0	56	0	56	56	56
6.4	Little Hadham	0	0	0	10	19	0	29	19
6.5	Much Hadham	5	5	0	19	10	0	24	15
6.6	Widford	15	0	0	29	15	0	29	15
6.7	Stanstead Abbots	0	0	0	0	0	12	12	12
7.1	Dicket Mead	0	4	0	8	0	0	13	21
7.2	Welwyn St Mary	0	0	0	14	0	28	14	28
7.3	Lockleys	0	71	0	0	0	71	0	0
7.4	Watton-at-Stone	0	0	0	0	10	10	0	0
7.5	Ayot St Lawrence	67	0	33	33	33	33	33	0
	All Sites	**7**	**10**	**7**	**24**	**14**	**15**	**17**	**9**
	Reece Mean (1995)	**6**	**12**	**6**	**31**	**20**	**16**	**19**	**12**
	Walton Mean (2012)†	**8**	**11**	**6**	**34**	**28**	**30**	**40**	**19**

Table 7.3: Proportions of coins from Hertfordshire sites/parishes by Reece Periods with the British Mean (Reece 1995) and PAS Mean (Walton 2012). †Figures exclude the coins from Richborough.

REECE PERIODS												
9	**10**	**11**	**12**	**13**	**14**	**15**	**16**	**17**	**18**	**19**	**20**	**21**
4	13	7	4	194	241	11	27	228	101	61	2	20
4	16	4	10	387	270	6	10	43	41	39	2	17
4	11	8	9	234	178	9	23	157	90	59	0	22
13	0	26	66	237	53	26	40	13	40	0	0	0
0	77	0	0	385	77	0	0	77	0	0	0	0
0	0	0	91	818	0	0	91	0	0	0	0	0
2	2	2	5	163	126	13	42	301	210	88	1	13
0	35	26	18	35	18	0	9	35	26	0	0	0
0	59	29	0	206	235	0	0	29	15	15	0	0
0	59	0	0	147	118	0	0	29	0	0	0	0
0	0	0	31	185	92	0	62	246	92	31	31	15
7	11	7	7	305	259	25	110	75	11	14	0	0
16	0	0	0	97	129	0	16	194	532	0	0	0
0	3	3	0	147	106	7	106	427	55	55	0	24
0	13	26	13	276	105	26	66	171	132	40	0	13
0	10	0	0	365	298	77	87	96	48	0	0	10
48	0	0	0	238	143	48	0	238	95	48	0	0
0	23	0	0	182	341	45	23	227	23	46	0	23
0	0	0	33	67	133	67	0	267	67	67	0	33
65	65	0	0	0	32	32	161	161	0	32	0	0
0	7	7	0	89	154	10	38	171	106	175	0	99
31	31	8	8	180	211	23	31	133	16	148	8	23
0	0	0	0	343	200	0	57	286	86	29	0	0
36	107	0	36	286	107	179	36	36	0	0	0	36
0	40	0	40	440	120	0	80	120	40	0	0	0
13	0	0	0	173	227	13	67	187	160	93	0	0
11	8	3	5	271	128	43	51	255	40	114	3	3
9	11	9	9	96	80	31	36	194	114	189	25	98
9	18	3	6	88	74	29	50	135	115	179	38	127
0	30	0	0	364	121	30	91	152	61	91	0	61
0	31	0	16	266	125	16	47	266	78	94	31	16
0	0	0	0	353	59	59	118	59	59	0	0	0
0	8	20	43	307	98	4	20	189	4	197	0	28
0	0	0	0	400	200	0	0	133	0	133	0	133
0	0	12	24	271	71	24	59	235	12	212	12	35
7	16	4	14	340	156	20	44	152	59	131	0	8
6	22	6	11	230	197	25	52	180	47	159	0	14
6	9	2	15	278	113	22	32	263	87	109	2	9
0	0	28	0	0	167	56	139	444	56	83	0	0
0	80		40	160	120	40	40	160	40	0	0	0
0	43	0	64	21	149	21	64	426	106	21	0	0
0	31	0	31	406	156	31	125	94	63	0	0	0
0	19	6	6	294	88	13	19	175	81	13	6	50
0	0	0	0	88	147	29	29	265	88	235	0	59
0	0	0	0	278	167	0	111	222	0	0	0	0
10	10	19	39	221	135	87	87	212	87	19	0	0
5	0	5	10	141	141	19	112	330	63	92	5	0
0	29	0	15	265	206	0	0	132	29	191	0	29
12	12	0	12	140	128	47	81	384	116	35	0	0
21	38	17	8	295	321	8	25	177	38	4	0	0
14	0	0	0	194	69	14	14	361	97	153	0	0
0	0	0	0	143	71	0	71	286	143	143	0	0
10	10	10	10	212	71	61	91	323	121	61	0	0
0	0	0	0	200	233	33	100	167	33	0	0	0
5	**12**	**6**	**9**	**226**	**173**	**16**	**38**	**205**	**103**	**82**	**3**	**21**
5	**15**	**7**	**8**	**144**	**121**	**17**	**44**	**246**	**98**	**118**	**5**	**50**
6	**16**	**7**	**10**	**137**	**111**	**22**	**43**	**235**	**89**	**110**	**4**	**32**

	REECE PERIODS									
Region	**1**	**2**	**3**	**4**	**5**	**6**	**7**	**8**	**9**	**10**
1a Ver	64	99	75	234	136	125	131	76	31	87
1b Ver Hint	13	13	12	44	24	40	39	16	2	13
1c Ver Hint	3	1	3	11	7	8	7	5	2	4
1 Ver All	80	113	90	289	167	173	176	97	35	104
2 Sarratt	1	3	1	4	3	1	0	1	2	2
3 Cow Roast	1	11	5	17	9	8	11	6	5	10
4 Lil & Off	1	1	0	4	4	6	9	5	5	3
5 Baldock	15	29	13	41	27	33	52	11	19	49
6 Br & Ware	3	6	3	13	16	8	17	11	3	7
7 Welwyn	2	2	1	4	2	5	5	7	7	10
All sites	103	165	113	372	228	234	271	138	76	185
All but 1a	39	66	38	138	92	109	140	62	45	98
All villas	5	10	5	20	14	15	14	13	8	19
PAS coins	30	11	13	44	30	34	53	19	25	46

	REECE PERIODS									
Region	**1**	**2**	**3**	**4**	**5**	**6**	**7**	**8**	**9**	**10**
1a Ver	7	11	8	25	15	14	14	8	3	9
1b Ver Hint	23	23	21	78	43	71	70	29	4	23
1c Ver Hint	5	2	5	18	11	13	10	8	3	6
1 Ver All	8	11	9	28	16	17	17	9	3	10
2 Sarratt	32	97	32	129	97	32	0	32	65	65
3 Cow Roast	2	22	10	34	18	16	22	12	10	20
4 Lil & Off	2	2	0	9	9	13	20	11	11	7
5 Baldock	5	9	4	13	8	10	16	3	6	15
6 Br & Ware	4	9	4	19	24	12	25	16	4	10
7 Welwyn	4	4	2	9	4	11	11	16	16	22
All sites	7	10	7	24	14	15	17	9	5	12
All but 1a	6	10	6	21	14	17	21	9	7	15
All villas	4	8	4	17	12	13	12	11	7	16
PAS coins	9	3	4	13	9	10	16	6	7	14

Table 7.4: Coins from Hertfordshire Regions (1a–8) by Reece Periods. Top: by count; bottom: per mill.

REECE PERIODS											
11	**12**	**13**	**14**	**15**	**16**	**17**	**18**	**19**	**20**	**21**	**Total**
46	64	2086	1778	96	264	1908	1165	609	11	156	9241
7	6	121	101	7	36	44	13	7	2	1	561
3	2	123	100	17	47	183	69	24	0	11	630
56	72	2330	1979	120	347	2135	1247	640	13	168	10432
0	0	0	1	1	5	5	0	1	0	0	31
3	3	80	85	11	20	81	37	71	1	33	508
1	2	115	65	17	24	110	27	50	1	1	451
19	50	791	411	75	142	622	239	471	28	120	3257
4	9	137	90	20	45	173	50	47	2	12	676
5	3	113	96	10	20	109	31	20	0	0	452
88	139	3566	2727	254	603	3235	1631	1300	45	334	15807
42	75	1480	949	158	339	1327	466	691	34	178	6566
9	7	306	243	23	92	252	86	35	2	12	1190
14	47	867	483	97	185	744	218	364	6	27	3357

REECE PERIODS										
11	**12**	**13**	**14**	**15**	**16**	**17**	**18**	**19**	**20**	**21**
5	7	226	192	10	29	207	126	66	1	17
13	11	216	180	13	64	78	23	13	4	2
5	3	195	159	27	75	291	110	38	0	18
5	7	223	207	12	33	205	120	61	1	16
0	0	0	32	32	161	161	0	32	0	0
6	6	158	167	22	39	159	73	140	2	65
2	4	255	144	38	53	244	60	111	2	2
6	15	243	126	23	44	191	73	145	9	37
6	13	203	133	30	67	256	74	70	3	18
11	7	250	212	22	44	241	69	44	0	0
6	9	226	173	16	38	204	103	82	3	21
6	11	225	145	24	52	202	71	105	5	27
8	6	257	204	19	77	212	72	29	2	10
4	14	258	144	29	55	222	65	108	2	8

	PHASE					PHASE			
Region	A	B	C	D	**Total**	A‰	B‰	C‰	D‰
1a: Verulamium	1168	3864	360	3849	**9241**	127	418	39	417
1b: Closer Hinterland	229	222	43	67	**561**	408	396	77	119
1c: Further Hinterland	56	223	64	287	**630**	89	394	101	456
1: All	1453	4309	467	4203	**10432**	139	413	45	403
2: Sarratt	18	1	6	6	**31**	581	32	194	194
3: Cow Roast	89	165	31	223	**508**	175	325	61	439
4: Lilley & Offley	41	180	41	189	**451**	90	393	90	418
5: Baldock	358	1184	217	1475	**3257**	110	369	67	454
6: Braughing & Ware	100	227	65	284	**676**	148	336	96	420
7: Welwyn	53	209	30	160	**452**	117	462	66	354
Total	**2112**	**6293**	**857**	**6545**	**15807**				
Average						**134**	**398**	**54**	**414**

Table 7.5: Coins by phases ABCD for regions (see text for details).

	PHASE					PHASE			
Region	A	B	C	D	**Total**	A‰	B‰	C‰	D‰
1a Verulamium town	1168	3864	360	3849	**9241**	127	418	39	417
All non-Verulamium	944	2429	497	2696	**6566**	144	369	76	411
PAS	366	1350	282	1359	**3357**	109	402	84	405
Villas	139	549	115	387	**1190**	117	461	97	325

Table 7.6: Coins by phases ABCD for comparison of various sub-groups (see text for details).

The coin totals (see Table 7.2) can, following Reece (1995: 183), be converted to per mill figures for comparison (see Table 7.3). In addition, I have employed Reece's division of the period into four broader parts (Reece 1987: 89ff):

> A: All Roman coins, Republican and Imperial, up to AD 260.
>
> B: Coins from AD 260–96, predominantly base-silver and bronze 'radiates'.
>
> C: Coins, mostly bronze *nummi*, struck after Diocletian's reforms,
>
> AD 294/6–330.
>
> D: Coins, mostly silver *siliquae* and bronze *nummi*, from AD 330–402.

7.4 Commentary on site finds

7.4.1 Hertfordshire and the national average

At a very broad level, one can compare the profile for coin-finds in Hertfordshire against the national averages as determined by Richard Reece (1995) and Philippa Walton (2012; for her totals, see final row of Table 7.4). Fig. 7.4 shows how, overall, the profile for Hertfordshire (all coins and PAS coins only) closely follows that of Britain as a whole. This immediately shows the broad similarity in profile between the PAS data and the other datasets, confirming in broad terms the validity of the PAS data in statistical analysis.

Until 260 Hertfordshire's level of coin-loss is quite similar to the national average, although the PAS finds are lower in several instances; this is probably because of the large proportion of coins excavated at Verulamium, where early coins are better represented than on rural sites, which is where PAS coins are generally found. The Flavian peak (Period 4: AD 69–96) is distinctive at urban sites such as Verulamium. However, for PAS finds the first major peak tends to be in Period 7 (AD 138–61), which is the case for Hertfordshire (Moorhead 2013: 92; Walton 2012: 35, fig. 13).

In the second half of the third century (Periods 13–14: AD 260–96) Hertfordshire rises well above the national average. However, in the fourth

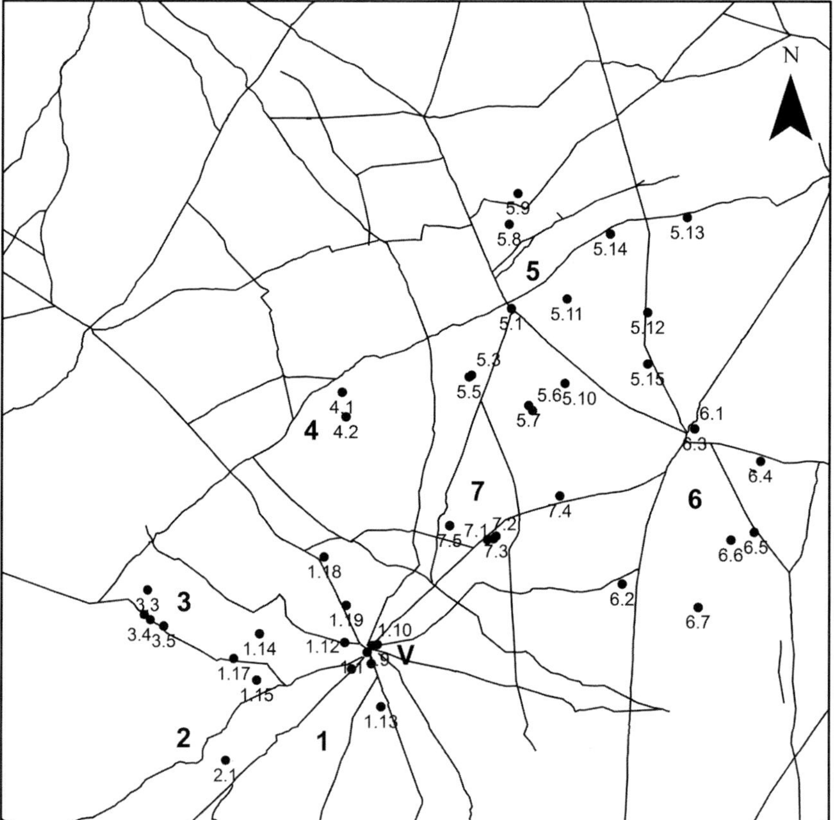

Figure 7.3: Map showing sites and parishes from Hertfordshire with Roman assemblages (sites and regions numbered according to Appendix 2). V = Verulamium. Map © Philippa Walton.

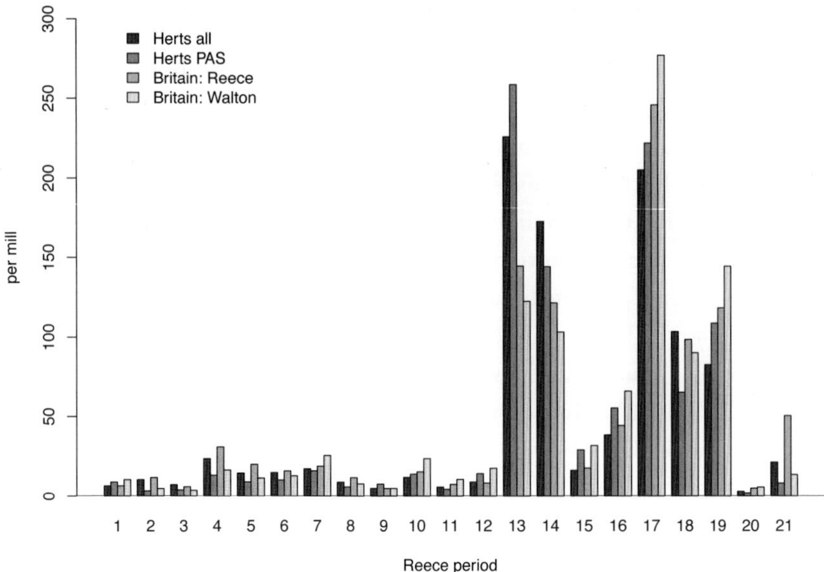

Figure 7.4: Bar chart showing all Hertfordshire finds and all Hertfordshire PAS finds (per mill) against Richard Reece's (1995) and Philippa Walton's (2012) national averages.

century (Periods 17–21: AD 330–402) Hertfordshire lags behind the British average. This overall profile, with a stronger representation in the third century and a drop-off in the fourth century, tends to occur on urban sites across the province. In Hertfordshire it occurs on many rural sites as well as at Verulamium and therefore, in superficial terms, the coin finds from Hertfordshire have an urban feel. This is a phenomenon shared by other counties in the south-east, such as Essex, Surrey, Sussex and much of Kent. It is in marked contrast to many counties to the west, such as Hampshire, Wiltshire and Gloucestershire, which have much higher proportions of fourth-century coins (Moorhead 2001b: 90–95; Reece 1980–82: 62–3).

This analysis is supported by considering Richard Reece's phases (see Tables 7.5–7.6 and Fig. 7.5). The high proportion of phase B coins ('radiates') to phase D coins (mostly *nummi*) is an urban phenomenon, noted by Reece both nationally and for Hertfordshire (Reece 1984: 11–17; 1987: 88–94). If one plots the Hertfordshire regions according to the ratio of B to D coins (see Fig. 7.5) they all fall within the same area as the large towns (*civitas* capitals) in Reece's analysis (1987: 93, Fig. 5.8) except for the Closer Hinterland of Verulamium (no. 1b), which has very few fourth-century coins, and Sarratt (no. 2), which is poorly represented in both periods. What is most interesting is that the villa sites present a more urban profile than Verulamium itself (see Fig. 7.10)! This does underline the urban nature of the coin profile from the county noted by Reece (1980–82: 62–3).

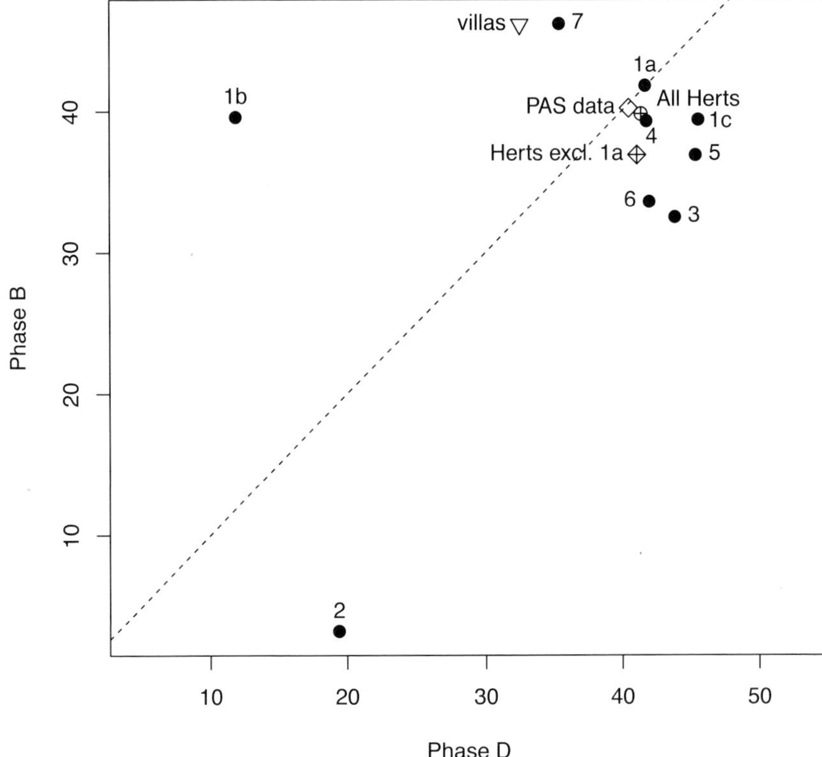

Figure 7.5: Scattergram showing percentages of Period B (AD 260–96) against Period D (AD 330–402) coins. Solid points are the regions used in Appendix 7.2, other points as labelled. Dashed line represents equal numbers of phases B and D.

However, I feel that the ABCD tool is slightly too simplistic for the purposes of this article, because it does not differentiate between proportions of coins for AD 330–64 versus AD 364–402 – these are grouped together in Phase D. As we will see below, the proportions of coins for 364–402 are important factors for grouping sites and regions.

However, although this superficial analysis might provide a broad indication of the nature of currency use in the county in the Roman period, one has to consider smaller regions and individual sites within the county because, as we shall see, there is greater local variation that makes the picture more complex. It is to these regions that I now turn.

7.5 Regions

7.5.1 Verulamium and its hinterland

This region really comprises three groups: the 9,241 coins excavated in Verulamium; 561 coins from the immediate hinterland; and 630 pieces from

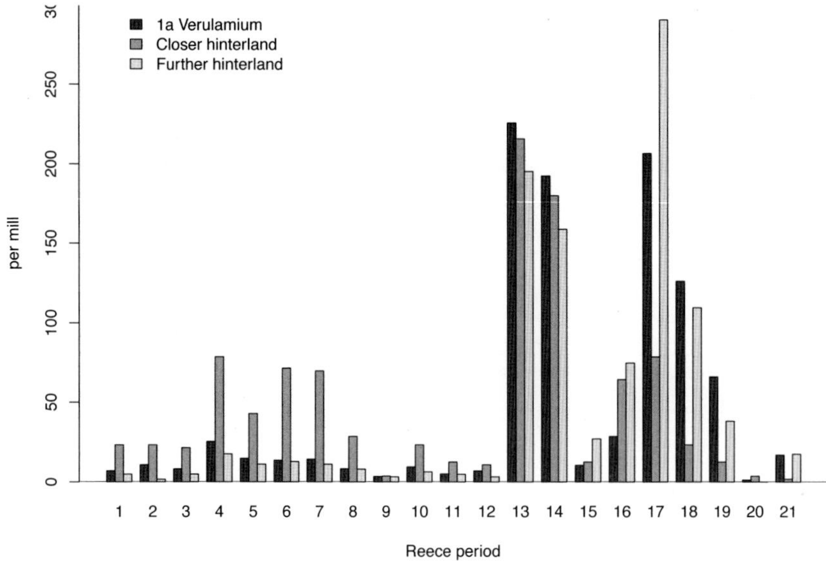

Figure 7.6: Bar chart showing Verulamium town finds (Region 1a), Closer Hinterland finds (Region 1b) and Further Hinterland finds (Region 1c).

the further hinterland (Fig. 7.6). Richard Reece has shown that the Verulamium profile is quite normal for a Romano-British town, the most distinct diagnostic feature being the ratio of radiate coins (B: 418‰) to fourth-century pieces (D: 417‰; Reece 1984: 11–17, 1987: 94). It should be added that Verulamium's urban signature would be even stronger if the coins from the theatre site, which show a much higher proportion of fourth-century coins than the rest of the town (Reece 1987: 90–91), were not included. The two hinterland groups share similar proportions of radiate coins (B: 396‰ and 394‰), but there are two major differences. The immediate hinterland (1b) shows a higher loss of pre-AD 260 coins, although this is largely due to the finds from King Harry Lane cemetery. The further hinterland has a greater peak in Period 17 (AD 330–48), typical for rural sites, although for the rest of the fourth century its profile is similar to that of Verulamium, suggesting the use of a similar currency pool. However, there is a notable downturn in coin loss in the immediate hinterland in the fourth century, a phenomenon which can be seen to be contrary to the evidence from some other towns, such as Canterbury (Moorhead *et al.* forthcoming). However, the two hoards or votive deposits from extramural sites at Verulamium should be noted (see hoards 45 and 47). All sites have low coin loss in the Valentinianic period (19: AD 364–78), even the 88‰ at Verulamium Theatre being far below the national average of 118‰ (Reece 1995). Only 10 of the 19 assemblages have Theodosian coins, none of these coming close to the national average. Put

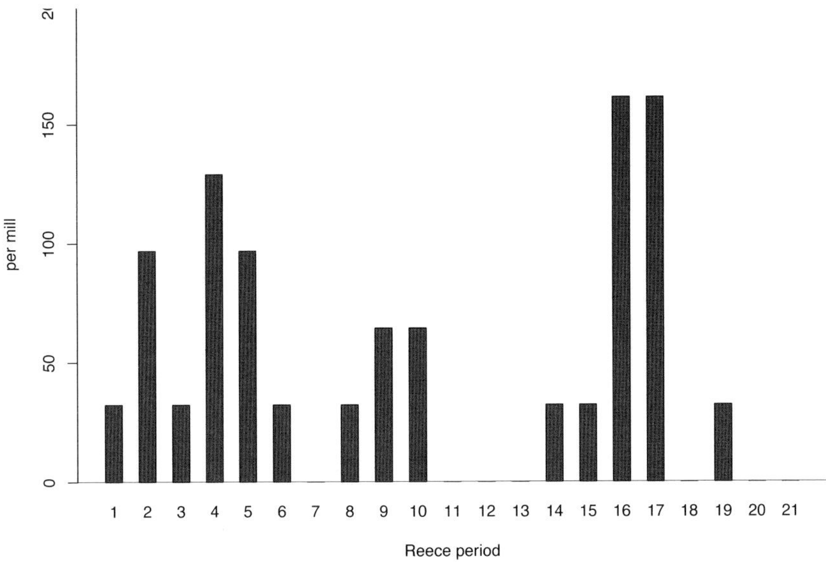

Figure 7.7: Bar chart showing Sarratt (Region 2) finds.

simply, the highest coin-loss seen in Verulamium and its hinterland runs coin-loss up until the end of the third century, with a significant decline in the volume of coinage lost in the fourth century.

7.5.2 Sarratt

Sarratt lies close to the road that runs south-west from Verulamium, and Roman remains have been recorded from the parish (Page 1914: 163). However, the only coin record is the 31 coins recorded with the PAS (Fig. 7.7). These coins have an unusually strong bias to the early phase (A: 581‰), with a weaker showing for the late third and fourth centuries (C: 194‰; D: 194‰). This might be significant, but perhaps only because there is sometimes a preference for recording earlier, often larger and more interesting, coins by detectorists. Further research of the PAS finds from Sarratt is definitely needed.

7.5.3 Cow Roast

Cow Roast, in the parish of Wigginton, has been subject to much archaeological investigation and Richard Reece (1980–82) has produced a thorough report on the coins from the Orchard and Marina sites (Fig. 7.8). Reece suggests that the settlement 'moves quickly on the road to economic importance once the effects of the conquest period have been assimilated', but that the lower proportion of fourth-century coins suggests that it 'loses its prosperity or coin use before the

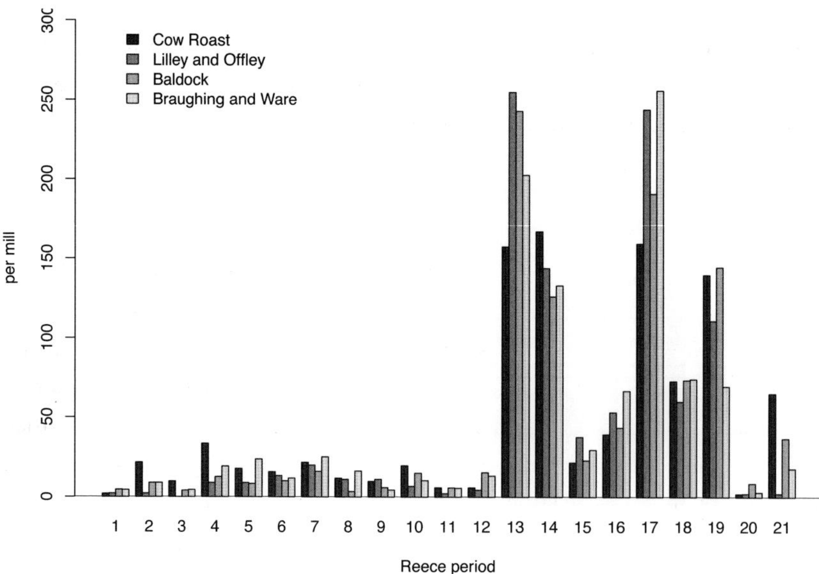

Figure 7.8: Bar chart showing coin finds from Cow Roast (Region 3), Lilley and Offley (Region 4), Baldock (Region 5) and Braughing and Ware (Region 6).

rest of the province (p63)'. I agree with the former, but not the latter. Both sites are weak in the period AD 330–348, when most rural sites peak (171‰ and 133‰ versus the British average of 246‰), but they are strong in the Valentinianic period (AD 364–78; 175‰ and 148‰ versus a national average of 118‰) and have a significant number of Theodosian coins (AD 388–402; 99‰ and 23‰ versus 50‰). Indeed, with the exception of Baldock (Guest, unpublished listing; Site 5.2), the Cow Roast Orchard site has the highest proportion of Theodosian coins from the county. The PAS coins from Berkhamsted range from the first to late fourth centuries, but the sample of 28 is rather too small for meaningful comment. The 35 PAS coins from Aldbury are all late third- and fourth-century.

7.5.4 Lilley and Offley

These two parishes lie between Cow Roast (section 7.5.3) and Baldock (section 7.5.5). It appears that only the PAS provides significant coin records for this region, with 75 coins from Lilley and 376 from Offley (Fig. 7.8). Both assemblages cover the full period of Roman occupation. Overall they tend to have a slightly stronger showing for radiate (B: 393‰) to fourth-century coins (D: 418‰) than is usual for rural sites. However, until AD 378 there are still a healthy number of coins; after AD 378 there is a collapse, with only two Theodosian coins from Offley. This might be because Theodosian bronze coins are small and often poorly struck, and can be difficult to identify.[7] Overall, the profile for Lilley and

Offley fits neatly with those of the Cow Roast region to the south-west and the Baldock region to the north-east. Whatever the precise significance of the coin profiles, the recording of these assemblages does provide an impetus for further research in the area.

7.5.5 Baldock

After the Verulamium region, the Baldock region has the largest number of site finds, with 3,210 coins from 15 assemblages (Fig. 7.8). The overall profile is quite similar to that for the Cow Roast region, with a strong showing for radiates (B: 366‰), a slightly depressed proportion for Period 17 (192‰), and another strong showing for the House of Valentinian (AD 364–78; 146‰). Theodosian (AD 388–402) coins are found on most sites, but are exceptionally numerous only on the Baldock excavations (Groups 5.1 and 5.2: 98‰ and 126‰).

7.5.6 Braughing and Ware

The Braughing and Ware region, with 676 coins from seven assemblages, has a similar profile to Cow Roast, Lilley and Offley, and Baldock up until AD 348 (Figs 7.8–7.9). However, with the exception of Foxholes Farm (site 6.2), Much Hadham (6.5) and Widford (6.6), there is a major collapse in coin loss in the Valentinianic period (19: AD 364–78). This fall-off in overall coin loss in AD 364–78 is a phenomenon that the Braughing and Ware region shares with that of

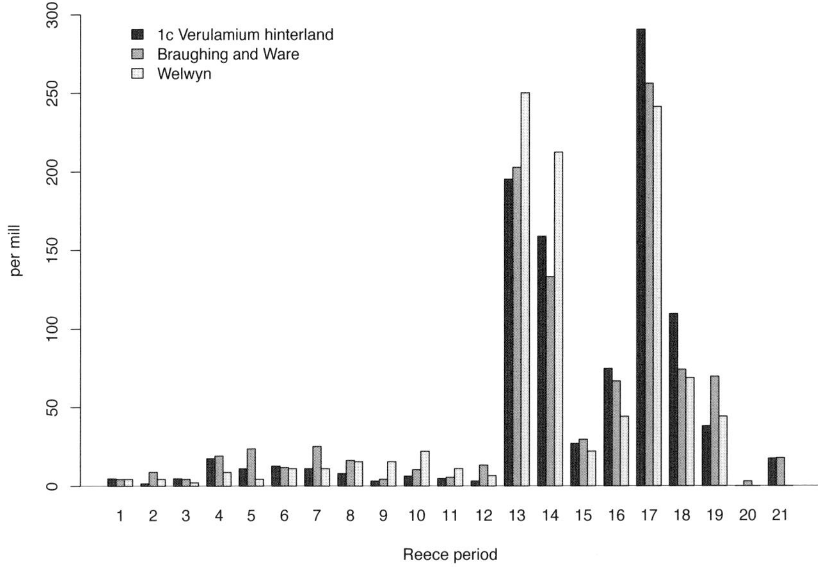

Figure 7.9: Bar chart showing coin finds from Verulamium Further Hinterland (Region 1c), Braughing (Region 6) and Welwyn (Region 8).

Welwyn and the Further Hinterland of Verulamium to the south-west (Fig. 7.9). Theodosian (21: AD 388–402) coins are found in large proportions at Puckeridge and Foxholes Farm (sites 6.1 and 6.2), but are absent from four of the assemblages.

7.5.7 Welwyn

Dicket Mead villa is strong in the radiate period (B: 616‰), but much weaker in the fourth century, collapsing in the Valentinianic and Theodosian periods (AD 364–402, Fig. 7.9). Welwyn St Mary, by contrast, is much stronger in the fourth century, with a Valentinianic peak well above the national average (153‰ compared to 118‰), although with no later coins. Watton-at-Stone peaks strongly in the mid-fourth century (AD 330–48: Period 17, 323‰), but tails off in the later part, with no Theodosian coins.

7.5.8 Villas

Although not a region, it is important to consider villas as a group in this analysis. Although one or two villas show some exceptional peaks in coin loss (Gadebridge in Period 17, AD 330–48; Park Street in Period 18, AD 348–64), the overall profiles for the eight villas in this study (Gorhambury, Park Street, Gadebridge, Boxmoor, Northchurch, Ninesprings, Dicket Mead and Lockleys) are remarkably similar. It is interesting, too, how similar their joint profile is to that of Verulamium, underlining how they present a typically urban, rather

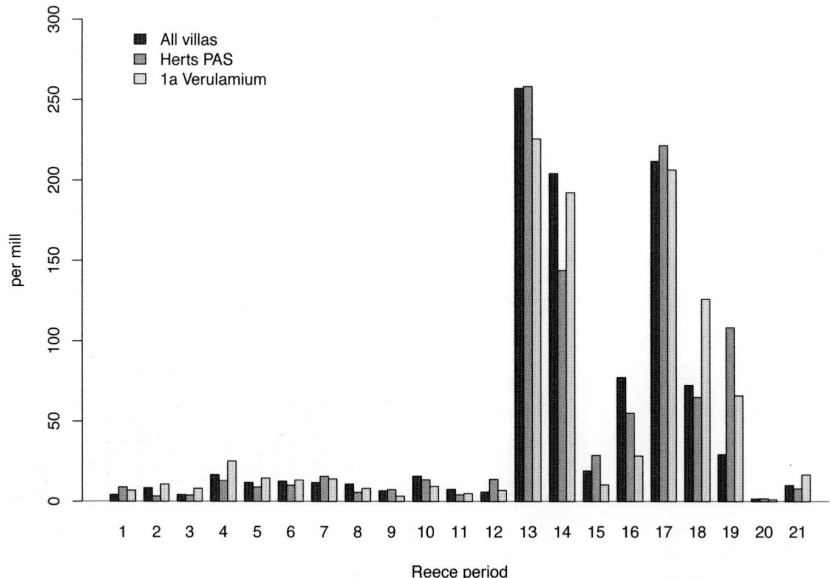

Figure 7.10: Bar chart showing coin-loss for villa sites, PAS assemblages and Verulamium.

than rural, profile (Fig. 7.10). This is almost certainly largely due to the apparent demise of several villas in the middle decades of the fourth century – Gadebridge Park, Boxmoor and Gorhambury (Curteis 1994–6: 10). Furthermore, it is known that the Hertfordshire villas never attained the same size and wealth as those in the West Country (Niblett 1995: 82). There is a general collapse in coin loss in the Valentinianic period (19: AD 364–78, 254‰) that is even greater than that at Verulamium (659‰). Only three villas record finds of Theodosian coins (21: AD 388–402) – Gadebridge Park, Boxmoor and Ninesprings.

7.5.9 Summary for regions

It is immediately clear that these profiles for regional coin-loss do tend to suppress greater variation among specific assemblages, which is why I have provided full data for all of the assemblages so that readers can reinterrogate the material in different ways. However, I would argue that some general patterns can be traced. Only a quick glance at Table 7.5 shows how, in general, the regions share the same overall proportions of coins by period, with only Verulamium's Closer Hinterland (1b) and Sarratt (2) diverging greatly from the normal range of values. Futhermore, Fig. 7.11 shows how Verulamium has a broadly similar profile to the rest of Hertfordshire. Until AD 296 the homogeneity of Hertfordshire is striking, especially in the radiate Phase B. Also, at a glance, the proportions for coins of Phase D are remarkably uniform. There is no doubt that, in the

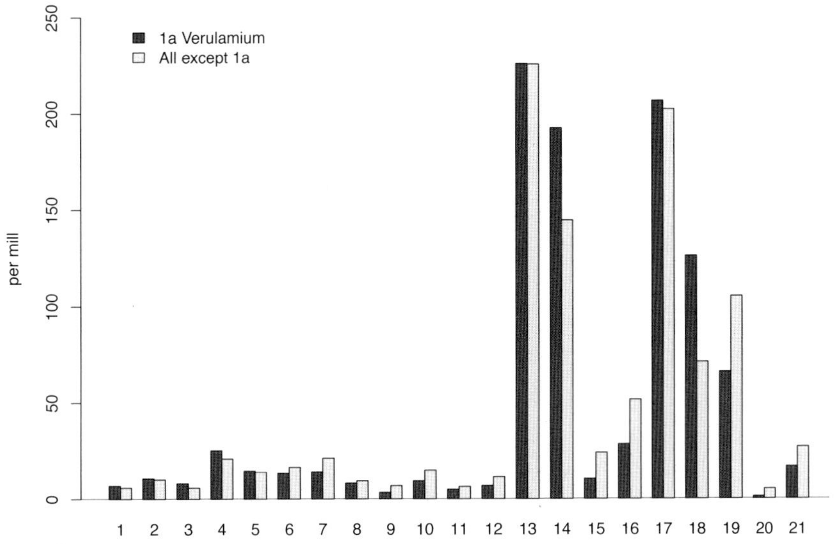

Figure 7.11: Bar chart showing Verulamium town (Region 1a) against all other Hertfordshire regions (1b–8).

fourth century, Hertfordshire's proportion of coin-loss drops significantly when compared with many other parts of Britannia, notably to the west. A relationship with the west might just be reflected in the higher proportions of fourth-century coins from Verulamium's Further Hinterland (1c, D: 456‰), Cow Roast (3, D: 439‰) and Baldock (5, 454‰) regions. However, as I mentioned above, the broad categorisation of coins in Phase D, AD 330–402, masks important details, especially in Hertfordshire. As the reader will have noted in my discussion above, where sites and regions do really vary in coin-loss is in the Valentinianic and Theodosian periods (AD 364–402), to which I will now turn.

7.6 The Valentinianic (AD 364–78) and Theodosian (AD 388–402) periods[8]

As I mentioned above, some distinctive patterns emerge in the late fourth century. I have been interested for a long time in coin-loss across Britain in the Valentinianic period (Period 19: AD 364–78; Moorhead 2001b: 90–95; Moorhead 2009: 156–8; Moorhead and Stuttard 2012: 227; Moorhead 2013: 198). At Verulamium and in its hinterland the numbers of Valentinianic coins are low, only the coins from Verulamium Theatre (88‰) surpassing the Hertfordshire average of 82‰. However, there are several regions in Hertfordshire where there are significant peaks in coin-loss in the Valentinianic period (Fig. 7.12). Although the two Cow Roast sites have a generally depressed fourth-century coin-loss, they both have peaks in the Valentinianic period which are above the national average (175‰ and 148‰ against 118‰). Moving north-eastwards, although the totals at Lilley (4.1) and Offley (4.2) (93‰ and 114‰) are below the national average, they are still above the average for Hertfordshire (82‰). It is in the Baldock region that most of the sites with high proportions of Valentinianic coins cluster: Baldock (5.1), 189‰; Baldock (5.2), 179‰; Boxfield Farm (5.6), 197‰; Lobs Hole (5.7), 133‰; Hinxsworth (5.8), 212‰; Ashwell (5.9), 131‰; and Clothall (5.10), 158‰. Furthermore, a further three sites are above the Hertfordshire average: Ninesprings villa (5.3–5.4), 91‰ and 94‰; Wallington (5.10), 109‰; and Buckland (5.11), 83‰. To the south and east there are many fewer sites with high proportions of Valentinianic coins: Foxholes Farm (7.1), 235‰; Widford (7.2), 191‰; Welwyn St Mary (8.2), 153‰; Lockleys villa (7.3), 143‰; and Much Hadham (6.5), 92‰. It is also interesting to note that nine of the 20 assemblages listed above have been recorded with the PAS, highlighting the importance of PAS data in helping to determine regional patterns in artefact loss.

I have identified that high proportions of Valentinianic coins are found in particular parts of Britain: in the West Country counties of Somerset, Dorset, Wiltshire, Hampshire, Gloucestershire and Oxfordshire; in some assemblages in Buckinghamshire and Northamptonshire which link with sites around the Wash; and, further north, in Lincolnshire, Nottinghamshire and East Yorkshire (Moorhead 2001b: 90–95). In the south-east (Essex, much of Kent, Surrey and Sussex) and the north-west Valentinianic coins are much scarcer, their presence often being noted in numbers only on military sites, as at Caernarvon, for example (Reece 1991: no. 121). The Valentinianic assemblages in Hertfordshire are mostly on the Icknield Way, clustered between Cow Roast and Baldock, which does suggest that these sites are linked in a monetary sense to the west and north, where Valentinianic coins are much more common, rather than to Verulamium, where such coins are much scarcer. However, it is interesting to note the important hoard of Valentinianic *nummi* from Kings Langley (hoard no. 44). It is the most easterly hoard of its kind, the bulk of large Valentinianic hoards coming from the West Country (Moorhead 2001b: 92, table 3).

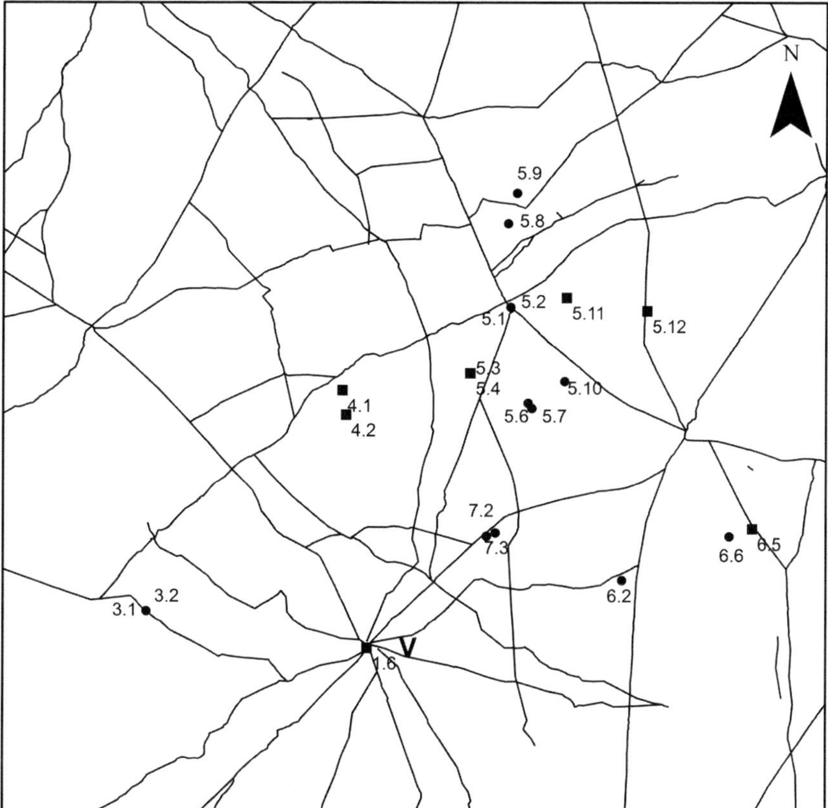

Figure 7.12: Hertfordshire sites with a proportion of Valentinianic coins (Period 19: AD 364–78) above the average for Hertfordshire (88‰) [squares] and the national average (118‰) [circles]. V = Verulamium. Map © Philippa Walton.

I have argued that the presence of large numbers of Valentinianic bronze coins represents official activity. In this case, I believe that the Roman authorities (military and procuratorial) were concerned to extract taxes in kind (the *annona militaris*) from particular regions of the country. We know that Julian went to great lengths to export grain from Britain to Germany in the late 350s and I have no reason to believe that the export of foodstuffs did not continue into the Valentinianic period.[9] Therefore, I would argue that farmland along the Icknield Way was a target for such activity in a way that much of the region around Verulamium was not.

Finds of Theodosian coins (Period 21: AD 388–402) in Hertfordshire are only half of that of the national average (24‰ as opposed to 50‰). They are found in small numbers in and around Verulamium, although two Theodosian-period hoards are recorded from close to the town (nos 44–45). Mirroring

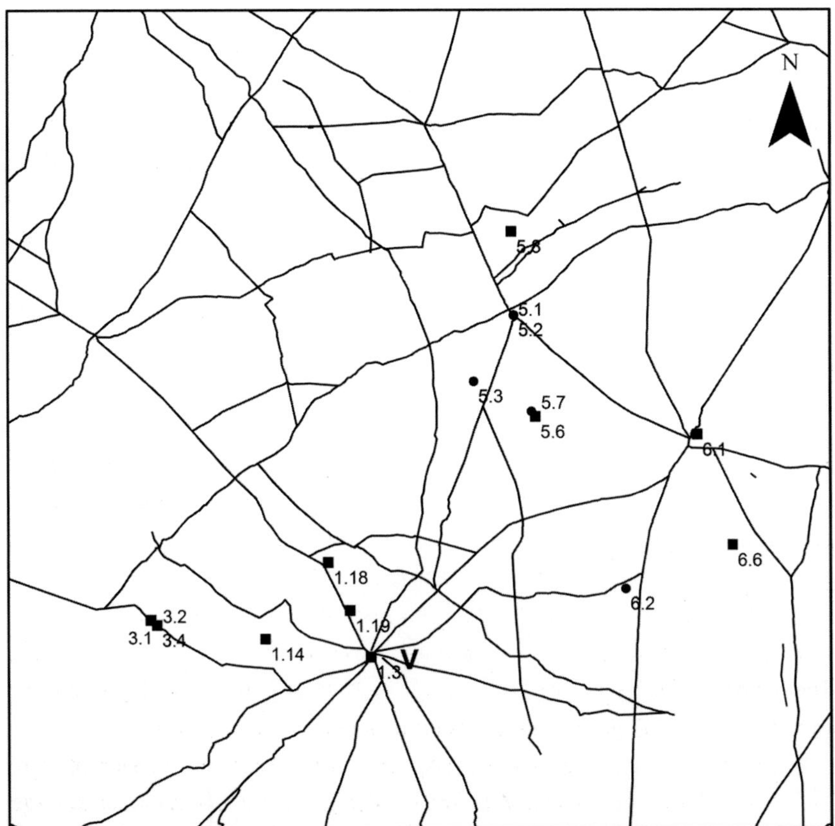

Figure 7.13: Hertfordshire sites with a proportion of Theodosian coins (Period 21: AD 388–402) above the average for Hertfordshire (21.1pm) [squares] and the national average (50.25pm) [circles]. Map © Philippa Walton.

the Valentinianic coin pattern, a number of sites along the Icknield Way have Theodosian pieces, a few in high numbers: Cow Roast (3.1), 99‰; Baldock (5.2), 126‰; Ninesprings villa (5.3), 61‰; and Lobs Hole, 133‰ (Fig. 7.13). Again, to the south and east there are many fewer pieces, with eight out of eleven sites having no Theodosian coins whatsoever. However, at Puckeridge (6.1) there is 50‰ and at Foxholes Farm 59‰. Philippa Walton has shown how the distribution of Theodosian coin finds shrinks from previous periods, often down to nodal points on the road system (2012: 104–5). This does suggest that *nummi* were now used only really in urban and military contexts, being generally eschewed on rural settlements (Moorhead and Walton 2014). In this case it can be argued that the Icknield Way remained a major artery and that settlements such as Puckeridge/Braughing and Verulamium were still important centres; three of the four known Theodosian hoards came from the St Albans region (hoards nos 45, 47 and 48).

In addition to the recent discovery of a late gold hoard near Verulamium (no. 48) with a *terminus post quem* of AD 408, it should be noted that single finds of seven late Roman gold *solidi* have been recorded from the county, dating from AD 379–402 (Bland and Loriot 2010: 169–70, nos 241–7). Finally, although this article is concerned with assemblages, mention should be made of two bronze *nummi* of Valentinian III (AD 425–55), struck *c.* AD 425–35, which have been found near St Albans (Abdy and Williams 2006: 31, nos 57 and 60). Only three other coins of this late date are known from the rest of Britain – from Richborough, Wroxeter and Dunstable (Abdy and Williams 2006: 31–2, nos 58, 59 and 61) – making the St Albans pieces even more significant.

7.7 Conclusions

As noted above, most coin finds, in terms of both hoards and site finds, come from the north and west of the county, around the Chilterns. To the south and east, in the London and Boulder Clay zones, only three outlying hoards (nos 13, 18 and 39), and no significant site assemblages, have been found.

In the early period, AD 41–260, the majority of coins are found at major centres, mostly by excavation: Verulamium, Cow Roast, Baldock and Braughing. The majority of early hoards are found in the same areas, suggesting that these were the regions where there was most intensive coin use at the time.

However, in the radiate Phase B (AD 260–96) there is an explosion of coin-loss across the entire county, with many sites exceeding the national average. This does confirm the 'urban' nature of the coin profile for the county of Hertfordshire as a whole. This had already been noted by Richard Reece, but it is interesting that the picture remains largely the same with the addition of 23 PAS assemblages. Furthermore, this is the period with the highest proportion of coin hoards from the county.

There is a downturn in the number of hoards from the fourth century. Although a few sites have coin records which peak in the mid-fourth century, the county is generally depressed at a time when most rural regions to the west and north have high coin-loss. This is a pattern which is more akin to Essex, Surrey, Sussex and much of Kent. However, in the Valentinianic period (AD 364–78), many sites, mostly along the Icknield Way, have a high proportion of coin-loss which links them in a monetary sense to the West Country, Northamptonshire, counties around the Wash, Lincolnshire and East Yorkshire. In contrast, Verulamium and its environs appear to be linked to the south-east, where Valentinianic coins are in general scarcer.

Finally, in the Theodosian period (AD 388–402), a large number of sites are not represented, but high proportions at sites on the Icknield Way and in the Braughing region and three coins hoards from near to Verulamium suggest that, at least at nodal points, coinage was still being used. The importance of Verulamium in the last years of Roman Britain is shown by the recent discovery of over 159 gold *solidi* from Sandridge and the recording of 2 *nummi* of Valentinian III from near to St Albans.

I hope that this short overview will provide some insights into the nature of Roman currency in Hertfordshire; if nothing else, it provides a dataset for others to interrogate and against which to compare new finds.

7.8 Acknowledgements

I am grateful to Eleanor Ghey for providing vital information about hoards from Hertfordshire, especially the unpublished ones from Ashwell (Ghey forthcoming). I must also extend thanks to Julian Watters and David Thorold for all of their work recording coins for the Portable Antiquities Scheme. I would also like to thank Philippa Walton for producing the maps and Kris Lockyear for producing the graphs, and for his patience.

7.9 References

Abdy, R. and Minnitt, S. (2002), 'Shapwick Villa, Somerset', *Coin Hoards from Roman Britain* 11, pp. 169–233.

Abdy, R. and Williams, G. (2006) 'A Catalogue of Hoards and Single Finds from the British Isles, c. AD 410-675' in Cook, B. and Williams, G. (eds) (2006), *Coinage and History in the North Sea World, c.500–1250* (Leiden), pp 12–73.

Bland, R. and Loriot, X. (2010), *Roman and Early Byzantine Gold Coins found in Britain and Ireland*, Royal Numismatic Society Special Publication No. 46 (London).

Curteis, M. (1994–6), 'The coinage of Ninesprings Roman villa, Great Wymondley', *Hertfordshire Archaeology* 12, pp. 7–11.

Davies, J.A. and Gregory, A. (1991), 'Coinage from a *Civitas*: a survey of Roman coins found in Norfolk and their contribution to the archaeology of the *Civitas Icenorum*', *Britannia* 22, pp. 65–101.
Ghey, E. (forthcoming), 'The coins', in R. Jackson and G. Burleigh, *Dea Senuna: Treasure, Cult and Ritual at Ashwell, Herts* (London).
Guest, P. (2005), *The late Roman gold and silver coins from the Hoxne Treasure* (London).
Guest, P. and Wells, N. (2007), *Iron Age and Roman Coins from Wales* (Wetteren).
Harper, P. (2010), 'Stylistic Links among Copies of Bronze Coins of Claudius I found in Britain and Spain', *Numismatic Chronicle* 170, pp. 105–14.
Kenyon, R. (1987), 'The Claudian coinage', in N. Crummy (ed.), *The Coins from the Excavations in Colchester, 1971–9*, Colchester Archaeological Report 4 (Colchester), pp. 24–41.
Kenyon, R. (1992), 'The coins from the Culver Street and Gilberd School sites', in Crummy, P. (1992) (ed.), *Excavations at Culver Street, the Gilberd School and Other Sites in Colchester, 1971–85*, Colchester Archaeological Report No. 6 (Colchester), pp 290–308.
Moorhead, T.S.N. (2001a), 'Roman Coin finds from Wiltshire', MPhil thesis, University College London.
Moorhead, T.S.N. (2001b), 'Roman coin finds from Wiltshire', in P. Ellis (ed.), *Roman Wiltshire and After* (Devizes), pp. 85–105.
Moorhead, T.S.N. (2009), 'Three Roman coin hoards from Wiltshire terminating in the coins of Probus (AD 276–82)', *Wiltshire Archaeological and Natural History Magazine* 102, pp. 150–59.
Moorhead, T.S.N. (2013), *A History of Roman Coinage in Britain* (Witham).
Moorhead, T.S.N. and Stuttard, D. (2012), *The Romans Who Shaped Britain* (London).
Moorhead, T.S.N., and Walton, P. (2014), 'Coinage at the end of Roman Britain', in Haarer, F.K. with Collins, R., Fitzpatrick-Matthews, K.J., Moorhead, S., Petts, D. and Walton, P.J. (eds) (2014), *AD 410: The History and Archaeology of late Roman and post-Roman Britain* (London), pp. 99–116.
Moorhead, T.S.N., Anderson, I. and Walton, P. (forthcoming), 'The Roman coins from the excavations at Whitefriars, Canterbury', in A. Hicks and M. Houliston, *Whitefriars, Canterbury. Excavations 1999–2003* (Canterbury).
Niblett, R. (1995), *Roman Hertfordshire* (Wimborne Minster).
Page, W. (ed.) (1914), *VCH Hertford*, vol. 4 (London).
Penhallurick, R.D. (2009), *Ancient and Early Medieval Coins from Cornwall and Scilly*, Royal Numismatic Society Special Publication 45 (London).
Reece, R. (1972), 'Roman coins found on fourteen sites in Britain', *Britannia 3*, pp. 269–76.
Reece, R. (1983), 'The coins from the Cow Roast, Herts. – a commentary', *Hertfordshire Archaeology* 8, pp. 60–66.
Reece, R. (1984) 'The Coins', in S.S. Frere, *Verulamium Excavations III* (Oxford), pp. 3–17.
Reece, R. (1987), *Coinage in Roman Britain* (London).
Reece, R. (1991), *Roman Coins from 140 Sites in Britain* (Cirencester).
Reece, R. (1995) 'Site-Finds in Roman Britain', *Britannia* 26, pp. 179–206.
Robertson, A. (2000), *An Inventory of Romano-British Coin Hoards*, Royal Numismatic Special Publication 20 (London).
Shotter, D. (1990), *Roman Coins from North-West England* (Lancaster).
Shotter, D. (1995), *Roman Coins from North-West England. First Supplement* (Lancaster).
Shotter, D. (2000), *Roman Coins from North-West England. Second Supplement* (Lancaster).

Shotter, D. (2011), *Roman Coins from North-West England. Third Supplement* (Lancaster).
Thorold, D. (2013), 'The Sandridge Hoard', *Searcher* 329 (January 2013), p. 16.
Walton, P. (2012), *Rethinking Roman Britain: Coinage and Archaeology* (Wetteren).

Notes

1 I am aware that this number could probably be increased with the inclusion of other finds not included in this study, such as the excavation coins from Ashwell (Ghey forthcoming), but I believe this sample to be satisfactory for providing an overview of coinage in Hertfordshire. When this article was about to go to press Adrian Chadwick and Eleanor Ghey kindly drew my attention to a hoard of 147 coins, ranging from *c.* AD 273 to *c.* AD 383, found in the excavations at King's Park, St Albans, in 2002. They were not submitted to the Treasure process, hence their not being entered on to our hoards database. This hoard has been added to Appendix 1 as No. 50.

2 Appendix 1 has been created by the editor by merging the data provided by Moorhead (this chapter) and Wythe (the following chapter) along with a small number of additional addenda and corrigenda. The numbering of the hoards in the two chapters has been standardised, but no attempt has been made to update the text or the figures discussed therein.

3 There were 260 Mark Antony *denarii* out of 9,238 coins in the Shapwick Hoard (Abdy and Minnitt 2002).

4 Hoxne (Suffolk) has 577 gold coins (Guest 2005); Eye (Suffolk) reputedly had over 600 gold pieces (Robertson 2000: no. 1620); for Sandridge, see Thorold (2013).

5 Nos 22 and 23 may be from the same find.

6 Data taken from <www.finds.org.uk> June 2013.

7 When identifying large assemblages of detector finds there are normally some Theodosian coins, but it is not uncommon to have very few or even none.

8 Although AD 378–88 is the earlier Theodosian period, it is a period of minimal coin-loss in Britain. The coins of the later Theodosian period, AD 388–402, are much more numerous and are much more meaningful to use in statistical analysis.

9 For sources for Julian's export of grain from Britain, see Moorhead and Stuttard 2012: 206–8.

CHAPTER 8

Archaeology and the Roman coin hoards of Hertfordshire

Dave Wythe

8.1 Introduction

The following paper has two specific and related aims: the first is to reassess the process through which we define a coin hoard, and the second is to take the results of that reassessment and apply them to a group of hoards – in this case, Roman coin hoards discovered in Hertfordshire. Arguably, this makes the current paper somewhat different to the vast majority of numismatic studies, where the emphasis has often been on the structure or contents of the hoard.[1] While this may seem like a somewhat unusual approach, it is arguably more appropriate for a non-numismatic publication.

8.2 The data

The principal source of data is Robertson's *An Inventory of Romano-British Coin Hoards* (2000). The findspots are shown in Figure 7.2. The quality of the information contained within the *Inventory* is, as Richard Reece (2002: 70) observed, somewhat variable, with considerably more information being available for those hoards which closed before the end of the third century and significantly less being provided for fourth-century hoards. It has been necessary, therefore, to return to the original source material, such as the *Numismatic Chronicle* (*NC*) and the relevant excavation reports, to obtain the necessary information either on the coins themselves or on the nature of the hoards and their findspots, which is essential to this paper.

For those hoards discovered subsequent to the publication date of Robertson's *Inventory* (2000), information has been obtained from the various editions of the NC and from the Portable Antiquities Scheme (PAS) database

(<www.finds.org.uk>). This information has in turn been supplemented by the more detailed reports in the *Coin Hoards of Roman Britain* series, edited by staff from the Coins and Medals department of the British Museum and published initially by the British Museum as occasional papers, and now more recently by Moneta (see references in Appendix 1).

The hoards themselves have been listed in Appendix 1 (p. 337) in order of the latest coin found in the hoard. Each hoard has been given a sequential reference number by which it is identified in the current paper. The total number of hoards included in the study is 46.[2]

8.3 What is a coin hoard?

Rather than simply processing the above body of data into a series of groups which can then be analysed and compared with other similar, or even contrary, bodies of data, it is perhaps worth exploring just what constitutes a coin hoard and, likewise, what we are in danger of erroneously treating or failing to treat as a coin hoard.

The question, however, of what precisely defines a coin hoard is not so easily answered. John Casey (1986: 51) argued:

> For practical purposes the minimum size of a hoard is just two coins and the qualifying factor is that the coins should have been brought together in a deliberate manner.

While Reece (2002: 67) offered the following definition:

> A coin hoard from the Roman period consists of money that was buried or set aside … It consists of coins which may vary from the high value of one gold piece all the way down to a few scruffy bronze coins.

While both definitions allow for there to have been no deliberate intention of retrieval, Casey is quite specific over the minimum number of coins required before the term 'hoard' can justifiably be applied. Reece's definition, however, recognises the that value does not have to be a key indicator of a hoard.

More importantly, neither Casey nor Reece see burial as an essential part of the definition of a coin hoard. Certainly, the word 'burial' appears in Reece's definition, but it is clearly linked to the phrase 'or set aside'. Burial, therefore, irrespective of the reasons why retrieval did not occur, simply becomes the process through which we learn that the hoard existed or it entered the archaeological record. It is not in itself a defining quality of hoards.

8.3.1 Coin hoards and the Treasure Act

The Treasure Act (1996) offers the following definitions of what constitutes treasure, and specifically its relevance to coins. Under Section 1 (1) (a) it states:

> (ii) when found, is one of at least two coins in the same find which are at least 300 years old at that time and have that percentage [10% of weight] of precious metal; or
> (iii) when found, is one of at least ten coins in the same find which are at least 300 years old at that time.

While clearly hoards of Roman coins are going to exceed 300 years in age, it is worth exploring the question of how far this particular definition of treasure has subsequently been used to define a hoard in recent years, particularly where finds recorded under PAS are concerned.

Four of the hoards recovered from Hertfordshire have fewer than 10 non-precious metal coins (nos 5, 17, 24, 27), and all of these were recovered under excavation conditions. Only one hoard of fewer than 10 coins has been recorded during the period subsequent to the introduction of the Treasure Act – a hoard of two Republican *denarii* that is defined as a hoard primarily because of the proximity of the coins to each other (no. 1).

Hoards of fewer than 10 non-precious metal coins may well have been discovered in Hertfordshire over the course of the 18 years since the introduction of the act; however, their failure to fit neatly into the category of treasure may well mean that they have potentially been treated as individual stray finds rather than as hoards.

8.3.2 The closure date of a coin hoard

It is important to distinguish between the closure date of a hoard and the burial date of a hoard (Lockyear 2012: 203–7; Lockyear forthcoming). The closure date of a hoard is the date of the most recent coin in the hoard, unless dating has been obtained through other methods, such as associated small finds or the container itself. Strictly speaking, this is actually a *terminus post quem* for the hoard, or the date after which coins ceased to be added to the hoard (Robertson 1974: 15). The level of wear on a coin can provide some additional information on when the hoard was closed, with those in mint condition more likely to have been withdrawn from circulation earlier or sooner than those which are worn. It should be noted, though, that the most recent coin in the hoard is not necessarily the same as the last coin added to the hoard.

The burial date of the hoard can be any time after the last or latest coin was added. This is frequently hard to ascertain with any confidence and it has not been unreasonable for both archaeologists and numismatists to assume that hoards were buried some time shortly after their closure date. Evidence from the Bredon Hill hoard, however, which contained 3,874 coins and was closed in the late third century, but was subsequently recovered from a fourth-century deposit, has demonstrated either that a hoard could either have been closed some considerable time before it was finally buried (in this case 70 years) or that late third-century coins could continue to be hoarded during the course of the fourth century and also prove to be the latest coins included in a hoard (Nash 2012). The Bredon Hill evidence is a strong reminder that the closure date of a hoard is no guide to its burial date.

8.3.3 Site finds or scattered hoards?

Nick Ryan (1988: 34), in his study on fourth-century coinage, argued that the number of coins recovered as site finds or stray finds were, in his opinion, 'quite incompatible with conceivable rates of accidental loss'. This argument was based on the fact that comparable volumes of coin-loss to that in the Roman period are not found until the early modern period. This, in turn, led Ryan to further dismiss both the difficulty of finding coins lost accidentally during the Roman period and also differing excavation techniques as factors in the number of coins recovered (Ryan 1988: 34). Instead, he argued that:

> Deposited material, particularly that in surface and near-surface layers, can be and frequently has been subject to considerable disturbance and scattering. Despite this, the idea of the scattered hoard is less commonly used than might be expected in attempts to explain widespread scatters of roughly contemporary material. (Ryan 1988: 34)

Ryan then questioned the value of studies which relied upon the patina of the coins in order to identify hoards from site finds, preferring instead the detailed recording of the spatial patterning of coins. In considering site finds, it was his conclusion that 'the possibility of deliberate deposition, even of deliberate disposal, must be given serious consideration' (Ryan 1988: 35).

For Ryan such deliberate deposition involved coins either being discarded, simply because they had ceased to have any monetary value, or being buried as votive deposits. Sadly he does not state whether or not surface corrosion or the spatial distribution of such coins can assist in identifying the one from the other, or either from accidental losses in general.

While the scattered hoard theory has some viability and the question of deliberate deposition is certainly one we will return to (see Section 8.7, below), it is worth noting that precious metal coins are overwhelmingly recovered within hoards, and that, if Ryan's theory were correct, considerably more would be mis-recorded as site finds.

In conclusion, one might be forgiven for thinking that it is impossible to distinguish site finds or single or small groups of finds from coin hoards, but there are several indicators that we can look for that can assist in this process. These can be defined as follows:

Was there a container? This is not to argue that all hoards must have containers; however, the use of a container of some kind, recovered either complete, near-complete, broken, or even just evidenced either by the existence of nails which could have once held together a wooden box or by the staining or otherwise discolouring of the coins all strongly suggest a process whereby coins were deliberately brought together and stored for a purpose.

The patina of the coins. Despite Ryan's objections, noted above, the patina can be a useful indicator and similarities or dissimilarities between the patinas of various groups of coins should be recorded and noted, especially where there is some doubt (or even if there is initially no doubt) over how the coins in question entered the material record. The value of recording and studying the patina is commented on further below (see Section 8.5, below).

The spatial distribution of the coins. While this may be particularly useful when attempting to distinguish between scattered hoards and site finds, it should be noted that there are no rules or formulae which can be applied that can then be used to define a scattered hoard, other than considering whether or not the site finds consisted of precious metals, and this is not a foolproof method. Indeed, it is worth noting that the idea of the scattered hoard is now being supplanted in favour of the 'market' theory, whereby certain spatial distributions of coins are being used to argue that the location of the finds had been a market, at which sites a widespread loss of coinage had resulted from a large number of monetary-based transactions over the course of various decades (for an example see Bidwell and Snape 2002: 275–9).

The find spot. Where the coins were found is particularly important and forms a key part of some of the arguments made in the current paper (see Sections 8.5–8.7, below, for a fuller discussion of this important aspect of hoarding and identifying a hoard).

8.4 Hoard types

The discovery of hoards led in turn to the definition of various types of hoards – emergency, savings and purse (or circulation). These definitions were based primarily on the motivations behind the composition of the hoard and the forces or events which had led both to their initial burial, from fear in the case of emergency hoards to accidental loss in the case of purse (or circulation) hoards, and their subsequent non-recovery.[3] Reece (2002: 72) was somewhat scathing of such distinctions, stating that: 'This is not so much wrong, as absolutely pointless.' The basis of Reece's argument was that, unless it was possible to make such distinctions based on the contents of the hoard alone, then these various types existed nowhere except in the mind of the numismatist. Despite the fact that savings hoards should, theoretically, contain coins of greater value or, where precious metal coins were concerned, greater purity, and purse hoards should, arguably, consist of small collections of coins accidentally lost, Reece (2002: 72) nevertheless observed:

> No one who has talked about such hoards has provided any methods of identifying the one from the other, and no studies on the analysis of hoards has shown any major distinguishable groupings within their composition.

8.4.1 The structure of a coin hoard

Kris Lockyear's work on the structure of a coin hoard was subsequently used to explore the question of different hoard types. Lockyear (1993: 368) noted that a coin hoard can theoretically be divided into three sections, which here I call the 'tail', the 'torso' and the 'nose', as illustrated in Figure 8.1. The 'tail' includes the oldest coins in the hoard. These would have been circulating the longest and could therefore be expected to be relatively rare in comparison to later coins. The 'torso' represents those coins which are in current circulation when the hoard is being formed, or which can be said to have formed the bulk or majority of the coinage available to the hoarder from which he could extract coins to hoard. The 'nose' of the hoard includes the most recent issues, slowly entering circulation but insufficient, in quantitative terms, to form a majority, or a significant proportion, of the current coin available to the hoarder. Guest (1994: 29) has also subscribed to this tripartite division of a hoard.

Guest subsequently used variations of Lockyear's model as the initial basis for his analysis of hoards buried throughout the western Roman Empire. A key part of that study was its exploration of the evidence for the existence of various hoard types, and his conclusions are worth noting (1994: 260):

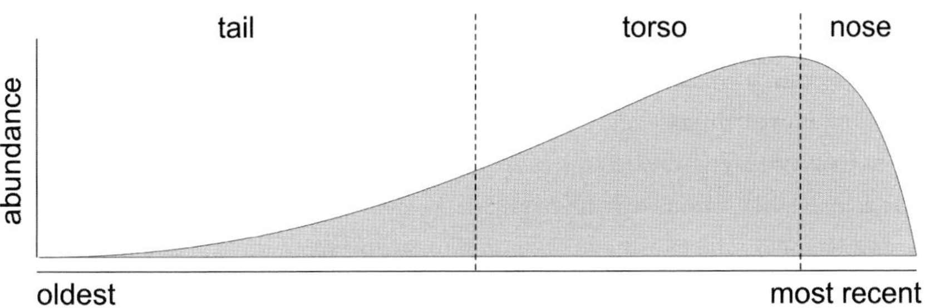

Figure 8.1: Theoretical structure of a coin hoard.

> There is very little evidence to support the suggestion that various types of hoards, such as Savings or Emergency hoards, existed during the Roman period.

Guest was thus able to conclude that the majority of hoards were therefore purse (or circulation) hoards (1994: 261). Of course, it can be added that just because the hoards studied did not fit into modern, preconceived notions of what an emergency hoard or a savings hoard would or should look like or where they should be buried, this does not in itself automatically mean that they are, by default, purse (or circulation hoards). Guest (1994: 263) recognised this when he added: 'the possibility exists that a proportion of hoards are in fact ritual deposits rather than temporary storage of wealth'.

In conclusion, while the idea of differing hoard types has had a long currency in numismatics, studies such as that conducted by Guest have slowly been eroding some of these theories, while forthright thinking, such as that offered by Reece and quoted above, has also done much to change views on this subject. I would argue, however, that while Reece is correct to emphasise that the contents of a hoard should be the principal data that we work with when conducting such analyses, there are other archaeological indicators that we can use which provide us with equally valuable information.

8.5 Possible hoards

As noted above, there are four indicators that we can apply to a group of coins, and that evidence from any should be sufficient to define that group of coins as a hoard. Where a group of coins fails to show any of these indicators then we should question whether or not we are dealing with a coin hoard.

Based on a failure to demonstrate any of these indicators, 15 of the hoards listed (nos 1, 4, 5, 13, 15, 20, 24, 25, 26, 32, 36, 37, 40, 42, 49) should be classified as probable rather than certain or definite. This is not an inconsiderable proportion of the total listed, nearly a third, and it is worth considering some of these hoards in a little more detail, together with the reasons why they should not be classed as certain.

One of the hoards (no. 32) initially sounds quite promising – a series of coins in a small embossed urn – but Robertson's analysis, which suggests that the two latest coins were potentially intruders, must throw some doubt on whether or not the remainder formed a genuine hoard or whether the whole was simply a personal collection of coins which had been stored in a Roman vase by their original owner. A potentially similar hoard (no. 42) was simply subsumed into the general coin collection of the Ashwell museum, so little evidence exists that it was a genuine hoard.

A number of finds made by metal detectorists demand closer inspection: one hoard, with no recorded container, was found in three batches (no. 37), while another hoard, or group of coins, again with no recorded container, was found over an indistinct area of land over a two-year period (no. 13). In addition to this, far too little is known about a third hoard for it to be comfortably included (no. 20).

A further hoard was found as the result of illegal metal detecting over the scheduled site at Aldbury (no. 26). The fact that this hoard was linked to another from the area (no. 25), which itself had been found with metal, pottery and animal remains, all strongly suggestive of site finds rather than a hoard, must in turn throw similar doubt on whether or not the former group of coins (no. 26) was in fact a hoard or also simply site finds. Neither of the hoards were found in containers.

Connected to this category are two further possible hoards (nos 1, 40) that have been defined as such based simply on a balance of probabilities or the proximity of the coins. Clearly, given the inclusion of the previously noted hoards (particularly nos 13, 25, 26 and 37), phrases such as 'balance of probabilities' and 'proximity of the coins to one another' are decidedly ambiguous.

While it may appear easy to criticise metal detectorists and the value of personal collections, the information obtained from excavations is not always as detailed as might be expected or hoped for: very little is known of the small three-coin hoard (no. 5) recovered from the secondary floor of Room 33, Insula XIV at Verulamium by Sheppard Frere, which is recorded in the dating evidence for the period of the building in question but not noted in the published text. The same can also be said of the eight-coin hoard recovered from the levelling clay 'and miscellaneous material' of Room 3, Building III, Insula III at Verulamium by Wheeler, together with at least 16 other coins all dating to the end of the third century (no. 24). Finally, Frere (1983: 98) notes that the burial of a small hoard of eight *denarii* and one *antoninianus*, recovered from outside Room 3 Insula XIV at Verulamium in a fifth-century context, 'is difficult to explain' (no. 15). His description of the burial suggests that this hoard could have been buried considerably earlier, and that its appearance in a fifth-century context was the consequence of disturbance resulting from the collapsed debris of the building. While this, of course, cannot be confirmed, two of the hoards (nos 15, 24) do strongly suggest the redeposition of individual coins into new contexts rather than the burial of hoards. It is worth adding, however, that both excavators, Wheeler and Frere, had provided sufficient in the way of information for doubts to be raised and discussed rather than relying on the simple evidence of the group of coins or hoard itself. The likeliest hoard is Frere's collection of *denarii* which appeared in a fifth-century context (no. 15). It is worth noting that under the terms of the Treasure Act (as quoted above) two of the hoards discussed here would not even qualify as such (nos 5, 24).

In every instance – misjudged personal collections, questionable metal detectorist finds and doubtful excavation finds – one of the indicators that should have been considered further, and could arguably have resolved the issue, is that of the patina of the coins recovered. This has been touched on above, but is worth raising again, firstly, because a lack of sufficient work or recorded information has thrown doubt on the integrity of nearly a third of the hoards – although this would be their integrity as hoards, not as genuine coins – and, secondly, because the body of data from Hertfordshire also includes a hoard which could only be identified from the group of site finds precisely by studying the patina of the coins (no. 28). The Great Wymondley villa hoard exists purely because of work conducted on the condition of the coins (Curteis 1992: 122). It can therefore be argued that, while recording and studying the patina of the coins may keep us busy in dismissing hoards from the list, it could keep us equally busy in the discovery of new and confirmed hoards.

8.6 The importance of location

Where a hoard was found can tell us at least as much about it as can the coins that it contains. The Bredon Hill example – already discussed above, and which, when taken in isolation from its findspot, is simply another late third-century coin hoard to be added to the ever-increasing inventory – provides intriguing dating evidence once the archaeology surrounding the find is brought into consideration. While Hertfordshire doesn't quite offer any examples which match Bredon – that we are aware of – what it does have are a number of hoards where the findspot tells us more about why the hoard was buried than the coins themselves do. All the hoards in question were recovered during excavations at Verulamium.

The hoard of late third-century barbarous radiates recovered from Insula XIX during the excavations conducted by Frere offers an opportunity to explore the idea that hoards, as a means by which people saved, were fairly common and that some, such as this one, found their way into the archaeological record seemingly by accident (no. 30). Frere's (1983: 130) observations on this hoard strongly suggest that it was initially buried elsewhere, perhaps in the wall or roof of the building, and was dislodged during demolition. Of course it remains equally possible that demonetisation of the coins made their original owners simply lose interest in their hoard, something which may have affected large numbers of late third-century coin hoards.

Two further hoards, both of which were also closed in the late third century (nos 33, 34), were recovered from Building I Insula V (Wheeler and Wheeler 1936: 110), suggesting that they were initially buried and then later sealed by the next layer, because they had been either forgotten by their owners or discarded if, as with the hoard recovered from Insula XIX, their original owners had decided that the coins themselves were now worthless and not worth the effort of retrieval. It can also be tentatively argued that the hoards represented what could conceivably be argued was some form of foundation offering or deposit, deliberately buried at a point where retrieval, without demolition of the building itself or tearing up of the floors, would have been impossible.

The hoard of nearly 800 barbarous radiates (no. 31) recovered from under the cement floor of the theatre stage (Kenyon 1935: 236) may also be a foundation deposit. Certainly the evidence as presented indicates that the hoard was placed beneath the stage during the reconstruction process immediately prior to the construction of the stage itself, so it is unlikely to be a hoard which the owner buried and then forgot about or accidentally lost.

While it is tempting to view the evidence offered by both Wheeler and Kenyon as irrefutable proof that coins, in the form of hoards, were being used as foundation deposits certainly at the end of the third century, if not at other times during the Roman period, it is worth remembering that both excavations belong to the same period (the early 1930s) and also used the same techniques (the Wheeler baulk and trench method), and that evidence from later investigations, in which more modern excavation techniques and methods of recording finds were employed, has so far not been forthcoming.

8.7 Votive deposits

While the question of some hoards forming votive deposits or cult offerings has never been doubted (e.g., Grierson 1975: 136; Reece 2002: 71), the identification of such hoards has frequently been determined as much by the location of the hoards themselves as by any other factor.[4] The most notable exception to this rule is the hoard recovered at Frome in Somerset in 2010 (Moorhead *et al.* 2010: 36).

Plate 1.1: Welwyn Roman Baths (photograph: Kris Lockyear).

Plate 1.2: St Helens church, Wheathampstead (photograph: Kris Lockyear).

Plate 2.1: Merle Rook and her diaries (photograph: Tony Rook).

Plate 2.2: Excavations at Great Humphreys (photograph: Tony Rook). Back row, from left to right: Richard Balley, Kris Lockyear, Mike Heasman, Lewis Orchard, Jenny Searle and Merle Rook; in front, Jack Parker.

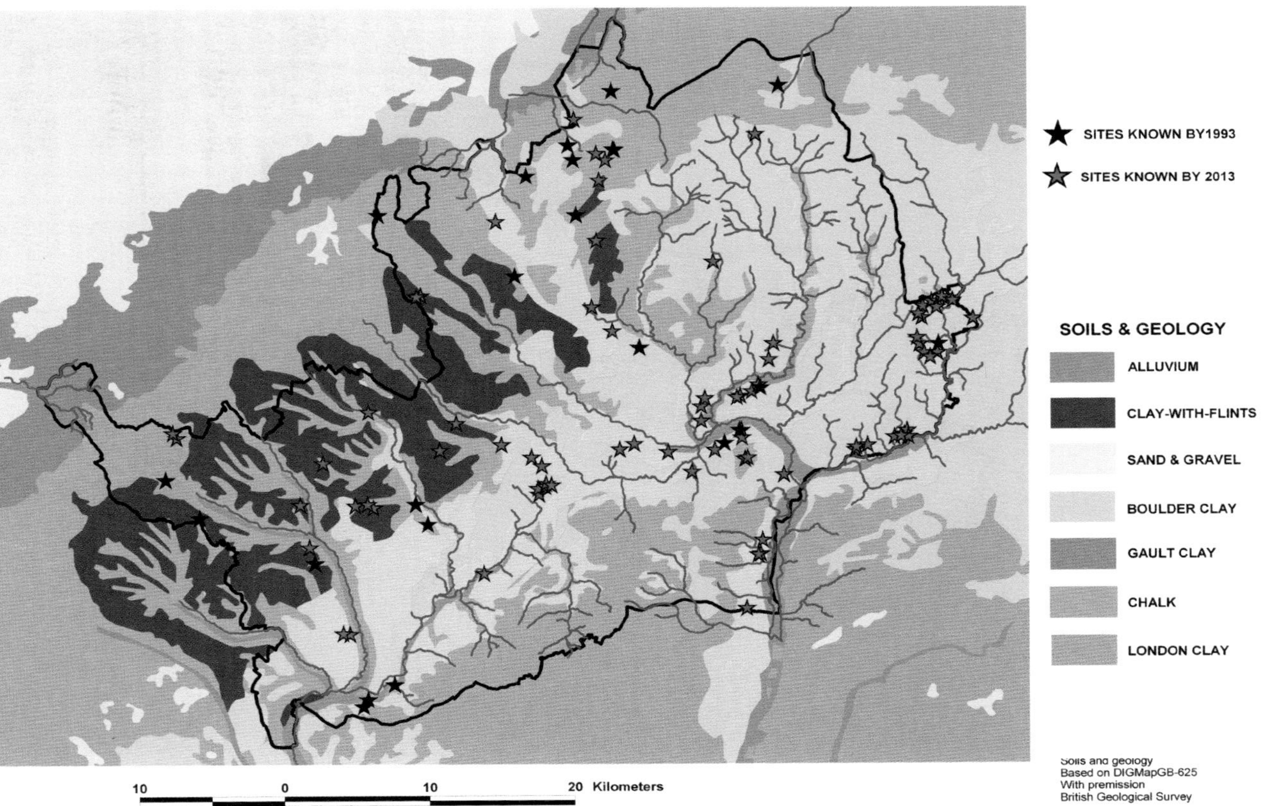

Plate 3.1: Map of sites showing those found before and after 1993 against background of soils/geology and rivers. Ordnance Survey data © Crown Copyright 2015 OS 100056350.

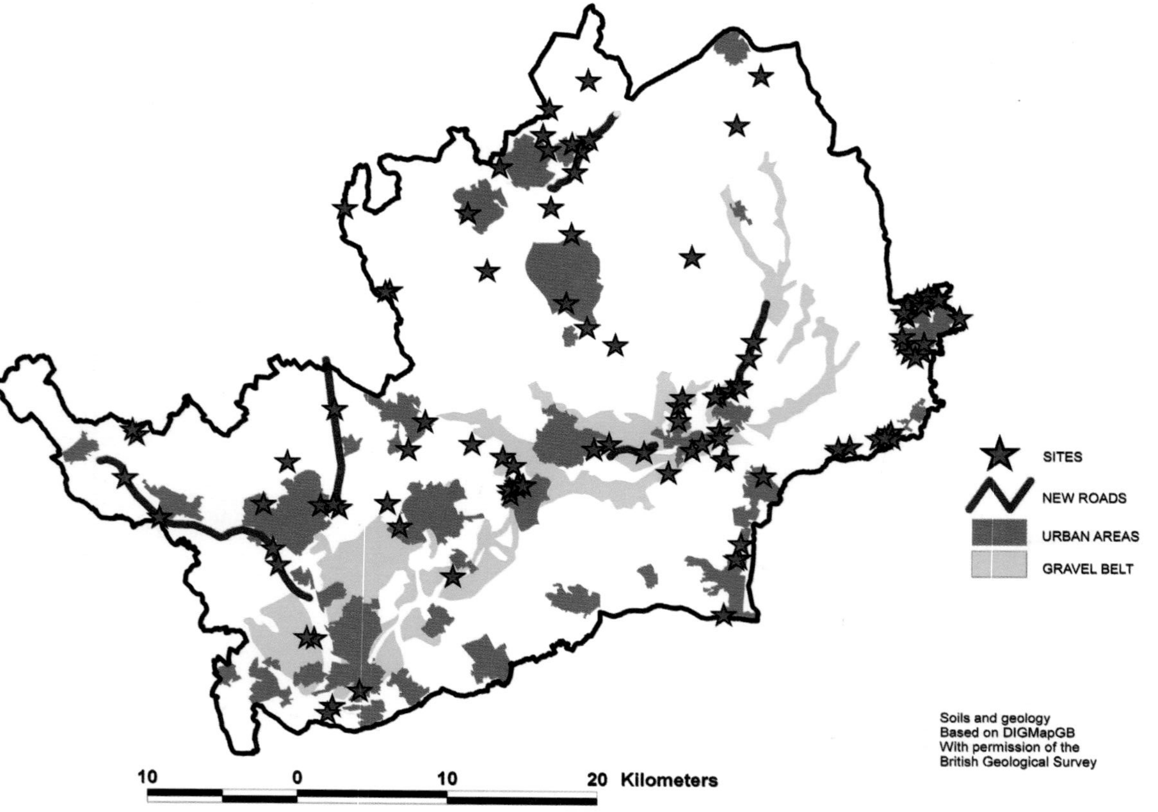

Plate 3.2: Map of all sites against indicators of development pressure. Ordnance Survey data © Crown Copyright 2015 OS 100056350.

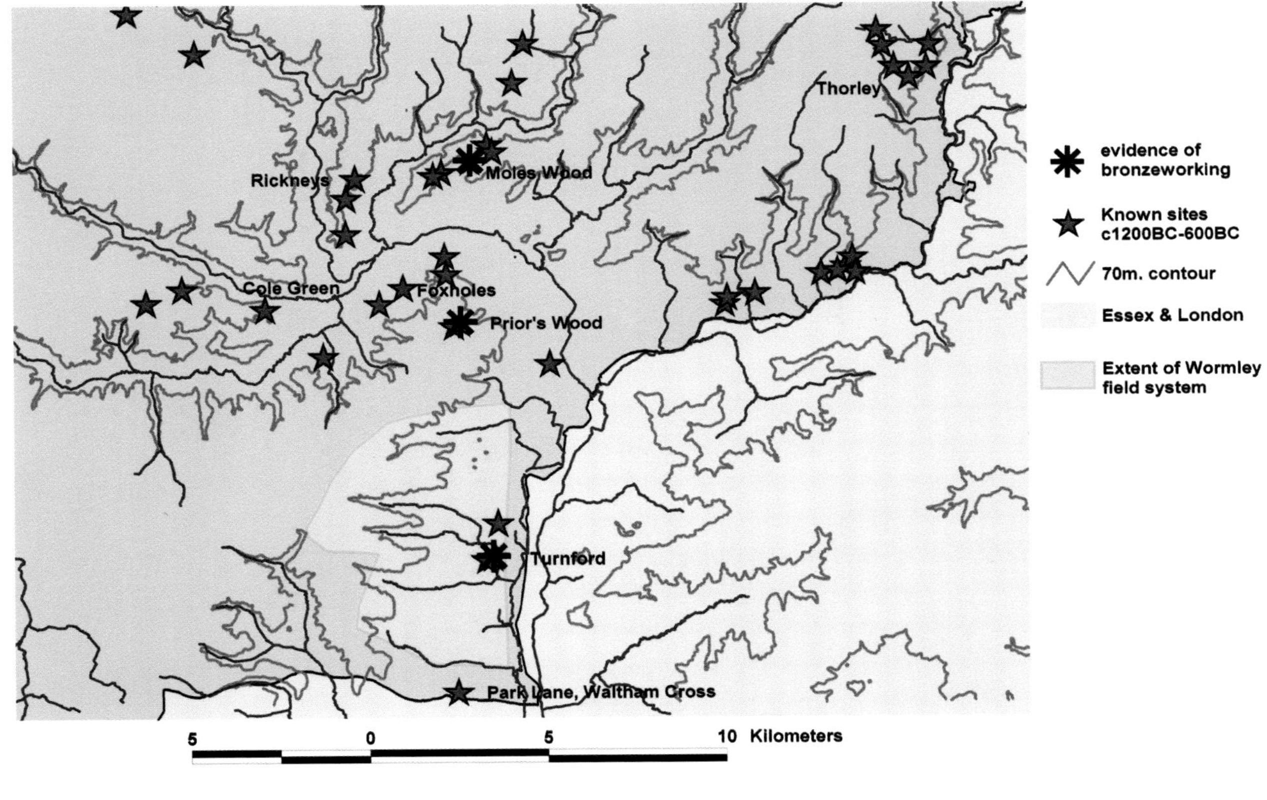

Plate 3.3: Map of the late Bronze Age–earliest Iron Age evidence along the Hertfordshire side of the river Lea valley and its tributaries, indicating key sites mentioned in text. Ordnance Survey data © Crown Copyright 2015 OS 100056350.

Plate 4.1: Third millennium BC structure at Clothall Common, Baldock, in 1989 (photograph: North Herts Museum).

Plate 4.2: The Neolithic burial enclosure east of Baldock under excavation in 2003 (photograph: Albion Archaeology).

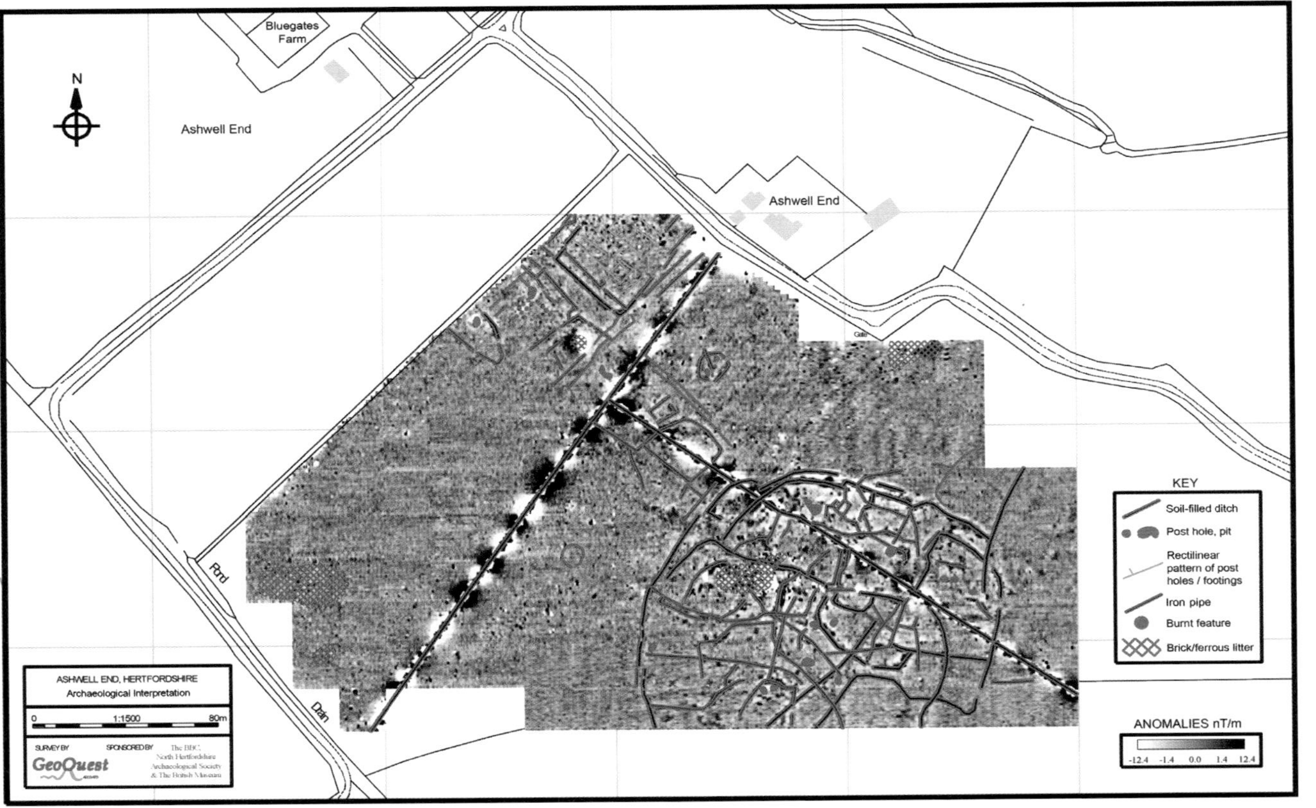

Plate 5.1: Interpretation of geophysical survey of settlement features around the temple treasure hoard and ritual feasting site at Ashwell End. Survey by Prof. Mark Noel of GeoQuest Associates, 2004, reproduced with permission. Ordnance Survey data © Crown Copyright 2015 OS 100056350.

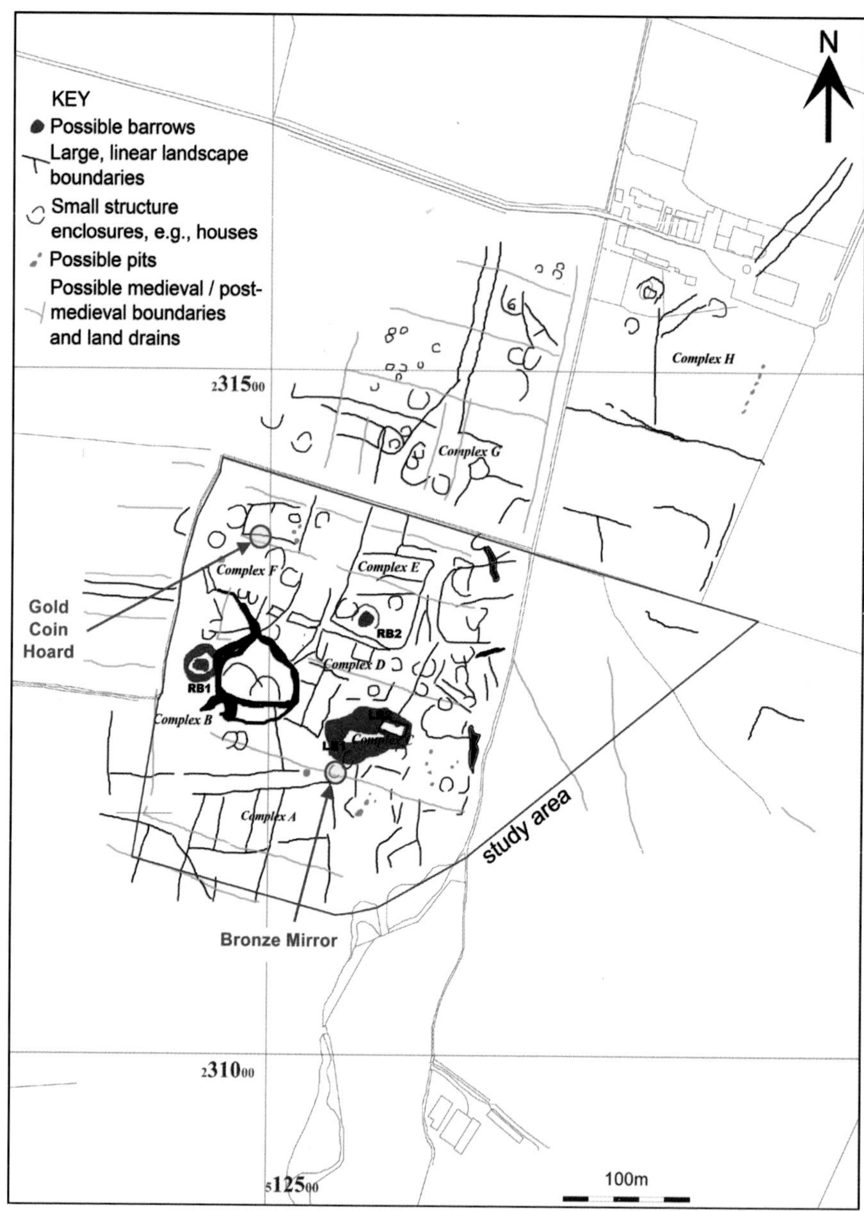

Plate 5.2: Plan of cropmarks at Pegsdon Common Farm, Shillington, Bedfordshire (from Thorpe and Wells 2003, Fig. 2). Reproduced with the kind permission of Albion Archaeology. Ordnance Survey data © Crown Copyright 2015 OS 100056350.

Plate 10.1: Finds from the burials at Turners Hall Farm; centre left is the strainer bowl with its zoomorphic spout. © St Albans Museums Service.

Plate 10.2: The villa building at Turners Hall Farm under excavation. © St Albans Museums Service.

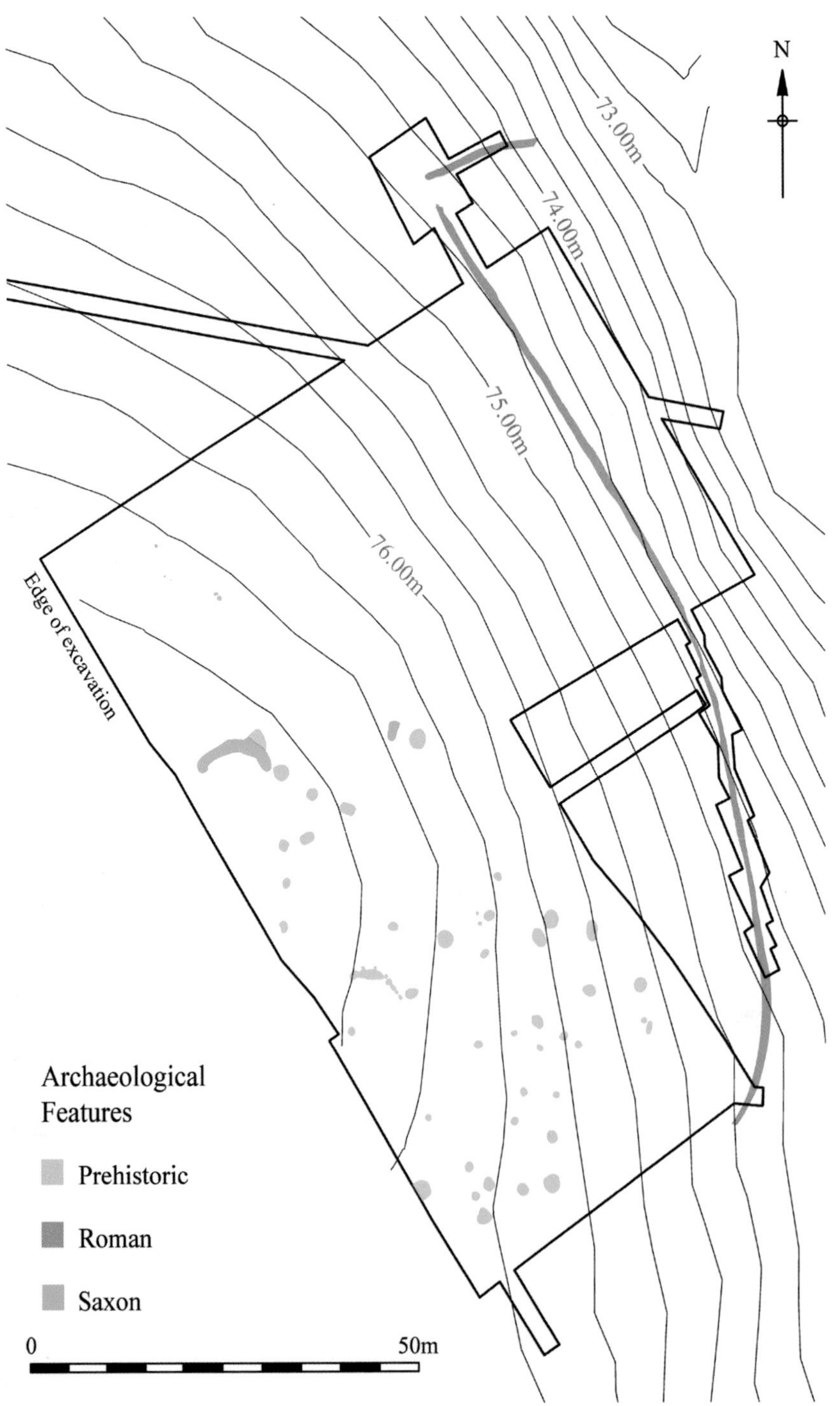

Plate 11.1: Phase plan of features recorded during the excavations at Station Road, Watton-at-Stone (see text for details). Ordnance Survey data © Crown Copyright 2015 OS 100056350.

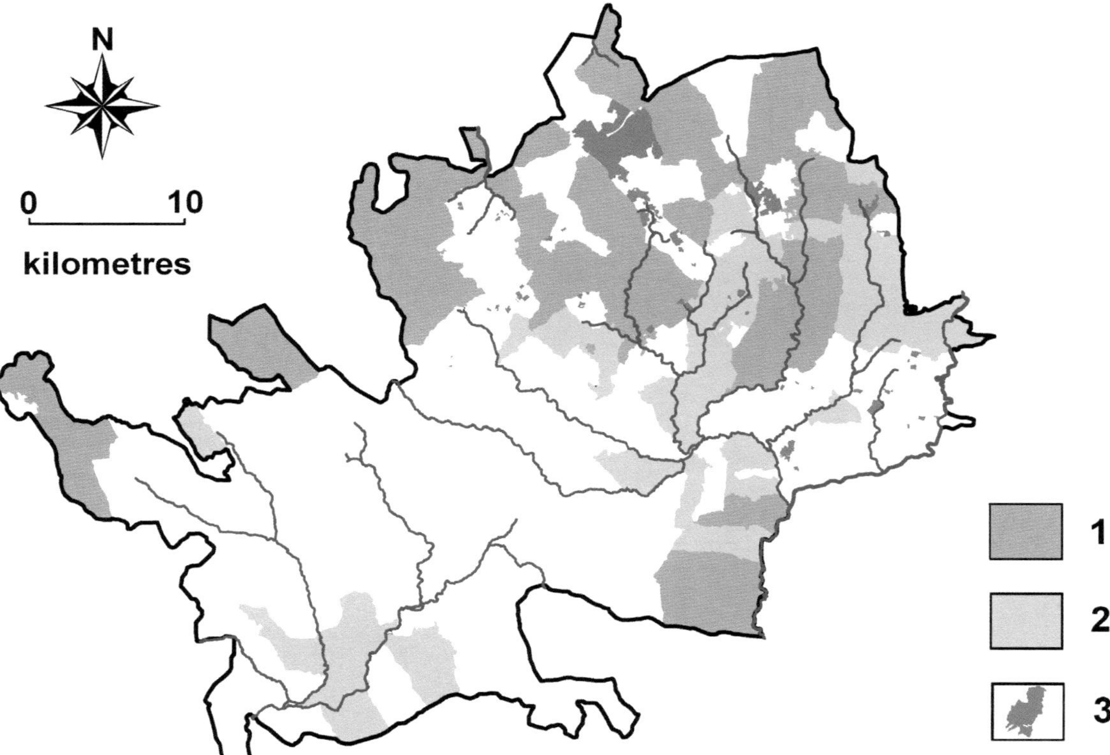

Plate 13.1: Parliamentary enclosure in Hertfordshire. 1. Parishes with enclosure acts which included some open-field arable, and which affected a total area of more than 500 acres (c.200 hectares); 2. parishes with enclosure acts which included some open-field arable, and which affected a total area of 500 acres or less; 3. surviving areas of open field in c.1800.

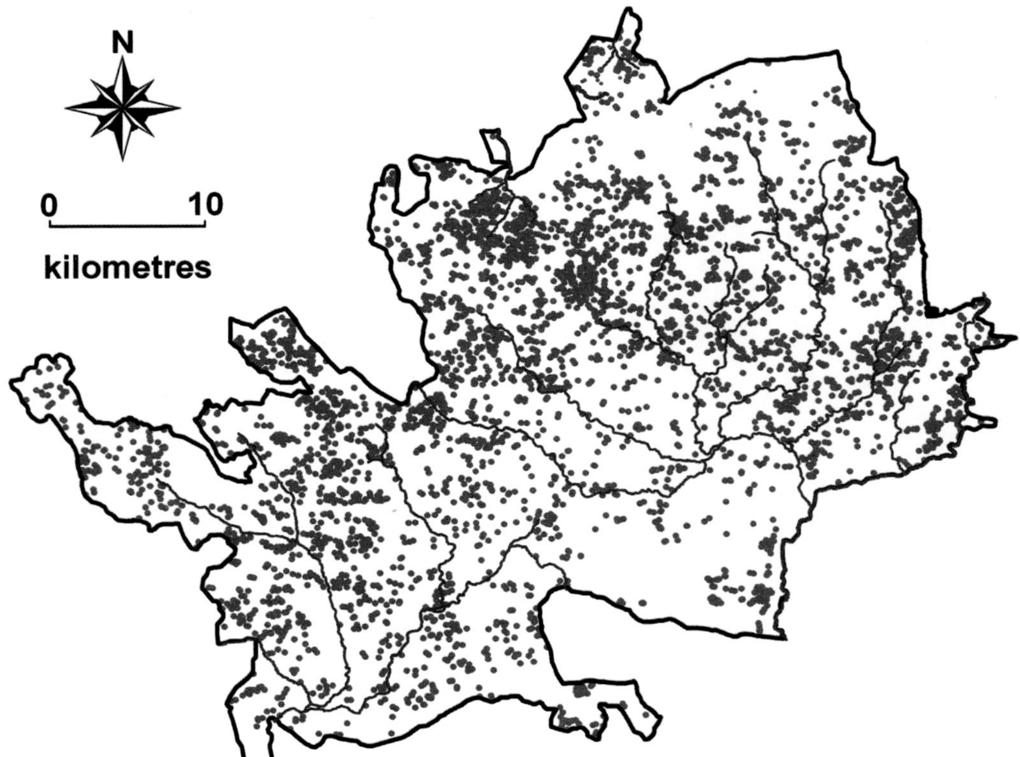

Plate 13.2: Distribution of field boundaries created by piecemeal enclosure in Hertfordshire. The dots mark the mid-points of all boundaries with the smooth, continuous curves or sinuous forms characteristic of this kind of early informal enclosure shown on the late nineteenth-century first edition Ordnance Survey 6 inches: 1 mile maps of the county.

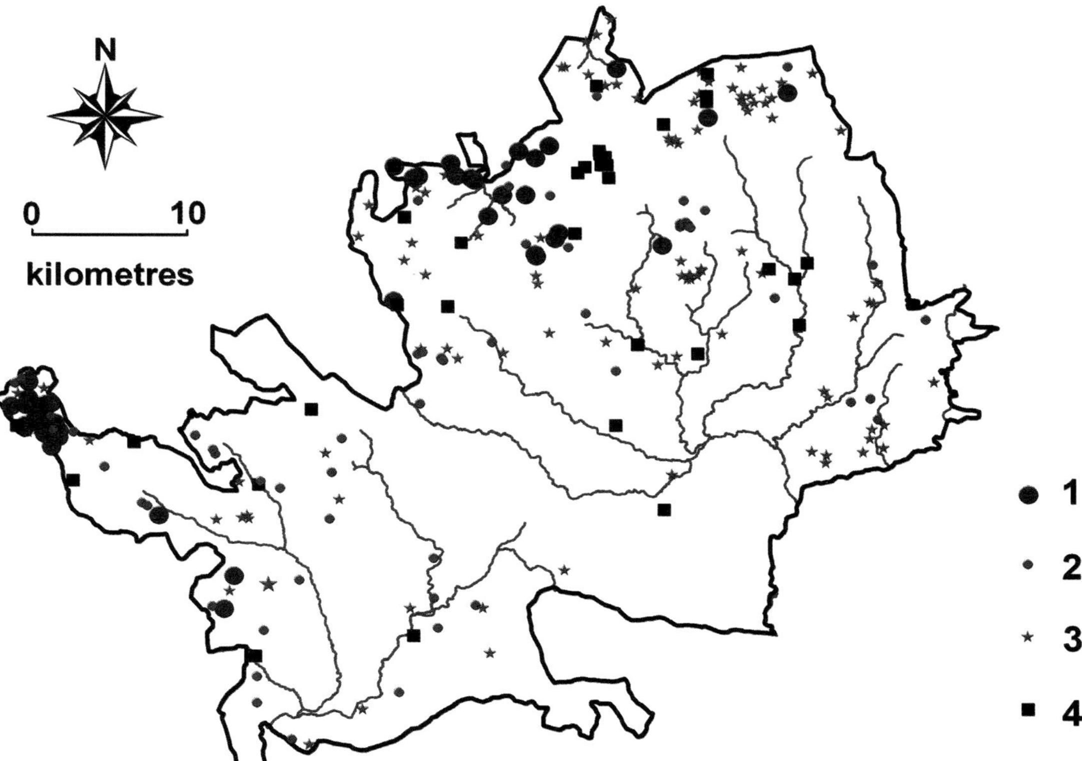

Plate 13.3: Archaeological evidence for open-field agriculture in Hertfordshire. 1. Clear, high-backed broad ridge and furrow; 2. ridge and furrow which is faint, eroded, vestigial or of uncertain form; 3. cropmark, soilmark or parchmark evidence for ploughed-out ridge and furrow, balks etc.; 4. strip lynchets. Based on the HHER. With amendments and additions by the author.

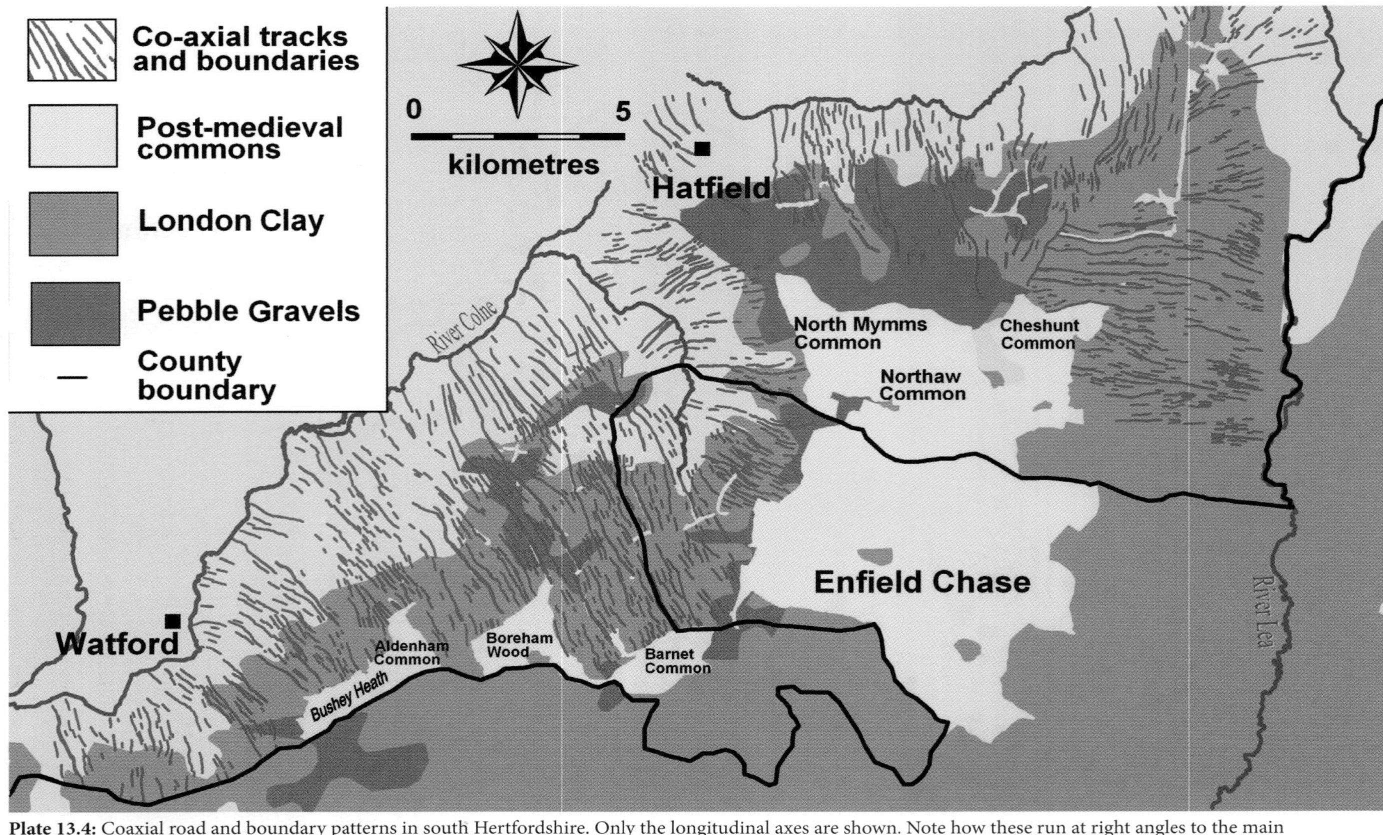

Plate 13.4: Coaxial road and boundary patterns in south Hertfordshire. Only the longitudinal axes are shown. Note how these run at right angles to the main watercourses, up onto the poor soils formed in London clay and pebble gravel.

Plate 14.1: A boar shaking acorns from a young oak pollard from the *Tacuinum sanitatis*, c.1400 (Bibliothèque de Rouen). Source: <http://commons.wikimedia.org/wiki/File:Tacuin_Gland15.jpg>, accessed 25 August 2013.

Plate 14.2: Detail of a plan of the manor of Great Barwick, Standon, by Hollingworth, 1778, showing pasture and arable fields and woodland lying west of the Old North Road (top of picture), just north of High Cross. North is to the left. The trees are colour coded as follows: 'Timber – The Oak distinguished in Green, Elm in Red, Ash in Yellow; The Pollards in Black.' Pollards fill the boundary hedgerows and perhaps some field margins too. Reproduced by kind permission of Hertfordshire Archives and Local Studies (HALS A/2832 and A/2833).

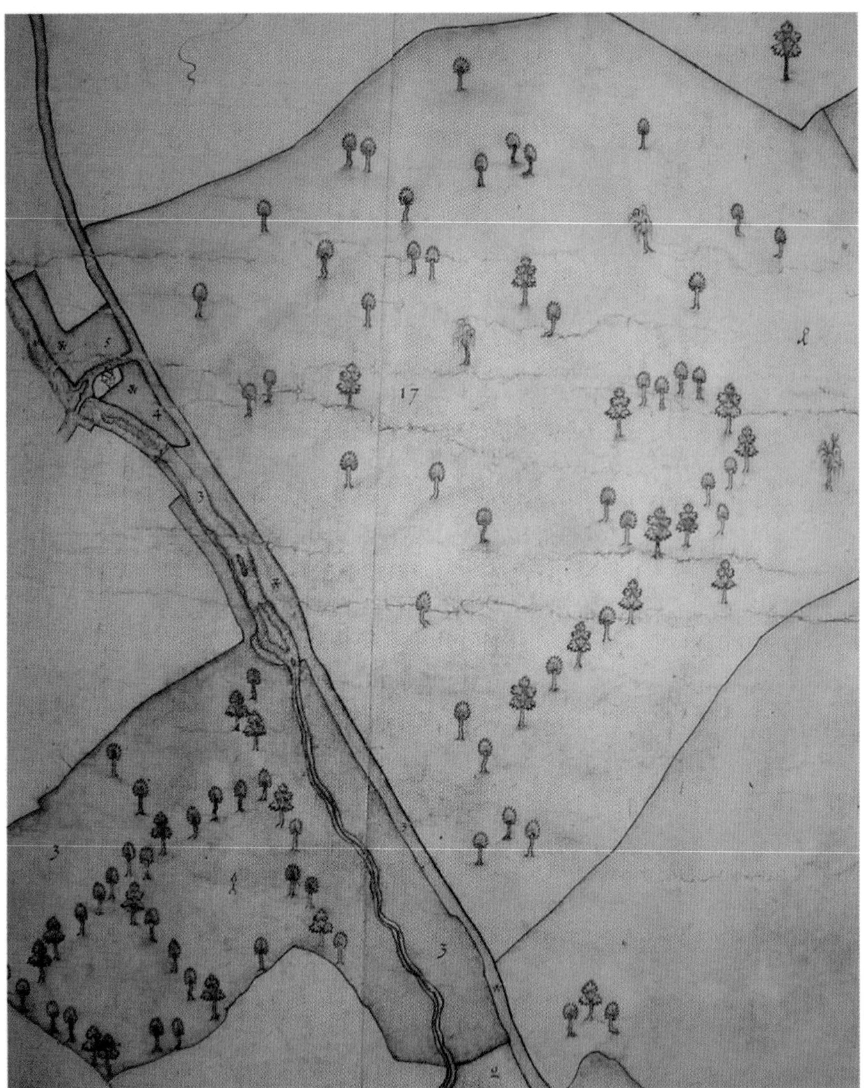

Plate 14.3: Detail of a map of the manor of Digswell, 1599, showing fields bordering the river Mimram and the road from Hertford. A mix of maiden trees and pollards is depicted within a large field of wood-pasture to the right of the road and, to the left, pollards predominate in what appear to be former hedgerows. North is towards the bottom left of the photograph. Reproduced by kind permission of Hertfordshire Archives and Local Studies (HALS DE/P/P1 map of the manor of Digswell, 1599).

Such hoards can be formed using one of two methods: the first involves large numbers of individuals each depositing no more than a single coin or several coins which, over a course of decades, and in some cases centuries, can slowly accumulate into large hoards of tens of thousands of coins, while the second involves a single individual or family group amassing a number of coins, saved perhaps over the course of several or more years, and then dedicating them as a single offering to a particular cult. In the case of Frome, Sam Moorhead, Anna Booth and Roger Bland theorised that the 52,503 coins which made up the hoard could just as easily have been the combined wealth of a community as it could the possession of a single individual or family (Moorhead *et al.* 2010: 36). The coins in the hoard are clearly stratified and show a complex series of additions (Moorhead *et al.* 2010: 11).

In terms of the current study, the Frome hoard raises two important questions: what evidence is there to genuinely support the argument that the hoard was votive in nature? And how far can that evidence then be applied to the hoards from Hertfordshire?

8.7.1 The first Treasure Act?

Hadrianic legislation preserved in the Institutes of Justinian may offer some support to the idea of Frome, together with other hoards, being votive in nature. The relevant parts are worth citing in full:

> It hath been allowed by the emperor [H]Adrian, in pursuance of natural equity, that any treasure, which a man finds in his own lands, shall become the property of the finder, and that whatever is casually found, in a sacred or religious place, shall also become the property of him who finds it. But if a person not making it his business to search, should fortuitously find a treasure in the ground of another, the emperor hath granted the half of such treasure to the proprietor of the soil, and half to the finder. (Justinian *Institutes*, Book II, Title I, XXXIX)

While it may be reasonably doubted how far it was possible to enforce such legislation, the removal of valuable items from sacred or religious places does appear not only to have occurred on a sufficiently regular basis but also to have been considered socially acceptable, so that some form of legislation was deemed necessary by Hadrian not to prevent it but, rather, to define ownership of the items themselves. This, of course, somewhat flies in the face of arguments, such as Reece's, which view the removal of such items as unacceptable (Reece 2002: 71).[5]

While explanations for the appearance of unusable miniatures, broken pottery sherds and, potentially, unusable coinage at votive sites is beyond the remit of the current paper, the Hadrianic legislation would certainly explain why a community or an individual seeking to make a votive offering which consisted primarily of valuable, useable coinage, might seek to hide that deposit where it would be unlikely to be found by any unscrupulous passers-by.

8.7.2 Votive deposition in Hertfordshire

While Hertfordshire cannot match Frome in terms of the number of coins recovered in a single hoard, it can certainly provide a total of seven hoards which, like Frome, appear to have been both contained in pots and buried in isolated parts of (what was likely to have been) the rural Roman landscape (nos 2, 14, 22, 38, 39, 44, 46).

In addition to this, two further hoards (nos 21, 47) offer evidence of watery deposition of a votive nature, not dissimilar to that previously noted at Piercebridge (Walton 2008: 286–93). In the case of one of the hoards (no. 47), its discovery on the site of a Roman river bed together with other artefacts initially led the excavator to believe that they could be rubbish (Frere 1983: 281). A further two hoards (nos 11, 12) appear to have been buried close to the edge of a river; however, it remains possible that the topography of the landscape might have changed significantly in the 1,800 years since the hoards were closed. As the former was recovered in a pot and the latter with evidence of what was probably a wooden container they are, however, unlikely to have been examples of watery deposition.

Finally, two further votive hoards deserve to be mentioned: the small purse hoard recovered in the grave of a child in excavations at King Harry's Lane just outside Verulamium (no. 6) and the probable votive deposit discovered at the villa at Gadebridge Park (no. 41). This, like those hoards cited above (nos 21, 47), is a further example of watery deposition of a votive nature (Curnow 1974: 107).

8.8 Conclusions

The principal aim of this paper has been to produce a series or list of criteria by which we might define a coin hoard and then to test those criteria against the list of hoards recovered from Hertfordshire. The results have proven interesting.

Of the 46 hoards originally listed, 15 can be described as only probable or possible hoards, based on their failure to fulfil or meet any of the listed criteria. This number is a sizeable proportion of the whole; nevertheless, it is worth bearing in mind Guest's (2005: 29) comments regarding differences between the patterns of hoarding in Britain and elsewhere in the Roman Empire:

> Britain, for example, has produced 62% of all early fifth-century precious metal treasures, and 58% of all hoards containing silver coins from the period 300–500. Britain's prominence as a focus of large-scale hoarding also extends

> to bronze coins: 24% of all bronze hoards from the empire come from Britain, twice as many as have been recovered from any other region.

A possible initial conclusion, therefore, is that we here in Britain are, contrary to Ryan's opinions noted above, treating too many site finds as hoards.

On the basis of the evidence from Frome and sites such as the river Tees at Piercebridge, together with legislation dating to the Hadrianic period, an additional 16 hoards were described as potentially votive in nature: that is, hoards which would have been concealed without any intention of retrieval by their owners, either buried in fields or deposited in water. This provides some clarity in comparison with Guest's somewhat generalised comment regarding votive deposition cited above. It also raises the spectre of Ryan's argument regarding scattered hoards once again, and the question of whether or not individual stray finds recovered from fields could in fact be scattered votive deposits on the Frome model. If so, what implication could that have for the interpretation of the Treasure Act (1996)?

Based simply on the archaeological evidence surrounding their burial and the nature of their discovery, 15, less than a third of the overall total, can now be discussed as hoards which were buried by their owners with the intention of retrieval. Of these, none date to the first century; two date to the second century (nos 7, 8) and are both *denarius* hoards; 10, of which the majority are *antoniniani* and barbarous radiates, date to the third century (nos 16, 17, 18, 19, 23, 27, 28, 29, 30, 35); and three, one of which is a group of 159 *solidi*, date to the latter half of the fourth century (nos 43, 45, 48). This forms a new picture of the evidence based on the archaeology of the hoards themselves and potentially provides a new mechanism for organising the data for analysis in the future.

8.9 References

Abdy, R.A. (2002), *Romano-British Coin Hoards* (Oxford).

Allason-Jones, L. and Mackay, B. (1985), *Coventina's Well: a shrine on Hadrian's Wall* (Hexham).

Bidwell, P. and Snape, M. (2002), 'The History and Setting of the Roman Fort at Newcastle upon Tyne', *Archaeologia Aeliana*, fifth Series, 31, pp. 251–84.

Bourne, R.J. (2001), *Aspects of the Relationship between the Central and Gallic Empires in the Mid to Late Third Century AD with Special Reference to Coinage Studies*, British Archaeological Reports International Series 963 (Oxford).

Casey, P.J. (1986), *Understanding Ancient Coins: An Introduction for Archaeologists and Historians* (London).

Creighton, J.D. (1992), 'The Circulation of Money in Roman Britain from the First to Third Century', PhD thesis (University of Durham).

Curnow, P.E. (1974), 'The Coins', in David S. Neal, *The Excavation of the Roman Villa in Gadebridge Park Hemel Hempstead 1963–8*, Reports of the Research Committee of the Society of Antiquaries of London 31 (London), pp. 101–22.

Curteis, M. (1992), 'Ninesprings Roman Villa, Great Wymondley, Hertfordshire', in R. Bland (ed.), *Coin Hoards of Roman Britain Vol. IX*, (London), pp. 122–4.

Davies, J.A. (1988), 'Barbarous Radiates: a study of the irregular Roman coinage of the 270s and 280s AD from southern England', PhD thesis (University of Reading).

Frere, S. (1983), *Verulamium Excavations Vol. II*, Reports of the Research Committee of the Society of Antiquaries of London 41 (London).

Grierson, P. (1975), *Numismatics* (London).

Guest, P.S.W. (1994), 'A Comparative Study of Coin Hoards from the Western Roman Empire', PhD thesis (University of London).

Guest, P.S.W. (1997), 'Hoards from the end of Roman Britain', in R. Bland and J. Orna-Ornstein (eds), *Coin Hoards from Roman Britain Vol X* (London), pp. 411–23.

Guest, P.S.W. (2005), *The Late Roman Gold and Silver Coins from the Hoxne Treasure* (London).

Kenyon, K. (1935), 'The Roman Theatre at Verulamium, St. Albans', *Archaeologia* 34, pp. 213–61.

Lockyear, K. (1991), 'Simulating coin hoard formation', in K. Lockyear and S.P.Q. Rahtz (1991), *Computer Applications and Quantitative Methods in Archaeology 1990*, British Archaeological Reports International Series 30 (Oxford), pp. 195–206.

Lockyear, K. (1993), 'Coin hoard formation revisited ...', in J. Andresen, T. Madsen and I. Scollar (eds), *Computer Applications and Quantitative Methods in Archaeology 1992* (Aarhus), pp. 367–76.

Lockyear, K. (2007), *Pattern and Process in Late Republican Coin Hoards, 157–2 BC*, British Archaeological Reports International Series 1733 (Oxford).

Lockyear, K. (2012), 'Dating coins, dating with coins', *Oxford Journal of Archaeology* 31/2, pp. 191–211.

Lockyear, K. (forthcoming), 'The Coin Hoards of the Roman Republic database: the history, the data and the potential', *The American Journal of Numismatics*.

Moorhead, S., Booth, A. and Bland, R. (2010), *The Frome Hoard* (London).

Nash, D. (2012), *The Bredon Hill Roman Coin Hoard* <http://www.whub.org.uk/cms/museums-worcestershire/bredon-hill-roman-coin-hoard.aspx>, accessed 1 August 2014.

Reece, R. (1988), *My Roman Britain* (Cirencester).

Reece, R. (2002), *The Coinage of Roman Britain* (Stroud).

Robertson, A. (1974), 'Romano-British coin hoards; their numismatic, archaeological and historical significance', in J. Casey and R. Reece (eds), *Coins and the Archaeologist* (Oxford), pp. 12–36.

Robertson, A. (2000), *An Inventory of Romano-British Coin Hoards*, Royal Numismatic Society Special Publication 20 (London).

Ryan, N. (1988), *Fourth-Century Coin Finds from Roman Britain, A Computer Analysis*, British Archaeological Reports British Series 183 (Oxford).

Sauer, E. (2005), *Coins, cult and cultural identity: Augustan coins, hot springs and the early Roman baths at Bourbonne-les-Bains*, Leicester Archaeology Monographs 10 (Leicester).

Walker, D.R. (1988), 'The Roman Coins', in B. Cunliffe (ed.), *The Temple of Sulis Minerva at Bath Volume 2: The Finds from the Sacred Spring* (Oxford), pp. 281–358.

Walton, P. (2008), 'The Finds from the River', in H.E.M. Cool and D.J.P. Mason (eds), *Roman Piercebridge, Excavations by D.W. Harding and Peter Scott 1969–1981* (Durham), pp. 286–93.

Wheeler, R.E.M. and Wheeler, T.V. (1936), *Verulamium: A Belgic and two Roman Cities*, Reports of the Research Committee of the Society of Antiquaries of London 11 (London).

Notes

1 See Bourne (2001) for coinage of the Gallic Empire and Central Empire dating to the end of the third century; Creighton (1992) for first- and second-century *denarii* and *sestertii* and third-century *antoniniani*; Davies (1988) for barbarous radiates; Guest (1994) for the Western Roman Empire; Guest (1997) for hoards closing in the late fourth century; Guest (2005) for early fifth-century precious metal hoards; and Lockyear (2007) for Republican denarii.

2 Three hoards used by Moorhead (this volume) have been excluded from this study as information was not available at the time of writing. Editorial note: Appendix 1 has been created by merging Moorhead's and Wythe's data with the addition of a small number of addenda and corrigenda.

3 For a fuller discussion of hoard types see Abdy (2002: 9), Casey (1986: 55–7), Grierson (1975: 130–36) and Lockyear (1991).

4 See Allason-Jones and Mackay (1985) for the coins recovered from Coventina's Well on Hadrian's Wall; Sauer (2005) for the Augustan coins recovered from the bath house and hot spring at Bourbonne-les-Bains; Walker (1988) for the coins recovered from the Sacred Spring at Bath; and Walton (2008) for the coins recovered from the river Tees at Piercebridge.

5 The example in question, which refers to the removal or theft of flowers from a cemetery to be taken to an aunt in hospital, is surprising, not least because of Reece's documented insistence that we cannot judge the values and actions of the past by the moral standards applicable to the present (see Reece 1988 for a fuller discussion).

CHAPTER 9

The Iron Age and Roman site at Broom Hall Farm, Watton-at-Stone: a preliminary report

Kris Lockyear

9.1 Background

Broom Hall Farm lies on the 80m OD contour above the river Beane to the east of the village of Watton-at-Stone (Fig. 9.1). A dry valley runs north–south just to the west. The bedrock is chalk with a drift geology of boulder clay (diamicton of the Lowestoft formation) or mid-Pleistocene glaciofluvial sands and gravels.[1] A number of archaeological sites are known in the area and are plotted in Figure 9.1, including the Saxon site at Watton-at-Stone (Boyer *et al.*, this volume).

Attention was drawn to the site at Broom Hall Farm[2] when, in late 1975 or early 1976, farmer John Wallace of Broom Hall Farm, Watton-at-Stone, found a stamped amphora rim on his land not far from the farm buildings (*WASNews* [Newsletter of the Welwyn Archaeological Society] Spring 2006: 5). The amphora is a transitional Dressel 1a/1b in Peacock's (1971) fabric 3 and has an unusual *planta pedis* stamp (see Fig. 9.5, no. 1; C. Green, pers. comm.).[3] This find was seen to be potentially significant owing to the association of Dressel 1a/1b amphorae with high-status late Iron Age sites such as the Baldock, Welwyn and Welwyn Garden City 'chieftain' burials (Stead 1967; Stead and Rigby 1986). Following a meeting on site on 3 February 1976[4] Tony Paccito undertook a small excavation in Middle Field in freezing winter conditions (Fig. 9.2; J. Wallace, pers. comm.), funded by the British Museum (*WASNews* Spring 2006: 5). Unfortunately, we have been unable to locate any records of this excavation, although it is thought that at least one Samian vessel was found (*WASNews* Spring 2006: 5).

Although the Welwyn Archaeological Society has been active in the general area since the early 1970s it was not until 2005/6, when Andy Wight of the North

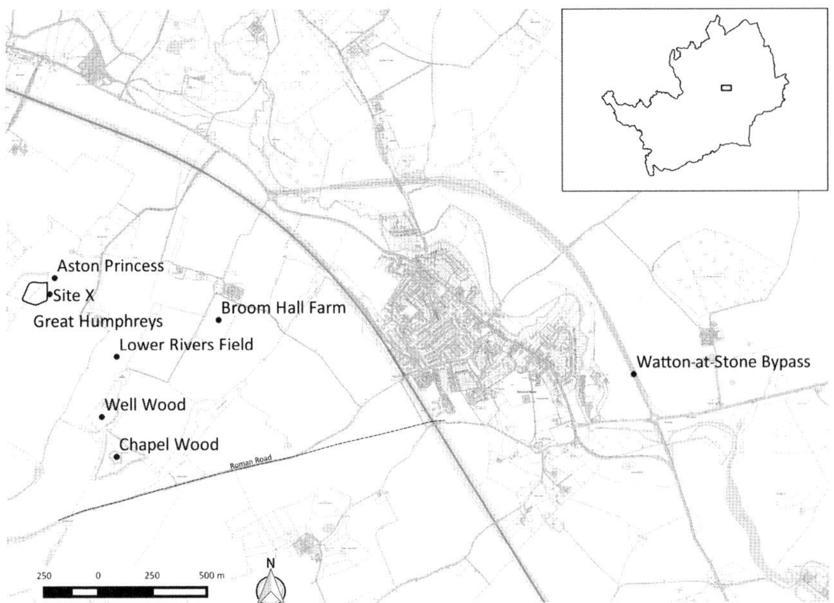

Figure 9.1: Location of Broom Hall farm and nearby sites. Map by Ellen Shlasko. Ordnance Survey data © Crown Copyright 2015 OS 100056350.

Herts Charity Metal Detector Group began to recover Iron Age and Roman finds from Cartway (see Fig. 9.2), that our attention was drawn back to the site. WAS plotted Andy's finds from that season precisely, using a total station, and showed that the distribution was concentrated along the boundary between Cartway and Six Acres. The finds, which now include more than 100 coins, have all been reported to the PAS. As well as the coins (Appendix 2, site 7.4), which will be discussed in more detail below, Andy found various weights, probably from steelyard balances, a spatula handle in the form of Minerva, brooches and parts of keys and locks. The finds other than Roman coins are listed in Section 9.5, below.

In 2007 I was asked to teach a short field course in geophysics for students from UCL. As Cartway was under crop it seemed worthwhile to survey along the eastern side of Six Acres – which is under grass – closest to where the finds were recovered. Both resistance and magnetometry surveys were conducted and these located two linear features which ran south-west–north-east on diverging paths (Fig. 9.2, nos 1–2). These two features were sectioned by Tony Rook in the autumn of 2008 and proved to be two ditches: no. 1 contained very early Roman pottery and no. 2 contained fourth-century ceramics. In 2010 I was asked to run a second course and so the area in Six Acres was expanded. The initial results from the course led to the rest of the field being surveyed during the

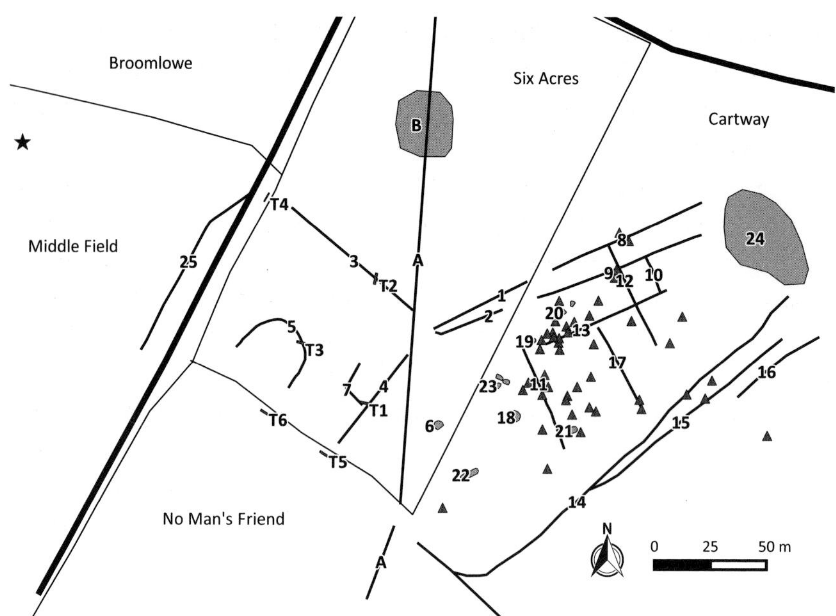

Figure 9.2: Site plan. Geophysical survey interpretation labelled A, B and 1–25; trenches T1–T6; triangles are metal detected finds; star is approximate find spot of amphora rim and BM excavation. Map by Ellen Shlasko. Field boundaries traced from satellite imagery.

spring of 2010 by WAS and three trial trenches being excavated in the autumn of that year. In 2011/2 further small surveys in Middle Field and No Mans Friend were undertaken, as well as the excavation of a further three trenches. A magnetometry survey of Cartway and No Man's Friend was undertaken in 2013 as part of the *Sensing the Iron Age and Roman Past* project.[5]

Although work on the site is still ongoing a preliminary report is offered here. A discussion of the geophysical surveys will be followed by the results of the trial trenches. Lastly, a discussion of the site offers some tentative preliminary conclusions.

9.2 The geophysical survey

The initial surveys in 2007 consisted of magnetometry using a dual Bartington Grad-601 at 0.5m transects and four readings per metre, and resistance survey using a TRCIA resistance meter at one-metre intervals. Both surveys indicated the existence of the two linear features (Fig. 9.2, nos 1 and 2) noted above. The surveys undertaken during the course in 2010 used the same equipment and settings. The magnetometry survey of the rest of Six Acres, including the re-survey of some parts, was completed during 2010, again using a Bartington dual Grad-601 at 0.5m spacing and four readings per metre. This survey revealed three further linear features (Fig. 9.3 and see Fig. 9.2, nos 3–5). In 2011 both a magnetometry survey in Middle Field, this time at eight readings per metre, and a resistance survey failed to reveal any convincing features. In 2012 a resistance survey limited to the border of set-aside in No Man's Friend also failed to locate further features.

The next major survey was in 2013 as part of the *Sensing* project. A Foerster Ferex four-sensor cart-based magnetometer, which enables rapid survey at 0.5m transect spacing and 10 readings per metre, was used. This system allowed us to survey a significant proportion of Cartway in the spring of 2013 and a large section of No Man's Friend in the autumn. A composite plot of the 2010, 2011 and 2013 surveys is given in Figure 9.3, with the interpretation given in Figure 9.2.

Within Six Acres the most obvious features are the modern ones: a defunct metal water pipe which runs north–south across the site and the area of modern disturbance around the concrete base (Fig. 9.2, A and B). The two ditches which run diagonally (Fig. 9.2, nos 1 and 2) appear to peter out to the west, although the noise from the metal water pipe makes this hard to be sure. Three further ditches can be clearly seen: no. 3 runs east–west, no. 4 runs north–south and no. 5 is the horseshoe-shaped feature in the south-west corner. The two new linear features appear to meet at right angles, although this is obscured by the water pipe, and our working hypothesis is that they form two sides of a quadrilateral enclosure with an oval or horseshoe-shaped feature inside. Other than the linear features, there is remarkably little in the way of other obvious features. A large sub-circular feature

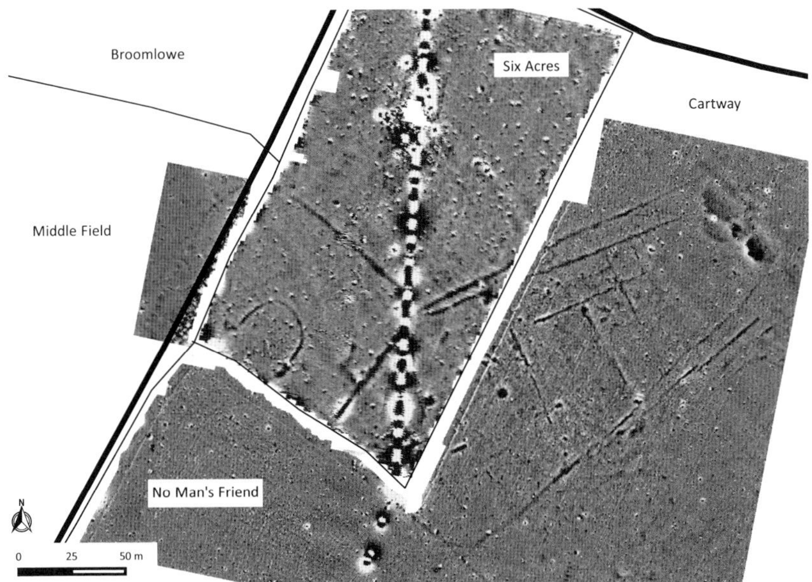

Figure 9.3: Magnetometry survey results. Map by Ellen Shlasko. Field boundaries traced from satellite imagery.

(no. 6) may be a pit, although it is about 6m across, and there is a less well-defined feature that perhaps forms a corner (no.7) which joins the ditch (no. 4).

The survey in Cartway and No Man's Friend revealed a number of linear features. The two originally seen in Six Acres clearly continue (nos 8–9). In addition, there are at least eight new linear features (nos 10–17) forming a series of almost rectangular enclosures or fields. Overlying the metal-detected finds on the survey results reveals a close correlation with the linear features. There are a number of probable pits (nos 18–21 and others), one of which is extremely large, *c.*6.5m in diameter, and strongly magnetic (–10nT to +15nT). There is also an elongated feature (no. 22) which is 2m by 10m with a magnetic range of –8nT to +10nT, as well as three features close to the hedge line (no. 23). The large feature at the northern edge of the survey (no. 24) is a filled-in pit, probably a post-medieval digging for gravel or clay.

The survey in No Man's Friend is a puzzle, as it does not show any archaeological features. The north–south ditch (no. 4) does not appear in the data, nor does the horseshoe-shaped feature (no. 5). Have these features been ploughed away, or did they not go into this field? Alternatively, does the southern edge of the enclosure lie under the hedgerow?

A preliminary survey in Middle Field also does not show any clear features. The 'noise' on the eastern edge is the modern track. The faint line visible at no. 25 is suspiciously parallel to the track and hedgerow and is likely to be an artefact caused by ploughing. A more extensive survey using the Foerster Ferex system is planned.

Although the resistance survey in Six Acres does show pipeline A and linear features 1 and 2, in general resistance survey is not very successful in this area. This is probably because the varied nature of the underlying drift geology creates broad-scale patterning in the data against which it is usually hard to discern archaeological features.

9.3 The excavations

As a result of the 2010 surveys WAS decided to excavate three 5m by 1m trial trenches in the autumn of 2010 (Fig. 9.2, T1–T3). The aim of these trenches was to (a) confirm that the geophysical data does indeed represent ditches and (b) recover dating material. Isobel Thompson kindly examined the ceramics from these three trenches as well as from the Iron Age ditch dug by Rook in 2008. In the following, the forms refer to Thompson's (1982) corpus and the identifications and comments are derived from her report (2011).

In general, the stratigraphy was hard to distinguish clearly. The boulder-clay fills of the features were similar to the soils through which they were cut. With a few exceptions, only the presence of some finds and occasional charcoal flecks allowed the layers to be distinguished. In the following discussion context numbers for fills are in parentheses (e.g., (104)) and those for cuts are in square brackets (e.g., [109]).

Trench 1 was intended to section the north–south ditch no. 4, but we seem to have hit the junction between this feature and no. 7, which appears to be later Roman. The stratigraphy consisted of layers sloping from west to east (Fig. 9.4), with the majority of pottery coming from (104). Small pieces of pottery continued to turn up to a depth of 1.6m, at which point the trench was closed. The ceramics were, in general, rather scrappy and broken up and are clearly a secondary deposit. They included sherds of a B2–2 rippled jar rim, a large B3–10 jar (Fig. 9.5, no. 5), at least three storage jars (C6–1) and a jug handle (G6), as well as later Roman material.

Trench 2 sectioned the east–west ditch, no. 3. The ditch was 2.25m wide and 1.5m deep. A lens of darker soil with frequent flecks of charcoal (203) was probably partly responsible for the clear magnetic response from the survey and was the only indication of the boundary between context (201) and the underlying context (204), which was the main fill of the ditch from whence most of the finds derive (Fig. 9.4). Context (204) consisted of a compact yellow-brown clay and appears to be largely weathered boulder-clay similar to the subsoil. The finds included a fragment of a Dressel 1b amphora handle, some residual prehistoric flint-gritted ware, fragments of large cordoned jars (B3–1 and B3–6, Fig. 9.5, nos 3–4), other jars (C7–2, Fig. 9.5, no. 2), a cordoned bowl (D2–1) and two 'scraps' of Roman pottery. The finds from context (201) were, in contrast, much more scrappy and contained more Roman material. Context (202), which underlies (204), was possibly the subsoil at the time the ditch was cut which has then weathered into the ditch, making it impossible to see the cut line. No finds were recovered from that context.

Trench 3 sectioned the horseshoe-shaped feature, no. 5. Time constraints prevented us from completing the excavation but the ditch was at least 2.3m wide and 1.5m deep. Virtually all the finds came from an upper fill (303), which was 1.5m wide and about 0.3m deep. Although this fill looked similar to (203) it differed in that virtually all the finds from this trench derive from it, and not from the underlying fill (305). Layer (303) contained at least two C-3 plain jars with a turned-in rim and one C7-1 jar. The underlying layer (305) was fairly sterile weathered boulder-clay. Time did not allow us to bottom this feature completely. Thompson (2011) suggests that this deposit is slightly earlier than those in Trenches 1 and 2, perhaps even late 1st century BC.

Trench 4 was opened in the autumn of 2011 on the eastern edge of Middle Field and was 4.0m long and 0.5–0.6m wide (Fig. 9.2). It was hoped that by

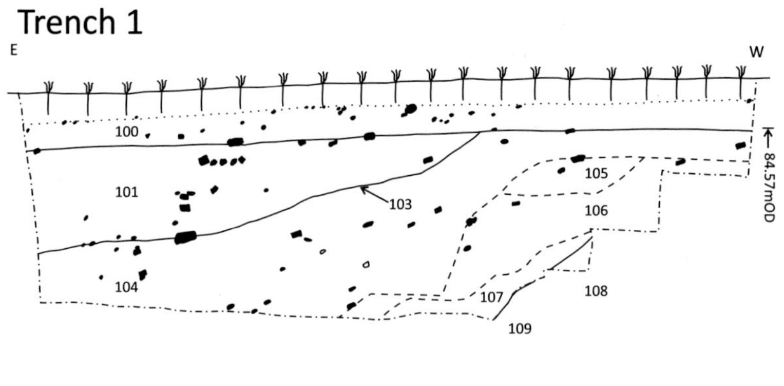

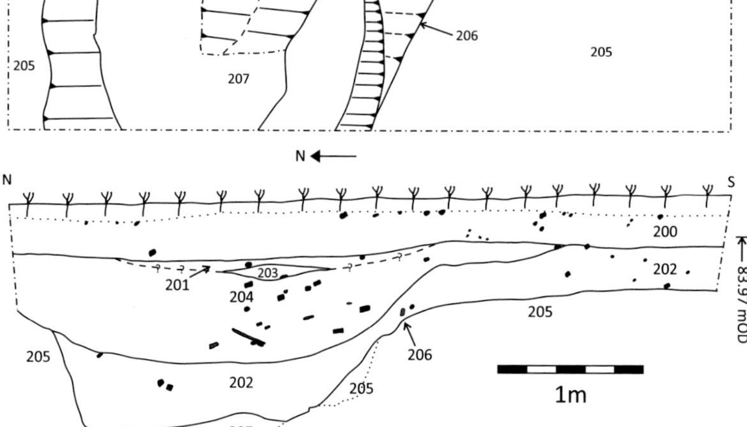

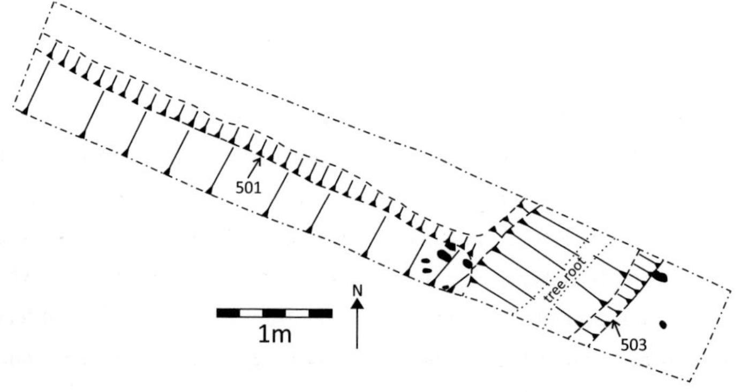

Figure 9.4: North facing section of Trench 1 (1:50); Trench 2: plan of excavation (1:50); Trench 2: west facing section (1:50); Trench 5: plan (1:75).

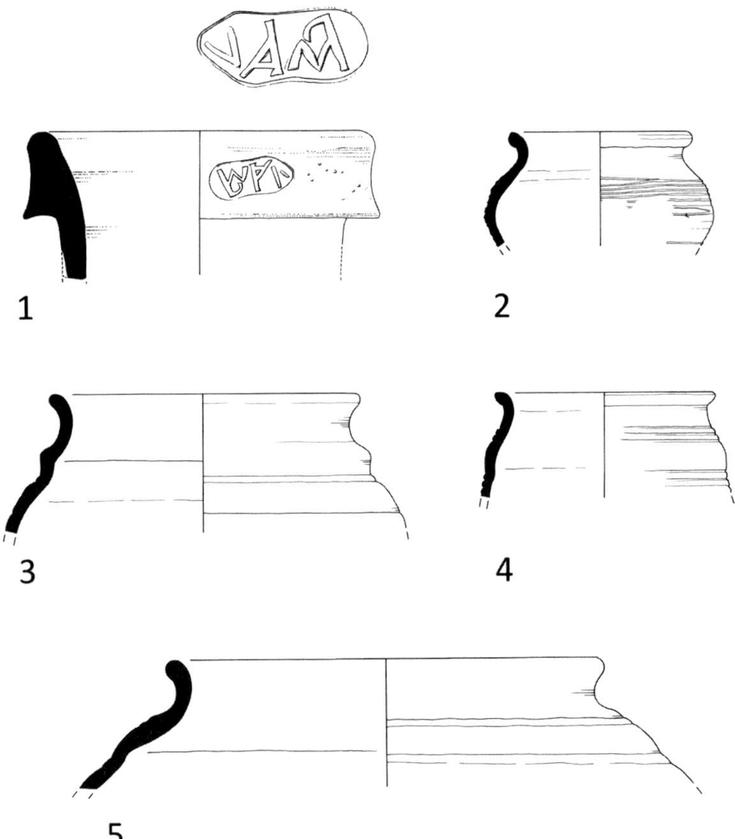

Figure 9.5: Ceramics from Broom Hall Farm. 1: Dressel 1a/1b amphora rim with stamp (drawn by Chris Green); 2: context 204, form C7-1; 3: context 204, form B3-1, possibly B3-6; 4: context 204, form B3-1; 5: context 104, form B3-10. Vessels 2–5 drawn by Frances Saxton. Scale: 1:4, stamp detail reversed and at 1:2.

cutting a small trench within the drainage ditch that runs alongside the track we might be able to detect where the east–west linear feature no. 3 runs into Middle Field. Unfortunately, no features were recovered and the only finds were two residual sherds of late Bronze Age flint-tempered pottery.

Trenches 5 and 6 were excavated during 2012 and were 5.6m by 0.9m and 5.0m by 0.85m respectively (Fig. 9.2). As the set-aside in No Mans Friend was subsidised by English Nature we had to keep our trenches very close into the hedge. It was hoped to section the north–south ditch no. 4 in Trench 5 where it crossed into No Man's Friend. Unfortunately, tree roots following the cut features made it difficult to be sure of the stratigraphy but we appeared to have a shallow cut [501] running east–west along the hedge line and a second shallow cut [503] running north–south (Fig. 9.4). Virtually no finds were recovered. We assumed at the time that [501] represented a bedding trench for the hedge and that [503] was a continuation of the north–south ditch. The results of the 2013 survey (discussed above), however, throw some doubt on this initial interpretation. Neither cut seems to be of the scale of the 'enclosure' ditches: [503] was only about 1.0m wide and 0.8m deep and, although we could not determine the width of [501] because it was parallel to our trenches, its observed depth was only 0.3m. Compared to [206], which was 2.25m wide and 1.5m deep, these features seem very ephemeral.

Trench 6 was intended to section the horseshoe-shaped feature no. 5 but the only cut found was a continuation of the supposed bedding trench for the hedge [601]. Again, this ran parallel to the trench and its observed depth was only 0.35m.

Trenches 1–3 were successful in showing that the linear features seen in the geophysical survey were indeed ditches with organically enhanced fills. The majority of the finds were rather battered and are likely to be secondary deposits. Unfortunately, the primary fills were devoid of finds. It is likely, however, that these features date to the late Iron Age/early Roman period: that is, approximately from the middle of the first century AD. It is possible, but unlikely, that the cuts could be earlier or later in date. Trenches 1 and 2 both contained a little residual Neolithic/Bronze Age material, which is not uncommon in the area, although a Bronze Age awl and a Mesolithic tranchet adze have been found in Cartway.[6] Even the handle of a Dressel 1b amphora found in [204] would have been residual by the time it was deposited in the ditch. Similar is true for the material from Rook's excavation of feature no. 2.

The other feature sectioned by Rook, no. 1, contains fourth-century pottery including a Nene Valley base and a flanged rim bowl (C. Lewis, pers. comm.). Similar material has been observed on the surface of Cartway in the area where the metal-detected finds originate.

9.4 Discussion

So far we have had the opportunity to excavate features only within Six Acres, where we have established that the 'enclosure' probably dates to the late Iron Age–Roman transitional period, and that one of the two diagonal ditches, no. 1, is broadly contemporary with it. The second ditch, no. 2, or at least the fills from it, date some centuries later. The enclosure, if that is what it is, has an area of at least 6,300m^2 (0.63ha). A parallel to this enclosure that came to mind initially was the Iron Age phase of the Hayling Island temple (Smith 2001: 40–44). That enclosure, however, is only about 1,600m^2 and the internal structure has a diameter of 10m compared with 28m here. Indeed, given its size and the depth of the ditch it seems unlikely that the central feature at Broom Hall Farm is part of a circular structure. An alternative parallel is the Iron Age shrine site at Fison's Way, Thetford (Gregory 1992). The inner enclosure is a more comparable size (5,600m^2) but the outer enclosure is much larger (35,750m^2). The inner circles, however, were roundhouses with a diameter of *c.*14m. It would seem, therefore, that neither of these sites presents a close analogue to Broom Hall Farm.

The National Mapping Project report for Hertfordshire identified 27 square enclosures ranging from 484m^2 to 16,900m^2 and 163 rectangular enclosures ranging from 60m^2 to 40,800m^2 which may be of the correct date (RCHME 1992). Unfortunately, most of these are not illustrated and nor do the lists of sites provide areas or a concordance with the HHER. The more recent report on the NMP for Essex (Ingle and Saunders 2011) provides a more useful discussion. Although there are some comparable sites, such as Elmdon (11,200m^2) or Oldmoor (3,456m^2), the circular features inside are, again, likely to be roundhouses, with that at Elmdon having a diameter of 20m and that at Oldmoor being 12m across. The horseshoe-shaped ditch is hard to parallel.

Hunn's (1996) corpus lists 102 enclosures from Hertfordshire. Figure 9.6 shows the distribution of these sites with the addition of Broom Hall Farm, Datchworth Green, Great Humphreys and Lower Sacombe. The Broom Hall Farm enclosure appears to be a 'regular, single ditched, short quadrilateral

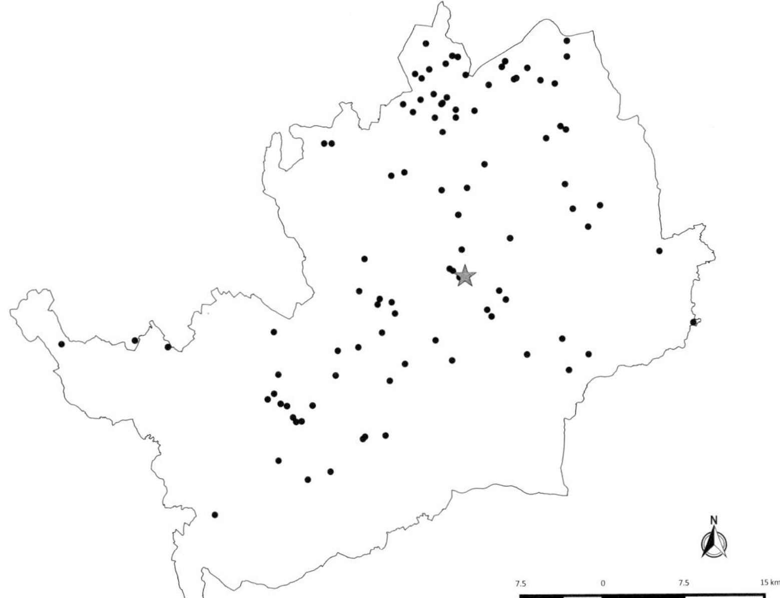

Figure 9.6: Distribution of Iron Age and Roman enclosures in Hertfordshire (redrawn from Hunn 1996 by Ellen Shlasko). Broom Hall farm is marked by a star. Contains Ordnance Survey data © Crown Copyright and database right 2014.

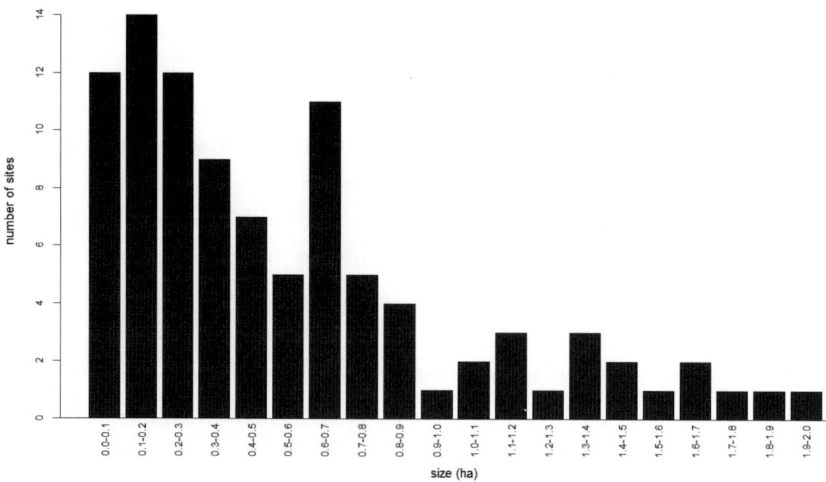

Figure 9.7: Size distribution of enclosures in Hertfordshire (redrawn from Hunn 1996, Table 2).

enclosure' according to Hunn's typology (1996: 7); these form 18.4 per cent of those he studied. The enclosure from Ware (HHER 1147; Hunn 1996: 20 and fig. 4) seems closely comparable in shape, size (5,600m^2) and general location, but is known only from aerial photographic evidence. Figure 9.7 shows the size distribution of enclosures in Hunn's study. The distribution is, as one would expect, skewed to the right, but with a peak that doesn't fit the trend at 0.6 to 0.7ha, exactly the class into which Broom Hall falls. Thus, apart from the unusual horseshoe-shaped central feature, the site would be fairly 'normal' for the period.

The complex of ditches in Cartway, however, appears to be a series of small infields and enclosures for a Roman farmstead, and can be paralleled by sites such as Lexden Lodge or Hill Farm in Essex (Ingle and Saunders 2011: fig. 3.14) or Hunn's (1996: 7) 'regular single-ditched sub-divided quadrilateral enclosures', such as HHER 4195 at Hertingfordbury (Hunn 1996: 26 and fig. 6).

Turning to the finds, Thompson (2011) notes that, in terms of the style of the grog-tempered ceramics (Fig. 9.5), the site's main connections were eastwards towards Braughing, where most of the specific parallels are to be found, rather than towards Verlamion/Verulamium to the west. Thus, the B3–1 jar from context (104) has parallels with vessels from Skeleton Green (Partridge 1981: fig. 41, nos 7–8) and the C3 jar from (303) can be compared with one from Braughing in the Henderson Collection (Partridge 1981: fig. 129, no. 41).

The metal-detected coin evidence is discussed in terms of the broad pattern by Moorhead (this volume). The data from this site is illustrated in Figure 9.8. From this we can see that there is very little coin-loss until period XIII, the early radiate period (AD 260–75), and that the earlier part of the fourth century is well represented, although there are no coins from periods XX or XXI. This

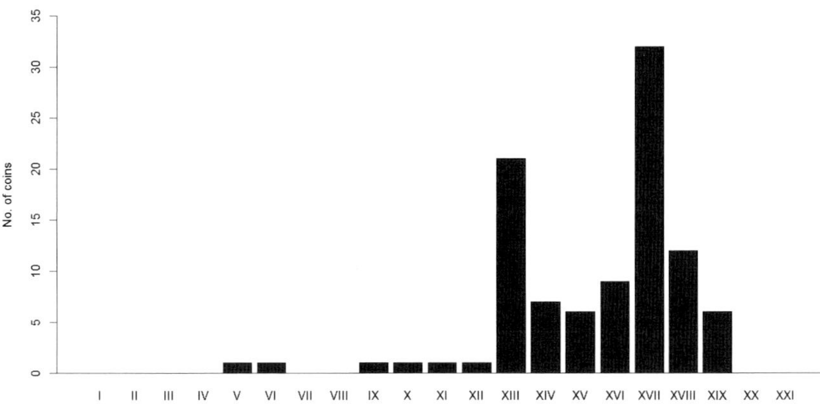

Figure 9.8: Bar chart showing coin-loss from Broom Hall Farm by Reece period. For dates of the periods see Moorhead, this volume.

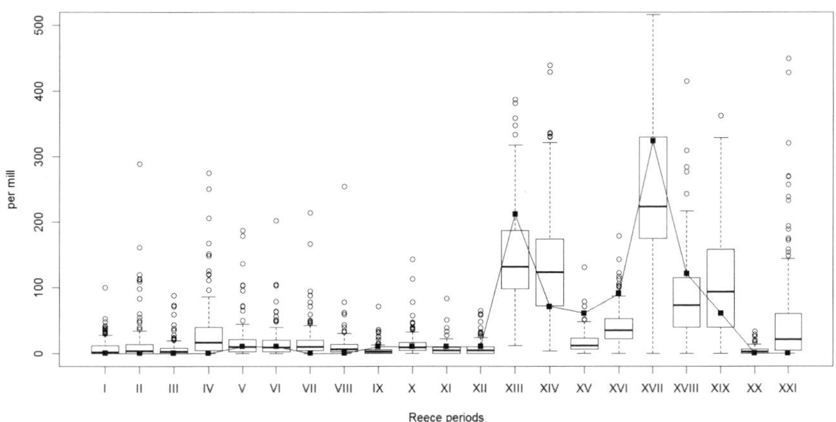

Figure 9.9: The boxplots show the range of values in per mills for the 140 sites published by Reece (1991), with 50% of the values lying within the central box and the median indicated by the line. The Broom Hall Farm pattern is indicated by the filled squares joined by a continuous line. The y-axis has been truncated at 500‰.

pattern should, however, be compared to the British background. In Figure 9.9 the data from Reece (1991) has been shown as a series of box-and-whisker plots where the median for each period is indicated by the horizontal line, the range of the middle 50 per cent of the values is shown by the box, and outliers are shown by the open circles. On to this has been plotted the figures for Broom Hall Farm, shown by the solid squares and a continuous line. As can be seen, the values follow the background pattern with the exception of above average numbers of coins from periods XV and XVI. The coin-loss pattern is, therefore, fairly unremarkable. It does have, however, *more* coins than is usual for a 'rural' site. The possible temple site at Hinxworth has only 85 coins (Table 7.2, no. 5.8,

Figure 9.10: A selection of the finds from Cartway found by Andy Wright. (half size). All photographs © the Portable Antiquities Scheme.

see also Burleigh, this volume), and the known ritual site at Ashwell has the greatest number of PAS finds from Hertfordshire, with 954 (Table 7.2, no. 5.9). One must also remember that the two Iron Age coins found at Broom Hall Farm are omitted from these lists.

The other finds on the PAS database from the site are listed in Section 9.5, below, and a selection is illustrated in Figure 9.10. It is interesting to see that, of the five possible brooch fragments found, four are early and only one find could be part of a late brooch. This contrasts with the late coinage, but is not entirely surprising as brooch loss in general is less in the fourth century than the first and second. The fragments of keys and locks are, however, an interesting group, as are the various steelyard weights, although these are notoriously hard to date.

The site at Broom Hall Farm will continue as the focus for the work for WAS for the next few years and any conclusions made here are very preliminary. The geophysical evidence, along with the two Dressel 1 amphora fragments and the Iron Age coins, suggest that at the very end of the Iron Age and/or in the earliest years of the Roman province a rather special Iron Age site was to be found here. Whether this site was of a ritual nature is hard to say given how few late Iron Age 'cult' sites are known, and the similarities to those that are known may be illusory. The site is very close to the probably contemporary large enclosure at Great Humphreys which is, however, very different in form, with an irregular plan and deep ditches.

This early part of the site goes out of use during the first century and a 'normal' Roman farmstead develops alongside it. The earthworks for the earlier site may well have remained visible, as ditch no. 1 appears to respect them. It seems likely that medieval or post-medieval ploughing finally levelled the features. The site is likely to have been occupied when the small cremation cemetery at Lower Rivers Field 450m to the west-south-west was in use and when the Iron Age ditch enclosure at Great Humphreys was used for dumping rubbish in the fourth century.

The site appears to go out of use by about the 380s, a few years after the abandonment of the villa at Hooks Cross, 1.5km to the north-west (see Appendix 2, site 7.8), as no period XX or XXI coins are found. The roadside settlement just to the east of Watton-at-Stone, 2km away (Appendix 2, sites 7.6 and 7.7), lasts into period XXI, as does the enclosure at Great Humphreys, 950m to the west (Appendix 2, site 7.9, Rook and Lockyear, this volume). What happens in the chronological gap between this site and the Saxon burials at Watton-at-Stone (Boyer *et al.*, this volume), a kilometre to the south-east, is as yet unknown, although the survival of the field system and the road clearly shows that the area continued to be occupied and exploited in this period.

One last aspect of this site deserves note. Despite the active involvement of WAS in this small area for 30 years, new sites such as that at Broom Hall Farm continue to be found. This site does not appear on any aerial photographs, although some possible new sites nearby were detected in the 2010 survey (Cox 2013). Community archaeological groups have the luxury of working in, and getting to know, an area at a level of detail that commercial units would love to be able to achieve. Collaboration between statutory bodies, universities, community groups and commercial archaeology is clearly the best route to follow.

9.5 Catalogue of PAS finds (except Roman coins)

The following list was derived from the PAS database. Many of the identifications are preliminary.

BH-C91368 Mesolithic flint tranchet adze

BH-1C3697 Bronze Age awl

BH-C94852 Iron Age coin, heavily worn

BH-E11516 Iron Age coin, a heavily worn bronze of Tasciovanus

BH-2CF638 Part of a Roman key

BH-1CB5C3 Part of a Roman key

BH-CB77D5 Part of a Roman lock pin, (Fig. 9.10)

BH-CB55B4 Part of a Roman lock pin

BH-2D1574 Part of a Roman lock pin

BH-57C9D5 Incomplete copper alloy object, possibly a lid from a jug

BH-DE9894 Copper alloy dolphin, perhaps part of a Roman bronze lamp handle , (Fig. 9.10)

BH-DCAB15 Fragment of a brooch, possibly a late Roman crossbow brooch

BH-2CC212 Early Roman brooch, possibly a Colchester type , (Fig. 9.10)

BH-1C8103 A copper-alloy Colchester type two-piece brooch of 1st century AD date, (Fig. 9.10)

BH-DC7E23 Copper alloy T-shaped brooch, late 1st to mid-2nd century, (Fig. 9.10)

BH-2CDA47 Fragment of a copper alloy plate brooch, probably 2nd century

BH-CB9385 Copper alloy decorated bracelet fragment, late Roman

BH-1C5A42 A fragment of a copper-alloy flat-section bracelet of probable 4th century AD date

BH-DE1662 Harness fitting, possibly a late Iron Age or early Roman terret ring, (Fig. 9.10)

BH-DDC670 Mount, possibly from horse harness; uncertain date, possibly Roman?

BH-1D40B5 Mount, Roman, 'military style', (Fig. 9.10)

BH-2D40D1 Possible copper alloy Roman harness link

BH-2EE223 Bronze Roman spatula handle in the form of Minerva, (Fig. 9.10)

BH-CC0282 Roman steelyard weight, 107g

BH-CBEB77 Roman steelyard weight, 112g
BH-9EB1D3 Roman steelyard weight, 333g
BH-1B6098 Lead steelyard weight of probable Roman date, 355g, (Fig. 9.10)
BH-1B8823 Probable Roman steelyard weight, 693g
BH-1B44A0 Possible Roman steelyard weight, 59g
BH-468C67 Lead weight of uncertain date, 610g
BH-9F2420 Copper alloy plate rim, possibly Roman
BH-CCE0A1 Medieval token
BH-1CFB45 A slightly corroded zoomorphic mount of probable 13th century AD date
BH-1A0356 Medieval strap fitting
BH-1BFBB2 Uncertain copper-alloy object, possibly a medieval mount
BH-DE45A3 Medieval or post-medieval buckle
BH-9EF102 Medieval or post-medieval weight; 43g
BH-DE5595 Post-medieval cloth seal
BH-1BE3E0 Medieval lead spindle whorl 39g
BH-1BC1C5 ditto, 20g
BH-22FF08 Medieval weight; 28g
BH-22F0E2 ditto; 32g
BH-1B0F93 ditto; 43g

9.6 Acknowledgements

First and foremost I would like to thank John Wallace for allowing us access to his land for this project and many others in the past. I would also like to thank the members of WAS and the Community Archaeology Geophysics Group (CAGG) for all their contributions to the project, especially Clare Lewis who, as well as helping with the surveys and excavations, provided valuable comments on the Roman ceramic assemblages; Jim West, especially for helping with the survey of No Man's Friend in less than ideal conditions; and Jon Wimhurst, Lewis Orchard, Les Maher, Nick Tracken and Jenny Searle. Isobel Thompson very kindly reported on the pottery from Trenches 1–3 and SA08. Chris Green provided helpful information on the 1976 amphora find, as well as providing the drawing. Frances Saxton drew the rest of the pottery at very short notice. Ellen Shlasko drew the maps using QGIS. Andy Wight kindly loaned me his finds and helped us plot those from the first season in detail.

9.7 References

Cox, C. (2013), 'Interpretation of aerial photographs for archaeology in Hertfordshire, 2010–2013 HER update; final report', Air Photo Services unpublished report.

Gregory, A. (1992), *Excavations in Thetford, 1980–82: Fison Way*, East Anglian Archaeology 53 (Norwich).

Hunn, J.R. (1996), *Settlement patterns in Hertfordshire: a review of the typology and function of enclosures in the Iron Age and Roman landscape*, British Archaeological Reports British Series 249 (Oxford).

Ingle, C. and Saunders, H. (2011), *Aerial Archaeology in Essex: the role of the National Mapping Programme in interpreting the landscape*, East Anglian Archaeology 136 (Chelmsford).

Partridge, C. (1981), *Skeleton Green: a late Iron Age and Romano-British site*, Britannia Monograph 2 (London).

Peacock, D.P.S. (1971), 'Roman amphorae in pre-Roman Britain', in M. Jesson and D. Hill (eds), *The Iron Age and its Hill-forts*, University of Southampton Monograph Series 1 (Southampton), pp. 161–88.

Reece, R. (1991), *Roman Coins from 140 sites in Britain* (Cirencester).

RCHME (Royal Commission on the Historical Monuments of England) (1992 [2011]), *Crop Marks in Hertfordshire. A report for the National Mapping Programme*, PDF version 2011 available from <https://www.english-heritage.org.uk/professional/research/landscapes-and-areas/national-mapping-programme/hertfordshire-nmp/>, accessed 18 August 2014.

Smith, A. (2001), *The Differential Use of Constructed Sacred Space in Southern Britain, from the Late Iron Age to the 4th Century AD*, British Archaeological Reports British Series 318 (Oxford).

Stead, I.M. (1967), 'A La Tène III Burial at Welwyn Garden City', *Archaeologia*, second series, 101, pp. 1–62.

Stead, I.M. and Rigby, V. (1986), *Baldock: The Excavation of a Roman and Pre-Roman Settlement, 1968–72*, Britannia Monograph Series 7 (London).

Thompson, I. (1982), *Grog-tempered 'Belgic' pottery in south-eastern England*, British Archaeological Reports British Series 108 (Oxford).

Thompson, I. (2011), 'Late Iron Age pottery from two sites at Broomhall Farm, Datchworth, Herts, 2008–10 (site codes BH10, SA08)', Welwyn Archaeological Society unpublished report.

Notes

1 Data from the British Geological Survey's 'Geology of Britain viewer', available at <http://www.bgs.ac.uk/discoveringGeology/geologyOfBritain/viewer.html?src=topNav>, accessed 1 September 2014.

2 Unfortunately, over time the site has been given several names derived from the field names. We have decided to standardise with 'Broom Hall Farm'. WAS site codes used are SA and BH followed by the year of excavation: e.g., SA08, BH10. The field names are given in Fig. 9.2.

3 Note that Sealy (2009) is critical of the use of the traditional 1a and 1b division.

4 Entry in Merle Rook's diary: 'Tony cycled to Datchworth and met Ian Stead. Adrian [Havercroft] and Chris [Saunders] were there too. Tony Pasito [*sic*] used a metal detector.'

5 <hertsgeosurvey.wordpress.com>, accessed 1September 2014.

6 PAS find no. BH-1C3697.

CHAPTER 10

'Out of town and on the edge?': evaluating recent evidence for Romanisation within the Verulamium region

Simon West

For when great Julius in an earlier age
Describes the island closely all his page
Is full of river fords and forest tracks.
But towns, he says, the island wholly lacks
Save one, a tortuous burrow without name,
Though famous afterwards as Verulam.
And this was true. But when mighty hand
Of Roman law had ordered all the land,
Then within walls where once the camps had been
Markets and homes secure and spacious lawns were seen.

(Adam Fox, *Old King Coel* 1937, Bk 1, Vs 2)

10.1 Introduction

While at school I was taught all about the Romans. I was taught that they arrived by boat in AD 43 (in a school assembly I was to be the standard bearer who first jumped off the ship to lead the invasion, but I went on holiday instead and missed my first starring part!) and that they wore togas, had roads, villas and an army, and built a wall, but I cannot remember anything else. Sometime later the Romans left, and then there were the Tudors. Later I settled in St Albans to begin my new career as an archaeologist and everything came crashing down. The first crash happened between 1991 and 1993 as a result of the excavations undertaken by Dr R. Niblett at Folly Lane. Subsequently, since 2006, when I was appointed District Archaeologist, there has been a multi-site pile-up of the results from commercial and public archaeology. It became obvious that the story I was taught between the ages of 9 and 12 was far too simple.

'Romanisation' is a term used to describe the change from a 'Celtic'-based society to one recognisably 'Roman'. Both terms, 'Celtic' and 'Roman', have posed difficulties as to definition, and the concept of 'Romanisation' is quite controversial (e.g., Barrett 1997; Freeman 1993; James 2001; Millett 1990). In this paper I will attempt to simplify the definitions. Here 'Roman' is defined as meaning 'that which is recognisably influenced by continental, Mediterranean influenced, contacts' and 'Celtic' as 'that which has a pre-Roman ancestry', although the latter could easily be 'Romanised' and party to both cultures. Therefore, even before we begin, there is already a degree of ambiguity! 'Roman', at least superficially, appears to be attributable to a specific group of individuals, although the people included in this group varies over time. 'Celtic' is much more nebulous and non-specific (Collis 2003; James 1999). For argument's sake, I will take the term to mean those tribes with a cultural affinity in north-west Europe that predates the Roman invasion. Whatever may be said about the term, it is a useful word for a differentiated, but generally accepted, north-west pan-European culture. Further, 'Romanisation' is defined here as the process of change when these two cultures interact, although whether by acculturalisation, creolisation or any other means is probably not important for the purposes of this paper. I am adopting what has been characterised as the 'weak' definition of the term (Keay and Terrenato 2001b: ix). Indeed, one has to ultimately question how far this process had embedded itself by AD 400, as it appears to have rapidly diminished in the following few decades to nothing, or merely a vestige of its former self, according to whether continuity is or is not argued for by an author.

Commercial archaeology through the planning process, unlike public archaeology, rarely allows for a structured research process by site. However, most sites can be matched to overarching research priorities (e.g., James and Millett 2001) and, for every project, a priority or priorities can be fashioned. Ultimately, however, we are nearly always at the mercy of the developers and where they want to build. Therefore, it is incredibly important that someone has an overall view of the results of these projects and has the time to be able to synthesise this work. To this end I am fortunate to be able to draw on the work of Dr R. Niblett, who has carried out work and extensive research in the St Albans District, and of my planning colleagues at the County Council and farther afield. Their help with the larger context of what is being uncovered in this small but significant part of Britain is invaluable. On the other hand, with public archaeology and local excavations it is easier to target sites which one hopes will examine hypotheses as part of a broader research agenda.

Commercial and public archaeology since 1991 have afforded us the opportunity to look again at known sites as well as visiting new ones. The Folly Lane excavations uncovered evidence for early occupation at the ceremonial site overlooking Verulamium. There has also been an opportunity to reassess the early Roman bath house just inside Verulamium at the 'Six Bells' in the programme *Rory's Pub Dig*. We have been able to look at the longer-term implications of 'Romanisation' for the elite at Turners Hall Farm, Wheathampstead, at which were found several rich burials and a villa. At Friar's Wash, excavations with *Time Team* uncovered evidence for a pre-Roman, or at least an early Roman, temple structure. Interestingly, this structure appears to have undergone the same destruction process as the mortuary house at Folly Lane. While at Folly Lane this took place just within the 'Roman' period, there appear to have been pre-Roman ancestral connotations in this practice. It is these sites which have come to illustrate the slow process of 'Romanisation', although in the case of the Roman masonry building at the 'Six Bells' the evidence now points to a later building, possibly a *mansio*, and not the first masonry Roman bath house in Britain. This new evidence better matches with our understanding of the development of Verulamium as part of a gradual process of 'Romanisation', rather than one of immediate imposition.

The history of the early Roman period is given to us by the classical sources. Put simply, we know that Caesar came to Britain twice, in 55 and 54 BC, that further incursions were contemplated by Augustus and Caligula, and that Claudius finally came across the channel in AD 43. Exactly, how, where and with whom the Romans came is debated, but we have this basic skeleton of history. This skeleton is a resource on which to hang the archaeology of this period, but it can also be a straightjacket if everything is forced into this episodic narrative. It has been argued that the Roman invasion was a long and partially indirect process, possibly beginning as far back as 200 BC. Objects from the Mediterranean world had been penetrating, in a variety of ways, into the Celtic heartland for many years (Roberts 1995; Szabó 1995). In this way, the process involving south-east Britain began with the development of Rome as a Mediterranean power with its trading networks, first around the western Atlantic seaboard and latterly up the northern European river systems. The development of these contacts has been broken down into a series of phases. First, and slowly from *c.*200 BC to *c.*60 BC, there was a period of contact involving the 'Celtic' world and its social elite through trade and gift exchange (Carver 2001: 4). This was formalised in the Caesarian episode of *c.*60–*c.*50 BC when direct contact led to an irrevocable change. Cicero gives an immediate account of the conclusion of the Caesarian incursion in his letter to his brother:

> The outcome of the war in Britain is eagerly awaited; for it is well known that the approaches to the island are set round with walls of wondrous mass. It has also become clear that there isn't an ounce of silver in the island, nor any prospect of booty except slaves. I don't suppose you're expecting any of them to be accomplished in literature or music!
>
> Cicero, *Ad Atticum* IV, 16, 7 (tr. Ireland 1996: 34)

Shortly afterwards Caesar wrote to him from near Dover. Britain had been settled; hostages had been taken but no booty, and a tribute imposed. The army was now being withdrawn (Cicero, *Ad Atticum* IV, 18, 5; tr. Ireland 1996: 35).

Finally, from *c.*50 BC to *c.* AD 43, there is the impact period. This latter phase is illustrated by Strabo:

> At present, however, some of the chieftains there, having gained the friendship of Caesar Augustus through embassies and paying court to him, have set up votive offerings on the Capitolium and have almost made the whole island Roman property.... on the imports from Gaul – these consist of ivory chains, necklaces, amber, glassware, and other such trinkets ...
>
> Strabo IV, 5, 3 (tr. Ireland 1996: 37)

Evidence to date for the St Albans District suggests that the area was bypassed by this earliest phase of contact. It is only after the Caesarian period that things began to change, at least for the elite, and it is the elite that are the subject of this paper. Below them, 'Romanisation' becomes visible archaeologically only through a system of gift exchange and slow downward cultural transformation, and even then only small quantities of finds are recovered.

I see this process as inevitable, and, if the above description is accurate, as showing a high level of integration of, at the least, the chieftain society of south-east Britain into the Roman political and cultural system (*cf.* Creighton 2000). The Roman world was expanding and had not reached its limits. The Celtic world of south-east Britain now viewed the Romans across only 20 miles of sea, and, inevitably, there was to be contact. It has been argued that in Hertfordshire this is evident at Braughing/Puckeridge, where the number and types of Roman Mediterranean imports fluctuates with the interest that the Roman state had for Britain (S. Bryant, pers. comm.). For example, Caesar Augustus appears to have thought about an invasion on at least three occasions, and Caligula even got to the coast with an army, only to have them pick up sea shells on the sea shore (Dio Cassius LIX, 25, 1–3, tr. Ireland 1996: 42–3), but this event may have initiated the building of the lighthouse at Boulogne (Jones 2013: 7). At these points in time there may be more imports available, but these times of interest are tempered in AD 9 by the loss of Varus and his legions in the Teutoborg Forest, which brought about a period of introspection for the Empire. Adminius, Cunobelinus' son, was banished and went to Caligula (Suetonius, *Caligula* 44, 46, tr. Ireland 1996: 42). Adminius may have returned to Britain under Claudius and may have been an ally, and it has been suggested that he was buried at Folly Lane (R. Niblett, pers. comm.). Further afield, the possibility has been raised that there was a pre-invasion military presence – perhaps a *vexillatio* of the Roman army (possibly auxiliaries) – at Fishbourne, Sussex (Creighton 2006: 54–61). At Colchester the Temple of Claudius was a very early and definitively 'Roman' artefact, which is presumably why it took much of the brunt of the Boudiccan attack (Crummy 2001).

10.2 Pre-Roman developments in the St Albans region

At St Albans the development of 'Celtic' society, possibly out of a later Bronze Age one, is evidenced by the growth of the system of hillforts and cross dykes dominating the Chiltern ridge. Hunn (1994, 22) suggests that 'The Aubrey's bivallate promontory fort [Fig. 10.1], as part of this system, possibly acted as a seasonal communal enclosure' for access in spring to the rich river pastures and an autumnal focus for rounding up fattened animals. By the later Iron Age there is the *oppidum* at Wheathampstead (Wheeler and Wheeler 1936), which is traditionally the location of Cassivellaunus' defeat by Caesar on his second incursion into Britain.

A late Iron Age burial was recovered at Batford (Harpenden East) railway station in the nineteenth century when the railway was put through (Fig. 10.1, no. 5; Bagshawe 1928). The Batford burial dates to the first few decades following Caesar, when the putative *oppidum* at Wheathampstead has been argued to be moving to Verlamion. Although we have only scraps of material (now in Luton Museum), they suggest that this burial, of chieftain status, was insular in its cultural outlook. Its bucket-handled escutcheons and turned shale vessels from Dorset indicate access to long-distance internal trade but not direct international contact. Mattingly (2006: 57), however, argues that the use of a lathe to turn shale vessels and of a fast wheel to turn pottery was a product of cultural contact.

The first evidence for occupation at the *oppidum* of Verlamion was found at the King Harry Lane cemetery (Stead and Rigby 1989), which dates to around 15 BC, or perhaps as early as 25 BC if the brooches are used to date the early

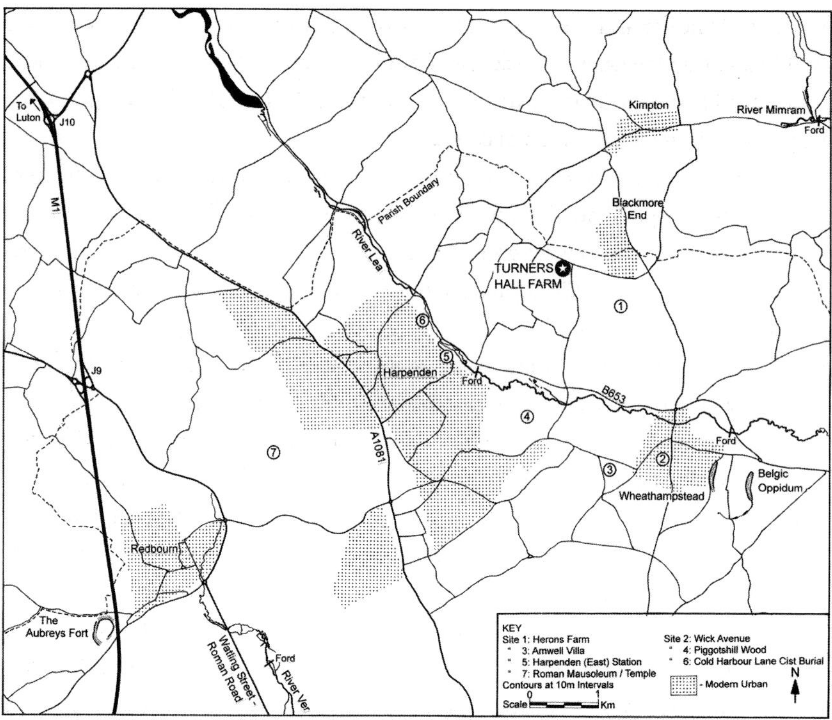

Figure 10.1: Turners Hall Farm and nearby sites. © Simon West. Ordnance Survey data © Crown Copyright 2015 OS 100056350

burials (R. Niblett, pers. comm.). The site at Wheathampstead appears to go out of use as Verlamion develops, probably under Tasciovanus, who had coins minted with the legends VER or VERLAMIO. However, occupation in and around Wheathampstead continues into the Roman period, notably in the valley below the *oppidum* (Saunders and Havercroft 1980–82), where late Iron Age coins have been recovered. Nearby, at Wick Avenue to the west (Fig. 10.1, no. 2; HHER 9795), a site was excavated which revealed a ditch – in which was found an unusually large bronze unit of Tasciovanus – and evidence for metalworking and burial.

A particular style of local pottery (Thompson, this volume; Thompson 1982) began around the period of the Caesarian incursions and slowly developed in fabric and form throughout the last and first decades BC/AD. This grog-tempered pottery is characteristic of late Iron Age/early Roman sites locally. It would appear to have developed from a grog-tempered insular form to a more Romanised form with sand and grog, and possibly into the later sand-tempered Verulamium Region White Ware industry which supersedes it by AD 70/80. Whether this development was stimulated in local potters by the incoming Romans or whether new potters took over a pre-existing industry is impossible to distinguish at present. The grog-tempered tradition is visible at the Wheathampstead *oppidum* in the Wheeler trenches (Wheeler and Wheeler 1936) and appears to date to the Caesarian period *c.*50 BC, but by the time of Wick Avenue and Turners Hall Farm it has developed into a sand and grog fabric with some 'Romanised' forms. This development may have been stimulated by external contact.

Other pottery types such as *mortaria* are completely alien to the pre-Roman culture prior to the invasion. They were a specific vessel used for a uniquely Roman type of food preparation even if the overall 'activity' is universal (Meadows 1997: 25–6). *Mortaria* developed in our area with Verulamium Region White Ware from the 50s but took over as the dominant fabric in the 70s and 80s AD. This shows the gradual move to a Roman lifestyle and the creation of a British form of that lifestyle as *mortaria* were popular in Britain.

This is one of those recurring themes. There is change, but it is slow and gradual, and archaeologically it could be argued to go almost unnoticed in our area. We know from the written sources, and archaeology's desperate attempts to prove the location of an invasion, that there was such a momentous event, but that it had no immediate impact in our area (see Thompson, this volume). Even the process of meeting the first 'Roman' would have been a highly significant occasion, one possibly distinguished by feasting, but one feast is not tangibly dissimilar to many before or many thereafter, at least for a while. The status of the Folly Lane burial is rivalled only by the earlier one at Lexden, Colchester, with its silver medallion of Augustus (Foster 1986; Laver 1927). These two burials appear to be of a significantly higher status than the 'chieftain' level burials which appear to emulate them, and they fulfil most of the points suggested by Struck (2000: 85) that demonstrate high status: there was a significant and complicated funeral process and monumental funerary architecture (tumulus and temple), the body was possibly laid out, there were valuable objects and the grave was located very prominently.

10.3 Key sites for studying change in the region

10.3.1 Folly Lane and the *oppidum* and Roman town

The inclusion in the Folly Lane burial of items that could relate to a rider and a member, or ex-member, of the Roman auxiliary cavalry in the form of a decorative bridle bit, a strap distributor and a long chain mail coat is indicative of a significant member of the late Iron Age aristocracy (Fig. 10.2). In addition, the remains of a possible couch were also recovered from the burial (Niblett 1995: 267–71). This couch was possibly an early Italian import with turned decorative elements in ivory, copper alloy strips, rivets, small domed bosses and iron spindles, and may have been a diplomatic gift. The majority of the couch fragments, with the chain mail coat, bridle bit and so on, were recovered from the 'burial' alongside and above the demolished funerary house. The couch appears to have been part of the cremation ritual rather than part of the more generalised burial ritual, which resulted only in partial and broken objects, as opposed to pyre objects, fully or partially burnt, broken or otherwise. The former were included in the funerary house or in its back fill; the latter range from complete but fire-damaged to almost fully destroyed, as with the droplets of metal (such as the silver) in the fill of the burial or on the chain mail coat. Together, these suggest a highly significant individual buried in 'Celtic' style but with a Romanised flavour to the burial goods (Niblett 1999). What may be significant is the lack of weaponry. However, the terminus of a firedog may in fact be the horned anthropomorphic end of a Celtic sword, as it appears too robust and curved when compared with the firedog terminals from the Welwyn burial, although this may be a product of the funerary (and taphonomic) process. In addition, the location, overlooking late Iron Age Verlamion/Roman Verulamium, and its later veneration, with a classic Romano-British temple, indicates a long-term use

Figure 10.2: The chain mail from the Folly Lane burial with small globules of silver adhering; chain mail may have been a 'Celtic' invention. © St Albans Museums Service.

of the site. Anyone going back and forth to Colchester along the main road or looking across the river up to the slopes above Verulamium would have seen the burial tumulus and its temple dominating the skyline.

The evidence for the early development of the site at Verlamion is limited to the excavated burial site at King Harry Lane (Fig. 10.3; Stead and Rigby 1989) and evidence from the bottom of trenches excavated in the Roman town. These appear to indicate a site centred on one (Central Enclosure; Niblett and Thompson 2005: 32–4), or two (Annex; Niblett and Thompson 2005: 34) enclosures in the valley bottom and various enclosures along the valley tops, as at Gorhambury and the King Harry Lane development. Enclosing the *oppidum* is a system of dykes and, within that, a system of ditches (Wheeler Ditch and Folly Lane Ditch; Niblett and Thompson 2005: 27 and 30); the former define the *oppidum*, the latter divide it internally. The dyke system is not a complete defensive circuit, but does appear to use the natural terrain to best advantage and channel activity to entrances/openings. It may even be that the dyke system, defining the location of the Roman town in its south-west corner, is part of this earlier Iron Age setup and was not originally constructed until after the final invasion, or indeed, that it is much later and contemporary with the third-century walls. Part of the possible annex ditch was seen during the Verulamium Museum Extension excavation in 1997 on the footprint of the Museum entrance. A geophysical survey was undertaken and pottery retrieved from the top of the ditch suggests a first-century AD date for its infill. In addition, over the ditch but below the later road and in its foundations coins were retrieved, suggesting that the main thoroughfare through the Roman town did not become a reality until, at the earliest, the 70s. This would neatly fit with the dedication of the Basilica in its first large masonry form in AD 79 (Niblett and Thompson 2005: 83). The deflection of this main thoroughfare (Watling Street) may also be significant, as the Basilica appears to sit in the earlier central enclosure, thereby respecting its location but at the same time showing Roman authority.

10.3.1 Turners Hall Farm

Turners Hall Farm (Fig. 10.1) is the site of two Roman burials, a villa and a bath house, and has evidence for occupation dating from the middle Iron Age to the later Roman period. Of particular interest is the development of the landscape from a late Iron Age farmstead to the Roman villa estate.

This site was initially the subject of an excavation undertaken by Archaeological Solutions (then the Hertfordshire Archaeological Trust) on the route of a gas pipeline which cut across this field from north to south and uncovered a small sunken building, partial evidence for a second structure (to

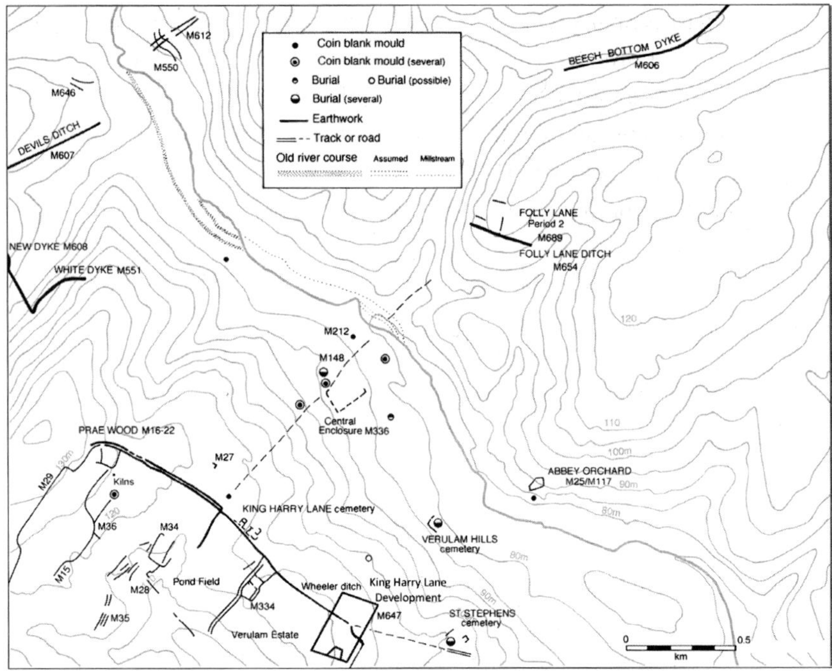

Figure 10.3: Late Iron Age features in the Verulamium area showing the extent of the *oppidum*, with the site at the King Harry Lane Development bottom centre. © R. Niblett.

become the bath house) and, at the southern edge, a series of apparently isolated pits containing coin pellet moulds (McDonald and Pearson n.d.). In 2002 two metal detectorists who had been informed of the earlier finds were scanning the 'Roman field' when they found the two cremation burials (Plate 10.1). This find was followed by several years of excavations (2002–2006), initially undertaken to put the detector finds into context, but subsequently continued as a community excavation (Fig. 10.4).

Finds and features dating from the late Iron Age include a series of pits containing coin pellet moulds, several 'ritual' pits and a series of ditches defining enclosures and trackways. The pits were perhaps the most significant features, as only three sites in Hertfordshire have produced evidence for minting coins: the Verlamion *oppidum*, Braughing/Puckeridge and Turners Hall Farm. They suggest significant status for this site, as only 'official' sites would have been allowed to mint coins. The field more generally has also produced bronze and silver late Iron Age coins, including some of Tasciovanus. Although it is impossible to connect the two, it is tempting to see these coins as being produced and lost in the same area. There was also a large roundhouse close to the later villa, but this has not been securely dated and could date from the Bronze Age to late Iron Age, although pottery sherds from the fill of the eaves drip gully suggests the latter.

By the early Roman period the main site ditches appear to have been infilled. Pottery from the primary deposits in their base include the ubiquitous grog-tempered types and would suggest a date for infilling before Verulamium Region White Ware became common in the 70s. The main ditch close to the villa also appears to have been deliberately infilled, as rubbish loss and a charcoal layer is sealed beneath a more solid clay layer that may represent the bank. This did not silt into the ditch but was deliberately deposited.

Over the top of this ditch a Roman villa was constructed (Plate 10.2). It was composed of 10 ground-floor rooms on a solid flint-in-trench foundation. The

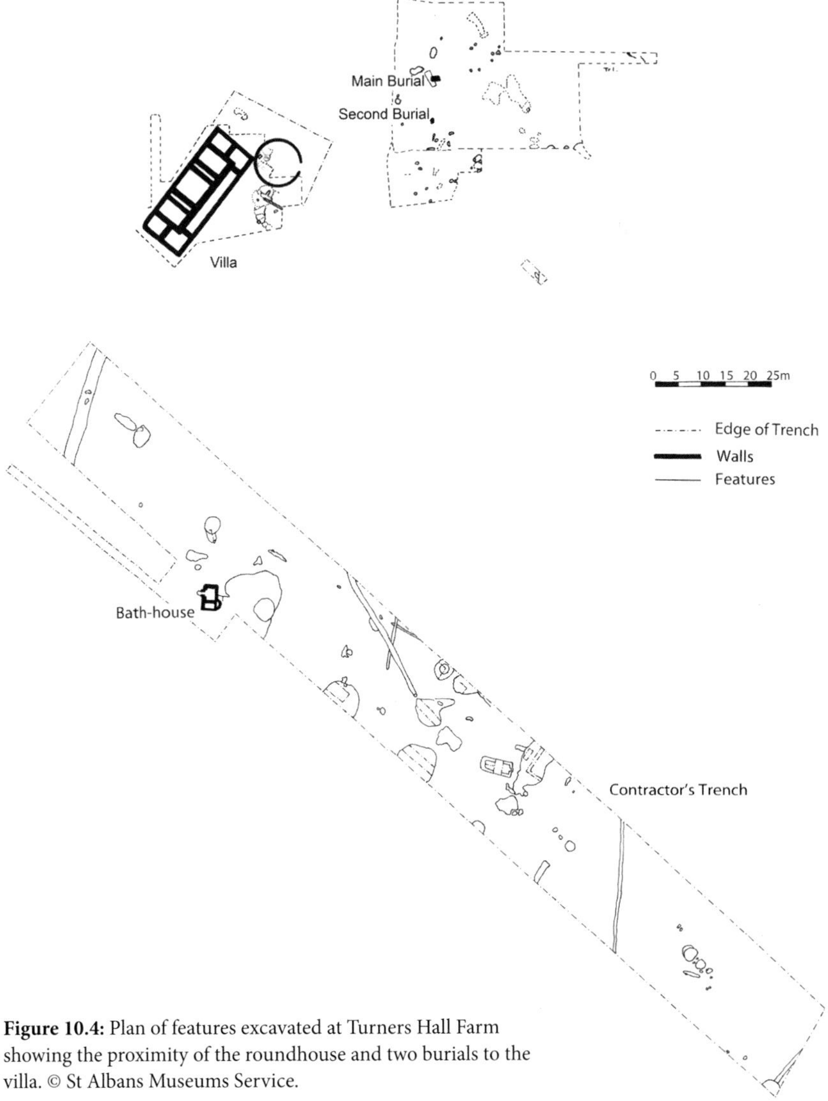

Figure 10.4: Plan of features excavated at Turners Hall Farm showing the proximity of the roundhouse and two burials to the villa. © St Albans Museums Service.

foundation was reinforced with a concrete layer where it cut through the ditch but not elsewhere, so the builders were clearly aware of the ditch. It has been speculated at Verulamium that these simple timber structures were the result of an army presence, but equally the structure would require no further knowledge of woodworking than what had gone previously (Niblett 1999: 64; *cf.* Millett 1990). Associated with the villa, some 70m to the south-east, is a small three-roomed bath house with a timber warm room, a masonry hot room and a plunge pool sufficient for two or three people. The corner of the bath house was first seen during the gas pipeline excavation.

Evidence from the demolition of the villa suggests that it had a tile roof and painted plaster walls. There was no evidence for a hypocaust, although there was circumstantial evidence for an upper storey in the form of two narrow rooms flanking the main central one. Three further rooms were located at either end of the villa and the whole was almost symmetrical across the middle of the central axis.

At around the time that the villa and bath house were demolished two cremation burials were interred approximately 70m to the south-east. The main burial cuts a small late Iron Age ditch, but otherwise both burials are not closely associated with features. The burials contain the finest bronzes of their type (M. Henig, pers. comm.) and the overall assemblage represents a complete dining service (Plate 10.1). Other significant finds from the main burial include 35 iron arrowheads (three probably set up as arrows on one side of the main grave, the rest contained in a textile bag or wrap on the other side), five small woodworking planes possibly in a box, three blades (killing, chopping and skinning blades perhaps representing a hunting kit?), textiles, pottery (Samian and otherwise), glass jugs and jars, bronze vessels (including a spouted strainer bowl) and an open lamp or lamp holder. Struck (2000: 96), quoting Millett (1990: 35–8), states that the late pre-Roman Iron Age elite in Britain projected their image as warriors, hunters and social drinkers. At Turners Hall Farm the last two are evident. The first may be absent owing to the prohibition of weapons in the non-military environment, although there were hunting knives.

Evidence from the fill of the burial suggests that it gradually silted up, rather than being backfilled, presumably through a wooden structure enclosing the body. Evidence in the form of mineral replacement deposits on the largest bronze bowl indicate that at least part of the floor of the grave was covered with grass or hay. Taken together, the Samian vessels form a table setting for four individuals with a cup, bowl and platter each, and it was the Samian vessels that provided a *terminus post quem* for the burials. Two of the vessels contain stamps dating to the middle of the second century; one in particular dates to *c.* AD 140–*c.*155

and is of the potter or workshop of CINNAMUS. This is the latest dated vessel in the two grave groups. The cremations have been researched by Jackie McKinley. Unfortunately, the main burial was heavily disturbed by the detectorists, but evidence suggests that it may have been in a small chest decorated with bronze rings and lion masks at the north end. The second burial was more intact and was contained inside a crushed square glass jar in the centre of the burial. McKinley has suggested that the main burial was 'possibly' and the second burial was 'probably' female. These females were aged between 20–45 (main burial) and 35–50 (second burial) (McKinley 2003: 1). In addition, the main burial contained a spouted strainer bowl. Strainer bowls are often associated with wine drinking and are frequently found with amphorae in graves. For example, the Welwyn Garden City burial (Stead 1967), on display in the British Museum, contains five amphorae and a strainer bowl. However, the Welwyn Grave B, which also contained amphorae, had no strainer bowl (Smith 1911–12). Interestingly, Folly Lane also contained amphorae but in that case the sherds, from Dressel type 2–4 or Haltern 67, were distributed on the floor of the funerary house. The Lexden Tumulus, perhaps the only equivalent to the Folly Lane burial, also contained amphora sherds, enamelled bronze objects and chain mail (Rigby 1995: 254–5), although it appears to have been disturbed in antiquity and again when originally excavated in 1928.

The site at Turners Hall Farm appears to be fairly straightforward. However, the finding of coin pellet moulds, the construction of a villa over an Iron Age field system and the inclusion of two high-status burials with their finery point to an interesting political dimension to the site. The coin pellet moulds – assuming that that is their function – are a rare find. The minting of coins is probably linked to the royal family of the time, as minting coins, unless undertaken illegally, would have been controlled from the top of society. This suggests a high-status site presumably with an individual(s), of equivalent (chieftain?) status, in control. Despite the Roman invasion there is little change until the site is redesigned in the latter half of the first century. It is tempting, but not impossible, to see the influence of the Boudiccan Revolt in this change. The native hierarchy are left to themselves to run the area, but finally realise that the Romans are not going away, and begin to adopt aspects of 'Roman' material culture. This is observed in the location of the villa over an earlier enclosure, demonstrating 'Roman' precedence over the original native set-up. In addition, the burials are firmly illustrative of a 'Romanised' elite, but within the burial are elements that hark back to an earlier pre-invasion past.

The finds are key to our understanding of the context of the burials. In particular, the spouted wine strainer bowl is illustrative of an earlier cultural influence. These bowls, with their mesh strainer behind a spout, appear to have two main distribution areas: south-east England and the west bank of the Rhine. They date from the end of the first century BC to the first century AD. Other spouts and strainer bowls include a spout from Felmersham (early first century AD; Kennet 1970; Watson 1949), an outlier at Łęg Piekarski (deposited later first century AD and possibly British in origin; May 1971: 256; Megaw 1963) and the spout from Kirmington, Lincolnshire (May 1971). The Łęg Piekarski find is from one of three chieftains' burials all containing Roman imports including two silver skyphoi in Tomb 2 and two lesser-quality skyphoi from Tomb 3.

The obvious parallel for the Turners Hall Farm strainer bowl is in the Welwyn Garden City burial, but this is earlier (last quarter of the first century BC), and does not appear to be as well designed as the Turners Hall Farm example. Strainer bowls as an artefact pre-date the Roman invasion and are, following the Caesarian invasion, associated with chieftain burials. They may be a response to the introduction of additives to wine, either to alter its flavour or to make it more palatable:

> The practice in Africa is to soften any roughness with gypsum, and also in some parts of the country with lime. In Greece, on the other hand, they enliven the smoothness of their wines with potter's earth or marble dust or salt or seawater, while in some parts of Italy they use resinous pitch for this purpose, and it is the general practice both there and in the neighbouring provinces to season must with resin; in some places they use the lees of older wine or else vinegar for seasoning. (Pliny, *Nat Hist.* xiv, 24)

In addition, wine and wine strainers had secondary functions as a medicine and medicinal infuser respectively. Evidence for celery has been found in one strainer (M. Henig, pers. comm.) and artemisia (wormwood) was discovered at Stanway, presumably for the infusion of a bitter medicine (Wiltshire 2007).

There is no evidence for a strainer (or an amphora) in the Batford burial, but they begin to show up just before the end of the first century BC. At first they appear to be 'cobbled together' artefacts (such as the Welwyn Garden City example), possibly being created via the modification of an existing bowl. By the time of the Turners Hall Farm strainer, however, all the elements appear to be a cohesive whole, with the bowl, strainer, spill plate and spout all integrated. It may, nevertheless, still be an ancestral object. Although the origin of these vessels is in the pre-Roman Iron Age, even if ultimately they have Mediterranean ancestry, the insular forms appear to be a response to the increase in contact with Rome. There appears to be a cultural shift at chieftain level and above towards emulating a Mediterranean lifestyle, although this emulation of Roman lifestyle probably never penetrated far down in society. Sealey (1999) has suggested that these strainers were used for serving beer, as there is no classical link between wine additives and the 'Celts'. However, the lower levels of society were probably using ceramic strainers or cloth for this purpose; the latter would be unlikely to leave any trace, while the former are present in the archaeological record. In the case of the Turners Hall Farm strainer, even a mid-first-century date would make it a century old before it was deposited, and thus perhaps the oldest object in the grave. The entire grave assemblage, while heavily 'Romanised', is suggestive of a 'Celtic' ancestry, with its strainer bowl and emphasis on feasting – which, although a Roman practice, was also a Celtic pastime. The inclusion of arrows, arrowheads, hunting knives and planes may also hint at an other than 'Roman' lady, assuming the objects were personal to her and not burial gifts.

10.3.2 The King Harry Lane development

In 2011–12 work on the King Harry Lane development produced preliminary evidence for the growth of the Iron Age and Roman towns. A development of more than 100 houses was proposed for an open space in the Iron Age *oppidum* and subject to an evaluation which initially located the 'Wheeler Ditch' (Wheeler and Wheeler 1936: 41–2, Niblett and Thompson 2005: 27–9), although this later had to be confirmed. Fortunately, it was decided to almost completely strip the site, allowing for a 'map and record'-type project undertaken by Foundations Archaeology. Various development requirements, such as the need to provide access for services from the lower to upper parts of the site across the Wheeler Ditch and the requirement for a large soakaway, also enabled sections of features to be fully excavated.

During the stripping various features not observed in the evaluation also came to light, the earliest of which were late Bronze Age/early Iron Age pits full of burnt material. Samples of the burnt flint were taken for thermoluminescent dating and preliminary results gave three dates: two from Feature [1003] gave a date of 2900–2000 BP and Feature [1023] gave a date of 3600–2800 BP (900–1 BC and 1600–800 BC respectively). A ditch and cobbled surface of the late Iron Age were orientated towards the entrance in the 'Wheeler Ditch', where cremation burials were interred. At the highest point of the site a rectangular ditch, which also extended to the south-west beyond the boundary of the site, ran to the north-east into the development.

Dr R. Niblett suggested that, based on the angle of a trackway located in St Stephen's cemetery (Fig. 10.3), the original line of Watling Street did not go towards the *oppidum* but diverted towards the entrance in the Wheeler Ditch. In the development, a shallow hollow-way with a cobbled surface was recorded on the same alignment. This hollow-way petered out and a short length of palisade trench took its place. These two features were contemporary, as demonstrated by a silty fill, which was present over the cobbled surface and ran into the base of the ditch. The ditch then became part of the larger late Iron Age/early Roman enclosure entrance system. Cutting into the top of the Wheeler Ditch was one of three burials which appear to be either of the latest Iron Age or the early Roman period. In addition, a bronze coin hoard was deposited in the short length of palisade ditch; this will provide a *terminus post quem* for the entire Iron Age *oppidum* ditch system in this area. This has implications for the final transformation from an Iron Age ditched landscape to a Romanised one. The results are keenly awaited.

A collection of more than 100 lead slingshots was found many years ago at Windridge Farm near Verulamium (Greep 1987), although the collection was possibly much larger and examples were for sale in an antique centre in Harrogate in 2011. This type of slingshot is generally thought to be first century AD and military in origin. This has potentially significant implications, if both these factors are correct, for the location of a military presence, even if only temporary in nature.

At the top, southern, end of the development site was a rectilinear enclosure with a V-shaped ditch possibly infilled in the first century AD. The ditch entered the development site from back gardens beyond. Apart from one small undated burnt feature there was nothing of significance in the enclosure, perhaps suggesting a temporary use.

10.3.3 M25 widening

In 2010 the widening of the M25 provided an unexpected opportunity to excavate a series of early pottery kilns near Bricket Wood, to the south of Verlamion/Verulamium. The work was undertaken by Oxford Archaeology and produced a landscape possibly dating from the late Bronze Age to the modern period, as some of the ditches appeared on the first edition Ordnance Survey maps. The potential of continuity through 3500 years seems unlikely, however. The kilns appeared in a cluster in Area D, immediately to the south-east of Junction 21a, and were excavated as the ground was going to be reduced. Although only one feature contained pedestals associated with a pottery kiln, three of the four were a very similar keyhole shape; a fourth was sub-circular, but the fills were similar. It is suggested that the features were a series of kilns, each being used for one or more firings before being cannibalised to make the next. The features were dug into the ground and lined with clay; surviving streaks in the clay were produced by fingers. In the best-preserved kiln a quantity of pottery in two different fabrics was recovered. Although this was not definitively from the last firing of the kiln it is suggestive of the last use, as the kiln was then backfilled, presumably with locally produced (on-site?) material.

The early kilns, with their single chamber and single flue, have been suggested by Swan (1984) to represent 'Romanisation'. She argues that, originally, potters were itinerant, using portable kiln furniture in clamps, but that they then changed to a more settled lifestyle, firing in semi-permanent kilns. This process, which began in the early first century AD, took a century to complete and may have been instigated following the Conquest by potters moving from an insular 'Belgic' technique to a more universal one, with particular reference to Roman dining habits.

10.3.4 Friar's Wash

Time Team came to St Albans on 10–12 June 2008 to look at a site at Friar's Wash, close to Junction 9 of the M1 (Fig. 10.1, J9; Wessex Archaeology 2009). The site is approximately 7km north-north-west of Verulamium, on the opposite side of the Ver valley to Roman Watling Street. They had chosen the site owing to an aerial photograph taken by James Brown in 1976 (Fig. 10.5). It appeared to show two Romano-British temples, a further square feature immediately to the south and, to the east, a circular structure. In addition, there was a series of triple ditches, a sub-circular enclosure and many other features, probably including pits and ditches, as well as a possible farmstead at the north end of the field around an existing farm. Previously, in 1965, Roman building remains were ploughed up, and, following the aerial photography in 1976, Harpenden and District Local History Society recovered a small assemblage of Romano-British material during fieldwalking on the site. Although the work was undertaken for the *Time Team* programme, owing to the quality and significance of the remains the results were written up subsequently by Wessex Archaeology (2009). The site has gone to English Heritage for scheduling.

The results of the project included two Romano-British temples, one temple mausoleum and a rectangular building which may have been associated with the temples, or another temple (Fig. 10.6). In addition, there was a series of three, possibly Bronze Age, ditches, the ditch to a curvilinear enclosure, and within, but stratigraphically earlier than the *cella*, a series of postholes which may be significant. The finds included a dispersed coin hoard and a stone 'head'.

The excavation of one quadrant of one of the *cellae* produced a sequence of deposits very similar to that from the end of the funerary house at Folly Lane (discussed above). Beneath the fill in the *cella* were at least three postholes, although, as three-quarters of the internal area was not excavated, there may

Figure 10.5: Aerial photograph of the site at Friar's Wash taken by James Brown in 1976. © St Albans Museums Service.

have been up to nine. The level with the postholes had been deliberately covered by a turf layer within which were located large flint and puddingstone boulders. At Folly Lane the demolition sequence of the funerary house appeared to contain large puddingstone boulders, possibly used in the demolition of the house, which were then all covered, and the pit infilled, by turf, possibly collected from a large area with a variety of natural habitats. The demolition of the funerary house at Folly Lane took place around AD 55 at the same time as the burial. If this sequence can be translated to Junction 9 then a similar date may be postulated, with the posthole structure possibly being a late Iron Age or early Roman timber temple or shrine. The location of this structure towards one side of the curvilinear enclosure may suggest that there is something of significance in the centre, possibly of an earlier date still, which this structure respected. With the later building of two or more temples this veneration continued, albeit in a more 'Romanised' fashion, thereby illustrating continuity. In addition, the stone

Figure 10.6: One of the temples under excavation by *Time Team*. Two postholes of the timber structure are visible in the cella, with large puddingstone and flint boulders against the corner of the structure. © St Albans Museums Service.

'head' may have links to a 'Celtic' head cult, which directly refers back to Folly Lane. The latter appears to go out of use as a religious site when Christianity and the cult of St Alban emerged. Traditionally, St Alban was executed by decapitation and, ultimately, the founding of the abbey under Offa in the eighth century secured the purported location as a focus for the cult. Although the site at Folly Lane goes out of use, at Junction 9 the site appears to continue until the end of Roman Britain, as a coin of the Emperor Eugenius was found during the *Time Team* excavation. Early Christianity was very much a town religion, which could be better promoted and controlled in the urban environment, away from the *pagani* and their unruly habits.

10.3.5 Six Bells

It has been accepted since the 1970s that the Roman building in Insula XIX under the Six Bells public house was one of the, if not the, earliest masonry building in Verulamium and that it was a bath house (Niblett and Thompson 2005: 85). However, in July 2011 work carried out for another television programme, *Rory's Pub Dig*, in two trenches in the car park at the Six Bells can now question this hypothesis, although there can be no firm conclusions and more work is required. The work was carried out by Archaeology South-East, a division of the Centre for Applied Archaeology, UCL, for Oxford Scientific Films between 11 and 15 July 2011 for a pilot of the TV programme which became part of the series (Hopkinson 2011). The original work took place in 1974–5, when the pub was extended. The work took place in deep trenches, which for health and safety reasons could not be fully recorded. The results of this project were written up as a typescript and the structure was identified as a bath house. In addition, coin pellet moulds were recovered from a clay exterior to the building, as was evidence for a burnt timber structure, originally recorded as a building but later changed to a drain. In conjunction with the programme makers, it was decided that two trenches were to be excavated: one at the front of the site to investigate the possibility of discovering more pellet moulds and recovering more context for them, and another at the rear of the car park to examine the potential length and complexity of the building previously recorded.

In the event, Trench 1, at the front of the site, identified a large circular feature. It had heavily fire-scorched edges and a decayed chalk deposit at the base but no additional pellet moulds. The circular feature was interpreted as a post-medieval lime kiln thought to have gone out of use during the eighteenth or nineteenth century. If the interpretation of the lime kiln is correct, and the work undertaken by Archaeology South-East would suggest that this is a good possibility, then it would imply that there has been a lot of ground make-up in this area. Normally, a lime kiln is charged from the top and emptied from the bottom, meaning that, if this feature is a kiln, the ground has been raised by up to 1m. This poses problems for the location of the coin pellets, which appear to have been in the same clay that surrounded the kiln. More work is required, however, as the location of the original find of the moulds was not covered by Trench 1, and there may be stratigraphic differences in the intervening space.

Trench 2, at the rear of the site, contained two abutting Roman walls, one of which shared the same alignment as the north-west–south-east wall of the earlier excavations under the public house; the other wall was at right angles to this one. Internal Roman floor surfaces were also identified associated with these walls. A deposit of painted plaster filled one of the rooms. It was face down, as it had fallen from a wall or ceiling. These Roman levels had been sealed by a post-medieval deposit that was cut by a number of refuse pits and postholes which were beneath a deep Victorian garden soil and, finally, the car-park surface.

The location of the 'bath house' is just inside the third-century walls in Insula XIX, by the north-east gate. The building would appear to be related to this entrance and the contemporary road system. As we have seen, the road system may be later first-century at the earliest, and the north-east gate to Colchester may be quite late, as the original road may have gone through the north gate and then across Folly Lane by the ceremonial enclosure. If this is the case it would immediately question the date of the masonry bath house, although it does not provide a definitive answer in this regard. The bath house was originally thought to have had an ambulatory around it, created when two walls creating the walkway were added to the swimming pool. Trench 2 appears to have uncovered these walls, but now with a cross wall cutting across the ambulatory. This means that the ambulatory cannot be circumferential around the pool, and would also appear to negate the theory that this structure was a temple. The time duration of the excavation allowed the Roman building only to be uncovered, and did not permit any investigation of that structure. Further work on the archive from the original project might suggest an answer as to its date. Originally the timber structure was thought to be an early building, but because the makeup around the masonry building was first century in date, it would be problematic to suggest that it could be both an early building that was replaced by a masonry one, which was then heavily damaged by Boudicca, but limped on for a couple of decades and *still*, stratigraphically, one of the last features surviving in the insula. It is more likely that the original hypothesis holds true. There was a first-century timber building that was burnt by Boudicca. When the masonry building was created and the pool area excavated to depth to provide a substantial pitched tile foundation, much of the material was dumped on the outside – material the original excavators used to date the masonry building. This would fit the development sequence of Verulamium, where the masonry buildings are post-Boudiccan. This structure could still have a pool and be of two phases and have suffered fire damage, during either the mid-second-century fire or another, later one. The concept of a temple or bath house has to be questioned, but as a masonry structure, contemporary or later than the third-century gated entrance to the town, it could be a *mansio*, possibly with its own bath house.

This project adds to our knowledge of the 'Romanisation' of the Verulamium region negatively. It possibly redates an anomaly in the archaeological record so that it better fits the theory of gradual change and corresponds with the overall development of Verulamium. Although not identified as a *mansio*, its form, location, quality of decoration and date are highly suggestive of one. It is a building which needs further investigation.

10.4 Conclusion

It is inevitable that a momentous event such as the invasion of 'Celtic' Britain by the 'Romans', and Britain's early development thereafter, should be an obsession for some archaeologists, whether their obsession is to find the first location of the invasion or the first evidence for 'Roman' activity in Britain, or to definitively find Boudiccan deposits and her burial site (as opposed to mid-first-century fire episodes). However, it should be up to the archaeologist to tell the story and, given all of our biases, for us to present the evidence so that it can be scrutinised. To this end I suggest that, for this small area of Britain, the Roman invasion had little or no impact on daily life at first: AD 42 came and went, AD 43 came and went, AD 45 came and went … AD 59 came and went … and in AD 60 Boudicca came … but the Romans didn't go. Many changes may have taken place as a new power took up the reins of running the St Albans area and it is, in all probability, largely the elite that will have felt this change. Most of this would have left no archaeological evidence and possibly, for the vast majority of 'Celts', would have had little effect except an increase in taxation. Real change in Verulamium occurs after the Boudiccan Revolt, with the realisation that the incomers were not going to be defeated and go away. At this point the British elite, while still retaining their ancestry, become British 'Romans', if they were not already so. It was not until the third century that things really began to change. At this point the province became much more integrated into the running of the Empire, and things were done differently. For example, basilicas appear to undergo a functional change – metalworking is often found taking place in them – if not go into terminal decline, and the burial record suggests that there was a new elite with new styles of burial. Whether there was a cultural change or a new intervention by other 'Romans' is impossible to distinguish at present. However, limited evidence from oxygen isotope analysis may suggest a new ethnically different male elite along with this new way of doing things.

Folly Lane proves, as far as it is possible to prove, that the pre-Roman elite were still running Verlamion/Verulamium into the Roman period. At Turners Hall Farm the chieftain elite survive until at least the mid-second century, but they still hark back to their Celtic ancestral roots. The King Harry Lane site hints at changes, and will ultimately date the end of the internal landscape system of the *oppidum* of Verlamion, as a bronze coin hoard (Appendix 1, no. 50) was located in the top of the ditch leading from the end of the trackway towards the Wheeler entrance, while there was a cremation burial in the top of one of the Wheeler ditches. At Junction 9 of the M1 the temple site may have begun as a late Iron Age or early Roman temple; it was a location continually venerated for 400 years, that was Romanised and integrated, and that may have remained stubbornly pagan. At the Six Bells a structural anomaly may not be so, and the status quo, of timber structures not being replaced by masonry 'Roman' ones until after Boudicca, may be maintained. We know historically that the Romans invaded, and we know that things changed, but archaeologically these events are elusive at Verulamium, if not non-existent for several generations after the Roman invasion.

To summarise the recent evidence, the process of Romanisation was a gradual one which appreciably began only around the time of the Caesarian incursions but did not come to full fruition until long after the Boudiccan Revolt in AD 60/61. It was only the outcome of this event that forced some of the Celtic elite to come to terms with the Roman invasion; the Romans were not going away, so they made the most of it. However, it was not all one-sided, as they did not disregard from where they had come and were still demonstrating their Celtic ancestry well into the second century, albeit by this time with a very 'Romanised' flavour. Following on from this period there are hints at changes, with new taxation systems and a new ethnic elite from outside the Celtic world. This new elite were from parts far afield, and there is some evidence emerging from oxygen isotope analysis that the new elite burials, with their new rite of inhumation, were composed of 'other' Romans.

10.5 References

Bagshawe, T.W. (1928), 'Early Iron Age objects from Harpenden', *Antiquaries Journal* 8, pp. 520–22.

Barrett, J.C. (1997), 'Romanization: a critical comment', in D. Mattingly (ed.), *Dialogues in Roman Imperialism. Power, Discourse and Discrepant Experience in the Roman Empire*, JRA Supplementary Series 23 (Portsmouth RI), pp. 51–66.

Carver, E. (2001), *The Visibility of Imported Wine and its Associated Accoutrements in Later Iron Age Britain*, British Archaeological Reports British Series 325 (Oxford).

Collis, J. (2003), *The Celts. Origins, Myths and Inventions* (Stroud).

Creighton, J.D. (2000), *Coins and Power in Late Iron Age Britain* (Cambridge).

Creighton, J.D. (2006), *Britannia. The creation of a Roman province* (London and New York).

Crummy, P. (2001), *City of Victory*, revised reprint (Colchester).

Foster, J. (1986), *The Lexden Tumulus: a re-appraisal of an Iron Age burial from Colchester, Essex*, British Archaeological Reports British Series 156 (Oxford).

Freeman, P.W.M. (1993), '"Romanisation" and Roman material culture', *Journal of Roman Archaeology* 6, pp. 438–5.

Greep, S.J. (1987), 'Lead sling-shot from Windridge Farm, St Albans and the use of the sling by the Roman Army in Britain', *Britannia* 18, pp. 183–200.

Hopkinson, D. (2011), *An Archaeological Evaluation at The Six Bells public house, St Michael's Street, St Albans, Hertfordshire*, Archaeology South-East Report No. 2011190 (Portslade). doi: 10.5284/1012022.

Hunn, J. (1994), *Reconstruction and Measurement of Landscape Change*, British Archaeological Reports British Series 236 (Oxford).

Ireland, S. (1996), *Roman Britain. A Sourcebook*, 2nd edn (London and New York).

James, S. (1999), *The Atlantic Celts: Ancient people or modern invention?* (London and Madison).

James, S. (2001), '"Romanization" and the peoples of Britain', in Keay and Terrenato, (2001), pp. 77–89.

James, S. and Millett, M.J. (2001), *Britons and Romans: advancing an archaeological agenda*, Council for British Archaeology Research Report 125 (York).

Jones, R. (2013), *The Lighthouse Encyclopedia: The Definitive Reference*, 2nd edn (Guildford).

Keay, S. and Terrenato, N. (eds) (2001a), *Italy and the West. Comparative Issues in Romanization* (Oxford)

Keay, S. and Terrenato, N. (2001b), 'Preface', in Keay and Terrenato, (2001), pp. ix–xii.

Kennet, D.H. (1970), 'The Felmersham Fish-head Spout: a suggested reconstruction', *The Antiquaries Journal* 51, pp. 86–8.

Laver, P.G. (1927), 'The excavation of a Tumulus at Lexden, Colchester', *Archaeologia* 76, pp. 241–54.

McDonald, T. and Pearson, A. (n.d.), 'Two Rural Romano-British Settlements in Hertfordshire: Turners Hall Farm & Sandridge', Hertfordshire Archaeological Trust (Hertford) unpublished report.

McKinley, J.I. (2003), 'Wheathampstead, Hertfordshire: Cremated Bone Reports', Verulamium Museums unpublished report.

Mattingly, D. (2006), *An Imperial Possession: Britain in the Roman Empire* (London).

May, J. (1971), 'An Iron Age Spout from Kirmington, Lincolnshire', *Antiquaries Journal* 51, pp. 253–9.

Meadows, K.I. (1997), 'Much ado about nothing: the social context of eating and drinking in early Roman Britain', in C.G. Cumberpatch and P.W. Blinkhorn (eds), *Not so much a pot, more a way of life* (Oxford), pp. 21–35.

Megaw, J.V.S. (1963), 'A British Bronze Bowl of the Belgic Iron Age from Poland', *Antiquaries Journal* 43, pp. 27–37.

Millett, M.J. (1990), *The Romanisation of Britain* (Cambridge).

Niblett, R. (1995), 'A Chieftain's Burial from Verulamium', in Swaddling et al. (1995), pp. 267–71.

Niblett, R. (1999), *The excavation of a ceremonial site at Folly Lane, Verulamium, Britannia* Monograph 14 (London).

Niblett, R. and Thompson, I. (2005), *Alban's Buried Towns. An assessment of St Albans' archaeology up to AD 1600* (Oxford).

Rigby, V. (1995), 'Italic Imports in Late Iron Age Britain: A Summary of the Evidence from "Chieftain Burials"', in Swaddling et al. (1995), pp. 253–61.

Roberts, H.E. (1995), 'Imports into Denmark from Pre-Roman and Roman Italy', in Swaddling et al. (1995), pp. 291–304.

Saunders, C. and Havercroft, A.B. (1980–82), 'Excavations on the Line of the Wheathampstead By-Pass, 1974 and 1977', *Hertfordshire Archaeology* 8, pp. 11–31.

Sealey, P.R. (1999), 'Finds from the Cauldron Pit', in N.R. Brown, *The Archaeology of Ardleigh, Essex: Excavations 1955–1980*, East Anglian Archaeology 90 (Chelmsford), pp. 117–24.

Smith, R.A. (1911–12), 'On late Celtic antiquities discovered at Welwyn, Herts', *Archaeologia* 63, pp. 1–30.

Stead, I.M. (1967), 'A La Tène burial at Welwyn Garden City', *Archaeologia* 101, pp. 1–62.

Stead, I.M. and Rigby, V. (1989), *Verulamium: The King Harry Lane Site*, English Heritage Archaeological Report 12 (London).

Struck, M. (2000), 'High status burials in Roman Britain (first–third centuries AD) – potential interpretation', in J. Pearce, M. Millett and M. Struck (eds), *Burial, Society and Context in the Roman World* (Oxford), pp. 85–96.

Swaddling, J., Walker, S. and Roberts, P. (eds) (1995), *Italy in Europe: Economic Relations 700 BC–AD 50*, British Museum Occasional Paper 97 (London).

Swan, V. (1984), *The Pottery Kilns of Roman Britain*, RCHME Supplementary Series 5 (London).

Szabó, K. (1995), 'Italian Bronze Vessels in Transdanubia before the Roman Conquest', in J. Swaddling, S. Walker and P. Roberts, *Italy in Europe: Economic Relations 700 BC–AD 50*, British Museum Occasional Paper 97 (London), pp. 273–89.

Thompson, I.M. (1982), *Grog Tempered 'Belgic' Pottery of South-Eastern England*, British Archaeological Reports British Series 108 (Oxford).

Watson, W. (1949), 'Belgic Bronzes and Pottery found at Felmersham-on-Ouse, Bedfordshire', *Antiquaries Journal* 29, pp. 37–61.

Wessex Archaeology (2009), *Friars Wash, Redbourn, Hertfordshire. Archaeological Evaluation and Assessment of Results*, Wessex Archaeology Report 68735.01 (Salisbury).

Wheeler, R.E.M. and Wheeler, T.V. (1936), *Verulamium. A Belgic and two Roman cities*, Research Reports of the Society of Antiquaries of London 11 (Oxford).

Wiltshire, P.E.J. (2007), 'Palynological analysis of the organic material lodged in the spout of the strainer bowl', in P. Crummy, S. Benfield, N. Crummy, V. Rigby and D. Shimmin, *Stanway: an Elite Burial Site at Camulodunum*, *Britannia* Monograph 24 (London), pp. 394–8.

CHAPTER 11

Prehistoric pits and an Anglo-Saxon hill-top cremation cemetery at Station Road, Watton-at-Stone

Peter Boyer, Katie Anderson, Tom Woolhouse, Barry Bishop and Berni Sudds, with contributions from Nina Crummy and Dr Jean-Luc Schwenninger

11.1 Introduction

The site at Station Road (Hertfordshire Site Code HSRW11), on the west side of the village of Watton-at-Stone (centred on NGR TL 2980 1908), occupied an 'L-shaped' area of approximately 3.8ha (Figs 11.1–11.2).

The site occupies superficial Mid Pleistocene glaciofluvial deposits of sands and gravels, overlying the Cretaceous Upper Chalk (British Geological Survey 1979; SSEW 1983). It is located on raised ground on the west side of the valley of the river Beane, some 600m from the river. The surface elevation rises from *c.*73m OD in the east to a high point of 77m OD on the west side of the site (Plate 11.1). The landscape continues to rise gently further to the west, but the western edge of the site effectively forms a plateau overlooking the river valley. It was on this higher ground that most of the archaeological remains were located.

The most significant archaeological remains encountered comprised a dispersed swathe of prehistoric pits and a group of early Anglo-Saxon features, including cremation burials and part of a possible mortuary structure. In addition, two ditches forming part of a later Romano-British (third century AD or later) field system were recorded at the eastern edge of the main excavation areas (Plate 11.1). The field ditches were aligned parallel with and perpendicular to the course of the Roman road from Verulamium, which forded the river Beane at Watton-at-Stone and is projected to have crossed the

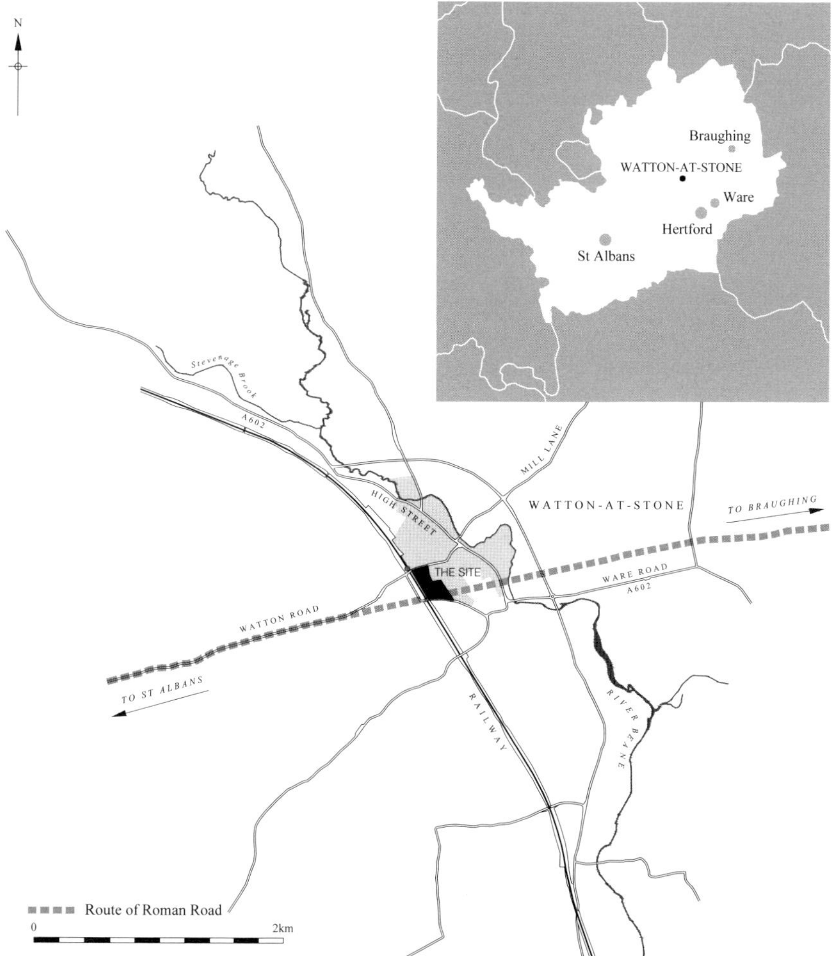

Figure 11.1: The location of the site. Ordnance Survey data © Crown Copyright 2015 OS 100056350.

development site, although no trace of the road was encountered in evaluation trenches positioned to identify its course (Watton Road, Figs. 11.1 and 11.2). One ditch extended downslope to the east; the more extensive ditch (Group 201[1]) approximately followed the contours of the hillside (on or just below 75m OD) and continued to be utilised, at least in part, into the early Anglo-Saxon period. Details of the excavation and sampling methodologies, full descriptions of all the archaeological features identified and full specialist finds and environmental reports can be found in the Assessment Report (Boyer 2012), available at the HHER. The finds and archive from the site have been deposited at Hertford Museum.

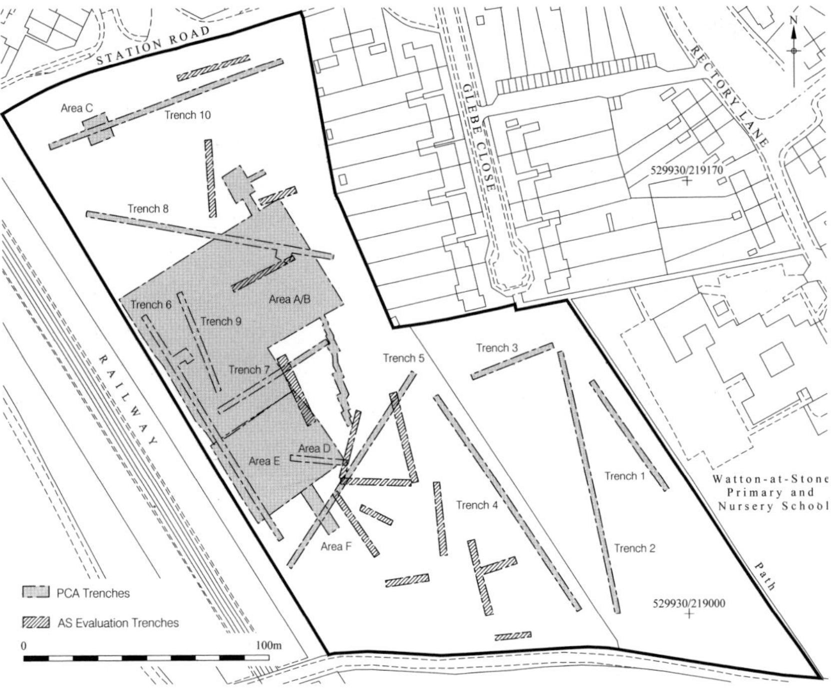

Figure 11.2: The trench locations. The first phase of evaluation trenches were excavated by Archaeological Solutions (Smith 2008), the second set of trenches and the open areas by Pre-Construct Archaeology. Ordnance Survey data © Crown Copyright 2015 OS 100056350.

11.2 The prehistoric pits

Although a small assemblage of struck flint dating to the Mesolithic period was recovered during the course of the investigations this occurred exclusively within later features. The earliest archaeological features were a dispersed swathe of 42 pits (Plate 11.1 and Fig. 11.3) which, based on their character and the finds recovered, are all likely to be prehistoric. In total, 20 of the 42 pits were excavated, comprising those features located in areas most likely to be damaged or destroyed by construction.

The pits were located on the high ground in the central western part of the site and covered an area measuring *c.*65m from north-west to south-east by 38m from north-east to south-west, extending beyond the western limit of excavation. They varied in size and character; diameters ranged from 0.99m to 2.80m, with most in excess of 1.50m wide, and depths from 0.30m to 2.05m. The fill sequences showed differing patterns. Shallow pits less than *c.*1.00m deep tended to contain only single fills, while deeper pits contained between two and five fills. The fills of many of the pits were fairly homogeneous, comprising compact yellowish-brown to grey-brown sandy silts with moderate to common flint inclusions.

The pits can best be described as forming a swathe or loose cluster, with no clear pattern in their distribution apart from their shared location on the higher ground. That said, it is of note that, with the exception of pits [301] and [311], none of the pits was intercutting or overlapping, suggesting that the locations of existing pits were not only visible but also respected. This adds weight to the view that the pits were broadly contemporary with one another, and while this does not mean that they were all dug or open at exactly the same time, their locations are likely to have been visible when new pits were being dug. The similarity in fills across many of the pits perhaps further supports the view that they were contemporary.

It is not possible to assign specific dates to most of the pits because the associated finds assemblages are very limited: pottery and struck flint were recovered from just 12 pits (Table 11.1). The lithic assemblage is predominantly earlier Neolithic in date (see Bishop, below); however, much of this material is likely to be residual. The condition of the pottery also limits any definitive dating, with the majority of the assemblage comprising sherds with very broad possible date ranges of Neolithic to Iron Age (Percival 2012).

Based on the composition of the finds assemblages, one pit is certainly Neolithic in date, with a further four pits tentatively dated as Neolithic. Large sub-circular pit [307], which was 2.00m in diameter and 1.10m deep, was located

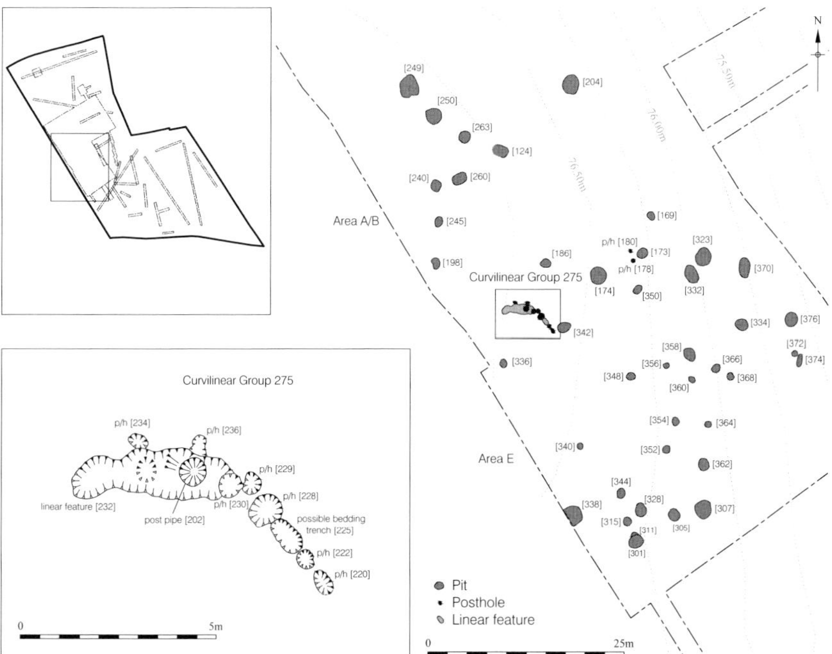

Figure 11.3: Prehistoric features.

towards the southern edge of the open area. It contained two fills, the upper of which produced a sizable assemblage of worked flint typologically indicative of Neolithic manufacture (see Bishop, below). Although the small, undiagnostic assemblage of flint-tempered pottery can be only broadly dated as Neolithic to early Iron Age (Percival 2012, see below) a Neolithic date is most likely given the homogeneous composition and date of the associated struck flint.

Four further pits, [301], [305], [311] and [332], mostly located close to [307], also produced small flint and pottery assemblages indicative of a possible Neolithic date. That said, these three are dated to the Neolithic with some caution, as although some of the worked flint from these features is also typologically Neolithic, other pieces are more ambiguous, with the pottery assemblages again suggesting only a broadly prehistoric date of Neolithic to early Iron Age. All of these pits were large, measuring between 1.09m and 2.44m in diameter and 0.52–2.05m deep. Pit [301] contained five fills and had a clay lining at the base, suggesting that it was a storage pit.

A group of pits excavated in the central part of the pit swathe included three that contained worked flint assemblages and pottery. Two large pits [173] and [186] produced small assemblages of struck flint of Neolithic to early Bronze Age date. The pits measured 1.52m and 1.57m in diameter and 0.85m and 1.50m deep, respectively. Both contained two fills, with finds present in both fills of pit [173] and the upper fill of [186]. Nearby pit [174] was larger than the other two

	Struck flint		Prehistoric pottery		Other finds
Pit	**No.**	**Flint date**	**No.**	**Wt (g)**	
[173]	6	N–EBA	11	19	
[174]	8	N–MBA	13	48	
[186]	5	N–EBA	3	2	1 cattle tooth
[204]	2	M/EN	7	6	1 burnt flint
[240]	1	N–EBA			
[245]	1	U/D	8	28	1 burnt flint
[260]	1	N–EBA	9	11	5 burnt flints
[301]	15	N–BA	13	37	
[305]	13	N–BA	10	11	
[307]	20	N	18	70	4 burnt flints
[311]	1	N	3	3	
[332]	6	N			2 burnt flints
Total	**79**		**95**	**235**	

M=Mesolithic, EN=Early Neolithic, N=Neolithic, EBA=Early Bronze Age, MBA=Middle Bronze Age, BA=Bronze Age, U/D=Undated

Table 11.1: Summary of finds from the prehistoric pits.

features, measuring 2.15m in diameter by 1.40m deep and containing three fills, all of which produced small struck flint and pottery assemblages, although these are, again, chronologically undiagnostic.

Three pits in the north-western part of the cluster contained small struck flint assemblages; two of these also contained sherds of pottery. Sub-circular pits [260] and [240] both yielded lithic material exhibiting Neolithic traits, while a sherd of flint-tempered pottery with possible impressed decoration, possibly of late Neolithic date, was recovered from the former. Pit [245], to the south of these, was in excess of 1.30m deep and produced sherds of pottery broadly datable as prehistoric, along with a single flint artefact of possible later prehistoric date. The north-easternmost of the pits, [204], was another large feature that was circular in plan with a diameter of 1.98m and a depth of 1.18m. One of its secondary fills produced struck flint with Mesolithic or early Neolithic technological traits and pottery broadly datable as prehistoric. The upper fill also produced prehistoric pottery.

An interesting group of features (Group 275) was located in the central western part of the site and approximately centrally within the pit cluster (Fig. 11.3 inset). This comprised a short curvilinear trench [232], associated with a number of postholes, which were cut both into and next to [232] and together formed a curvilinear arrangement. This group of features is indicative of a post-built structure, possibly serving as a windbreak, hunting bluff or temporary shelter. Seven very small fragments of prehistoric pottery (7g) were found in one of the postholes but cannot be closely dated.

11.3 Struck flint *by Barry Bishop*

Archaeological investigations at the site resulted in the recovery of 82 struck flints, along with unworked burnt flint fragments and a small quantity of fragments of other stone. All metrical information follows the methodology established by Saville (1980). The assemblage derives from a number of different contextual groups. A small quantity, comprising three struck pieces, was recovered from Roman or later features and can be considered residually deposited. The bulk of the assemblage, consisting of 79 pieces, was recovered from 12 pits that have been dated to the prehistoric period.

No truly chronologically diagnostic pieces are present, but, overall, the assemblage is relatively homogeneous and can be dated to the Neolithic period based on its technological attributes. It is dominated by flakes but also contains 10 blades (12.2% of the total) and many of the flakes are either narrow or have blade-like dorsal scars, which may indicate that at least some date to the early Neolithic. Four cores are also present, along with eight retouched implements, the latter having all come from a single feature, pit [307].

11.3.1 Pit [307]

Pit [307] contained the largest and probably the most internally consistent of the individual assemblages. Its fill contained 20 struck pieces, in variable but mostly good condition, all made from a very similar mottled grey/black flint and possibly from a single nodule, although none of the pieces could be refitted.

This assemblage includes 10 flakes and two blades, the remainder consisting of retouched implements; no cores are present. The flakes are mostly thin and narrow and represent knapping waste, including core shaping and trimming flakes along with broken pieces. Only a single decortication flake is present, suggesting that the raw materials were dressed elsewhere. Even if this does represent a single episode of knapping, only a small portion of what must have been produced is present, suggesting that the assemblage has been selected from a larger accumulation.

Eight pieces (40% of the total) are retouched and a few others may have been utilised, but any traces of this are obscured by subsequent damage. The retouched pieces include four edge-trimmed flakes, an end-scraper, a spurred flake or piercer and two serrates. The edge-trimmed flakes all have fine marginal retouch along various parts of their lateral edges but otherwise vary considerably in shape and size. The scraper is made on a thick and partially cortical flake with moderately steep convex, slightly invasive retouch around its distal end. Its working edge is rather chipped and uneven, suggesting that it was used on hard materials. The spurred implement consists of a short flake, the left lateral margin of which has been modified with abrupt bifacial retouch to form a small broad point. The tip and other parts of the point are abraded, again indicating that it was used like an awl on relatively hard materials. One of the serrates was made on a narrow flake that has been serrated along its right lateral margin; the other is a large and predominantly cortical flake measuring 86mm in length that has been serrated along its left, non-cortical, lateral margin. This also has abrupt retouch at its distal end, possibly to aid holding; the flake fits very comfortably into the hand, with the cortex acting as 'padding'. The serrations on both are fairly coarse, at around eight per centimetre.

A small quantity of burnt flint and a burnt quartz pebble fragment were also recovered from this pit. The quartz pebble may have been found as an erratic in the glacial deposits that are common in the area, although its selection, burning and inclusion within the pit could indicate that it had symbolic or ceremonial associations of some kind (Darvill 2002).

The struck flint assemblage from this pit is typologically, technologically and materially homogeneous and can be dated to the Neolithic period. It is in relatively good condition and contains a high proportion and wide range of retouched implements, also consistent with certain Neolithic deposition practices (e.g., Garrow 2006; Lamdin-Whymark 2008; Thomas 1999). Given the nature of the flint assemblage, the most obvious interpretation of the pit is that it is Neolithic and contemporary with the flintwork it contains.

11.3.2 Other pits

Eleven other pits also contained struck flint. While some of these features may also have been contemporary with their flintwork, their assemblages have a different character and contrast, to greater or lesser extents, with that from pit [307].

The pits produced variable quantities of struck flint: four contained only single pieces, while only two, pits [301] and [305], produced more than 10, these containing 15 and 13 pieces respectively. These pieces consist mainly of flakes struck from nodules of different colours, textures and cortex, indicating multiple episodes of production. Their mostly rather chipped condition indicates that a period of time had elapsed between manufacture and eventual deposition, suggesting that they were either residually introduced into the features or had been 'middened' or otherwise 'kicking around' for some time prior to final incorporation within the pits.

Pit [301] produced the largest assemblage. This is also technologically consistent and at least the majority of pieces can be dated to the Neolithic period. Most pieces are in a rather chipped condition and, although some of the flakes may have been struck from the same cobble, overall a number of different raw materials are represented. The assemblage comprises only knapping waste, including flakes and blades, with no retouched implements or cores present. One of the blades may have been serrated but this cannot now be confidently distinguished from subsequent damage. Pit [305] also produced a relatively large assemblage of 13 pieces, all or most of which are likely to date to the Neolithic period. They exhibit noticeable edge chipping, which is more consistent with residual incorporation, although it is possible that the assemblage could have been deliberately middened for some time prior to deposition. The assemblage consists entirely of knapping debris and includes a core with few potentially useable pieces still present. The core has two platforms set at right angles and weighs 55g. It had produced a number of flakes and possibly blades.

11.3.3 Significance

Most, if not all, of the struck flint recovered during the excavations can be dated to the Neolithic period and the bulk of this to the early Neolithic. Taken together, it represents all stages in the reduction sequence, although the distribution of pieces from individual stages is uneven; for example, all of the certainly retouched pieces come from a single feature, pit [307].

11.4 Other finds

A total of 105 sherds (243g) of hand-made, overwhelmingly flint-tempered prehistoric pottery was recovered from the pits and other prehistoric features (a short ditch [232] and a posthole [228] in Group 275), with a further 13 sherds (12g) collected from later features (analysed in Percival 2012). The pottery from the pits is in very poor condition, with a very low mean weight of just 2.5g. Several of the sherds are burnt, indicating that the pottery had spent some time exposed on the ground surface before eventual deposition in pit fills. The 'scrappy' assemblage is prehistoric but is otherwise not closely datable owing to both the small size and the poor condition of the sherds and to the lack of diagnostic forms. The exception to this is a single rim sherd recovered from a Saxon pit [206], which has distinctive fingernail impressions to the rim top and is almost certainly earlier Iron Age. The dating of the remainder of the assemblage remains tentative. The pottery found in the pits and other features is more enigmatic, though it is possible that this assemblage, too, is of earlier Iron Age date. Two cattle bones were also recovered from the pits: a skull fragment from [249] and a loose mandibular molar from [186].

11.5 Discussion of the prehistoric phase

Since the finds assemblages from the pits do not provide conclusive answers regarding the features' date and function, regional parallels for pit-dominated prehistoric sites may be instructive. There are several comparable sites in Hertfordshire, including Aldwick Iron Age Settlement in Barley, which, although larger in scale, produced a similar repertoire of features consisting of more than 100 pits and a curvilinear feature (Cra'ster 1961). As at Watton-at-Stone, there were very few instances of pits cutting one another, suggesting that they were mostly broadly contemporary. The sizes of the pits – between 0.79m and 3.05m in diameter and up to 1.70m deep – were comparable. Perhaps the most interesting difference between the two sites is that the finds assemblage from the Aldwick pits was much more substantial, with many described as rubbish pits owing to the quantities of pottery and animal bone present.

A further parallel can be seen at the Baldock Bypass in north Hertfordshire, which produced, among other features, swathes of pits spanning the prehistoric period. Some were Neolithic in date and apparently remained partially open for considerable periods of time. Several other pit clusters were late Bronze Age to middle Iron Age in origin (Phillips 2009). However, as with the Aldwick examples, many of the pits recorded in the Baldock Bypass excavations produced large quantities of pottery and animal bone indicative of the disposal of refuse/midden material, evidence that is lacking at Watton-at-Stone.

Overall, both the range of activities and the depositional history represented by the prehistoric pits at Watton-at-Stone are difficult to reconstruct. The pit most likely to date to the Neolithic period, [307], suggests an episode of tool production followed by the deliberate deposition of selected, in particular retouched, pieces within the pit relatively soon after their manufacture and use. Some of the other pits, notably [301], could also date to the Neolithic. However, the composition and condition of the associated flintwork indicates a different depositional pattern, with the flintworking waste having been middened or otherwise stored for some time prior to portions of it being selected for eventual deposition within pits, a practice noted at other Neolithic sites (e.g., Garrow *et al.* 2006; Lamdin-Whymark 2008). At least one of the larger pits, [301], appears to have had a clay lining and was probably originally used for storage.

The ambiguous nature and dates of the pits and the relative lack of finds are interesting. This is especially the case when compared to contemporary sites that yielded larger assemblages of finds. The fills and finds in many of the pits at Baldock Bypass and Aldwick were interpreted as deriving from the clearance of surface middens once the pits had ceased to be used for storage. Therefore, while the dimensions of many of the Watton-at-Stone pits suggest an original storage function, the limited quantities of finds from both the pits and the site as a whole implies that there were no large midden deposits on the site. The prehistoric activity may thus have been sporadic and seasonal rather than permanent and settled. The topographic position of the site – on a hilltop overlooking a river valley – is a favourable location for a settlement.

11.6 The Anglo-Saxon cremation cemetery

The most significant phase of activity on the site took place during the early Saxon period, when the site was occupied by a cremation cemetery that possibly extended westwards beyond the excavation (Fig. 11.4).

The most noteworthy feature dating to this phase was a curvilinear ditch (Group 273), which was re-cut on at least one occasion and then backfilled with a number of artefact-rich and burnt deposits. In common with the prehistoric pits, this was located on the high ground at the western edge of the site. The original cut of the feature, [271], extended for no more than 5m from the south-eastern terminus, was an average of 0.45m deep and contained a single fill. The recut of the ditch [255] was 8.5m long, up to 0.60m deep (though it became

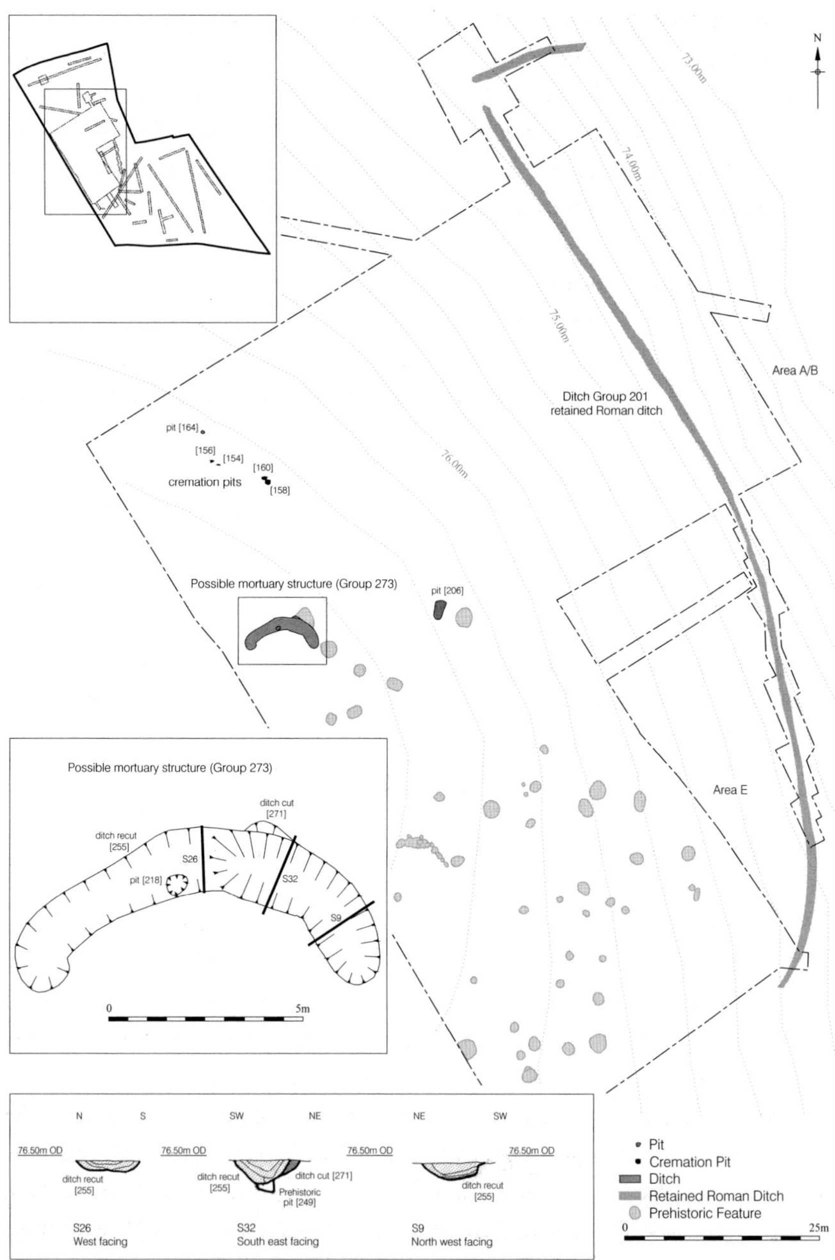

Figure 11.4: Saxon features.

shallower to the west) and had been backfilled with up to five different deposits at different points along its length, several of which were rich in organic material. Large sherds of early Saxon pottery were present within the backfills, including one large vessel which appeared to have been deposited complete from inside the area of the arc defined by the ditch. The pottery assemblage is almost unique in Hertfordshire and of considerable importance for Anglo-Saxon studies in the region (see Sudds, below).

The upper fill of the ditch, close to the eastern terminus, produced two late Roman coins, one of which is pierced, suggesting a secondary use (see Crummy, below). A further Roman coin was found in the upper fill of the central part of the ditch, while additional residual Romano-British material was found elsewhere within the feature. The ditch also yielded a fragment of a sandstone spindle whorl of probable Saxon date; spindle whorls were used as grave goods in the early Anglo-Saxon period, usually in female graves (Crummy 2007: 265). After backfilling of the ditch had commenced, but before it had been completed, a small pit [218] was apparently dug into secondary backfilling deposit (216), close to the southern edge of the ditch. This pit was circular in plan, measuring 0.60m in diameter and 0.23m deep. Its fill, (219), contained burnt material, including fragments of burnt bone, possibly from a cremation burial, although, owing to the size and condition of the bone fragments, it cannot be determined whether they are human or animal (Tierney 2012).

The rich and varied finds assemblage from the ditch strongly suggests a funerary function, perhaps as part of a (truncated) mortuary structure or shrine. The various fills of the ditch were extensively bulk-sampled, with three of the samples yielding fragments of burnt bone which further reinforce a funerary interpretation. A group of five pits located 10–20m to the north appear to have been contemporary with the ditch. Two of these are of particular note. Small pit [158] included a fill which contained extensive carbonised remains; it was 100 per cent sampled but no dateable artefacts were present. Small pit [160], immediately adjacent to this, also contained a burnt fill, below which were the broken remains of a large Saxon jar (Sudds, below). Although burnt bone was present only in small quantities in the former, it is probable that both of these features were heavily truncated Anglo-Saxon cremation burials. Three further pits, [154], [156] and [164], located a short distance to the north, are also likely to have been ploughed-out cremation burials of this date, although the quantity and quality of the associated burnt bone does not allow positive identification as either human or animal (Tierney 2012).

A sub-rectangular pit, [206], was located 15m east of the curvilinear ditch. It measured 2.45m by 1.20m and was 0.33m deep, with steeply sloping sides and a flattish base. The lower fill, (208), produced a small assemblage of early/middle Saxon pottery broadly contemporary with that recovered from the curvilinear ditch and cremation pit [160]. The upper fill, (207), produced a single residual early Iron Age sherd. The function of the pit is unclear; however, given its date and its position relatively close to other Anglo-Saxon features, it is possible that it also had a funerary/ritual function. A number of slots excavated through the extensive north–south-aligned Roman field ditch (Group 201) to the east also produced sherds of Saxon pottery, indicating that it continued to be utilised after the late Roman period and may even have formed an enclosure around the area of Saxon funerary activity.

11.7 The Saxon pottery *by Berni Sudds*

With the exception of a medieval south Hertfordshire greyware sherd and a single fifteenth- or sixteenth-century redware sherd, the post-Roman pottery assemblage is entirely of early Saxon date. A total of 368 sherds weighing 4609g and largely comprising a group of fragmented but semi-complete vessels in very good condition, was recovered. Owing to the scarcity of pottery of this date in the county, the discovery of such a convincing group of Saxon vessels is highly significant.

11.7.1 Fabric

The pottery was examined under ×20 magnification and divided into three broad fabric groupings on the basis of major or defining inclusion type. Further subdivisions were made under these groupings according to the presence of additional inclusions. Chemical provenance studies (using Inductively Coupled Plasma Atomic Emission Spectrometry) were beyond the remit of the current study but could prove informative in the light of further significant contemporary discoveries in the region, or as part of a broader research programme. A mnemonic code has been attributed to each fabric based upon major and minor inclusion type.

Chaff-tempered wares

Three broad fabric groupings were isolated among the chaff-tempered pottery from the site on the basis of the absence or presence and the size of quartz sand inclusions. These are very similar to the range identified at Mill Road and Foxholes Farm, both in Hertford (Partridge 1989; Sudds forthcoming a), and also to the major chaff-tempered groups from the London region (Blackmore with Vince 2008: 179; Blackmore 2012: 233–4).

ORG: Fine matrix with abundant chaff inclusions. Very rare sand (up to 0.7mm), iron oxide and calcareous inclusions.

FSORG: Fine sandy matrix containing abundant fine sand (up to 0.1mm) with moderate to abundant chaff inclusions. Rare flint and calcareous inclusions.

SORG: Moderate to abundant sand (mostly up to 0.3mm but occasionally up to 0.7mm), moderate to abundant chaff, rare flint and calcareous inclusions.

Sand-tempered wares

SANM: Abundant very fine sand (up to 0.3mm), occasional organic inclusions (or voids where burnt out), mica.

SANF: Abundant fine sand (up to 0.5mm), rare flint, iron oxide, mica, organic and calcareous inclusions.

Sandstone-tempered wares

The fabrics in this group are dominated by quartz or sand temper but contain occasional to moderate sandstone inclusions that distinguish them from the sand-tempered group, in addition to being generally coarser in composition. Three sub-fabrics have been identified, but with so few sherds these may simply reflect differences between individual vessels, as is probably the case with the sand-tempered group. Indeed, the CSST ORG group is comprised solely of the sherds of a single vessel spread across multiple deposits.

SSST: Abundant white and clear angular to sub-rounded quartz sand (up to 0.3mm but occasionally up to 1mm), moderate white sandstone (up to 2mm) and moderate organic inclusions (chaff?).

QSST: Moderate to abundant white, grey, clear sub-angular to rounded quartz (generally up to 1mm, occasionally up to 2mm), occasional fine-grained white sandstone (up to 2mm), occasional organic and calcareous inclusions.

CSST ORG: Abundant white, clear, iron-stained sub-angular to rounded quartz/quartz sand (up to 1mm), moderate organic (chaff) and stained or heat-altered (?) calcareous inclusions, occasional white sandstone fragments (up to 1mm).

With so little contemporary material for comparison in the vicinity it is difficult to gauge with any certainty how typical the assemblage might be in terms of fabric composition. To date in Hertfordshire individual Saxon sherds or vessels have been identified at Stevenage, Royston, Sawbridgeworth and Ware (Myres 1969: 104, 110; Partridge 1989: 177, Sudds forthcoming b) and the nearest early to middle Saxon assemblages are from Hertford, although these are relatively small in size (Foxholes Farm: Partridge 1989; Mill Road: Sudds forthcoming a). Interestingly, as is the case with the material from Mill Road and Foxholes Farm, the assemblage is dominated by chaff-tempered fabrics and compares fairly closely in composition to those sites (Table 11.2). Among the remaining fabrics from Watton-at-Stone, the quartz, sand, sandstone and mica inclusions, occurring in various combinations, can also be paralleled at Mill Road, and the flint temper at Foxholes Farm.

It has long been assumed that chaff-tempered wares, and some of the generic sand- and quartz-tempered wares, were produced in the locality of the settlements in which they were used (Blackmore and Vince 2012: 172; Hamerow 1993: 27–31; Laidlaw 1996: 88; Sudds 2005: 219). However, chemical analysis carried out on the chaff-tempered pottery from Lundenwic has revealed a more complex picture for the London region at least, where the wares used in the wic were made near the settlement but not within it (Blackmore and Vince 2012: 173). The same may be true of the Watton-at-Stone assemblage, although the pottery could just as easily have been manufactured in the associated settlement given the ready availability of the necessary materials. Similarly, although there are no outcrops of sandstone local to the area, just as in London, it is possible that some of these were locally produced using detrital sandstone from boulder clay, of which there is plenty in the immediate region (Blackmore 2012: 241–2; Blackmore and Vince 2008: 155; Blackmore and Vince 2012: 174; Ordnance Survey Geological Survey Sheet 239: Drift). Pottery production may thus have been local, regional or both. The discovery of further contemporary material in Hertfordshire, coupled with chemical analysis, is clearly required to better understand issues of provenance, trade and economy.

11.7.2 Form, surface treatment and use

Where diagnostic, the assemblage is comprised entirely of jar forms with rounded or sub-rounded profiles and simple upright rims (Fig. 11.5 right), although one everted rim was recovered from the fill of ditch [214] (217), part of Group 273. The majority of vessels demonstrate some form of surface treatment, typically smoothing, although a few are burnished. No other decoration was identified. At least one vessel, the CSST ORG burnished jar from fills (211) (212) (216) (257) and (259) of Group 273 (Fig. 11.5 left), has what appear to be heat-altered inclusions and a base that has been exposed to high temperatures, potentially indicating prior usage, perhaps in a domestic setting.

11.7.3 Distribution and function

The majority of the assemblage was recovered from the backfill of the semi-circular ditch in the west of the site (Group 273) and is comprised mainly of fragmented but semi-complete individual vessels. There are multiple instances of cross-joining between vessels from different fills of the ditch, perhaps indicating that the episodes of backfilling occurred in quick succession. Cross-joins were also

Code	Description	Date range (AD)	Sherd count	Weight (g)
Chaff-tempered wares				
ORG	Chaff-tempered ware	500–850	2	8
FSORG	Fine sand- and chaff-tempered ware	500–850	193	2620
SORG	Sand- and chaff-tempered ware	500–850	144	1782
Sand-tempered wares				
SANM	Very fine sand-tempered ware with mica	450–850	1	11
SANF	Fine sand-tempered ware	450–850	1	3
Sandstone-tempered wares				
SSST	Sand-, sandstone- and chaff-tempered ware	450–850	1	11
QSST	Quartz-tempered ware with sandstone, calcareous and chaff inclusions	450–850	13	53
CSST ORG	Quartz sand- and chaff-tempered ware with calcareous and sandstone inclusions	450–850	11	99

Table 11.2: The Saxon pottery: mnemonic fabric codes, descriptions and suggested date ranges.

observed between corresponding contexts from the evaluation and excavation phases of the investigation. Pit [160] contained the remains of a single fragmented large jar. The remainder of the assemblage was dispersed in the fills of the north–south-aligned late Roman ditch in the east of the excavation (Group 201) and in other postholes and pits. A minimum of 40 vessels may be represented, although with further reconstruction this figure is likely to be smaller. Table 11.3 summarises the distribution of the Saxon pottery.

In the absence of residues it is often difficult to reveal anything about the function to which vessels or assemblages were put, and this is particularly true of the Saxon period, where there is little specialisation of form. Nonetheless, a number of features of the Watton-at-Stone assemblage suggest a funerary interpretation. First, there are a large number of fresh conjoining sherds from a relatively small number of vessels, which is atypical of domestic activity but indicates that the vessels were initially deposited whole. Although the feature is truncated, this is particularly clear in pit [160]. Many of the vessels are also large, a feature noted in Saxon cremation cemeteries. Cremation vessels are often larger than their domestic counterparts, probably for symbolic rather than practical reasons (McKinley 1994: 85). The vessels are also, for the most part, well made and finished, with a few fine and competently potted examples. With a funerary perspective in mind, the fragmentation but clustering of the vessels from the backfilled ditch (Group 273) may suggest the remnants of disturbed, re-deposited cremations, particularly given the adherence of charcoal and cremated bone to unwashed surfaces (e.g., (213)).

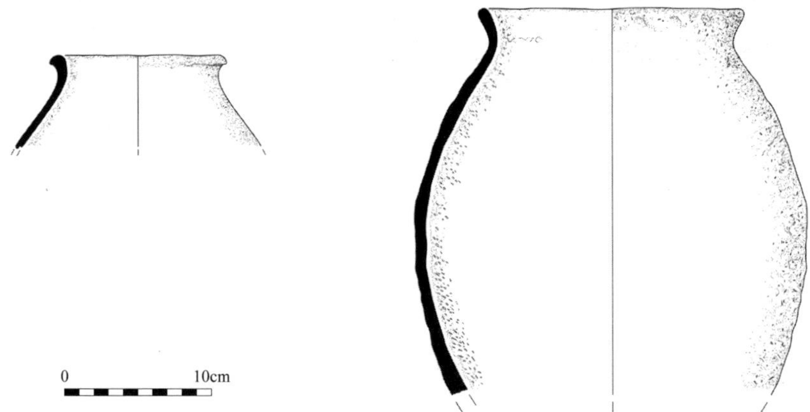

Figure 11.5: Saxon pottery. Left: vessel retrieved from contexts (211), (212), (216), (257), (259); Right: vessel retrieved from context (213).

11.7.4 Discussion

Interpretation of the Saxon assemblage from Watton-at-Stone is somewhat impeded by its relatively small size and, with the exception of spot finds and the two small settlement assemblages from Hertford, the lack of comparable material in the county. Some inferences can be made, however, and the questions raised by the assemblage are worth discussing with a view to future discoveries.

Given the small quantity of material for comparison in the locality, a broader regional view of the progression of fabrics and forms during the Anglo-Saxon period was assumed in order to help date the assemblage. In addition, owing to the regional significance of the assemblage, two sherds from the backfills of the curvilinear ditch ([255] (257) (259)) were sent for Optically Stimulated Luminescence (OSL) dating (see Schwenninger, below).

On the basis of fabric alone, specifically the dominance of organic temper (93% by number; 96% by weight), a date from the sixth to the eighth century would be suggested, as across much of central, eastern and southern Britain organic-tempered ware increased in importance during this period, becoming most prevalent in assemblages during the seventh century (Anderson 2003; Blackmore 2012: 233; Blackmore with Vince 2008: 179; Cotter 2000; Denham 1985a; 1985b; Hamerow 1987; 1993; Matthews and Chadwick-Hawkes 1985; Sudds 2005: 216; Wade 2009: 109). The absence of later, diagnostically middle Saxon fabrics, such as Maxey-type ware or Ipswich ware, could further indicate a date prior to the late seventh or early eighth century, when these regional 'industries' began, although the site is probably too far south to receive Maxey-type ware from Northamptonshire or Lincolnshire and, as a rural site at some distance from Ipswich, is not likely to have received Ipswich ware in any quantity.

	Feature Group								
Fabric code	**160**	**206**	**243**	**249**	**201**	**109**	**120**	**273**	**Totals**
By sherd count									
ORG								2	2
FSORG				5	1	11	36	140	193
SORG	52				16	5	3	68	144
SANM					1				1
SANF			1						1
SSST								1	1
QSST		8						5	13
CSST ORG								11	11
By weight (g)									
ORG								8	8
FSORG				13	16	56	497	2038	2620
SORG	70				10	123	33	946	1782
SANM					11				11
SANF			3						3
SSST								11	11
QSST		7						46	53
CSST ORG								99	99

Table 11.3: Fabrics by sherd count (top) and weight (bottom) by feature.

Turning to form, the potential danger of dating Saxon pottery on the basis of profile has been raised elsewhere (Arnold 1997: 17; Hamerow 1993), although it is generally apparent that the distinctive and pronounced forms of the fifth and sixth centuries became diluted as time passed (Myres 1977), with profiles becoming more slack or even straight-sided and ovoid, as at Mucking (Hamerow 1993: 44). The absence of pronounced carinated and biconical forms in the assemblage may indicate that a very early date is unlikely, as might the absence of any form of line, boss or stamped decoration, also considered to be early in date, although, again, not exclusively (Hamerow 1993: 45–56). Equally, the absence of low bulbous forms with tall necks, which appear during the seventh century, might preclude a later date, although these are more commonly associated with inhumation burial (for example, Kempston and Chamberlains Barn, Bedfordshire, and Melbourn, Cambridgeshire: A. Slowikowski, pers. comm.; Myres 1977: 27).

The rite of cremation itself, representing a regionally manifested cultural distinction, gradually disappeared towards the end of the early Anglo-Saxon period, giving way to inhumation by the seventh century (Boddington 1990: 179–81; Stoodley 2007: 154). This transition has long been held to represent a shift from pagan beliefs to Christianity but the reality may be rather more complex, resulting instead from the evolution of the landscape under pressures from social, economic and religious change (Boddington 1990: 196; Stoodley 2007: 160). The Synod of Hertford held in *c.* AD 672, if the correct Hertford, might on the face of it suggest that the region had converted to Christianity by this date, although the change is likely to have been much more piecemeal and localised, and dependent upon local factors, such as the establishment and growth of a manor or king's *tun* (Boddington 1990: 197). Whether a long-lived burial site encompassing the changeover (Castledyke, Lincolnshire: Drinkall and Foreman 1998; Kempston, Bedfordshire: A. Slowikowski, pers. comm.; Springfield Lyons, Essex: Tyler and Major 2005; Bloodmoor Hill, Suffolk: Dickens *et al.* 2005), or a new relocated site (Chamberlain's Barn, Bedfordshire: Hyslop 1963; Winnall, Hampshire: Meaney and Hawkes 1970), the character of seventh-century cemeteries across the region is quite consistently different, comprised solely of inhumations.

Together, this evidence broadly points to a date during the sixth to early seventh century, and perhaps more specifically a later sixth- or early seventh-century date. Interestingly, the OSL analysis provides dates of 1525 +/- 115 years before present for the sherd from Ditch Slot [255] fill (257) (*c.* AD 373 to *c.* AD 603) and 1515 +/- 125 years before present for the sherd from Ditch Slot [255] fill (259) (*c.* AD 373 to *c.* AD 623). The earlier part of this date range is irreconcilable with the fabric and form composition, as discussed above, but if accurate the latest date given would narrow the potential date range from the later sixth century to the earliest years of the seventh century, suggesting that the group represents a late early Anglo-Saxon cremation assemblage apparently dominated by chaff-tempered vessels.

The paucity of chaff-tempered pottery from Saxon cremation cemeteries in favour of finer sand- and mineral-tempered vessels has been noted by some commentators in the past (Brisbane 1981; Brown 1974). A contemporary decline in the rite of cremation just at the time when chaff-tempered pottery was becoming more widespread is apparent, but the absence of chaff-tempered vessels from sixth-century burials, where they would be expected at this date, was instead explained by a perceived segregation between the production of ritual and domestic pottery. Chaff-tempered pottery, due to its often crude forming and manufacture using agricultural by-products, was thought to have been made by the occupants of local settlements strictly for domestic use (Brown 1974). Conversely, funerary pottery was the result of ceremonial production, with vessels being made specifically for burial (Brisbane 1981) and even for specific individuals (Richards 1987).

Where comparison can be made between associated cemetery and settlement assemblages these hypotheses can no longer be substantiated, with virtually identical fabric compositions being observed in both contexts, as at Mucking (Hamerow 1993: 31) and Spong Hill (Brisbane 1984: 32). Although it is not possible to relate them directly to the current assemblage (as related settlements and cemeteries are usually found within 500–600m of each other; see Boddington 1990: 195), settlement assemblages local to Watton-at-Stone, namely from Hertford, some five miles to the south (Partridge 1989; Sudds forthcoming a), are very similar in composition, with chaff-tempered wares dominating. Indeed, chaff-tempered vessels evidently dominate sixth-century cemetery assemblages in the region, in addition to settlement groups (Mucking: Hamerow 1993: 31; Springfield Lyons: Tyler 2005: 120–21).

Furthermore, the difficulty of determining funerary versus domestic has long been known (Arnold 1997: 96), but a recent reappraisal of the pre-burial origins of cremation urns has pointed out that the deliberate production of vessels for burial is at best based on circumstantial evidence, as is the notion that they were selected from domestic stock (Perry 2011). Instead, it has been argued that a more individual approach is required where the pre-burial function of each vessel should be determined through use-alteration techniques. Where applied to the cremation cemetery at Cleatham, it was possible to conclude that the majority of vessels did demonstrate a pre-burial use, including fermentation (Perry 2011: 19). Thus, the likelihood is that they were not manufactured specifically for a burial but selected from the household. Through other correlations it was possible to establish that their previous function determined whether they were suitable for use as cinerary urns or for a particular individual (Perry 2011: 19).

The assemblage is too small and disturbed to determine whether this is the case at Watton-at-Stone. The vessels and cremated remains are no longer associated and, in any case, noted correlations would not be statistically viable in such a small group. Key culturally and socially diagnostic markers, such as decoration, are also absent. No attrition is evident inside the vessels but the pre-use of at least one, demonstrating a heat-altered base possibly from use on a fire, is apparent. Residue analysis could potentially prove fruitful, although, again, a larger dataset would be needed for this to be viable. The vessels exhibit some degree of variability in technological accomplishment, but there are not the extremes noted in other assemblages where very finely potted and decorated vessels appear alongside crudely formed plain examples. This may just reflect the late and limited date of the group (Sudds 2007; Tyler 2005). Aside from issues of pre-use and vessel selection, the variability seen elsewhere may reflect different levels of production and exchange in settlements, perhaps occurring contemporaneously. In the absence of chemical provenance studies it is impossible to be certain, but the Watton-at-Stone vessels do appear very similar to others found in the locality. Whether they were made in the household or within the settlement by a specific individual, or were exchanged in from outside, remains unknown.

It is quite possible, even likely, that the current assemblage forms part of a much larger, more long-lived cemetery falling beyond the limit of excavation. Chaff-tempered pottery dominates the latest phase of cremations at Springfield Lyons, some 25 miles to the east (Tyler 2005: 121, 185–6). In the same way, the vessels recovered from this site may represent the final phase of cremation at Watton-at-Stone, or perhaps a section of the cemetery used by a less affluent kin-group. The discovery of this material has raised more queries than can be answered until further contemporary material is excavated and analysed. Notwithstanding, the confirmation of the presence and character of a late early Anglo-Saxon funerary assemblage in Hertfordshire represents a very significant step forward regionally.

11.8 Luminescence dating *by Dr Jean-Luc Schwenninger*

11.8.1 Introduction

This report summarises the methodology and results of the Optically Stimulated Luminescence (OSL) dating analysis of the pot sherds (samples A and B) from Station Road, Watton-at-Stone. A separate palaeodose estimate was determined for each of the selected sherds from Ditch [255]: that from fill (257) (sample A) and that from fill (259) (sample B). The results were almost identical (3.86 ± 0.13 Gy for sample A and 3.83 ± 0.18 Gy for sample B). The calculations for the dating are based on the concentrations of radioisotopes within sample A (internal dose rate) and the surrounding sediment (external dose rate). The results of the OSL dating provide a mean age estimate of 1525 ± 115 years before 2013, giving a date range of *c.* AD 373 to *c.* AD 603. A summary of the OSL dating is presented in Table 11.4 and further details pertaining to the analyses may be found in Table 11.5.

11.8.2 Methodology

The concentrations of radionuclides within the fired clay matrix and the surrounding sediment were determined by laboratory-based inductively coupled plasma mass spectroscopy (ICP-MS). There is a good level of confidence in the OSL measurements and in the determination of the equivalent dose. The quartz extracted from both sherds was characterised by high sensitivity, good recycling, low thermal transfer and no feldspar interference, and the measurements resulted in a tightly clustered distribution of multiple palaeodose estimates.

Dose rate calculations are based on the concentration of radioactive elements (potassium, thorium and uranium) within the samples and were derived from elemental analysis by ICP-MS/AES using a fusion sample preparation technique. The final OSL age estimate includes an additional 2 per cent systematic error to account for uncertainties in source calibration. Dose rate calculations are based on Aitken (1985). These incorporated beta attenuation factors (Mejdahl 1979), dose rate conversion factors (Adamiec and Aitken 1998) and an absorption coefficient for the water content (Zimmerman 1971). The contribution of cosmic radiation to the total dose rate was calculated as a function of latitude, altitude, burial depth and average overburden density based on data from Prescott and Hutton (1994).

The OSL analysis was aimed at the measurement of the luminescence signal from coarse-sized quartz mineral grains (180–255μm) extracted from the sherds using standard preparation techniques, including wet sieving, HCl (10%) treatment to remove carbonates, HF treatment (48%) to dissolve feldspathic minerals and heavy mineral separation with sodium polytungstate. OSL measurements were made in an automated Risø luminescence reader equipped with an infra-red laser diode (870Δ 40nm) and blue (470Δ 40nm) LEDs (Bøtter-Jensen 1988; 1997; Bøtter-Jensen *et al.* 2000) using a SAR post-IR blue OSL measurement protocol (Murray and Wintle 2000; Banerjee *et al.* 2001; Wintle and Murray 2006).

A GG-420 cut-off filter was placed in front of the blue diodes to restrict stimulation light below 420nm reaching the photomultiplier tube. The emitted luminescence signal was filtered by a 7mm U-340 filter placed in front of the detector. A preheat regime of 240/220°C was adopted for all the measurements. The post-IR blue OSL dating procedure was designed to deplete any feldspar contribution to the OSL signal by preceding each OSL measurement with an Infrared Stimulated Luminescence (IRSL) measurement. The IR exposure reduces the size of feldspar contributions, besides providing an alternative means to determine the equivalent dose. The measurements did not reveal the presence of an IR signal and the absence of feldspathic components (which can suffer from anomalous fading of the IRSL and OSL signals) suggests that the measured OSL signal is dominated by quartz.

Field code	Lab. code	Burial depth (cm)	Water content (%)	Palaeodose (Gy)	Dose rate (Gy/ka)	Age estimate (years before 2013)
Sample A	X6069	60	5–15	3.86 ± 0.13	2.53 ± 0.16	1525 ± 115
Sample B	X6070	60	5–15	3.83 ± 0.18	(2.53 ± 0.16)	1515 ± 125
Mean [A+B]		60	5–15	3.84 ± 0.14	2.53 ± 0.16	1520 ± 120

Table 11.4: Results of the OSL dating.

Sample name	Sample A	Sample B	
Laboratory code	X6069	X6070	Mean
De (Gy)	3.86	3.83	3.84
Uncertainty	0.13	0.18	0.14
Grain size			
Min. grain size (mm)	180	180	180
Max grain size (mm)	255	255	255
External gamma-dose rate	1.11±0.11	1.11±0.11	1.11±0.11
Measured concentrations			
standard fractional error	0.050	0.050	0.050
% K	1.040	[1.040]	1.040
error (%K)	0.052	[0.052]	0.052
Th (ppm)	13.30	[13.30]	13.30
error (ppm)	0.66	[0.66]	0.66
U (ppm)	2.90	[2.90]	2.90
error (ppm)	0.14	[0.14]	0.14
Cosmic dose calculations			
Depth (m)	0.60	0.60	0.60
error (m)	0.20	0.20	0.20
Average overburden density (g.cm3)	1.90	1.90	1.90
error (g.cm3)	0.10	0.10	0.10
Latitude (deg.), north positive	52	52	52
Longditude (deg.), east positive	0	0	0
Altitude (m above sea-level)	73	73	73
Geomagnetic latitude	0.197	0.197	0.197
Dc (Gy/ka), 55N G.lat, 0 km Alt.	0.067	0.067	0.067
error	0.60	0.60	0.60
Cosmic dose rate (Gy/ka)	0.20	0.20	0.20
error	1.90	1.90	1.90
Moisture content			
Moisture (water / wet sediment)	0.100	0.100	0.100
error	0.050	0.050	0.050
Total dose rate, Gy/ka	2.53	2.53	2.53
error	0.16	0.16	0.16
OSL age estimate (years before 2013)	1525	[1515]	1520
error	115	[125]	120

Table 11.5: OSL dating and radioactivity data.

11.9 The metalwork *by Nina Crummy*

A small number of metal objects were recovered during the course of the investigations. Three late Roman coins were found in the fills of the curvilinear Saxon ditch (Group 273), two from slot [182] and one from slot [255]. One of those (SF 7) from [182] is a pierced issue of Constantine I dated to AD 330–35 (Hill and Kent 1972: fig. 15). It is not much worn and was probably removed from circulation by the middle of the century if not earlier. The other is a worn issue of the House of Valentinian, dated to within the period AD 364–78. The third coin is also of the House of Valentinian and is in very poor condition. The only other metal object from the Saxon ditch is a nail fragment from slot [214].

As no Roman coins were either stratified in Roman features or residual in post-medieval to modern topsoil on the site, it is highly unlikely that the three coins from the Saxon ditch fill are residual from disturbed Roman levels. Roman coins, particularly of the later third and fourth centuries, often occur in Anglo-Saxon settlements in eastern England, sometimes in considerable numbers, and they were also used as grave goods in Migration Period cemeteries. In some cases they seem to have been curated for their metal content, in others as curiosities, and some, especially those used as grave goods in the burials of children, were credited with amuletic properties (Crummy 2010: 72–3; King 1988; Meaney 1981: 213–16). Where there is little or no underlying Roman stratigraphy on these sites it is generally believed that the coins were collected from neighbouring Roman settlements. For example, many of the 289 Roman coins from the Anglo-Saxon village of West Stow, Suffolk, are likely to have been gathered from the nearby Roman small town at Icklingham (Curnow 1985: 76–7), while 46 from the Anglo-Saxon cemetery at Great Chesterford, Cambridgeshire, would almost certainly have come from the nearby Roman town and its immediate hinterland (Evison 1994: 27; Medlycott 2011: fig. 1.5). The Watton-at-Stone coins were probably similarly imported to the site in the early Anglo-Saxon period from a more concentrated area of Roman activity nearby.

The degree of wear on the two House of Valentinian issues and the perforation through the Constantinian coin both support the possibility of secondary usage. A feature of Roman coins on Anglo-Saxon sites is the numbers that have been pierced. Thirty-five of the West Stow coins were pierced, as well as three of those from Great Chesterford (Curnow 1985: 80–81; Evison 1994: 27). Evidence from Migration Period inhumations suggests that pierced coins were principally used on bead festoons, where they would have functioned as spangles, amulets, indications of status or a combination of all three (Evison 1994: 27; Hines 1984: 199–241; Walton Rogers 2007: 128, 132, 195). Coin SF 7 from Watton-at-Stone was probably used in this way, but pierced coins were also used as amulets in very late Roman burials (Crummy 2010: 69–74) and an earlier origin for the perforation through this coin cannot be entirely discounted.

11.10 Conclusions

The dating of prehistoric features on the site is restricted by the lack of diagnostic material, particularly the small fragments of flint-tempered pottery. However, the lithic assemblage strongly suggests a Neolithic presence, with at least one of the large pits dating to this period. The remaining pits can be only broadly dated as prehistoric. However, it seems likely that some, if not most, were Iron Age in date, given that there are numerous local and regional parallels for pit-dominated sites dating to this period, including Aldwick and Baldock Bypass in Hertfordshire (Cra'ster 1961; Phillips 2009), and Trumpington Park and Ride (Hinman 2004) and Harston Mill (O'Brien *et al.* forthcoming; O'Brien with Doel 2005) in Cambridgeshire. The exact functions of most of the pits also remain ambiguous. Evidence of clay lining in one pit suggests that it was originally utilised for storage. The small prehistoric finds assemblage implies that activity at the site was small-scale and intermittent, perhaps seasonal in character.

Sites of early and middle Saxon date are very rare across Hertfordshire. Partridge (1989: 177) reports a sixth-century saucer brooch being found at Watton-at-Stone, though the exact provenance is unclear and the artefact does not appear to be listed in the HHER. At Hertford, *c.*8km to the south of Watton-at-Stone, two sites have yielded features and finds of broadly contemporary date. At Foxholes Farm, to the south of the town (Partridge 1989), a number of elongated post-built structures, sunken-featured buildings (SFBs) and pits were recorded. Some of these features contained sherds of grass-tempered pottery. At Mill Road, east of the medieval town (Boyer forthcoming), a possible SFB was identified with residual middle Saxon pottery found across a wider area of the site in later medieval features. A single sherd of middle Saxon pottery was also found during recent investigations on a neighbouring site immediately to the west (Maher 2011). At nearby Ware a number of archaeological interventions have recorded early to middle Saxon activity in areas to the east of the Roman town (Kiln and Partridge 1994: 69–74).

To the north of the current site, there is known to have been an early Saxon settlement at Baldock, middle Saxon pottery has been recorded at Stevenage and Royston (Myres 1969: 104, 110), and an Anglo-Saxon burial is recorded at Furneux Pelham, to the north-east (Meaney 1964: 104). Further to the north-west, excavations in Letchworth have revealed a settlement that may have developed from as early as the mid-seventh century (Matthews and Burleigh

1989) and, in the vicinity, a small, scattered Saxon cemetery (Moss-Eccardt 1971). A possible Anglo-Saxon burial of mid-seventh-century date is also reported from the Wheathampstead area, to the south-west of Watton-at-Stone (Page 1902: 253–7), although the site was not fully recorded and just two vessels were salvaged. In recent years a number of finds of early and middle Saxon date, mostly from metal-detecting, have been reported to the PAS, but none appear to relate to a specific known settlement or other site.

Within the wider eastern region, Hertfordshire and, to some extent, Essex are notably lacking in sites of early and middle Saxon date, especially when compared with Norfolk and Suffolk, where literally hundreds of such sites have been identified (Wade 2000). The reasons for the extreme scarcity of identified early Anglo-Saxon sites in Hertfordshire compared with other eastern counties, including neighbouring Cambridgeshire and, particularly, Suffolk and Norfolk, are not clear. Mortimer Wheeler (1935) argued for the existence of a 'sub-Roman' enclave focused on London and parts of the south-east, which survived the withdrawal of the Roman army and central government and remained under British political control during the fifth and part of the sixth century. The area included in his 'sub-Roman triangle', free from Germanic influence, has since been eroded by the discovery of numerous early Anglo-Saxon cemetery and some settlement sites, particularly in Essex; nevertheless, the northern part of the triangle, roughly equating to Hertfordshire and southern Buckinghamshire, remains strikingly clear of evidence of Germanic material culture (Baker 2006: 10–11). Some positive evidence for continuing British control within this area comes from excavations at Baldock in the 1980s that found evidence for multiple phases of fifth-century and later sub-Roman stratigraphy associated with distinctively sub-Roman pottery (Fitzpatrick-Matthews 2010, 2012). The Watton-at-Stone cemetery indicates the presence of Anglo-Saxon material culture and burial practice in this part of Hertfordshire by the later sixth or beginning of the seventh century. Although it is of highly dubious value as a source for historical events, it is interesting to note that the Anglo-Saxon Chronicle records large territories in the Chilterns falling to the Saxons after the Battle of Bedcanford (usually presumed to be Bedford) in AD 571.

The early to middle Saxon evidence from the site has undoubtedly made a major contribution to the archaeology of this period within Hertfordshire. However, given the rarity of contemporary sites and the consequent lack of comparative pottery assemblages in the county it is difficult at this stage to place the site within a secure social and political context. It will, however, provide an important reference for future research when further contemporary sites are identified.

11.11 Acknowledgements

Pre-Construct Archaeology Ltd would like to thank Duncan Hawkins of CgMs Consulting for commissioning the work on behalf of Barratt Homes, North London. The staff of Barratt North London, in particular Peter Bloomfield, Andy Hunt, Ian Ritchie and Dave Talmadge, are to be thanked for their help and cooperation. Thanks also to Alison Tinniswood of the Historic Environment Unit, Hertfordshire County Council, for monitoring the fieldwork and for her help and advice during the course of the investigations. Thanks are due to the project manager Mark Hinman, who also coordinated the post-excavation programme. The author would like to thank all members of the post-excavation assessment team who have contributed to the post-excavation assessment and this report: Katie Anderson (Roman pottery), Barry Bishop (lithics), Nina Crummy (small finds), Val Fryer (environmental analysis), Sarah Percival (prehistoric pottery), Kevin Rielly (faunal remains), Dr Jean-Luc Schwenninger (Luminescence Dating Laboratory, Research Laboratory for Archaeology and the History of Art, University of Oxford), Lisa Snape (environmental processing), Berni Sudds (post-Roman pottery) and Aileen Tierney (cremated bone). Also many thanks to Josephine Brown and Hayley Baxter for their work on the illustrations in this report, Sandy Pullen for surveying and Strephon Duckering for photography. Finally thanks go to those who worked on site, whose contribution is greatly appreciated: Mark Beasley, Andy Brown, Karl Hanson, Richard Humphrey, Claire Jackson, Chris Montague, Lawrence Morgan-Sherbourne, Sandy Pullen, Gary Trimble and Matt Williams. This article was edited for publication by Katie Anderson and Tom Woolhouse.

11.12 References

Adamiec, G. and Aitken, M.J. (1998), 'Dose-rate conversion factors: new data', *Ancient TL*, 16, pp. 37–50.

Aitken, M.J. (1985), *Thermoluminescence Dating* (Orlando).

Anderson, S. (2003), 'Post-Roman pottery', in C. Gibson with J. Murray, 'An Anglo-Saxon settlement at Godmanchester, Cambridgeshire', *Anglo-Saxon Studies in Archaeology and History* 12, pp. 174–83.

Arnold, C.J. (1997), *An Archaeology of the Early Anglo-Saxon Kingdoms*, 2nd edn (London).

Baker, J.T. (2006), *Cultural Transition in the Chilterns and Essex Region, 350 AD to 650 AD*, Studies in Regional and Local History 4 (Hatfield).

Banerjee, D., Murray, A.S., Bøtter-Jensen, L. and Lang, A. (2001), 'Equivalent dose estimation using a single aliquot of polymineral fine grains', *Radiation Measurements* 33, pp. 73–94.

Blackmore, L. (2012), 'The pottery', in Cowie et al. (2012), pp. 226–56.

Blackmore, L. and Vince, A. (2008), 'Pottery supply', in Cowie and Blackmore (2008), pp. 153–6.

Blackmore, L. with Vince, A. (2008), 'Early Saxon wares', in Cowie and Blackmore (2008), pp. 176–93.

Blackmore, L. and Vince, A. (2012), 'Pottery', in Cowie t al. (2012), pp. 172–5.
Boddington, A. (1990) 'Models of Burial, Settlement and Worship: The Final Phase Reviewed', in E. Southworth (ed.), *Anglo-Saxon Cemeteries: a reappraisal* (Slough), pp. 177–99.
Bøtter-Jensen, L. (1988), 'The automated Riso TL dating reader system', *Nuclear Tracks and Radiation Measurements* 14, pp. 177–80.
Bøtter-Jensen, L. (1997), 'Luminescence techniques: instrumentation and methods', *Radiation Measurements* 27, pp. 749–68.
Bøtter-Jensen, L., Bulur, E., Duller, G.A.T. and Murray, A.S. (2000), 'Advances in luminescence instrument systems', *Radiation Measurements* 32, pp. 523–8.
Boyer, P. (2012), 'Assessment of Archaeological Investigations on Land at Station Road, Watton-at-Stone, Hertfordshire, SG14 3SH', Pre-Construct Archaeology Report 11189, unpublished report.
Boyer, P. (forthcoming), 'Archaeological watching brief and excavation at the former Council Depot, Mill Road, Hertford', *Hertfordshire Archaeology and History* 17.
Brisbane, M. (1981), 'Incipient markets for early Anglo-Saxon ceramics: variations in levels and modes of production', in H. Howard and E.L. Morris, *Production and Distribution: A Ceramic Viewpoint*, British Archaeological Reports International Series 120 (Oxford), pp. 229–42.
Brisbane, M. (1984), 'The inhumation pottery fabric analysis', in C. Hills, K. Penn and R. Rickett (eds), *The Anglo-Saxon Cemetery at Spong Hill, North Elmham, Part 3*, East Anglian Archaeology 21 (Norwich), pp. 29–32.
British Geological Survey (1979), *Legend for the 1:625,000 Geological Map of the United Kingdom (Solid Geology); Hertford* (Mansfield).
Brown, D. (1974), 'Problems of continuity', in T. Rowley (ed.), *Anglo-Saxon Settlements and Landscape*, British Archaeological Reports British Series 6 (Oxford), pp. 16–19.
Cotter, J.P. (2000), *Post-Roman Pottery from Excavations in Colchester, 1971–85*, Colchester Archaeological Report 7 (Colchester).
Cowie, R. and Blackmore, L. (2008) *Early and Middle Saxon Rural Settlement in the London Region*, Museum of London Archaeology Monograph 41 (London).
Cowie, R. and Blackmore, L. with Davis, A., Keily, J. and Rielly, K. (2002) *Lundenwic: Excavations in Middle Saxon London, 1987–2000*, Museum of London Archaeology Monograph 63 (London).
Cra'ster, M.D. (1961), 'The Aldwick Iron Age settlement, Barley, Hertfordshire', *Proceedings of the Cambridge Antiquarian Society* 54, pp. 22–46.
Crummy, N. (2007), 'Grave and pyre goods from the cremation burials', in Gibson (2007), pp. 238–350, p. 265.
Crummy, N. (2010), 'Bears and coins: the iconography of protection in late Roman infant burials', *Britannia* 41, pp. 37–93.
Curnow, P. (1985), 'The Roman coins', in S. West, *West Stow, the Anglo-Saxon village*, East Anglian Archaeology 24 (Ipswich), pp. 76–81.
Darvill, T. (2002), 'White on Blonde: quartz pebbles and the use of quartz at Neolithic monuments in the Isle of Man and beyond', in A. Jones and G. MacGregor (eds), *Colouring the Past: the significance of colour in archaeological research* (Oxford), pp. 73–93.
Denham, V. (1985a), 'The Saxon pottery', in H. Bamford, *Briar Hill: Excavation 1974–1978*, Northampton Development Corporation Archaeological Monograph 3 (Northampton), pp. 122–4 and microfiche.
Denham, V. (1985b), 'The Saxon pottery', in J.H. Williams, M. Shaw and V. Denham, *Middle Saxon Palaces at Northampton*, Northampton Development Corporation Archaeological Monograph 4 (Northampton), pp. 46–62.

Dickens, A., Mortimer, R. and Tipper, J. (2005), 'The early Anglo-Saxon settlement and cemetery at Bloodmoor Hill, Carlton Colville, Suffolk: a preliminary report', *Anglo-Saxon Studies in Archaeology and History* 13, pp. 63–79.

Drinkall, G. and Foreman, M. (1998), *The Anglo-Saxon Cemetery at Castledyke South, Barton-on-Humber*, Sheffield Excavation Reports 6 (Sheffield).

Evison, V. (1994), *An Anglo-Saxon Cemetery at Great Chesterford, Essex*, Council for British Archaeology Research Report 91 (York).

Fitzpatrick-Matthews, K.J. (2010), 'The experience of "small towns": utter devastation, slow fading or business as usual?' Paper presented at *AD 410. The End of Roman Britain*, conference held at The British Museum, 13 March 2010.

Fitzpatrick-Matthews, K.J. (2012), 'Defining fifth-century ceramics in North Hertfordshire', paper presented at *Roman Pottery in the Fifth Century AD*, conference held at Newcastle University, 7 June 2012.

Garrow, D. (2006), *Pits, Settlement and Deposition during the Neolithic and Early Bronze Age in East Anglia*, British Archaeological Reports British Series 414 (Oxford).

Garrow, D., Lucy, S. and Gibson, D. (2006), *Excavations at Kilverstone, Norfolk: an episodic landscape history*, East Anglian Archaeology 113 (Cambridge).

Gibson, C. (2007) 'Minerva: an early Anglo-Saxon mixed-rite cemetery in Alwalton, Cambridgeshire', *Anglo-Saxon Studies in Archaeology and History* 14, pp. 238–50.

Hamerow, H. (1987), 'Anglo-Saxon settlement pottery and spatial development at Mucking, Essex', *Berichten van de Rijksdienst voor bet Oudheidkundig Bodemondersock* 37, pp. 245–73.

Hamerow, H. (1993), *Excavations at Mucking 2: the Anglo-Saxon settlement. Excavations by M.U. Jones and W.T. Jones*, English Heritage Archaeological Report 21 (London).

Hill, P.V. and Kent, J.P.C. (1972), 'Part 1: the bronze coinage of the House of Constantine AD 324–346', in R.A.G. Carson, P.V. Hill and J.P.C. Kent, *Late Roman Bronze Coinage* (London), pp. 4–40.

Hines, J. (1984), *The Scandinavian character of Anglian England in the pre-Viking period*, British Archaeological Reports British Series 124 (Oxford).

Hinman, M. (2004), *Neolithic, Bronze Age and Iron Age Activity on Land Adjacent to Hauxton Road, Trumpington, Cambridge. Post Excavation Assessment of Evaluation and Excavation at Trumpington Park and Ride*, Cambridgeshire County Council Archaeological Field Unit Report 706 (unpublished report).

Hyslop, M. (1963), 'Two Anglo-Saxon cemeteries at Chamberlains Barn, Leighton Buzzard, Bedfordshire', *Archaeological Journal* 120, pp. 161–200.

Kiln, R.J. and Partridge, C.R. (1994), *Ware and Hertford. The story of two towns from birth to middle age* (Welwyn Garden City).

King, M.D. (1988), 'Roman coins from Anglo-Saxon contexts', in P.J. Casey and R. Reece (eds), *Coins and the Archaeologist*, 2nd edn (London), pp. 224–9.

Laidlaw, M. (1996), 'Pottery', in P. Andrews and A. Crockett, *Three Excavations along the Thames and its Tributaries, 1994: Neolithic to Saxon settlement and burial in the Thames, Colne and Kennet valleys*, Wessex Archaeological Report 10 (Salisbury), pp. 81–91.

Lamdin-Whymark, H. (2008), *The Residues of Ritualised Action: Neolithic depositional practices in the Middle Thames Valley*, British Archaeological Reports British Series 466 (Oxford).

McKinley, J.I. (1994), *The Anglo-Saxon Cemetery at Spong Hill, North Elmham. Part VIII: the cremations*, East Anglian Archaeology 69 (Dereham).

Maher, S. (2011), *Land at St Johns Street, Hertford, Hertfordshire, SG14 1RX: An Assessment of an Evaluation and Watching Brief*, Pre-Construct Archaeology Report 11057 (unpublished).

Matthews, C.L. and Chadwick-Hawkes, S. (1985), 'Early Saxon settlements and burials on Puddlehill, near Dunstable, Bedfordshire', *Anglo-Saxon Studies in Archaeology and History* 4, pp. 59–115.

Matthews, K.J. and Burleigh, G.R. (1989), 'A Saxon and early medieval settlement at Green Lane, Letchworth', *Hertfordshire's Past* 26, pp. 27–31.

Meaney, A.L. (1964), *Gazetteer of Early Anglo-Saxon Burial Sites* (London).

Meaney, A.L. (1981), *Anglo-Saxon Amulets and Curing Stones*, British Archaeological Report British Series 96 (Oxford).

Meaney, A.L. and Hawkes, S.C. (1970), *Two Anglo-Saxon Cemeteries at Winnall, Winchester, Hampshire*, Society for Medieval Archaeology Monograph 4 (London).

Medlycott, M. (2011), *The Roman Town of Great Chesterford*, East Anglian Archaeology 137 (Chelmsford).

Mejdahl, V. (1979), 'Thermoluminescence dating: beta-dose attenuation in quartz grains', *Archaeometry* 21, pp. 61–72.

Moss-Eccardt, J. (1971), 'An Anglo-Saxon cemetery at Blackhorse Road, Letchworth, Hertfordshire', *Bedfordshire Archaeological Journal* 6, pp. 27–32.

Murray, A.S. and Wintle, A.G. (2000), 'Luminescence dating of quartz using an improved single-aliquot regenerative-dose protocol', *Radiation Measurements* 32, pp. 57–73.

Myres, J.N.L. (1969), *Anglo-Saxon Pottery and the Settlement of England* (Oxford).

Myres, J.N.L. (1977), *A Corpus of Anglo-Saxon Pottery of the Pagan Period* (Cambridge).

O'Brien, L. with Doel, P. (2005), *Excavations at Harston Mill, Harston, Cambridgeshire. An Archaeological Excavation Interim Site Narrative*. Archaeological Solutions Report 1634 (unpublished report).

O'Brien, L. with Allen, M., Cowgill, J., Crummy, N., Gale, R., Guest, P., Jones, R., Last, J., Mills, P., Peachey, A., Phillips, C., Riddler, I., Scaife, R., Sudds, B., Thompson, P., Tingle, M. and Waldron,† T. (forthcoming), *Blood, Seeds and Soil: Bronze Age, Iron Age and Anglo-Saxon settlement and burial at Harston Mill, Cambridgeshire*, East Anglian Archaeology.

Page, W. (ed.) (1902), *VCH Hertfordshire*, vol. 1 (London).

Partridge, C. (1989), *Foxholes Farm: A Multi-Period Gravel Site* (Hertford).

Percival, S. (2012), 'Appendix 3: Prehistoric Pottery Assessment', in Boyer (2012), pp. 80–83.

Perry, G.J. (2011), 'Beer, butter and burial: the pre-burial origins of cremation urns from the early Anglo-Saxon cemetery of Cleatham, North Lincolnshire', *Medieval Ceramics* 32, pp. 9–22.

Phillips, M. (2009), *Four Millennia of Human Activity Along the A505 Baldock Bypass, Hertfordshire*, East Anglian Archaeology 128 (Bedford).

Prescott, J.R. and Hutton, J.T. (1994), 'Cosmic ray contributions to dose rates for luminescence and ESR dating: large depths and long-term time variations', *Radiation Measurements* 23, pp. 497–500.

Richards, J.D. (1987), *The Significance of Form and Decoration of Anglo-Saxon Cremation Urns*, British Archaeological Reports British Series 166 (Oxford).

Saville, A. (1980), 'On the measurement of struck flakes and flake tools', *Lithics* 1, pp. 16–20.

Smith, L. (2008), *Land at Station Road, Watton-at-Stone, Hertfordshire: An Archaeological Evaluation*, Archaeological Solutions Report 3181 (unpublished report).

SSEW (Soil Survey of England and Wales) (1983), *Soils of Eastern England (Sheet 4)* (Harpenden).

Stoodley, N. (2007), 'New perspectives on cemetery relocation in the seventh century AD: the example of Portway, Andover', *Anglo-Saxon Studies in Archaeology and History* 14, pp. 154–62.

Sudds, B. (2005), 'The Saxon pottery', in J. Murray with T. McDonald, 'An Anglo-Saxon settlement at Gamlingay, Cambridgeshire', *Anglo-Saxon Studies in Archaeology and History* 13, pp. 173–330, pp. 213–22.
Sudds, B. (2007), 'Vessels from the cremation and inhumation graves', in Gibson, pp. 238–350, pp. 255–61.
Sudds, B. (forthcoming a), 'The Saxon pottery', in Boyer (forthcoming).
Sudds, B. (forthcoming b), 'Saxon pottery', in I. Bright, 'Evidence of a Late Iron Age enclosure on land at Buntingford (between London Road & the A10 Bypass)', *Hertfordshire Archaeology and History.*
Thomas, J. (1999), *Understanding the Neolithic: a revised second edition of rethinking the Neolithic* (London).
Tierney, A. (2012), 'Appendix 8: Cremated Bone Assessment', in Boyer (2012), pp. 93–4.
Tyler, S. (2005), 'Discussion of the grave- and pyre-goods: Pottery', in Tyler and Major (2005), pp. 117–22.
Tyler, S. and Major, H. (2005), *The Early Anglo-Saxon Cemetery and Later Saxon Settlement at Springfield Lyons, Essex*, East Anglian Archaeology 111 (Chelmsford).
Wade, K. (2000), 'Anglo-Saxon and Medieval (Rural)', in N. Brown and J. Glazebrook (eds), *Research and Archaeology: a Framework for the Eastern Counties, 2. Research Agenda and Strategy*, East Anglian Archaeology Occasional Paper 8 (Norwich), pp. 23–6.
Wade, K. (2009), 'Pottery vessels', in C. Scull, *Early Medieval (Late 5th–Early 8th Centuries AD) Cemeteries at Boss Hall and Buttermarket, Ipswich, Suffolk*, Society for Medieval Archaeology Monograph 27 (Leeds), p. 109.
Walton Rogers, P. (2007), *Cloth and Clothing in Early Anglo-Saxon England, AD 450–700*, Council for British Archaeology Research Report 145 (York).
Wheeler, R.E.M. (1935), *London and the Saxons* (London).
Wintle, A.G. and Murray, A.S. (2006), 'A review of quartz optically stimulated luminescence characteristics and their relevance in single-aliquot regeneration dating protocols', *Radiation Measurements* 41, pp. 369–91.
Zimmerman, D.W. (1971), 'Thermoluminescent dating using fine grains from pottery', *Archaeometry* 13, pp. 29–50.

Notes

1 Throughout this paper archaeological context numbers for cuts are given in square brackets thus: [301], and fills are indicated by normal parentheses: (260). As part of the post-excavation process contexts are joined into stratigraphic 'groups' which are also numbered.

CHAPTER 12

Hertfordshire hundreds: names and places

John Baker

12.1 Introduction

From the time that the Anglo-Saxons started to write down their laws, and as far as we know from the very beginning of the Anglo-Saxon period, governance in England was carried out at public assemblies, described variously as *mæþel*, *þing* or *(ge)mōt* (Abt 1; Hl 10; Hu; Liebermann 1903: 3, 10, 192; Whitelock 1979: 391, 395, 429–30). These were the venues for, among other matters, the resolution of disputes and the administration of justice, and they served communities that were, presumably, rooted within well-established territories. We know that by the tenth century such districts and their courts at one level were called hundreds (or wapentakes in parts of England subject to especially intense Scandinavian influence), that they met every four weeks, normally in the open air, and that all freemen were required to attend. They were the cornerstone of English judicial administration and part of an administrative hierarchy that included the shires themselves, which held their own twice-yearly moots. In many cases, hundredal courts were probably already the focus for a wide range of other financial, social, economic and political activities: collection of tax revenues, military mustering, the buying and selling of goods and chattels and so on (Anderson 1939b: 184, 213–14; Pantos 2004: 166–70; Baker 2014). Thus the study of these districts and in particular their meeting places can shed light on the evolution of early medieval English governance, the nature of Anglo-Saxon socio-political interaction and the development of an administrative geography that survived in modified form into the modern period. This paper addresses such themes with particular reference to three of Hertfordshire's medieval hundreds (Fig. 12.1) and by considering some of the place-name evidence for public assembly in the landscape and for the types of activity that took place at such gatherings.

In fact it is only with the compilation of the Domesday survey in 1086 that we get a reasonably detailed picture of this administrative structure. In Domesday Book, shires are divided into hundreds or wapentakes, the number of which can vary significantly from shire to shire. For the present analysis, three key pieces of information become available in a systematic way from this time: the vills included in each hundred; the hidage values of the hundreds; and, of course, their names. The first two of these are important in establishing the size and shape of the districts, but the third is of great significance in identifying the sites of public gatherings, since most hundreds seem to have been named after the chief manor of the district or after the site at which hundredal assemblies took place. By identifying these sites we are able better to analyse them and their environs archaeologically and toponymically, so this third piece of information is also crucial in understanding the activities that took place at such sites and their evolving role in the judicial, administrative and social lives of the hundreds. Beyond the hundred names themselves, a number of other place-names are indicative of public assembly, and these may sometimes also preserve evidence of the locations where the freemen of the hundreds met. In some instances the names of meeting places or the microtoponymy of their immediate surroundings can reveal a great deal about the types of activity that took place there; sometimes simply locating the site of meetings allows a better appreciation of the way in which hundredal territories were created. A close examination of the Hertfordshire hundreds and their meeting places may help us towards a better understanding of the evolutionary processes behind the Domesday shire.

This article explores some of the ways in which place-names, when used alongside the evidence from other disciplines, can contribute to our understanding of the administrative geography of medieval Hertfordshire in two important areas. Firstly, they can help in locating the places where hundredal assemblies took place, especially in cases where this is a question of some complexity; secondly, they can help in identifying other meeting places that appear to have existed outside the hundredal system as it appears at the time of Domesday, and in exploring the possible origins of these sites. It will then discuss the implications of this evidence and its significance for our understanding of the development of the shire. In Hertfordshire we are fortunate that various studies have helped to identify and contextualise the hundred meeting places (notably the various volumes of the *Victoria County History*; Gover *et al.* 1938; Anderson 1939b, 25–33; Meaney 1994; 1997; Williamson 2010), but detailed and focused analysis can still refine widely accepted interpretations and address a number of unanswered questions about the processes behind the selection of assembly sites.

12.2 Locating hundred meeting places

The locations of some hundred meeting places are, on the face of it, easy to identify, especially when a hundred was apparently named from the site at which meetings took place. Broadwater hundred, for instance, met near the point where the road from London to Baldock was joined by that from Hertford—a place still known as Broadwater and recorded as *Bradwater Asshe* in 1390, when the sheriff's tourn was held there (Anderson 1939b: 27–8). By this time, and indeed already in the eleventh century, a large part of the judicial business of the hundred was dealt with at what became known as the sheriff's tourn, a biannual meeting of the full hundred (Jewell 1972: 49–50, 163; Loyn 1984: 147; Warren 1987: 203–4), so that, although it need not have taken place at the

Figure 12.1: Hertfordshire's hundredal geography at the time of Domesday, with the location of sites named in the text. 1. Broadwater; 2. Odsey; 3. Wickham Hill; 4. Edwinstree; 5. Spellbrook; 6. Wakeley; 7. Plaistowes; 8. Metley Hill; 9. The Frith; 10. Segham Assh. Drawn by Stuart Brookes. SRTM: <http://www2.jpl.nasa.gov/srtm/>; UCL Landscapes of Governance.

traditional hundred meeting place, it seems likely that in practice it often did. In this instance, then, both place-name and documentary evidence point to a single site. Such clear identifications are not invariably to be expected, however, and are not always straightforward. The meeting place of Odsey hundred in northern Hertfordshire, for example, is likely to have been in the vicinity of Odsey in Guilden Morden parish, which is on the Icknield Way (Anderson 1939b: 25–7; Meaney 1994: 82–3); yet Guilden Morden is in Cambridgeshire, rather than Hertfordshire, which raises interesting questions about the choice of meeting-place. Three specific difficulties that confront attempts to identify hundred meeting places in Hertfordshire and elsewhere are exemplified by Edwinstree, *Daneis* and Braughing.

12.2.1 Edwinstree hundred

In some cases the feature that gave its name to a hundred has since disappeared or ceased to be known by that name, so the name of the hundred has effectively disappeared on the ground, along with the best means of securely identifying its meeting place. Trees, mounds and stone monuments, all common meeting place markers, are especially vulnerable to destruction or removal over time. This is the case with Edwinstree hundred (*Edwinestrev hvnd'* 1086; Anderson 1939b: 33) in eastern Hertfordshire, the name of which, meaning 'Edwin's tree', does not survive as a local toponym to the present day and is not closely located in the historical record. Identification of the site relies on the triangulation of circumstantial evidence. Firstly, a *boscum de Edwynebrugge* is mentioned in an Assize Roll of 1278 (Anderson 1939b: 33; Page 1914: 3),[1] either in Brent or Furneux Pelham. Anderson noted that the hundred of Edwinstree was mentioned in the same roll, and thought it likely that both places took their first element from the same person and were close together. Since the hundred was called *Eddiford* in the time of Henry VI (Gover *et al.* 1938: 169), a closer equation of the two names seems reasonable. Place-names in *ford* sometimes interchange with names in *brycg*, and it is also of course conceivable that the river was crossed here at various times by both a ford and a bridge. In Furneux Pelham a field adjacent to Violets Lane was known in modern times as Meeting Field (Fig. 12.2), and it has been suggested that *Eddiford* was the ford on the Ash in Violets Lane (Gover *et al.* 1938: 168–9; Williamson 2010: 113).

The situation is complicated, however, by the existence of a place-name Mutfords (*terra de Mutforde* t. Ed 3, *cf.* Richard de *Mutford* 1327) about four kilometres to the west, in Little Hormead (Anderson 1939b: 33; Gover *et al.* 1938: 180). Since it occurs only in late spellings, the final *s* of the name is probably pseudo-manorial – added to the name due to a misinterpretation of Mutford as

Figure 12.2: Edwinstree, showing Meeting Field, Mutfords and Hare Street. Drawn by Stuart Brookes. © Crown Copyright and Landmark Information Group Limited (2013). All rights reserved (1876–7).

a family name rather than a toponym – so this is almost certainly an instance of Old English (OE): *(ge)mōt-ford*: 'assembly ford'. If the two sites were a little closer together it would be easy to assume they both referred to meetings at the same spot, but they are sufficiently distant to make such an assumption awkward at best. An alternative solution is to view *(ge)mōt-ford* as 'the ford on the way to the meeting place', but this seems unsatisfactory. In the first place, presumably a number of other fords on the way to the meeting might have been labelled in the same way; and, secondly, OE *(ge)mōt* place-names often seem to denote a feature at the actual site of assembly, such as a mound (OE *(ge)mōt-hlāw* or *beorg*). The existence of two meeting places within four kilometres of each other and within the same hundred requires a better explanation.

The misleading toponym in this instance may in fact be Meeting Field. Meeting House field names often commemorate the presence of nonconformist chapels (Field 1993: 200), and it is worth noting that Meeting Field in Long Melford, Suffolk (almost on the Essex county boundary), is near to Independent and Methodist chapels (first edition Ordnance Survey County Series 1:2500 Suffolk, 1886), Meeting Green in Wickhambrook is next to a Congregational chapel (first edition Ordnance Survey County Series 1:2500 Suffolk, 1885, sheet 33053101) and The Meetings (Farm) in Little Tew (Oxfordshire) is probably also associated with nonconformity.[2] In Furneux Pelham a Primitive Methodist Chapel is shown directly to the south of the junction of The Street and Violets Lane, and therefore close to Meeting Field. Accepting that occasional reuse, conscious or otherwise, of earlier sites of assembly by nonconformist congregations is a possibility, it is nevertheless clearly problematic to assume that the gatherings recalled in such place-names were necessarily judicial. Meeting Field is in any case a modern place-name – indeed, Meaney (1994: 75) notes its absence from the enclosure and tithe maps of Furneux Pelham – and may well owe its existence to the local Methodist congregation rather than an earlier hundredal moot.

Although the vills of Furneux and Brent Pelham are mentioned in connection with 'the wood of *Edwynesbrugg*', the precise location of the latter is unknown (Page 1914: 3). If 'Edwin's Bridge' was an alternative name for 'Edwin's Ford', it may have been a reference to the hundred rather than the river-crossing itself.[3] In that case, it is unnecessary to assume that the wood in question was immediately adjacent to 'Edwin's Bridge', and, while it is likely to have been close to the Pelhams, it need not have been located entirely within the bounds of the modern parishes of Furneux or Brent Pelham. The westernmost boundary of Furneux Pelham is still two kilometres away from Mutfords, but the wood might well have occupied the apex of the Ash/Quin interfluve, straddling that boundary. It is certainly conceivable that *Edwynesbrugge* was itself further to the west. There is, moreover, no certainty that the *Edwynestre* mentioned in an Assize Roll of the same date was actually in one of the Pelhams.

In the case of Edwinstree, the place-name evidence seems equivocal; but, when examined within a wider context, the modern place-name Meeting Field turns out not to be conclusive evidence for the location of a hundred meeting place on the river Ash near Violets Lane. Given that the evidence for associating *Eddiford* with a crossing of the Ash is also circumstantial, Mutfords – a place-name on record since the medieval period with an etymology clearly indicating the presence of assemblies – provides a much more likely location for the hundred moot. A better interpretation might therefore be to take *Edwynesbrugge* and the recorded hundred name *Eddiford* to be references to a single crossing of the river Quin or of Little Hormead Brook, and **(ge)mōtford,* 'assembly ford', surviving in the modern place-name Mutfords, to refer also to one of those crossings. Edwinstree must then have been nearby, and the hundred meeting place would have been close to the road running north from Braughing to Barkway. About a mile away is the settlement known as Hare Street. This place-name goes back to OE *here-strǣt* or 'army road', and indicates the presence of an important routeway, perhaps the road from Braughing itself (Gover *et al.* 1938: 179–80). Finally, a tumulus called Bummers Hill, marked a short distance to the north of Mutfords,[4] might have provided a convenient platform for pronouncements – such features are often associated with hundred meeting places (Anderson 1934: xxxiii–xxxiv, 1939b: 192–3, 197–8; Adkins and Petchey 1984; Meaney 1997: 212–16).

12.2.2 *Segham Assh*

In the case of the Domesday hundred of *Daneis*, later known as Dacorum, the name of the hundred seems not to provide a clue to the location of its meeting place. It is traditionally taken to be the Middle English (ME) word *Daneis*, 'a Dane' or 'Danes' (Kurath *et al.* 1956–2001, *sub* Daneis), with the post-Conquest name simply a Latin rendering based on the misapprehension that Dacians were to be identified with Danes (Skeat 1904: 69; Gover *et al.* 1938: 25). The name thus apparently describes the Danish nature of the hundred (the justification for which is unclear and beyond the bounds of the present discussion), rather than making reference to the place where assemblies were held. Identification of that site, therefore, has to rely on other sources.

Fowler (1890–91: 17–18) raised the idea that meetings of Tring hundred and then Dacorum (which eventually absorbed some of the vills formerly in Tring) were held at the Frith (*le Fryth* 1291; cf. Gover *et al.* 1938: 28) on Berkhamsted Common, the name of which he derived from OE *friþ*, 'peace, protection'. In a sense, the location would have been suitable for this, since Berkhamsted Common was probably close to the boundary between *Daneis* and Tring hundreds, but Fowler's assertion is unhelpful as far as the Domesday or early post-Conquest meeting place of *Daneis* is concerned. Soon after the Norman Conquest William I created the Honour of Berkhamsted, drastically reducing the jurisdiction of Tring hundred (Page 1902: 234–45). Although recorded references to that hundred continue to 1191, the Honour of Berkhamsted was, at least in the thirteenth century, referred to as a hundred in its own right (1230×1294; Anderson 1939b: 29) and the Frith was presumably not part of Dacorum until the end of the thirteenth century at the earliest – indeed, Fowler (perhaps following Clutterbuck 1815: 276 and Skeat 1904: 69) believed this merger to have taken place under Edward III in the fourteenth. Before that time *Daneis* seems most unlikely to have met at the Frith, and on these grounds Page (1902: 141–2) dismissed the identification. In any case, the range of early forms is more consistent with the etymology proposed by Gover *et al.* (1938: 28, 254), who take it to be OE *fyrhðe*, 'wooded land', rather than Fowler's *friþ*. A simplex place-name meaning 'peace' is anyway unlikely, and it was principally this second interpretation that led in the first place to Fowler's connection of the name with the peace-securing role of public assembly.

At present, the best suggested identification for the meeting place of *Daneis*/Dacorum is the lost place called *Segham Assh*.[5] This is where the sheriff's tourn was held, according to a record of March 1381, and, since the hundred was in royal hands, Page argued (quite reasonably) that the hundred court might have been held at the same place (Maxwell Lyte 1895: 608; Page 1902: 141–2 and n. 12). The bounds of Flamstead and of Wheathampstead (S 912; S 1031; Crick 2007: 178–89) mention a *secgham*, 'rushy hemmed-in land or water-meadow', which has been identified with seventeenth-century references to *(an Ashe Tree called) Segam ashe* and *(a laune called) segame laune*, probably located on Watling Street near to the present junction of the A5 and M1, on the edge of Harpenden and Redbourn parishes (Munby 1973: 4–6 and fig. 2; Rumble 1977: 9). The '*Ashe Tree called Segam ashe*' seems very likely to have stood on the same site as the fourteenth-century *Segham Assh*, whether or not the actual ash tree had been replaced in the intervening centuries; Munby (1973: 5–6) pointed out the appropriateness of this site as a hundred meeting place. Invaluable though Munby's careful work in locating *Segham Assh* is, it should nevertheless be noted that the site is that of the sheriff's tourn rather than the hundred moot. While the probability that the two events were held at the same venue is extremely high (the similar use of Broadwater has already been noted above), and the absence of a strong alternative for the *Daneis* meeting place compelling, a measure of caution is nevertheless required. Meetings at *Segham Assh* are not attested until 300 years after the Domesday survey, and an unequivocal link between the hundred of *Daneis* and this meeting place is therefore lacking.

12.2.3 Braughing

Hundreds consisting of a folk or district name are also potentially problematic, as are those apparently named from their chief manors. In the first case, the name of the folk or district might not provide specific enough information for the identity of the assembly site to be ascertained. In the second case, the traditional meeting-place may have been adjacent to or distant from the manorial centre. Anderson, for instance (1934: xxix–xxxi; 1939a: 79–80, 83–84, 86–88, 90–91, 92–99) showed that hundreds might bear more than one name, reflecting appurtenance to a central vill on the one hand, and location of meetings on the other, so that being named from a vill does not mean that a hundred also met at that location. In his examples, Ermington Hundred, so called from the royal vill of that name, was also in the eleventh century known as *Allerige* Hundred, presumably from its meeting-place (see also note 3); while the Domesday hundred of *Dippeford*, named from the royal vill of Diptford, came to be known from the twelfth century as Stanborough and held its meetings at Stanborough

Brake in the east of the hundred.[6] In other circumstances, both manor and meeting-place might take their names from the same landscape feature.

Braughing belongs to both of these difficult categories. It is an entirely reasonable assumption that the hundred of Braughing was named after the significant Domesday vill of the same name (Williamson 2010: 113), but the vill itself takes its name from what seems to have been a folk-group—the **Brahhingas* or 'people of *Brahha*' (Gover *et al.* 1938: 189).

In this instance, the meeting-place of the hundred can be identified by other means. Rowe and Williamson (2013: 65) take it to have been on Wickham Hill, site of a Romano-British small town just to the south-west of Braughing, where coin finds suggest continued use into the late medieval period. This location fits neatly with a range of place-name and topographical evidence — most obviously, of course, the fact that the hundred is called Braughing and might be expected to be close to the medieval settlement that bears the name. According to fourteenth-century Court Rolls (Page 1912: 291; Anderson 1939b: 33), the sheriff's tourn was at that time held at Puckeridge, perhaps indicating the location of the hundred's meetings. The settlement of Puckeridge is in the north of Standon parish and the present Braughing/Standon boundary runs over Wickham Hill. It is worth noting that it is not unusual for hundred meeting-places to be close to parish boundaries (Pantos 2003). This alone would probably explain the reference to Puckeridge. However, although the settlement of Puckeridge lies along the Puckeridge Tributary which feeds into the Rib north of Standon, its name (*Pucherugge* 1294; Gover *et al.* 1938: 198) means 'goblin ridge' (OE *pūca* + *hrycg*).[7] It is possible that the referent is the raised strip running north from Puckeridge and west of the River Rib, along which the Standon/Braughing parish boundary runs and of which Wickham Hill occupies the northern section. In other words, Wickham Hill might well have been the northern end of the ridge described in the name Puckeridge. Short (1987) has demonstrated that Braughing and Standon were probably originally part of a single administrative unit, perhaps the earlier territory of the **Brahhingas*. The fact that their mutual boundary runs over Wickham Hill suggests, as Williamson (2010: 126–28) observes, that the former Roman town was a focal point for this folk group. Although the first reference to meetings at Puckeridge is late, it might preserve an earlier tradition echoing the examples of *Allerige* and *Dippeford* in Devon, where meetings took place on Puckeridge but the hundred was also named after its chief vill of Braughing; or indeed after the folk-group that traditionally occupied this part of Hertfordshire.

However, Gover *et al.* (1938: 189) suggest that the meetings of Braughing hundred were 'at or near Braughing, possibly at Ford Bridge'. Ford Bridge (so-called at least since 1606) is where the road heading south-west from

Braughing crosses the river Rib, but Gover *et al.* cite no basis for its association with meetings of the hundred. They may, however, have been guided by a thirteenth-century form *Brachingeford*, which they connect with Ford Bridge, and which might suggest that this was originally 'the ford of the **Brahhingas*' (Gover *et al.* 1938: 191 n. 1). The name alone is not proof that hundred meetings were ever held at Ford Bridge, but there is a direct parallel with nearby Armingford hundred in Cambridgeshire, named from 'the ford of the **Earningas*', probably Arrington Bridge (Anderson 1934: 104). In the latter case Arrington Bridge is thought to have been the hundred meeting place, even though microtoponymic evidence shows that other places within the hundred also had a tradition of hosting assembly, perhaps at a different period (Meaney 1994: 70; Reaney 1943: 50–51; Cam 1963 [1930]: 172). Ford Bridge is approximately 500m from the Standon/Braughing boundary on Wickham Hill, and might well have formed part of the landscape of assembly here – contemporaneously with Wickham Hill or not. In other words, Braughing assemblies may have made use of a more extensive zone incorporating Wickham Hill and Ford Bridge, or meetings may have taken place at the two separate sites at different times.[8]

12.2.4 Discussion

Locating with precision the sites at which hundredal assembly took place can be extremely challenging. Indeed, since the approximate location of several of these hundred moots has long been known, this detailed analysis of the evidence for locating them might seem unnecessarily pedantic – how much difference to our understanding of Hertfordshire's administrative evolution does it make, for example, to place the meetings of Edwinstree a few kilometres to the west of Meeting Field? In answer to this it can be said that the more precisely we can locate such meetings the better our chances of understanding how landscape was used as part of the judicial process, what variety of functions took place at assembly sites and how the meeting places of Hertfordshire compare with those in neighbouring counties and in other parts of the country. To take a very simple example, Odsey, which gave its name to Odsey hundred, is located at the foot of Gallows Hill (*Gallowhill* 1676; Gover *et al.* 1938: 160). Because the location of the hundred meeting place is relatively accurately defined, it is not unreasonable to suppose that Gallows Hill was a topographically prominent place of execution associated with the judicial functions of Odsey, at least from the early modern period.

In the case of Edwinstree, the proposed alternative site of judicial assemblies may provide an invaluable insight into the way that meeting places evolved as foci for more than just judicial functions. Somewhere within Great Hormead parish, and perhaps in the vicinity of Hare Street, was the place known as *Langeport*

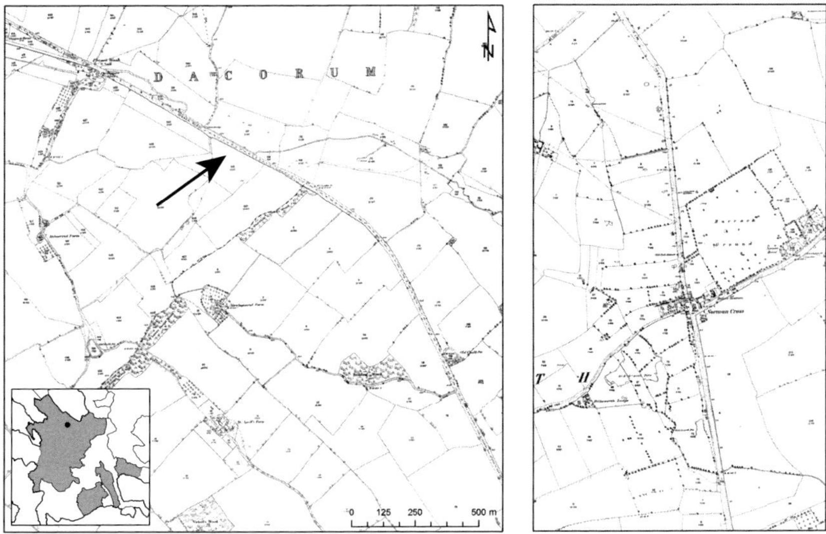

Figure 12.3: Comparison of the location of *Segham Assh* and Normancross hundred meeting places. Drawn by Stuart Brookes. © Crown Copyright and Landmark Information Group Limited (2013). All rights reserved. (1876–7)

(Gover *et al.* 1938: 179–80). This is a recurrent place-name compound meaning 'long market-place'. Ekwall (1936: 180–82) drew attention to the select group of *Langport* place-names (only eleven survive as major names or are recorded in or before Domesday), suggesting that they were periodically used markets consisting of rows of booths stretching out along a main road. This, he argued, would explain their occasional occurrence well away from major centres and the fact that so many of them seem to have disappeared. Although the compound is relatively rare in place-names, it is notable that at least six (seven, if Edwinstree met near Mutfords) can be directly associated with hundred meeting places (Baker 2014: 1499). The presence of a periodically used assembly site may well have been an important stimulus for the appearance of markets of this kind. The co-existence of markets and meeting places is otherwise not frequently attested, although a notable coincidence of meeting places and towns, especially town gates, may hint at it (Baker 2014: 1499–1501; Baker and Brookes 2014),[9] and by the late tenth century the buying of livestock had to be witnessed either by the borough or the hundred (IV Eg 10; Liebermann 1903: 212; Whitelock 1979: 436). This juxtaposition of assembly sites such as Edwinstree and occasional markets therefore adds to our picture of the nature of hundred meeting places and the propensity for commercial activities to arise in the vicinity of a small number of them.

At a wider level this detailed re-evaluation is crucial if further analysis of the characteristics of assembly sites is to be undertaken in order to refine and extend our understanding of site-types and to build on the important work of Meaney (1997), Pantos (2002) and others. Edwinstree, positioned near to Mutfords, falls into a very large category of meeting places located beside major routeways – in this case perhaps a road known as *here-strǣt* – and may, like many similar sites, have made use of a tumulus as a marker or an element of the ceremonial topography of the site (Baker and Brookes 2015). Odsey and *Segham Assh* may belong to the same category. The latter finds a very close parallel in the meeting place of Normancross hundred in Huntingdonshire (Fig. 12.3). Both are located next to Roman roads and are very close to major realignments of those routeways, a feature that perhaps aided recognition of the meeting location. The characteristic of close proximity to a major road might be thought a natural feature of meeting places, but is not shared by all; and many such sites are not situated centrally to their districts – Odsey being a prime example. It is conceivable that such sites were selected not by locals but by a higher authority determined to choose locations most convenient for officials. Location of sites such as *Segham Assh* and Normancross next to marked changes in the topography of major arterial routeways may indeed suggest that they were being made distinctive and easily identifiable to people travelling longer distances along those roads, rather than to locals with a more nuanced appreciation of local terrain. In the case of Edwinstree, the location of that meeting place in the portion of the hundred that seems, earlier, to have been part of the Braughing estate (Short 1987: esp. maps 1 and 3) may be further evidence of late reorganisation of the administrative geography.

Braughing poses more complicated problems. If Wickham Hill was indeed the early focus of the people called the **Brahhingas* and later served as the meeting place of the hundred that bore their name, it provides an important glimpse of the *longue durée* of some local assembly sites, connecting the judicial arrangements of late Anglo-Saxon and post-Conquest Hertfordshire with much earlier administrative or even 'tribal' arrangements. In that context, it should perhaps be compared with other pre-English sites that served a similar purpose – Badbury and Eggardon in Dorset, Borough Hill in Fawsley hundred, Northamptonshire, and so on – where the placement of assembly within ancient enclosures may have been part of a deliberate assertion of legitimacy and association with earlier structures of authority (Baker and Brookes forthcoming). On the other hand, the occurrence of a possible **Brahhingaford* (Ford Bridge) and the tantalising possibility that this too was a focus of hundredal moots, potentially finding a parallel in nearby Armingford, casts the hundred in a slightly different light. Ford Bridge would easily fall into the category of roadside meeting places discussed above; but its proximity to both Wickham Hill and Braughing minster might bear comparison with another group of similarly configured sites where the location of the meeting place just outside a centre of power probably helped to delineate different zones of jurisdiction and to articulate power relationships (Baker and Brookes 2014). In any case, it is noteworthy that, while the nucleus of settlement and presumably the administrative centre of gravity in Braughing moved to the site of the minster, a tradition of assembly at the old tribal centre, which was perhaps specifically thought of as relating to the **Brahhingas*, may have been preserved into the late medieval period. The hundred arrangements in this instance may, therefore, reflect a much earlier organisation of local administrative geography – that of an early or middle Anglo-Saxon folk-grouping centred on a Roman and pre-Roman settlement, perhaps even the successor of a Romano-British territory based on Braughing. In Hertfordshire, it is worth noting that Hitchin half hundred seems to have similar origins as part of the territory of the Tribal Hidage *Hicce* (e.g., Friel 1982).

12.3 Two non-hundredal meeting places

The names of the Hertfordshire hundreds, as recorded in Domesday Book, are invaluable for identifying their meeting places for the very reason that the districts are often named after sites of assembly. However, place-names can help to identify additional meeting places commemorated by elements that refer to the act of assembly or to activities associated with the gathering of large groups of people. Such place-names may provide evidence of other systems of governance that existed at another time or occupied a different level of administration from the hundredal arrangements of late Anglo-Saxon England.

12.3.1 Spellbrook

A first example once again involves Braughing hundred. In the parish of Sawbridgeworth is a hamlet called Spellbrook, one of the 12 late medieval districts of the parish (Page 1912: 332–47). The name is first recorded as *Spelebrok* in 1287 and derives from OE *spell* 'speech' and *brōc* 'stream'. Gover *et al.* (1938: 195) note the possibility that meetings were held there at some time – that is, in the thirteenth century or earlier. Their slight caution is probably unnecessary given the evidence for the use of OE *spell* in connection with known assembly sites. It occurs as the first element in two relatively nearby hundred names – Spelthorne in Middlesex (Anderson 1939a: 56; Gover *et al.* 1942: 11) and Spelhoe in Northamptonshire (Gover *et al.* 1933: 131–2; Anderson 1934: 122). It also occurs several times in minor place-names located close to probable hundred meeting places. It is compounded with OE *beorg* in the names of Sperberry Hill, St Ippolitts, thought to have been the meeting place of Hitchin hundred (*Speleburwe* 1203; Gover *et al.* 1938: 14); Spelsbury Farm (*Spelsbury* 1773) in Wiltshire, adjacent to Dunworth Farm, which gave its name to Dunworth hundred (Gover *et al.* 1938: 14; 1939: 197–8); and Spelsbury Barn (*Spellborough* 1698) in Gloucestershire, just above Kiftsgate Court in Kiftsgate hundred (Smith 1964: 250). Although Spellbrook's compound of *spell* and *brōc* is unusual, it can be compared with Tingrith in Bedfordshire, a name derived from OE *þing* 'assembly' and *riþ* 'stream', referring to a brook that runs by the meeting place of Manshead hundred (Mawer and Stenton 1926: 112–13, 134–5).

At the time of Domesday Sawbridgeworth and therefore, presumably, Spellbrook were in Braughing hundred, but the 'speech stream' cannot be connected with the meeting place of the hundred. In the eleventh century the vills that made up the hundred were grouped into two arms (Fig. 12.1). One of these was based on the Rib valley and constituted much of the reconstructed territory of the middle Anglo-Saxon estate of Braughing (Short 1987; Rowe and Williamson 2013: 64, fig. 3.4); the other occupied the north-west part of the Stort valley. The two branches joined at their south-western ends but were separated for most of their lengths by the valley of the river Ash, most of which was within the southern salient of Edwinstree hundred.[10] As discussed above, the meeting place of Braughing hundred was in the vicinity of Puckeridge, fairly high up the Rib valley, while Spellbrook is close to the northern tip of the Stort branch.

The context for the assembly site commemorated in the name of Spellbrook may help uncover its original purpose. The stream referred to by the name runs from Thorley into the Stort, which it joins opposite Wallbury hillfort. The Stort here forms the boundary between Hertfordshire and Essex, and is crossed by Spellbrook bridge. There has been a crossing here at least since the end of the fourteenth century (Powell *et al.* 1983: 113–24) and the river could be forded just two kilometres upstream at Twyford, so it is possible that it was fordable near Spellbrook from early times. Spellbrook might therefore be close to an important early crossing of the Stort and passage between Hertfordshire and Essex, and might have been an early shire or multiple-shire meeting place, perhaps used for more important judicial business, or for the mustering of substantial forces. Other place-names in OE *spell* are known to occupy similar positions between hundreds and shires; for instance, *Spelbeorhge* (another instance of *spell-beorg*), from an admittedly spurious eleventh-century charter (Sawyer 1968: no. 907), lies adjacent to Ring Hill Camp, at the boundaries of Cambridgeshire, Essex and Hertfordshire (Reaney 1935: 530 n. 1; Hesse 1994: 135–7). *Spelbeorhge* seems likely, therefore, to have served as a place of assembly for a district that was not one of the late Anglo-Saxon hundreds, and might even have been supra-hundredal, consisting of three different shires. Spellbrook might occupy a similar administrative position.

On the other hand, the boundary between Essex and Hertfordshire as it stands may well be a construct of a later period. If medieval diocesan boundaries are a good guide to early political units, as is widely accepted, then the kingdom of the East Saxons incorporated the eastern edge of Hertfordshire (Short 1987: 10; Williamson 2010: 90–100); and, in any case, it seems likely that the shires as outlined in the Domesday survey were a creation of the late Anglo-Saxon period (Taylor 1957: 24–5; Baker and Brookes 2013). In that case, Spellbrook cannot have been on the shire boundary before, perhaps, the tenth century.

At least two possible alternatives present themselves. It is conceivable that an earlier (pre-shire) territorial organisation included a territory based on the river Stort and centred on Wallbury, with judicial meetings taking place at Spellbrook, just across the river from and under the view of the hillfort. It is worth noting the similar proximity of *Spellbeorhge*, discussed above, to Ring Hill camp. At some point before the compilation of the Domesday survey a large part of this territory was amalgamated with a substantial portion of that of the **Brahhingas* to form a new hundred. On the other hand, Spellbrook might have served as a moot during the late Anglo-Saxon or post-Conquest period. Given the idiosyncratic geographical configuration of Braughing hundred, it is possible that Spellbrook acted as a second assembly site, which alternated with Wickham Hill as the primary site of judicial assembly, acted as a subsidiary moot for the people of the Stort valley, held different functions from Wickham Hill or even, for a time, replaced Wickham Hill. In the end, the various possible uses of Spellbrook are not mutually exclusive. Perhaps it does mark the site of an early Anglo-Saxon tribal meeting place, later used both as a multi-shire moot and an alternative assembly site for Braughing hundred; but no certainty is possible.

12.3.2 Wakeley

The reconstructed Domesday hundredal geography of eastern Hertfordshire shows a remarkable configuration of boundaries where Broadwater, Odsey, Edwinstree and Braughing adjoin (Fig. 12.1). Of potential significance is the way in which the boundaries seem to contort so that all four hundreds converge on the small ancient parish of Wakeley.[11] Wakeley itself is in Edwinstree hundred, but its parish borders Odsey hundred to the north-west, the hundred of Braughing to the south-east and that of Broadwater to the south-west, which has an extraordinary salient of land jutting between Edwinstree and Odsey and stretching along the Roman road that forms Wakeley's boundary here. Moreover, Westmill is the only part of Braughing hundred on the western side of the probable Anglo-Saxon diocesan boundary between London and Leicester, and therefore outside the territory of the East Saxons, while Wakeley is one of only five Edwinstree vills on the Leicester (Middle Anglian or Mercian) side of the same divide (*cf.* Williamson 2010: 95–9). Indeed, the western projection of Edwinstree hundred occupies a large section of what may formerly have been the Braughing estate (Short 1987; Williamson 2010: 126–8). There is a sense that, during the creation of the administrative geography of this area, efforts were made to provide access to Wakeley from all four hundreds.

A word of caution about this reconstruction is required. Domesday reveals which vills belonged to each hundred in the eleventh century, but the precise contemporary boundaries of those vills are not known, and in some cases vills may have been separated by stretches of land over which rights were shared, rather than by firm linear divisions. Even allowing for a rationalisation of all divisions into notional borders, it is generally only from modern parish and township boundaries that approximations to their extent can be made. On the whole, it is likely that local boundaries were relatively stable and represent in broad terms the divisions that existed in the medieval period, even if they have changed in minor detail. Use of these boundaries allows the Domesday hundredal territories to be drawn, with the provisos noted here, and, where hundredal boundaries are concerned, minor changes at township level are unlikely to have a dramatic impact on their overall shape. It could also be argued, conversely, that the boundaries of the four hundreds converge on Great Munden parish; but the meaning of the place-name Wakeley adds to the sense that this was the focus of the boundaries.

Wakeley is recorded in the Domesday survey as *Wachelei*, a name consisting of the OE elements *wacu*, 'a watch, a wake' and *lēah*, 'woodland clearing' (Gover *et al.* 1938: 210). Ekwall (1936: 189–90) suggested that *wacu* place-names commemorated sites where periodic festivals were held – in other words, assembly sites of some kind.[11] This strongly suggests that it held a wider significance, and perhaps one that would have been respected when the hundreds were created. At the very least, Wakeley may have served a role as meeting place for the parishes immediately in its vicinity, but it is not unreasonable to suggest that it was an important communal site for all four hundreds. What function it served is difficult to say, but any administratively central role went unrecorded in 1086 and it does not seem to have retained a socially focal position subsequently. The place-name, of course, existed already in the eleventh century, and might well have been coined many years – centuries perhaps – before that. In any case, the communal role that it suggests Wakeley once held must belong to an earlier period and had perhaps already ceased by the time of the Domesday survey. It may, in that case, have been the centre of a community and its territory that pre-dated the laying out of the hundreds in this part of Hertfordshire and perhaps pre-dated some of the early territories outlined by Williamson (2010: 125–41), since it stands on the reconstructed boundary between the estates of Braughing and Bennington – territories characterised in Williamson's view by two folk-groups with similar types of name: the **Brahhingas* discussed above and the **Beningas* or 'people of the River Beane'.[13] Given the potential antiquity of the tribal territory of the **Brahhingas*, its possible origin as a subdivision of a larger unit is certainly worthy of further examination, perhaps with reference to groupings of hundreds in other parts of the country, such as Kent (Brookes 2011).

12.3.3 Discussion

Place-names such as Spellbrook and Wakeley highlight the complexity of Hertfordshire's administrative past. They hint at multiple phases of territorial organisation and at different scales of judicial authority. They are certainly not the only names across the county that indicate the former presence of communal assemblies. Gover *et al.* (1938: 259) note an unlocated *Spelthorn* or 'speech thorn', Coates (1978) suggests that Metley Hill in Wallington, one of the parishes that make up the hundred of Odsey, might go back to OE *(ge)mōt-lēah*, 'assembly clearing'. Plaistowes in St Stephens, right on the border between Domesday *Daneis* and Albanstow, is one of at least two Hertfordshire instances of the OE compound *pleg-stōw*, '(gathering) place for sport',[14] and therefore records some kind of site of communal assembly (Gover *et al.* 1938: 98).[15] In the last case, the location of a minor place-name Daneswick, probably more or less in the centre of the *pleg-stōw*, is of particular note. This is first recorded as *Danes oke* (1512; Gover *et al.* 1938: 100) and might go back to ME *daneis-oke*, 'Danish oak-tree' or perhaps '*Daneis* oak-tree'. The connection with *Daneis* hundred, in the light of the uncertainty otherwise surrounding its meeting place, is hard to avoid and raises difficulties and implications beyond the bounds of the present discussion; for the present purposes, it highlights the vast potential of this kind of approach.[16]

Importantly, these place-names confirm what might be suspected: that the hundredal system of the Domesday shire was just one more stage in a longer-term evolution of local administrative geography which built on and re-drew earlier judicial districts, some perhaps of very early origin, and was soon overtaken by subsequent phases of administrative realignment. Such reorganisation could involve the amalgamating of earlier territories, as perhaps happened in the case of Braughing (Williamson 2010: 114); the fossilisation, albeit in reduced form, of earlier 'folk'-groupings such as the **Brahhingas* and possibly the **Beningas*; and perhaps, for example, at Odsey, *Segham Assh*, Edwinstree and Ford Bridge, the creation by a central authority of new territories with meeting places selected for the convenience of officials rather than local inhabitants. We might think of such territorial constructs as artificial, but it is questionable whether any administrative territory can be entirely organic in its development, and there must be an element of artifice in any delineation of units of this kind. On the other hand, the example of Wakeley, together with that of Plaistowes, suggests either that earlier territories had sometimes to be dismantled in order to create the hundredal system or that some hundreds were clustered together and carried out certain functions or activities in unison.

12.4 Conclusions

By analysing the names of Hertfordshire's hundreds, and examining them within their local landscape and against the wider background of meeting places across the country, it is possible to understand more about their origins and evolution. The meeting places preserved in the Domesday survey and exemplified in the Hertfordshire cases discussed here seem to consist of a patchwork of different kinds of assembly site: ancient survivals alongside recent innovations, traditional territorial foci, negotiated locales of communal activity, imposed venues for official business, manorial centres and so on. The functions they held before, at and after that time may have included commercial, military and even recreational ones alongside the judicial, although evidence of this kind tends to be later and more piecemeal. Certainly there are sites recorded in the Domesday survey that seem to have been known for other kinds of gathering. All of this gives the impression that the hundredal system of the late eleventh century was a still-evolving rationalisation of several different levels and fields of communal activity, and of recurrent phases of territorial reorganisation. The partial survival of earlier units provides a tantalising glimpse of what may have gone before.

Firm conclusions are impossible, but the evidence from Hertfordshire provides an indication that the Domesday shire was not the first major administrative division laid out in this area. Around Wakeley, a sizeable unit incorporating at least the middle Anglo-Saxon estates of Braughing and Bennington may have occupied much of the east of Hertfordshire before the restructuring that resulted in the Domesday hundreds; and, given the location of Plaistowes, something similar may have existed to the west, including what later became the hundreds of *Daneis* and Albanstow, which are, in any case, thought to have been late divisions of an earlier unit (Gover *et al.* 1938: 26; Anderson 1939b: 28–9; Williamson 2010: 106). The plethora of place-names that make reference to public assembly of one kind or another, but cannot always be associated with hundredal moots, may also be symptomatic of major reconstitutions of the administrative landscape. At the very least, the occurrence of such place-names suggests that other administrative layers – chronological, hierarchical or functional – existed and that the landscape of assembly is a complicated one at all levels – a landscape that we can hope to understand only through the application of a multidisciplinary methodology.

12.5 Acknowledgements

The research underpinning this article took place as part of the Leverhulme Trust-funded 'Landscapes of Governance' project. I am grateful to my colleagues on that project, and especially to Stuart Brookes, for help, support and ideas.

12.6 References

Adkins, R.A. and Petchey, M.R. (1984), 'Secklow Hundred Mound and Other Meeting-place Mounds in England', *Archaeological Journal* 141, pp. 243–51.

Anderson, O.S. (1934), *The English Hundred-Names*, vol 1, Lunds Universitets Arsskrift 30/1 (Lund).

Anderson, O.S. (1939a), *The English Hundred-Names: The South-Western Counties*. vol 2, Lunds Universitets Arsskrift 35/5 (Lund).

Anderson, O.S. (1939b), *The English Hundred-Names: The South-Eastern Counties*, vol 3, Lunds Universitets Arsskrift 37/1 (Lund).

Baker, J. (2014), 'The Toponymy of Communal Activity: Anglo-Saxon Assembly Sites and their Functions', in Tort I Donada, J. (2014) (ed.), *Els noms en la vida quotidiana. Actes del XXIV Congrés Internacional d'ICOS sobre Ciències Onomàstiques. Annex. Secció 7*, published online, <http://www.gencat.cat/llengua/BTPL/ICOS2011/cercador.html>, pp. 1498–1509 accessed 12 November 2014.

Baker, J. and Brookes, S. (2013), 'Governance at the Anglo-Scandinavian interface: hundredal organization in the southern Danelaw', *Journal of the North Atlantic. Special Volume 5. The Assembly Project: Meeting Places in Northern Europe AD 400–1500*, pp. 76–95.

Baker, J. and Brookes, S. (2014), 'Outside the gate: sub-urban legal practices in early medieval England', *World Archaeology* 45/5, pp. 747–61.

Baker, J., and Brookes, S. (2015), 'Developing a field archaeology of outdoor assembly in early Medieval England', *Journal of Field Archaeology* 40.

Baker, J. and Brookes, S. (forthcoming), *Landscapes of Governance: legal geographies and political order in Anglo-Saxon England, AD 400–1066*.

Brookes, S. (2011), 'The Lathes of Kent: a review of the evidence', in S. Brookes, S. Harrington and A. Reynolds (eds), *Studies in Early Anglo-Saxon Art and Archaeology: Papers in Honour of Martin G. Welch*, British Archaeological Reports British Series 527 (Oxford), pp. 156–70.

Cam, H. (1963 [1930]), *The Hundred and the Hundred Rolls* (London).

Clutterbuck, R. (1815), *The History and Antiquities of the County of Hertford*, vol 1 (London).

Coates, R. (1978), 'The linguistic status of the Wandlebury giants', *Folklore* 89/1, pp. 75–8.

Crick, J. (ed.) (2007), *Charters of St Albans*, Anglo-Saxon Charters 12 (Oxford).

Crossley, A. (ed.) (1983), *A History of the County of Oxford: Volume 11: Wootton Hundred (northern part)*, Victoria County History (Oxford).

Ekwall, E. (1936), *Studies on English Place-Names* (Stockholm).

Ekwall, E. (1960), *The Concise Oxford Dictionary of English Place-Names*, 4th edn (Oxford).

Field, J. (1993), *A History of English Field names* (London and New York).

Fowler, H. (1890–91), 'Berkhampstead Castle', *Transactions of the St Albans and Hertfordshire Architectural and Archaeological Society* 8, pp. 17–28.

Friel, I. (1982), 'The Hicce – an Anglo-Saxon tribe of the Hitchin area', *Hertfordshire's Past* 13, pp. 2–18.

Gelling, M. and Cole, A. (2000), *The Landscape of Place-Names* (Stamford).

Gover, J.E.B., Mawer, A. and Stenton, F.M. (1933), *The Place-Names of Northamptonshire* (Cambridge).

Gover, J.E.B., Mawer, A. and Stenton, F.M. (1938), *The Place-Names of Hertfordshire* (Cambridge).

Gover, J.E.B., Mawer, A. and Stenton, F.M. (1939), *The Place-Names of Wiltshire* (Cambridge).

Gover, J.E.B., Mawer, A. and Stenton, F.M. (1942), *The Place-Names of Middlesex* (Cambridge).

Hesse, M. (1994), 'The Anglo-Saxon bounds of Littlebury', *Proceedings of the Cambridge Antiquarian Society* 83, pp. 129–39.

Jewell, H.M. (1972), *English Local Administration in the Middle Ages* (Newton Abbot).

Kristensson, G. (1995), *A Survey of Middle English Dialects 1290–1350: The East Midland Counties* (Lund).

Kurath, H. *et al.* (1956–2001), *Middle English Dictionary* (Ann Arbor). <http://quod.lib.umich.edu/m/med/med_ent_search.html>, accessed 25 September 2013.

Liebermann, F. (ed.) ([1903] 1960), *Die Gesetze der Angelsachsen*, Band 1, reprinted 1960 (Halle).

Longman, G. (1977), 'The Origin of Watford', *Hertfordshire's Past* 2, pp. 7–11.

Loyn, H.R. (1984), *The Governance of Anglo-Saxon England 500–1087* (London).

Mawer, A. and Stenton, F.M. (1926), *The Place-Names of Bedfordshire and Huntingdonshire* (Cambridge).

Maxwell Lyte, H.C. (ed.) (1895), *Calendar of the Patent Rolls Preserved in the Public Record Office, Preserved under the Superintendence of the Deputy Keeper of the Records, Richard II. A.D. 1377–1381* (London).

Meaney, A. (1994), 'Gazetteer of Hundred and Wapentake Meeting-places of the Cambridge Region', *Proceedings of the Cambridge Antiquarian Society* 82, pp. 67–92.

Meaney, A. (1997), 'Hundred Meeting-places in the Cambridge Region', in A.R. Rumble and A.D. Mills (1997), *Names, Places and People: an Onomastic Miscellany in Memory of John McNeal Dodgson* (Stamford), pp. 195–233.

Mills, A.D. (1980), *The Place-Names of Dorset Part II* (Cambridge).

Munby, L. (1973), *Wheathampstead and Harpenden Volume I: The Settlement of Wheathampstead and Harpenden* (Harpenden).

Page, W. (ed.) (1902), *VCH Hertford*, vol. 1 (London).

Page, W. (ed.) (1908), *VCH Buckingham*, vol. 2 (London).

Page, W. (ed.) (1912), *VCH Hertford*, vol. 3 (London).

Page, W. (ed.) (1914), *VCH Hertford*, vol. 4 (London).

Pantos, A. (2002), 'Assembly-Places in the Anglo-Saxon Period: Aspects of Form and Location', DPhil thesis (University of Oxford).

Pantos, A. (2003), '"On the edge of things": the boundary location of Anglo-Saxon assembly sites', *Anglo-Saxon Studies in Archaeology and History* 12, pp. 38–49.

Pantos, A. (2004), 'The location and form of Anglo-Saxon assembly-places: some "moot points"', in A. Pantos and S. Semple (eds), *Assembly Places and Practices in Medieval Europe* (Dublin), pp. 155–80.

Powell, W.R., Board, B.A., Briggs, N., Fisher, J.L., Harding, V.A., Hasler, J., Knight, N. and Parsons, M. (eds) (1983), 'Parishes: Great Hallingbury', *A History of the County of Essex: Volume 8* (1983), pp. 113–24. http://www.british-history.ac.uk/report.aspx?compid=63846, accessed 25 September 2014.

Reaney, P.H. (1935), *The Place-Names of Essex* (Cambridge).

Reaney, P.H. (1943), *The Place-Names of Cambridgeshire and the Isle of Ely* (Cambridge).

Rowe, A., and Williamson, T. (2013), *Hertfordshire: A Landscape History* (Hatfield).

Rumble, A. (1977), 'The Wheathampstead (Herts.) charter-bounds, A.D. 1060: a corrected text and notes on the boundary-points', *Journal of the English Place-Name Society* 9, pp. 6–12.

Sawyer, P. (1968), *Anglo-Saxon Charters: an annotated list and bibliography*, Royal Historical Society Guides and Handbooks 8 (London).

Short, D. (1987), 'Braughing: a possible Saxon estate?', *Hertfordshire's Past* 23, pp. 8–15.

Skeat, W.W. (1904), *The Place Names of Hertfordshire* (Hertford).

Smith, A.H. (1956), *English Place-Name Elements Part II (JAFN–YTRI)* (Cambridge).

Smith, A.H. (1964), *The Place-Names of Gloucestershire Part I* (Cambridge).

Taylor, C.S. (1957), 'The origin of the Mercian shires', in H.P.R. Finberg (ed.), *Gloucestershire Studies* (Leicester), pp. 17–51.

Warren, W.L. (1987), *The Governance of Norman and Angevin England 1086–1272* (London).

Whitelock, D. (ed.) (1979), *English Historical Documents, c.500–1042*, 2nd edn, English Historical Documents 1 (London).

Williamson, T. (2010), *The Origins of Hertfordshire*, 2nd edn (Hatfield).

Wright, J. and Wright, E.M. (1928), *An Elementary Middle English Grammar*, 2nd edn (London).

Notes

1 'In the 13th century the hundred court still met on a plot of ground called 'Edwynestre['], which was held by the sheriff and was worth 1*d.* per annum. Unfortunately there is no direct evidence as to where this plot was situated. At the same date, however, there is mention of 'the wood of Edwynesbrugg['], and as the vills of Furneux Pelham and Brent Pelham were presented for not making suit in connexion with a murder in this wood, it seems probable that Edwinsbridge was in their neighbourhood and perhaps also Edwin's Tree' (Page 1914: 3, citing Assize Roll 313 (6&7 Edw.I), m. 44 and m. 46).

2 'Baptists were first mentioned in 1771, and in 1778 Edward Drake, a labourer, registered his house for meetings and taught 10 Anabaptists there. From that time the strength and persistence of nonconformity in Little Tew distinguished it from its larger neighbour [Great Tew]' (Crossley 1983: 247–58).

3 Hundreds could have more than one name simultaneously, as discussed below, and these seem to have been sufficiently interchangeable to have occurred in very similar contexts. The alternative hundred-names Ermington and *Allerige* in Devon, for example, both occur in the Geld Rolls (Anderson 1939a: 92).

4 Without attestations earlier than the first edition OS 25' (1878) and 6' (1883) County Series (viewed at Edina Digimap), the etymology of Bummers Hill, which was not discussed by Gover *et al.* (1938), is not transparent.

5 Page (1908: 141–2 and n. 12, citing Maxwell Lyte 1895: 608).

6 In Dorset, the alternative hundred names *Celeberge* and Loosebarrow might refer to the same place (Mills 1980: 54–55).

7 Smith (1956: 74, 83), following Ekwall (1960 and earlier editions), takes the second element to be an unrecorded OE **ric* 'a narrow strip'; but the run of early forms does not especially favour such an interpretation (cf. Gelling and Cole 2000: 191, 214).

8 As will become clear in the second part of this essay, Braughing hundred also contained at least one other place where communal gatherings took place.
9 In this context, the development of Watford following the granting of a market very close to the meeting place of Cashio hundred is worth noting (Longman 1977).
10 All of the rivers mentioned in this section are included in Fig. 12.1, but it proved impossible to add river-names without cluttering the map too much. The rivers Rib and Ash can be seen running through the north-western part of Braughing Hundred and the southern salient of Edwinstree Hundred, respectively. The Stort is the unnamed river that forms the eastern boundary of the south-eastern part of Braughing Hundred and of the shire itself.
11 Fig. 12.1 shows the location of the remaining settlement of Wakeley.
12 The proximity of Wateringplace Green, just along the Roman road in Ardeley (*loc. Voc. The Watering place* 1495; Gover *et al.* 1938: 152), at least suggests the presence of a supply of water nearby, and may indicate that this was still a naturally good stopping-place in the fifteenth century.
13 Although Ekwall (1960: 37) took this view of the name, it must be admitted that the forms for Bennington do not necessitate such an interpretation, and the editors of the EPNS survey for Hertfordshire preferred an alternative derivation (Gover *et al.* 1938: 121). Derivation of Bennington from an original **Beningatūn* – 'farm or estate of the people of the river Beane' gains some support if it does belong together with Bengeo, as suggested by Williamson (2010: 129; cf. Gover *et al.* 1938: 215).
14 Plaistowes is *Plasters* 1679; cf. William de *Pleystouwe* 1307. A rather later-recorded place-name, Playstow (*Play Stowe c.*1840) is in Barley, on the eastern edge of the county (Gover *et al.* 1938: 98, 175).
15 What kind of sport this refers to is difficult to say. Displays of athletic or martial prowess, contests arranged for pleasure or to settle disputes, and simple military training are all possibilities.
16 Caution is needed, of course. In Hertfordshire *danes* could also be the outcome of OE *denu* – 'valley' (ME dene, pl. and gen.sg. *denes*), and there is indeed a small, dry valley here (Kristensson 1995: 35–6, 188, Map 5; Wright and Wright: 1928, 140).

CHAPTER 13

The fields of Hertfordshire: archaeological, documentary and topographic investigations

Tom Williamson

13.1 Open fields in Hertfordshire

Landscape historians sometimes describe the medieval countryside of lowland England in terms of a somewhat simplistic, yet nevertheless useful, dichotomy between 'champion' and 'woodland' areas. The former, which dominated a broad swathe of England running from Yorkshire through the Midlands to the south coast, were landscapes of nucleated settlements and extensive 'open fields' (Homans 1941; Rackham 1986: 4–6, 164–79; Roberts and Wrathmell 2000; Williamson 2003: 91–118). The holdings of individual farmers took the form of a multiplicity of unhedged strips which were intermingled and scattered evenly through the territory of each township or village, and there were few, if any, enclosed fields other than village tofts. Farming was organised on highly communal lines and, in particular, one of the two or three great fields into which the arable was divided lay uncultivated or 'fallow' each year, to be grazed in common by the village livestock. In 'woodland' areas, in contrast, settlement was more dispersed, featuring numerous small hamlets and isolated farms as well as villages, and farming tended to be carried out on a more individualistic basis.

Hertfordshire, fortunately for those who study its landscape, falls astride this broad regional division (Fig. 13.1). A narrow strip in the north, lying on or below the chalk escarpment – from Tring in the west to Barley in the far north-east – formed the southern edge of the 'champion' zone. Early maps, such as that for Ickleford, surveyed in 1771 (HALS DE/Ha/P1), show landscapes of clustered settlement and extensive open fields (Fig. 13.2). There were some apparent deviations from Midland practices. Groups of strips orientated in the same

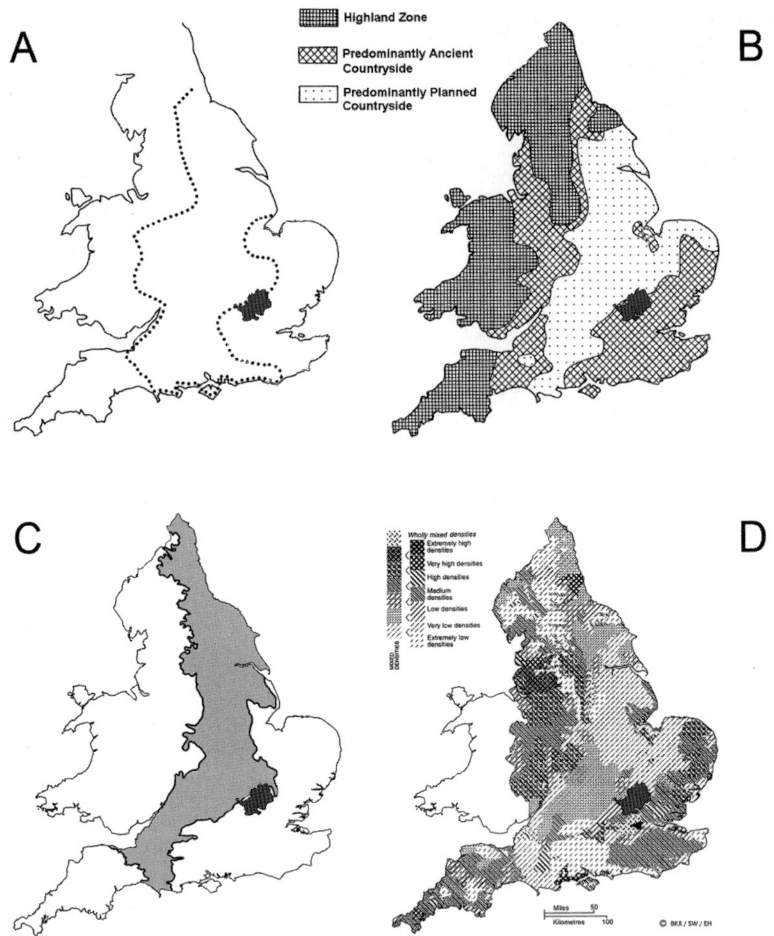

Figure 13.1: Landscape regions in England, with the area of Hertfordshire superimposed. (a) The boundaries of Howard Gray's 'Midland System', the classic form of two- or three-field open-field agriculture; (b) Oliver Rackham's distinction between the 'planned' and the 'ancient' countryside: that is, between areas of generally late enclosure, comprising the former 'champion' lands, and areas of early enclosure and more irregular field systems; (c) the 'Central Province', of nucleated settlement and well-developed open-field farming, as defined by Brian Roberts and Stuart Wrathmell (2000); (d) densities of dispersed settlement, as mapped by Roberts and Wrathmell (2000), showing the dominance of nucleated settlements within the Midland 'champion' zone.

direction – which functioned as the basic unit of cropping in such field systems – were here called 'shotts' rather than 'furlongs', as was usual in the Midlands. More notably, in most Hertfordshire villages by the eighteenth century the arable was organised not into the two or three fields usual in Midland villages but into four or more. Ashwell, for example, had four fields when finally enclosed in 1863 – Quarry Field, Claybush Field, Redland Field and North Field – all roughly

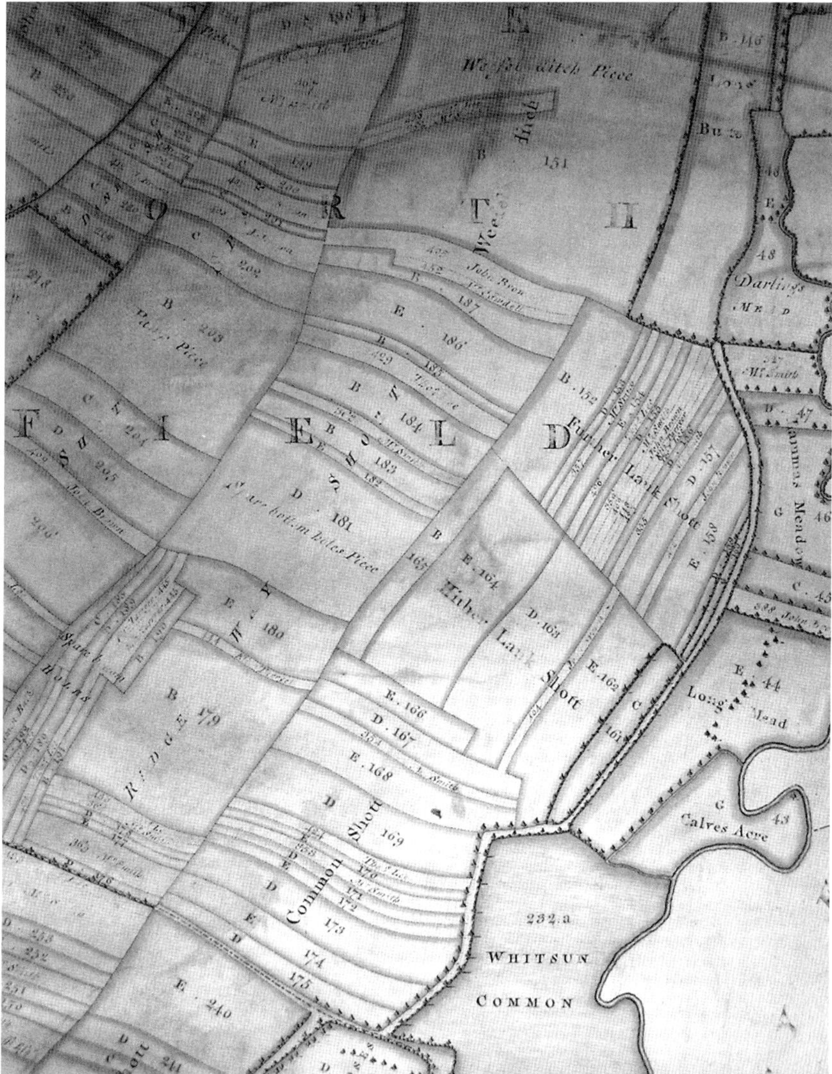

Figure 13.2: Part of the open fields of Ickleford, as shown on a map of 1771. Note the sinuous shapes of the open field strips, the piecemeal enclosures within the fields with similarly sinuous boundaries and the use of the term 'shott' in place of the more usual 'furlong'. HALS DE/Ha/P1: Plan of the Manor and Parish of Ickleford and other lands.

the same size (HALS QS/E9). Ickleford, similarly, had four named fields when mapped in 1771, as had Great Wymondley in 1811, while Pirton had no less than seven when enclosed in 1818 (HALS DE/Ha/P1). These kinds of arrangements were not universal, however, and the hamlet of Walsworth, in Hitchin, for example, cultivated three fields when enclosed in 1767. In some cases they may have been the consequence of post-medieval reorganisation of the cropping boundaries, perhaps resulting from the adoption of new crops and rotations. Norton certainly had three fields in the seventeenth century but four at the time of enclosure in 1796 (HALS DP/75/3/1; HALS QS/E54).

On heavier soils, especially on the Gault clays to the north of Tring, open fields were often enclosed and laid to pasture in the course of the fifteenth, sixteenth and seventeenth centuries. But in most 'champion' parishes they were only finally swept away by parliamentary enclosure acts in the late eighteenth and early nineteenth centuries, to be replaced by landscapes of large, straight-sided fields in private occupancy, bounded by hawthorn hedges. One of the curious features of the county, however, is that in a number of places – Hitchin, Bygrave, Wallington and Clothall – open fields still survived, unenclosed, into the late nineteenth or even twentieth centuries (Plate 13.1). The historian Gilbert Slater discussed those at Clothall and Bygrave in his book *The English Peasantry and the Enclosure of Common Fields* of 1907, while Hitchin's fields formed a major part of Frederick Seebohm's analysis of open-field farming in *The English Village Community* of 1883 (Slater 1907; Seebohm 1883). The Victoria County History (VCH) in 1912 likewise described the appearance of the fields at Bygrave and Clothall at some length:

> Between Baldock and Clothall Church lies Clothall Field, containing about 600 acres, a 'common-field' of open arable land famous for its barley, and divided into irregular strips by 'balks', or narrow banks of grass, sometimes grown with bushes ... On the hill-side the scarped terraces, or 'lynches', form a distinctive feature of the parish. The high ridges between these terraces have the appearance of artificial defences, but are in reality due to the custom of turning the sod down-hill in ploughing. (Page 1912: 220)

13.2 'Woodland' Hertfordshire

Although champion landscapes could thus be found in this northern strip of Hertfordshire, most of the county comprised 'woodland' countryside with a more dispersed pattern of settlement, featuring numerous isolated farms and hamlets – often grouped around commons or small greens – as well as villages. It is sometimes supposed that in such areas all the land was farmed 'in severalty' – that is, as enclosed, hedged fields – from an early date. But, as Roden (1973) and others showed many decades ago, while enclosed land did dominate many such districts in medieval times, in others much or even most of the land lay in open fields, although these usually took rather different forms to those found in the 'champion' areas. They were usually interspersed, to varying degrees, with enclosed land; in most parishes there were large numbers of named 'fields', often associated with particular hamlets; and the holdings of individual farmers were usually clustered in restricted parts of a township rather than being widely and evenly scattered across its area, as was normal in 'champion' landscapes. In general, as Roden noted, 'irregular' open fields of this kind were most extensive and continuous where large tracts of light, freely draining land could be found. In King's Walden, for example, there were 30 separate 'fields', the largest occupying the slopes of wide chalk valleys (Roden 1973: 331). In some cases, and especially in the north-east of the county – where the boulder clay plateau was extensively dissected by streams and rivers – they covered particularly large areas (Fig. 13.3), and here many parishes were only finally enclosed, like most in the 'champion' regions, by parliamentary acts (Plate 13.1). Indeed, a few areas still remained open, as in the Mundens, as late as the 1880s. Elsewhere in the county, however – on the Chiltern dipslope, in the Vale of St Albans and in the south – open fields had largely disappeared from most parishes by the time that the earliest maps were made, in the seventeenth and eighteenth centuries.

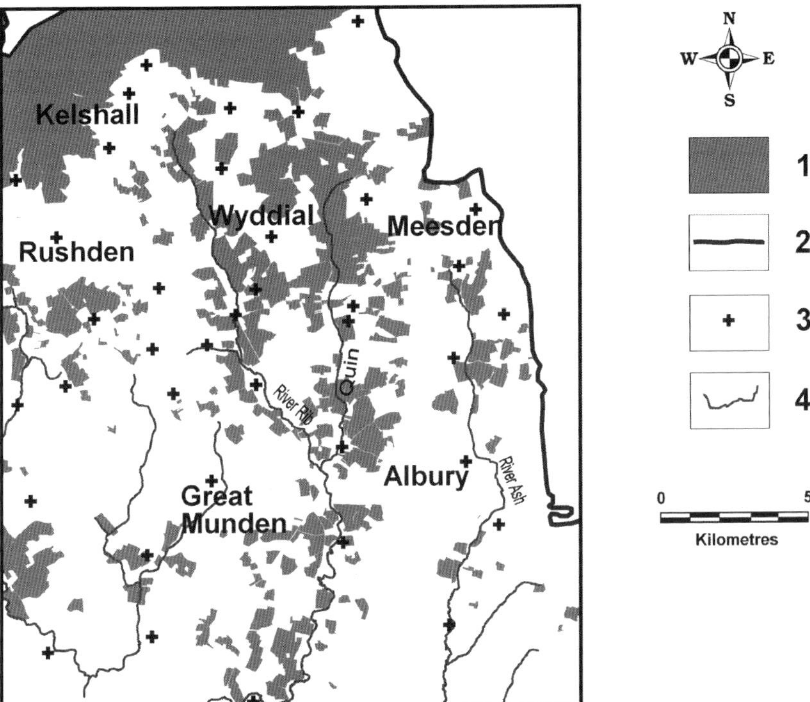

Figure 13.3: Open fields in the claylands of north-east Hertfordshire. 1. Areas of open field shown on the earliest available maps for the parishes in question (for sources see Rowe and Williamson 2013); 2. county boundary; 3. parish churches; 4. principal watercourses. Note how the largest areas of open arable tend to be found in the major river valleys. The continuous area of open field in the north of the figure represents the edge of the 'champion' on the chalk escarpment.

In such places, the evidence of early extents and surveys sometimes testifies to their former extent. An example from Hemel Hempstead, dated 1523 but apparently based on one drawn up in the late Middle Ages, thus describes around 7000 acres of land, of which 3000 lay in open fields (Munby 1977: 165). In Shenley, in the valley of the Colne, an extent of 1276 describes how much of the demesne lay in three great fields in the vicinity of the parish church and manor house – 136½ acres in Adgranosfeld, 134½ in 'Shenlefeld', and 118½ in 'Westfeld' (Barton 1981: 27). In other places, however, the former presence of open arable has to be deduced by employing a rather wider range of documentary evidence, including leases and references in court rolls. In Bushey, for example, a few kilometres to the west of Shenley, a document drawn up as late as 1825 refers to a number of unhedged parcels lying within the fields called Bournehall Bottom, Church Bottom, Great Grove Field, Little Grove Field, Skippetts, Upper and Lower Wardells, Little Broadfield, Upper Rye Hill and Barn Croft Field, all in the north of the parish, some of which were described as 'dispersed lands in the Common Field of Bushey' (BL Phillips MS 82742). Some at least of these fields contained intermixed properties of both the main manors, Bournehall and Bushey: indeed, it is probable that this circumstance explains why some memory of ancient arrangements still persisted as late as this, for a map of the parish surveyed in 1799 leaves no doubt that these unhedged parcels were by this time entirely notional in character (HALS DP/26/29/2). Earlier, in the mid-seventeenth century, there are references to strips lying 'in a furlong and in another furlong and in a third furlong and the balks' – that is, narrow unploughed strips lying between the individual arable lands – within Broadfield (HALS 54807). In addition, there are numerous medieval references, in the court rolls of the two manors, to particular pieces of land lying *in campo* – 'in the field'; to 'acres' or 'parcels' lying 'in' various fields; and to the presence of 'balks'. The element 'shott' also appears in 10 of the field names recorded on the 1799 parish map. They are concentrated on the lighter land in the north and the middle of the parish, and are absent from the heavy London clay soils in the south: the same is true of the various other references to open fields, at least where the location of the lands in question can be identified.

Documentary evidence thus suggests the widespread presence of 'irregular' open fields throughout Hertfordshire in the Middle Ages, especially on the better-drained land. Such fields were probably already in existence by the time of Domesday (many, as in King's Walden, are associated by name with hamlets representing Domesday manors) but they continued to be created, altered and adapted into the twelfth and perhaps thirteenth centuries – one of the fields in Stocking Pelham, for example, was called 'Assett Field', almost certainly from the

Old French word *assart*, meaning 'woodland clearance'. It is, however, difficult to obtain a clear idea from scattered documentary sources just how widespread such fields may have been or how much ground they might have covered. Further light can, however, be thrown on this problem by combining topographical and archaeological approaches.

13.3 Topographic evidence for open fields

When open fields disappeared before the seventeenth century this was usually through the process of 'piecemeal' enclosure, a series of private agreements which led to the gradual amalgamation, through purchase and exchange, of groups of contiguous open-field strips and their subsequent fencing or hedging (Yelling 1977: 11–29). This type of enclosure, because it involved the establishment of boundaries along the margins of groups of strips, tended to preserve in simplified form the essential layout of the old open landscape. As Figure 13.2 shows clearly, open-field strips were usually slightly curving or sinuous in plan, sometimes taking the form of a shallow 'reversed S', caused by the way that the ploughman moved to the left with his team as he approached the headland at the end of the strip in order to avoid too tight a turning circle (Eyre 1955).

Although boundary patterns like this were mainly the consequence of piecemeal enclosure, they could be created in other ways. Parliamentary enclosure is the most familiar and most important method by which the common arable of a township could be extinguished at a stroke, through a single enclosure 'event', but there were other, earlier ways in which this was achieved: where a single owner managed to acquire all the land in a parish or township, for example, or where the principal proprietors agreed to enclose their fields. Such processes probably account for the removal of open fields in several of Hertfordshire's smaller 'champion' parishes, such as Newnham (388 hectares), Letchworth (350), Radwell (302) and Caldecote (a mere 134 hectares) (Rowe and Williamson 2013: 46–9). Some of these pre-parliamentary forms of 'general' enclosure – to adopt Yelling's terminology – also involved the establishment of hedged boundaries along the margins of furlongs or smaller groups of strips. For the purposes of ascertaining the likely former extent of open arable in the county, however, the *precise* manner in which these slightly sinuous or smoothly curving boundaries came into existence is of little relevance. It is their number and distribution which are important (Plate 13.2).

At first sight it might appear paradoxical that boundaries of this kind are comparatively rare in most of the 'champion' area of the county, especially on the chalk, but this is simply because much of the open land here survived into the late eighteenth or nineteenth century when, as already noted, it was enclosed by parliamentary acts, producing the kinds of rigidly linear field patterns already described. The densest concentration lies a little to the south of the true 'champion', in the broad lowlands of the Hitchin gap between Hitchin and Stevenage, on soils formed in chalk and glacial gravels. In most of the river valleys cutting through the boulder clays in the east of the county this kind of boundary is also common, except in those of the Quin and the Rib, where the particularly extensive but irregular open fields around places such as Braughing and Standon (see Fig. 13.3) were largely removed by parliamentary acts. In the west of the county, on the dipslope of the Chilterns, such boundaries are also widespread, although again with a clear tendency to cluster on the lighter soils, in the principal valleys cutting through the clay-with-flints and plateau drift. In the centre and south of the county, in contrast, such evidence for open-field cultivation is sparser: thinly scattered across the glacial sands and gravels within the Vale of St Albans; more clustered where chalk, or the sands and clays of the Reading and Upnor formations, are exposed in the valleys of the Lea and Colne; and only sporadically found on the heavy, acidic soils formed in the London clay.

We need to be cautious in our use of such evidence. The identification of particular kinds of field pattern is, to some extent, a subjective exercise on which mapping confers a measure of spurious objectivity. In addition, archaeological approaches to the analysis of modern field patterns sometimes fail to emphasise sufficiently the extent to which field patterns can be redrawn after the initial enclosure of the landscape. In particular, eighteenth- and nineteenth-century landowners were sometimes keen to 'modernise' the irregular, archaic field patterns on their estates, creating landscapes which are reminiscent of those created by parliamentary enclosure. In Bushey, for example, the *majority* of boundaries shown on the parish map of 1799 in the northern third of the parish, on light soils beside the Colne, had been uprooted – realigned, or removed altogether – by the time the Ordnance Survey six-inch map was surveyed in 1886. We should also note that many of the gaps in the distribution shown in Plate 13.2 simply reflect the absence, by the late nineteenth century, of field boundaries of any kind. Some districts were extensively wooded and landscape parks occupied around 8 per cent of the county's total land area, while, on the highest ground in the Chilterns and on the pebble gravels in the far south of the county, vast tracts of common land existed which were either enclosed by parliamentary acts (creating networks of rectilinear fields) or, in a few cases, still survived at the time the first edition Ordnance Survey maps were surveyed. Like all distribution maps, in other words, Plate 13.2 needs to be treated with a measure of caution. This said, it provides a reasonable indication of the extent and distribution of the early enclosure of open fields, and thus of open fields themselves; and it suggests that some open-field arable probably existed in every Hertfordshire parish in the Middle Ages.

13.4 The archaeological evidence for open fields

A second method of ascertaining the extent of open-field agriculture across the county is to use archaeological evidence. The most familiar 'signature' of open-field cultivation is 'ridge and furrow', comprising parallel and slightly sinuous earthwork ridges preserved under permanent pasture (D. Hall 1982, 1995: 39–42). The HHER contains numerous references to such remains extending well beyond the 'champion' areas of the county, with examples recorded even on the heavy London clays in the far south. HERs, particularly that for Hertfordshire, are a wonderful resource but need to be treated with caution. In practice archaeologists employ the term 'ridge and furrow' for a number of rather different kinds of earthwork. We need, in particular, to make a distinction between 'broad rig', in which each ridge is between five and ten metres in width; and so-called 'narrow rig', where each ridge is typically between three and five metres wide (D. Hall 1982; 1995: 38–40; Sutton 1965: 104, 107; Bowen 1961: 67).

It is the former type that is closely related to open-field agriculture, although some enclosed land was also cultivated in this manner. Each ridge usually coincided with a strip or 'selion' within the open fields. Strips were ploughed individually, as an elongated spiral, starting on the perimeter; and because medieval farmers used a plough with a fixed share and mouldboard this procedure served to repeatedly move soil towards the middle of the strip (Kerridge 1973: 31–2; Hall 1995: 40). To some extent, ridging was thus a simple consequence of cultivating land in narrow strips. But not all open fields were ploughed in ridges, especially on light, thin soils, where continual movement of soil towards the centre of the individual 'lands' would expose the infertile subsoil at the margins. In such circumstances farmers 'ploughed out' every few years, or in alternate years (Sutton 1965: 103–5). That is, they reversed the direction of cultivation, ploughing the strip in an anti-clockwise direction and thus redistributing earth outwards once again, a practice adopted in the fallow year even in areas where strips *were* ridged (Hall 1995: 40). The high-backed ridge and furrow – at least a third of a metre in height – which is characteristic of heavy soils in the Midland counties was thus at least in part created intentionally, to improve drainage. This type of earthwork, until the Second World War, carpeted large areas of the ground in Midland districts, a consequence of the fact that, following enclosure of the open fields, large areas were laid to permanent pasture (Harrison *et al.* 1965). Reconversion to arable and reseeding of pastures during the second half of the twentieth century has rendered these earthworks relatively rare.

Narrow rig, which is fairly common in Hertfordshire, is rather different. Ridges with a width of between three and five metres are too narrow to represent open-field strips, and they appear to have been formed by ploughing within enclosed fields. It is often suggested that earthworks of this kind are of eighteenth- or nineteenth-century date, and it is certainly true that in some contexts – as in areas of moorland in the north and west of England – they can be associated with the expansion of arable cultivation on to marginal land during the Napoleonic Wars, when French blockades pushed grain prices to unprecedented levels (Woodside and Crow 1999: 127). On the other hand, excavated examples in Chelmsford in nearby Essex have been firmly dated to the medieval period (Drury 1981). Most Hertfordshire examples appear to be of post-medieval date, although probably in general pre-dating the period of the Napoleonic Wars. Narrow rig preserved under grass in the George VI Recreation Ground in Bushey, for example, lies within fields which had already been laid to pasture by 1799 and have not been ploughed up subsequently (Fig. 13.4). Narrow rig is mainly found on the London clays in the south of the county and on the decalcified boulder clays soils of the Hornbeam Association around Stevenage, although occasional examples also occur on the chalky boulder clays, as in the park at Weston. Such an association with clay soils suggests that, like 'true' ridge and furrow, narrow rig was primarily intended to improve drainage.[1] A number of early agricultural writers refer, in fact, to ploughing enclosed land in 'stetches' – narrow and often impermanent ridges – and in a Hertfordshire context William Ellis, writing in 1742 about Bushey, in the south of the county, describes how farmers:

> Prepare their Ground and sow their Wheat in a quite different manner to what we do in the Western parts of Hertfordshire, because here they lie rather wetter, and their Soil is more a clayey Loam than ours, which obliges them to sow their Wheat in 3 or 4 Bout lands. (Ellis 1742: 106)

In other words, ploughing was carried out with three or four furrows laid one way and three or four another, to create a low ridge.

The HHER does not consistently distinguish between these two kinds of ridging. The well-preserved examples of narrow rig, with a width of *c.*3.5 metres, in the mown grass areas of Cheshunt Park are thus simply described as 'medieval' ridge and furrow (HHER 13306). On Plate 13.3 I have attempted to remove those examples of narrow rig known to me, or clearly visible on

Figure 13.4: Typical 'narrow rig', with a wavelength of *c.*3.7 metres, preserved in the turf of the George VI Recreation Ground, Bushey.

aerial photographs, leaving only 'true' ridge and furrow likely to be associated with open-field cultivation, but in the absence of an extensive programme of fieldwork there is little doubt that a number of instances have slipped through this net. Moreover, some examples with a width of *c.*5 metres might legitimately be placed in either class.

Further distinctions within the HHER records of 'ridge and furrow' can also be usefully made. Firstly, much is described as 'slight', 'possible', 'visible in low light', 'remnant', 'traces' or 'eroded'. While some of these records do unquestionably represent high-backed broad rig, largely but not entirely destroyed by post-enclosure ploughing at right angles, most almost certainly mark where land was ploughed in strips, but without a deliberate attempt to build high-backed ridges. In Plate 13.3 I have thus tried to distinguish between this kind of low, often scarcely visible ridging, and 'true' ridge and furrow on the Midland pattern. Secondly, much of the 'ridge and furrow' is represented only by cropmarks, soilmarks or (more rarely) parchmarks. Most such records – unsurprisingly, given the character of cropmark formation – come from light, freely draining land. Just under half are actually from thin chalk soils of the kind, as noted, where ridging was usually avoided. Where lands were ridged, adjacent selions were usually separated by a deep furrow sometimes termed a 'water-furrow'. But where lands were ploughed flat, or only slightly ridged, they were usually separated by narrow unploughed 'balks' such as those described by the VCH in its account of Clothall quoted above. Much, although not of course all, of the 'ridge and furrow' recorded as soil or cropmarks probably represents ploughed-out balks, rather than ridge and furrow *sensu stricto*, and I have therefore represented such records with a third symbol on Plate 13.3. In one sense, of course, such a distinction is somewhat pedantic: most of these features, even if they do indeed represent ploughed-out balks, are nevertheless – like true ridge and furrow – evidence for open-field cultivation.[2]

As well as various kinds of ridging, and the cropmarks of ploughed-out balks, open fields are also represented archaeologically in Hertfordshire by the earthworks called strip lynchets, sometimes referred to in the literature as 'cultivation terraces'. These were created by ploughing land in strips lying parallel with the contours, something which usually only occurred on steeper slopes (Sutton 1965: 106; Bowen 1961: 40–46; Kerridge 1973: 36). Years of cultivation ensured that the soil and subsoil were removed and eroded on the uphill side of each strip, creating level or near-level 'steps' which might then, in some cases, have been deliberately accentuated in order to create level areas for ploughing. All known Hertfordshire examples of these earthworks are shown on Plate 13.3: other kinds of lynchet, as for example where soil has simply been eroded and redeposited along the line of a hedged boundary, have been omitted.

In broad terms, the distribution of the archaeological evidence supports that of maps, documents and topographic analysis in suggesting that open-field cultivation was strongly concentrated in the champion north of the county; was widespread in the northeast, mainly but not exclusively on the lighter soils cutting through the boulder clay plateau; and was also widespread, although perhaps less common, on the dipslope of the Chilterns in the west of the county. In the south of the county open-field agriculture was more limited, being largely restricted to the major valleys where light soils formed in underlying chalk or the sands and light clays of the Lambeth Group were exposed. The map also shows, however, that there were important variations in the distribution of the main archaeological 'markers' of open-field agriculture.

Unsurprisingly, strip lynchets are concentrated in the north, on steep chalk slopes in the champion countryside around Baldock. Elsewhere they are thinly scattered, usually occurring where steep-sided valleys cut through overlying drift and chalk is exposed, as with the fine series to the west of Sarratt church, in the Chess valley. True 'broad rig', in contrast, is strongly associated with the Gault clays at the foot of the chalk escarpment, especially around Tring, forming part of a wider distribution on the heavy clays of the Midlands. Not only was such land in particular need of drainage but it was also often laid to grass following enclosure from the fifteenth century, thus preserving – at least until the twentieth century – extensive areas of this type of earthwork. Some examples are also found, more thinly scattered, in the belt of champion countryside between Hitchin and Ashwell, partly on Gault clay but also on outlying deposits of boulder clay lying at the foot of the escarpment. Especially striking are those on Norton Common in the middle of Letchworth Garden City, now partly engulfed in scrub and secondary woodland (Fig. 13.5). It might appear strange that common land should have been ploughed as part of the open fields but this was not, in fact, part of the traditional common grazing of the parish, but an area of former arable land which was (rather unusually) put aside for the use of the minor landowners when Norton was enclosed in 1796 (HALS QS/E54). The ridges were almost certainly last ploughed at this point in time, a useful reminder of the fact that, while we often describe ridge and furrow as 'medieval', the overwhelming majority represents land which was still being cultivated in the required manner in the seventeenth, eighteenth or even nineteenth centuries.

It is noteworthy that the distribution of 'slight' or 'eroded' ridge and furrow is different from that of upstanding, high-backed broad rig. Although examples are recorded from the 'champion' districts, earthworks of this type are more widely

Figure 13.5: Well-defined 'ridge and furrow' surviving on Norton Common, now in the centre of Letchworth Garden City.

scattered across the county, especially on the clay-with-flints of the Chiltern dipslope in the west. In part, as noted, slight ridges of this kind may represent high-backed ridges which have been eroded by a brief phase of cross-ploughing following enclosure and in this context it is important to note that, whereas land on the heavy Gault clays, where high-backed ridges are concentrated, was often laid to pasture following enclosure and remained unploughed until relatively recent times, on the Chiltern dipslope, in contrast, post-medieval land use was more mixed, with around three-quarters of the land being in tilth at the time the tithe award maps were surveyed in *c.*1840, for example. The fact that *some* high-backed ridges can be found in this area, as at Venus Hill in the south of Bovingdon (HHER 17293), would support such an interpretation. It is also probable, however, as already intimated, that much if not most of this scarcely visible ridging was never any higher, and represents the cultivation of land in strips in locations where drainage was not a major concern: the plateau clays of the dipslope are less susceptible to waterlogging than the heavy Gault clays at the foot of the escarpment.

The various sources of evidence thus agree in showing that in medieval Hertfordshire open fields were particularly extensive and 'regular' in character in the champion north of the county; widespread, but 'irregular' in form, across the north-east and the Chiltern dipslope, where they were most continuous on the lighter soils of the main valleys; and more thinly scattered in the centre and south, where such exposures were more limited. There is no space here to discuss the origins of such spatial variations in agrarian arrangements. The origins of open-field agriculture, and of regional variation in the landscape of medieval England more generally, continue to be areas of lively debate (recent contributions include Brown and Foard 1998; Jones 2011; Lambourn 2010; Lewis *et al.* 2002; Oosthuizen 2007; Rippon 2008; Roberts and Wrathmell 2002; Taylor 2002; Williamson 2003, 2013). It is often suggested that 'champion' landscapes developed in areas of early settlement and high population density, and that districts largely cleared and settled only in the twelfth or thirteenth centuries generally possessed landscape of 'woodland' type. While there may be some truth in this – as the comparative paucity of open fields on the heavy London clay soils, only really opened up for settlement after the Conquest, would suggest – it is only part of the story. The boulder clays in the east of the county, with their scattered hamlets and a mixture of enclosed land and 'irregular' open fields, were in fact more densely settled by the time of Domesday than many townships in the 'champion' areas, especially those on the Gault clays around Tring. Other factors, mainly but not exclusively environmental in character, also shaped medieval landscapes. The need to rapidly mobilise shared plough teams on certain kinds of clay soil, such as those formed in the sticky Gault clays, may have encouraged farmers to live in close proximity to one another and carefully coordinate their agricultural activities. Conversely, on particularly light soils, such as those on the escarpment, village living and communal farming may have been encouraged by the need to organise the movement of the great folding flocks required to keep the thin, leached soils in heart. Clustered settlements, and the complex field systems which went with them, may – in Hertfordshire as elsewhere – also have been encouraged by hydrological factors. Across most of the county drinking water was widely available from shallow wells, but in these northern districts, as across much of the scarp-and-vale countryside of the Midlands, reliable sources were much more limited. Good supplies could be obtained only from the springs at the junction of the Middle and Lower Chalk, the Lower Chalk and the Gault Clay from wells sunk in the boulder clay on the plateau above the escarpment, or in the intermittent patches of such clay at its foot. Farms were thus to some extent obliged to cluster, as cultivated land expanded out across the effectively waterless land around, so that holdings became steadily more intermixed, drawing farmers ever further into mutual cooperation (Williamson 2013: 184–206).

13.5 The archaeology of hedges

Whatever the determinants of open-field agriculture, and of its variant forms, in Hertfordshire much land lay from an early date in enclosed fields. Some of this comprised ring-fenced farms often associated with early manors, which had probably been brought into cultivation as early as that in the nearby open fields. Some, however, represented land assarted from the woods and wastes only in the course of the twelfth and thirteenth centuries (Rowe and Williamson 2013). Such fields generally have relatively irregular outlines, different from the gentle, smooth curves of those created by early piecemeal enclosure. In addition, enclosed landscapes – as should by now be clear – proliferated between the fifteenth and the eighteenth centuries as the open fields, especially those of 'irregular' form, were gradually enclosed. Most of the remaining open land in the county was converted into fields in the later eighteenth and early nineteenth centuries, when surviving open fields, and many areas of common 'waste', were removed by enclosure acts.

In Hertfordshire, as in other lowland counties, enclosed fields were mainly bounded, from medieval times, by hedges. These had to be rigorously managed, otherwise they would develop into a line of unconnected shrubs and trees, and in Hertfordshire this was often achieved by laying or plashing. Every 10 or 12 years, in the winter, the hedge was hacked back with a billhook but some of the principal stems were allowed to remain, cut roughly three-quarters of the way through and bent at an angle of 60 degrees or more, so that each overlapped its neighbour. When growth resumed a thick, impenetrable wall of vegetation was created (Muir and Muir 1997: 96–104). Where hedges were wider, however, they were treated as linear woods and coppiced – their constituent shrubs would simply be cut down, at intervals of between 10 and 20 years, usually to within a few centimetres of the ground (Rowe and Williamson 2013: 166–7). Such 'hedge rows' are commonly depicted on maps, and are described by a number of early commentators. James Parnell thus noted in 1769 how, in Hertfordshire,

> the oak and Elm hedgerows appear rather the work of Nature than Plantations generally Extending 30 or 40 feet Broad growing Irregularly in these stripes and giving the fields the air of being Reclaim'd from a general tract of woodland.
> (London School of Economics Coll. Misc 38/3 f.8)

The main purpose of hedges, whatever their precise form or mode of management, was to provide a stock-proof barrier, but they were also used as a source of firewood, as were the pollards which – as Anne Rowe describes elsewhere in this volume – were usually planted at intervals along them. Perhaps because of the proximity to fuel-hungry London, Hertfordshire farm leases from the seventeenth and eighteenth centuries place particular emphasis on the management of hedges and pollards, presumably to prevent over-cropping, restricting the frequency with which they could be cropped and sometimes insisting that pollards should only be lopped when the hedges in which they stood were plashed or otherwise 'new made'. A lease drawn up in 1657 for a farm in Ridge in Hertfordshire thus allowed the tenant 'to lopp all the pollard hasells maples sallows willows hawthorns & hornebeame trees growing in the severall hedges, fields, dells & hedgrows' provided that he 'lopp and cutt but one tenth part of all the pollards hasells, maples sallowes willowes hawthorns & hornbeams every year for and during the last nyne yeres' of the term (HALS D/ECd/E14).

In the 1960s the ecologist Max Hooper suggested that hedges could be roughly 'dated' by counting the number of shrub species which they contained in a standard 30-yard length. This was because most, he believed, had been planted with a single species, and subsequently acquired additional colonists through natural succession at a fairly uniform rate (Pollard *et al.* 1974: 79–85). Although the 'Hooper hypothesis' was widely accepted when first proposed, at least as a rough guide to a hedge's antiquity, a mass of evidence accumulated over subsequent decades leaves no doubt that it does not really work (see, for example, Barnes and Williamson 2006; Willmott 1980; J. Hall 1982). This is largely because early hedges were usually planted not with a single species but with several (Johnson 1978). Pehr Kalm, a Scandinavian visitor to England in 1748, noted how in the west of Hertfordshire hedges were planted with a mixture of hawthorn and sloe in addition to which the farmers 'set here and there, either at a certain distance or length from each other, or just as they please, small shoots of willows, beeches, ash, maple, lime, elm, and other leaf-trees' (Mead 2003: 116). Multi-species planting was common in part because it was difficult to access large quantities of good-quality hedging thorn but mainly because of the way that hedges were used as a source of fuel, which encouraged the planting of species such as ash, oak, elm, hazel, hornbeam and maple. Useful species might also be added some time *after* hedges had been planted. Arthur Young thus described in the early nineteenth century how the need for firewood in the county had 'induced the farmers to fill the old hedges everywhere with oak, ash, sallow and with all sorts of plants more generally calculated for fuel than fences' (1804: 50). Even if hedges did indeed acquire new 'colonists' at a relatively even rate, as Hooper believed, counting the number of species that a particular hedge now contains can tell us little about its age if we do not know how many species it was originally planted with. Eighteenth- and nineteenth-century hedges contain fewer species than older examples in part because they have had less time to acquire colonists, but also because, by this time – with the spread of coal use among the wealthier elements in society and the development of large commercial nurseries – it had become fashionable to plant single-species hedges of hawthorn or blackthorn, or hedges featuring a combination of both – hedges which might be managed by regular trimming rather than by vigorous laying. The connection between this change and the greater availability of coal as the transport infrastructure of the country improved was made clear by Young in a Hertfordshire context when he described how a thorn hedge, maintained by regular trimming, was 'a mere luxury and ornament, and has nothing profitable to recommend it. Hedges thus cease to be the collieries of a country' (1804: 52).

In 1977 a number of short papers published in *Hertfordshire's Past* described local attempts at using Hooper's method in generally negative terms (Dulley *et al.* 1977). David Short, for example, examining hedges in the area around Ashwell, suggested that it should be treated with caution and noted how two hedges bounding a parliamentary enclosure road not much more than a century old contained an average of five and six species per 30 yard length respectively (Dulley *et al.* 1977: 22–3). Hedges planted in the eighteenth and nineteenth centuries – dominated by thorn, and with relatively few other species – can to some extent be distinguished from multispecies hedges mainly (although not exclusively) planted before *c.*1750. But any further refinements in 'dating' along these lines are impossible, for reasons which should by now be clear. Much of the variation in species-content within the county, moreover, is related more to environmental factors than to age. On the damp, fertile boulder clays in the east mixed and often species-rich hedges are common, containing hazel, maple and dogwood, with significant quantities of ash, elm, hawthorn and blackthorn, and with scattered examples of hornbeam, wayfaring tree and spindle. In the Chilterns hedges containing a similar range of shrubs are common on the more calcareous ground, but on the acidic Plateau Drift dogwood and spindle are rare, hazel more common than maple, and the total number of species present fewer. In the south of the county the most diverse hedges likewise occur on more calcareous ground, as where chalk is exposed in major valleys. On the heavy, acidic London clays even medieval hedges often boast no more than four or five species in a 30-metre length, for blackthorn and elm tend to out-compete other shrubs, suckering vigorously and gradually spreading sideways along the hedge.

13.6 Relict fields and 'coaxial landscapes'

The discussion so far has assumed that Hertfordshire's fields – whether open or enclosed – are of medieval or post-medieval date. But a number of historians have argued that in some places field patterns might have much earlier origins. In 1885 Seebohm thus discerned (on what now seems very thin evidence) traces of 'a Roman holding' in the layout of the fields of Great Wymondley, while in 1962 R.H. Reid suggested that the semi-regular arrangement of fields at Reed was the remains of Roman 'centuriation' (Seebohm 1883; Reid 1962). Such ideas were given particular prominence in the neighbouring county of Essex in the 1970s and 1980s when Warwick Rodwell and Paul Drury noted that in some

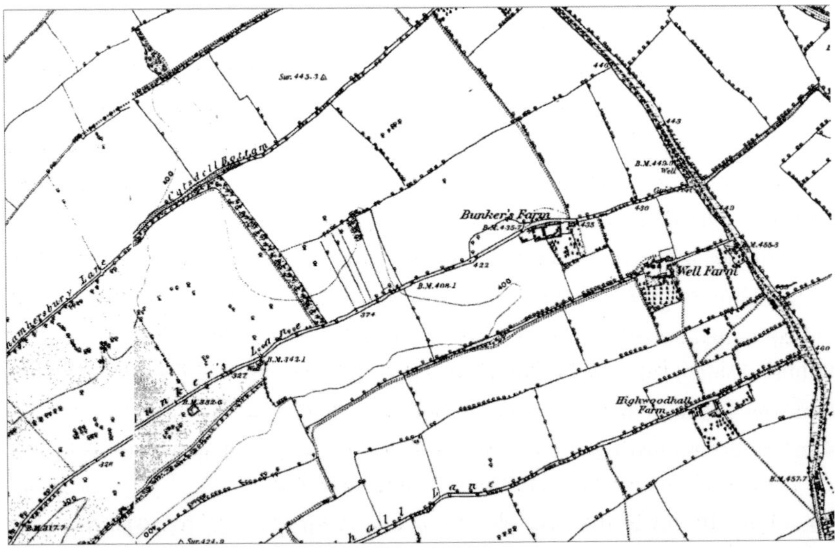

Figure 13.6: Coaxial field pattern in the west of Hemel Hempstead, as shown on the first edition Ordnance Survey 6 inches: 1 mile map.

districts patterns of fields could be found which, because they shared a common orientation across areas significantly larger than the vills or manors of the Middle Ages, appeared to have been planned in some earlier period, probably the Roman or later Iron Age (Rodwell 1978; Drury and Rodwell 1980). They also noted how, at places such as Little Waltham, Roman military roads appear to slice through the modern field pattern in a way analogous to a railway line or bypass, leaving awkward corners, in such a manner as to suggest that the fields were earlier. Subsequent work elsewhere identified other 'relict landscapes', many of which closely resembled a kind of planned prehistoric field system known, in the form of cropmarks or upstanding walls or earthworks, from a number of areas in England, most notably Dartmoor. These so-called 'coaxial' landscapes have a dominant 'grain', with axes running for a longer distance in one direction than another, so that they resemble in plan rather wavy and irregular brickwork (Fig. 13.6). Field patterns of this kind, extending over wide areas of countryside, have been identified in parts of Norfolk and Suffolk, in western and in south-eastern Cambridgeshire and in the Arrow valley of Shropshire, around Hergest and Lyonshall (Williamson 1987; 1998; Davison 1990; Hesse 1992; Oosthuizen 1998; 2003; Harrison 2002; White 2003: 37–47, 73–5). Some examples appeare to be visibly 'slighted' by Roman military roads; more generally, their antiquity seems to be confirmed by the fact that they generally extend over several parishes and townships, the boundaries of which join, leave and rejoin their principal axes in such a manner as to suggest that their basic frameworks at least were in place by the eleventh or twelfth centuries, when parishes became fixed in the landscape.

The idea that co-axial landscapes represent fragments of prehistoric systems of land division which have somehow survived to the present is accepted by many archaeologists. Indeed, Hertfordshire's 'Historic Landscape Characterisation' itself includes coaxial fields as a distinctive kind of field pattern, the accompanying text speculating on their possible prehistoric origins (Dyson-Bruce *et al.* 2006). Prehistoric or Roman origins have been suggested for such landscapes in the area around Arkley, in the far south of the county, and in Aldenham (Hunn 2004: 115–18; Brown 1992). The present author, working with Stewart Bryant and Brian Perry, has himself argued for the extreme antiquity of such field patterns in the area around Broxbourne and Wormley (Bryant *et al.* 2005). In reality, these distinctive landscapes probably have more complex histories: rather than dating from a single 'period' they are the result of many centuries of development, and their distinctive form is largely a consequence of the natural topography.

Most Hertfordshire examples of 'coaxial field systems' are found in the west of the county, on the Chiltern dipslope, or in the south, on the poor soils derived from London clay and pebble gravels. Early maps and surveys suggest that some of their constituent fields have always been enclosed and farmed in severalty; others, however, seem to have originated through the early piecemeal enclosure of open fields. Either way, these landscapes are invariably orientated at right angles to major rivers, their long axes running up the sides of the valley slopes and far out onto the interfluves, always from lower ground to higher (Plate 13.4). Many of their main elements, it should also be noted, were or are formed by roads and tracks, rather than by boundaries per se, especially on the London clays.

It is striking that the two areas characterised by these distinctive landscapes were, at the time of Domesday, the most sparsely populated in the county. They carried extensive tracts of woodland and pasture in Anglo-Saxon times, exploited by settlements concentrated in the principal valleys. It was here, on lighter land, that the main areas of arable land were located. The sparsely settled uplands, in contrast, were exploited as woodland and grazing, and it seems likely that the systems of parallel tracks developed because there was a recurrent pattern of movement between lower and higher ground, as wood and timber were brought from uplands down to valley settlements, and as livestock – including pigs – were repeatedly driven to the upland woods and pastures and back again. Yet at the same time it is probable that these landscapes did not originate solely as networks of lanes. Some of their prominent elements may have served as boundaries, dividing the upland woods and grazing grounds between different groups living in the principal valleys. Whatever their precise character, such lines or axes must initially have formed a rather sparse pattern. Only in the course of the later Saxon and early post-Conquest periods, as the population rose and more intensive forms of land use developed, were these loose networks gradually infilled with fields, the boundaries of which replicated their dominant 'grain'. The coaxial landscape in the area around Wormley and Broxbourne is particularly interesting in this respect (Bryant *et al.* 2005). While partly defined by field boundaries and roads, some of the main elements of the 'system' comprise earthworks surrounding, and subdividing, the ancient hornbeam woods of the district. The areas thus enclosed are much larger than the hedged fields lying outside the woods, suggesting that originally the landscape comprised a network of tracks and rather large enclosures suitable for grazing and the management of woodland, much of which was only later infilled with smaller fields (Bryant *et al.* 2005: 14). The expansion of cultivation, in the south of the county particularly, petered out as the poorest soils of the uplands – those formed on pebble gravels – were reached, and here vast tracts of common land survived until the nineteenth century, the coaxial landscapes clearly stretching out, as it were, to reach them (Plate 13.4).

Hertfordshire's coaxial landscapes are thus best understood as the footprint left by ancient economies which were based on the extensive exploitation of large territories, within which a high proportion of the land area was occupied by woodland and pasture; and also by the subsequent mode of their fragmentation, as population rose in the course of the Middle Ages. The same is probably true of similar landscapes found in other parts of England, and this has important implications for how we establish the antiquity of such arrangements. If, in their earliest phases, they were really networks of tracks and broad axes of movement, rather than true field systems, they clearly cannot be 'dated' by the fact that they are crossed, at an oblique angle, by a Roman military road. The original relationship was not between the road and a dense network of fields, but rather between the road and a widely spaced pattern of parallel lanes and boundaries. The tracks could just as easily post-date as pre-date the Roman road; their orientation was decided by local topography, by the need to connect two places by a straight line, or a series of lines. In fact, neither the Chiltern coaxials nor those funnelling in towards the southern uplands are in fact obviously 'slighted' by Roman military roads in this manner. The best example of such apparent superimposition in Hertfordshire comes from an area well known to Tony Rook – the elevated tract of countryside to the north-east of Welwyn, bounded by the rivers Mimram to the south and west and Beane to the east.

The Roman road running east from Welwyn to join Ermine Street just to the north of Colliers End visibly 'slights' the field pattern between Datchworth and Watton, leaving all kinds of awkward angles, some of which – even following large-scale 'simplification' of the landscape in the later twentieth century – are still noticeable today (Fig. 13.7). Tony in fact noticed this unusual arrangement back in the 1970s, although he never (to my knowledge) got as far as publishing his observations. Although the field pattern itself lacks the kind of rigid parallelism that may allow us to classify it as a 'coaxial system', the overall impression is of a Roman road cutting obliquely through an earlier, semi-regular, organised landscape. When we examine the wider landscape context, however, the situation becomes more complex.

The higher ground between the rivers is occupied by heavy and acidic soils of the Hornbeam Association, contrasting with the well-drained and neutral loams of the valley sides (Hodge *et al.* 1984). Large tracts of woodland and common land occur here, the latter – before the early nineteenth century – more extensive than today. The area's early role as a more continuous tract of upland wood-pasture is clear from the character of parish boundaries. Welwyn, Digswell and Datchworth were interdigitated in complex ways and a detached portion of Knebworth formed an island within Datchworth, embracing an isolated farm whose name – Swangley, 'the clearing of Swan's people' – still recalls its woodland origins (Rowe and Williamson 2013: 22). Evidently, late in the Saxon period a formerly intercommoned tract of land was shared between these parishes. Roads and boundaries seem to funnel up towards the core of the woodlands from the surrounding lower ground, and the boundaries and lanes apparently 'slighted' by the road should be seen in this context – their alignment is in part related to the direction of slope, but mainly shaped by the recurrent direction of movement from low ground to higher (Fig. 13.7). The Roman road, in contrast, takes a direct route, oblivious of topography.

Hertfordshire's coaxial landscapes do not, therefore, represent – in any straightforward and unproblematic manner – the remains of prehistoric field systems. This said, certain of their primary elements, making up their basic frameworks of parallel roads and boundaries, may nevertheless be very old. An excavation within Cheshunt Park, more or less in the centre of the area occupied by the coaxial system around Broxbourne and Wormley, revealed ditches conforming in orientation to the surrounding landscape which contained first- and second-century pottery (Ely and Edwards 2003). On the other side of the county excavations carried out in 2000 at The Grove, just to the north

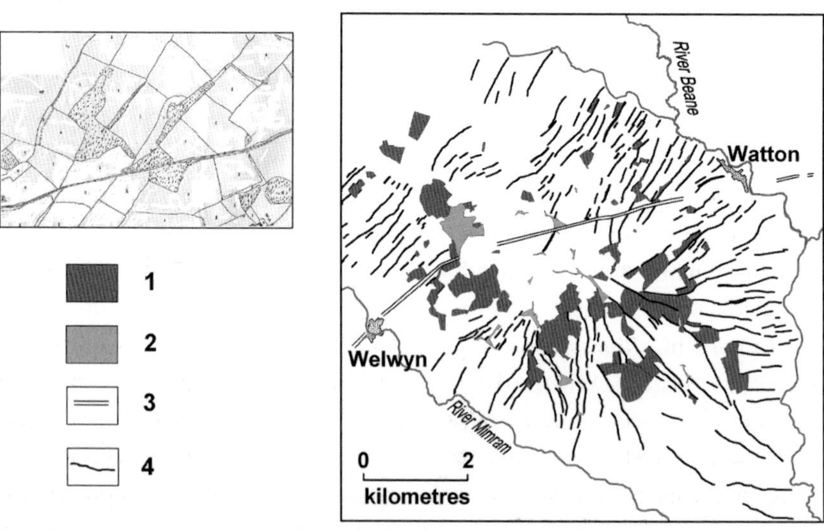

Figure 13.7: Roman road and early boundaries between Watton and Datchworth. The tithe award map for Watton (inset, left) appears to cut obliquely through an earlier field pattern of irregular coaxial form. The extract shown represents the area in the centre of the larger figure; examined against a wider landscape canvas it can be seen that the main boundaries 'slighted' by the Roman road have orientations determined by the local topography, running from lower ground to higher. 1. Principal areas of early woodland surviving in the nineteenth century; 2. commons; 3. Roman road; 4. selected lanes and boundaries.

of Watford, revealed lost elements of the local coaxial field pattern which had been removed when the landscape park was laid out here in the 1760s, several of which contained, in their basal fills, sherds of unabraded Iron Age pottery (Le Quesne *et al.* 2001). The late Iron Age and Roman landscape surveyed by Angus Wainwright, preserved as earthworks within woodland and common land on the Ashridge estate north of Berkhamsted, comprised a pattern of loosely parallel hollow-ways leading to small islands of enclosures and settlements surrounded by wide areas of apparently undivided land (Morris and Wainwright 1995). The layout of these features fits in neatly with the coaxial patterns of lanes and field boundaries in the wider landscape, and shows clearly the kind of early landscape from which these presumably evolved.

13.7 Conclusion

Hertfordshire's medieval fields may thus have developed, in some places at least, within ancient frameworks: but for reasons which still remain unclear they developed in a variety of different ways. In a strip of countryside lying on and below the chalk escarpment, extensive and continuous areas of open field emerged, probably by the eleventh century, which were farmed on highly communal lines from nucleated settlements. Where such land lay on chalk, individual strips were separated by unploughed grass balks and sometimes – on the steeper slopes – developed as lynchets or terraces. On the heavier soils, in contrast, especially on the Gault clays near Tring, the individual lands were usually ploughed as high-backed ridges. Some of this latter land was enclosed and laid to grass between the fifteenth and the eighteenth centuries – usually in small townships, dominated by a single landowner – but in larger places, and especially on the chalk, the landscape often remained open until enclosure by parliamentary act and some open fields, as at Bygrave and Clothall, survived into the twentieth century.

Outside this 'champion' belt of the county settlement developed in a more dispersed manner but open fields – albeit of 'irregular' form – were more widespread in medieval times than is often assumed, especially where the soils were comparatively light, in the principal valleys. They were interspersed with areas of enclosed land farmed in severalty, and with areas of woodland and grazing, all of which were mainly concentrated on the interfluves between the principal valleys. The area of enclosed land in the county gradually increased over time, as open fields were enclosed piecemeal, but where open arable was most extensive – in the larger valleys cutting through the boulder clay plateau in east Hertfordshire – it often survived until parliamentary enclosure in the eighteenth and nineteenth centuries and occasionally, as in the champion area, into the twentieth century. Parliamentary enclosure also created networks of fields at the expense of the county's larger commons, although, once again, a few survived, now used mainly as recreational spaces. In addition to the progress of enclosure, there were innumerable piecemeal changes – field patterns, in Hertfordshire and elsewhere, do not usually have 'dates', but histories. Of particular note was the widespread redrawing of field patterns by improving landlords in the eighteenth and nineteenth centuries, something which affected the east and the south of the county in particular. The most recent change has been the wholesale simplification of the landscape in the second half of the twentieth century, caused by large-scale mechanisation and the adoption of arable monocultures, which has affected the boulder clays of the north-east especially badly. Here, around two-thirds of the hedges have been removed since the 1950s, and those that remain are often poorly managed; in some parishes the proportion is higher, over 80% having been destroyed in Aspenden, for example.[3] Hedges and fields have also been lost on some scale in the south and west of the county through progressive urbanisation and suburbanisation since the later nineteenth century, although to a remarkable extent the broad outlines of the earlier agricultural landscape have often been maintained in the disposition of roads and property boundaries.

The story I have briefly sketched out in the foregoing pages needs further testing and refinement. Some issues are in particularly urgent need of research, and could usefully be addressed by local historians and archaeologists. More attention needs to be given to differentiating 'true' ridge and furrow in the archaeological record from 'narrow rig', and the latter needs to be more accurately dated. The true extent and character of open arable in medieval times needs to be assessed by detailed research into well-documented sample areas, in the south and centre of the county especially. Of particular interest is the survival of open fields at so many places into the late nineteenth century. Why did this happen – and what became of such fields eventually? This remains a rich field of research, for both professionals and 'amateurs'.

13.8 Acknowledgements

I would like to thank Isobel Thompson of the Hertfordshire County Council Historic Environment Unit for being, as usual, immensely generous with HHER data; Hertfordshire Archives and Local History, for permission to reproduce figure 13.2; and my old friend Anne Rowe, for reading and commenting on an earlier draft of this chapter and for supplying Figure 13.5.

13.9 References

Barnes, G. and Williamson, T. (2006), *Hedgerow History: ecology, history and landscape character* (Oxford).

Barton, P. (1981), *Manorial Economy and Society in Shenley: a Hertfordshire manor in the 13th and 14th Centuries* (Hertford).

Bowen, H.C. (1961), *Ancient Fields* (London).

Brown, T. and Foard, G. (1998), 'The Saxon Landscape: a Regional Perspective', in P. Everson and T. Williamson (eds), *The Archaeology of Landscape* (Manchester), pp. 67–94.

Brown, W.N. (1992), 'A Roman Settlement in Aldenham?', *Hertfordshire's Past* 33, pp. 4–5.

Bryant, S., Perry, B. and Williamson, T. (2005), 'A "Relict Landscape" in South-East Hertfordshire: Archaeological and Topographic Investigations in the Wormley Area', *Landscape History* 27, pp. 5–15.

Davison, A. (1990), *The Evolution of Settlement in Three Parishes in South East Norfolk*, East Anglian Archaeology 49 (Dereham).

Drury, P. (1981), 'Medieval 'narrow rig' at Chelmsford and its possible implications', *Landscape History* 3, pp. 51–8.

Drury, P. and Rodwell, W. (1980), 'Settlement in the Later Iron Age and Roman Periods', in D.G. Buckley (ed.), *The Archaeology of Essex to AD 1500*, Council for British Archaeology Research Report 34 (London), pp. 59–75.

Dulley, F., Burleigh, G., Sawford, B., Rowe, S. and Short, D. (1977), 'Hedges and local history', *Hertfordshire's Past*, 3 pp. 15–24.

Dyson-Bruce, L., Bryant, S. and Thompson, I. (2006), *Historic Landscape Character: County Report for Hertfordshire* (Hertford).

Ellis, W. (1742), *The Modern Husbandman* (London).

Ely, K.D. and Edwards, K. (2003), 'Cheshunt Park, Hertfordshire: an Archaeological Evaluation by the Time Team', unpublished report (Bristol).

Eyre, S.R. (1955), 'The curving plough-strip and its historical implications', *Agricultural History Review* 3, pp. 80–94.

Hall, D. (1982), *Medieval Fields* (Princes Risborough).

Hall, D. (1995), *The Open Fields of Northamptonshire* (Northampton).

Hall, J. (1982), 'Hedgerows in West Yorkshire: the Hooper method examined', *Yorkshire Archaeological Journal* 54, pp. 103–9.

Harrison, M.J., Mead, W.R. and Pannett, D.J. (1965), 'A Midland Ridge and Furrow Map', *Geographical Journal* 131, pp. 366–9.

Harrison, S. (2002), 'Open Fields and Earlier Landscapes: six parishes in south-east Cambridgeshire', *Landscapes* 3, pp. 35–54.

Hesse, M. (1992), 'Fields, Tracks and Boundaries in the Creakes, South Norfolk', *Norfolk Archaeology* 41, pp. 305–24.

Hodge, C.A.H., Burton, R.G.O., Corbett, W.M., Evans, R. and Searle, R.S. (1984), *Soils and their Use in Eastern England* (Harpenden).

Homans, G.C. (1941), *English Villagers of the Thirteenth Century* (Cambridge, MA).

Hunn, J. (2004), *Tyttenhanger: excavation and survey in the parish of Ridge* (Oxford).

Johnson, W. (1978), 'Hedges: a review of some early literature', *Local Historian* 13, pp. 195–204.

Jones, R. (2011), 'The Village and the Butterfly: Nucleation out of Chaos and Complexity', *Landscapes* 11, pp. 25–46.

Kerridge, E. (1973), *The Farmers of Old England* (London).

Lambourn, A. (2010), *Patterning Within the Historic Landscape and its Possible Causes* (Oxford).

Le Quesne, C., Capon, L. and Stevens, T. (2001), 'Post-excavation assessment of The Grove Estate, Watford', unpublished report, Hertfordshire County Council Environment Department.

Lewis, C., Mitchell-Fox, P. and Dyer, C. (2002), *Village, Hamlet and Field: Changing Settlements in Central England* (Macclesfield).

Mead, W.R. (2003), *Pehr Kalm: a Finnish visitor to the Chilterns in 1748* (Aston Clinton).

Morris, M. and Wainwright, A. (1995), 'Iron Age and Romano-British Settlement and Economy in the Upper Bulbourne Valley, Hertfordshire', in R. Holgate (ed.), *Chiltern Archaeology: recent work* (Dunstable), pp. 68–75.

Muir, R. and Muir, N. (1997), *Hedgerows: their history and wildlife* (London).

Munby, L. (1977), *The Hertfordshire Landscape* (London).

Oosthuizen, S. (1998), 'Prehistoric fields into medieval furlongs? Evidence from Caxton, South Cambridgeshire', *Proceedings of the Cambridgeshire Antiquarian Society* 86, pp. 145–52.

Oosthuizen, S. (2003), 'The roots of common fields: linking prehistoric and medieval field systems in west Cambridgeshire', *Landscapes* 4, pp. 145–52.

Oosthuizen, S. (2007), 'The Anglo-Saxon kingdom of Mercia and the origins and distribution of common fields', *Agricultural History Review* 55, pp. 153–80.

Page, W. (ed.) (1912), *VCH Hertford*, vol 3 (London).

Pollard, E., Hooper, M.D. and Moore, N.W. (1974), *Hedges* (London).

Rackham, O. (1986), *History of the Countryside* (London).

Reid, R.H. (1962), 'Reed: a topographical problem', *Hertfordshire Past and Present* 3, pp. 19–24.

Rippon, S. (2008), *Beyond the Medieval Village: The Diversification of Landscape Character in Southern Britain* (Oxford).

Roberts, B.K. and Wrathmell, S. (2000), 'Peoples of wood and plain: an exploration of national and local regional contrasts', in Hooke, D. (2000) (ed.) *Landscape: the richest historical record* (London), pp. 85–95.

Roberts, B.K. and Wrathmell, S. (2002), *Region and Place: A Study of English Rural Settlement* (London).

Roden, D. (1973), 'Field systems of the Chilterns and their environs', in A.R.H. Baker and R.A. Butlin (eds), *Studies of Field Systems in the British Isles* (Cambridge), pp. 325–76

Rodwell, W. (1978), 'Relict landscapes in Essex', in H.C. Bowen and P.J. Fowler (eds), *Early Land Allotment* (Oxford), pp. 89–98.

Rowe, A. and Williamson, T. (2013), *Hertfordshire: A Landscape History* (Hatfield).

Seebohm, F. (1883), *The English Village Community* (London).

Slater, G. (1907), *The English Peasantry and the Enclosure of the Open Fields* (London).

Sutton, J.E.G. (1965), 'Ridge and furrow in Berkshire and Oxfordshire', *Oxoniensia* 29, pp. 99–110.

Taylor, C. (2002), 'Nucleated Settlement: A View from the Frontier', *Landscape History* 24, pp. 53–71.

White, P. (2003), *The Arrow Valley, Herefordshire: Archaeology, Landscape Change and Conservation* (Hereford).

Williamson, T. (1987), 'Early coaxial field systems on the East Anglian boulder clays', *Proceedings of the Prehistoric Society* 53, pp. 419–31.

Williamson, T. (1998), 'The "Scole-Dickleburgh field system" revisited', *Landscape History* 20, pp. 19–28.

Williamson, T. (2004), *Shaping Medieval Landscapes: Settlement, Society, Environment* (Oxford).

Williamson, T. (2013), *Environment, Society and Landscape in Early Medieval England: time and topography* (Woodbridge).
Willmott, A. (1980), 'The woody species of hedges with special reference to age in Church Broughton, Derbyshire', *Journal of Ecology* 68, pp. 269–86.
Woodside, R. and Crow, J. (1999), *Hadrian's Wall: an historic landscape* (London).
Yelling, J.A. (1977), *Common Field and Enclosure, 1450–1850* (London).
Young, A. (1804), *General View of the Agriculture of Hertfordshire* (London).

Notes

1 Little if any surviving ridge and furrow on the London clays appears to be of 'broad' form. However, an illustration of *c.*1735 by Badeslade of Totteridge Park, on London clay in the far south of the county, appears to show an area of well-defined ridge and furrow, although its magnitude is difficult to assess and it might represent narrow rig.

2 This said, there are grounds for believing that some of these cropmarks have other origins: parallel lines might represent eighteenth- or nineteenth-century field drains, which were often spaced at around seven metres – similar to the width of broad rig.

3 Based on a random sample of ten one-kilometre by one-kilometre squares, and on a generous definition of what constitutes a hedge. The figures are: 8.8km reduced to 3.8km (TL3429); 6.4km reduced to 0.7km (3427); 7.8km reduced to 2km (3826); 8.5km reduced to 0.46km (4125); 9.9km reduced to 5.6km (4319); 16.4km reduced to 5.3km (4418); 10.8km to 6.1km (4223); 6.1km to 1.3km (3718); 7.1km to 4.1km (3334); and 9.1km to 4.4km (3232).

CHAPTER 14

Pollards: living archaeology

Anne Rowe

14.1 Introduction

Old pollarded trees are among the most ancient living features in our countryside and most trees over two centuries old are former pollards (Barnes and Williamson 2011: 5). As well as being venerable and sometimes awe-inspiring, they are usually of great ecological value and also provide valuable evidence of past landscape management practices. The branches of a pollard all grow from the same point on the trunk of the tree, generally between two and three metres above the ground. This is the point where, from a young age, the tree was repeatedly 'beheaded' – the crown lopped off and then allowed to regrow before being cut again. The process is essentially the same as that for coppicing trees but with the latter the branches, or poles, are cut at or near ground level. The advantage of pollarding is that grazing animals cannot reach the tender new shoots that appear after lopping. So pollards are ideally suited to growing in hedgerows and also in the dual-purpose habitat known as wood-pasture, where livestock or deer graze the pasture beneath well-spaced trees which, because they are regularly beheaded, are relatively small, with compact crowns. Although managed primarily as a naturally renewable source of wood for fuel, pollards could also be cut to supply leafy fodder or other wood products requiring relatively small poles. Many of our native tree species respond well to being repeatedly lopped in this way, often over the course of several centuries, the trunk (or bolling) developing over time into a relatively short, stout, cylinder (often hollow) topped by a compact crown of small branches. While actively managed these pollards are physically very stable structures but, with the decline of pollarding from the late eighteenth century onwards, their branches have grown unchecked, making the trees 'top heavy' and vulnerable to high winds: many have been lost in recent decades (Fig. 14.1; Petit and Watkins 2003: 164–8, 171). Most survivors today are oaks and the majority are to be found

Figure 14.1: An old oak pollard in Weston Park which collapsed in the winter of 2011/12.

in old hedgerows or marking former field boundaries. But these venerable oaks give us a misleading impression of the ancient practice of pollarding and of the appearance of the countryside in the past; recent research – both archival and in the field – reveals a more complex picture.

There will no doubt always have been a number of large, hoary old trees of the kind with which we are familiar today, but the majority of pollards in earlier centuries would have been considerably smaller: their branches – or poles – were probably lopped with a billhook rather than with an axe and perhaps while standing on the ground or on a short ladder. The early fifteenth-century illustration of an oak pollard and the sixteenth-century illustration of pollarding in Plate 14.1 and Figure 14.2 provide a better indication of the size of tree we should envisage.[1] In addition to the huge number growing in hedgerows, many pollards were managed in wood-pastures, which ranged in size from narrow belts around the margins of enclosed fields to those covering hundreds of acres, both within medieval deer parks and extending over vast areas of common grazing land. Wood-pasture commons covered extensive areas of Hertfordshire until the late eighteenth century, featuring especially in the north-west on the Chiltern hills and in the south and south-east of the county on the London clay-covered 'Southern Uplands'. This paper examines the evidence of pollards growing on Hertfordshire's farmland, in deer parks and other enclosures, and on

Figure 14.2: Detail from a woodcut illustration in a book by Georgius Agricolas, *De re metallica libri XII*, Basel, 1556. Source: <http://commons.wikimedia.org/wiki/File:Georgius_Agricola_Erzsucher.jpg>, accessed 25 August 2013.

commons from the medieval period onward. Unfortunately the evidence is very patchy, both geographically and chronologically, and there is very little evidence for pollards in the medieval period outside deer parks. Records of farmland trees start to become available from the sixteenth century and evidence for pollards on commons is especially abundant for the seventeenth century, but only for the south-eastern corner of the county. Here, the documentary record shows that in some places hornbeam pollards were growing in remarkably high densities, creating an interesting variant of the traditional wood-pasture landscape.

14.2 Farmland pollards

Most pollards were grown in hedgerows around fields and provided a constantly renewable source of fuel for local inhabitants, for whom wood, in a county with no reserves of coal or peat, was a vital resource. A survey of Olives Farm, Hunsdon, in 1556 provides one of our earliest detailed records of the number, value and management of farmland trees.[2] Growing in the hedgerows around the enclosed fields of the 174.5-acre farm were 403 oak trees that were being grown for their timber rather than being managed as pollards for wood fuel. These oaks were valued at between 2s and 8s per tree; most were worth 2s 6d or 2s 8d, but nine trees were worth 8s each. The total value of the timber oaks was £63 6s 4d. In addition to the timber oaks, the hedgerows also contained 493 pollards, which the surveyor listed as follows:

> 12 are worth 10d the pollard which is 10s
> 116 at 8d the pollarde which is 77s 4d
> 86 at 12d the pollarde which is £4 6s
> 132 at 16d the pollarde which is £8 16s
> 41 at 18d the pollard which is 61s 6d
> 40 at 20d the pollard which ys 66s 8d
> 40 at 2s the pollarde which is £4
> 26 at 2s 4d the pece which is 60s 8d
> Total value of the pollards £30 18s 2d

The range in values recorded by the surveyor suggests that the trees were managed on a 12-year pollarding cycle, with 40 trees lopped each year. On the neighbouring manor of Stanstead Abbots, also surveyed in 1556, the timber oaks were only small and consequently assigned the same value (20d each) as the pollards: 'growinge disparsed in severall groves and hedgerowes 187 tymber trees beinge yonge okes and pollardes valued one with another at xx d the tree in thole xv li xi s viii d'.[3] On Napsbury manor near St Albans in 1569 were 14 fields of pasture (172.9 acres) containing 158 pollards, 13 arable fields (238.6 acres) containing 338 pollards and 5 fields of meadow (29.75 acres) containing 21 pollards.[4]

Seventeenth- and eighteenth-century surveys of farmland trees also record large numbers of pollards and the way in which hedgerow pollards were to be managed was usually set down in farm leases of the period because, while the landlord remained the owner of the bolling, the tenant was often entitled to use the lops. A 12-year lease of Aspenden Hall Farm in 1745 is typical and specifies that the new tenant, Elizabeth Sibley, shall not:

- Lopp or Topp and Pollard Trees growing in or near any of the hedges … but when such hedges shall be plashed or new made …
- And shall & will do her … utmost endeavour to keep & preserve the said hedges trees & all other the Wood and Timber growing on the premises from being cropped or damaged by Cattle or otherwise …
- And also shall not nor will Lopp any of the Pollard Trees cut any of the Wood or new make any of the hedges growing on the premises under nine or above twelve years growth & then only at seasonable times of the year …
- Nor shall or will Lopp or Topp any Trees but such only as have been heretofore Lopped or Topped
- Nor shall or will stock Grub up Cut down Head Trim Prune or damage any of the stubbs or timber or timber like trees growing on the premises nor cut down any of the Pollard Trees …[5]

The importance of farmland trees to landowners is also made clear from the way that they were carefully portrayed on estate maps from the sixteenth to the nineteenth centuries. Not only were trees individually depicted, but some surveyors even colour-coded them to indicate the different species of timber tree – oak, elm or ash – or to indicate that a tree was a pollard.[6] The species of the pollards was generally not recorded – it was evidently not important (Plate 14.2). On some maps the pollards are depicted growing around the margins of fields and it is not clear whether that was in fact where they were growing or whether they were actually growing in the adjacent hedge. Analysis of these estate maps from the eighteenth and early nineteenth centuries shows that in north-east Hertfordshire over 60 per cent of the farmland trees were pollards, a figure which would no doubt have been higher in earlier centuries (Rowe and Williamson 2013: 171). The highest densities of hedgerow pollards were recorded in the south-east of the county. On the 89-acre Hammond Street Farm, Cheshunt, in 1650 there were '927 lopt Pollardes of oake Ash and Hornebeame'.[7] Assuming the majority of these were growing on the 48 acres (19 hectares) of enclosed fields on the farm, the density was about 19 pollards per acre. At Wormley West End Farm in Wormley in 1784, there were, spread fairly evenly through the 28 fields, which covered just 94 acres (38 ha), no fewer than 1,358 pollards (about 14 per acre), as well as 131 oak, 14 ash and 3 elm trees.[8] The record of hornbeam pollards on Hammond Street Farm is unusual: the few documents which do record the species of pollards on farmland suggest that they were most commonly elm, followed by ash and then oak. Hornbeam was rarely recorded on farmland but, as we shall see, in the south-east of the county at least, it was often the most frequent pollarded tree on commons (Rowe and Williamson 2013: 171).

14.3 Pollards in deer parks

The earliest parks were usually enclosed from areas of wooded manorial 'waste' (uncultivated land), often near the margins of the manor and parish, in the twelfth and thirteenth centuries. They were exclusive private enclosures stocked with deer and, because a park was an expensive asset, the cost of maintenance was commonly recorded in the manorial accounts. But a well-managed park could also be a source of income, primarily through sales of wood and timber. Translating the few medieval manorial accounts that have survived can be problematic, not least because the bailiff who usually compiled them wrote in Latin and used words whose meanings are now obscure or ambiguous. For example, *loppare* is the Latin verb meaning 'to cut off' or 'trim' and is used to record the cutting of branches from a tree. *Croppa* is usually translated as 'crop', 'harvest' or 'harvest of trees felled for timber', but it also appears to refer to pollarding, as it is frequently used in relation to a specific number of trees and it seems unlikely that the trees were being felled, partly because the price per tree is fairly constant and relatively low. Thus the bailiff's accounts for the manor of Little Hadham record the sales of 90 'cropp' de hernebem' in the park in 1375/6, 140 'croppees de hernebemes' in 1376/7 and 36 'croppys de herbemes' in the park in 1379/80, all of which sold for 2½d per tree or per 'crop'. In 1377/8 103 'loppes de hernebem' were sold, also for 2½d each, which seems to suggest that the words *cropp* and *lopp* were both used to record pollarding (Rowe 2009: 34).

The only park in the county for which comprehensive manorial accounts are known to survive from the medieval period is the deer park belonging to the bishops of Ely at Little Hadham. Oak was the only species recorded in this park in the early fourteenth century and 112 trees were pollarded in 1331/2. Later in the century far fewer oaks were being pollarded – for example, 13 in 1368/9 and just 4 in 1379/80 – and it appears that the oaks had been replaced as a source of wood by hornbeams – 132 trees called 'hernebems' were sold in the park for 2d each in 1374/5.[9] Hornbeam makes a similar appearance, albeit significantly later, in the records of the manors of Knebworth and Great Munden. Quantities of 'loppes' were being sold each year from the parks at Knebworth in the early fifteenth century but the species of tree being pollarded was not recorded. Later in the century, in 1482, the 'loppes' of 13 hornbeams in Knebworth's great park were sold; the bailiff recorded them as 'trees called hornebeme' as though the name was new to him.[10] Two decades earlier the 'lopp and cropp' of 'trees called Harinebeme' sold from the park at Great Munden was similarly recorded in the manorial accounts as if it was a novelty.[11] So there is a suggestion in these records that hornbeam was perhaps being deliberately introduced to Hertfordshire's deer parks during the fourteenth and fifteenth centuries, early trend-setters being the bishops of Ely, in whose accounts for the manor of Little Hadham the phrase 'trees called hornbeam' appears in 1375. The main Hertfordshire estate of the bishops, however, was at Hatfield, where the (considerably sparser) records paint a more complex picture.

About 2000 acres of land between Hatfield and Newgate Street village had been enclosed to create deer parks by the bishops of Ely in the parish of Hatfield before 1222 (Rowe 2009: 108–12, 114). Large quantities of charcoal were sold from the estate in 1396, although the accounts do not record whether the wood was derived from coppice or pollards, nor the species of tree, but an additional sum of 16s 6d was received from the sale of the 'cropp' of 102 hornbeam pollards in the little park.[12] However, a survey carried out in 1538, when Henry VIII acquired the manor of Hatfield, makes no reference to hornbeams. The great park (*c.*1860 acres) was said to contain 2000 oaks and beeches valued at 8d each, while the 350-acre middle park (the former little park) contained 2000 oaks and beeches valued at 8d each which were said to be worth 33s 4d yearly to sell.[13] The low valuation of 8d per tree, and the annual sale value, suggests that these 12,000 trees were all pollards. Given the puzzling omission of any reference to hornbeams – which reappear in the records in great numbers a century later – the possibility that the Tudor surveyor mistook hornbeams for beech trees has to be considered.

Oak dominates the records of parkland pollards in the mid-sixteenth century: the deer park at Hertingfordbury contained 1547 oak trees, 547 of which were pollards or dotards (an old, decayed pollard) worth 4s each in 1553;[14] numerous oak pollards were also recorded in the parks at Cheshunt and Kings Langley;[15] in Sayes Park, Sawbridgworth, there were 97 'pollarde okes and asshes reserved for the Farmor'. In the parks at Hunsdon in 1556 the parkland trees were mostly oaks (750 in the great park, 140 in the little park and 60 in the pond park, with 60 ash and four 'wyches') but it is not clear whether these were pollards or timber trees; almost certainly pollards were the 'woodgrounds set with maple, thornes, hasell, hornebeame and oke'.[16] However, in the parks at The More, Rickmansworth, described as 'well stored with pollards' in 1556, the dominant trees were hornbeams and maples.[17]

By the middle of the seventeenth century there appears to have been a significant change in the number of pollards growing in some parks. In 1650 the 670-acre Cheshunt Park contained 8693 'lopt Pollards of horne beame and oake' (13 per acre) valued at £663 17s 10d (just over 1s 6d each).[18] A further 613 'old Dotrills and Hallow trees good for little save for the fieringe' were valued at 10s per tree, £306 10s in total, which suggests that these old pollards were considerably larger than the trees which were still being lopped.[19] Large numbers of trees were also recorded in the nearby Theobalds Park in 1650 but the records of pollards are largely confined to those parts of the park which had been enclosed from the neighbouring commons of Cheshunt, Northaw and Enfield Chase by James I *c.*1612–22.[20] Unlike Cheshunt Park, which had been established by about 1280, Theobalds Park was a much more recent creation, first established *c.*1580 by Lord Burghley around his new house at Theobalds and subsequently expanded by his son, Robert Cecil and then, on a much larger scale, by James I (Rowe 2009: 78, 82; 2012: 38–9). It seems unlikely that large numbers of pollards would be established within the king's new park in the early seventeenth century, so the pollards recorded by the Parliamentary surveyors in 1650, after the execution of Charles I, are more likely to be a valuable record of the trees remaining on the former commons and will be discussed further below (p.310). Research by Peter Austin suggests that significant changes had been made to the tree composition of the surviving medieval parkland at Hatfield by the early seventeenth century. Much of the former Great Park had been disparked by Robert Cecil, Lord Salisbury, when he became the owner of the Hatfield estate at the beginning of the seventeenth century and records from 1626 indicate that the oak and beech pollards had been partly replaced by thousands of small hornbeam pollards valued at just 9½d each (Austin 2013: 143). Using figures recorded in a survey of 1669, Austin estimates that there were over 8000 hornbeam pollards in the 350-acre Middle Park – 'about 24 trees per acre' – in addition to 810 beech pollards and 539 oak pollards (Austin 2013: 146).

These pollards were growing in 20 named areas of the park and the average value of the hornbeams was about 2s, with significantly higher values for the beech and oak pollards. The dense plantations of small hornbeam pollards suggested by the Hatfield records are similar to those which appear to have been planted on areas of common land in the south-east of the county (discussed below).

14.4 Pollards in other enclosed wood-pasture

Pollards were also grown within private enclosures other than deer parks, but documentary evidence for their management is difficult to find before the sixteenth century. Many of the sources relate to rabbit warrens, which, like deer parks, were 'elite' features which could be created only by manorial lords. A survey of Hertingfordbury warren in 1553 recorded 260 pollards and dotards each valued at 16d, which the farmer of the warren had 'used to crop for his fuel'.[21] Some of our earliest maps record trees – and pollards – in remarkable detail and depict them growing in situations which would look very odd to modern eyes. One of the oldest (and most beautiful) maps in the Hertfordshire Archives, for example, records the manor of Digswell in 1599 and shows pollards – and a few unpollarded 'maiden' trees – growing in fields of wood-pasture close to the river Mimram (Plate 14.3).[22] In the adjacent manorial rabbit warren most of the trees are portrayed as 'maidens' but there is also a group of trees which have been pollarded, probably to provide dried leafy hay – supplementary winter fodder for the rabbits – and fuel for the warrener. A plan of the Cole Green estate of 1704 similarly distinguishes between timber trees and pollards, both in the hedgerows and within fields.[23]

14.5 Pollards on commons and wastes

Some of the best-documented wood-pasture commons were in the south-east of the county, where they survived until relatively recently. The largest was in the parish of Northaw and covered 2,150 acres when enclosed in 1806.[24] Growing on the common was an unrecorded number of hornbeams which were lopped every 20 years in late medieval times for the benefit of St Albans abbey, which held the manor.[25] In 1556 the 'common wood' of Northaw was reported to be 'seven miles compass' and the 'loppes and shreddinges' of the hornbeams provided William Clarke, the steward, bailiff and woodward of the manor, with sufficient income to pay his yearly rent of £56.[26] In addition to the hornbeams there were 100 oak pollards valued at 2s each and 4072 timber oaks worth a total of £549 6s.[27] Northaw common was joined to the west by Mymwood common and to the east by Cheshunt common (also known as Cheshunt Wood), forming an area of conjoined common land which extended over 19 square kilometres and survived into the late eighteenth century. To the south these commons were bordered by Enfield Chase in Middlesex, another huge common, which covered 33.8 square kilometres when enclosed in 1777 (Rowe and Williamson 2013: 129).

The documentary evidence suggests that hornbeam pollards were prevalent on these commons by at least the sixteenth century. In addition to those on Northaw common, a 1545 woodward's account records 14 'dottard hornebemes' in the common wood of Chesthunt, then held by Henry VIII, which were sold for 3s 8d (just over 3d each on average).[28] But, by the seventeenth century, the number of hornbeam pollards in particular appears to have increased markedly. The parliamentary survey of Theobalds Park of 1650 records the individual areas of the park which had been enclosed from each of the surrounding commons when James I expanded the park in the early seventeenth century, effectively 'fossilising' the trees growing on those commons within the new parkland. The 149 acres enclosed from Cheshunt common contained '4798 lopt pollards and hollow dotrills and horne beame' valued at 2s per tree (£479 16s). Of the 475 acres of Enfield Chase enclosed into the park in 1611, 140 acres were said to be 'Indifferentlie well planted with lopt Pollards hollow Dotrills hornebeame and oake worth each acre £5 5s' (£735 in total). Also standing on the former Chase were '418 trees of Beach and Horne beame of severall sortes and severall prises'; with an average value of 6s, these were probably larger trees sparsely scattered over the remaining 335 acres of the Chase.[29] The description of the 140 acres of the former Chase as 'Indifferentlie well *planted*' (my italics) is interesting. The 336 acres of Northaw common which were taken into the park included '132 acr[es] reasonable well *planted* with Lopt pollards hornebeame, oaken Dotrills and hollow trees' valued at £6 per acre (£792), and the 149 acres of the former Cheshunt common were also described as 'beinge *planted* with wood'. Aside from the interesting possibility that these trees had indeed been deliberately planted, the figures provided allow us to calculate the density of the trees on this part of Cheshunt common as about 32 trees per acre.

It is possible that the use of the word 'planted' by the seventeenth-century surveyor was simply a figure of speech and it might be assumed that the dominant tree species growing on any particular common is the incidental result of the interaction of natural features (such as soil and microclimate) and human intervention over many centuries – either direct cropping of the trees and shrubs for fuel or by the grazing of domestic livestock (the effects varying with the different grazing habits of cows, sheep, horses, etc., and with stocking densities). But the chances of any unprotected tree seedling growing to maturity on a well-used common must have been remote and evidence found by Patsy Dallas in Norfolk shows that some trees on commons were deliberately planted and, presumably, protected from grazing animals until big enough to survive. For example, at Pulham in south Norfolk the tenants of the manor were said to have planted and cropped the trees on the common near their houses since 'time out of mind' in 1600, and at Gressenhall and elsewhere in Norfolk there is evidence dating from the sixteenth to the early nineteenth centuries for tenants' holding rights to 'plantings' of trees on the common adjacent to their properties (Dallas 2010: 26–30). Conclusive proof of tree planting on commons in Hertfordshire is yet to be found but there is a growing body of evidence for dense stands of hornbeam pollards on commons in the south-east of the county, apparently quite different in character from those found by Dallas in Norfolk. One plausible explanation for these stands is that plantations of hornbeams were deliberately established on parts of the commons and subsequently pollarded in

Year	No. of transactions	Price per hundred heads	Heads lopped	Total income from sale of pollard heads
1658	48	£1 13s 4d	5045	£91 17s 8d
1659	30	£1 13s 4d	3034	£48 14s 8d
1660	22	£1 13s 4d	2500	£41 13s 4d
1661	19	£1 13s 4d	1800	£30
1662	18	£1 13s 4d	1550	£25 16s 8d
1663	16	£1 13s 4d	1250	£20 16s 8d
1664	13	£1 13s 4d	1400	£23 6s 8d
1665				no account for this year
1666	64	£2	6272	£125 10s
1667	57	both	6290	£119 4s
1668	20	£1 13s 4d	6200+	£133 18s (at least)[1]
1669	36	£2	3630 or 8652	£99 13s 10d (includes Wood Green and 'Rayes Gravill Pitts Hill'). Higher figure includes 'Larance hill' and 'Sand Pitts'[2]
1670	52	£2	4425	£90
1671	28	£2	2675	£54 19s
1672	34	£2	2800	£57 4s
1673	57	£2	3550	£71
1674	52	£2	3050	£61
1675	64	£2	2875	£57 10s
1676	62	£2	3200	£65 10s
1677	83	£2 4s	4950	£108 19s
1678	95	£2 4s	6400	£145 16s

Notes

1. There was a hiatus in the accounts in this year due to the death of Sir Richard Lucy, lord of the manor.
2. An extra entry in the account records a further 5667 heads but 645 of these at Wood Green had already been counted.

Table 14.1: Sales of pollard heads on Cheshunt Common recorded in the woodwards' accounts for the manor of Cheshunt in the seventeenth century.

order to increase the supply of wood or charcoal – perhaps to supply the London fuel market. Analysis of a variety of documentary records for Cheshunt in the later seventeenth century sheds some light on the management of the hornbeam pollards on Cheshunt common at that time.

At the end of the seventeenth century there were said to be 24,000 hornbeam pollards growing on 1186 acres of Cheshunt common (an average density of approximately 20 per acre)[30] and, unusually, the lord of the manor owned not only the trunks but also the pollard heads. Detailed woodwards' accounts covering two decades from 1658 show that purchasers were buying large quantities of heads at a set price and lopping the trees themselves (see Table 14.1).[31] The total number of pollard heads lopped and sold each year varied widely from 1250 to 6400, with no discernible cyclical pattern. Over the 20-year period 1658–78 purchases of 100 pollard heads were the quantity most frequently recorded (about half of the transactions) in the annual accounts, but the figures suggest that this percentage was starting to decline by 1678, when only 42 per cent of the buyers bought 100 heads. This is partly explained by a marked increase in the number of purchasers over the 20-year period, with a corresponding decrease in the number of heads bought in each transaction. In 1658 and 1668 just 11 per cent and 3 per cent, respectively, of the pollards cut were sold in quantities of 50 or fewer heads; in 1678 almost 40 per cent of the heads were sold in these smaller quantities. The price of the wood sold rose by 32 per cent between 1658 and 1678, reflecting the general trend in the price of underwood in eastern England (Rackham 2003: 167).[32]

The names of many of the people buying pollard heads on Cheshunt common recur regularly in the woodwards' accounts, often annually. A comparison of the lists of purchasers with the names recorded in the Cheshunt hearth tax returns of 1662–3 and 1664–5 and on a parish survey of 1669 shows clearly that the pollard heads were purchased almost entirely by the local inhabitants and, presumably, for their own consumption.[33] Of the 63 buyers recorded in 1666, all but 14 can be identified in these contemporary sources; seven of the unidentified 14 share surnames with others in the parish and were probably also local residents. These buyers were the poorer inhabitants of the area: all but a handful had just three or fewer hearths in their cottages and nine (14 per cent) were classified as paupers – too poor to pay the hearth tax – in 1664. Most of the buyers lived in the area known (significantly) as Cheshunt Woodside, in small secondary settlements – such as Hammonds End and Goffs Lane – bordering the common, rather than in the more affluent areas of primary settlement closer to the river Lea such as Churchgate and Waltham Cross Street. The heads of 100 pollards may seem a large quantity of wood for a single household to lop and consume in a year, but if the trees were small (as in Plate 14.1 and Fig. 14.2) and cut on a short cycle of six or seven years the quantity was perhaps not as large as we might imagine. Of course, it is possible that reselling some of the wood they had lopped provided a valuable source of income for some purchasers but presumably only for a small minority, or the competition would have driven the resale price down too low to make it worthwhile.

The fact that most purchases were of 100 heads, or a multiple or fraction thereof, raises a number of questions. Was 100 heads the average fuel requirement for the poorer household in Cheshunt? Or were the trees planted in rows or blocks of 50 or 100 trees? References to particular locations on the common suggest that the pollards were not evenly distributed but perhaps concentrated in groves or plantations. The account for 1668, records the pollards lopped at Wood Green, 'Rayes Gravill Pitts Hill' and 'Larance hill', but also those lopped in three numbered 'shots', a term normally associated with common arable fields (a bundle of strips cropped as a single unit). When combined together, these tenuous scraps of evidence – the use of the word 'shot', the regular purchases of pollard heads in units of 50 or 100 and the description of trees being 'planted' on areas of common – all provide supporting evidence for the theory that hornbeams were deliberately planted in dense stands on parts of these extensive commons in south-east Hertfordshire with the intention of producing a regular crop of wood from the common while still enabling the commoners to exercise their traditional grazing rights.

Establishing plantations on common land can have been possible only with the approval of – and probably at the instigation of – the lord of the manor who owned it. This seems particularly clear at Cheshunt because it was the lord of the manor who was gaining income from the sale of the pollard heads in the seventeenth century.[34] The same man was also lord of the neighbouring manor of Broxbourne, where there is also evidence for dense stands of hornbeam pollards, not only on Broxbourne common but also on roadside greens and verges – relatively small areas of common land or manorial 'waste' surviving from the medieval period – which appear to have been planted by the end of the sixteenth century. Similarly, the manor of Hoddesdonbury included large numbers of pollards on its part of Broxbourne common and on neighbouring Cowheath common, as well as on various smaller greens in the seventeenth century: the tenant of Hoddesdonbury farm was entitled to lop the pollards on Martins Green and Cowheath common in 1613, as was Sir Henry Monson, the lessee in 1671, when 1108 pollards were lopped on the latter (Austin 2013: 150).[35] Wood accounts for 1633 and 1645 record the sales of the heads of around 2500 pollards from Goosegreen and 'Redhill Street' (Ermine Street) and a survey in 1649 recorded 2086 pollards on

Martins Green and on the part of Broxbourne common belonging to the manor of Hoddesdonbury (Austin 2013: 150). Most of the pollards on the Broxbournebury and Hoddesdonbury estates appear to have been managed on a 12-year cropping cycle and the fact that it was the manorial lords who owned the wood lopped from pollards on the commons is good evidence that they (or their predecessors) were responsible for planting the trees in the first place.

14.6 Dating the hornbeam plantations

There appears to be no good evidence for the creation of these hornbeam 'plantations', but there are indications that it may have occurred in the second half of the sixteenth century. Although it is clear that there were pollards on the commons before the sixteenth century there is little evidence for their management, and wood sales in the middle of the sixteenth century were generally of coppice wood, sold by the acre, rather than of pollards – although, as previously noted, 14 dottard hornbeams were sold in 1545. By the beginning of the seventeenth century, however, there were dense stands of hornbeam pollards on both Cheshunt and Northaw commons, and on the 'greens and highway waste' of the Cecil estates in the Broxbourne area (Austin 2013: 150). William Cecil, later Lord Burghley, who acquired property between Hoddesdon and Waltham Cross from the 1560s, was certainly keen to maximise income from his woodlands, instituting new methods of woodland management and keeping good records (Austin 1996).[36] He also appears to have promoted the cultivation of pollards on his estates: when he acquired the manor and farm of Hoddesdonbury there had been barely enough pollards and wood to provide the farmer with sufficient fuel and wood for his everyday needs and yet, a century later, there was said to be 'a vast number of pollards on the farm' (Austin 2013: 149).[37] Burghley may well also have sought to improve the productivity of the commons and manorial 'wastes' between Hoddesdon and Cheshunt by planting pollards on the numerous wayside greens belonging to his manors of Perriers, Baas, Geddings and Hoddesdonbury – thereby enabling commoners to continue grazing their animals on the greens but also growing wood for his own profit. His ideas and methods may well have been shared with his neighbour Sir Henry Cock, who lived at Broxbournebury and also owned the manor of Cheshunt (Page 1912: 432, 447). Sir Henry was prominent in the Elizabethan court and, in his role as Cofferer of the Royal Household, he probably worked closely with Lord Burghley, the Queen's chief minister; perhaps the two men shared ideas on increasing wood production by establishing more pollards on their neighbouring estates. In addition, we have already noted the appearance of similarly dense plantations of hornbeam pollards within the former parkland on the Hatfield estate, acquired by Burghley's son, Robert Cecil, at the beginning of the seventeenth century. It is possible that the hornbeams were established in the late sixteenth century when the estate belonged to Queen Elizabeth – perhaps on the recommendation of Lord Burghley – or by Robert Cecil, immediately upon acquiring the estate from James I in 1607.

The motivation for creating the hornbeam plantations must have been to increase wood production while, both on the commons and in the parks, maintaining the pasture for grazing animals. The density of the tree-planting may well have reduced the quality of the pasture but this was perhaps mitigated to some extent in some places by a short pollarding cycle. Forestry experts maintain that the main reason for growing hornbeam was as a source of fuel, but whether the increased wood production in south-east Hertfordshire was primarily to supply local fuel needs or to increase the production of charcoal for sale further afield is not clear. Charcoal production, much of it destined for the London market, had been an important element of woodland management in south-east Hertfordshire from the medieval period. Records from 1368 onwards show that charcoal was regularly taken to the city by pack-horse and cart from both Cheshunt and Hatfield (Galloway *et al.* 1996: 454). Charcoal worth over £64 was made and sold on the Hatfield estate in 1396, charcoal worth nearly £15 was sold from the manor of Cheshunt in 1435–6 and, on the manor of Enfield, just over the county boundary in Middlesex, charcoal sales in 1444–5 were worth £60.[38] There was clearly still a market for charcoal in the later sixteenth century, as Lord Burghley's wood accounts detail sales totalling over £130 from just three of his manors in 1580: 1572 sacks of charcoal from Cowheath Wood on the manor of Hoddesdonbury, 5457 sacks from Derrys Grove on the manor of Perriers and 786 sacks (plus another 784 sacks delivered to Burghley's mansion at Theobalds) from Fryersfeild Grove on the manor of Beaumond Hall.[39] But the sources are often frustratingly opaque on whether the wood burnt in the charcoal kilns had come from coppiced woodland or from pollards and most, if not all, of the charcoal sold from these manors in 1580 was probably derived from the former.

Charcoal, being lighter and of a higher calorific value, was always more economical to transport than wood and its production in south-east Hertfordshire was no doubt influenced by the London market. But by the sixteenth century coal from Newcastle was being used in London, replacing wood and charcoal as the 'general fuel' in the capital by 1600 (Galloway *et al.* 1996: 455). The availability of coal in Hertfordshire was greatly increased as a result of an act passed in 1571 to make the river Lea navigable for barges as far as Ware. Water transport was considerably cheaper than the pack-horses which had, until then, carried the large quantities of malt and grain from Hertfordshire to the London breweries and, in addition, the barges returned from London laden with coal and iron bound for Stanstead, Ware and Hertford (Pam 1970: 7). Sea-coal from Newcastle became increasingly important as fuel in the county in the second half of the seventeenth century and probably became the fuel of choice for the wealthier inhabitants of Cheshunt and Waltham Cross, towns that lay alongside the river Lea and, consequently, had lower added transport costs. Pehr Kalm, a Finn who visited England in 1748, observed that coal was widely burned in villages within a 14-mile radius of London, but 'in places to which they had not any flowing water to carry boats loaded with coals' the population continued to burn wood (Kalm 1892: 137–8).[40] Firewood prices rose rapidly in the early seventeenth century but then remained very stable until the 1790s. Transport costs are likely to have been critically important: it is estimated that carting firewood just three miles in seventeenth-century England doubled its price (Warde 2006: 28–57). This, then, would have ensured that the pollard heads sold on Cheshunt Common – and elsewhere in the district – were almost entirely for local consumption.

14.7 The decline of pollarding

The hornbeam pollards on Cheshunt common disappeared at a relatively early date. At the end of the seventeenth century the lord of the manor, Sir Henry Monson of Broxbournebury, sold the pollards in order to have the trees cut down and removed.[41] His motives are unclear. He was making a good income from the pollards and the price of wood in the region was rising (Table 14.1). One possibility is that he hoped to enclose Cheshunt common and thought that felling the pollards was a necessary first step towards that end. In fact, the common was not to be enclosed for another century. Whatever Monson's motives, the loss of this major source of fuel must have had a significant impact on the poorer inhabitants of Cheshunt. In 1699 eight labourers and one weaver from Cheshunt (almost all of whom appear on the lists of buyers of the pollard heads two decades earlier) appeared in court indicted for 'forcibly and riotously assembling and entering the close called Cheshunt Common, otherwise Chesthunt Woodside, the property of Sir Henry Monson, Bart.', and assaulting, threatening and obstructing those employed by Monson to fell the trees.[42]

Regular pollarding continued in other places well into the eighteenth century – including on the manor of Broxbourne, which was also held by Sir Henry Monson and his descendants. The pollards on Broxbourne common were lopped every 12 years until at least 1777–8, but, crucially perhaps, the price of the pollard heads here had always been variable, perhaps reflecting variations in the quantity and quality of the wood, unlike the price of heads sold on Cheshunt common, which was presumably fixed by manorial custom.[43] The species of the pollards on Broxbourne common is not recorded but most of the surviving pollards in the area today are hornbeams. In 1748 Pehr Kalm described the great tract of undulating common land which existed 'between Cheshunt and Bell Bar', south of Hatfield, as follows:

> Common ling grew on it abundantly. It was covered with tufts of ling, between which bracken flourished and swamps abounded. But there was scarcely any grass. Sheep grazed here. In places *Carpinus* (hornbeam) grew fairly densely to a height of six feet, and the tops of it were cut for fuel. Otherwise it was of no particular use. (Mead 2003: 43–4)

Pollarding started to become unfashionable among the landowning classes from the late eighteenth century: few new pollards will have been created after that time and most pollards will not have been cut for over a century (Petit and Watkins 2003: 164–8, 171). Most pollarded trees we see today are likely to be at least 200 years old and the very oldest specimens probably date from the medieval period (Barnes and Williamson 2011: 5). By the nineteenth century pollards were viewed as ugly and utilitarian: William Cobbett, travelling north to Ware in 1822, noted: 'All the trees are shabby in this country [Hertfordshire]; and the eye is incessantly offended by the sight of pollards' (Tomkins 1998: 78). Many had already been felled, however, and estate maps from the beginning of the nineteenth century show that almost all of the pollards depicted on the maps of Digswell manor and around Cole Green, Hertingfordbury, a century or two earlier had disappeared. Vast numbers of pollards were felled unrecorded, but some are commemorated in place- or field-names on the tithe maps and awards of about 1840 and on the first edition Ordnance Survey maps of about 1880 (see Fig. 14.4).

14.8 Pollards as archaeological evidence

The majority of pollards that survive today are in hedgerows – or mark the course of former hedgerows – but there are also important concentrations of pollards, particularly older specimens of oak, in old parkland. Wood-pasture commons had all but disappeared from Hertfordshire by the nineteenth century, most falling victim to grazing pressure (which prevented saplings becoming established), enclosure and 'improvement', and felling for timber and firewood. The dense concentrations of hornbeam pollards have also, with a few notable exceptions, disappeared. But the few isolated groves of hornbeam pollards which have managed to survive provide valuable evidence of an aspect of the history of the landscape which might otherwise have been lost.

Figure 14.3: Some of the hornbeam pollards surviving beside the Roman road Ermine Street (known as 'Redhill Street' in the seventeenth century) to the west of Hoddesdonpark Wood. Trees were pollarded here in 1633 and 1645.

Figure 14.4: Detail of first edition Ordnance Survey sheet XXXVI, 6 inches to the mile, 1883, showing part of Broxbourne Woods. Although the Ordnance Survey map does not differentiate between maiden and pollarded trees, the individual tree symbols shown on the strips of land bordering Pembridge Lane and Whitestubbs Lane (the parallel lane further south), as well as those on Coldhall Green and on the common labelled 'Emanuel Pollards' – many of which are depicted in straight lines – are likely to have been pollards at the time the map was surveyed. Reproduced by kind permission of Hertfordshire Archives and Local Studies. HALS DE/Ha/P1)

Hornbeam pollards can still be seen growing alongside Ermine Street where it borders the west side of Hoddesdonpark Wood (Fig. 14.3) and further south, on and around Martins Green. Nearby, in Broxbourne Woods, is a surviving fragment of the former Broxbourne common, where, as we have seen, regular lopping of the pollards was recorded until 1778. The 4.3 acres of today's common support an old oak pollard but no pollarded hornbeams and yet, in the field adjoining the north side of the common and also to the west, hidden within the depths of a pine plantation dating from the 1960s–70s, there are a number of not very big, but old, hornbeam pollards, some of which appear to have been pollarded much more recently than 1778. These trees provide clear evidence of the former extent of Broxbourne common, which once covered at least 60 acres but which appears to have been 'unofficially enclosed' by the lord of the manor around 1870 (Rowe and Williamson 2013: 138, 155). Of particular interest is the fact that an aerial photograph taken in 1971 suggests that the pollards stood in straight lines; surviving upstanding, or recently fallen, hornbeams within today's pine plantation also appear to be in straight lines, providing further evidence that

Figure 14.5: The grove of hornbeam pollards at the west end of Knebworth Park, thought to date from the early eighteenth century and photographed in 2005. Pollarding was reinstated in 1991 after a gap of about 60 years.

Figure 14.6: Hornbeam pollards planted on strip lynchets in the early eighteenth century in part of the pleasure grounds of Tewin House, Tewin.

they were originally established as a plantation.[44] Trees, almost certainly pollards, were also depicted growing in straight lines on the first edition Ordnance Survey map on the greens alongside Pembridge Lane and Whitestubbs Lane in Broxbourne Woods, and also on the west side of the common called Emanuel Pollards (Fig. 14.4).

The best surviving grove of hornbeam pollards in the county, containing over 520 trees, can be seen at the western end of Knebworth Park, alongside the B656 (Fig. 14.5). According to a study by Warrington and Brookes in the 1990s the pollards had an estimated age of 250 years (± 50 years) and were last pollarded between the two World Wars.[45] Pollarding was reinstated from 1991 and the density of the trees is about 38 per acre. It is believed that they provided fuel for the brick kiln located nearby in the park which, like the grove of trees, is shown on an estate map of 1731.[46]

Another surviving grove of about 20 hornbeam pollards, this time at Tewin, provides evidence of an interesting phase of landscape reorganisation from the early eighteenth century. These trees appear to have been planted in the pleasure grounds of a remarkable mansion called Tewin House rebuilt from 1715 for Major General Joseph Sabine. In the course of laying out the landscape around his house Sabine persuaded the lord of the manor to sell him Church Field, lying south of the church, the steeper slopes of which had been terraced to form strip lynchets. These slopes bordered a steep-sided valley which carried the main highway south from Tewin village and past Tewin House to the river Mimram. Having obtained permission from the Court of Chancery to divert this road away from his house, Sabine incorporated Church Field into his pleasure grounds, which were set in a large rabbit warren dating from at least the early seventeenth century. Rabbits were still considered high-status animals in the early eighteenth century and warrens frequently featured in views from the homes of the social elite. The strip lynchets of the former arable field were planted up with rows of hornbeams which were subsequently pollarded – perhaps to provide 'leafy hay' to feed the rabbits in the winter months and as a source of fuel. Tewin House and its gardens were dismantled at the beginning of the nineteenth century, so it is likely that the surviving hornbeams are 300 years old and perhaps were pollarded only for the first century of their existence (Fig. 14.6).

These surviving groves of hornbeam pollards at Knebworth and Tewin appear to have been planted in the eighteenth century and were perhaps among the last groves to be established in the county. Those on Broxbourne common and nearby alongside Ermine Street may be older. Doubtless other groups of hornbeam pollards survive unnoticed in quiet corners of the countryside, possibly now hidden within areas of woodland. Good places to start looking might be Hook Wood, near Northaw; Harmergreen Wood, north of Digswell; and Blackfan Wood, near Bayford (James 2009: 117). The research into Hertfordshire's pollards so far leaves a number of questions unanswered, not least of which relate to the proposed 'hornbeam plantations' on commons: how widespread were they? Were they found in many parts of the country? Do they just extend into Essex (Hainault and Epping Forests, for example) and Middlesex (Enfield Chase, Stanmore common), or did they perhaps form a band around London? Or were they just a feature of the estates owned and influenced by one remarkable and enterprising man – William Cecil, Lord Burghley?

14.9 References

14.9.1 Primary sources

Hatfield House Archives (HHA), Hatfield
Box E/11 woodward's accounts, 1576–80
Court Rolls 11/4 Little Hadham, fo. 91, 1374/5
General 55/18 A particular of the farm late in lease to Sir Henry Monson
Hatfield Manor Papers I, p. 265

Hertfordshire Archives and Local Studies (HALS), Hertford
10996 A/B Notes in case concerning cutting down of trees on Cheshunt common, n.d.
63741 bailiff's account for the manor of Enfield, 1444–5
A/2832 and A/2833 Plan of The Manor of Great Barwick with Little Barwick, Cooks, Standon Green and Shepherd's Hill Farm, Standon, 1778
Aerial photomap No. 704, 1971
B86 manor of Broxbourne account book, with Cheshunt (mainly sales of timber), 1657–94
D/EB2067B/E24 'A note of suche woodes as apperteyned to the monasterie of St Albons', *c.*1485–*c.*1509
D/EX810/T1 printed Act for Inclosing Northaw Common, *c.*1806
DE/B1767/M1 survey and custumal of Cheshunt, 1669
DE/Bb/E26 Broxbourne wood accounts, 1719–95
DE/Bb/E27 timber survey of farms and tenements on the Broxbournebury estate, 1784
DE/Cd/E101 lease of Aspenden Hall Farm, 1745
DE/Cr/125/2 Plan of the Liberty and Manor of Cheshunt together with that part of Theobalds Park within the Parish of Northaw in the County of Hertford, and also that part of Theobalds Park within the Parish of Enfield in the County of Middlesex, 1785
DE/H/P16 Plan of Stockers & Pearces Farms in Thorley and Sawbridgeworth, 1807
DE/P/P1 map of the manor of Digswell, 1599
DE/P/P4 map of the estate of William Cowper, 1703–04
Estate map, 1731
Gorhambury Deeds X.I.2
K124 bailiff's account for Knebworth, 1481–2
KCAR/6/2/034 account for the manor of Cheshunt, 1435–6
King's College, Cambridge
Knebworth House collection

The National Archives: Public Record Office (TNA:PRO), Kew
E179/248/23 Hearth tax returns Cheshunt 1662–3
E179/375/33 Hearth tax returns Cheshunt 1664–5; E315/391 survey of Hertfordshire manors, lands and possessions of King Philip and Queen Mary, 1556
E315/457 Sales of wood in divers counties 35 Hen VIII, 1543–4, Hertfordshire
E315/458 Accounts etc. of sales of woods, 1544–5
E317/Herts/15 rental of the manor of Beaumond Hall, 1649
E317/Herts/16 Parliamentary survey of Cheshunt Park, 1650
E317/Herts/24 Parliamentary survey of Theobalds manor, 1650
E317/Herts/27 Parliamentary survey of Theobalds Park, 1650
LR2/216 Land Revenue Miscellaneous Book 216
SC6/867/17 account for Great Munden, *c.*1460

14.9.2 Secondary sources

Archer, P.C. (1923–4), *Historic Cheshunt* (Cheshunt).
Austin, P. (1996), 'The leasing of Lord Burghley's Hoddesdon woods in 1595. An insight into woodmanship', *Hertfordshire's Past* 41, pp. 11–21.
Austin, P. (2013), 'Pollards in early-modern South East Hertfordshire', *The Local Historian* 43/2, pp. 138–58.
Barnes, G. and Williamson, T. (2011), *Ancient Trees in the Landscape: Norfolk's arboreal heritage* (Oxford).
Dallas, P. (2010), 'Sustainable environments: common wood pastures in Norfolk', *Landscape History* 31/1, pp. 23–36.
Galloway, J.A., Keene, D. and Murphy, M. (1996), 'Fuelling the city: production and distribution of firewood and fuel in London's region, 1290–1400', *Economic History Review* 49/3, pp. 447–72.
Hunn, J.R. (1994), *Reconstruction and Measurement of Landscape Change*, British Archaeological Reports British Series 236 (Oxford).
James, T. (2009), *Flora of Hertfordshire* (Welwyn Garden City).
Kalm, P. (1892), *Kalm's Account of his Visit to England on his Way to America in 1748*, trans. J. Lucas (London).
Mead, W.R. (2003), *Pehr Kalm: a Finnish visitor to the Chilterns in 1748* (Aston Clinton).
Page, W. (ed.) (1912), *VCH Hertford*, vol 3 (London).
Pam, D.O. (1970), *Tudor Enfield. The Maltmen and the Lea Navigation*, Edmonton Hundred Historical Society Occasional Paper New Series 18 (Edmonton).
Petit, S. and Watkins, C. (2003), 'Pollarding trees: changing attitudes to a traditional land management practice in Britain, 1600–1900', *Rural History* 14/2, pp. 157–76.
Rackham, O. (2003), *Ancient Woodland* (Dalbeattie).
Rowe, A. (2009), *Medieval Parks of Hertfordshire* (Hatfield).
Rowe, A. (2012), 'Hertfordshire's lost water gardens 1500–1750', in D. Spring (ed.), *Hertfordshire Garden History vol. II: Gardens pleasant, groves delicious* (Hatfield), pp. 31–59.
Rowe, A. and Williamson, T. (2013), *Hertfordshire: A Landscape History* (Hatfield).
Tomkins, M. (1998), *So that was Hertfordshire: travellers' jottings 1322–1887* (Hertford).
Warde, P. (2006), 'Fear of Wood Shortage and the Reality of the Woodland in Europe, *c.*1450–1850', *History Workshop Journal* 62/1, pp. 28–57.
Warrington, S. and Brookes, R.C. (1998), 'The growth of hornbeam *Carpinus betulus* following the reinstatement of pollard management', *Forest and Landscape Research* 1, pp. 521–9.

Notes

1 See also photographs of pollards near Sluis in the Netherlands showing trees just after pollarding in 2007 and again two years later at <http://commons.wikimedia.org/wiki/File:Newly_pollarded_near_Sluis.JPG> and <http://commons.wikimedia.org/wiki/File:Pollarded_trees_near_Sluis_two_years_later_April_2009_cropped_to_match_last_times_more_or_less.jpg> accessed 18 August 2014.
2 TNA:PRO E315/391 survey of Hertfordshire manors, lands and possessions of King Philip and Queen Mary, 1556, p. 83. Also recorded 'growynge uppon the premysses' (presumably not in hedgerows) were twenty-three ash trees worth either 20d or 2s each and wiches worth 2s, 3s and 8s each.
3 TNA:PRO E315/391 survey of Hertfordshire manors, lands and possessions of King Philip and Queen Mary, 1556.
4 Hunn (1994: 241–2), citing HALS Gorhambury Deeds X.I.2, kindly brought to my attention by John Dent.
5 HALS DE/Cd/E101 lease of Aspenden Hall Farm, 1745.
6 Most notably in Hertfordshire a series of estate maps by Hollingworth including, for example, HALS A/2832 and A/2833 Plan of The Manor of Great Barwick with Little Barwick, Cooks, Standon Green and Shepherd's Hill Farm, Standon, 1778 and DE/H/P16 Plan of Stockers & Pearces Farms in Thorley and Sawbridgeworth, 1807.
7 TNA:PRO E317/Herts/24 Parliamentary survey of Theobalds manor, 1650, p. 37.
8 HALS DE/Bb/E27 timber survey of farms and tenements on the Broxbournebury estate, 1784.
9 HHA Court Rolls 11/4 Little Hadham, fo. 91, 1374/5.
10 HALS K124 bailiff's account for Knebworth, 1481–2.
11 TNA:PRO SC6/867/17 account for Great Munden, *c.*1460.
12 HHA Hatfield Manor Papers I, p. 265.
13 Page (1912: 99) citing Rentals and Surveys R. Herts, 276; TNA:PRO LR2/216 Land Revenue Miscellaneous Book 216.
14 Austin (2013: 144) citing TNA:PRO Duchy of Lancaster 43/3/38. There were also 70 ash trees valued at 10s each.
15 TNA:PRO E315/457 Sales of wood in divers counties 35 Hen VIII, 1543–4, Hertfordshire (49 were lopped in Cheshunt park and 60 in Langley park).
16 TNA:PRO E315/391 survey of Hertfordshire manors, lands and possessions of King Philip and Queen Mary, 1556.
17 TNA:PRO E315/391. fo. 8v survey of Hertfordshire manors, lands and possessions of King Philip and Queen Mary, 1556.
18 TNA:PRO E317/Herts/16 Parliamentary survey of Cheshunt Park, 1650.
19 Dotrill, dodderel and dottard were all synonyms for pollards (Petit and Watkins 2003: 160).
20 TNA:PRO E317/Herts/27 Parliamentary survey of Theobalds Park, 1650, p. 11.
21 Austin (2013: 144) citing TNA:PRO Duchy of Lancaster (DL) 43/3/38.
22 HALS DE/P/P1 map of the manor of Digswell, 1599.
23 HALS DE/P/P4 map of the estate of William Cowper, 1703–4.
24 HALS D/EX810/T1 printed Act for Inclosing Northaw Common, *c.*1806.
25 HALS D/EB2067B/E24 'A note of suche woodes as apperteyned to the monasterie of St Albons', *c.*1485–*c.*1509.
26 The £56 rent included 20s for a limekiln in the common wood.
27 TNA:PRO E315/391 survey of Hertfordshire manors, lands and possessions of King Philip and Queen Mary, 1556. The timber oaks were valued as follows: 'one thousand

are valued at 6s the oke one other thousand at 3s 4d the oke one other Thousand at 2s 6d the oke and five hundreth at 16d a pece and five hundreth thre score and twelve at 6d the oke'.

28 TNA:PRO E315/458 Accounts etc. of sales of woods, 1544–5.

29 TNA:PRO E317/Herts/27 Parliamentary survey of Theobalds Park, 1650, p. 11; the 418 beech and hornbeam trees were valued at £124 6s 8d.

30 HALS 10996 A/B Notes in case concerning cutting down of trees on Cheshunt common, n.d.; the density figure is based on the stated area of the common in 1785 of 1186.5 acres, which had changed little since 1669 [HALS DE/Cr/125/2 Plan of the Liberty and Manor of Cheshunt together with that part of Theobalds Park within the Parish of Northaw in the County of Hertford, and also that part of Theobalds Park within the Parish of Enfield in the County of Middlesex, 1785; DE/B1767/M1 survey and custumal of Cheshunt, 1669].

31 HALS B86 manor of Broxbourne account book, with Cheshunt (mainly sales of timber), 1657–94.

32 The first price rise in Cheshunt coincided with a change in ownership of the estate – Sir Richard Lucy died in April 1667.

33 TNA:PRO E179/248/23 Hearth tax returns Cheshunt 1662–3; E179/375/33 Hearth tax returns Cheshunt, 1664–5; HALS DE/B1767/M1 survey and custumal of Cheshunt, 1669; TNA:PRO E317/Herts/15 rental of the manor of Beaumond Hall, 1649.

34 HALS 10996 A/B Notes in case concerning cutting down of trees on Cheshunt common, c.1695; the tithes on the sales of the pollard heads had been commuted to a composition of £5 per year by this time.

35 HHA General 55/18 A particular of the farm late in lease to Sir Henry Monson; HALS B86 manor of Broxbourne account book, with Cheshunt (mainly sales of timber), 1657–94.

36 Most of the woodwards' accounts are in the Hatfield House Archives.

37 HHA General 55/18 A particular of the farm late in lease to Sir Henry Monson.

38 HHA Hatfield Manor Papers I, p. 265; King's College, Cambridge KCAR/6/2/034 account for the manor of Cheshunt, 1435–6; HALS 63741 bailiff's account for the manor of Enfield, 1444–5.

39 HHA Box E/11 woodward's accounts, 1576–80.

40 Cheshunt is fourteen miles from Charing Cross in London.

41 HALS 10996 A Notes in case concerning cutting down of trees on Cheshunt common, *c.*1695.

42 Archer (1923–4: 150), citing *Hertfordshire Sessions Rolls*: AD 1699. No. 311.

43 HALS DE/Bb/E26 Broxbourne wood accounts, 1719–95.

44 HALS Aerial photomap No. 704, 1971.

45 Warrington and Brookes (1998: 522) showed that the average girths of the pollards in five compartments ranged between 1.26m and 1.48m (calculated from stated mean diameters of 40cm and 47cm).

46 Knebworth House collection.

CHAPTER 15

Dig where we stand

Sarah Dhanjal, Andrew Flinn,
Kris Lockyear and Gabriel Moshenska

15.1 Introduction

In recent years there has been a growing concern within the university sector for 'public engagement'. At University College London (UCL) two projects were established as part of the Arts and Humanities Research Council's (AHRC) *Research for Community Heritage* programme, a strand within the cross-Research Council (RCUK) *Connected Communities* initiative. The first, which ran across 2011–12, was entitled *Dig Where We Stand: Developing and Sustaining Community Heritage* (DWWS), and forms the principal subject of this paper. The second, entitled *Continuing to Dig: supporting and sustaining innovative community heritage projects in London and the South East*, ran across 2012 and 2013.

In a wider context, 'Connected Communities' research is 'designed to help us understand the changing nature of communities in their historical and cultural contexts and the role of communities in sustaining and enhancing our quality of life'. Within this there is a 'Research for Community Heritage' strand, which aims to 'research with communities, not on communities', and was a partnership with the Heritage Lottery Fund (HLF) to encourage relationships between university researchers and community groups in order to develop 'innovative collaborative or co-produced community heritage research projects'.[1]

The initial DWWS project undertook several activities, two of which are reported in more detail below. The *Continuing to Dig* project was one of 21 multidisciplinary university teams nationally funded by the AHRC to support the community heritage research activities of groups funded by the HLF, including the Welwyn Archaeological Society (WAS). In a specially designed stream of funding – 'All Our Stories' grants worth £3000–£10,000 – the HLF funded some 500 community-based groups to conduct heritage research. The

DWWS team included UCL-based researchers from archaeology, archives, history, oral history, cultural heritage, digital humanities, public geography, film studies and museum studies, all united by an interest in community-based heritage and in engaging our disciplines and our research with people outside the university.[2]

The project took its name and inspiration from the Swedish author and activist Sven Lindqvist's influential *Gräv där du står* (1978) and his English article of the same title in *Oral History* (1979). Lindqvist wrote that history was dangerous and important 'because the results of history are still with us' and argued that, because it was crucial that workers (and others) should carry out their own research, it was essential for someone to facilitate that process by providing guidance on the techniques and methods of historical research. He thus produced *Dig Where You Stand*, 'a handbook which would help others, especially workers[,] to write these factory histories in their own neighbourhoods and their own places of work', and toured Sweden (and later the UK) addressing factory groups and Workers' Educational Association meetings on the workers undertaking factory community-based research.

In a similar fashion DWWS aimed to work with HLF-funded groups to enable them to develop and implement their research ideas, offering training in particular research skills where necessary and encouraging a more holistic approach to community-based heritage research by bringing together the different elements (e.g., archaeology, archive research, oral history and digital technology). The team were particularly interested in working with projects which sought to encourage greater participation by young people in community heritage activities. Lindqvist's work and slogan were inspirational and appropriate for the team not only because they linked the use of archaeology and other research methods and materials to a better understanding of the history of where communities 'stood' but also because they emphasised the significance of history, the importance of people participating in the telling of their own histories and the fact that the tools used by academic historians for rigorous community or factory-based historical research could be made available to all via handbooks, workshops and as web resources.

Over the course of 2012–13 DWWS ran a number of events, including a Community Heritage workshop ('Starting to Dig'), a week-long training excavation at Hendon School, an archaeology summer school in find identification and archiving (run jointly by UCL and WAS), and numerous presentations at community history-focused conferences, including the Community Archives conference at UCL in 2012. The team also worked with a number of groups advising them on their applications to the HLF, held one-to-one surgeries and delivered workshops on heritage research techniques such as oral history, archival research, exhibition practice and preservation of finds with grant holders. Finally, DWWS also worked in a more sustained fashion with 10 to 15 groups on the actual delivery of their projects.

Although, in the main, our collaboration has been in the tradition of Lindqvist in terms of exchanging skills and expertise rather than truly engaging in the co-development of new and innovative community-based heritage research, we did also work with many of the groups, especially those involving young people, to do historical, archival, oral history and archaeological research. In some cases (such as Mental Fight Club[3] and AldaTerra[4]) the team were able to develop relationships which we hope will lead to further innovative community heritage research in the future. In terms of a final outcome, many of the groups were able to use the techniques, equipment and good practice guidance that DWWS were able to offer to produce community-based heritage research considerably enhanced from their original intention. For example, one project, Hoxton Hall's 'Stories of Shoreditch',[5] reported that they had 'greatly benefited' from the guidance and conversations with DWWS on oral history and particularly on the ethics of recording and display. This had resulted in both 'a project that is of real relevance to the community of Shoreditch and our organisation' and learning that was now embedded in the organisation and would contribute to their future heritage and archive work. Naturally there were problems and challenges involved in this sort of programmed (as opposed to organic) collaboration and although there does not seem to be any immediate plan for the AHRC and the HLF to repeat the experiment, DWWS allowed university researchers and community-based heritage and archive groups to get to know one another and work together, and, we hope, seeded relationships which will develop and sustain themselves over the coming years.[6]

The remainder of this paper will focus on two archaeological activities undertaken during the first year of the project: the Hendon School Community Archaeology Project and the Handling Archaeological Finds course.

15.2 The Hendon School Community Archaeology Project

The Hendon School Community Archaeology Project (HSCAP) ran from 2006 to 2012, in its final year under the auspices of DWWS. From the outset the project was a collaboration between Hendon School, a state secondary school in Barnet, north London, the Institute of Archaeology at UCL and the Hendon and District Archaeological Society (HADAS). The project was instigated by Maria Phelan, a UCL archaeology graduate employed at Hendon School, with Sarah

Dhanjal and Jenny Stripe, then the Widening Participation and Diversity team at the Institute of Archaeology.

A plaque on the front of Hendon School declares that the school was built on the site of Hendon House, home of John Morden, an Elizabethan cartographer. Even before excavation began on the HSCAP we knew that this information was wrong. The oldest parts of the school buildings date to 1914. As we have discovered through map regression and documentary research, the earlier house, demolished in 1909, sat not under the school but some way to the west, and the school and its playing fields are situated on what were the ornamental gardens. In addition, it was John Norden (1548–1625) – not Morden – who built Hendon House, and it is still uncertain whether or not the house on Brent Street was indeed the 16-hearth mansion that he disparagingly described as his 'poore house in Hendone'. Norden was an early cartographer, best remembered for his monumental *Speculum Brittaniae* (published from 1593). Certainly the house was built at some point in the sixteenth century and, following the restoration in 1660, it belonged to Jeremy Whichcote, Solicitor General to the Elector Palatine. The Whichcote family later sold the house to Sir William Rawlinson, Commissioner of the Great Seal, and it later served as a mental hospital before being abandoned and finally demolished in 1909.

Figure 15.1: Sarah Dhanjal teaching section drawing to students at Hendon School.

The HSCAP had two sets of aims: one learning-focused and one research-focused. The learning aims of the project were:

1. First and foremost, to provide the students at Hendon School with an opportunity to take part in an archaeological excavation, while learning about the archaeological process (Fig. 15.1), the history of their school and the area around it.
2. To provide UCL students with experience in carrying out public engagement activities.
3. To help fulfil HADAS's and the Institute of Archaeology's commitments to education and widening participation in archaeology.

These formed the basis for the community archaeology element of the project, and the outcomes are discussed in more detail below. The archaeological research aims of the project, based on previous historical research and archaeological excavations in the general area by HADAS and others, were to address the following questions:

1. Is there any residual evidence of prehistoric activity?
2. Considering the proximity to various Roman roads, is there evidence of Roman activity?
3. Excavations in the area have uncovered considerable Anglo-Saxon material; is there any evidence of similar remains here?
4. Is there any evidence of activity in the area between its mention in Domesday and the construction of the house?
5. What evidence remains for the different phases of the rebuilding of the house up to the demolition in 1909?

The archaeological findings have been somewhat unexpected. The excavation of more than ten evaluation trenches around the perimeter of the school field over the course of the project has recovered a considerable amount of material. While no evidence for prehistoric activity on the site and very few finds from the Roman period or from the early phases of Hendon House have been discovered, considerable quantities of medieval ceramics dating to the period 1170–1350 were found. This assemblage of more than 200 sherds, together with possible evidence for structures, was recovered from two trenches on the eastern side of the field in 2010 and 2011. These are locally significant findings, indicating a hitherto-unknown focus of activity during this period.

The learning and community engagement aspects of the project evolved over the years. The initial focus was on providing an intensive introduction to archaeology to students from two groups: young people deemed at risk of social exclusion and those deemed 'gifted and talented'. This combination was surprisingly successful in the first year of the project, but in subsequent years the focus has been broadened to students from across Years 7 and 8 (aged 11–13).

The balance between accessibility and meaningful participation was a source of disagreement in the organisation of the project: in brief, in several years of the project the school prioritised giving the greatest number of students the opportunity to take part in the excavation for a limited time of a few hours, while the archaeological team preferred giving a smaller group of students – perhaps those who expressed a specific interest – a longer and more detailed introduction to archaeology. For this reason the number of students and the nature of their training experience varied across the years of the project.

At the core of the learning strategy was the aim of providing students with a pleasurable and interesting experience as well as an understanding of archaeological fieldwork, with a focus on excavation and artefact cleaning but also with a clear understanding that archaeology is about more than just digging. Each group's introduction to the site included looking at a series of maps and aerial photographs to provide a background in the history and topography of the site and to contextualise the excavation work. Where possible we provided the students with opportunities to use surveying and geophysical equipment. In the fourth year of the project we reviewed the learning format of the project and created a small handbook for the students to use while working on the site. The handbook covered topics such as stratigraphy, excavation techniques, finds processing and drawing and archaeological planning and surveying. This wide range of activities provided many links to the curriculum. While this was not the aim of the project, it illustrates the potential for archaeology to support young people's learning and demonstrates the relevance of curriculum subjects in real-world settings.

Feedback on the project from students, teachers and parents was overwhelmingly positive from the very beginning. For most of the participants the project met its modest aim of providing both an interesting and unusual learning experience and a basic understanding of archaeological excavation. This seems to have been a pleasurable experience for the overwhelming majority of participating students, not least as the alternative was usually normal classroom study at the very end of the summer term. For the HADAS members and UCL staff and students who ran the project it was an overwhelmingly fun and positive experience (dark moments notwithstanding), and for many of us an excellent grounding in the practice of community archaeology. Most gratifying of all was the small number of Hendon School students for whom participation in the project acted as a springboard to greater scholarly aspirations, particularly in history and archaeology.

15.3 The Handling Archaeological Finds course

This course was run by WAS and UCL as part of the DWWS project. In contrast to the Hendon School project, it was aimed at a much more mature age group. 'Community archaeology', under the guise of local archaeological societies, has a long history. Prior to the development of commercial units in the 1970s and 1980s local groups could call upon the expertise of university academics to help analyse their finds assemblages. As expertise in finds research has, at least in part, shifted to the commercial sector and academics are under much greater time and funding constraints than previously, it is increasingly difficult to get specialist reports written within the budget of small local groups. Unfortunately, it is much easier to get volunteers to help with excavation than with post-excavation. The aim of the course was to introduce 'community' archaeologists to the basics of finds processing and to this end a week-long programme was developed. Clearly, a day's training is insufficient to master the appropriate skills, but it was hoped that the course participants would gain a basic understanding of the processes and the issues involved. All the work undertaken during that week used WAS's archive of finds as the basis for the practical work.

Figure 15.2: Louise Martin of the Institute of Archaeology, UCL, teaches Jenny Searle of the Welwyn Archaeological Society animal bone analysis.

Despite some unavoidable last-minute changes, the course was a success. Anna Doherty (Archaeology South-East) and Clare Lewis (WAS) ran a day looking at pottery, including identification and quantification. The Society's excavations at Great Humphreys (Rook and Lockyear, this volume) and Lower Sacombe provided ample material on which to work, included some sherds of Southern British Glazed Ware, an unusual Roman green-glazed pottery, from the latter site. Clare Lewis has been running the 'Pottery Group' at Mill Green Museum (Welwyn Hatfield Museum Service) once a month. Her team are currently reanalysing the material from the Grange cemetery, Welwyn (Rook 1973).

Louise Martin (Fig. 15.2) from UCL ran a day looking at animal bones, again mainly from the Datchworth Green site, which included two complete cow skeletons. Louise has also supervised an undergraduate dissertation based on the animal bones from Great Humphreys.

James Hales, a conservator from UCL, taught 'first aid for finds', especially techniques for packing finds safely. This session also enabled the course participants to handle a variety of 'small finds' from various excavations. WAS members are now in the process of repacking finds from past excavations in plastazote and crystal boxes.

Kris Lockyear (WAS/UCL) and Frances Saxton (independent illustrator) taught a day on the basics of drawing and photographing finds, including pottery and other objects. Lastly, a day looking at the processing of small finds included repacking the coins from the excavations at the Watton-at-Stone bypass site, while at the same time catagorising them according to Richard Reece's 21 periods (see Moorhead, this volume) and then comparing them with other coins lists published by Reece (1991).

The course thus not only had educational aims but also gave WAS the opportunity to repackage and assess their finds archive.

15.4 Conclusions

In this paper we have concentrated on the two courses run as part of the original project. Subsequent work, such as Kris Lockyear's project undertaking geophysical surveys with community groups,[7] will be published elsewhere in due course.

The difficult 'next step' is to continue to build these contacts. The efforts, however, must go both ways. A good example of collaboration, for example, is to enable students to undertake dissertation research on bodies of material held by local societies. For example, the cremations from Lower Rivers Field (see Lockyear, this volume, chapter 9) were analysed by Emily Esche (2010) for her undergraduate dissertation. In this way, students, staff and community groups all benefit. Building and sustaining these contacts is, we believe, a valuable step for both 'community heritage' groups and for universities.

15.5 References

Esche, E. (2010), 'The cremations from Lower Rivers Field', *WAS News*, (Spring 2010), p. 3.

Lindqvist, S. (1978), *Gräv där du står: hur man utforskar ett job* (Stockholm).

Lindqvist, S. (1979), 'Dig Where You Stand', *Oral History* 7/2, pp. 24–30.

Reece, R. (1991), *Roman Coins from 140 Sites in Britain*, Cotswold Studies IV, provisional edition (Cirencester).

Rook, T. (1973), 'Excavations at the Grange Romano-British Cemetery, Welwyn, 1967', *Hertfordshire Archaeology* 3, pp. 1–30.

Notes

1 RCUK Connected Communities: <http://www.ahrc.ac.uk/Funding-Opportunities/Research-funding/Connected-Communities/Pages/Connected-Communities.aspx> and the AHRC Research for Community Heritage: <http://www.ahrc.ac.uk/Funding-Opportunities/Research-funding/Connected-Communities/Pages/HLF-All-Our-Stories-Initiative.aspx>, both accessed 30 August 2014.

2 This research was funded by grants from the AHRC's Research for Community Heritage fund. The UCL Dig Where We Stand team comprised Principal Investigator (Andrew Flinn), Co-Investigators (Gabriel Moshenska, Kris Lockyear, Beverley Butler), researchers (Sarah Dhanjal, Tina Paphitis, Anna Sexton) and other UCL team members (Ego Ahaiwe, Caroline Bressey, Debbie Challis, Lee Grieveson, James Hales, Louise Martin, Gemma Romain, Chris O'Rourke and Melissa Terras). More details of the project activities can be found at <http://blogs.ucl.ac.uk/dig-where-we-stand/>, last accessed 30.8.14.

3 <http://mentalfightclub.com/>, accessed 30 August 2014.

4 <http://aldaterra.com/>, accessed 30 August 2014.

5 <http://www.hoxtonhall.co.uk/>, accessed 30 August 2014.

6 A review of the AHRC Research for Community Heritage programme (2013) is available to download from <http://www.ahrc.ac.uk/News-and-Events/News/Documents/AHRC%20Research%20for%20Community%20Heritage%20accessible.pdf>, accessed 30 August 2014.

7 <hertsgeosurvey.wordpress.com>, accessed 30 August 2014.

APPENDIX 1

Roman coin hoards from Hertfordshire

Sam Moorhead and Dave Wythe

Editorial note: Sam Moorhead and Dave Wythe had created *corpora* of hoards from Hertfordshire independently. The information provided in each overlapped, obviously, but, as befits the aims of their two papers, differed in detail. It was decided, therefore, to consolidate their data into a single *corpus* and to standardise the reference numbers in their two papers. As a result, Moorhead's paper utilises hoards 1-48, whereas Wythe's paper excludes hoards 3, 9 and 10, as the data was not publicly available at the time, but includes no. 49. Hoard 50 was reported subsequently to both these papers, and hoard 51 is mentioned by Burleigh, this volume.

A number of editorial decisions had to be made in the creation of this combined *corpus*. In particular, the manner in which the *terminus post quem* was cited varied, again due to the aims of the differing papers. I have, therefore, given Moorhead's general date, followed by Wythe's more exact date based on the latest possible date of the hoard.

References of the form 2012 T528 refer to cases dealt with under the current Treasure legislation. References of the form BH-130685 are to the entries in the Portable Antiquities Scheme database.[1]

1. Northchurch, near Cow Roast

Date of discovery	2012
Terminus post quem	Mark *Antony* (32-31 BC)/31 BC
Number of coins	2
Composition	Two worn silver 'legionary' *denarii* of Mark Antony, 32-31 BC. 'Legionary' *denarii* of Mark Antony remained in circulation into the third century AD, so given the condition of these coins they were almost certainly lost or buried after the Claudian Conquest of AD 43.
Circumstances	Found by metal-detectorists; considered a hoard based on proximity; no container.
Reference	2012 T528; BH-130685/BH-12F905

2. Ayot St Lawrence

Date of discovery	1851
Terminus post quem	Tiberius (AD 14–37)/AD 37
Number of coins	*c.*200
Composition	Twenty silver *denarii* reported from the Republic to Tiberius.
Circumstances	Found by workmen widening a ride in Prior's Wood; found in pot.
Reference	Robertson (2000, no. 11); Evans (1851–2)

3. Ashwell

Date of discovery	2002
Terminus post quem	Claudius/Nero
Number of coins	8
Composition	Eight copper-alloy contemporary copies of Claudian *asses* found in excavation.
Reference	Ghey (forthcoming)

4. Hemel Hempstead

Date of discovery	1852
Terminus post quem	Vespasian (AD 69–79)/AD 73
Number of coins	19
Composition	Nineteen silver *denarii* – Republican to Vespasian.
Circumstances	Found at various times in a field north-west of Hemel Hempstead; no container.
Reference	Robertson (2000, no. 67); Evans (1852: 397–8); Curnow (1974: 120–22)

5. Verulamium, Insula XIV, Room 33

Date of discovery	1957–60
Terminus post quem	Titus (AD 80–81)/AD 80
Number of coins	3
Composition	Two copper-alloy *asses* of Vespasian; one copper-alloy *dupondius* of Titus.
Circumstances	Found in secondary floor; no container.
Reference	Robertson (2000, no. 88); Frere (1972: 52)

6. St Albans, St Stephen's Cemetery

Date of discovery	1984
Terminus post quem	Domitian, *c.* AD 90
Number of coins	4
Composition	Four coins, the latest a silver *denarius* of Domitian, found in excavation.
Circumstances	Found with other objects: four glass vessels, three flagons and a beaker, three iron objects; found in a purse.
Reference	Robertson (2000, no. 93); Frere (1985: 293)

7.Verulamium, Period II building, Insula XIV

Date of discovery	1958
Terminus post quem	Trajan (AD 112–17)/AD 117
Number of coins	50
Composition	Fifty silver *denarii* – Republican to Trajan.
Circumstances	Buried on the edge of a clay floor by a wooden partition which divided the room; no container.
Reference	Robertson (2000, no. 110); Kraay (1960); Frere (1972: 43, 53)

8. St Albans, Beech Bottom Dyke

Date of discovery	1932
Terminus post quem	Hadrian (117–38)/AD 138
Number of coins	41+

Composition	Forty-one silver *denarii* — Republican to Hadrian — were recovered from the original find for identification.
Circumstances	Found in the fill of the dyke; no container.
Reference	Robertson (2000, no. 145); Wheeler and Wheeler (1936: 17–18)

9. Ashwell

Date of discovery	2002
Terminus post quem	Hadrian (AD 119–28)
Number of coins	10
Composition	'Placed deposit' of two copper-alloy units of Tasciovanus and four of Cunobelin; one silver unit of the Iceni; one pierced *dupondius* of Claudius, one *as* of Vespasian and one *as* of Hadrian. The same Treasure find included a hoard of Iron Age coins only.
Circumstances	Found in excavation.
Reference	2002 T215 and Ghey (forthcoming)

10. Braughing

Date of discovery	1972
Terminus post quem	Lucilla (AD 164–9)
Number of coins	6
Composition	Six copper-alloy *sestertii* – two of Hadrian, three of Antoninus Pius, one of Lucilla, three of which fused together.
Circumstances	Found during excavations in the top layer of a pit; no container.
Reference	Shotter and Partridge (1988: 34)

11. Ashwell, Hinxworth

Date of discovery	1876
Terminus post quem	Marcus Aurelius (AD 161–80)/AD 180
Number of coins	500+
Composition	'more than 500 silver coins … Nero to Marcus Aurelius'.
Circumstances	Found close to a river and not far from Roman camp at Marborow or Arbury Banks; possible wooden container.
Reference	Robertson (2000, no. 234); Cussans (1870–1: 316)

12. Braughing, bank of river Rib

Date of discovery	1956
Terminus post quem	Marcus Aurelius (AD 170–71)/AD 171
Number of coins	61
Composition	Sixty-one silver *denarii* – Vespasian to Marcus Aurelius.
Circumstances	Found on the bank of the river Rib; found in pot.
Reference	Robertson (2000, no. 291); Carson (1957)

13. Potters Bar

Date of discovery	1994–5
Terminus post quem	Marcus Aurelius (AD 175–6)
Number of coins	95
Composition	95 silver *denarii* – Claudius to Marcus Aurelius.
Circumstances	Found by metal-detectorists in 1994 and more in 1995; no container.
Reference	Meadows *et al.* (1997)

14. Much Hadham

Date of discovery	1990
Terminus post quem	Geta (AD 210–11)/AD 211
Number of coins	165
Composition	129 silver *denarii*, Mark Antony to Geta; 36 copper-alloy *sestertii*, Nerva to Crispina.

Circumstances	Found by metal detectorists; found in pot.
Reference	Robertson (2000, no. 385A); Burnett (1992)

15. Verulamium, Insula XIV, Building 3

Date of discovery	1957
Terminus post quem	Elagabalus (AD 221)
Number of coins	8
Composition	Seven silver *denarii* – Antoninus Pius to Elagabalus; one silver radiate of Elagabalus.
Circumstances	Layer 3: in a pocket of dark soil in collapsed debris; burial in fifth-century context hard to explain; no container.
Reference	Robertson (2000, no. 400); Frere (1983: 98, 100)

16. Verulamium, outside NE Gate (Branch Road)

Date of discovery	1974
Terminus post quem	Elagabalus (AD 221)
Number of coins	21
Composition	Twenty-one silver *denarii* terminating with Elagabalus.
Circumstances	Found in alluvium covering fallen wall-plaster on floor of small cold plunge bath; found with seal box.
Reference	Robertson (2000, no. 401); Wilson (1975: 258–60)

17. Verulamium, Eastern Tower

Date of discovery	1932?
Terminus post quem	Severus Alexander (AD 222–35)/AD 235
Number of coins	5
Composition	Five large copper-alloy *aes* – Titus to Severus Alexander.
Circumstances	Found in chalk repair to original cement floor; no container.
Reference	Robertson (2000, no. 407); Wheeler and Wheeler (1936: 62)

18. Brickendon, Brickendonbury

Date of discovery	1895
Terminus post quem	Trajan Decius and Herennius Etruscus (AD 249–51)/AD 250
Number of coins	432
Composition	387 silver *denarii* – Commodus to Gordian III; 45 silver radiates – Elagabalus to Herennius Etruscus.
Circumstances	Found during draining works; no pot but all buried in a small recess; no container.
Reference	Robertson (2000, no. 465); Evans (1896: 191–208)

19. Stevenage, Chells Manor

Date of discovery	1986
Terminus post quem	Postumus (AD 260–69)/*c.* AD 269
Number of coins	2,579
Composition	387 silver *denarii* – Septimius Severus to Gordian III; 2,192 silver radiates – Caracalla to Postumus.
Circumstances	Found during trial-trenching of a settlement site; found in jar.
Reference	Robertson (2000, no. 485); Bland (1988)

20. Kings Langley II

Date of discovery	1957-2006
Terminus post quem	Postumus (AD 260-69)/AD 269
Number of coins	16+1
Composition	Sixteen radiates – Postumus, one uncertain radiate.
Circumstances	No container.
Reference	2006 T370; Abdy (2007)

21. Bourne End, Hemel Hempstead (River Bulbourne, Berkhamsted)

Date of discovery 1976
Terminus post quem Claudius II/Victorinus (AD 268–70)
Number of coins 39 (excluding coin of Magnentius).
Composition Five silver and base radiates – Gordian III to Claudius II/Victorinus; twenty-nine copper-alloy *sestertii* – Hadrian to Postumus; four copper-alloy *asses* – Claudius to Antoninus Pius; one uncertain *sestertius* or *as*; one coin of Magnentius.
Circumstances Recovered from a small area of 25 square feet in a river, coins worn by water; no indication of other finds; no container.
Comments The coin of Magnentius appears to be intrusive. It was found away from the rest of the group and is very worn.
Reference Robertson (2000, no. 533); Burnett (1977)

22. Welwyn, Glebe Road

Date of discovery 1961
Terminus post quem Quintillus (AD 270)
Number of coins 149
Composition Four silver *denarii* of Septimius Severus and Severus Alexander; one silver *drachma* of Julia Domna (Caesarea, Cappadocia); 144 silver and base radiates, Gordian III to Quintillus.
Circumstances Dug up in Glebe Road, Welwyn; found in pot.
Reference Robertson (2000, no. 549); Carson (1969)

23. Verulamium, Eastern Tower on Western Wall

Date of discovery 1932
Terminus post quem Tetricus I and II (AD 271–4)
Number of coins 52
Composition Fifty-two base radiates – Postumus to the Tetrici.
Circumstances Found during excavation of eastern tower, in earlier debris; no container.
Reference Robertson (2000, no. 566); Wheeler and Wheeler (1936: 62)

24. Verulamium, Building III, 2

Date of discovery 1932?
Terminus post quem Tetricus I and II (AD 271–4)
Number of coins 8
Composition Eight base radiates – Gallienus (sole reign) to the Tetrici.
Circumstances Found in levelling of final reconstruction; no container.
Reference Robertson (2000, no. 567); Wheeler and Wheeler (1936: 95)

25. Tring/Aldbury, Moneybury Hill

Date of discovery 1870
Terminus post quem Tetricus I and II (AD 271–4)
Number of coins 116
Composition One copper-alloy unit of Cunobelinus; two silver *denarii* of Vespasian and Septimius Severus; 78 copper-alloy *aes* from Claudius to Philip I; 28 cast *aes* from Vespasian to Otacilia Severa; eight base radiates of Gallienus (sole reign) to the Tetrici.
Circumstances Found with metal, animal remains and pottery; possible site finds; possible container.
Comments Coins from nos 25 and 26 were considered to represent two hoards, but it is equally likely that they represent votive activity.
Reference Robertson (2000, no. 568); Evans (1870)

26. Tring/Aldbury, Moneybury Hill

Date of discovery	1977
Terminus post quem	Tetricus I and II (AD 271–4)
Number of coins	29 (excluding *dupondius* of Nerva)
Composition	Seventeen regular and twelve 'barbarous' radiates – Postumus to the Tetrici; one *dupondius* of Nerva.
Circumstances	Disturbed illegal metal-detecting over scheduled Roman site; no container.
Comments	See no. 25. The *dupondius* is argued to be extraneous.
Reference	Robertson (2000, no. 556); Davies (1982)

27. Verulamium, Building XIV, 5

Date of discovery	*c.*1958
Terminus post quem	Victorinus or Tetricus I (AD 269–74)
Number of coins	4
Composition	Four base radiates – Salonina to Victorinus or Tetricus I.
Circumstances	Found in cellar of building, latest occupation levels; found in a bronze-bound wooden box.
Reference	Robertson (2000, no. 636); Frere (1972: 106)

28. Ninesprings Villa, Wymondley

Date of discovery	*c.*1940
Terminus post quem	Tetricus I and II (AD 271–4)
Number of coins	67
Composition	Sixty-seven base radiates (61 listed) – Gallienus (sole reign) to the Tetrici.
Circumstances	Recovered from villa; possible container.
Reference	Robertson (2000, no. 637); Curteis (1992); Curteis (1994–6: 10–11)

29. Northchurch Villa, Northchurch

Date of discovery	1975
Terminus post quem	Aurelian (AD 270–5)/AD 275
Number of coins	27
Composition	Twenty-seven silver and base radiates – Gordian III to Aurelian.
Circumstances	Found during excavation (Pit A, Room 2); possible container.
Reference	Robertson (2000, no. 720); Curnow (1974–6: 19)

30. Verulamium, Insula XIX

Date of discovery	1960
Terminus post quem	*c.* AD 275–*c.* AD 280
Number of coins	90
Composition	Ninety copper-alloy radiate copies.
Circumstances	Found in clay and rubble filling of a shallow cellar (might have fallen from wall or roof; no evidence that it had been buried there); no container.
Reference	Robertson (2000, no. 798); Mattingly (1971); Frere (1983: 130)

31. Verulamium, Theatre

Date of discovery	1933?
Terminus post quem	*c.* AD 280–*c.* AD 285
Number of coins	*c.*796
Composition	*c.*180 copper-alloy radiate copies, clipped fragments and blanks; 616 copper-alloy radiate minims.
Circumstances	Found in the stage of theatre; no container.
Comments	The context of the hoard suggests a burial date close to *c.* AD 300.

Reference Robertson (2000, no. 797); Kenyon (1935: 236–7); Wheeler and St. John O'Neil (1937)

32. Verulamium

Date of discovery 1749
Terminus post quem Diocletian and Maximian (AD 286–94)
Number of coins 343
Composition 343 base silver radiates from Valerian I to Diocletian and Maximian. Two intruders, copper alloy *nummi* of Magnentius and Valens.
Circumstances From a personal collection; possibly in a ceramic 'vase'.
Reference Robertson (2000, no. 833); copy of manuscript catalogue in British Museum

33. Verulamium, Building V, 1

Date of discovery 1932?
Terminus post quem Carausius (AD 286–93)/AD 293
Number of coins 36
Composition Thirty-six base radiates – Gallienus to Carausius
Circumstances Found in fire-blackened deposit of debris; found with jet bead; no container.
Reference Robertson (2000, no. 844); Wheeler and Wheeler (1936: 110)

34. Verulamium, Building V, 1, Room 19

Date of discovery 1932?
Terminus post quem Carausius (AD 286–93)/AD 293
Number of coins 19 or 20
Composition Nineteen or twenty base radiates of Carausius.
Circumstances Found near footings of wall, believed buried before wall constructed; no container.
Reference Robertson (2000, no. 845); Williams (1990)

35. Verulamium, Theatre stage

Date of discovery 1933–4
Terminus post quem Carausius (AD 286–93)/AD 293
Number of coins 144
Composition One copper-alloy as of Marcus Aurelius; two silver radiates of Philip I and Trajan Decius; 141 base radiates of Gallienus (sole reign) to Carausius (including barbarous radiates).
Circumstances Found in period iv make-up of stage; no container.
Reference Robertson (2000, no. 846); Kenyon (1935: 236–7)

36. Verulamium

Date of discovery 1959
Terminus post quem Carausius (AD 286–93)/AD 293
Number of coins 10
Composition Ten base radiates 'which may be possibly be part of a small dispersed Carausian hoard'.
Circumstances No container.
Reference Robertson (2000, no. 847); Shiel (1977: 70, no. 5)

37. Chipperfield, Scatterdells Wood

Date of discovery 1972
Terminus post quem Maximian I (AD 307–8); Constantine I (AD 307)/AD 307
Number of coins 67
Composition Sixty-seven copper-alloy nummi of the Tetrarchy, AD 294–307/8.

Circumstances	Found in three batches by metal-detectorists; no container.
Reference	Robertson (2000, no. 989); Carson (1974)

38. Ashwell, Arbury Banks

Date of discovery	*c.*1914
Terminus post quem	Constantine II (AD 317–25)/*c.* AD 325
Number of coins	11+?
Composition	Eleven copper-alloy nummi – one of Constantine I and 10 of Constantine II.
Circumstances	Dug up in a field; found in pot.
Reference	Robertson (2000, no. 1093); Westell and Applebaum (1932: 266)

39. Chorleywood, Stag Lane, Reservoir

Date of discovery	1977
Terminus post quem	Constantius II and Constans (AD 347–8)
Number of coins	4337 plus 21 fragments
Composition	One copper-alloy radiate of Divus Claudius; one copy of a copper-alloy radiate of Tetricus; 4335 copper-alloy nummi from Divus Constantius (AD 307–8) to VICTORIAE DD AVGGQ NN (AD 347/8) including 247 further imitations.
Circumstances	Found during construction of new reservoir; found in pot.
Reference	Robertson (2000, no. 1234); Burnett (1979)

40. Standon

Date of discovery	2010
Terminus post quem	House of Constantine (AD 337/40)
Number of coins	38
Composition	Two copper-alloy radiates and thirty-six nummi to GLORIA EXERCITVS (one standard).
Circumstances	Considered a hoard based on balance of probabilities; no container.
Reference	2010 T533; ESS-OE9427; Ghey (2011)

41. Hemel Hempstead, Gadebridge Villa excavations

Date of discovery	1968
Terminus post quem	Magnentius (AD 351–3)/AD 353
Number of coins	173
Composition	Ten copper-alloy radiates and 163 nummi to Magnentius, mostly House of Constantine.
Circumstances	Possible votive deposit; found with a variety of bronze artefacts; no container.
Reference	Robertson (2000, no. 1321); Curnow (1974, listed on pp. 115–17)

42. Ashwell

Date of discovery	1934
Terminus post quem	Magnentius (AD 350–3)/AD 353
Number of coins	13
Composition	Thirteen copper-alloy nummi of Magnentius.
Circumstances	Found in bag of assorted coins found over time by a farm labourer; no container.
Reference	Robertson (2000, no. 1326A)

43. St. Stephens, Park Street Villa excavation

Date of discovery	1943–5
Terminus post quem	Constantius II or Constans (AD 355–63)/*c.* AD 355
Number of coins	17

Composition One copper-alloy radiate of Tetricus II(?); sixteen copper-alloy nummi of Constantius II and Constans, ending with FEL TEMP REPARATIO falling horseman types.
Circumstances Found lying among burnt debris over southern flue of hypocaust in Rm. V; found with large lump of copper; no container.
Reference Robertson (2000, no. 1269); O'Neil (1945: 57); St. J. O'Neil, (1945: 60–2)

44. Kings Langley I

Date of discovery 1984
Terminus post quem House of Valentinian (AD 378)
Number of coins 1550
Composition Four copper-alloy radiates, 135 copper-alloy nummi, AD 300–364, and 1415 copper-alloy nummi of the House of Valentinian (AD 364–78).
Circumstances Found by metal-detectorists; found in pot.
Reference Chameroy (2009)

45. Verulamium, Extramural Site 1956R

Date of discovery 1956
Terminus post quem Gratian (AD 367–83)
Number of coins 28
Composition Two copper-alloy radiates and twenty-six copper-alloy nummi of the House of Constantine and Valentinian.
Circumstances Found in wooden box.
Reference Robertson (2000, no. 1415); Frere (1983: 280)

46. Cheshunt

Date of discovery *c.*1904
Terminus post quem Gratian (AD 367–83)
Number of coins *c.*280
Composition Seventeen copper-alloy radiates and seven nummi – House of Constantine and House of Valentinian – were listed in VCH IV, Robertson examined twenty coins (fourteen radiates and six nummi) in Hertford Museum.
Circumstances Found in pot.
Comments The earlier coins were in good condition, the later ones poor condition. Moorhead wonders if this was not a radiate or a Constantinian hoard with later intruders added to the archive.
Reference Robertson (2000, no. 1436); Page (1914: 152–3)

47. Verulamium, extramural water meadow excavation

Date of discovery 1956
Terminus post quem House of Theodosius (AD 388–402)/AD 402
Number of coins 249
Composition 249 late Roman copper-alloy coins.
Circumstances Found with a silver spoon and other objects on site of Roman river bed; initially thought to be votive, Frere later thought they could be rubbish; no container.
Comments Frere (1957: 14–15) gives a total of 249 coins, but only 94 are listed by Frere (1983).
Reference Robertson (2000, no. 1648); Frere (1957: 14–15); Frere (1983: 280–1)

48. Sandridge, St Albans

Date of discovery 2012
Terminus post quem Arcadius and Honorius (AD 408)
Number of coins 159

Composition	159 gold solidi from Valentinian II (AD 375–83) to Arcadius and Honorius (AD 394/5–408)
Circumstances	Found by metal-detectorist, no precise details on location made public; area excavated after initial find; no container and the coins appeared spread as if disturbed by ploughing, although now in a wood.
Reference	2012 T674; BH-D67AF4

49. Royston

Date of discovery	*c.*1833
Terminus post quem	*c.* AD 140
Number of coins	*c.*3+
Composition	'several coins of Claudius, and Vespasian, and Faustina....'
Circumstances	Recovered by workmen, found with skeletons; no container.
Comments	Although listed by Robertson as in Hertfordshire, the site actually lies over the county boundary.
Reference	Robertson (2000, no. 190)

50. King's Park, Verulamium

Date of discovery	2011 or 2012
Terminus post quem	AD 378–83
Number of coins	147
Composition	One third-century radiate, 146 fourth-century nummi of which 120 date to AD 364–78
Circumstances	Found during archaeological excavations on the basal silts of a late Roman re-cut of the 'Wheeler ditch' which forms part of the Iron Age *oppidum*; no container, 141 coins closely grouped, '6 coins were found, re-deposited by the excavation process, in the immediate vicinity.'
Reference	Wells (2013)

60. Ashwell, Arbury Banks

Date of discovery	Unknown
Terminus post quem	Unknown
Number of coins	Unknown
Composition	Unknown
Circumstances	The HHER refers to a second coin hoard found at Arbury banks but consultation of the original publication refers only to 'some coins' being found.
Reference	HHER 1322; Beldam (1856–59: 285)

References

Abdy, R. (2007), 'Kings Langley II, Hertfordshire', *Numismatic Chronicle* 167, p. 251.

Beldam, J. (1856–59), 'Memoir on some excavations which he had recently made at the Arbury Banks, near Ashwell, Hertfordshire', *Proceedings of the Society of Antiquaries of London*, First Series 4: 285–91.

Bland, R.F. (1988), 'Stevenage Hertfordshire', in R.F. Bland and A.M. Burnett (eds), *The Normanby Hoard and other Roman Coin Hoards from Roman Britain* (London).

Bland, R.F. (ed.) (1992), *The Chalfont Hoard and other Roman Coin Hoards*, Coin Hoards from Roman Britain 9 (London).

Burnett, A.M. (1977), 'Bourne End (1976)', *Coin Hoards* 3, pp. 77–8.

Burnett, A.M. (1979), 'The Hamble and Chorleywood hoards and the Gallic coinage of AD 330–335' in R.A.G. Carson and A.M. Burnett (eds), *Recent Coin Hoards from Roman Britain* (London), pp. 41–98.

Burnett, A.M. (1992), 'Much Hadham, Hertfordshire', in Bland (1992), pp. 73–80.
Carson, R.A.G. (1957), 'The Braughing Treasure Trove of Roman *denarii*', *Numismatic Chronicle* Sixth Series 17, p. 239.
Carson, R.A.G. (1969), 'The Welwyn Treasure Trove of Roman *denarii*', *Numismatic Chronicle* Seventh Series 9, pp. 143–4.
Carson, R.A.G. (1974), 'Chipperfield (Herts.) Treasure Trove', *Numismatic Chronicle* Seventh Series 14, pp. 182–4.
Chameroy, J. (2009), 'Kings Langley', in R. Abdy, E. Ghey, C. Hughes and I. Leins (eds), *Coin Hoards from Roman Britain Vol. XII,* Moneta 97 (Wetteren), pp. 316–30.
Curnow, P.E. (1974), 'The Coins', in D.S. Neal, *The Excavation of a Roman Villa in Gadebridge Park, Hemel Hempstead, 1963–8* (London), pp. 101–22.
Curnow, P.E. (1974–76), 'The Coins', in D.S. Neal, 'Northchurch, Boxmoor and Hemel Hempstead station: the excavation of three Roman buildings in the Bulbourne Valley', *Hertfordshire Archaeology* 4, pp. 1–135, pp. 18–19.
Curteis, M. (1992), 'Ninesprings Roman Villa, Great Wymondley, Hertfordshire', in Bland (1992), pp. 122–4.
Curteis, M. (1994–1996), 'The coinage of Ninesprings Roman villa, Great Wymondley', *Hertfordshire Archaeology* 12, pp. 7–11.
Cussans, J.E. (1870–71), *History of Hertfordshire, vol I* (Hertford). Reissued 1972 by E.P Publishing (Wakefield).
Davies, J.A. (1982), 'A Roman coin hoard from Moneybury Hill, Pitstone, Buckinghamshire', *Records of Buckinghamshire* 24, pp. 176–8.
Evans, J. (1851–52), untitled notice in 'Miscellanea', *Numismatic Chronicle* 14, pp. 83–4.
Evans, J. (1852), 'Account of Roman Remains found at Box Moor, Herts.', *Archaeologia* 34/2, pp. 394–8.
Evans, J. (1870), 'Note on a hoard of coins found on Pitstone Common, near Tring, 1870', *Numismatic Chronicle* New Series 10, pp. 125–32.
Evans, J. (1896), 'Roman coins found at Brickendonbury, Hertford', *Numismatic Chronicle* Third Series 16, pp. 191–208.
Frere, S.S. (1957), 'Excavations at Verulamium 1956: Second Interim Report', *The Antiquaries Journal* 37, pp. 1–15.
Frere, S.S. (1972), *Verulamium Excavations*, vol. 1 (London).
Frere, S.S. (1983), *Verulamium Excavations*, vol. 2 (London).
Frere, S.S. (1985), 'Roman Britain in 1984. I. Sites explored', *Britannia* 16, pp. 251–316.
Ghey, E. (2011), 'Standon Area, Hertfordshire, 4 September 2010', *Numismatic Chronicle* 171, p. 419.
Ghey, E. (forthcoming), 'The coins', in Ralph Jackson and Gilbert Burleigh, *Dea Senuna: Treasure, Cult and Ritual at Ashwell, Herts,* vol 2 (London).
Kenyon, K.M. (1935), 'The Roman Theatre at Verulamium, St. Albans', *Archaeologia* 84, pp. 213–61.
Kraay, C.M. (1960), 'A hoard of *denarii* from Verulamium, 1958', *Numismatic Chronicle* Sixth Series 20, pp. 271–3.
Mattingly, H.B. (1971), 'The Verulamium (1960) Hoard of "Barbarous Radiates"', *Britannia* 2, pp. 196–9.
Meadows, A., Orna-Ornstein, J. and Williams, J. (1997), 'Potters Bar, Hertfordshire', in R.F. Bland and J. Orna-Ornstein (eds), *Coin Hoards from Roman Britain Vol. X* (London), pp. 116–20.
O'Neil, H.E. (1945), 'The Roman villa at Park Street, near St Albans, Hertfordshire', *Archaeological Journal* 102, pp. 21–110.
Page, W. (ed.) (1914), *VCH Hertford*, vol. 4 (London).

Robertson, A. (2000) *An Inventory of Romano-British Coin Hoards*, Royal Numismatic Society Special Publication 20 (London).

St. J. O'Neil, B.H. (1945), 'The coins', in H.E. O'Neil, 'The Roman villa at Park Street, near St Albans, Hertfordshire', *Archaeological Journal* 102, pp. 21–110, pp. 59–62.

Shiel, N. (1977), *The episode of Carausius and Allectus: the literary and numismatic evidence*, British Archaeological Reports British Series 40 (Oxford).

Shotter, D.C.A. and Partridge, C.R. (1988), 'Roman coins', in T.W. Potter and S.D. Trow, *Puckeridge-Braughing, Hertfordshire: The Ermine Street Excavations, 1971–1972. The Late Iron Age and Roman settlement,* Hertfordshire Archaeology 10 (Hertford), pp. 30–34.

Wells, N.A. (2013), 'The coins', in A. Hood, *King's Park, King Harry Lane, St Albans, Hertfordshire. NGR: TL 1355 0625. Archaeological monitoring and excavation; Phase 2 Post-excavation assessment*, Foundations Archaeology Report No. 888 (Swindon), unpaginated.

Westell, W.P. and Applebaum, E.S. (1932), 'Romano-British Baldock: past discoveries and future problems', *Journal of the British Archaeological Association* New Series 38, pp. 235–77.

Wheeler, R.E.M. and Wheeler, T.V. (1936), *Verulamium. A Belgic and two Roman Cities*, Research Reports of the Society of Antiquaries of London 11 (Oxford).

Wheeler, T.V. and St. J. O'Neil, B.H. (1937), 'A hoard of radiate coins from the Verulamium Theatre', *Numismatic Chronicle* Fifth Series 17, pp. 211–28.

Williams, H.P.G. (1990), 'A small Carausian hoard from the Wheeler excavations at Verulamium', *British Numismatic Journal* 60, pp. 130–31.

Wilson, D.R. (1975), 'Roman Britain in 1974. I. Sites explored', *Britannia* 6, pp. 221–83.

Notes

1 <finds.org.uk>

APPENDIX 2

Excavation coins and PAS finds from Hertfordshire

Sam Moorhead

Editor's note: entries marked † are editorial additions to the *corpus* and have not been included in the figures or discussions in Moorhead's paper.

Region 1a: Verulamium excavations

1.1 Lord Verulam collection: 2,602 coins (Reece 1984; Reece 1991: no. 7)
1.2 Wheeler excavations, 1934–5: 1,635 coins (O'Neil 1936; Reece 1984; Reece 1991: no. 8)
1.3 Frere excavations, 1955–61: 1,636 coins (Reece 1984; Reece 1991: no. 6)
1.4 Verulamium excavations in Insula XIII, 1986–88: 76 coins (Greep 2006: 167–70)
1.5 Verulamium excavations in Insula II, 1986–88: 17 coins (Greep 2006: 171)
1.6 Verulamium excavations in Insula III: 12 coins (Greep 2006: 172)
1.7 Verulamium Theatre excavations: 3,268 coins (Reece 1984; Reece 1991: no. 9; after S. Keay lists)
See hoards 5, 7, 15, 17, 23–4, 27 and 30–36

Region 1b: Verulamium closer hinterland

1.8 King Harry Lane cemetery excavations: 122 coins (Reece 1989a)
1.9 Folly Lane cemetery excavations: 66 coins (Reece 1999)
1.10 Branch Road bath house excavations: 34 coins (Reece 1999)
1.11 St. Michael's, St. Albans, PAS finds: 65 coins
1.12 Gorhambury Villa excavations: 310 coins (Curnow 1990)
See hoards 6, 16, 45 and 47

Region 1c: Verulamium further hinterland

1.13 Park Street Villa excavations: 62 coins (O'Neil 1945); see also hoard no. 43
1.14 Gadebridge Park villa excavations: 297 coins (Curnow 1974; Reece 1991: no. 104); see also hoard no. 41
1.15 Boxmoor Villa excavation and stray finds: 76 coins (Page 1914: 156). I have estimated period totals from summary list so statistics are not precise
1.16 Boxmoor Villa excavations 1966–70: 105 coins (Curnow 1974–6: 99–101)
1.17 Hemel Hempstead, PAS finds: 21 coins
1.18 Friars Wash, Redbourn temple excavations: Time Team and Wessex Archaeology:

48 coins (Wessex Archaeology 2009)

1.19 Redbourn, PAS finds: 30 coins
See hoards 4, 8, 20–1, 41, 43–4 and 48

Region 2: Sarratt

2.1 Sarratt, PAS finds: 31 coins See hoard 39

Region 3: Cow Roast and environs

3.1 Cow Roast excavations (Orchard site): 292 coins (Reece 1980–82; Reece 1991: no. 77)
3.2 Cow Roast excavations (Marina site): 128 coins (Reece 1980–82; Reece 1991: no. 78)
3.3 Aldbury, PAS finds: 35 coins
3.4 Berkhamsted, PAS finds: 28 coins
3.5 Northchurch Villa excavations: 27 coins (Curnow 1974–6: 18–19); see also hoards nos 1 and 29
See hoards 1, 25–6 and 29

Region 4: Lilley and Offley

4.1 Lilley, PAS finds: 75 coins
4.2 Offley, PAS finds: 376 coins
No hoards recorded

Region 5: Baldock and environs

5.1 Baldock settlement excavations, 1968–72:[1] 449 coins (Curnow 1986)
5.2 Baldock settlement excavations by Albion Archaeology: 340 coins (Peter Guest, unpublished list)
5.3 Ninesprings villa excavations 1884: 13 coins (Page 1914: 171); 23+ coins from the general vicinity (Page 1914: 171): I have estimated totals for periods from these summary lists, but statistics cannot be precise
5.4 Ninesprings Villa excavations, 1921–2, Great Wymondley: 64 coins (Curteis 1994–1996)
5.5 Mounds east of St Mary's Church, Great Wymondley: 17 coins (Page 1914: 169). I have estimated period totals from a summary list so statistics are not precise
5.6 Boxfield farm settlement excavations, Chells: 254 coins (Corney 1999)
5.7 Lobs Hole settlement excavations, Stevenage: 16 coins (Curteis 2006)
5.8 Hinxworth, PAS finds: 85 coins
5.9 Ashwell, PAS finds: 954 coins
5.10 Clothall, PAS finds: 366 coins
5.11 Wallington, PAS finds: 540 coins
5.12 Buckland, PAS finds: 36 coins
5.13 Barley, PAS finds: 25 coins
5.14 Therfield, PAS finds: 47 coins
5.15 Buntingford, PAS finds: 32 coins
See hoards 3, 9, 11, 19, 28, 38 and 42

Region 6: Braughing and Ware

6.1 Puckeridge settlement excavations, 1975–79: 160 coins (Shotter and Partridge 1988)[2]
6.2 Foxholes Farm settlement excavations: 34 coins (Reece 1989b)
6.3 Braughing, PAS finds: 18 coins
6.4 Little Hadham, PAS finds: 104 coins
6.5 Much Hadham, PAS finds: 206 coins
6.6 Widford, PAS finds: 68 coins

6.7 Stanstead Abbots, PAS finds: 86 coins
6.8† Ware: 819 coins (Reece 1991: no. 82)
See hoards 10, 12, 14, 18, 40 and 46

Region 7: Welwyn and environs
7.1 Dicket Mead Villa, excavations: 237 coins (Reece 1983–86)
7.2 Welwyn St Mary's: 72 coins (included in Reece 1983–86)
7.3 Lockleys Villa, excavations: 15 coins (Allen 1938)
7.4 Watton-at-Stone, PAS finds: 99 coins
7.5 Ayot St Lawrence, PAS finds: 30 coins
7.6† Watton-at-Stone by-pass excavations: 119 coins (Reece 1991: no. 83)
7.7† Watton-at-Stone by-pass metal detecting: 526 coins (Reece 1991: no. 84)
7.8† Hooks Cross villa excavations: 47 coins (identifications by Reece, list Lockyear, pers. comm.)
7.9† Great Humphreys excavations 1979–82: 60 coins (identifications by Reece, list Lockyear 1987: 38–40)
See hoards 2 and 22

References

Allen, D.F. (1938), 'Coins', in J.B. Ward-Perkins, 'The Roman Villa at Lockleys, Welwyn', *Antiquaries Journal* 18, pp. 351–2.

Corney, M. (1999), 'Coins', in C.J. Going and J.R. Hunn, *Excavations at Boxfield Farm, Chells, Stevenage, Hertfordshire*, Hertfordshire Archaeological Trust Report 2 (Hertford), pp. 40–44.

Curnow, P.E. (1974), 'The Coins', in D.S. Neal, *The Excavation of a Roman Villa in Gadebridge Park, Hemel Hempstead, 1963–8* (London), pp. 115–17.

Curnow, P.E. (1974–6), 'The Coins', in D.S. Neal, 'Northchurch, Boxmoor, and Hemel Hempstead Station: The excavation of three Roman buildings in the Bulbourne valley', *Hertfordshire Archaeology* 4, pp. 18–19, 99–101.

Curnow, P.E. (1986), 'Roman Coin Lists', in I.M. Stead and V. Rigby, *Baldock: The Excavation of a Roman and Pre-Roman Settlement, 1968–72, Britannia* Monograph Series 7 (London), pp. 99–107.

Curnow, P.E. (1990), 'The Coins', in D.S. Neal, A. Wardle and J. Hunn, *Excavation of an Iron Age, Roman, and Medieval Settlement at Gorhambury, St Albans*, English Heritage Archaeological Report 14 (London), pp. 105–12.

Curteis, M. (1994–96), 'The coinage of Ninesprings Roman villa, Great Wymondley', *Hertfordshire Archaeology* 12, pp. 7–11.

Curteis, M. (2006), 'Coins', in J. Hunn, *Lobs Hole, Stevenage: A Romano-British Farmstead* (Letchworth), pp. 106–7.

Greep, S. (2006), 'The Coins', in R. Niblett, W. Manning and C. Saunders, 'Verulamium: Excavations within the Roman Town 1986–88', *Britannia* 37, pp. 167–72.

Lockyear, K. (1987), 'A Survey of the Antiquities of Great Humphreys and their Relation to other sites in Hertfordshire,' BA dissertation (University of Durham).

Page, W. (ed.) (1914), *VCH Hertford*, vol 4 (London).

Reece, R. (1980–82), 'The coins from Cow Roast, Herts. – a commentary', *Hertfordshire Archaeology* 8, pp. 60–66.

Reece, R. (1983–86), 'The coins', in T. Rook, 'The Roman Villa site at Dicket Mead, Lockleys, Welwyn', *Hertfordshire Archaeology* 9, pp. 143–5.

Reece, R. (1984), 'The Coins', in S.S. Frere, *Verulamium Excavations III* (Oxford), pp. 3–17.

Reece, R. (1989a), 'The Roman coins and their interpretation', in I.M. Stead and V. Rigby, *Verulamium: the King Harry Lane site* (London), pp. 12–15.

Reece, R. (1989b), 'The Roman Coins', in C.R. Partridge, *Foxholes Farm. A multi-period gravel site* (Hertford), pp. 143–4.

Reece, R. (1991), *Roman Coins from 140 Sites in Britain* (Cirencester).

Reece, R. (1999), 'The Coins', in R. Niblett, *The Excavation of a Ceremonial Site at Folly Lane, St Albans* (London), pp. 229–33.

Shotter, D.C.A. and Partridge, C.R. (1988), 'Roman coins', in T.W. Potter and S.D. Trow, 'Puckeridge-Braughing, Herts.: The Ermine Street Excavations, 1971–1972', *Hertfordshire Archaeology* 10, pp. 30–34.

St.J. O'Neil, B.H. (1936), 'Roman coins', in R.E.M. Wheeler and T.V. Wheeler, *Verulamium. A Belgic and two Roman Cities*, Research Reports of the Society of Antiquaries of London 11 (Oxford), pp. 227–39.

St.J. O'Neil, B.H.(1945), 'Coins', in H. O'Neil, 'The Roman Villa at Park Street, near St. Albans, Hertfordshire: Report on the Excavations of 1943–5', *The Archaeological Journal* 102, pp. 59–62.

Wessex Archaeology (2009) *Friars Wash, Redbourn, Hertfordshire, Archaeological Evaluation and Assessment of Results,* Wessex Archaeology Report 69735.01 (Salisbury).

Notes

1 This includes a private collection of coins found at Baldock.

2 This list does not contain the six coins that probably make up Hoard 10. Note Page's (1914: 151) reference to thousands of coins being found south of Larks Hill when the railway cutting was made in the nineteenth century – Iron Age, Augustus to Constantine I, 30 Carausius and Allectus. These probably comprise hoards, site-finds and even votive deposits, none of which can be reconstructed.

Index

References to figures given in *italics*.